TORTS AND COMPENSATION

PERSONAL ACCOUNTABILITY AND SOCIAL RESPONSIBILITY FOR INJURY

Concise Edition
Eighth Edition

■ ■ ■

Dan B. Dobbs

Regents Professor and Rosenstiel Distinguished Professor of Law Emeritus
James E. Rogers College of Law
The University of Arizona

Paul T. Hayden

Thomas V. Girardi Professor of Consumer Protection Law
Loyola Law School, Los Angeles
Loyola Marymount University

Ellen M. Bublick

Dan B. Dobbs Professor of Law
James E. Rogers College of Law
The University of Arizona

AMERICAN CASEBOOK SERIES®

WEST ACADEMIC
PUBLISHING

American Casebook Series is a trademark registered in the U.S. Patent and Trademark Office.

© 2009 Thomson Reuters
© 2013 LEG, Inc. d/b/a West Academic Publishing
© 2017 LEG, Inc. d/b/a West Academic
    444 Cedar Street, Suite 700
    St. Paul, MN 55101
    1-877-888-1330

West, West Academic Publishing, and West Academic are trademarks of West Publishing Corporation, used under license.

Printed in the United States of America

ISBN: 978-1-63460-818-3

To Dan Dobbs, whose work sets the standard.—P.T.H. & E.M.B.

To Diane, without whom my accomplishments would be fewer and far less meaningful.—P.T.H.

To Daniel, Harrison and David, with love. Looking forward to the next chapter.—E.M.B.

PREFACE TO THE CONCISE EIGHTH EDITION

This casebook is a teaching tool. As with our previous editions, we present challenging contemporary cases and issues, without straying too far from the classic cases and the core of lawyering—thoughtful analysis and criticism. We want to engage students without mystifying them, and—with the contributions of the professors who teach our book—to spark a lifelong interest in law in general and in tort law in particular.

This book deals centrally with injuries to persons, and reading about and discussing such serious matters can be difficult. But we have always approached torts by trying to present the reality of conflicts in tort law and we continue to do so in this edition. Tort law is about real people and real injuries, and the cases in this book reflect that reality. Of course, much of the reality is leavened at times by the absurd and unexpected. A torts class using this book will be more than an exercise in solemn analysis of tragic situations; our experience tells us that smiles and laughter are neither rare nor inappropriate as students and professors discuss the cases. We believe a good book will challenge students, yet provide a good time when possible.

While the foundation of tort law is timeless, the common law, by its very nature, has never been static. Tort law is largely *state* law, which means that for every new legal question that arises, courts in various states will provide different answers and perspectives. Thus tort doctrine itself is continually being produced by our great experiment in federalism. Even within single states, we can see courts evolve in the way they apply their old legal doctrines or develop new law. Our casebook tries to reflect this dynamic process. Thus this edition includes developments in cases, topics and academic commentary that have occurred in the last few years. There are many new main cases, many new case abstracts and hundreds of citations to newer cases.

Our primary criterion in selecting cases for inclusion in this book is whether they provide opportunities for analysis and for strengthening important lawyering skills such as reading, interpretation, evaluation and synthesis of legal materials. This book has never been merely a collection of illusory "majority rules." We hope students using this book will realize early on that both the cases and the notes aim to sharpen students' intellectual skills and enhance their understanding of legal process, as well as impart information.

Our Concise Edition attempts to present the core of tort law in personal injury and property damage cases in a shorter form that makes it possible to teach the central materials in a four-hour course. We have achieved this more streamlined coverage by cutting some cases, some case abstracts, and much note material from the standard edition. We have also reduced some entire chapter sections to much briefer text. Finally, we have focused the Concise edition almost exclusively on the tort law of physical injuries to persons and property, reducing the standard edition's explorations of both the alternatives to tort law (workers' compensation, public compensation systems and no-fault insurance) and economic and dignitary torts to mere "awareness" coverage.

A Note on Editing Conventions

The main "cases" reproduced in this (and almost any) casebook are opinions of judges, usually at the appellate levels. Such opinions are rarely succinct. They almost always include a good deal of matter on procedure and discuss many legal arguments that are not relevant to the ideas we want to highlight and develop. They also usually include many citations to cases as precedent or persuasive example. Editing is therefore necessary.

When we omit text in opinions, we indicate the omission by ellipses. Sometimes we summarize portions of a judicial opinion in our own language; we put that in brackets. We don't usually mark out omissions of citations of precedent and academic commentary at all, because such citations are so prevalent that every page would be cluttered with dots if we did. We likewise omit footnotes in opinions without marking the omission; when we retain footnotes we also retain their original numbering. Finally, in quoted materials, we usually omit any internal quotation marks to make materials more readable.

This edition contains numerous citations to the Restatements of Torts, and sometimes to the Restatements of Agency or other areas of relevant law. The Restatements of the Law in various editions are the product of the American Law Institute, a private law-reform group founded in 1923. The Restatements are not themselves law, but have proven quite influential with courts, many of which have voluntarily adopted the black-letter rules these Restatements contain. The newest torts Restatements are designated as the Restatement (Third) of Torts, with subtitles to indicate the particular area covered—for instance, Liability for Physical and Emotional Harm, or Products Liability.

We hope that professors and students alike will learn from and enjoy the many thoughtful and thought-provoking cases and materials presented here.

PAUL T. HAYDEN
ELLEN M. BUBLICK

March 2017

ACKNOWLEDGMENTS

We owe real thanks to many people who aided our work on this edition. Thanks to Jayme Weber, who served as Assistant Editor for the book, and whose insights and suggestions have helped make this edition the best to date. Thanks also to David Jacobs for his careful edits of many, many chapters. One of our great good fortunes with this book has been the ability to collaborate with so many fine torts scholars from around the country who teach this work and share suggestions to improve it. For thoughtful suggestions about potential changes to the Eighth Edition we thank Beau Baez, Bari Burke, Tony Dillof, David Eggert, Jay Feinman, Antonio Gidi, John LaVelle, Miranda McGowen, John Noyes, Stefan Padfield, Deana Pollard, and Chris Robertson. Paul gives kudos to the research librarians at Loyola Law School, under the leadership of Dan Martin and Laura Cadra. Ellen also thanks Maureen Garmon for effective design of research structures, Barbara Lopez for help with the manuscript, and Barbara Atwood and David Marcus for assistance with issues of procedure. Paul and Ellen give special thanks to Dan Dobbs for his vision, his hard work, his advice, and his friendship. All of us thank our students, past and present, who continue to inspire and engage us. We also thank the outstanding professionals at West Academic, who have always been supportive of our efforts and a great a pleasure to work with.

SUMMARY OF CONTENTS

———————

PART 6. LIMITING THE DUTY OF CARE BASED ON RELATIONSHIPS OR THEIR ABSENCE

PART 7. SPECIAL TYPES OF HARM

PART 8. THE EBB AND FLOW OF COMMON LAW STRICT LIABILITY FOR PHYSICAL HARMS

PART 9. PRACTICALITIES AND VALUES

PART 10. ALTERNATIVES TO TORT LAW

PART 11. ECONOMIC AND DIGNITARY TORTS

TABLE OF CONTENTS

PART 9. PRACTICALITIES AND VALUES

PART 10. ALTERNATIVES TO TORT LAW

PART 11. ECONOMIC AND DIGNITARY TORTS

TABLE OF CASES

The principal cases are in bold type.

———

TABLE OF CASES

Sacco v. High Country Indep. Press, Inc., 499

Sacramento, County of v. Lewis, 59

Sadler v. PacifiCare of Nev., 660

Safeway Stores, Inc. v. Nest-Kart, 635

Safford Unified Sch. Dist. #1 v. Redding, 60

Sagebrush Res., LLC v. Peterson, 57

Saleh v. Titan Corp., 385

Salica v. Tucson Heart Hosp.– Carondelet, L.L.C., 194

Salinas v. Vierstra, 287

Salinetro v. Nystrom, 181

Sallee v. Stewart, 333

Saltsman v. Sharp, 324

Sama v. Hannigan, 399

Samples v. Florida Birth-Related Neurological Injury Comp. Ass'n, 665

Samson v. Nahulu, 250

Sands ex rel. Sands v. Green, 299

Sanislo v. Give Kids the World, Inc., 277

Santa Barbara, City of v. Superior Court, 278

Santana v. Rainbow Cleaners, 466

Santana v. Zilog, Inc., 507

Santiago v. First Student, Inc., 149

Saucier ex rel. Mallory v. McDonald's Rests. of Mont., Inc., 78

Schaefer v. Amer. Family Mut. Ins. Co., 523

Schenk v. Schenk, 366

Schirmer v. Mt. Auburn Obstetrics & Gynecology Assocs., Inc., 513

Schoenfeld v. Quamme, 389

School of Visual Arts v. Kuprewicz, 56

Schork v. Huber, 514

Schroeder v. St. Louis County, 397

Schroeder v. Weighall, 364

Schuster v. Altenberg, 465

Schuster v. City of New York, 393

Sciarrotta v. Global Spectrum, 290

Scott v. Harris, 59

Scott v. James, 171

Scott v. Matlack, Inc., 116

Scott v. Universal Sales, Inc., 457, 465

Scurti v. City of New York, 324

Sears v. Morrison, 219

Seattle Western Industries, Inc. v. David A. Mowat Co., 427

Sebra v. Wentworth, 53

Second Judicial District Court, County of Washoe, State v., 403

Self v. Executive Comm. of Ga. Baptist Convention, 346

Senkus v. Moore, 325

Sepaugh v. LaGrone, 370

September 11 Litigation, In re, 230, 666

Sernovitz v. Dershaw, 512, 514

Service Cos., Inc. v. Estate of Vaughn, 50

Service Oil, Inc. v. Gjestvang, 56

Severn Peanut Co., Inc. v. Indus. Fumigant Co., 429

Sexton, Commonwealth v., 397

Shanks v. Upjohn Co., 594

Shantigar Found. v. Bear Mountain Builders, 646

Sharon P. v. Arman, 449

Shaw v. Jendzejec, 507

Shearer, United States v., 389

Shearin v. Lloyd, 295

Sheffer v. Carolina Forge Co., 472, 533

Shelton v. Kentucky Easter Seals Soc., Inc., 318, 331

Shen v. Leo A. Daly Co., 50

Shepherd v. Gardner Wholesale, Inc., 99

Sheppard-Mobley v. King, 508

Sheward, State v., 634

Shin v. Ahn, 292

Shine v. Vega, 356

Shipley v. City of New York, 497

Shipley v. Williams, 349

Shirley v. Glass, 472

Shoemake v. Fogel, Ltd., 371

Shore v. Maple Lane Farms, LLC, 52

Show v. Ford Motor Co., 595

Shuler v. Garrett, 355

Shuler v. United States, 383

Shull v. Reid, 510

Sibbing v. Cave, 209

Siegel v. Ridgewells, Inc., 486

Simmons v. Porter, 278

Simpson v. Roberts, 507

Sinclair v. Block, 345

Sinsel v. Olsen, 458

Siruta v. Siruta, 266

Sivit v. Village Green of Beachwood, 671

Skinner v. The London, Brighton and South Coast Railway Company, 165

Slack v. Farmers Ins. Exch., 638

Slone v. Gen. Motors Corp., 617

Smaxwell v. Bayard, 458

Smith v. Borello, 508

Smith v. Cote, 512

Smith v. Finch, 125, 142

Smith v. Lockheed Propulsion Co., 572

Smith v. Massey-Ferguson, Inc., 279

Smith v. Smith, 372

Smith v. Toney, 491

Smith v. United States, 388, 523

Smith v. Whitaker, 524

TORTS AND COMPENSATION

PERSONAL ACCOUNTABILITY AND SOCIAL RESPONSIBILITY FOR INJURY

Concise Edition
Eighth Edition

PART 1

A FIRST LOOK AT TORTS

...

CHAPTER 1

TORT LAW: AIMS, APPROACHES, AND PROCESSES

∎ ∎ ∎

§ 1. WHAT IS TORT LAW?

Tort as wrongdoing. Torts are wrongs recognized by law as grounds for a lawsuit. These wrongs include an intentional punch in the nose and also a negligent car wreck. They include medical malpractice and some environmental pollution. The list of tortious wrongs is very long. All torts involve conduct that falls below some legal standard. In almost all cases, the defendant is in some sense at fault, either because he intends harm or because he takes unreasonable risks of harm.

Harm required. In all tort cases, the defendant's wrong results in a harm to another person (or entity, such as a corporation), that the law is willing to say constitutes a legal injury. The injured person is said to have a "cause of action," that is, a claim against the person who committed the tort. This claim can be pursued in court. Most of the cases in this book involve some kind of physical injury or threat of physical injury. Some torts, however, involve harm that is purely commercial and others involve intangible harm such as harm to reputation.

Torts, crimes, and contracts. A breach of contract is often grounds for a lawsuit, but a breach of contract is often not considered to be a tort at all. It must ordinarily be redressed under the rules for contracts, not the rules for torts. Some torts are also crimes. A punch in the nose is a tort called battery, but it may also be a crime. Sometimes a defendant who attacked the plaintiff is prosecuted criminally and is also held liable to the plaintiff for the tort. The two fields of law often overlap. However, they are not identical. Some acts that cause no harm at all to individuals might be crimes but not torts. Conversely, some acts cause harm and are torts but not crimes. That is because criminal law aims at vindicating public interests, while tort law aims at vindicating individual rights and redressing private harms.

Non-tort systems. Physical injuries inflicted by one person upon another are commonly addressed by tort law, but there are alternatives to tort law. Toward the end of this book, several chapters consider alternatives such as workers' compensation systems, which require employers to buy insurance and to pay for all on-the-job injuries even when

3

the employer is not at fault. Non-tort systems are important for tort lawyers and also for those who wish to understand the way society deals with injuries. However, for now we are going to concentrate on the way injuries are addressed under tort law.

Common questions in tort law. Much of the law of torts is concerned with three questions: (1) what conduct counts as tortious or wrongful? (2) Did the conduct cause the kind of harm the law will recognize? (3) What defenses can be raised against liability if the defendant has committed a tort? The answers to these questions turn in part on why we have tort law and what its aims are.

§ 2. THE GOALS OF TORT LAW

A. SOME BROAD (AND CONFLICTING) AIMS

DOBBS, HAYDEN & BUBLICK, THE LAW OF TORTS
Vol. 1 §§ 10–14 (2d ed. 2011)

§ 10 Justice, policy, and process aims of tort law in summary

. . . *Morality or corrective justice.* Particular aims of tort law are usually erected under one of two large systems of thought. The first bases tort law on moral responsibility or at least on some idea that the defendant has in some important way wronged the plaintiff. It attempts to hold defendants liable for harms they wrongfully caused and no others. Good social effects may result when courts act to right the wrongs done by defendants, but in this system of thought that is not the point of imposing liability. Liability is imposed instead when and only when it is "right" to do so. As stated in a decision of the House of Lords, "The overall object of tort law is to define cases in which the law may justly hold one party liable to compensate another." *Fairchild v. Glenhaven Funeral Servs.,* [2002] 3 All E.R. 305, 2002 WL 820081 (H.L. 2002).

Social utility or public policy. The second large system of thought reverses the emphasis; it bases tort law on social policy or a good-for-all-of-us view. Social policy may coincide with justice in particular cases, but the dominant concern is not justice to the individual; it is to provide a system of rules that, overall, works toward the good of society.

Potential conflicts. The first two ways of looking at tort law are usually regarded as antithetical to each other. Although justice and policy often point to the same result, they do not always do so, and when they do not, one of these views must prevail or both must be compromised. The legal process view might also conflict with the aims of justice or those of policy.

Suppose a city, facing a raging and spreading fire, attempts to create a firebreak by blowing up a row of houses. Because time is critical, the city insists upon doing so before the plaintiff, who owns one of the houses, can remove his furniture. When the whole thing is over, the plaintiff claims damages from the city for the value of the furniture he could have saved. The city has acted for the good of its residents generally, but the plaintiff is the one who pays the costs. If the city's action is to be judged by a standard of social policy, some jurists might say the city should not be liable. On the other hand, if it is judged by corrective justice standards, the city should pay for the damage it caused in blowing up the houses. Otherwise, the city would get the advantage of its action (whatever that advantage might be) but would pay none of the costs. There are more subtle examples, but this one is enough to suggest the potential conflict between a decision based upon (supposed) social policy and one based upon justice to the individual. . . .

§ 11 Corrective justice, distributive justice, and policy

. . . For lawyers arguing cases, the question is not likely to be whether judges must wholly exclude policy or wholly exclude justice. Instead, advocacy requires lawyers to show judges why one approach or the other is most appropriate for the particular case. . . .

§ 12 Fault and other normative bases for liability

. . . *Fault and justice.* Tort law imposes liability upon defendants for conduct the law treats as wrong. In most instances, the conduct adjudged as wrong can be viewed as morally faulty conduct: it is intentional misconduct or at least unreasonably risky conduct likely to cause harm to others. In these cases, tort law seems to be commensurate in a general way with corrective justice ideals. The defendant's fault is a wrong that has harmed the plaintiff in some recognizable way; tort law, by subjecting the wrongdoer to a judgment that can be enforced against his assets, can put the accounts right between the parties.

Conversely, it can be argued that in a corrective justice scheme, it would be wrong to impose liability upon a defendant who is not at fault in causing the plaintiff's harm. Society may wish to compensate injured people by the use of public funds, but it cannot justly force one innocent individual to compensate another.

These views emphasize individual accountability for fault, accompanied by individual freedom to act without fault. They are consistent with an ideal of social responsibility for victims, however; they do not speak against government compensation for victims when the defendant is not at fault, only against compensation by the faultless defendant.

Strict liability and corrective justice. When tort law imposes liability without fault, does it go beyond the principle of corrective justice? At least *some* strict liability seems commensurate with corrective justice. For example, suppose a long-standing custom in our neighborhood permits any neighbor to borrow garden equipment from any other neighbor, but the custom is equally strong that if the equipment is damaged or lost while in the borrower's possession, the borrower must make the loss good. Suppose I borrow your lawnmower and without my fault it is damaged when a truck backs over it in my driveway. A rule that imposes liability upon me would be a strict liability rule because I was not at fault. Even so, liability seems to accord with corrective justice so long as you and I both know of the custom. . . . Whatever is to be said of strict liability theories of corrective justice, the great majority of tort cases turn on some kind of perception that the defendant is at fault in a significant way. At least for those cases, tort law begins with ideals of justice, even if those ideals may be modified by pragmatic, process, or policy considerations in particular cases.

§ 13 Compensation, risk distribution, fault

Compensation. Compensation of persons injured by wrongdoing is one of the generally accepted aims of tort law. Payment of compensation to injured persons is desirable. If a person has been wronged by a defendant, it is just that the defendant make compensation. Compensation is also socially desirable, for otherwise the uncompensated injured persons will represent further costs and problems for society. . . .

. . . *[R]isk distribution or loss spreading.* . . . [S]ome commentators have argued that tort liability should be strict or expansive in order to secure compensation for more injured persons. Some defendants if not all were seen as good "risk distributors" who should be liable for any harms they cause regardless of fault because they can "distribute" the costs of paying compensation. This means that some defendants, such as products manufacturers, could pay compensation for injuries they cause and then recoup some or all of those costs by raising the price of products. In this view, each individual purchaser of the products will pay a tiny fraction of the costs of injuries inflicted by those products and the injured person will not be compelled to bear the entire cost alone. Loss would thus cause less social dislocation. At the same time, an enterprise would be forced to internalize losses typically generated by the business itself.

Limited acceptance of risk distribution arguments. The common law of tort has not in fact generally adopted views that compensation is more important than corrective justice or that liability should be strict. Distribution arguments and strict liability have gone hand in hand, but only in certain kinds of cases. They have not supplanted fault as the most common basis for tort liability. . . .

§ 14 Fostering freedom, deterring unsafe conduct; economic analysis

Deterrence. Courts and writers almost always recognize that another aim of tort law is to deter certain kinds of conduct by imposing liability when that conduct causes harm. The idea of deterrence is not so much that an individual, having been held liable for a tort, would thereafter conduct himself better. It is rather the idea that all persons, recognizing potential tort liability, would tend to avoid conduct that could lead to tort liability. They might sometimes engage in the conduct in question, but only if they would get more out of it than the tort liability would cost. . . .

Deterrence: justice or social policy? Both systems of thought that emphasize justice and those that emphasize social policy goals can agree that deterrence is acceptable, but the two approaches might call for deterring quite different conduct. If you focus on conduct that is wrongful in the sense of being unjust to an individual, you might regard any given act as wrongful even though it is economically useful in society. If you focus on social policy, you might want to forgive defendants who cause harms by their socially useful activities. . . .

Economic analysis. [O]ne particular kind of social policy consideration is the economic one. If economics is defined broadly enough to include a consideration of all human wants and desires, then perhaps all social policies are in a sense economic policies. . . .

NOTE

Further reading. Many writers have analyzed tort law's goals and methods. Major contributions and differing views about justice vs. deterrence (or moral vs. economic analysis) are discussed in Gary T. Schwartz, *Mixed Theories of Tort Law: Affirming Both Deterrence and Corrective Justice,* 75 TEX. L. REV. 1801 (1997). For a more recent look at the tensions, see Lawrence A. Cunningham, *Traditional Versus Economic Analysis: Evidence from Cardozo and Posner Torts Opinions*, 62 FLA. L. REV. 667 (2010). There is also an admirably succinct summary in William E. Nelson, *From Fairness to Efficiency: The Transformation of Tort Law in New York,* 1920–1980, 47 BUFF. L. REV. 117 (1999). David A. Fischer, *Successive Causes and the Enigma of Duplicated Harm,* 66 TENN. L. REV. 1127 (1999), concludes that when courts have been forced to choose between the goals of fairness and efficiency, they have opted for fairness. Louis Kaplow and Steven Shavell argue in *Fairness versus Welfare*, 114 HARV. L. REV. 961 (2001), that courts err whenever they accord independent weight to notions of fairness such as corrective justice, and instead should focus on individual well-being. The materials in this book may help you determine for yourself whether either of these conclusions is well-founded.

B. APPROACHES IN ACTION: THE ROLE OF FAULT

A great deal can be said about approaches to tort law and its goals, but for those without experience in reading actual cases and encountering actual tort problems, the goals are so abstract that they almost elude the grasp. The best approach may be to keep the goals or approaches in mind while reading cases.

VAN CAMP V. MCAFOOS
156 N.W.2d 878 (Iowa 1968)

BECKER, JUSTICE.

This case comes to us on appeal from the trial court's action in sustaining defendant's motion to dismiss. We are therefore limited to what can be gleaned from the pleadings.

In Division I of her petition plaintiff sues Mark McAfoos alleging in pertinent part, "That at said time and place defendant Mark McAfoos was operating a tricycle on said public sidewalk, and drove the tricycle into the rear of the plaintiff without warning, striking the right leg of the plaintiff thereby causing an injury to the Achilles' tendon of that leg.

"That as a direct and proximate cause of the defendant's action, plaintiff's tendon was injured and subsequently required surgery. . . ." [In another part of the petition the plaintiff alleged that Mark was three years, one month old.]

The trial court sustained the motion to dismiss as to Division I stating in part, "It is not alleged that the defendant was negligent. It is not alleged that the action of the defendant was willful or wrongful in any manner. Under these circumstances it is difficult to see how the Division as now set out states any basis upon which the plaintiff could recover."

The question presented is, did plaintiff plead a cause of action. . . .

I.   Plaintiff's sole assignment of error as to Division I is "The trial court erred in failing to recognize categories of tort liability other than negligence, in evaluating the pleading in plaintiff's first division."

. . . She stands firmly on the proposition that invasion of her person is in itself a wrong and she need plead no more. We do not agree. . . . In essence plaintiff urges a person has a right not to be injuriously touched or struck as she lawfully uses a public sidewalk. She was injuriously struck by Mark. Therefore Mark is liable. She argues that no more need be pleaded. It follows that no more need be proved in order to justify submission of the case. Plaintiff's posture satisfies us she would have us impose liability without fault. We are not prepared to extend this concept to childish acts (by children).

II.   Plaintiff's reply brief states "If the absence of a single word or conclusory label remains the *sine qua non* of pleading a valid cause of action, we have restored today's jurisprudence to the specious procedural formalism of the 18th Century common courts."

The trial court's ruling was not a return to legal formalism. Plaintiff makes it abundantly clear she insists on a right to recovery by proof of an accident caused by another, independent of fault or wrong doing. Where an essential element of the cause of action is missing, the question is not what may be shown under the pleading but whether a cause of action has been pled.

. . . Unless and until we are ready to recognize liability without fault for otherwise innocent childish actions, fault must be discernible in the pleading and in proof. Intentionally wrongful or negligently wrongful use of the tricycle is neither pled nor can it be made out from the bare allegation defendant "operated a tricycle on said public sidewalk and drove the tricycle into the rear of the plaintiff without warning." . . .

III. Plaintiff cites many cases from other jurisdictions holding a child of tender years may be liable *in tort. Garratt v. Dailey*, 46 Wash. 2d 197, 279 P.2d 1091. All of the foregoing cases involve the fault concept. Many turn on the question of whether the child could be guilty of the fault charged but each case has fault as one of the essential elements of liability. We need not disagree with those authorities. Whatever her motive, plaintiff has chosen to plead in such a way as to avoid bringing herself within the scope of those cases. . . .

Affirmed.

NOTES

1. **Overview.** Casebook editors may select cases and materials with more than one purpose in mind. At any given point, several themes may be in progress. *Van Camp* displays both a substantive and a procedural theme. The substantive or tort law theme has to do with the grounds for liability. The procedural theme has to do with how a tort cause of action is pleaded in court. In this case, why does the court consider only "what can be gleaned from the pleadings"? Most cases in this book will raise a number of issues that require analysis and further thought. Notes like these should help you develop that analysis or furnish related information.

2. **Historical strict liability and the rules today.** From the early days of tort law, about the 13th century until perhaps as late as the 18th century, anyone who acted affirmatively and directly (like Mark McAfoos) might be held liable for harm done, even though he was not at fault. In these cases the plaintiff used a form of action for suing called *Trespass*. The plaintiff would win unless the defendant had some special defense, called justification or excuse. An example of a defense would be self-defense. If the harm caused was indirect, on the other hand, the defendant was not responsible unless he was at fault in some way. If Mark McAfoos had left his tricycle on the walk and the plaintiff had bumped into it in the dark, this would have been an indirect harm and even in the early English law Mark would not have been liable without fault. Cases of indirect harm required the plaintiff in that period to

select a form of action for suing called *Trespass on the Case*, or just *Case*. Does *Van Camp* implicitly or expressly reject the older rule that a defendant can be liable for direct harms even in the absence of fault?

3. **What is fault?** What would it take to show fault in *Van Camp*? Suppose McAfoos said that he ran into Ms. Van Camp on purpose because he wanted to hear her get angry. If McAfoos caused the accident, how could it have happened without his fault? In *Van Camp,* the court upheld the dismissal of plaintiff's claim because no fault had been pleaded—neither "intentionally wrongful" nor "negligently wrongful" use of the tricycle. Both intentional misconduct and negligent misconduct can be forms of fault. Specific tort claims require pleading particular types of fault.

4. **Tort law and the states.** With few exceptions, tort law is made by the courts and legislatures of the various states, not by the federal government. When you read *Van Camp* how can you tell which state court wrote the opinion? If *Van Camp* tells us that fault is required to maintain a battery claim in Iowa, do we know whether fault is required in Illinois?

5. **Evaluation of the legal rule.** How does the rule or principle in *Van Camp* stack up against the aims of tort law? Is the fault-based rule in *Van Camp* just? Does it reflect socially desirable standards of deterring wrongdoing and compensating injured persons? What other sort of rule could the court have adopted? Evaluation of bases for a legal rule and alternatives to it is important to lawyers. It is one process by which lawyers begin to formulate legal arguments.

6. **Grasping a principle.** *Van Camp* involved a child on a tricycle. But the principle or reason behind the case might apply to many other situations. One function of a lawyer is to recognize the possibility of applying the principle of a case to a new set of facts. Try it:

(a) H becomes angry with his wife, W, and repeatedly hits her with his fist, breaking her jaw and bruising her face. Would the principle or idea in *Van Camp* either establish or exclude liability?

(b) The defendant's yard has a tree near the sidewalk. The tree appears to be sound and healthy, but in fact it is rotten and it blows over in a wind. It strikes a passerby. Can you predict from *Van Camp* whether a court would impose liability?

§ 3. IMPLEMENTING TORT LAW'S GOALS WITH DAMAGES AWARDS

In a few cases the remedy for a tort is an injunction. That is, the court will order the defendant to cease committing a tort such as a nuisance or a continuing contamination of the plaintiff's land. In the overwhelming majority of injury cases, however, the remedy is compensatory damages, an award of money to compensate the injured person for the harms caused by the defendant's tortious conduct.

DILLON V. FRAZER

678 S.E.2d 251 (S.C. 2009)

JUSTICE PLEICONES.

[Noel Dillon, a Canadian resident, sustained injuries in a car accident in Greenville, South Carolina when his co-worker Neil Frazer ran a stop sign in a car in which Dillon was a passenger.] Dillon was transported by ambulance to a hospital, where it was determined that he had eight fractured ribs on his right side and two on his left, a fractured sternum, a fractured clavicle, a fractured left thumb, and a punctured lung. He was admitted to the hospital where he remained for two days. Once back in Canada, Dillon received physical therapy. The remainder of his care was covered by the Canadian Health System and those costs were not sought in this action.

Due to his punctured lung, Dillon was not medically able to fly back to Canada until the Friday following his release from the hospital. He did not return to work for at least 10 weeks. Initially, Dillon returned to full-time work, but performed fewer overtime hours than prior to his injuries. Dillon testified that, prior to the accident, he worked roughly between 900 and 1,100 hours of overtime and double time each year. He stated that, after the accident, the number of hours he was able to work diminished.

[Because Frazer admitted liability, the only questions for the jury concerned the amount of damages due Dillon.] All told, Dillon's hospital care in Greenville amounted to $10,518. Dillon also claimed $320 for EMS transportation to the hospital and $1,188 in physical therapy bills. In addition to compensation for medical care, Dillon also contended that he was entitled to $509,168 in lost past and future earnings, including $101,350 in lost wages from the date of injury to the estimated trial date and $407,818 for the post-trial period, based on calculations by Dillon's expert.

During deliberations, the jury sent questions to the judge asking whether any compensation had been paid to Dillon by a third party. [The judge instructed the jury that their questions were irrelevant, and that they should "disregard matters relating to third party payment of medical bills."] The jury awarded Dillon $6,000. . . . Dillon moved for a new trial *nisi additur* or in the alternative, for a new trial absolute as to damages only. The trial court granted Dillon's motion for *additur* and increased the damages by $15,000, bringing the total amount of damages to $21,000. [It] denied all other motions.

Dillon argues on appeal that the trial court erred by not granting a new trial absolute as to damages. We agree. The trial court has sound discretion when addressing questions of excessiveness or inadequacy of verdicts, and its decision will not be disturbed absent an abuse of discretion. "The trial court must grant a new trial absolute if the amount of the verdict is grossly inadequate or excessive so as to shock the conscience of the court and clearly indicates the figure reached was the result of passion, caprice, prejudice, partiality, corruption or some other improper motive. The failure of the trial judge to grant a new trial absolute in this situation amounts to an abuse of discretion and on appeal this Court will grant a new trial absolute." Vinson v. Hartley, 477 S.E.2d 715 (S.C. Ct. App. 1996). When considering a motion for a new trial based on the inadequacy or excessiveness of the jury's verdict, the trial court must distinguish between awards that are merely unduly liberal or conservative and awards that are actuated by passion, caprice, prejudice, or some other improper motive. . . .

Dillon presented evidence of over $500,000 in damages as a result of the accident. While Frazer contested portions of Dillon's claim, unchallenged testimony at trial established the following damages: $10,518 in medical bills, $320.00 for EMS transportation to the hospital, $1,188 in physical therapy bills, and $18,000 in lost wages and overtime pay. This totals $30,026 in undisputed damages.

We find the jury verdict of $6,000 irreconcilably inconsistent with the unchallenged evidence presented at trial. [The disparity between the award and the admitted damages goes beyond a merely conservative award and suggests that the jurors were motivated by improper considerations] . —

[handwritten margin note: Doctrine of Invisible Error]

[handwritten margin note: Jury not doing their job by assessing the evidence]

No plausible reason for the amount of the verdict has been advanced. For these reasons, the trial court erred in not granting Dillon's motion. . . . Since Frazer admitted liability, we remand for a new trial ~~on damages~~ only.

NOTES

1.   **Compensatory damages components.** The injured person usually has the burden of proving that the defendant is liable. In *Dillon* the defendant admitted liability. Once liability is proved or admitted, a plaintiff is entitled to recover compensatory damages caused by the defendant's tortious conduct. Upon proper proof, a plaintiff is entitled to compensation for (1) lost wages or lost earning capacity, (2) medical expenses, (3) pain and suffering endured, including mental or emotional pain, and (4) any special or particularized damages that do not fit neatly within the other categories. The plaintiff can recover not only for such losses that have already occurred, but also for such losses that are reasonably certain to occur in the future, if the evidence demonstrates the likelihood of such future losses. See 3 DOBBS, HAYDEN & BUBLICK, THE LAW OF TORTS § 479 (2d ed. 2011).

The gist of the damages rules is that the defendant has wrongfully reduced the plaintiff's net assets, tangible and intangible, and should be required to restore them. Are the compensatory damages rules consistent with some or all of the broad goals of tort law?

2.   **Evidence of payments made by third parties.** The trial court in *Dillon* told the jury to disregard any payments to the plaintiff from anyone other than the defendant. This was proper under what is called the collateral source rule, pursuant to which such payments (like insurance payments) are irrelevant to the jury's damages award against the defendant. This sometimes complex rule, followed by many states, is further explored in Chapter 26. For now, it is enough to explain that the rule does not usually result in any windfall to the plaintiff but instead simply preserves an insurance company's rights to recoup from the tortfeasor the payments the insurer made to the plaintiff, a practice called subrogation. See 3 DOBBS, HAYDEN & BUBLICK, THE LAW OF TORTS § 482 (2d ed. 2011).

3.   **Judge and jury.** Determining the amount of damages is the jury's job, but as you can see from *Dillon* the trial judge and the appellate judges have important roles to play in the final outcome. Once the jury has fixed damages, can an aggrieved party win simply by arguing that the jury got the amount wrong? Is that what happened in *Dillon*? How does a judge tell when a jury has based its award on some improper consideration?

4.   **Judicial powers: additur, remittitur, and new trial.** Following an insufficient award of damages in a jury trial, a state court trial judge has the power to deny the plaintiff's motion for a new trial on the condition that the defendant consents to pay an increased award of damages; this power is called *additur*. The judge's power to deny defendant's motion for new trial if plaintiff remits part of an excessively high award is called *remittitur*. The trial judge also has the power, and sometimes the duty to order a new trial on damages, as you can see in *Dillon*. Why was the trial judge's use of the *additur* power in *Dillon* not adequate to correct the jury's lower award? What does evidence produced at trial have to do with a compensatory damages award?

5.   **Measuring pain and suffering.** One difficulty in assessing proper compensation is that for many of us, our main assets are not in the form of money or property but in the form of good health and freedom from pain. Although pain is not quantifiable, freedom from pain has economic value. We can see that in the expenditures people make to gain pleasure and avoid pain. You could also imagine that someone offered you money for the right to break your leg. If you would accept such an awful offer at all, you would almost certainly demand even more money if the break would entail pain. The amount of money you would demand to suffer pain is not the measure of a tortfeasor's liability (he is only liable for reasonable compensation, not what you would demand). Even so, if freedom from pain is an intangible asset, pain inflicted by a defendant represents a real loss and should be compensated somehow. How does the jury know how much to award for pain and suffering?

6.   **Attorney's fees.** One of the most important institutional rules covering most litigation in the United States is that a losing party is not required to pay the winning party's attorney's fees as a line-item. Under this so-called American Rule, each party pays its own attorney's fees, win or lose, unless some special statute or law allows for fee-shifting. As a result, the

almost universal system of litigation finance in this country is that plaintiffs' attorneys in torts cases are paid by contingent fees: they are paid nothing if they lose, and a percentage of the recovery if they win. The percentage may vary from around 25% to 40%, sometimes higher. The percentage may sound high, but considering the lawyer's investment of time and effort and the fact that the lawyer will be paid nothing in some cases, such fees are usually not a bad deal for the client who could not afford to pay a lawyer otherwise. State rules of professional responsibility prohibit lawyers from charging or collecting fees that are unreasonable, excessive or unconscionable. *See* ABA MODEL RULES OF PROFESSIONAL CONDUCT 1.5(a) (prohibiting unreasonable fees).

Given that a plaintiff's lawyer is likely to be paid a percentage of the damages obtained, why isn't the plaintiff left short of money for medical expenses and lost wages and earning capacity in every case?

7. **Criticisms of damages.** You may have heard or read many criticisms of tort law—that it is out of control, that Americans litigate trivial matters, that they are greedy, and that they seek something for nothing. No doubt greed shows up in lawsuits as well as in corporate board rooms and elsewhere. However, it is important to know that the studies available do *not* support the claim that litigation by individuals has increased or that juries often run amok. A 2008 report issued by the Bureau of Justice Statistics estimates the median award in tort cases at $24,000, slightly lower than the $35,000 median award in contract cases. In all cases, only 4% of plaintiffs received awards over one million dollars. In addition, from 1992 to 2005 the number of tort cases decreased by 40%. Did plaintiffs fare better with juries rather than judges? Quite to the contrary. *See* Lynn Langton & Thomas H. Cohen, BUREAU OF JUSTICE STATISTICS, U.S. DEP'T. OF JUSTICE, NCJ 223851, CIVIL BENCH AND JURY TRIALS IN STATE COURTS, 2005 (October 2008).

8. **Calculating plaintiff's losses: an example.** In *Estevez v. United States*, 72 F. Supp. 2d 205 (S.D.N.Y. 1999), the defendant's employee carelessly caused a car accident that injured a two-year old child. The child was hospitalized for weeks and underwent surgeries to repair his aorta, kidney and bowel as well as some arteries and veins. In addition, the child had to wear a spinal fracture brace and was placed on breathing and feeding tubes for a period of time. Because of the injuries, he faced increased risks for future medical problems, required increased medical monitoring, and could anticipate a shortened work life expectancy. The court awarded $138,000 in past hospital and medical costs, $85,415 for future cardiac procedures, $1,800 for needed x-rays of his leg, $40,000 for orthotic devices he would need over the course of a lifetime, $11,700 for tendon lengthening surgery, $93,600 for physical therapy, $432,887 in lost wages for a 6.67 reduced work-life expectancy, $500,000 for past pain and suffering and $750,000 for future pain and suffering (an award that the court said amounted to "little more than $10,000 per year for a permanent limp and leg shortening, a damaged spine, potential abdominal adhesions, risk of infection of the Gortex patch [on the aorta], and the continued discomfort of medical monitoring and associated procedures." After plaintiff's total award of $1,993,902 was reduced by 25% for attorney fees, his

total adjusted award was $1,511,052. Although tort damage amounts may sound quite high, so far as pecuniary damages go, each item must be proved. Actual costs to the victim can be quite high when you calculate future costs of medical treatment and lost wages.

9. **Punitive damages.** In a few cases, juries are permitted to award punitive damages in addition to compensatory damages. Virtually all states authorize punitive damages only when a tortfeasor has acted maliciously or willfully or wantonly in causing injury. Punitive damages are intended to provide a measure of added deterrence and punishment for the wrongdoer's serious misconduct. They are measured not by what the plaintiff has lost, but rather by what will punish the particular defendant given the seriousness of wrongdoing, among other factors. *See Qwest Servs. Corp. v. Blood*, 252 P.3d 1071 (Colo. 2011) (upholding punitive damages award of $18 million against utility company found by the jury to have acted willfully and wantonly in failing to maintain a utility pole that collapsed and seriously injured a lineman). Punitive damages are explored in greater detail in Chapter 26.

NOTE: POPULAR CONCEPTIONS AND MISCONCEPTIONS—THE McDONALD'S CASE

You should be cautious about forming judgments about all tort law based upon anecdotes or media presentations rather than an understanding of the whole tort system. One case that grabbed media attention and continues to generate criticism involved a large judgment for a woman who was burned by scalding coffee she got at a McDonald's drive-through. Sitting in the car, she held the container between her legs to take the top off and the coffee spilled. It was hot enough to inflict third degree burns—which covered her groin and genital area. Third degree burns can burn entirely through the skin and vessels and all the way to the bone. She was hospitalized, underwent skin grafts, had excruciating pain, and was permanently disfigured. She asked McDonald's to pay her $11,000 hospital bills, but McDonald's refused. She hired an attorney who demanded $90,000 in damages, but McDonald's refused that, too. Her lawyer then filed a suit and discovered that McDonald's intentionally kept its coffee hot enough to inflict third degree burns and in fact had known of at least 700 people who had been burned by its scalding coffee. Shriner's Burn Center had published warnings to the fast food industry about the severity of the burns from coffee at this temperature. The lawyer now demanded more in compensatory damages, and sought punitive damages as well. At trial, after hearing all of the evidence, the jury awarded the plaintiff $200,000 in compensatory damages, reduced to $160,000 because it decided that she was partly at fault in causing her own injuries. The jury then added $2.7 million in punitive damages, based on a finding that McDonald's was reckless or even malicious. While this was a large sum, it represented only about two days' of McDonald's revenues from coffee sales. The judge reduced the punitive award to $480,000, leaving the plaintiff with a total damages award of $640,000.

Media and web commentators often present a different picture. They often leave out the fact that most of the award was in the form of punitive damages—meant to punish, not to compensate, that the punitive damages award was reduced as part of the ordinary mechanisms of tort law (the judge's review), and that the coffee was not merely "hot," but capable of great harm, which it in fact caused quite needlessly. You can still read comments on the web in essence saying that "an old woman" spilled coffee on herself and got something for nothing, omitting to note that the jury reduced the compensatory damages by $40,000 for the plaintiff's supposed fault in spilling the coffee, and perhaps betraying a contempt for "old women." You'll want to judge for yourself, but as professionals we should base our analyses on more facts than appear in the popular media. You can find a summary of the McDonald's case in Mark B. Greenlee, *Kramer v. Java World: Images, Issues, and Idols in the Debate over Tort Reform,* 26 CAP. U. L. REV. 701 (1997).

CHAPTER 2

READING TORTS CASES AND UNDERSTANDING TRIAL PROCEDURE

▪ ▪ ▪

§ 1. LOOKING FOR FACTS, RULES, AND REASONS

Reading cases to understand principles and predict law. This course presents real cases that involve individuals and sometimes organizations as plaintiffs, defendants, lawyers, and judges. The "cases" in this book are actually the explanations judges give for the legal decisions that they make. By carefully reading these judicial explanations, called opinions, good lawyers can learn the governing legal principles of tort law. They can also envision what other legal rules could develop from these principles. Why are these skills important? One reason is that in the United States, tort law develops through a common law system. That means a court decision in an individual case not only serves to resolve that case, but creates a rule to be followed in future cases. In order to make professional estimates about likely outcomes of a case, an attorney will need to be able to read and understand prior case law. Also, an attorney who wishes to construct a sound legal argument must be able to compare the case before her with prior legal cases and principles.

Facts. The facts of a case are likely to influence the judge in deciding on appropriate legal rules. If the case is about a four-year-old who causes harm, the judge's observations about "the liability of children" may really be observations only about the liability of very young children. The facts that influence the judge's decision may be an explicit part of the case or an implicit part of the judge's reasoning. The scope of a rule will require interpretation on your part, and it means that you must understand the facts in the case very well indeed. When you identify the important facts of a case be sure to include all facts necessary to the judge's decision and to the legal elements of the case. For example, if a cause of action requires proof of actual physical harm, the fact that the defendant's achilles tendon was injured and required surgery will be an important fact to record. You may also include facts that demonstrate the overall context of the case and facts helpful to remembering the case.

Procedural posture. Reading cases well requires attention to both the substantive legal issues raised by the parties and the legal procedures through which those issues are raised. The legal procedure that triggered

[handwritten margin note: law students learn through reading appellate opinions]

17

the court's ruling is important to understanding the substantive legal rule of the case—did the lower court dismiss the plaintiff's complaint before any evidence had been gathered, grant summary judgment for the defendant after reviewing all the material facts, or reverse a judgment against the defendant after a full trial and verdict? The allocation of decision-making power between judge and jury is a major process element in many tort cases. Suppose: (1) The defendant files a motion saying the judge should dismiss the plaintiff's claim without letting a jury decide it, but the judge denies the motion and lets the jury decide. (2) The jury decides for the defendant. (3) The judge upholds the jury's verdict. Process values explain this sequence. In item (1), by refusing to dismiss the case the judge is not saying that the plaintiff should win. The judge is saying instead that the decision on the particular issue in light of the facts stated should be made by the jury, not by the judge. So the jury's verdict either way will be upheld on those particular facts. In other cases, judges will take the case away from the jury, allocating power to themselves instead of the jury. The appropriate role of judge and jury is often a basic concern in applying legal rules. Typically, judges decide issues of law and juries resolve issues of fact. A reader of cases must pay attention to which procedure triggers the appeal. One example of a statement about the procedure of a case might be "summary judgment granted by the trial court and upheld by the appellate court."

Issues. The substantive issue raised by the litigants as shaped by the court will also affect the holding. It is helpful to recognize both the procedural issue—"should the trial court's motion for summary judgment be upheld?"—and the substantive question presented to the court—"is intent to harm required to show a battery?" Often the substantive issue will be the primary focus of analysis in classes other than procedure.

Holding. The holding of the court is the court's response to the issues raised by the parties. The procedural form of the holding might be as simple as "reversed." However, a fuller statement of the holding might also include the rule of law the court stated in response to the substantive issue raised in the case. For example, a statement of a holding that includes both the procedural holding and the rule of the case might be "Reversed, for the defendant; a battery cannot be proved without proof that the defendant intended harm or offense." The rules of law established by the court concerning the substantive issues, sometimes referred to as "the rules of a case," are helpful because they may be used to resolve similar cases later on. Sometimes a judge clearly earmarks a rule. More often, you must interpret what you read.

Reasoning. The rules in most judicial decisions are interpreted in part by following the judge's reasoning. Ideally, the judge's reasoning explains why the rule exists (or why the judge is creating the rule) and how it applies to the case. The judge's reasoning may include analogies to other cases or legal doctrines, reference to persuasive authorities like the Restatement or prominent treatises, and discussion of fairness or policy concerns. What the judge emphasizes in reasoning about the rule tells you a great deal about what the rule is and what its limits might be. Be sure to note the reasoning of arguments made in concurring and dissenting opinions as well as the majority's explanation.

Application of rules. Often, in the common law, attorneys are asked to apply the rule and reasoning of a decided case to a new factual situation or hypothetical. Although rules found in yesterday's cases will help resolve today's disputes, they usually will not do so simply or directly. You will find you must reason about how the rule is to be applied in other fact scenarios, including your client's situation.

Evaluation. After you read the case, take time to think about how the case you read relates to other cases you have examined. What does the case add? Why is it significant? Is the rule of the case just? Does it promote useful policy aims? Is the reasoning sound? Are there alternative solutions that would be preferable in terms of principle and policy? Does the rule of the case work effectively with other rules you have studied? This is your chance to reflect on connections between cases and the wisdom of rules as a whole.

Rules point lawyers to evidence required and arguments available. Frequently, the rules in yesterday's cases do not actually resolve today's disputes at all. Instead, their most important function is to point to evidence that lawyers will need to gather for a trial and to arguments lawyers will need to construct in presenting a claim or in defending it.

§ 2. PROCEDURES AT TRIAL

Facts are determined by a trial court)

Since a judge's decision about tort law will come within a particular procedural context, it is necessary to have a basic understanding of trial procedure.

Trial procedure can be complicated, but the basic plan of a trial is very simple. It is designed to resolve two kinds of disputes. The first kind of dispute is about the facts, about what happened. Almost all trials involve at least some factual dispute. The second kind of dispute is about the law. Most trials also involve disputes about what the legal rules are, or how they should apply to the particular case.

Below you will find a list of trial procedures. Although we've listed these procedures in the order in which they typically arise in a trial, some of the procedures—the ones marked with an asterisk—are the main procedural devices that raise the legal issues that appear in the tort cases in this book. The procedures that most frequently raise legal issues reflect the judge's role as a gatekeeper who screens out whole cases, preventing the evidence or the case from being considered by the jury. One of the first questions lawyers are likely to ask when they evaluate a new case is: Can this case get to the jury?—meaning, will the judge screen the case out or will the jury be permitted to make the ultimate decision in the case?

For our discussion here, it may be helpful to imagine a very simple kind of case in which the plaintiff contends that the defendant struck him. Defendant denies this completely. How does this get to court and what happens there?

Complaint. Plaintiff's lawyer, having investigated the applicable law and facts, writes up a document called a complaint or petition. This document states the facts as claimed by the client. This document is formally filed with the court (in the court clerk's office) and a copy is served on (delivered to) the defendant, sometimes by an officer of the court such as the sheriff or the federal marshal. In most courts today, electronic filing is available and may be mandatory.

*The Motion to Dismiss or Demurrer. If the defendant believes that the plaintiff's complaint does not state facts that show a good legal claim, the appropriate response is to file a motion to dismiss the complaint for failure to state a claim upon which relief can be granted. This is a Rule 12(b)(6) motion under the Federal Rules of Civil Procedure. The effect of this motion is to say to the judge, "Take all the facts stated in the complaint as if they were proved; even so, they do not show a valid legal claim."

Since the facts alleged are temporarily assumed to be true for purpose of considering this motion, there is no factual dispute. The issue raised is one of law, for the judge to decide, not the jury. Suppose plaintiff's lawyer wrote up, filed and served a complaint stating not that the defendant struck the plaintiff, but instead that the defendant frowned at the plaintiff. Frowning is not a tort, so defendant's motion to dismiss would be sustained.

Notice that the motion to dismiss comes at a very early stage of the case—it comes before any time has been invested in developing proof or calling a jury.

Answer. If the defendant has not moved to dismiss the complaint, or if the defendant's motion to dismiss is denied, the defendant must file a document taking a position on the complaint. Very often it is an "answer." An answer usually disputes some of the factual claims of the plaintiff. For example, if plaintiff's complaint states "Defendant struck the plaintiff in the face," the defendant might answer saying she denies that she struck the plaintiff. This reveals what facts are in dispute between the parties. Because the dispute is about the facts, the parties will gather evidence for presentation to a jury.

Discovery. Discovery is the portion of the case in which both parties gather information about the underlying claims. For example, the defendant might depose the plaintiff in order to obtain new information or reveal inaccuracies. Did the plaintiff seek medical treatment after the event? What did the plaintiff tell the doctor at the time? Discovery is not limited to gathering information from the parties. The parties may also seek information from others who know about the event. For example, if other people were in the room at the time that the defendant allegedly struck the plaintiff, the parties might interview those witnesses (sometimes under oath) and ask what they saw. The parties can investigate facts through written requests for documents as well as oral interviews. For example, either party could ask for written records of the plaintiff's doctor visit.

The Motion for Summary Judgment. The motion to dismiss assumes all the facts stated in the complaint are true and argues that, even so, the complaint fails to show a good legal claim. On the other hand, the summary judgment motion, which occurs after the parties have gathered facts during the process of discovery, is based on a developed set of facts. If the moving party, almost always the defendant, shows that (1) there is no real dispute about important facts and (2) on the undisputed facts, the law compels judgment for the defendant, summary judgment will be granted.

Suppose the parties go through discovery and the plaintiff states, "he hit me," while the defendant states, "I did not." The defendant cannot get summary judgment because the truth of the fact he asserted is important to the controversy and is directly disputed by the plaintiff. It will be for the jury to decide which party is speaking truthfully. Even if one party has more witnesses than another, the dispute of fact is still for the jury to resolve.

Pretrial briefs and motions in limine. After a case is set for trial, the parties may want the judge to decide beforehand whether to include or exclude certain types of evidence and whether particular legal rules will apply. The parties may file motions or briefs asking the judge to shape the trial in a particular way. For example, in a motion in limine the defendant might ask the trial judge to keep out evidence that the defendant struck another person five years earlier on the ground that evidence of the earlier incident might prejudice the jury against the defendant.

Selection of a jury. When the case comes up for trial, prospective jurors are questioned by the judge and perhaps by the lawyers to determine whether they are biased about issues in the case or about one of the parties. Lawyers may "strike" or eliminate some prospects. Of those who remain, 12 (or sometimes six or eight) are then "put in the box" as jurors for the particular case.

Opening statements. At this point the judge will ask the plaintiff's lawyer to state the case for the plaintiff. This is not an argument but a preliminary view of the testimony the plaintiff will put on. Then the defendant's lawyer will make a similar opening statement.

Plaintiff's case. Next the plaintiff's attorney calls the first witness. By asking questions, the lawyer elicits answers that establish what the witness knows about the facts relevant to the case. After the witness is questioned by the plaintiff's lawyer, the defendant's lawyer has an opportunity to cross-examine the witness, by asking questions that may put the matters in a different light, or may give them a different emphasis, or may show that the witness was mistaken, lying, or biased. The two examinations of the witness thus can give the jury a basis for judging how much the witness really knew and how credible the witness might be. This process continues as the plaintiff's attorney calls each of the plaintiff's witnesses in turn.

*The Motion for Directed Verdict. Defendants usually move for a directed verdict (referred to as a motion for judgment as a matter of law in federal courts) at the end of the plaintiff's evidence and again when the defendant's evidence is completed. Such motions assert that the proof offered by the plaintiff is legally insufficient to warrant a jury's verdict for the plaintiff. More rarely, a plaintiff might move for directed verdict, but such a motion is seldom granted in view of the plaintiff's burden of proof.

The judge considers the evidence in the light most favorable to the plaintiff. That is, the judge takes into account all the reasonable inferences the jury would be allowed to draw from the testimony. Considering all the evidence in this light, the judge will grant the motion for a directed verdict if a jury of reasonable persons could not differ on the evidence, or if the facts taken in this favorable light do not establish any legal claims. A directed verdict should be denied if there is room for reasonable jurors to disagree. This almost always involves some interaction of fact and law—do the facts, taken in a light favorable to the plaintiff, establish the elements required by law?

A motion for directed verdict is somewhat similar to a summary judgment motion, with a similar standard, but it is based on the *evidence produced in full at the trial.*

Defendant's case. When all of the plaintiff's witnesses have been examined and cross-examined, the defendant puts on witnesses who give the defense side of the story. After each witness is examined by the defense counsel, the plaintiff's counsel cross-examines.

*Objections to Evidence and Offers of Evidence. Not only before the trial, but also during the trial, the parties can object to evidence that is presented. Evidence that is not relevant to help prove any element involved in the case should be excluded by the judge, especially if the evidence is likely to mislead the jury or to be "prejudicial." A trial judge's admission of

evidence over objection, or her refusal to admit evidence because of objection, raises legal issues.

Closing arguments. Plaintiff's lawyer, then defendant's lawyer, then plaintiff's lawyer in rebuttal, will make closing arguments to the jury. These are arguments, not statements of fact. They are aimed at persuading the jury, on the basis of the testimony, that one side or the other should be believed.

*Proposed Jury Instructions and Objections to Them. Instructions are the trial judge's statements of law to the jury. They tell the jury what it must consider and what facts must be found to exist before the plaintiff can recover, or before a defense applies. Instructions must accurately state the law. Lawyers must actively object to instructions they feel are incorrect statements of law, or propose instructions of their own. Once the judge listens to each party's suggested instructions and decides which are appropriate, the judge instructs or "charges" the jury. Thus, a judge might instruct the jury that if it finds that the defendant intentionally struck the plaintiff with intent to harm, it should bring in a verdict for the plaintiff. Notice that this leaves the fact-finding to the jury and the legal rules to the judge. Since an instruction is supposed to represent a correct statement of the law, and one on which the jury will act, an erroneous statement of the law would be ground for appeal.

Jury verdict. After receiving instructions from the judge, the jury members talk with each other and consider whether the evidence presented in the trial meets or does not meet the legal rules articulated by the judge. The jury reaches a verdict on the plaintiff's claim, and when applicable decides on an appropriate remedy. For example, if the jury finds that the defendant struck the plaintiff in a way that provides the plaintiff with a recognizable claim against the defendant, the jury might also award the plaintiff a sum of money it deems fair compensation.

*The Motion J.N.O.V.—A Renewed Motion for Judgment as a Matter of Law. The post-trial motion for judgment notwithstanding the verdict (also referred to as a renewed motion for judgment as a matter of law in federal courts) is a virtual renewal of the motion for directed verdict. (N.O.V. is for the Latin *non obstante veredicto*, meaning notwithstanding the verdict.) The motion asserts that the evidence is not legally sufficient to justify a jury verdict for the plaintiff. A judge who is unwilling to grant a directed verdict before the jury reaches its decision may grant a J.N.O.V. after the verdict is reported. There may be several reasons for this. For example, the judge may firmly believe the jury will find for the defendant even without a directed verdict. Another possibility is that the judge wants to have a jury verdict in case that can simply be reinstated if the appellate court reverses on appeal.

The legal issue presented by the J.N.O.V. motion is the legal sufficiency of the evidence. It should be decided according to the same standard that governs the directed verdict motion: that no reasonable jury could have arrived at the verdict.

The Motion for New Trial. The parties are entitled not only to a trial but to one that is carried out without any serious legal error. Either attorney may therefore file a motion for a new trial due to error(s) made in the first one. If the judge agrees that an error was made and that there is a strong possibility the error prejudiced the jury, a new trial should be granted.

A second kind of new trial motion is unique. This asks the judge to grant a new trial, not because of error, but because the verdict is against the weight of the evidence or because the damages award was unconscionably high (or possibly unconscionably low). These motions really ask the judge to use something like discretion. The judge cannot substitute herself for the jury and make the ultimate decision in the case merely because she differs from the jury about what is right. Still, the judge does have considerable power to grant a *new trial*. If a new trial is granted, a new jury will hear the evidence. Judges do not often grant such motions, although they do sometimes grant a remittitur when they view damages as excessive, conditioning the denial of the new trial motion on plaintiff's consent to receive a lower amount of damages than granted by the jury.

Appeals. When a case has been resolved by a judge or jury, a party may ask a higher court to review the determination. Typically, state court systems have two levels of courts of appeal—intermediate appellate courts and a state supreme court. If an intermediate appellate court affirms the trial court's ruling, the non-prevailing party can accept the appellate court ruling or appeal further to the state supreme court. The tort issue can be appealed further to the United States Supreme Court. It is unusual for tort cases to be resolved by the United States Supreme Court because tort law is generally state law for which state courts are considered the final arbiter.

When an appellate court reverses a lower court's decision, the case typically returns to the place it left off in the trial process. For example, if the trial court dismisses the plaintiff's complaint and the court of appeals reverses the dismissal, the plaintiff will not necessarily prevail in the case. Instead, the case will be returned to the lower court and the defendant will have to answer the complaint, after which the discovery process will begin, and so forth.

REFERENCES: THOMAS A. MAUET & DAVID MARCUS, PRETRIAL (9th ed. 2015); STEVEN H. GOLDBERG & TRACY WALTERS MCCORMACK, THE FIRST TRIAL (WHERE DO I SIT? WHAT DO I SAY?) IN A NUTSHELL (2d ed. 2009).

PART 2

INTENTIONAL TORTS

■ ■ ■

CHAPTER 3

INTENTIONAL TORTS TO
PERSON OR PROPERTY

■ ■ ■

Every type of tort claim has its own *elements*, or particular points that a plaintiff must prove in order to succeed on that claim. A plaintiff must first allege facts comprising these required elements—in other words, a "prima facie case," or a case good "on the face of it." If the plaintiff does not, the judge will dismiss the complaint. But making allegations is not enough to win. The plaintiff must then go on to *prove* the prima facie case of some particular tort. The plaintiff bears the burden of proof on each element, meaning if the plaintiff fails to prove a prima facie case, the defendant will win even without putting on a defense. In this chapter we will explore the required elements of a number of intentional tort claims. In the next chapter we will see a number of defenses that may allow the defendant to escape liability even where a prima facie case has been proved.

There are many types of tort claims. Conceptually, one way to organize these claims is to group them along two dimensions—the interests they protect, and the levels of culpability they require. In terms of interests, tort actions can protect against (1) physical injury to person or property; (2) dignitary and emotional harm; and (3) economic harm. With respect to culpability, tort rules may impose liability for intentional wrongdoing (intent or malice), negligence (lack of reasonable care), and even when the defendant is guilty of no fault (strict liability). Our exploration of tort claims begins with causes of action that protect against intentional physical injuries.

§ 1. BATTERY

A. ELEMENTS

SNYDER V. TURK

627 N.E.2d 1053 (Ohio Ct. App. 1993)

RICHARD K. WILSON, JUDGE. . . .

[Defendant was a surgeon performing a gall-bladder operation. The procedure did not go well. Evidence would permit these findings: The defendant became frustrated with the operation itself and with the plaintiff, a scrub nurse in the operating room. Defendant's perception was that the plaintiff was making mistakes and complicating an already difficult procedure. The defendant finally became so exasperated when the plaintiff handed him an instrument he considered inappropriate that he grabbed her shoulder and pulled her face down toward the surgical opening, saying, "Can't you see where I'm working? I'm working in a hole. I need long instruments." The nurse sued for battery but the trial court granted a directed verdict for the surgeon.]

The parties agree that a "battery" is defined as an intentional, unconsented-to contact with another. The appellee contends that there is no liability for the commission of a battery absent proof of an intent to inflict personal injury. Dr. Turk further contends that the directed verdict was properly granted on the battery liability issue because of the absence of evidence that he intended to inflict personal injury. . . .

A person is subject to liability for battery when he acts intending to cause a harmful or offensive contact, and when a harmful [or offensive] contact results. Contact which is offensive to a reasonable sense of personal dignity is offensive contact. . . .

A motion for a directed verdict assumes the truth of the evidence supporting the facts essential to the claim after giving the nonmovant the benefit of all reasonable inferences from the evidence and refers the application of a reasonable-minds test to such evidence. It is in the nature of a demurrer to the evidence.

Applying the above test we believe that reasonable minds could conclude that Dr. Turk intended to commit an offensive contact. The first assignment of error is sustained.

(handwritten margin notes: alleged battery by; Nurse sued for battery but trial court granted a directed verdict for surgeon; rule of law (courts reasoning); impact facts; (D) Surgeon argues; Rule; ← element used in favor of P; Courts judgment; (woman) (male nurse))

COHEN V. SMITH
648 N.E.2d 329 (Ill. App. Ct. 1995)

JUSTICE CHAPMAN delivered the opinion of the court:

Patricia Cohen was admitted to St. Joseph Memorial Hospital ("Hospital") to deliver her baby. After an examination, Cohen was informed that it would be necessary for her to have a cesarean section. Cohen and her husband allegedly informed her physician, who in turn advised the Hospital staff, that the couple's religious beliefs prohibited Cohen from being seen unclothed by a male. Cohen's doctor assured her husband that their religious convictions would be respected.

During Cohen's cesarean section, Roger Smith, a male nurse on staff at the Hospital, allegedly observed and touched Cohen's naked body. Cohen and her husband filed suit against Nurse Smith and the Hospital. The trial court allowed defendants' motions to dismiss. We reverse.

(handwritten bottom note: Cohen (P) sues Smith (D) for observing + touching C's naked body → TC grants D's motion to dismiss → P appeals)

In reviewing a motion to dismiss for failure to state a cause of action, the court must view all well-pleaded facts in the light most favorable to the plaintiff. A trial court may dismiss a cause of action for failing to state a cause of action, based solely on the pleadings, only if it is clearly apparent that no set of alleged facts can be proven which will entitle a plaintiff to recovery. . . .

The Restatement (Second) of Torts provides that an actor commits a battery if: "(a) he acts intending to cause a harmful or offensive contact with the person of the other or a third person, or an imminent apprehension of such a contact, and (b) a harmful [or offensive][1] contact with the person of the other directly or indirectly results." (Restatement (Second) of Torts, § 13 (1965).) Liability for battery emphasizes the plaintiff's lack of consent to the touching. "Offensive contact" is said to occur when the contact "offends a reasonable sense of personal dignity."

Historically, battery was first and foremost a systematic substitution for private retribution. (W. Prosser & Keeton, Torts § 9, at 41 (5th ed. 1984) (Prosser).) Protecting personal integrity has always been viewed as an important basis for battery. "Consequently, the defendant is liable not only for contacts which do actual physical harm, but also for those relatively trivial ones which are merely offensive and insulting." This application of battery to remedy offensive and insulting conduct is deeply ingrained in our legal history. As early as 1784, a Pennsylvania defendant was prosecuted for striking the cane of a French ambassador. The court furthered the distinction between harmful offensive batteries and nonharmful offensive batteries. "As to the assault, this is, perhaps, one of that kind, in which the insult is more to be considered than the actual damage; for, though no great bodily pain is suffered by a blow on the palm of the hand, or the skirt of the coat, yet these are clearly within the definition of assault and battery, and among gentlemen too often induce duelling and terminate in murder." (Respublica v. De Longchamps (Pa.1784), 1 Dall. 111, 1 L.Ed. 59, in Gregory, Kalven, & Epstein, Cases & Materials on Torts 904–905 (1977).). . . .

Although most people in modern society have come to accept the necessity of being seen unclothed and being touched by members of the opposite sex during medical treatment, the plaintiffs had not accepted these procedures and, according to their complaint, had informed defendants of their convictions. This case is similar to cases involving Jehovah's Witnesses who were unwilling to accept blood transfusions because of religious convictions. Although most people do not share the Jehovah's Witnesses' beliefs about blood transfusions, our society, and our courts, accept their right to have that belief. Similarly, the courts have consistently recognized individuals' rights to refuse medical treatment

---

[1] The editors of this casebook inserted the bracketed words, which appear in Restatement § 18.—Eds.

even if such a refusal would result in an increased likelihood of the individual's death.

A person's right to refuse or accept medical care is not one to be interfered with lightly. . . . Accepting as true the plaintiffs' allegations that they informed defendants of their religious beliefs and that defendants persisted in treating Patricia Cohen as they would have treated a patient without those beliefs, we conclude that the trial court erred in dismissing both the battery and the intentional infliction of emotional distress counts.

Judgmt

NOTES

1.   **Elements.** What are the elements of a cause of action for battery? What sources would you look to in order to find these elements?

2.   **Lack of intent to harm.** Perhaps the paradigm of battery is an intentional punch in the nose. The defendant in *Snyder* argued that he lacked an intent to harm the plaintiff physically, yet the court held against him. Looking closely at the required elements of battery, why isn't this a winning argument?

3.   **Plaintiff not physically harmed.** Under the Restatement rule quoted in *Cohen,* can a plaintiff state a claim for battery even without showing physical harm? If the plaintiff did not suffer physical harm, what must the plaintiff prove? *That he was offensive contact*

4.   **Testing the rules.** How should the following cases be resolved?

    a.   The plaintiff's employer was engaged in teasing and horseplay with an automobile condenser that had been electrically charged, giving employees a mild shock. He shocked the plaintiff, who was trying to avoid it. The plaintiff, quite unexpectedly, developed a serious nerve problem that required surgery. *Caudle v. Betts,* 512 So. 2d 389 (La. 1987).   *intent, offensive contact*

    b.   Plaintiffs' employer refused to allow plaintiffs to bring their own meals to work or let them leave the workplace for meals. Plaintiffs let the employer know that because of religious reasons they could not eat beef-pork meatballs. The employer said it would switch to turkey meatballs, which it did, but it then switched back to beef-pork without letting the employees know. *Kumar v. Gate Gourmet, Inc.,* 325 P.3d 193 (Wash. 2014). *See also* RESTATEMENT (THIRD) OF TORTS: INTENTIONAL TORTS TO PERSONS § 103 illus. 6 (Tentative Draft No. 1, 2015).

5.   **Bodily contact.** Neither harm nor offense would be sufficient for a claim in the absence of bodily contact. There is often no dispute in a case whether contact occurred between the plaintiff and the defendant; think again of the punch in the nose example. But does "contact" mean that the defendant's body directly touches the plaintiff's body? Imagine a defendant who fires a bullet into the plaintiff's body and seeks to escape liability for battery on the

ground that there was no touching. Reasoning from the purposes of battery law, would courts accept the defendant's argument? Now consider a defendant who shakes the limb of a tree on which the plaintiff is sitting, but does not touch the plaintiff. A classic case on this point is *Fisher v. Carrousel Motor Hotel, Inc.*, 424 S.W.2d 627 (Tex. 1967). The plaintiff, Fisher, was a mathematician attending a meeting on telemetry equipment. He and the others at the meeting adjourned for lunch in the defendant's hotel. As the plaintiff was about to be served, he was approached by the manager, who "snatched the plate from Fisher's hand and shouted that he, a Negro, could not be served in the club." The court said: "[T]he intentional grabbing of plaintiff's plate constituted a battery. The intentional snatching of an object from one's hand is as clearly an offensive invasion of his person as would be an actual contact with the body." *See also Reynolds v. MacFarlane*, 322 P.3d 755 (Utah 2015).

6. **What counts as contact?** Would it be "contact" if a talk-show host blew cigar smoke in the face of an anti-smoking advocate in order to humiliate him? *See Leichtman v. WLW Jacor Communications Inc.*, 634 N.E.2d 697 (Ohio 1994) (yes—tobacco smoke, as particulate matter, has the physical properties capable of making contact). What about being touched by light or sound waves? Your noisy neighbor bombards you with loud music every night—battery?

7. **The new tort of purposeful infliction.** Should liability for an intentional tort turn on physical contact? Battery liability has always depended upon this. However, the Restatement Third of Torts recently adopted a new tort of "purposeful infliction of bodily harm." The tort is established if: "(a) the actor purposely causes bodily harm to the other, either by the actor's affirmative conduct or by the actor's failure to prevent bodily harm when the actor has a duty to prevent such harm; and (b) the other does not effectively consent to the otherwise tortious conduct of the actor." What if a neighbor visits elderly E's house and as E has a heart attack and reaches for the phone to call emergency assistance, the neighbor deliberately moves the phone out of E's reach? Would the new tort apply then? What if a defendant does something that is not wrongful in itself—for example, moves a chair from the office of an employee with a bad back—but does it hoping to cause the employee back pain? Should this otherwise legitimate conduct become actionable because of the defendant's bad intent? Is there any problem with conditioning suit on wrongful intent in the absence of objectively wrongful action?

8. **Procedure: directed verdict in *Snyder*.** The defendant in *Snyder* persuaded the trial court to grant a directed verdict in his favor. The court of appeals reversed. Does that mean the plaintiff won the case?

9. **Procedure: motion to dismiss in *Cohen*.** The plaintiff in *Cohen* prevailed in overturning the trial court's dismissal. What if, on remand, the plaintiff cannot produce evidence that Nurse Smith knew of Patricia Cohen's wishes? *See Mullins v. Parkview Hospital, Inc.*, 865 N.E.2d 608 (Ind. 2007) (medical technician student intubated the plaintiff and caused harm but did not know plaintiff refused consent to have students participate in her care).

NOTE: DAMAGES FOR BATTERY

1. *No need for physical harm.* What damages may be recovered by a plaintiff who prevails on a battery claim? Battery is one of the so-called "trespassory torts," that group of torts (also including assault, false imprisonment, and some property torts) that are accomplished by the use of some physical force and are regarded as harmful in and of themselves. These torts "are actionable even if the plaintiff has no proven physical harm." 1 DOBBS, HAYDEN & BUBLICK, THE LAW OF TORTS § 28 (2d ed. 2011). Sometimes it is said that with these trespassory torts, damages are "presumed" to flow from the tort itself. Does the history of the tort of battery, as recited above in *Cohen*, help explain why this is the rule?

2. *Nominal damages.* A plaintiff who suffers only trivial harm or offense may still be entitled to some money. In *Leichtman*, cited above in Note 7, the court wrote, "No matter how trivial the incident, a battery is actionable, even if damages are only one dollar."

3. *Economic damages.* If the intentional contact causes damages such as medical expenses or lost wages or earning capacity, those damages are readily recoverable upon proper proof. *See Hough v. McKiernan*, 101 A.3d 853 (R.I. 2014) (evidence presented at trial justified $925,000 for battery victim who suffered a swollen skull, a piece of which had to be removed and stored in his abdomen for three months before being put back in place, and who had to relearn how to walk and talk).

4. *Pain and suffering and emotional distress damages.* When emotional distress results from a trespassory tort like battery, damages for the distress are readily recoverable whether or not the plaintiff has suffered physical harm. How are such damages measured? As one court said, the plaintiff who proves assault or battery can recover "compensatory damages for bodily pain, humiliation, mental anguish and other injuries that occur as a necessary and natural consequence of the tortious conduct. There is no fixed measure or standard available to the trier of fact in determining the measure of damages for pain and suffering. The measure of damages is simply that which is fair and reasonable." *A.R.B. v. Elkin*, 98 S.W.3d 99 (Mo. Ct. App. 2003). A battery that is offensive but not physically harmful, then, can give rise to a substantial damages award. *See, e.g., Whitten v. Cox*, 799 So. 2d 1 (Miss. 2000) (affirming compensatory damage awards of $50,000 for one plaintiff and $30,000 for another when the defendant menaced them with a gun and threatened to throw one of them into a river while handcuffed).

5. *Punitive damages.* In addition to compensatory damages, courts may allow punitive damages against an intentional tortfeasor who is guilty

trial court dismissed action and plaintiff appealed

pages 33-41

of "malice" or wanton misconduct. *See Carpentier v. Tuthill*, 86 A.3d 1006 (Vt. 2013).

B. TAKING A CLOSER LOOK AT "INTENT"

GARRATT V. DAILEY

279 P.2d 1091 (Wash. 1955)

HILL, JUSTICE. . . .

Brian Dailey (age five years, nine months) was visiting with Naomi Garratt, an adult and a sister of the plaintiff, Ruth Garratt, likewise an adult, in the back yard of the plaintiff's home, on July 16, 1951. It is plaintiff's contention that she came out into the back yard to talk with Naomi and that, as she started to sit down in a wood and canvas lawn chair, Brian deliberately pulled it out from under her. The only one of the three persons present so testifying was Naomi Garratt. (Ruth Garratt, the plaintiff, did not testify as to how or why she fell.)

The trial court, unwilling to accept this testimony, adopted instead Brian Dailey's version of what happened, [concluding that Brian moved the chair without the purpose to affect the plaintiff, but rather to sit in it himself, and that when he saw the plaintiff about to sit where the chair had been, he tried unsuccessfully to move it back. Consequently, he had no purpose to cause contact.] *(Trial court's reasoning)*

It is conceded that Ruth Garratt's fall resulted in a fractured hip and other painful and serious injuries. To obviate the necessity of a retrial in the event this court determines that she was entitled to a judgment against Brian Dailey, the amount of her damage was found to be $11,000. Plaintiff appeals from a judgment dismissing the action and asks for the entry of a judgment in that amount or a new trial.

The authorities generally, but with certain notable exceptions, state that when a minor has committed a tort with force he is liable to be proceeded against as any other person would be.

In our analysis of the applicable law, we start with the basic premise that Brian, whether five or fifty-five, must have committed some wrongful act before he could be liable for appellant's injuries. . . .

It is urged that Brian's action in moving the chair constituted a battery. . . . A battery would be established if, in addition to plaintiff's fall, it was proved that, when Brian moved the chair, he knew with substantial certainty that the plaintiff would attempt to sit down where the chair had been. If Brian had any of the intents which the trial court found, in the italicized portions of the findings of fact quoted above, that he did not have, he would of course have had the knowledge to which we have referred. The mere absence of any intent to injure the plaintiff or to play a prank on her

---

Handwritten margin notes:

- (P)
- Trial court believe Dailey's version & testimony and ruled in Dailey's favor. Therefore dismissed action and P appealed
- Trial court didn't except P testimony that Brian deliberately pulled the chair from under her
- (P) Ruth Garratt injuries
- authorities state
- §[court] explain that Brian's action in moving the chair would a constitute battery if
- Issue - Whether B's moving of the chair be liable for battery

or to embarrass her, or to commit an assault and battery on her would not absolve him from liability if in fact he had such knowledge.

Without such knowledge, there would be nothing wrongful about Brian's act in moving the chair and, there being no wrongful act, there would be no liability.

While a finding that Brian had no such knowledge can be inferred from the findings made, we believe that before the plaintiff's action in such a case should be dismissed there should be no question but that the trial court had passed upon that issue; hence, the case should be remanded for clarifications of the findings to specifically cover the question of Brian's knowledge, because intent could be inferred therefrom. If the court finds that he had such knowledge the necessary intent will be established and the plaintiff will be entitled to recover, even though there was no purpose to injure or embarrass the plaintiff. If Brian did not have such knowledge, there was no wrongful act by him and the basic premise of liability on the theory of a battery was not established.

It will be noted that the law of battery as we have discussed it is the law applicable to adults, and no significance has been attached to the fact that Brian was a child less than six years of age when the alleged battery occurred. The only circumstance where Brian's age is of any consequence is in determining what he knew, and there his experience, capacity, and understanding are of course material. . . .

The cause is remanded for clarification, with instructions to make definite findings on the issue of whether Brian Dailey knew with substantial certainty that the plaintiff would attempt to sit down where the chair which he moved had been, and to change the judgment if the findings warrant it. . . .

NOTES

1. **Subsequent history of the case.** On remand, the trial court found that the plaintiff was in the act of sitting down when Brian moved the chair, and that Brian knew this. On the basis of the substantial certainty test, the judge found for the plaintiff. This was affirmed on the second appeal, *Garratt v. Dailey*, 304 P.2d 681 (Wash. 1956).

2. **Defining intent.** What is the definition of intent accepted by the *Garratt* court? Imagine that defendant hates the plaintiff, sees him at a distance and hurls a stone, hoping to hit the plaintiff but believing that success is extremely unlikely. The stone does in fact hit the plaintiff, however. Is this a battery? Is the intent involved the same intent on which Brian Dailey was held liable? The Restatement Third of Torts defines intent to produce a consequence as either a "purpose of producing that consequence" or "knowing that the consequence is substantially certain to result." RESTATEMENT (THIRD) OF TORTS: LIABILITY FOR PHYSICAL AND EMOTIONAL HARM § 1 (2010).

3. **Distinguishing intent from negligence.** Legal fault usually takes the form of intent or the form of negligence. Negligence is a large subject, to be considered beginning in Chapter 5. In general, negligence is conduct that creates an unreasonable risk of harm. Driving too fast would be an example.

4. **Reckless, willful and wanton conduct.** Between intent and negligence, courts sometimes identify another level of fault—willful and wanton, or reckless conduct. The Restatement Third counsels that: "[w]hen a person's conduct creates a known risk that can be reduced by relatively modest precautions," that conduct should be considered reckless rather than simply negligent. RESTATEMENT (THIRD) OF TORTS: LIABILITY FOR PHYSICAL AND EMOTIONAL HARM § 2 cmt. a (2010); *see also Doe v. Hartford Roman Catholic Diocesan Corp.*, 119 A.3d 462 (Conn. 2015) ("[r]ecklessness requires a conscious choice of a course of action either with knowledge of the serious danger to others involved in it or with knowledge of facts which would disclose this danger to any reasonable man, and the actor must recognize that his conduct involves a risk substantially greater . . . than that which is necessary to make his conduct negligent"). While line-drawing can be difficult, courts sometimes must distinguish recklessness or wanton misconduct from intent or negligence for certain rules of damages or different statutes of limitation.

5. **Levels of intent.** Can you distinguish between *Garratt v. Dailey* intent on the one hand and negligence or recklessness on the other? Test it out: Defendant became highly intoxicated and drove his car on the wrong side of the highway, causing a head-on collision that seriously injured the plaintiff. Is that *Garratt v. Dailey* intent, recklessness or just negligence?

NOTE: CHILD LIABILITY

1. *General rule.* As recognized in *Garratt v. Dailey*, in most states children may be liable for torts they commit as long as the injured plaintiff can prove the required elements, including intent. That is, in most states a child cannot escape tort liability simply because of young age. *See, e.g., Bailey v. C.S.*, 12 S.W.3d 159 (Tex. App. 2000) (four-year old may be liable for battery, as "there is currently no specific age at which minors are immune from liability for intentional torts as a matter of law"). Does *Van Camp v. McAfoos* (Chapter 1) stand in opposition to this general rule?

2. *Young children.* In some states, however, particularly young children are "conclusively presumed to be incapable of harmful intent." Under the "rule of sevens," age seven is frequently used as the cut-off point. *See, e.g., DeLuca v. Bowden*, 329 N.E.2d 109 (Ohio 1975); *cf. Carey v. Reeve*, 781 P.2d 904 (Wash. Ct. App. 1989) (children under six cannot form the intent to harm others).

3. *Other solutions.* Will small children always be liable in states that do not grant blanket immunity to children under a particular age? Notice

that the child's age would be relevant to show either that he could not or did not form an adequate intent to touch, to offend, or to harm.

NOTE: PARENTAL LIABILITY FOR THE TORTS OF THEIR MINOR CHILDREN

Why should a person injured by the tortious action of a child not just sue the child's parents and seek damages from them? The answer is that such a lawsuit is possible only if a statute authorizes such a suit—in which case the statutory requirements for recovery must be met—or if the parents are themselves at fault in some way. That is, the common law rule is that parents are not vicariously liable for the torts of their children simply by virtue of being parents.

Statutes imposing liability on parents for their children's torts exist in virtually every state, but they are usually limited in two significant ways: First, the child's tort must have been committed willfully or wantonly. Second, the damages that may be obtained are limited. Some states cap damages at a very low amount, while others are less restrictive. *Compare* CONN. GEN. STATS. ANN. § 52–572 (capping damages at $5,000 for injury to persons or property) *with* FLA. STAT. ANN. § 741.24 (providing no cap on damages for theft and destruction of property but limiting recovery to the amount of actual damages incurred).

Plaintiffs who sue parents for the parents' own fault will often allege that the parents negligently supervised their child, and that this caused the plaintiffs' harm. Such claims are very difficult to win. Indeed, such a claim failed in *Van Camp v. McAfoos* (Chapter 1) because the plaintiffs did not prove that the parents were at fault. Why might such a claim fail?

If parents often are not legally liable for a child's torts, how can the injured plaintiff hope to see any money in a suit against a child? Often the parents' insurance policy may well cover minor children living in the household. Such a policy would pay any judgment rendered against the child.

(D)   (P)

WHITE V. MUNIZ
999 P.2d 814 (Colo. 2000)

JUSTICE KOURLIS delivered the Opinion of the Court. . . .

In October of 1993, Barbara White placed her eighty-three year-old grandmother, Helen Everly, in an assisted living facility, the Beatrice Hover Personal Care Center. Within a few days of admission, Everly started exhibiting erratic behavior. She became agitated easily, and occasionally acted aggressively toward others. [A physician concluded that

Caregiver (Muniz) sued ~~Everly~~ brought suit for
assault and battery against Defendants which include Everly
(old lady) and White (grandniece)

CH. 3
INTENTIONAL TORTS TO
PERSON OR PROPERTY
37

she had progressive dementia, loss of memory, impulse control and judgment, a degenerative dementia of the Alzheimer type.]

Facts of Case

On November 21, 1993, the caregiver in charge of Everly's wing asked Sherry Lynn Muniz, a shift supervisor at Hover, to change Everly's adult diaper. The caregiver informed Muniz that Everly was not cooperating in that effort. This did not surprise Muniz because she knew that Everly sometimes acted obstinately. Indeed, initially Everly refused to allow Muniz to change her diaper, but eventually Muniz thought that Everly relented. However, as Muniz reached toward the diaper, Everly struck Muniz on the jaw and ordered her out of the room.

[Muniz sued Everly and White as her representative for assault and battery. After the evidence was presented, the trial judge instructed the jury in part as follows.]

trial judge instructed the jury in part

The fact that a person may suffer from Dementia, Alzheimer type, does not prevent a finding that she acted intentionally. You may find that she acted intentionally if she intended to do what she did, even though her reasons and motives were entirely irrational. However, she must have appreciated the offensiveness of her conduct.

which means understanding the wrongfulness of her actions

Court of Appeals Judgment

Muniz's counsel objected to the last sentence of the instruction, claiming that it misstated the law. [The jury found for Everly and White. The Court of Appeals held the instruction to be error and reversed.]

ISSUE

The question we here address is whether an intentional tort requires some proof that the tortfeasor not only intended to contact another person, but also intended that the contact be harmful or offensive to the other person.

State courts and legal commentators generally agree that an intentional tort requires some proof that the tortfeasor intended harm or offense. See W. Page Keeton et al., Prosser and Keeton on the Law of Torts § 8 (5th ed.1984); Dan B. Dobbs, The Law of Torts § 30 (2000). According to the Restatement (Second) of Torts [§ 13],

What State courts and legal commentators generally agree

(1) An actor is subject to liability to another for battery if

    (a) he acts intending to cause a harmful or offensive contact with the person of the other or a third person, or an imminent apprehension of such a contact, and

    (b) an offensive [or harmful] contact with the person of the other directly or indirectly results. . . .

[Historically,] the actor had to understand that his contact would be harmful or offensive. See Keeton, supra, § 8; Dobbs, supra, § 29. The actor need not have intended, however, the harm that actually resulted from his action. Thus, if a slight punch to the victim resulted in traumatic injuries,

In Restatement of torts
② actor had to
understand his contact would be

Single phrase — intention
cause contact
that is harmful or
offensive

the actor would be liable for all the damages resulting from the battery even if he only intended to knock the wind out of the victim.

Juries may find it difficult to determine the mental state of an actor, but they may rely on circumstantial evidence in reaching their conclusion. No person can pinpoint the thoughts in the mind of another, but a jury can examine the facts to conclude what another must have been thinking. For example, a person of reasonable intelligence knows with substantial certainty that a stone thrown into a crowd will strike someone and result in an offensive or harmful contact to that person. Hence, if an actor of average intelligence performs such an act, the jury can determine that the actor had the requisite intent to cause a harmful or offensive contact, even though the actor denies having such thoughts.

More recently, some courts around the nation have abandoned this dual intent requirement in an intentional tort setting, that being an intent to contact and an intent that the contact be harmful or offensive, and have required only that the tortfeasor intend a contact with another that results in a harmful or offensive touching. Under this view, a victim need only prove that a voluntary movement by the tortfeasor resulted in a contact which a reasonable person would find offensive or to which the victim did not consent. These courts would find intent in contact to the back of a friend that results in a severe, unexpected injury even though the actor did not intend the contact to be harmful or offensive. The actor thus could be held liable for battery because a reasonable person would find an injury offensive or harmful, irrespective of the intent of the actor to harm or offend. . . . .

Because Colorado law requires a dual intent, we apply here the Restatement's definition of the term. As a result, we reject the arguments of Muniz and find that the trial court delivered an adequate instruction to the jury.

Operating in accordance with this instruction, the jury had to find that Everly appreciated the offensiveness of her conduct in order to be liable for the intentional tort of battery. It necessarily had to consider her mental capabilities in making such a finding, including her age, infirmity, education, skill, or any other characteristic as to which the jury had evidence. We presume that the jury "looked into the mind of Everly," and reasoned that Everly did not possess the necessary intent to commit an assault or a battery.

A jury can, of course, find a mentally deficient person liable for an intentional tort, but in order to do so, the jury must find that the actor intended offensive or harmful consequences. As a result, insanity is not a defense to an intentional tort according to the ordinary use of that term, but is a characteristic, like infancy, that may make it more difficult to prove the intent element of battery. Our decision today does not create a special rule for the elderly, but applies Colorado's intent requirement in the context of a woman suffering the effects of Alzheimer's. . . .

[Jury verdict reinstated.]

––––––––––––

WAGNER V. STATE, 122 P.3d 599 (Utah 2005). While waiting in a department store customer-service line, plaintiff Tracy Wagner was suddenly attacked from behind by Sam Geise, a mentally disabled patient who was brought to the store and accompanied by State employees as a part of a state mental health treatment program. Wagner sued the State for failing to supervise Geise. By statute, the State could not be liable for the patient's conduct if that conduct "arose out of battery." In her suit against the state, plaintiff asserted that Geise's conduct was *not* a battery. The trial court disagreed and dismissed plaintiff's Complaint, and the court of appeals affirmed. The Wagners argue that Mr. Giese's attack could not legally constitute a battery because battery requires the actor to intend harm or offense through his deliberate contact, an intent Mr. Giese was mentally incompetent to form. The State, on the other hand, argues that the only intent required for battery is simply an intent to make a contact. *Held*, affirmed.

"Utah has adopted the Second Restatement of Torts to define the elements of [battery], including the element of intent. . . . [We] agree with the State that only intent to make contact is necessary. . . . We hold that the actor need not intend that his contact be harmful or offensive in order to commit a battery so long as he deliberately made the contact and so long as that contact satisfies our legal test for what is harmful or offensive. . . . [A dual intent rule is practically unworkable.] For example, a man who decides to flatter a woman he spots in a crowd with an unpetitioned-for kiss, one of the examples of battery Prosser provides, would find no objection under the Wagners' proposed rule so long as his intentional contact was initiated with no intent to injure or offend. He would be held civilly liable for his conduct only if he intended to harm or offend her through his kiss. A woman in such circumstances would not enjoy the presumption of the law in favor of preserving her bodily integrity; instead, her right to be free from physical contact with strangers would depend upon whether she could prove that the stranger hoped to harm or offend her through his contact. So long as he could show that he meant only flattery and the communication of positive feelings towards her in stroking her, kissing her, or hugging her, she must be subjected to it and will find no protection for her bodily integrity in our civil law."

NOTES

1. **Single vs. dual intent.** As you can see, the state courts are split on whether battery requires a plaintiff to prove merely that the defendant

intended to touch, or rather that the defendant intended to harm or offend by touching. Courts that adopt a single intent rule and courts that adopt a dual intent rule both trace the origins of those rules to the Restatement Second of Torts and to Dean Prosser's treatise, which suggests that those authorities are themselves less than clear on this requirement.

2. **When contact is intended but harm or offense is not.** Single intent favors plaintiff recoveries when the defendant caused a harmful or offensive contact but the plaintiff cannot prove that the defendant intended the harm or offense. In what kinds of cases might this matter? Look at *White* and *Wagner*. In both cases, because of mental disabilities, the plaintiffs might be unable to prove that the defendants who caused harmful contact actually intended the harm. In many other cases, as when a defendant punches a plaintiff in the nose, the difference between single and dual intent will not matter. The Restatement Third of Torts adopts a single intent rule because the rule "affords greater protection to the plaintiff's interest in bodily integrity" and is consistent with a number of cases, particularly in the medical battery context. However, the Restatement acknowledges that "a dual-intent approach is more consistent with the view that liability for battery should exist only when the actor is especially culpable." RESTATEMENT (THIRD) OF TORTS: INTENTIONAL TORTS TO PERSONS § 102 cmt. b (Tentative Draft No. 1, 2015).

3. **An example.** The Restatement Third of Torts provides the following illustration:

> Stephanie approaches Carol, a new coworker in her office, from behind. "You look tense!" Stephanie declares, and immediately begins giving Carol a vigorous neck massage. When Carol objects, Stephanie promptly ends the massage. The massage injures Carol's neck and requires her to miss several weeks of work. Stephanie is subject to liability to Carol for battery.

Id. cmt. b, illus. 2. Do you agree with the Restatement's conclusion that Stephanie should be subject to liability for battery?

4. **Justice and policy.** The issue of whether the single or dual intent rule is preferable has provoked strong reactions from judges. *See White v. University of Idaho*, 797 P.2d 108 (Idaho 1990) (Bistlin, J., dissenting) ("The Court's opinion has a chilling effect on any thought of ever again tapping a dancing gent on the shoulder to ask, 'May I?' Today it is learned that so doing is a battery even though no harm or offense is intended. One lives and learns."). Scholars have also disputed the point. Compare Kenneth W. Simons, *A Restatement (Third) of Intentional Torts?*, 48 ARIZ. L. REV. 1061 (2006) (advocating for single intent), with 1 DOBBS, HAYDEN & BUBLICK, THE LAW OF TORTS § 35 (2d ed. 2011) (supporting a dual intent rule).

5. **Applications.** How would the single and dual intent rules play out in these cases?

     a. Plaintiff gave her male supervisor a gift of Christmas cookies. The supervisor thanked her and told her she never ceased to amaze him. He then hugged her in a way that seemed too intimate to the plaintiff. *Balas v. Huntington Ingalls Indus., Inc.*, 711 F.3d 401 (4th Cir. 2013).

b.   A law professor who had been at odds with his colleague grabs the other professor's shoulder in a "strong and tight fashion." See *Gerber v. Veltri*, 2016 WL 4468065 (N.D. Ohio 2016).

———————

NOTE: LIABILITY OF THE MENTALLY IMPAIRED

Why is a mentally impaired person potentially liable for an intentional tort at all? When a defendant intends to harm the plaintiff but does so because of "insanity" (which remains the proper legal term), ordinary rules of battery apply. The usual American view is that insanity does not excuse one from tort liability. In *Polmatier v. Russ*, 537 A.2d 468 (Conn. 1988), defendant Russ shot his father-in-law Arthur Polmatier, causing his death. Russ was found not guilty by reason of insanity on a murder charge in criminal court, but in the tort action, a judgment was entered for the plaintiff. The court held that the judgment against defendant was appropriate even though Russ could not make a rational choice, and shot his father-in-law for "crazy" or schizophrenic reasons (including Russ' beliefs that Polmatier was a spy for the red Chinese and that Russ was a supreme being who could make his bed fly out of the window). According to the court "[a]n insane person may have an intent to invade the interests of another, even though his reasons and motives for forming that intention may be entirely irrational." Because Russ intended to shoot Polmatier, plaintiff was entitled to prevail. *intent doesn't have to be rational to constitute as intent*

Not all countries hold the insane liable for intentional torts. The German Civil Code § 827, for instance, excludes civil responsibility for one who is unable to exercise free will, except where he caused his own temporary disability by use of alcohol or similar means. Other countries are more nuanced still. In Mexico, for example, the Código Civil para el Distrito Federal § 1911 provides that the incompetent person is liable *unless* some other person such as a guardian is liable.

Should people with diminished mental capacity be held to the same rules of liability as others? If you were writing a statute to resolve the problem of injury caused by insane persons, would you want to consider any other options besides liability or non-liability? Many states have enacted crime victims' compensation statutes, through which the state creates a fund for partial victim compensation. *See* Charlene Smith, *Victim Compensation: Hard Questions and Suggested Remedies*, 17 RUTGERS L.J. 51 (1985). Would this be a good solution for the problem?

———————

Handwritten margin note (top): P brough suit against D for injuries; The DC granted D motions for summary judgment on limitations grounds pg 42-48

BASKA V. SCHERZER, 156 P.3d 617 (Kan. 2007). Celeste Baska had given her daughter Ashley, a high school senior, permission to organize a scavenger hunt and party. Around midnight, a fight broke out between Harry Scherzer, Jr. and Calvin Madrigal. Baska yelled at the boys to stop fighting. When they did not, Baska placed herself between them and was punched in the face, losing several teeth and receiving injuries to her neck and jaw. Baska sued Madrigal and Scherzer for personal injuries. In depositions, both Madrigal and Scherzer testified that they did not intend to strike or injure Baska. Instead, each testified that it was his intent only to strike and injure the other defendant. Madrigal and Scherzer then filed motions for summary judgment based on the one-year statute of limitations for assault and battery. [The statute of limitations for negligence actions was longer and would not have barred the plaintiff's claim]. *Held*, motions granted; Baska's cause of action was an action for assault and battery, not negligence. The court explained: "[T]he doctrine of transferred intent states that '[t]he tort of battery or of assault and battery may be committed, although the person struck or hit by the defendant is not the one whom he intended to strike or hit.' The comments to the Restatement (Second) of Torts, in describing the intent necessary for battery, explain:

'The intention which is necessary to make the actor liable [for civil battery] is not necessarily an intention to cause a harmful or offensive contact or an apprehension of such contact to the plaintiff himself or otherwise to cause him bodily harm. It is enough that the actor intends to produce such an effect upon some other person and that his act so intended is the legal cause of a harmful contact to the other. It is not necessary that the actor know or have reason even to suspect that the other is in the vicinity of the third person whom the actor intends to affect and, therefore, that he should recognize that his act, though directed against the third person, involves a risk of causing bodily harm to the other so that the act would be negligent toward him.' Restatement (Second) of Torts § 16, comment b (1964). . . .

The undisputed facts in this case show that the defendants intended to strike and cause harm to one another. When Baska intervened and stepped between the two boys, she was 'unintentionally' struck by punches intended for the defendants. Had the defendants struck each other and brought suit, they would be liable to one another for assault and battery. Under the doctrine of transferred intent, which has long been recognized in this state, the fact that the defendants struck the plaintiff does not change the fact that their actions (punching) were intentional. . . . [Failure to initiate her action within one year of the fight bars her action by reason of the one-year statute of limitations.] The trial court correctly granted defendant's motion for summary judgment."

Handwritten margin notes (left): Defendants explain their side of thing / Rule / Restatement (Second) / Court reasoning / under doctrine of transferred intent

Handwritten note (bottom): Supreme court held trial court correctly granted motions for summary judgment because of P's failure to initiate her action within one year of the fight

NOTES

1. **Transferred intent.** The doctrine of transferred intent has wide acceptance. This case demonstrates one form of transferred intent. How would you state the rule?

2. **The extended liability principle.** The defendant who commits an intentional tort, at least if it involves conscious wrongdoing, is liable for all damages caused, not merely those intended or foreseeable. We will call this the extended liability principle. This principle actually explains the result in most transferred intent cases, as where the defendant intends a battery to one person and then accidentally causes a battery to another as well. *See* Osborne M. Reynolds, Jr., *Transferred Intent: Should its "Curious Survival" Continue?*, 50 OKLA. L. REV. 529 (1997). No doubt there is a limit to this principle, however.

3. **Accepting or rejecting the rule in light of policy rationales.** If the purpose of the transferred intent rule is to afford broad recovery to people injured in situations in which harms were at least to some extent intended, might courts choose to employ the transferred intent rule only when the rule would effectuate those policies? See Vincent R. Johnson, *Transferred Intent in American Tort Law*, 87 MARQ. L. REV. 903 (2004).

4. **The irony of transferred intent.** Sometimes, classifying a tort as an intentional tort may help the plaintiff. For example, judgments in intentional tort cases may be more difficult for a defendant to discharge in bankruptcy. However, the Restatement Third of Torts calls it "somewhat ironic" that "intentional torts are generally deemed considerably more serious than torts of mere negligence," and yet "in certain circumstances the plaintiff is worse off if the tort committed against the plaintiff is classified as intentional rather than negligent." RESTATEMENT (THIRD) OF TORTS: LIABILITY FOR PHYSICAL AND EMOTIONAL HARM § 5 cmt. a (2010). How could a plaintiff be worse off with a judgment against the defendant for an intentional tort in contrast to a negligent or reckless tort?

5. **The effects of classifying a tort as intentional.** One reason plaintiffs are worse off when the tort against them is classified as intentional is that many insurance policies pay judgments for negligent and reckless acts, which are considered "accidents," but do not cover intentional torts, which are not, thereby limiting the plaintiff's potential source of recovery. *See, e.g., Tibert v. Nodak Mut. Ins. Co.*, 816 N.W.2d 31, 37 (N.D. 2012) (noting that the court has "repeatedly held that an intentional acts exclusion precludes coverage for the natural and probable consequences of an intentional act"). Also, an insurance company may seek declaratory judgment that the insured's conduct was intentional rather than negligent, freeing the insurer from any duty to defend or indemnify the insured. *See, e.g., QBE Ins. Corp. v. Jinx-Proof Inc.*, 6 N.E.3d 583 (N.Y. 2014*)*. Similarly, a government may have waived immunity for some negligent acts but retained immunity for intentional torts. *See City of Watauga v. Gordon*, 434 S.W.3d 586 (Tex. 2014). Another reason is that statutes of limitations for intentional torts are often shorter than are statutes

of limitations for negligent torts. *Raddin v. Macalaster Educ. Found., Inc.*, 175 So. 3d 1243 (Miss. 2015) (one-year statute of limitations barred battery claims against prep school dean). Because of these adverse effects for plaintiffs, plaintiffs sometimes try to "underplead" intentional tort cases and style them as claims for negligence. *See* Ellen Smith Pryor, *The Stories We Tell*, 75 TEX. L. REV. 1721 (1997).

§ 2. ASSAULT

CULLISON V. MEDLEY
570 N.E.2d 27 (Ind. 1991)

KRAHULIK, JUSTICE.

Dan R. Cullison (Appellant-Plaintiff below) petitions this Court to accept transfer of this cause in order to reverse the trial court's entry of summary judgment against him and in favor of the Appellees-Defendants below (collectively "the Medleys"). . . .

According to Cullison's deposition testimony, on February 2, 1986, he encountered Sandy, the 16-year-old daughter of Ernest, in a Linton, Indiana, grocery store parking lot. They exchanged pleasantries and Cullison invited her to have a Coke with him and to come to his home to talk further. A few hours later, someone knocked on the door of his mobile home. Cullison got out of bed and answered the door. He testified that he saw a person standing in the darkness who said that she wanted to talk to him. Cullison answered that he would have to get dressed because he had been in bed. Cullison went back to his bedroom, dressed, and returned to the darkened living room of his trailer. When he entered the living room and turned the lights on, he was confronted by Sandy Medley, as well as by father Ernest, brother Ron, mother Doris, and brother-in-law Terry Simmons. Ernest was on crutches due to knee surgery and had a revolver in a holster strapped to his thigh. Cullison testified that Sandy called him a "pervert" and told him he was "sick," mother Doris berated him while keeping her hand in her pocket, convincing Cullison that she also was carrying a pistol. Ron and Terry said nothing to Cullison, but their presence in his trailer home further intimidated him. Primarily, however, Cullison's attention was riveted to the gun carried by Ernest. Cullison testified that, while Ernest never withdrew the gun from his holster, he "grabbed for the gun a few times and shook the gun" at plaintiff while threatening to "jump astraddle" of Cullison if he did not leave Sandy alone. Cullison testified that Ernest "kept grabbing at it with his hand, like he was going to take it out," and "took it to mean he was going to shoot me" when Ernest threatened to "jump astraddle" of Cullison. Although no one actually touched Cullison, his testimony was that he feared he was about to be shot throughout the episode because Ernest kept moving his hand toward the gun as if to draw the revolver from the holster while threatening Cullison to leave Sandy alone.

As the Medleys were leaving, Cullison suffered chest pains and feared that he was having a heart attack. Approximately two months later, Cullison testified that Ernest glared at him in a menacing manner while again armed with a handgun at a restaurant in Linton. On one of these occasions, Ernest stood next to the booth where Cullison was seated while wearing a pistol and a holster approximately one foot from Cullison's face. Shortly after the incident at his home, Cullison learned that Ernest had previously shot a man. This added greatly to his fear and apprehension of Ernest on the later occasions when Ernest glared at him and stood next to the booth at which he was seated while armed with a handgun in a holster.

Cullison testified that as a result of the incident, he sought psychological counseling and therapy and continued to see a therapist for approximately 18 months. Additionally, Cullison sought psychiatric help and received prescription medication which prevented him from operating power tools or driving an automobile, thus injuring Cullison in his sole proprietorship construction business. Additionally, Cullison testified that he suffered from nervousness, depression, sleeplessness, inability to concentrate and impotency following his run-in with the Medleys. . . .

[Cullison sued the Medleys for a number of torts, including assault. The defendants moved for summary judgment on all claims. The trial court granted the motion and the appeals court affirmed.]

In count two of his complaint, Cullison alleged an assault. The Court of Appeals decided that, because Ernest never removed his gun from the holster, his threat that he was going to "jump astraddle" of Cullison constituted conditional language which did not express any present intent to harm Cullison and, therefore, was not an assault. Further, the Court of Appeals decided that even if it were to find an assault, summary judgment was still appropriate because Cullison alleged only emotional distress and made no showing that the Medleys' actions were malicious, callous, or willful or that the alleged injuries he suffered were a foreseeable result of the Medleys' conduct. We disagree. (we = SC of Indiana)

It is axiomatic that assault, unlike battery, is effectuated when one acts intending to cause a harmful or offensive contact with the person of the other or an imminent apprehension of such contact. It is the right to be free from the apprehension of a battery which is protected by the tort action which we call an assault. As this Court held approximately 90 years ago in *Kline v. Kline* (1901), 158 Ind. 602, 64 N.E. 9, an assault constitutes "a touching of the mind, if not of the body." Because it is a touching of the mind, as opposed to the body, the damages which are recoverable for an assault are damages for mental trauma and distress. "Any act of such a nature as to excite an apprehension of a battery may constitute an assault.

It is an assault to shake a fist under another's nose, to aim or strike at him with a weapon, or to hold it in a threatening position, to rise or advance to strike another, to surround him with a display of force. . . ." W. PROSSER & J. KEETON, PROSSER AND KEETON ON TORTS § 10 (5th ed. 1984). Additionally, the apprehension must be one which would normally be aroused in the mind of a reasonable person. *Id.* Finally, the tort is complete with the invasion of the plaintiff's mental peace.

The facts alleged and testified to by Cullison could, if believed, entitle him to recover for an assault against the Medleys. A jury could reasonably conclude that the Medleys intended to frighten Cullison by surrounding him in his trailer and threatening him with bodily harm while one of them was armed with a revolver, even if that revolver was not removed from the . . . holster. Cullison testified that Ernest kept grabbing at the pistol as if he were going to take it out, and that Cullison thought Ernest was going to shoot him. It is for the jury to determine whether Cullison's apprehension of being shot or otherwise injured was one which would normally be aroused in the mind of a reasonable person. It was error for the trial court to enter summary judgment on the count two allegation of assault. . . .

[Reversed in part and remanded.]

NOTES

1. **Applying *Cullison*.** In *Raess v. Doescher*, 833 N.E.2d 790 (Ind. 2008), "defendant [a cardiovascular surgeon], angry at the plaintiff about reports to the hospital administration about the defendant's treatment of other perfusionists [individuals who operate the heart/lung machine during open heart surgeries], aggressively and rapidly advanced on the plaintiff with clenched fists, piercing eyes, beet-red face, popping veins, and screaming and swearing at him. The plaintiff backed up against a wall and put his hands up, believing that the defendant was going to hit him, '[t]hat he was going to smack the s**t out of me or do something.' Then the defendant suddenly stopped, turned, and stormed past the plaintiff and left the room, momentarily stopping to declare to the plaintiff 'you're finished, you're history.'" Under *Cullison*, would these facts, if proved, entitle the plaintiff to recover on the assault claim?

2. **Assault and battery.** "Assault" has a technical meaning in tort law. Newspapers may use the term as a euphemism for sexual battery. Even judges may use the term assault to mean a battery. But the two torts are different. One can find cases, especially older ones, that say, "Every battery necessarily involves an assault." *McGlone v. Hauger*, 104 N.E. 116 (Ind. Ct. App. 1914). Can this be an accurate formulation? Suppose the defendant struck a sleeping plaintiff with a baseball bat. Would that be an assault? See *Koffman v. Garnett*, 574 S.E.2d 258 (Va. 2003), in which a 260-pound football coach slammed an unaware 144-pound 13-year-old student to the ground to demonstrate proper tackling technique.

3. **Apprehension.** What does "apprehension" mean? One common meaning of that word is "fear," and certainly the plaintiff in *Cullison* was probably fearful. But apprehension in the context of assault does not mean some generalized fear, but rather an awareness of an imminent touching that would be a battery if completed. *See* 1 DOBBS, HAYDEN & BUBLICK, THE LAW OF TORTS § 39 (2d ed. 2011). The Restatement Third of Torts now asks if "the actor intends to cause the other to anticipate an imminent, and harmful or offensive, contact with his or her person." RESTATEMENT (THIRD) OF TORTS: INTENTIONAL TORTS TO PERSONS § 105 (Tentative Draft No. 1, 2015).

4. **Actual or reasonable apprehension?** The *Cullison* court asks the jury to decide whether Cullison's apprehension that he would be shot was "one which would normally be aroused in the mind of a reasonable person." Should the question be whether a reasonable person would have anticipated an imminent harmful or offensive contact or whether Cullison himself did? The Restatement Third of Torts recommends a subjective standard except when the claim stems primarily from the defendant's words. *Id.* § 105 cmt. d. Also, to satisfy the test of offensive contact, a contact typically must offend a reasonable sense of personal dignity. *Id.* § 103.

5. **"Words alone."** Courts have sometimes said that words alone cannot count as an assault. But isn't it almost impossible to imagine words alone, divorced from any act at all? Suppose someone stands perfectly still at the entrance to a dark alley. He is masked and holding a gun. He says: "I am now going to shoot you dead." Surely this could be reasonably understood as a threat of imminent bodily harm. Maybe "words alone" is another shorthand or inaccurate statement. Perhaps it means that the plaintiff must reasonably apprehend an immediate touching and that in most cases words alone will not suffice to create such an apprehension. This is how the Restatement Third of Torts interprets the rule. *Id.* § 105 cmt. g.

6. **Words negating intent to effect immediate touching.** Sometimes acts seem threatening but the threat is countered by words. The defendant draws back his arm as if to strike, but at the same time he is saying "If the police officer were not here, I'd punch your nose." The words clearly mean he is *not* going to punch your nose. If there are no facts to make it reasonable to believe that the defendant will strike you in spite of the police officer's presence, this does not look like an assault.

7. **Words offering a choice of tortious alternatives.** Suppose the defendant says in a menacing way "I won't beat you to a pulp if you give me your basketball tickets; otherwise you are going to be pretty bloody." Is this an assault, even though the threatened battery can be avoided by complying with the aggressor's demands? *See also Gouin v. Gouin*, 249 F. Supp. 2d 62 (D. Mass. 2003).

8. **The meaning of "imminent."** To state a claim for assault, the plaintiff must have been placed in apprehension of an "imminent" harmful or offensive touching. What does that phrase mean? The Restatement Third of Torts says "imminent is not limited to immediate . . . [I]mminence means that

RS 48-58
51-58

the conduct will occur without significant delay." RESTATEMENT (THIRD) OF
TORTS: INTENTIONAL TORTS TO PERSONS § 105 cmt. e (Tentative Draft No. 1,
2015). In *Dickens v. Puryear*, 276 S.E.2d 325 (N.C. 1981), the plaintiff, a 31-
year-old man, "shared sex, alcohol and marijuana" with defendant's 17-year-
old daughter. The defendant and some of his friends lured the plaintiff into a
rural area, where they beat him, handcuffed him to a piece of farm machinery,
and threatened him with castration while brandishing knives. The court had
no problem labeling many of these acts as batteries and assaults. But the
defendant also "told plaintiff to go home, pull his telephone off the wall, pack
his clothes, and leave the state of North Carolina; otherwise he would be
killed." He was then freed, and sued the defendant almost three years later in
a North Carolina court. Was this last threat imminent for the purposes of
assault? What do you see as the strongest arguments on each side?

9. **Revisiting transferred intent.** In *Baska* (section 1.B above), the
defendant intended a battery against Person A but instead struck Person B
(the plaintiff), thus committing a battery on the plaintiff based on the doctrine
of transferred intent. A second form of transferred intent occurs when a
defendant intends to commit one tort and ends up committing another. As the
court held in *Nelson v. Carroll*, 735 A.2d 1096 (Md. 1999), one who intends an
assault but "touches this person in a harmful or offensive manner and claims
the touching was inadvertent or accidental, is liable for battery." *See also City
of Watauga v. Gordon*, 434 S.W.3d 586 (Tex. 2014) ("Liability in battery
moreover extends to harmful bodily contacts even though only offensive
contacts were intended").

§ 3. FALSE IMPRISONMENT

MCCANN V. WAL-MART STORES, INC.
210 F.3d 51 (1st Cir. 2000)

This case involves a claim for false imprisonment. On December 11,
1996, Debra McCann and two of her children—Jillian, then 16, and
Jonathan, then 12—were shopping at the Wal-Mart store in Bangor,
Maine. . . . [T]he McCanns went to a register and paid for their purchases.
One of their receipts was time stamped at 10:10 p.m.

As the McCanns were leaving the store, two Wal-Mart employees,
Jean Taylor and Karla Hughes, stepped out in front of the McCanns'
shopping cart, blocking their path to the exit. Taylor may have actually put
her hand on the cart. The employees told Debra McCann that the children
were not allowed in the store because they had been caught stealing on a
prior occasion. In fact, the employees were mistaken; the son of a different
family had been caught shoplifting in the store about two weeks before, and
Taylor and Hughes confused the two families.

Despite Debra McCann's protestations, Taylor said that they had the
records, that the police were being called, and that the McCanns "had to go

with her." Debra McCann testified that she did not resist Taylor's direction because she believed that she had to go with Taylor and that the police were coming. Taylor and Hughes then brought the McCanns past the registers in the store to an area near the store exit. Taylor stood near the McCanns while Hughes purportedly went to call the police. During this time, Debra McCann tried to show Taylor her identification, but Taylor refused to look at it. . . .

Although Wal-Mart's employees had said they were calling the police, they actually called a store security officer who would be able to identify the earlier shoplifter. Eventually, the security officer, Rhonda Bickmore, arrived at the store and informed Hughes that the McCanns were not the family whose son had been caught shoplifting. Hughes then acknowledged her mistake to the McCanns, and the McCanns left the store at approximately 11:15 p.m. . . .

The jury awarded the McCanns $20,000 in compensatory damages on their claim that they were falsely imprisoned in the Wal-Mart store by Wal-Mart employees. Wal-Mart has now appealed. . . .

Although nuances vary from state to state, the gist of the common law tort is conduct by the actor which is intended to, and does in fact, "confine" another "within boundaries fixed by the actor" where, in addition, the victim is either "conscious of the confinement or is harmed by it." . . .

While "confinement" can be imposed by physical barriers or physical force, much less will do—although how much less becomes cloudy at the margins. It is generally settled that mere threats of physical force can suffice, and it is also settled . . . that the threats may be implicit as well as explicit, and that confinement can also be based on a false assertion of legal authority to confine. Indeed, the Restatement provides that confinement may occur by other unspecified means of "duress." . . .

The evidence, taken favorably to the McCanns, showed that Wal-Mart employees . . . told the McCanns that they had to come with the Wal-Mart employees and that Wal-Mart was calling the police, and then stood guard over the McCanns while waiting for a security guard to arrive. The direction to the McCanns, the reference to the police, and the continued presence of the Wal-Mart employees (who at one point told Jonathan McCann that he could not leave to go to the bathroom) were enough to induce reasonable people to believe either that they would be restrained physically if they sought to leave, or that the store was claiming lawful authority to confine them until the police arrived, or both.

Wal-Mart asserts that under Maine law, the jury had to find "actual, physical restraint," a phrase it takes from [*Knowlton v. Ross*, 95 A. 281 (Me. 1915).] While there is no complete definition of false imprisonment by Maine's highest court, this is a good example of taking language out of context. In *Knowlton*, the wife of a man who owed a hotel for past bills

to leave is now considered a trespass. Also, if the landowner grants an entrant limited rights to enter, that does not give the entrant permanent rights. In *LeBlanc v. Snelgrove*, 133 A.3d 361 (Vt. 2015), the plaintiff granted a boathouse owner a limited right to enter a section of the plaintiff's property for the purpose of making repairs to the boathouse. That did not entitle the boathouse owner to build a permanent retaining wall several feet high and extending 25 feet onto the plaintiff's property.

3. **The object of intent.** The object of intent need not be "to trespass." It is enough that the defendant intended to enter the land. Once intent to enter is shown, the defendant does not escape liability merely because the defendant did not intend to harm the plaintiff's property or to interfere with the plaintiff's rights of possession. Similarly, it is no defense that the defendant reasonably believes that this is the defendant's own land or that there is a right to be there.

4. **Trespass and nuisance.** Many trespass cases also raise issues of nuisance, which is a separate tort. According to a passage from Dean Prosser the distinction between the torts of trespass and nuisance is that "trespass is an invasion of the plaintiff's interest in the exclusive possession of his land, while nuisance is an interference with his use and enjoyment of it. The difference is that between walking across his lawn and establishing a bawdy house next door; between felling a tree across his boundary line and keeping him awake at night with the noise of a rolling mill." *See Amaral v. Cuppels*, 831 N.E.2d 915 (Mass. App. Ct. 2005); *Shore v. Maple Lane Farms, LLC*, 411 S.W.3d 405 (Tenn. 2013).

5. **Tangible invasion.** Trespass historically requires a tangible invasion onto the plaintiff's property. *Mueller v. Hill*, 345 P.3d 998 (Idaho 2015) (defendant blasted rocks and debris onto land). Intangible intrusions, as by noise, odor or light alone, are dealt with as cases of nuisance. *Babb v. Lee Cty. Landfill SC, LLC*, 747 S.E.2d 468 (S.C. 2013); *see also Larkin v. Marceau*, 959 A.2d 551 (Vt. 2008) (pesticides that blew onto plaintiffs' land did not have any demonstrated physical impact on the plaintiffs' property).

6. **Remedies for trespass: damages.** Because trespass is another trespassory tort, a trespasser will be liable for at least nominal damages even if no physical harm is done. When the defendant's trespass physically damages the land, the plaintiff can get damages measured either by the cost of repair or by the diminution in the value of the premises resulting from the tort. However, compensatory damages must actually be compensatory. *Goforth v. Fifield*, 352 P.3d 243 (Wyo. 2015) (a $57,000 damage award for parking a camper and pickup truck on the plaintiff's property for an extended time was not an appropriate compensatory award). Upon proper proof the plaintiff can also get compensatory damages for loss of use of the land and for emotional distress or annoyance caused by the trespass. *See* 1 DOBBS, HAYDEN & BUBLICK, THE LAW OF TORTS § 56

(2d ed. 2011). South Carolina recently held that "damages for permanent trespass or nuisance in [the state] are limited to the full market value of the property." *Babb v. Lee Cty. Landfill SC, LLC*, 747 S.E.2d 468 (S.C. 2013). Could such a rule effectively permit private takings?

7. **Remedies for trespass: injunctive relief.** Where damages are inadequate, as where trespasses are continuing or will be repeated, the plaintiff may be entitled to an injunction to stop the trespassing or to force a trespasser to leave or remove something placed on the plaintiff's land. Where the defendant significantly disrupted the plaintiff's use and enjoyment of her property over a significant period of time, the plaintiff can obtain both an injunction (such as an order to remove an encroaching structure) and damages for diminution in value caused by that encroachment. *Banville v. Brennan*, 84 A.3d 424 (R.I. 2014) (ordering removal of defendant's building on plaintiff's land and upholding $50,000 award).

8. **Punitive damages.** Punitive damages may be awarded if the trespass is deliberate or "malicious." *See, e.g., Sebra v. Wentworth*, 990 A.2d 538 (Me. 2010) (defendants trespassed maliciously when they continued to use the plaintiff's driveway as an easement in disregard of a prior judgment).

9. **Extended liability.** The trespasser is liable for damages directly caused by his trespass, even if he never intended harm and could not foresee that harm. Suppose the defendant knows he is trespassing on a farm, and throws his cigarette into what appears to be a puddle of water. The "water" is really gasoline that leaked from a tractor, and it spreads a fire that burns down the farmer's barn. The extended liability rule makes the trespasser liable for loss of the barn.

10. **Hypotheticals.**

(a) An unidentified cat perches atop a fence that divides the Plunkett property from the Durfee property. The cat sets up an intolerable caterwauling in the middle of the night and Durfee hurls a shoe at the cat from her side of the line. The cat dodges and continues its serenade, but the shoe falls on Plunkett's property. Do these facts make a prima facie case of trespass?

(b) John Dangle took off from a mountain point in a hang-glider. He passed over Pergolesi's land at a height of 250 feet. Shortly thereafter a shotgun blast from an unidentified source ripped holes in the glider's surfaces and Dangle lost control. He landed safely in Burger's back yard. No damage was done to Burger's property. Is Dangle a trespasser as to either Pergolesi or Burger?

B. CONVERSION OF CHATTELS—TROVER

Dubbs steals Pedrick's watch. This is a conversion and Dubbs is a converter. He has, as it is said, "converted the watch to his own use." In other words, Dubbs has exercised substantial "dominion" over the watch and interfered with Pedrick's ability to control it. In such a case Pedrick can sue for the value of the watch at the time and place of the taking. In the earlier common law the form of action used to redress this conversion was known as *Trover*, and this is the word under which conversion cases are usually indexed even today.

NOTES

1. **Intent.** Conversion is an intentional tort. The defendant must intend to exercise substantial dominion over the chattel. See *Turdo v. Main*, 132 A.3d 670 (R.I. 2016) (defendant repossessed a truck on which payments under the contract were current; conversion claim was appropriate). But, as in the case of trespass to land, there is no requirement that the defendant be conscious of wrongdoing. One who takes another's watch in the honest belief that it is the person's own is still a converter if the dominion thus exercised is sufficiently substantial and the act interferes with another's right to exercise control. *See Kelley v. La Force*, 288 F.3d 1 (1st Cir. 2002) (even if police officers believed they were putting Pub into possession of its rightful owner, they still acted with intent to deprive plaintiff, the rightful owner of the Pub, of possession).

2. **How conversion is accomplished.** In each of the following cases, suppose the defendant reasonably but mistakenly believes he has a right to deal with the property.

(a) Defendant decides to burn his copy of a torts casebook and throws it in the fire. By mistake he got the plaintiff's copy instead.

(b) Defendant restaurant holds a coat checked by A and also one checked by B. By mistake defendant gives B's coat to A, who disappears and is never found. B's coat is far more valuable than A's.

(c) Defendant, honestly believing that Turvey has the right to sell a watch, buys it from him. The watch in fact was stolen from plaintiff.

3. **Substantial dominion.** One of the more difficult issues is what constitutes substantial dominion. It is clear that dominion is exercised in all the above cases, including where the property is damaged by the defendant. But in other cases defendant merely takes the property for a short period of time, as in the case of a joyride. If he takes a car for a joyride and it is destroyed in the process, he is no doubt liable. But suppose he takes it and returns it. Is this a conversion? These facts and many variations on them raise questions of degree. The American Law Institute concludes that it is all a matter of how serious the interference is. Since a finding of conversion will mean that the defendant pays the full value of the chattel, the ALI concluded that the

interference should be serious enough to justify imposing such liability and that a number of factors were important including:

(a) extent and duration of control;

(b) the defendant's intent to assert a right to the property;

(c) the defendant's good faith;

(d) the harm done; and

(e) expense or inconvenience caused.

See RESTATEMENT (SECOND) OF TORTS § 222A (1965). "Conversion would not apply where the '[i]ntention [is] good, the duration brief, the event harmless.'" *Loungee Conservancy v. Citimortgage*, 48 A.3d 774 (Me. 2012) (lender secured wrong home for foreclosure but provided access code to lockbox immediately upon notification of the error).

4. **New forms of property.** What types of property may be converted? The traditional common law rule was that conversion would lie only for tangible personal property. Thus neither land nor intangible property such as paper money or promissory notes could be converted. The rules today seem more liberal. *See* 1 DOBBS, HAYDEN & BUBLICK, THE LAW OF TORTS § 63 (2d ed. 2011). One can convert shares of stock or bonds and other documents which are strongly identified with the right itself. See also *Thompson v. UBS Fin. Servs., Inc.*, 115 A.3d 125 (Md. 2015). Cases have recognized some other expansions. Can a domain name be converted? *See Kremen v. Cohen*, 337 F.3d 1024 (9th Cir. 2003) (sex.com domain name). Courts have taken very different stances on whether copying and use of confidential data can be a conversion. Compare *American Biomedical Group, Inc. v. Techtrol, Inc.*, 374 P.3d 820 (Okla. 2016), with *Integrated Direct Marketing, LLC v. May*, 495 S.W.3d 73 (Ark. 2016) ("intangible property, such as electronic data, standing alone and not deemed a trade secret, can be converted if the actions of the defendant are in denial of or inconsistent with the rights of the owner").

5. **Serial conversions.** Dubbs steals Pedrick's watch, then sells the watch to Byer. Dubbs is a converter and so is Byer, since both have exercised substantial dominion and have intended to do so. Pedrick could sue either or both, though he could collect only once.

6. **Bona fide purchasers.** Byer in the preceding illustration is liable even if she buys in good faith, that is, even if she is a bona fide purchaser for value and without notice of Pedrick's rights. The theory is that Byer cannot purchase from Dubbs anything more than what Dubbs legally possesses. Dubbs has no title and thus cannot transfer title to Byer.

There is one special wrinkle in this rule. If Dubbs does not steal the watch but tricks Pedrick into selling it to him, then Dubbs *does* get title. Since Dubbs got it by a trick or fraud, Pedrick could go to court and have the sale voided; he could get his watch back because of Dubbs' fraud. However, he is not *required* to do this. He may do nothing at all and keep the money Dubbs paid him. At any rate, until Pedrick does go to court, Dubbs has title to the watch. This means that Dubbs could transfer title to someone else, including Byer. In this kind of case Byer would obtain good title and would *not* be a converter if she were a bona fide purchaser for value and without notice of Pedrick's rights. On the other hand, if Byer knew of the fraud practiced on Pedrick, and bought the watch anyway, she would also be a converter, along with Dubbs.

7. **The Uniform Commercial Code.** A comprehensive statute enacted in almost all states regulates many commercial dealings. One provision of the code covers this kind of case: Orwell takes his bike to the Merchant Bike Shop for repair. The bike shop repairs the bike but before Orwell returns, sells it to Dalzell. Under the rules stated above, Dalzell would be liable, since Merchant had no title to pass. The UCC, however, provides that if goods are entrusted to the possession of a merchant who deals in goods of that kind, the merchant has the legal power to transfer all the rights of the "entrustor." Is Dalzell liable or not? Suppose Orwell had stolen the bike, then taken it to Merchant for repair. Would Dalzell be liable?

8. **Remedies.** The usual remedy for conversion is damages, measured by the value of the chattel at the time of conversion. *See, e.g., Serv. Oil, Inc. v. Gjestvang*, 861 N.W.2d 490 (N.D. 2015); *Birchwood Land Co. v. Ormond Bushey & Sons, Inc.*, 82 A.3d 539 (Vt. 2013) (defendant did not move sand from construction site "to profit from its sale and mostly lost money on it," although the removal constituted conversion). At times, however, the value of the chattel fluctuates in the market, as in the case of shares of stock or commodities. The plaintiff, who has lost her property, may be forced to replace it in a rising market. If so, the time of conversion rule would be unfair. Some courts have accordingly permitted the plaintiff to recover the highest market value of the chattel that occurs within a reasonable time for replacement. The plaintiff might, instead of seeking value of the chattel, seek "replevin" or "claim and delivery," that is, an actual return of the chattel itself. This might also be possible in some instances through an injunction suit brought in equity. *See* 1 DOBBS, HAYDEN & BUBLICK, THE LAW OF TORTS § 73 (2d ed. 2011).

C. TRESPASS TO CHATTELS

SCHOOL OF VISUAL ARTS V. KUPREWICZ, 771 N.Y.S.2d 804 (Sup. Ct. 2003). The defendant, a former employee of the School of Visual Arts, allegedly caused large volumes of pornographic emails and unsolicited job applications to be sent to the plaintiff, resulting in depleted hard disk space, drained processing power, and other adverse affects on plaintiff's computer system. The school and its director of human resources brought suit against the defendant for trespass to chattels. In the trial court, *held—* motion to dismiss the trespass to chattels claim denied.

"To establish a trespass to chattels, [plaintiff] must prove that Kuprewicz intentionally, and without justification or consent, physically interfered with the use and enjoyment of personal property in [plaintiff]'s possession, and that [plaintiff] was harmed thereby. Thus, one who intentionally interferes with another's chattel is liable only if there results in harm to 'the owner's materially valuable interest in the physical condition, quality, or value of the chattel, or if the owner is deprived of the use of the chattel for a substantial time.' RESTATEMENT (SECOND) OF TORTS § 218, cmt. *e*. Furthermore, to sustain this cause of action, the defendant must act with the intention of interfering with the property or with knowledge that such interference is substantially certain to result. . . . The Court concludes that accepting these factual allegations as true, SVA has sufficiently stated a cause of action for trespass to chattels, and has alleged facts constituting each element of this claim. . . . It is important to note that by this decision, the Court does not hold that the mere sending of unsolicited e-mail communications will automatically subject the sender to tort liability. The Court merely concludes that . . . accepting [plaintiff]'s factual allegations of damage to its computer systems, the complaint states a valid cause of action for trespass to chattels."

NOTES

1.   **Elements.** Trespass to chattels involves something short of a conversion. Liability is based on actual damage, either in the form of actual harm to the chattel itself or an interference with the plaintiff's access or use. *See* 1 DOBBS, HAYDEN & BUBLICK, THE LAW OF TORTS § 60 (2d ed. 2011).

2.   **Hypotheticals.** Is there a trespass to chattel, a conversion, or no tort at all in the following cases?

(a)   Defendant pets the plaintiff's dog although the plaintiff has repeatedly told him not to do so. The dog is not harmed.

(b)   Defendant leans against the plaintiff's car.

(c)   Defendant takes the car for a joyride against the plaintiff's will, and puts the dog in the front seat with him.

(d)   Defendant, angered at the dog's barking, kicks the dog, then pushes the car over a cliff, causing substantial damages.

3.   **Expansions of the tort.** Trespass to chattels has traditionally involved the plaintiff's tangible chattel. "An actionable claim for trespass to chattels or personal property generally requires dispossession of the property, impairment of the condition, quality or value of the property, loss of use of the property, or other harm." *Sagebrush Res., LLC v. Peterson*, 841 N.W.2d 705 (N.D. 2014) (landowners who had complained about oil and gas operators' activities to a state commission did not cause dispossession, loss of use, or impairment of the property's value or condition; claim against landowners by operators failed). However, as in *School of Visual Arts,* some modern cases have held that clogging a company's email or computer systems with large amounts of unwanted email or other electronic interference can count as a trespass to chattels. *See, e.g., Compuserve Inc. v. Cyber Promotions, Inc.,* 962 F. Supp. 1015 (S.D. Ohio 1997) (unsolicited email and advertisements found to have damaged plaintiff's business reputation and goodwill); *Register.com v. Verio, Inc.,* 356

F.3d 393 (2nd Cir. 2004) (defendant's use of a "search robot" that could overtax plaintiff's servers); *but cf. Intel Corp. v. Hamidi*, 71 P.3d 296 (Cal. 2003) (sending spam email not a trespass to chattels where it interferes with neither possessor's use or possession of a legally protected right in the plaintiff's computer system itself). Recent cases continue to challenge unwanted email as trespass to chattels. *See, e.g., Beyond Sys., Inc. v. Kraft Foods, Inc.*, 777 F.3d 712 (4th Cir. 2015) (sending spam email would be a trespass to chattels under state statutes, but plaintiff consented, precluding recovery).

§ 5. FORCIBLE HARMS AS CIVIL RIGHTS VIOLATIONS

1. **An introduction to Section 1983.** We have pointed out that most tort law is the common law of various states. But there are a few federal statutes that create tort claims. One of the most important of those is found in the Civil Rights Act passed after the Civil War, 42 U.S.C.A. § 1983. The federal claims under that statute are usually known as "section 1983 claims." The facts involved in those statutory claims often closely parallel the common law claims we've seen in this Chapter, usually involving the direct application of force. Section 1983 in its entirety reads:

> Every person who, under color of any statute, ordinance, regulation, custom, or usage, of any State or Territory or the District of Columbia, subjects, or causes to be subjected, any citizen of the United States or other persons within the jurisdiction thereof to the deprivation of any rights, privileges, or immunities secured by the Constitution and laws, shall be liable to the party injured in an action at law, suit in equity, or other proper proceeding for redress.

2. **Coverage of section 1983.** Not all intentional tort claims will also constitute valid section 1983 claims, of course. Notice the parameters in the statute itself. First, a plaintiff has a section 1983 claim only where the defendant "acts under color of" state law. This means that the defendant must have exercised power made possible by state law; the typical defendant is a state officer, such as a police officer. However, "color of law" is broad enough to include off-duty officers and even some private persons who willingly participate in the use of state power. *Wittner v. Banner Health*, 720 F.3d 770 (10th Cir. 2013). Second, the plaintiff must prove not that the defendant committed a common law tort, but rather that the defendant subjected the plaintiff to a deprivation of federal rights, often rights guaranteed by the United States Constitution.

3. **Individuals and entities liable.** Section 1983 says a "person" may be liable under the statute. This means that individuals, as long as they are acting under color of state law, are subject to liability. The Supreme Court has also held that cities may be liable under section 1983, at least

under certain conditions. Because the statute refers only to those who act under color of *state* law, neither the federal government nor federal officers are subject to its terms—instead, special statutes and rules apply to federal governmental defendants.

4. **The most common constitutional bases for liability.** As noted above, a plaintiff can succeed on a section 1983 claim only by proving that the defendant has deprived her of some federally guaranteed right. The right might derive from a federal statute or the right might be based on the violation of a constitutional right. Three main provisions of the U.S. Constitution give rise to most section 1983 claims: (a) the Fourteenth Amendment's Due Process and Equal Protection Clauses; (b) the Fourth Amendment, which protects against unreasonable searches and seizures; and (c) the Eighth Amendment, which prohibits cruel or unusual punishment.

5. **Standards of care.** What it takes to prove a constitutional violation depends upon the particular provision involved. In the Fourteenth Amendment cases, a plaintiff must prove that the defendant's act "shocks the conscience of the court." *See, e.g., County of Sacramento v. Lewis*, 523 U.S. 833 (1998). In the Fourth Amendment context, the test is whether the defendant's search or seizure was "unreasonable," which normally means search or seizure either effected without a warrant or probable cause to believe a crime has been committed, or involving an unreasonable use of force. *See, e.g., Scott v. Harris*, 550 U.S. 372 (2007); *Graham v. Connor*, 490 U.S. 386 (1989). The Fourth Amendment's "reasonableness" standard means that officers using deadly force in an emergency may be found not to have violated a constitutional right at all. *See Partlow v. Stadler*, 774 F.3d 497 (8th Cir. 2014); *Krause v. Jones*, 765 F.3d 675 (6th Cir. 2014) (use of deadly force to subdue decedent was reasonable, given circumstances of decedent's pointing a gun at police). An Eighth Amendment violation turns on the court's interpretation of the term "cruel and unusual"; for example, the Court in *Hudson v. McMillian*, 503 U.S. 1 (1992), found prison guards violated plaintiff's Eighth Amendment rights by inflicting sadistic punishment. Cruel and unusual punishment may also be found where the conditions of confinement are especially harsh, or where necessary medical attention is denied to a person in custody.

6. **Why raise a section 1983 claim?** Many § 1983 cases involve actions that also constitute common law torts. *See, e.g., Morton v. Kirkwood*, 707 F.3d 1276 (11th Cir. 2013) (shooting an unarmed driver who raised his hands when he heard officer shout was use of excessive force in violation of the Fourth Amendment and a battery as well). If the facts of a case would allow a claim for a common law tort such as battery, assault, false imprisonment, trespass, or conversion, why would a plaintiff bring a section 1983 claim? Perhaps the most important reason is that another

section of the federal Civil Rights Act allows a prevailing plaintiff to recover her attorneys' fees from a losing defendant in a section 1983 case—something not available in the vast majority of common law tort claims. Second, the plaintiff may prefer a federal forum. The plaintiff may choose to bring a section 1983 case in either federal or state court. *See Haywood v. Drown,* 556 U.S. 729 (2009).

7. **Qualified immunity.** One significant disadvantage for a plaintiff in a § 1983 case is that a defendant is allowed to assert qualified immunity. *Messerschmidt v. Millender,* 565 U.S. 535 (2012). If a defendant raises the issue of qualified immunity, the plaintiff must show that the officer's conduct violated a constitutional right, and that the constitutional right was clearly established at the time of the violation. *Ryburn v. Huff,* 565 U.S. 469 (2012). Thus even where the defendant did violate the plaintiff's constitutional rights, the plaintiff will not prevail if the law protecting the plaintiff from the defendant's action was not "clearly established." *See, e.g., Safford Unified Sch. Dist. #1 v. Redding,* 557 U.S. 364 (2009) (no liability for public school principal whose strip search of the plaintiff violated her constitutional rights; qualified immunity applied because decisional law on propriety of strip searches was not clearly established at the time). Chapter 15 addresses these issues at greater length.

REFERENCES: 1 DOBBS, HAYDEN & BUBLICK, THE LAW OF TORTS §§ 28–79 (2d ed. 2011); DOBBS, HAYDEN & BUBLICK, HORNBOOK ON TORTS §§ 4.1–6.15 (2d ed. 2016).

CHAPTER 4

DEFENSES TO INTENTIONAL TORTS—PRIVILEGES

■ ■ ■

Even when the plaintiff states and proves facts sufficient to state a prima facie case for an intentional tort, the defendant might still prevail by proving a defense or privilege. The privileges explored in this chapter are for the most part affirmative defenses, meaning that the defendant has the burden of pleading and proving them. These defenses do not usually challenge the elements of the plaintiff's prima facie case; rather, they supply a legal reason or justification for the defendant's actions that render those actions non-tortious. We see three sets of privileges: first, those that attempt to justify the defendant's conduct as a response to the apparent misconduct of the plaintiff; second, the special case of consent; and third, the privileges of public and private necessity, which are based on policy rather than the plaintiff's apparent conduct or misconduct.

§ 1. PROTECTING AGAINST THE PLAINTIFF'S APPARENT MISCONDUCT

A. SELF-DEFENSE AND DEFENSE OF OTHERS

GRIMES V. SABAN
173 So. 3d 919 (Ala. 2014)

BRYAN, JUSTICE.

[Sarah Grimes sued Kristen Saban, alleging assault and battery. Grimes argued that the beating she sustained by Saban left her with head injuries, anxiety, migraines and a deformed nose. Saban argued that Grimes instigated the altercation "by uttering hateful words to Saban" and that Saban acted in self-defense. Saban moved for summary judgment, which the trial court granted.]

In its summary-judgment order, the circuit court stated:

"Findings

"In the early morning hours of August 29, 2010, Grimes and Saban, along with some mutual girlfriends, returned to Saban's apartment after a night of socializing at a local bar. As they sat in the kitchen discussing the night's events, an argument ensued between Grimes and Saban, which prompted Saban to leave the room, go upstairs to her bedroom, and lock her door.

"While in her room, Saban posted on Facebook, "No one likes Sarah, yayyyyy!" apparently in reference to Grimes. Sometime later, Grimes saw this post, became angry, went to Saban's bedroom and began yelling and pounding on the locked door, demanding the post be removed. When Saban opened the door to her bedroom and attempted to show Grimes her phone and that the post had been removed, Grimes advanced toward Saban, got within inches of Saban's face, and continued yelling. As Saban pushed Grimes away, Grimes grabbed Saban by the throat, and the physical altercation began.

"Conclusions

"Saban was in her home, locked in her bedroom, when Grimes sought out Saban and initiated the confrontation. Grimes's response to Saban's Facebook post was unreasonable and excessive. . . . When Saban opened the door to an angry Grimes within inches of her face, it was reasonable for Saban to believe imminent use of unlawful physical force by Grimes was about to be used against her. Saban had a right to be in her home, had no duty to retreat and had the right to stand her ground. Therefore, Saban was justified in using physical force to defend herself from what she reasonably believed to be the use of unlawful physical force by Grimes. Furthermore, Saban was justified in using a degree of force that she reasonably believed was necessary to repel Grimes's use and threat of physical force.

"Due to these facts, Alabama Code § 13A–3–23 presumes that Saban's actions were justified and necessary to repel the use of physical force against her. Grimes failed to present evidence to rebut this presumption. Therefore . . . Saban's Motion for Summary Judgment is hereby GRANTED. . . ."

Grimes appealed. Grimes argues that the circuit court erred in entering a summary judgment in favor of Saban because, she says, genuine issues of material fact exist as to whether Saban acted in self-defense, under § 13A–3–23, Ala. Code 1975. Section 13A–3–23 provides, in pertinent part:

(a) A person is justified in using physical force upon another person in order to defend himself or herself or a third person from what he or she reasonably believes to be the use or imminent use of unlawful physical force by that other person, and he or she may use a degree of force which he or she reasonably believes to be necessary for the purpose. . . .

Stand your ground law deadly force don't have to retreat

(b) A person who is justified under subsection (a) in using physical force, including deadly physical force, and who is not engaged in an unlawful activity and is in any place where he or she has the right to be has no duty to retreat and has the right to stand his or her ground.

(c) Notwithstanding the provisions of subsection (a), a person is not justified in using physical force if:

not justified if

issues P claims D did not fulfill

(2) He or she was the initial aggressor, except that his or her use of physical force upon another person under the circumstances is justifiable if he or she withdraws from the encounter and effectively communicates to the other person his or her intent to do so, but the latter person nevertheless continues or threatens the use of unlawful physical force.

(d) A person who uses force, including deadly physical force, as justified and permitted in this section is immune from criminal prosecution and civil action for the use of such force, unless the force was determined to be unlawful.

The [conclusions made by the trial court] . . . are supported by Saban's deposition testimony and the affidavits of [other friends present on the evening of the incident], which she attached to her motion for a summary judgment. However, they are disputed by Grimes's deposition testimony, which was attached to Grimes's brief filed in opposition to Saban's summary-judgment motion. . . .

conclusions by trial court are supported by Saban deposition testimony and affidavits of friends present in incid

Grimes testified in her deposition that after she banged on Saban's door, insisting that Saban take down the Facebook post, Saban opened the door and came out of her bedroom to show Grimes that the post had been removed. Grimes testified that [the two were in the hall and] . . . Grimes had backed away from Saban's door when Saban came out of her room. . . . Grimes also testified in her deposition that, after Saban told her that the Facebook post had been removed, she said to Saban "something to the effect of 'I don't care, okay, but we're done,' and I called her crazy." Grimes testified that Saban then used both of her hands and shoved Grimes into [an] open door frame. . . . According to Grimes, when she put her hands on Saban's throat and chest to push her away, Saban started punching her and hit her in the face more than five times."

Grimes testified that she went D to take down FB posting then said she doesn't care and called P crazy then P actually was crazy

Grimes testified that, after the first punch, she told Saban that she was calling the cops. Grimes stated: "I'm not sure how many blows were after that. I did not swing back. I know I had my arm up to defend myself. She had a grip on my hair. And we were somehow moving along the wall. . . . [A friend] at this point . . . tried to pull her off, and it wasn't working. And at some point, the closer we got towards the living room, [another friend], who was asleep, got up out of bed and they somehow managed to pull Saban off of me." . . .

→ P testified that she would call cops after D punched her first. P didn't swing back and only had arm up to defend herself

When viewed in the light most favorable to Grimes and when all reasonable inferences are drawn in favor of Grimes, Grimes's deposition testimony raises genuine issues of material fact as to whether Saban reasonably believed the use of force was necessary to defend herself against Grimes, whether Saban used a degree of force she reasonably believed was necessary, and whether Saban was the initial aggressor in the altercation.... Thus, the circuit court erred in entering a summary judgment in Saban's favor based on § 13A–3–23. In so holding, we should not be understood as expressing a view as to the merits of the underlying claims or affirmative defenses; we merely hold that there remain genuine issues of material fact for resolution by the fact-finder so as to preclude the entry of a summary judgment. REVERSED AND REMANDED.

NOTES

1. **Elements of the self-defense privilege.** The trial court in *Grimes* erred by crediting the defendant's story. Does that mean the plaintiff will prevail? Which party must prove that the defendant acted in self-defense? To whom must that party prove that she acted in self-defense?

2. **Provocation.** Provocation is generally not sufficient to raise the self-defense privilege. As you can glean from *Grimes*, insults and arguments, for example, do not justify a physical attack by the insulted defendant. How can we distinguish acts that create the reasonable appearance of an attack from mere provocation? What facts did the trial and appellate courts recite to support one conclusion or the other? In *Touchet v. Hampton*, 1 So.3d 729 (La. App. 2008), Touchet was terminated from his job at Hampton's car dealership, and left threatening phone calls on Hampton's answering machine. When Hampton went to Touchet's new place of business to tell him to stop the harassing phone calls, Touchet "quickly turned around in his chair" towards Hampton and yelled "F[--k] you." Hampton then struck Touchet several times. In Touchet's suit for battery, what result on Hampton's defense of self-defense?

3. **Mistake.** What if a defendant reasonably believes that he is being attacked, but is mistaken? Would a self-defense privilege still be available? *See* RESTATEMENT (SECOND) OF TORTS § 70 (1965).

4. **Excessive force.** The privilege extends only to the use of reasonable force. Any excessive force is unprivileged and the defendant is liable for it. A defendant who retaliates or continues the "defense" after the fight is over is likewise liable.

5. **Assault or imprisonment in self-defense.** The Restatement specifically recognizes that one may be privileged, given appropriate facts, to commit what otherwise would be an assault or a false imprisonment in self-defense. *See* RESTATEMENT (SECOND) OF TORTS § 67 (1965). One point of special interest is the rule in § 70 of the Second Restatement that the defendant may be privileged to put the plaintiff in apprehension of a harmful or offensive bodily contact even though the contact itself would not be privileged. Would

this authorize defendant to point a gun at the plaintiff to forestall a punch in the nose, even though the defendant would not be privileged to fire it?

6. **"Reasonable" deadly force.** The quantum of force considered reasonable in self-defense will vary with the facts. Is deadly force ever reasonable? The general rule is that the defendant's privilege to use that amount of force extends only so far as reasonably necessary to prevent death or serious bodily harm. *See First Midwest Bank v. Denson*, 562 N.E.2d 1256 (Ill. App. Ct. 1990) (upholding jury verdict for 67-year-old landlord who shot and killed evicted tenant whom landlord believed was about to push him down the stairs).

7. **Retreat**. The defendant who is attacked is usually not required to retreat or otherwise avoid the need for self-defense. When the defendant is threatened with force likely to cause death or serious bodily harm, the defendant is privileged to respond with reasonable deadly force. However, some states require reasonable retreat before deadly force is used when the defendant is not at home. *See, e.g.,* CONN. GEN. STATS. ANN. § 53a–19(b). Others have no such requirement.

8. **Statutes.** A number of states, as in *Grimes*, have adopted "Stand Your Ground" laws that remove the duty to retreat before using force in self-defense. These statutes allow an actor to use greater self-defense than permitted under traditional rules. *Ray v. Wal-Mart Stores*, Inc., 359 P.3d 614, 626–27 (Utah 2015). As of 2014, there were 18 states that granted civil immunity through such laws. *See* NAT'L TASKFORCE ON STAND YOUR GROUND LAWS, AM. BAR ASS'N, A REVIEW OF THE PRELIMINARY REPORT AND RECOMMENDATIONS 52–53 (2014). These statutes provide for immunity from civil liability. *See Pages v. Seliman-Tapia*, 134 So. 3d 536 (Fla. Dist. Ct. App. 2014) (defendant immune in suit for assault and battery, on ground that he had a reasonable fear for his disabled wife's safety in a parking-lot altercation with the plaintiff).

NOTE: DEFENSE OF OTHERS

At one time, the privilege to defend a person other than one's self was limited to defending family members and servants. This restrictive view has little support today. Most jurisdictions recognize that people may defend others on the same basis that they may defend themselves. For example, suppose a defendant sees A striking B. Believing that B is being attacked, the defendant seizes A and delivers a stunning blow. B then runs off. It turns out that A was a police detective attempting to carry out a lawful arrest which B was resisting. A sues the defendant for battery. Can the defendant claim a privilege? The rule embodied in the Restatement Second of Torts § 76 says yes, as long as the defendant's belief that B was being attacked and needed help was reasonable, even if mistaken, and the amount of force used was reasonable. Some courts, however, have held that a mistake, even a reasonable one, destroys the privilege, leaving the defendant liable for battery.

B. DEFENSE AND REPOSSESSION OF PROPERTY

KATKO V. BRINEY

183 N.W.2d 657 (Iowa 1971)

MOORE, CHIEF JUSTICE.

[Defendant Bertha Briney inherited an unoccupied farm house. For ten years there were a series of housebreaking events, with damage to this property. She and her husband boarded up the windows and posted no trespass signs and eventually they set up a shotgun trap in one of the rooms. The gun was rigged to an old iron bed, barrel pointed at the door. A wire ran from the doorknob to the trigger. It was pointed to hit the legs of an intruder. Mr. Briney admitted he was "mad and tired of being tormented," but said he did not intend to injure anyone. There was no warning of the gun. The plaintiff and one McDonough had been to the house before. They were looking for old bottles and jars. They broke into the house, and plaintiff started to enter the bedroom. The shotgun went off, and much of his right leg, including part of the tibia, was blown away. He spent 40 days in the hospital. The jury found for the plaintiff in the sum of $20,000 actual damages and $10,000 punitive damages.]

Plaintiff testified he knew he had no right to break and enter the house with intent to steal bottles and fruit jars therefrom. He further testified he had entered a plea of guilty to larceny in the nighttime of property of less than $20 value from a private building. He stated he had been fined $50 and costs and paroled during good behavior from a 60-day jail sentence. . . .

The main thrust of defendants' defense in the trial court and on this appeal is that "the law permits use of a spring gun in a dwelling or warehouse for the purpose of preventing the unlawful entry of a burglar or thief." . .

Instruction 6 stated: "An owner of premises is prohibited from willfully or intentionally injuring a trespasser by means of force that either takes life or inflicts great bodily injury; and therefore a person owning a premise is prohibited from setting out 'spring guns' and like dangerous devices which will likely take life or inflict great bodily injury, for the purpose of harming trespassers. The fact that the trespasser may be acting in violation of the law does not change the rule. The only time when such conduct of setting a 'spring gun' or a like dangerous device is justified would be when the trespasser was committing a felony of violence or a felony punishable by death, or where the trespasser was endangering human life by his act."

The overwhelming weight of authority, both textbook and case law, supports the trial court's statement of the applicable principles of law.

Restatement of Torts, section 85, page 180, states: "The value of human life and limb, not only to the individual concerned but also to society, so outweighs the interest of a possessor of land in excluding from it those whom he is not willing to admit thereto that a possessor of land has . . . no privilege to use force intended or likely to cause death or serious harm against another whom the possessor sees about to enter his premises or meddle with his chattel, unless the intrusion threatens death or serious bodily harm to the occupiers or users of the premises. . . . A possessor of land cannot do indirectly and by a mechanical device that which, were he present, he could not do immediately and in person." . . .

<u>Affirmed.</u> *Judgment*

[handwritten margin note: Court refers Restatement Torts]

NOTES

1. **Reasonable force.** Both the self-defense privilege and the privilege to defend property similarly allow a defendant to use "reasonable" force. Why, then, might the amount of force used be found to be excessive in one context but not another?

2. **Home invasion.** Would the case have been different if the trespasser had been entering the defendants' dwelling while the defendant was at home? Might a different common law privilege apply? *See Graves v. Trudell*, 765 N.Y.S.2d 104 (App. Div. 2003).

3. **Warnings and other barriers.** Would you favor a rule that permitted spring guns if there were large, clear warning signs? How about electrified fences or trained attack dogs? In deciding how to structure a rule on this subject, should you consider the possibility that a child or a police officer with a warrant might enter and be killed or grievously wounded if deadly force were permissible?

BROWN V. MARTINEZ
361 P.2d 152 (N.M. 1961)

[handwritten: P brought an action for injuries sustained when shot while stealing watermelons]

MOISE, JUSTICE.

[Plaintiff, a 15-year-old boy, and two other boys visited the defendant's garden patch for the purpose of stealing watermelons. On the next night, the boys returned to the defendant's farm for the same purpose. Hearing the boys in the patch, defendant came out of his house with a rifle, and called to the boys to get out. Seeing two boys running toward the southwest corner of the property, defendant fired the gun toward the southeast to scare them. However, plaintiff was in the southeast corner of the property and the bullet struck him in the back of the left leg. The trial court dismissed the plaintiff's claim.] *So P appeals*

[handwritten: trial court dismissed P (15 year-old boy, and two other boys) claim]

[handwritten top margin: I was use of a firearm to prevent trespass or theft a reasonable one]

[handwritten left margin: Court explains conduct (resort to firearms) is not excusable]

. . . Our examination of the authorities convinces us that the question of the reasonableness of resort to firearms to prevent a trespass or to prevent commission of an unlawful act not amounting to a felony is one of law for the court, and that such conduct is not excusable.

Dean Prosser in his Handbook of the Law of Torts, states the rule thus:

[handwritten left margin: When only property is threatened there is no privilege to use any force calculated to cause death or serious bodily injury]

"The reasonableness of the force used is usually a question of fact for the jury. But as in the case of self-defense, the law has marked out certain limitations. The force used must be of a kind appropriate to the defense of the property. A push in the right direction may be proper where a slap in the face is not. *And, since the law has always placed a higher value upon human safety than upon mere rights in property, it is the accepted rule that there is no privilege to use any force calculated to cause death or serious bodily injury where only the property is threatened.* The defendant may use the force reasonably necessary to overcome resistance and expel the intruder, and if in the process his own safety is threatened, he may defend himself, and even kill if necessary but in the first instance a mere trespass does not justify such an act." (Emphasis ours.)

[handwritten right margin: may use it only in self defense if genuine — it is]

[handwritten left margin: Court argues that no proof D felt threatened]

There is no suggestion in the proof here that appellee in any way felt his safety was threatened. Accordingly, under the facts as proven and found, the appellee acted improperly and is liable for injuries caused in using a gun in the manner he did, and with such unfortunate consequences, in order to drive away trespassers on his property, or to protect his watermelons, or to scare the intruders. . . .

[Reversed and remanded for a determination of damages.] *[handwritten: Court's judgm.]*

NOTES

1. **Privileged acts.** Did the defendant in *Brown* perform any unprivileged act? What tort did he intend? Does the law of transferred intent help the plaintiff here?

2. **Recapture of chattels.** You might see *Brown v. Martinez* as more about recapturing chattels (watermelons) than it is about defending property before the defendant has lost possession. Any privilege to regain possession of chattels is quite limited; in general, the owner must resort to the courts for a remedy rather than using self-help. *See* 1 DOBBS, HAYDEN & BUBLICK, THE LAW OF TORTS § 91 (2d ed. 2011). If the defendant acts in "fresh pursuit," however, he is privileged to use a reasonable amount of force to defend possession. The privilege is lost if the defendant is mistaken about the need for force—for example, if he is wrong about the fact that the plaintiff has actually taken the chattel. *Id.*; *see also* RESTATEMENT (SECOND) OF TORTS §§ 100, 103 (1965).

3. **Repossession of land.** Many courts, operating under statutes, invoke similar rules when the owner of land has lost or given up possession of

[handwritten bottom margin: however cases are divided and some allow owner to use force... When you lose land seek recovery in the courts]

his real property: he must seek recovery in the courts, not by use of force, even by the use of reasonable force. The cases are divided, however, and some permit the owner with right to possession to use force, limited always to reasonable force. *See* 1 DOBBS, HAYDEN & BUBLICK, THE LAW OF TORTS § 90 (2d ed. 2011).

C. ARREST AND DETENTION

GORTAREZ V. SMITTY'S SUPER VALU, INC.
680 P.2d 807 (Ariz. 1984)

FELDMAN, JUSTICE.

[Ernest Gortarez, age 16, and his cousin, Albert Hernandez, age 18, were shopping in defendant's store around 8:00 p.m. While Hernandez was paying for a $22.00 power booster in the automotive department, Gortarez picked up a 59-cent vaporizer used to freshen the air in cars. Gortarez asked the clerk, Robert Sjulestad, if he could pay for it in the front of the store when he finished shopping, and the clerk said yes. Sjulestad had a "hunch" that Gortarez was going to steal the vaporizer, and followed them around the store and watched them as they shopped. Sjulestad never saw them dispose of or pay for the vaporizer, and when they left the store told the assistant manager, Scott Miller, and the security guard, Daniel Gibson, that "[t]hose two guys just ripped us off." Gibson, Miller and two other store employees ran out of the store to catch Gortarez and Hernandez. Gibson confronted Hernandez and began to search him, without saying what he was looking for. Hernandez did not resist and kept denying that he had taken anything. When Gortarez saw Gibson grab Hernandez, he yelled at Gibson to leave his cousin alone. A struggle ensued and Gibson put Gortarez in a choke hold, holding him even after Gortarez told the men that he had left the vaporizer in the store. The two cousins were released after a check-out boy told the store employees that he had found the vaporizer in one of the "catch-all baskets" at an unattended check-out stand in the store. Gortarez required medical treatment for injuries suffered from the choke hold. He and his parents sued Smitty's and Gibson for false arrest and false imprisonment, assault, and battery. At the close of the evidence in a jury trial, the court directed a verdict for the defendants on the false arrest and false imprisonment count. The jury returned a verdict for Gibson on assault and battery. The court of appeals affirmed, and the plaintiffs appealed.]

Historical Perspective

At common law, a private person's privilege to arrest another for a misdemeanor was very limited. . . . Arizona has codified the common law. So far as relevant here, the statute provides that a private person may make an arrest for a misdemeanor when the person to be arrested has committed a misdemeanor amounting to a breach of the peace in the presence of the person making the arrest. Thus, [at common law and by statute, the privilege to arrest for misdemeanors without a warrant is limited to those misdemeanors which constitute a breach of the peace. [A mistaken belief that a breach of the peace has been committed does not confer a privilege under this statute.] In the case of misdemeanors such as shoplifting, there is no breach of the peace, and no common law privilege to arrest. [There is a common law privilege to use reasonable force to recapture a chattel "while in fresh pursuit," but the property owner must be correct that the person has stolen the chattel.]

Thus, privileges for misdemeanor arrest traditionally available at common law recognize no privilege to arrest for ordinary "shoplifting." Under this rule a shopkeeper who believed that a customer was shoplifting was placed in an untenable position. Either the shopkeeper allowed the suspect to leave the premises, risking the loss of merchandise, or took the risk of attempting to recapture the chattel by detaining the customer, facing liability for the wrongful detention if the person had not stolen merchandise.

As Prosser noted, shoplifting is a major problem, causing losses that range into millions of dollars each year. There have been a number of decisions which permit a business person for reasonable cause, to detain a customer for investigation. This privilege, however, is narrow; it is "confined to what is reasonably necessary for its limited purpose." . . .

The developing, common law "shopkeeper's privilege" described by Prosser was incorporated into the second Restatement of Torts with the addition of section 120A—Temporary Detention for Investigation:

One who reasonably believes that another has tortiously taken a chattel upon his premises, or has failed to make cash payment for a chattel purchased or services rendered there, is privileged, without arresting the other, to detain him on the premises for the time necessary for a reasonable investigation of the facts.

Comment (a) states that this section is necessary to protect shopkeepers from the dilemma we have just described. Comment (d) explains that the privilege differs from the privilege to use reasonable force to recapture a chattel, because it protects the shopkeeper who has made a reasonable mistake regarding the guilt of the suspect. As noted in Comment (g), the privilege is one of detention only.

We have not had occasion to pass upon the applicability of the Restatement rule. Instead Arizona has adopted the shopkeeper's privilege by statute, which provides in pertinent part:

C. A merchant, or his agent or employee, *with reasonable cause, may detain* on the premises *in a reasonable manner and for a reasonable time* any person suspected of shoplifting . . . *for questioning or summoning a law enforcement officer.*

D. Reasonable cause is a defense to a civil or criminal action against a peace officer, merchant or an agent or employee of such merchant for false arrest, false or unlawful imprisonment or wrongful detention.

A.R.S. § 13–1805 (emphasis supplied).

The trial court was evidently of the view that by the terms of subsection D, reasonable cause, alone, was a defense. We disagree; we believe that the statutory shopkeeper's privilege, like that described in the Restatement, involves all of the elements noted in subsection C. Subsections C and D of § 13–1805 must be read together. . . .

To invoke the privilege, therefore, "reasonable cause" is only the threshold requirement. Once reasonable cause is established, there are two further questions regarding the application of the privilege. We must ask whether the purpose of the shopkeeper's action was proper (*i.e.*, detention for questioning or summoning a law enforcement officer). The last question is whether the detention was carried out in a reasonable manner and for a reasonable length of time. If the answer to any of the three questions is negative, then the privilege granted by statute is inapplicable and the actions of the shopkeeper are taken at his peril. . . .

Reasonable Cause

. . . [F]or the purposes of this privilege, reasonable cause and probable cause seem equivalent. Reasonable cause is not dependent on the guilt or innocence of the person, or whether the crime was actually committed. *Tota v. Alexander's*, 314 N.Y.S.2d 93, 95 (1968). In *Tota,* the court stated that one may act on what proves to be an incorrect belief provided the facts show that the belief was reasonable. . . .

In the case at bench, the facts supporting reasonable cause are as follows: the clerk saw Gortarez with the item when he asked if he could pay for it at the front. The clerk followed the two young men through the store, and did not see them either deposit the item or pay for it as they left. Although the question of reasonable cause in the instant case may have been close we defer to the trial court's better opportunity to see and judge the credibility of witnesses and uphold it on the specific finding that conflicting inferences could not be drawn from the facts and that reasonable cause existed as a matter of law.

Purpose of the Detention

The statute provides this privilege for the express and limited purpose of detention for investigation by questioning or summoning a law enforcement officer. A finding of detention for the proper purpose could not have been made as a matter of law on the state of the evidence before the trial judge, since there was no evidence of either questioning or summoning of officers. At best, this was a question for the jury, because although there was no questioning, it is possible that the intent of the employee was to question or call officers.

Reasonableness of the Detention

Assuming there was reasonable cause for the detention, and that the detention was for a proper purpose, the privilege still may not attach if the merchant does not detain in a reasonable manner and for a reasonable time.... Comment (h) to § 120A of the Restatement (Second) of Torts states that ...

> Reasonable force may be used to detain the person; but ... the use of force intended or likely to cause serious bodily harm is never privileged for the sole purpose of detention to investigate, and it becomes privileged only where the resistance of the other makes it necessary for the actor to use such force in self-defense. In the ordinary case, the use of any force at all will not be privileged until the other has been requested to remain; and it is only where there is not time for such a request, or it would obviously be futile, that force is justified.

The Arizona statute is essentially a codification of the common law shopkeeper's privilege. The limitations on the use of force are obviously wise. We hold that the principle quoted is applicable to our statutory requirement that the detention be carried out in a "reasonable manner."

Under the restrictions given above, there was a question whether the use of force in the search of Hernandez, and, more importantly, in the restraint of Gortarez, was reasonable. There was no request that the two young men remain. No inquiry was made with regard to whether Hernandez had the vaporizer. Gibson testified that Hernandez gave no indication of resistance and made no attempt to escape. The possible theft of a 59 cent item hardly warrants apprehension that the two were armed or dangerous. There was, arguably, time to make a request to remain before Gibson seized Hernandez and began searching him. Also, there is no indication that such a request would *obviously* have been futile. The evidence adduced probably would have supported a finding that the manner of detention was unreasonable as a matter of law. At best, there was a question of fact; there was no support for the court's presumptive finding that as a matter of law the detention was performed reasonably.

Holding [The court erred in its findings on the reasonableness of both the purpose and the manner of detention.] This requires reversal and retrial. At the new trial evidence on the three issues should be measured against the principles set forth in this opinion. ...

NOTES

1. **The common law rule and statutes.** Many states have adopted statutes that codify the merchant's common law privilege. *See, e.g., Barkley v. McKeever Enters., Inc.*, 456 S.W.3d 829 (Mo. 2015) (en banc). These statutes are typically based on the reasonableness of the merchant's suspicion, as well as the time and manner of detention. Do flexible "reasonableness" standards provide sufficient guidance or should statutes state more specifically what a shopkeeper may or may not do?

2. **Mistake.** Under the common law rule and most statutes, the shopkeeper is privileged to act even if reasonably mistaken about the fact that the plaintiff has taken goods without paying. *See, e.g., Dillard Dep't Stores, Inc. v. Silva,* 148 S.W.3d 370 (Tex. 2004). A few states require the shopkeeper to be correct—that is, they do not allow the shopkeeper to utilize this privilege unless the plaintiff did actually take the goods in question. Would this be a better rule? *See Great Atl. & Pac. Tea Co. v. Paul,* 261 A.2d 731 (Md. 1970) (refusing to adopt the Restatement's rule on reasonable mistake). If Arizona had such a "no mistake" rule in place with regard to shoplifting, how might it have changed the analysis in *Gortarez*?

3. **Reasonable manner of detention.** The *Gortarez* court, in discussing the reasonableness of the manner of detention, makes note of the fact that the item believed stolen was of little value (a 59-cent vaporizer). How might the analysis differ if the item had been worth, say, $5,000? Even if the item believed stolen had been valuable, what other facts might lead a jury to conclude that the manner of the detention in *Gortarez* was unreasonable?

4. **A merchant's recapture of chattels.** The common law grants no special privilege to merchants to recapture chattels once possession has been lost; the rules we saw in the Notes after *Brown v. Martinez*, above, apply to merchants as well. Thus if a thief runs out of a store with a stolen item, the store's guard is privileged to recapture it if he does so immediately or in fresh pursuit and uses a reasonable amount of force. Once possession has been lost, however, the detective cannot forcibly recapture it from the thief a week later. The store instead will be forced to sue or to invoke criminal processes. 1 DOBBS, HAYDEN & BUBLICK, THE LAW OF TORTS § 91 (2d ed. 2011).

5. **Using force to detain trespassers.** What if a landowner threatens or uses force and detains a trespasser? In *Whitten v. Cox,* 799 So. 2d 1 (Miss. 2000), to get to land leased by a relative, the three plaintiffs drove a pickup truck onto land occupied legally by the defendant Whitten, who was a municipal judge. Whitten shouted for the truck to stop. When it did not, he fired several shots from a .45 caliber handgun—shooting out one of the back tires. Whitten, along with other men who were all armed with loaded assault rifles, told all three plaintiffs that they were under arrest for trespassing and handcuffed one of them, Cox. According to Cox, Whitten asked the two other plaintiffs whether they thought Cox could swim in the nearby bayou with those handcuffs on. Whitten and his companions escorted the three plaintiffs back to a camp Whitten occupied, and Whitten unsuccessfully tried to reach the

Sheriff. At this point Whitten recognized Cox as the brother of someone who leased neighboring property, and the plaintiffs were freed. The plaintiffs sued Whitten for battery, assault and false imprisonment. Whitten claimed he asserted a valid privilege to arrest and detain them as trespassers. The case went to a jury. According to the court, "If the force used in the arrest of a suspected misdemeanant [and trespassing is a misdemeanor] is unreasonable and excessive, this may render the arrest and detention invalid."

D. DISCIPLINE

Where children are permitted to sue parents for torts, parents still enjoy a privilege to discipline, and to use force and confinement to do so. The limits of this force are ill-defined. The Restatement says parents may use reasonable force as they reasonably believe necessary. *See* RESTATEMENT (SECOND) OF TORTS § 147 (1965); 1 DOBBS, BUBLICK & HAYDEN, THE LAW OF TORTS § 104 (2d ed. 2011). Courts have more commonly articulated standards for appropriate discipline in the context of the criminal law. In *Commonwealth v. Dorvil*, 32 N.E.3d 861 (Mass. 2015), the Massachusetts Supreme Court wrote: "we hold that a parent or guardian may not be subjected to criminal liability for the use of force against a minor child under the care and supervision of the parent or guardian, provided that (1) the force used against the minor child is reasonable; (2) the force is reasonably related to the purpose of safeguarding or promoting the welfare of the minor, including the prevention or punishment of the minor's misconduct; and (3) the force used neither causes, nor creates a substantial risk of causing, physical harm (beyond fleeting pain or minor, transient marks), gross degradation, or severe mental distress."

Those who are in charge of someone else's children also enjoy a similar disciplinary privilege. Teachers and school bus drivers are the most obvious examples. However, it may be that the teacher would not enjoy the same latitude for punishment that courts would recognize in a parent. Suppose a child is spanked by her parent for misbehavior and again by her teacher for additional misbehavior. Apart from local school board regulations affecting corporal punishment, what factors should a court consider in determining whether either the parent or the teacher is liable in tort?

What if "to calm him down" a teacher holds down on the floor a twelve-year-old child who has Asperger's syndrome? What if an 8-year-old with attention deficit disorder and mild mental retardation is repeatedly locked in a "seclusion room" by herself when she misbehaves at school? Some false imprisonment lawsuits have arisen from those sorts of responses.

E. OBSERVING PRIVILEGES

Many common law privileges have the effect of resolving the issues in the case by matter of reasonableness and degree. In self-defense, the issue is frequently whether the defendant reasonably believed that defense was necessary and then whether he used the amount of force reasonable to cope with the apparent threat. In the case of schoolroom punishment, teachers, being privileged to inflict some punishment, are liable only if they go too far. In false imprisonment cases a defendant might be privileged to detain for investigation for a short time, but not for long. All such cases involve matters of reasonableness and hence matters of degree.

Notice how those cases differ from cases in which a defendant commits a "kissing battery"—he kissed the plaintiff, a stranger, or touched the plaintiff in a private place. This is an offensive battery and it is no defense to say the touching did not last long, that the force used was minimal, or that the injury was not great. Thus in common law actions, there are cases in which "degree" is not important, and other cases in which, because the issue of privilege is injected, degree becomes quite significant.

§ 2. THE SPECIAL CASE OF CONSENT

Austin cooked a continental dinner for a new acquaintance, Berwyn, served in candlelight and accompanied by excellent French wines. After dinner the couple sat on the sofa listening to *Traviata* and sipping Benedictine and Brandy. The moment came, as it must in every scene of this sort, in which Austin drew closer and with parted lips looked in Berwyn's eyes. A kiss was imparted and Austin's hand caressed Berwyn's neck. Suddenly, to the surprise of everyone, there was a snap as a vertebra in Berwyn's neck broke. Neither Austin nor Berwyn knew that Berwyn had a congenital condition that made such an outcome possible.

This vignette illustrates several problems about the surprisingly complex "defense" of consent, but also suggests some common sense answers to some of those problems.

1. Berwyn testified: "I never consented to be touched at all, and in fact I was revolted at the idea." If the trier of fact believes this testimony, does it show there was no consent?

2. Was there anything to show there *was* consent?

3. Berwyn's lawyer argued to the trial judge: "Berwyn certainly did not consent to a broken vertebra even if there was consent to a kiss." What do you think of this argument? *Cf. Wulf v. Kunnath*, 827 N.W.2d 248 (Neb. 2015) (doctor who had a "light hearted" relationship with nurse thumped her on the back of her neck, resulting in aggravation of a preexisting disc injury).

4. Is consent really a "defense"? What practical matter would turn on the answer to this? *See Envtl. Processing Sys., L.C. v. FPL Farming Ltd.*, 457 S.W.3d 414 (Tex. 2015).

NOTE: RELATIONSHIP OF THE PARTIES

In real cases lawyers would want to know a great deal more about the facts. Would it impact the analysis if Berwyn had kissed Austin on the cheek when Austin arrived? What if Berwyn had kissed Austin on the lips? What if Berwyn worked for Austin and was told that the dinner was a meeting to discuss a potential promotion? Specific facts like these might be relevant to the issue of apparent consent. Maybe Austin can take it that consent is given by silence in some relationships but not in others. Maybe in some cases a person has no capacity to consent and the actor knows it. Suppose you are sedated and while sedated give "consent" to an operation. If the doctor knows you are heavily sedated should the doctor believe you have manifested consent? There may be some situations in which the power relationships between the parties affect the issue of consent.

ROBINS V. HARRIS, 769 N.E.2d 586 (Ind. 2002). As described by the appellate court, in *Robins v. Harris,* 740 N.E.2d 914, 917 (Ind. Ct. App. 2000), plaintiff Tammy Robins was a female inmate at a county jail and defendant Michael Soules was a new corrections officer on the third shift. According to Soules, when he met Robins she and another inmate, Martha Custer, flashed him by lifting up their shirts and exposing their breasts. Later that evening, Soules ordered a lock down, requiring all inmates to stay in their cells. Soules first summoned Custer out of her cell and upon her return then summoned Robins. He grabbed Robins by the arm and brought her into the shower room where she performed fellatio on him. Robins filed suit, alleging battery. Soules originally denied the allegations but two days later admitted to the sexual contact and resigned his position. He subsequently pled guilty to misdemeanor official misconduct in exchange for dismissal of a felony charge. In the tort action, Soules claimed he was not liable and raised an affirmative defense of consent. The court of appeals held that several parties were potentially subject to liability and that the inmate's alleged consent to the sexual contact was no defense. In the Indiana Supreme Court, "affirmed except as to the availability of the consent defense to the claim of battery," on which point the majority issued no opinion.

Sullivan, J., dissenting. "[T]he Court of Appeals said: 'We also note that consent is not available as a defense to Robins's sexual assault claim. Under I.C. § 35–44–1–5(b), a [jailer] may not claim consent as a defense for sexual misconduct with a detainee. Given Robins's general lack of autonomy as an inmate, it would be incongruous to withhold the defense of consent in the criminal context but to allow Soules the defense in a civil claim.' I agree with this analysis. Our Legislature has made a public policy determination that the position of authority a jailer holds over a prisoner dictates that there be no exception for consent in our criminal law to the rule against sexual contact between jailer and prisoner. Our state's civil law should further the public policy objective the Legislature has adopted in the criminal context."

NOTES

1. **Power relationships.** Should consent be an available defense when the relationship between the plaintiff and the defendant is inherently unequal as in the situation of jailer and prisoner? *See also, Grager v. Schudar*, 770 N.W.2d 692, 698 (N.D. 2009). Sexual conduct between guards and prisoners can also raise issues about whether the prisoners' civil rights have been violated. *See Graham v. Sherriff of Logan Cty.*, 741 F.3d 1118 (10th Cir. 2013). What about relationships that involve lesser power imbalances? For example, some state statutes forbid all sexual contact between mental health professionals and their patients. Under these statutes, the patient's consent is not legally effective to bar a claim against the therapist. *See Flores v. Santiago*, 986 N.E.2d 1216 (Ill. App. Ct. 2013). What about a relationship between a pastor and parishioner? *See Wende C. v. United Methodist Church*, 827 N.E.2d 265 (N.Y. 2005).

2. **Employers.** Should employers be permitted to claim that an employee who is dependent for a job, wage increase, or promotion consented to sexual intercourse? *See Reavis v. Slominski*, 551 N.W.2d 528 (Neb. 1996) (claim against employer based on sexual contact after an office New Year's Eve party). Federal statutes against employment discrimination forbid sexual harassment of employees. Employer conduct might count as a violation of those statutes, which are usually considered in advanced courses. You should be aware, however, that the damages awards under those statutes may be less attractive to the plaintiff in some instances than the common law awards.

3. **Incapacity to consent: minors.** Minors as a class are often thought to lack capacity to consent, although there is not a blanket rule that covers every situation; courts will sometimes look at the individual facts, to see if the particular minor has the experience and intelligence to consent to the particular act involved in the case. *See* 1 DOBBS, HAYDEN & BUBLICK, THE LAW OF TORTS § 109 (2d ed. 2011). Although courts are split, it is generally assumed that minors may consent to a number of touchings appropriate to their age. Probably two eight-year-olds can effectively consent to a football game in which touching is inevitable. Older minors can consent to more serious touchings, such as routine medical attention. The hospital emergency room that administers first aid to a 16-year-old with a broken arm is presumably protected from any claim of battery if the teenager consents. But many states impose criminal liability for sexual conduct with a minor. Many, though not all, states agree that a minor's consent is no defense in a civil action for such sexual contact, either. Should the age of the child claimed to have consented

matter? *See C.C.H. v. Philadelphia Phillies, Inc.*, 940 A.2d 336 (Pa. 2008) (alleged consent of 11-year-old child could not be a defense).

4. **Incapacity to consent: adults.** Incapacity of an adult is usually established only by showing that the particular adult could not manage his own affairs, or, in consent cases, that he did not understand the nature and character of the act. See *Saucier ex rel. Mallory v. McDonald's Rests. of Mont., Inc.*, 179 P.3d 481 (Mont. 2008) (employee who was mentally retarded engaged in a sexual relationship with her manager at McDonald's; genuine issue of material fact remained as to plaintiff's ability to consent).

KAPLAN V. MAMELAK, 162 Cal. App. 4th 637 (2008). A patient sued his doctor for medical malpractice and battery, claiming that the doctor operated on the wrong herniated disks in his back. The trial court granted the doctor's demurrer to the battery claim, and the jury found for the doctor on the malpractice claim. *Held*, reversed and remanded. A doctor who operates on a patient without that patient's consent commits a battery. Here the doctor "may have committed battery by operating on appellant's T6–7 and T7–8 disks when he did not have permission to operate on any disk other than T8–9." While "the law will deem a patient to have consented to a touching that, although not literally covered by the patient's express consent, involves complications inherent to the procedure, . . . a battery occurs if the physician performs a 'substantially different treatment' from that covered by the patient's expressed consent." These issues are for the jury, making the grant of demurrer improper.

NOTES

1. **Exceeding the scope of consent.** Many cases of "medical battery" involve allegations that the doctor exceeded the scope of the patient's consent. *See Duncan v. Scottsdale Medical Imaging, Ltd.*, 70 P.3d 435 (Ariz. 2003) (patient told the nurse that she would accept only non-synthetic demerol or morphine, and nurse assured her that only one of those particular drugs would be administered, however, synthetic drug was administered, causing complications; "general authorization of an injection does not defeat her battery claim because her consent was limited to certain drugs"). What about a hospital patient who consents to a blood draw without being told that it was for a non-medical law-enforcement purpose? *See O'Brien v. Synnott*, 72 A.3d 331 (Vt. 2013).

2. **Emergencies.** The ordinary rule—that it is battery when a doctor treats a patient without the patient's consent, or in excess of the scope of a patient's consent—may not apply when the doctor must act in an emergency and obtaining consent is not possible. *See, e.g., Kennedy v. Parrott*, 90 S.E.2d 754 (N.C. 1956) (finding implied consent for a doctor to "extend the operation to remedy any abnormal or diseased condition in the area of the original

incision" when the patient is incapable of giving consent and no one else with authority to consent is available).

3.   **Substituted consent.** An adult family member or guardian may be empowered to give consent on behalf of a minor or an incapacitated adult. The rule is easy enough to state, but many issues arise in real cases. In *Harvey v. Strickland*, 566 S.E.2d 529 (S.C. 2002), an adult patient, preparing for an operation, signed a form saying he refused to accept a blood transfusion for religious reasons. During the operation, the doctor determined that the patient needed a transfusion and called the patient's mother for permission, which she granted. When sued by the patient for battery, the doctor claimed that the patient had once said he would "consider" a transfusion. Can we say that this patient impliedly consented to substituted consent by his mother? The court said the case presented a jury question on that issue.

[handwritten margin note: Sometimes refer to health care proxy or "power of attorney"]

4.   **Incompetence to give or withhold consent.** What if a person is intoxicated at the time of emergency treatment—should the doctor be required to obtain consent? In *Miller v. Rhode Island Hospital,* 625 A.2d 778 (R.I. 1993), the plaintiff had consumed many, many drinks before he was in an automobile collision. The trauma team at the emergency room, fearing internal bleeding, insisted on performing a peritoneal lavage. When plaintiff objected, doctors strapped him to a gurney, anesthetized him and performed the lavage. The plaintiff sued for battery. The court thought that competence to consent (or refuse consent) should be measured by the plaintiff's ability to understand the condition, nature and effect of the proposed treatment or its rejection. When the plaintiff was unable to understand the nature of the treatment due to his intoxication, doctors were not required to attempt to obtain his consent.

DOE V. JOHNSON, 817 F. Supp. 1382 (W.D. Mich. 1993). Plaintiff Jane Doe alleged: Earvin Johnson, Jr., transmitted human immunodeficiency virus (HIV) to her through consensual sexual contact. Johnson knew or should have known that he had a high risk of being infected with HIV because of his promiscuous lifestyle. Nevertheless, he did not warn Doe of this high risk or inform her that he did in fact have HIV. Nor did he use a condom. Doe suffers from HIV now and will develop AIDS. On motion to dismiss the battery claim, *held,* motion denied. One who knows he has a venereal disease, and knows that his sexual partner does not know of his infection, commits a battery by having sexual intercourse.

[handwritten margin note: should have known because of promiscuous lifestyle; didn't use condom; inform P he had HIV]

NOTES

1.   **STDs.** Where the defendant knows he has a sexually transmitted disease but neither warns his sexual partner nor provides any protection, several cases have imposed liability. *E.g., Johnson v. Jones*, 344 P.3d 89 (Or. Ct. App. 2015) (genital herpes not revealed; consent obtained by material nondisclosure is not consent at all). In *Doe v. Johnson,* can you say that the defendant had the intent to touch in a harmful or offensive way? Remember to

distinguish intent from negligence. Is it relevant that Johnson claimed to have had unprotected sex with more than 2,000 partners? Is high-risk sexual activity enough to establish constructive knowledge? *Kohl v. Kohl,* 149 So. 3d 137 (Fla. Dist. Ct. App. 2014) (husband's extramarital relations with prostitutes is not enough to establish actual or constructive knowledge).

2.   **Consent procured by fraud.** Courts recognize that, in a general way, consent procured by fraud is not valid. Do you see how the outcome in *Doe v. Johnson* could be characterized as consent procured by fraud? If induced by false information, consent may not be valid even if one voluntarily participates in the touching. *See Hackett v. Fulton County Sch. Dist.*, 238 F. Supp. 2d 1330 (N.D. Ga. 2002).

3.   **Avoiding the effect of consent.** To avoid the effect of a manifested consent, the plaintiff's mistake must be "about the nature and quality of the invasion intended by the conduct." W. PROSSER & J. KEETON, PROSSER AND KEETON ON TORTS § 18 (5th ed. 1984). Eating a chocolate from a box of poisoned candy seems like a mistake about the nature and quality of the contact. Mistakes or misrepresentations about collateral matters such as price or timing do not nullify the consent. *See* 1 DOBBS, HAYDEN & BUBLICK, THE LAW OF TORTS § 111 (2d ed. 2011).

4.   **Revocation of consent.** Subject only to the slightest qualification, the plaintiff can revoke consent at any time by communicating the revocation to the defendant. Thus a landowner who has consented to another person's presence on the land could order the person to leave; if the visitor does not leave, he becomes a trespasser. A person who consents to intimate contact with another can have a change of heart and revoke consent; if that is communicated to the other person, any further contact would become tortious. *See id.* § 108.

5.   **Consent to crime.** When the plaintiff is injured during an illegal activity in which he has agreed to participate (such as an illegal boxing match), courts have struggled to find a consistent approach to the issue of consent. Some have held consent to a crime is invalid, so that the tort claim can proceed. Others have said that that the plaintiff's consent bars the tort claim. The Restatement's rule is that the plaintiff's consent is a bar just as in any other case. RESTATEMENT (SECOND) OF TORTS § 892C (1979). However, if the statute makes the conduct illegal in order to protect the plaintiff from her own consent, as might be the case with a statutory rape law for example, the plaintiff's consent should not bar her claim. Suppose a statute makes it unlawful to hire a child under 15 for work near industrial machinery. Should the child's consent be a bar? *See id*; 1 DOBBS, HAYDEN & BUBLICK, THE LAW OF TORTS § 116 (2d ed. 2011).

A Mini-Problem for Review

"On May 29, 2007, Mr. Christopherson [a supervisor at Prosper, Inc.] asked for volunteers for a new motivational exercise. He offered no explanation to his team members regarding the nature of the exercise. In his search for volunteers, Mr. Christopherson challenged the loyalty and determination of his team members. Mr. Hudgens volunteered to be a part of the exercise to prove his loyalty and determination. Mr. Christopherson then led his team members to the top of a hill near Prosper's office. Once on the hill, Mr. Christopherson ordered Mr. Hudgens to lie down, facing up, with his head pointed downhill. Mr. Christopherson ordered other team members to hold Mr. Hudgens down by his arms and legs. Mr. Christopherson then slowly poured water from a gallon jug over Mr. Hudgens's mouth and nose so that he could not breathe. Mr. Hudgens struggled and tried to escape but, at Mr. Christopherson's direction, the other team members held him down. After concluding the exercise, Mr. Christopherson instructed his team members that they should work as hard at making sales as Mr. Hudgens had worked at trying to breathe." *Hudgens v. Prosper, Inc.,* 243 P.3d 1275 (Utah 2010). Based on these facts, Mr. Hudgens filed a Complaint alleging a number of intentional torts. What intentional torts do you see? If the defendants argued that Mr. Hudgens consented to their conduct, how would you analyze that argument?

§ 3. PUBLIC AND PRIVATE NECESSITY

SUROCCO V. GEARY

3 Cal. 69 (1853)

MURRAY, CHIEF JUSTICE, delivered the opinion of the Court.

This was an action, commenced in the court below, to recover damages for blowing up and destroying the plaintiffs' house and property, during the fire of the 24th of December, 1849.

Geary, at that time Alcalde of San Francisco, justified, on the ground that he had the authority, by virtue of his office, to destroy said building, and also that it had been blown up by him to stop the progress of the conflagration then raging.

It was in proof, that the fire passed over and burned beyond the building of the plaintiffs', and that at the time said building was destroyed, they were engaged in removing their property, and could, had they not been prevented, have succeeded in removing more, if not all of their goods.

The cause was tried by the court sitting as a jury, and a verdict rendered for the plaintiffs, from which the defendant prosecutes this appeal under the Practice Act of 1850.

The only question for our consideration is, whether the person who tears down or destroys the house of another, in good faith, and under apparent necessity, during the time of a conflagration, for the purpose of

[Handwritten margin notes:]

Facts: D (Geary) had P['s] (Surocco) house destroyed in an effort to save many more buildings from a fire. P sued to recover for the damages to his property

P filed suit to recover damages sustained by the destruction of house

Public necessity

Also that benefit the society

trespass to land + house conversion; replevin; damages

(P) argued — prove that they could of saved more goods if not all

Judgment by jury. (σ was entered for P). D appealed

Issue

Issue — whether the person who tears down or destroys the house of another's in good faith, and under apparent necessity, during the time of a conflagration.

saving the buildings adjacent, and stopping its progress, can be held personally liable in an action by the owner of the property destroyed. . . .

The right to destroy property, to prevent the spread of a conflagration, has been traced to the highest law of necessity, and the natural rights of man, independent of society or civil government. "It is referred by moralists and jurists to the same great principle which justifies the exclusive appropriation of a plank in a shipwreck, though the life of another be sacrificed; with the throwing overboard goods in a tempest, for the safety of a vessel; with the trespassing upon the lands of another, to escape death by an enemy. It rests upon the maxim, Necessitas inducit privilegium quod jura privata."

The common law adopts the principles of the natural law, and places the justification of an act otherwise tortious precisely on the same ground of necessity.

This principle has been familiarly recognized by the books from the time of the saltpetre case, and the instances of tearing down houses to prevent a conflagration, or to raise bulwarks for the defense of a city, are made use of as illustrations, rather than as abstract cases, in which its exercise is permitted. At such times, the individual rights of property give way to the higher laws of impending necessity.

A house on fire, or those in its immediate vicinity, which serve to communicate the flames, becomes a nuisance, which it is lawful to abate, and the private rights of the individual yield to the considerations of general convenience, and the interests of society. Were it otherwise, one stubborn person might involve a whole city in ruin, by refusing to allow the destruction of a building which would cut off the flames and check the progress of the fire, and that, too, when it was perfectly evident that his building must be consumed. . . .

The counsel for the respondent has asked, who is to judge of the necessity of the destruction of property?

This must, in some instances, be a difficult matter to determine. The necessity of blowing up a house may not exist, or be as apparent to the owner, whose judgment is clouded by interests, and the hope of saving his property, as to others. In all such cases the conduct of the individual must be regulated by his own judgment as to the exigencies of the case. If a building should be torn down without apparent or actual necessity, the parties concerned would undoubtedly be liable in an action of trespass. But in every case the necessity must be clearly shown. It is true, many cases of hardship may grow out of this rule, and property may often in such cases be destroyed, without necessity, by irresponsible persons, but this difficulty would not be obviated by making the parties responsible in every case, whether the necessity existed or not.

The right to destroy property to prevent the spread of a conflagration has been traced to the highest law of necessity ex plain in a shipwreck

Common law adopts the principles of the natural law places justification on same ground of necessity

principle has been familiarly recognized by the books from the time of the saltpetre case

a house on fire which serve to communicate the flames is lawful to abate

Question who is to judge of the necessity of the destruction of property

Question is difficult to determine as owner of house judgment might be clouded

If a buildings be torn down without apparent or actual necessity parties would be liable for trespass

In every case necessity must be clearly shown. It is true hardship may grow out of this rule ex irresponsible persons

NOTES

1. **The common law rule and statutes.** Many states have adopted statutes that codify the merchant's common law privilege. *See, e.g., Barkley v. McKeever Enters., Inc.*, 456 S.W.3d 829 (Mo. 2015) (en banc). These statutes are typically based on the reasonableness of the merchant's suspicion, as well as the time and manner of detention. Do flexible "reasonableness" standards provide sufficient guidance or should statutes state more specifically what a shopkeeper may or may not do?

2. **Mistake.** Under the common law rule and most statutes, the shopkeeper is privileged to act even if reasonably mistaken about the fact that the plaintiff has taken goods without paying. *See, e.g., Dillard Dep't Stores, Inc. v. Silva,* 148 S.W.3d 370 (Tex. 2004). A few states require the shopkeeper to be correct—that is, they do not allow the shopkeeper to utilize this privilege unless the plaintiff did actually take the goods in question. Would this be a better rule? *See Great Atl. & Pac. Tea Co. v. Paul,* 261 A.2d 731 (Md. 1970) (refusing to adopt the Restatement's rule on reasonable mistake). If Arizona had such a "no mistake" rule in place with regard to shoplifting, how might it have changed the analysis in *Gortarez*?

3. **Reasonable manner of detention.** The *Gortarez* court, in discussing the reasonableness of the manner of detention, makes note of the fact that the item believed stolen was of little value (a 59-cent vaporizer). How might the analysis differ if the item had been worth, say, $5,000? Even if the item believed stolen had been valuable, what other facts might lead a jury to conclude that the manner of the detention in *Gortarez* was unreasonable?

4. **A merchant's recapture of chattels.** The common law grants no special privilege to merchants to recapture chattels once possession has been lost; the rules we saw in the Notes after *Brown v. Martinez*, above, apply to merchants as well. Thus if a thief runs out of a store with a stolen item, the store's guard is privileged to recapture it if he does so immediately or in fresh pursuit and uses a reasonable amount of force. Once possession has been lost, however, the detective cannot forcibly recapture it from the thief a week later. The store instead will be forced to sue or to invoke criminal processes. 1 DOBBS, HAYDEN & BUBLICK, THE LAW OF TORTS § 91 (2d ed. 2011).

5. **Using force to detain trespassers.** What if a landowner threatens or uses force and detains a trespasser? In *Whitten v. Cox,* 799 So. 2d 1 (Miss. 2000), to get to land leased by a relative, the three plaintiffs drove a pickup truck onto land occupied legally by the defendant Whitten, who was a municipal judge. Whitten shouted for the truck to stop. When it did not, he fired several shots from a .45 caliber handgun—shooting out one of the back tires. Whitten, along with other men who were all armed with loaded assault rifles, told all three plaintiffs that they were under arrest for trespassing and handcuffed one of them, Cox. According to Cox, Whitten asked the two other plaintiffs whether they thought Cox could swim in the nearby bayou with those handcuffs on. Whitten and his companions escorted the three plaintiffs back to a camp Whitten occupied, and Whitten unsuccessfully tried to reach the

Sheriff. At this point Whitten recognized Cox as the brother of someone who leased neighboring property, and the plaintiffs were freed. The plaintiffs sued Whitten for battery, assault and false imprisonment. Whitten claimed he asserted a valid privilege to arrest and detain them as trespassers. The case went to a jury. According to the court, "If the force used in the arrest of a suspected misdemeanant [and trespassing is a misdemeanor] is unreasonable and excessive, this may render the arrest and detention invalid."

D. DISCIPLINE

Where children are permitted to sue parents for torts, parents still enjoy a privilege to discipline, and to use force and confinement to do so. The limits of this force are ill-defined. The Restatement says parents may use reasonable force as they reasonably believe necessary. *See* RESTATEMENT (SECOND) OF TORTS § 147 (1965); 1 DOBBS, BUBLICK & HAYDEN, THE LAW OF TORTS § 104 (2d ed. 2011). Courts have more commonly articulated standards for appropriate discipline in the context of the criminal law. In *Commonwealth v. Dorvil*, 32 N.E.3d 861 (Mass. 2015), the Massachusetts Supreme Court wrote: "we hold that a parent or guardian may not be subjected to criminal liability for the use of force against a minor child under the care and supervision of the parent or guardian, provided that (1) the force used against the minor child is reasonable; (2) the force is reasonably related to the purpose of safeguarding or promoting the welfare of the minor, including the prevention or punishment of the minor's misconduct; and (3) the force used neither causes, nor creates a substantial risk of causing, physical harm (beyond fleeting pain or minor, transient marks), gross degradation, or severe mental distress."

Those who are in charge of someone else's children also enjoy a similar disciplinary privilege. Teachers and school bus drivers are the most obvious examples. However, it may be that the teacher would not enjoy the same latitude for punishment that courts would recognize in a parent. Suppose a child is spanked by her parent for misbehavior and again by her teacher for additional misbehavior. Apart from local school board regulations affecting corporal punishment, what factors should a court consider in determining whether either the parent or the teacher is liable in tort?

What if "to calm him down" a teacher holds down on the floor a twelve-year-old child who has Asperger's syndrome? What if an 8-year-old with attention deficit disorder and mild mental retardation is repeatedly locked in a "seclusion room" by herself when she misbehaves at school? Some false imprisonment lawsuits have arisen from those sorts of responses.

E. OBSERVING PRIVILEGES

Many common law privileges have the effect of resolving the issues in the case by matter of reasonableness and degree. In self-defense, the issue is frequently whether the defendant reasonably believed that defense was necessary and then whether he used the amount of force reasonable to cope with the apparent threat. In the case of schoolroom punishment, teachers, being privileged to inflict some punishment, are liable only if they go too far. In false imprisonment cases a defendant might be privileged to detain for investigation for a short time, but not for long. All such cases involve matters of reasonableness and hence matters of degree.

Notice how those cases differ from cases in which a defendant commits a "kissing battery"—he kissed the plaintiff, a stranger, or touched the plaintiff in a private place. This is an offensive battery and it is no defense to say the touching did not last long, that the force used was minimal, or that the injury was not great. Thus in common law actions, there are cases in which "degree" is not important, and other cases in which, because the issue of privilege is injected, degree becomes quite significant.

§ 2. THE SPECIAL CASE OF CONSENT

Austin cooked a continental dinner for a new acquaintance, Berwyn, served in candlelight and accompanied by excellent French wines. After dinner the couple sat on the sofa listening to *Traviata* and sipping Benedictine and Brandy. The moment came, as it must in every scene of this sort, in which Austin drew closer and with parted lips looked in Berwyn's eyes. A kiss was imparted and Austin's hand caressed Berwyn's neck. Suddenly, to the surprise of everyone, there was a snap as a vertebra in Berwyn's neck broke. Neither Austin nor Berwyn knew that Berwyn had a congenital condition that made such an outcome possible.

This vignette illustrates several problems about the surprisingly complex "defense" of consent, but also suggests some common sense answers to some of those problems.

1. Berwyn testified: "I never consented to be touched at all, and in fact I was revolted at the idea." If the trier of fact believes this testimony, does it show there was no consent?

2. Was there anything to show there *was* consent?

3. Berwyn's lawyer argued to the trial judge: "Berwyn certainly did not consent to a broken vertebra even if there was consent to a kiss." What do you think of this argument? *Cf. Wulf v. Kunnath*, 827 N.W.2d 248 (Neb. 2015) (doctor who had a "light hearted" relationship with nurse thumped her on the back of her neck, resulting in aggravation of a preexisting disc injury).

4. Is consent really a "defense"? What practical matter would turn on the answer to this? *See Envtl. Processing Sys., L.C. v. FPL Farming Ltd.*, 457 S.W.3d 414 (Tex. 2015).

NOTE: RELATIONSHIP OF THE PARTIES

In real cases lawyers would want to know a great deal more about the facts. Would it impact the analysis if Berwyn had kissed Austin on the cheek when Austin arrived? What if Berwyn had kissed Austin on the lips? What if Berwyn worked for Austin and was told that the dinner was a meeting to discuss a potential promotion? Specific facts like these might be relevant to the issue of apparent consent. Maybe Austin can take it that consent is given by silence in some relationships but not in others. Maybe in some cases a person has no capacity to consent and the actor knows it. Suppose you are sedated and while sedated give "consent" to an operation. If the doctor knows you are heavily sedated should the doctor believe you have manifested consent? There may be some situations in which the power relationships between the parties affect the issue of consent.

ROBINS V. HARRIS, 769 N.E.2d 586 (Ind. 2002). As described by the appellate court, in *Robins v. Harris*, 740 N.E.2d 914, 917 (Ind. Ct. App. 2000), plaintiff Tammy Robins was a female inmate at a county jail and defendant Michael Soules was a new corrections officer on the third shift. According to Soules, when he met Robins she and another inmate, Martha Custer, flashed him by lifting up their shirts and exposing their breasts. Later that evening, Soules ordered a lock down, requiring all inmates to stay in their cells. Soules first summoned Custer out of her cell and upon her return then summoned Robins. He grabbed Robins by the arm and brought her into the shower room where she performed fellatio on him. Robins filed suit, alleging battery. Soules originally denied the allegations but two days later admitted to the sexual contact and resigned his position. He subsequently pled guilty to misdemeanor official misconduct in exchange for dismissal of a felony charge. In the tort action, Soules claimed he was not liable and raised an affirmative defense of consent. The court of appeals held that several parties were potentially subject to liability and that the inmate's alleged consent to the sexual contact was no defense. In the Indiana Supreme Court, "affirmed except as to the availability of the consent defense to the claim of battery," on which point the majority issued no opinion.

Sullivan, J., dissenting. "[T]he Court of Appeals said: 'We also note that consent is not available as a defense to Robins's sexual assault claim. Under I.C. § 35–44–1–5(b), a [jailer] may not claim consent as a defense for sexual misconduct with a detainee. Given Robins's general lack of autonomy as an inmate, it would be incongruous to withhold the defense of consent in the criminal context but to allow Soules the defense in a civil

claim.' I agree with this analysis. Our Legislature has made a public policy determination that the position of authority a jailer holds over a prisoner dictates that there be no exception for consent in our criminal law to the rule against sexual contact between jailer and prisoner. Our state's civil law should further the public policy objective the Legislature has adopted in the criminal context."

NOTES

1. **Power relationships.** Should consent be an available defense when the relationship between the plaintiff and the defendant is inherently unequal as in the situation of jailer and prisoner? *See also, Grager v. Schudar*, 770 N.W.2d 692, 698 (N.D. 2009). Sexual conduct between guards and prisoners can also raise issues about whether the prisoners' civil rights have been violated. *See Graham v. Sherriff of Logan Cty.*, 741 F.3d 1118 (10th Cir. 2013). What about relationships that involve lesser power imbalances? For example, some state statutes forbid all sexual contact between mental health professionals and their patients. Under these statutes, the patient's consent is not legally effective to bar a claim against the therapist. *See Flores v. Santiago*, 986 N.E.2d 1216 (Ill. App. Ct. 2013). What about a relationship between a pastor and parishioner? *See Wende C. v. United Methodist Church*, 827 N.E.2d 265 (N.Y. 2005).

2. **Employers.** Should employers be permitted to claim that an employee who is dependent for a job, wage increase, or promotion consented to sexual intercourse? *See Reavis v. Slominski*, 551 N.W.2d 528 (Neb. 1996) (claim against employer based on sexual contact after an office New Year's Eve party). Federal statutes against employment discrimination forbid sexual harassment of employees. Employer conduct might count as a violation of those statutes, which are usually considered in advanced courses. You should be aware, however, that the damages awards under those statutes may be less attractive to the plaintiff in some instances than the common law awards.

3. **Incapacity to consent: minors.** Minors as a class are often thought to lack capacity to consent, although there is not a blanket rule that covers every situation; courts will sometimes look at the individual facts, to see if the particular minor has the experience and intelligence to consent to the particular act involved in the case. *See* 1 DOBBS, HAYDEN & BUBLICK, THE LAW OF TORTS § 109 (2d ed. 2011). Although courts are split, it is generally assumed that minors may consent to a number of touchings appropriate to their age. Probably two eight-year-olds can effectively consent to a football game in which touching is inevitable. Older minors can consent to more serious touchings, such as routine medical attention. The hospital emergency room that administers first aid to a 16-year-old with a broken arm is presumably protected from any claim of battery if the teenager consents. But many states impose criminal liability for sexual conduct with a minor. Many, though not all, states agree that a minor's consent is no defense in a civil action for such sexual contact, either. Should the age of the child claimed to have consented

matter? *See C.C.H. v. Philadelphia Phillies, Inc.*, 940 A.2d 336 (Pa. 2008) (alleged consent of 11-year-old child could not be a defense).

4. **Incapacity to consent: adults.** Incapacity of an adult is usually established only by showing that the particular adult could not manage his own affairs, or, in consent cases, that he did not understand the nature and character of the act. See *Saucier ex rel. Mallory v. McDonald's Rests. of Mont., Inc.*, 179 P.3d 481 (Mont. 2008) (employee who was mentally retarded engaged in a sexual relationship with her manager at McDonald's; genuine issue of material fact remained as to plaintiff's ability to consent).

KAPLAN V. MAMELAK, 162 Cal. App. 4th 637 (2008). A patient sued his doctor for medical malpractice and battery, claiming that the doctor operated on the wrong herniated disks in his back. The trial court granted the doctor's demurrer to the battery claim, and the jury found for the doctor on the malpractice claim. *Held*, reversed and remanded. A doctor who operates on a patient without that patient's consent commits a battery. Here the doctor "may have committed battery by operating on appellant's T6–7 and T7–8 disks when he did not have permission to operate on any disk other than T8–9." While "the law will deem a patient to have consented to a touching that, although not literally covered by the patient's express consent, involves complications inherent to the procedure, . . . a battery occurs if the physician performs a 'substantially different treatment' from that covered by the patient's expressed consent." These issues are for the jury, making the grant of demurrer improper.

NOTES

1. **Exceeding the scope of consent.** Many cases of "medical battery" involve allegations that the doctor exceeded the scope of the patient's consent. *See Duncan v. Scottsdale Medical Imaging, Ltd.*, 70 P.3d 435 (Ariz. 2003) (patient told the nurse that she would accept only non-synthetic demerol or morphine, and nurse assured her that only one of those particular drugs would be administered, however, synthetic drug was administered, causing complications; "general authorization of an injection does not defeat her battery claim because her consent was limited to certain drugs"). What about a hospital patient who consents to a blood draw without being told that it was for a non-medical law-enforcement purpose? *See O'Brien v. Synnott*, 72 A.3d 331 (Vt. 2013).

2. **Emergencies.** The ordinary rule—that it is battery when a doctor treats a patient without the patient's consent, or in excess of the scope of a patient's consent—may not apply when the doctor must act in an emergency and obtaining consent is not possible. *See, e.g., Kennedy v. Parrott*, 90 S.E.2d 754 (N.C. 1956) (finding implied consent for a doctor to "extend the operation to remedy any abnormal or diseased condition in the area of the original

"incision" when the patient is incapable of giving consent and no one else with authority to consent is available).

3. **Substituted consent.** An adult family member or guardian may be empowered to give consent on behalf of a minor or an incapacitated adult. The rule is easy enough to state, but many issues arise in real cases. In *Harvey v. Strickland*, 566 S.E.2d 529 (S.C. 2002), an adult patient, preparing for an operation, signed a form saying he refused to accept a blood transfusion for religious reasons. During the operation, the doctor determined that the patient needed a transfusion and called the patient's mother for permission, which she granted. When sued by the patient for battery, the doctor claimed that the patient had once said he would "consider" a transfusion. Can we say that this patient impliedly consented to substituted consent by his mother? The court said the case presented a jury question on that issue.

4. **Incompetence to give or withhold consent.** What if a person is intoxicated at the time of emergency treatment—should the doctor be required to obtain consent? In *Miller v. Rhode Island Hospital,* 625 A.2d 778 (R.I. 1993), the plaintiff had consumed many, many drinks before he was in an automobile collision. The trauma team at the emergency room, fearing internal bleeding, insisted on performing a peritoneal lavage. When plaintiff objected, doctors strapped him to a gurney, anesthetized him and performed the lavage. The plaintiff sued for battery. The court thought that competence to consent (or refuse consent) should be measured by the plaintiff's ability to understand the condition, nature and effect of the proposed treatment or its rejection. When the plaintiff was unable to understand the nature of the treatment due to his intoxication, doctors were not required to attempt to obtain his consent.

DOE V. JOHNSON, 817 F. Supp. 1382 (W.D. Mich. 1993). Plaintiff Jane Doe alleged: Earvin Johnson, Jr., transmitted human immunodeficiency virus (HIV) to her through consensual sexual contact. Johnson knew or should have known that he had a high risk of being infected with HIV because of his promiscuous lifestyle. Nevertheless, he did not warn Doe of this high risk or inform her that he did in fact have HIV. Nor did he use a condom. Doe suffers from HIV now and will develop AIDS. On motion to dismiss the battery claim, *held,* motion denied. One who knows he has a venereal disease, and knows that his sexual partner does not know of his infection, commits a battery by having sexual intercourse.

NOTES

1. **STDs.** Where the defendant knows he has a sexually transmitted disease but neither warns his sexual partner nor provides any protection, several cases have imposed liability. *E.g., Johnson v. Jones*, 344 P.3d 89 (Or. Ct. App. 2015) (genital herpes not revealed; consent obtained by material nondisclosure is not consent at all). In *Doe v. Johnson,* can you say that the defendant had the intent to touch in a harmful or offensive way? Remember to

distinguish intent from negligence. Is it relevant that Johnson claimed to have had unprotected sex with more than 2,000 partners? Is high-risk sexual activity enough to establish constructive knowledge? *Kohl v. Kohl,* 149 So. 3d 137 (Fla. Dist. Ct. App. 2014) (husband's extramarital relations with prostitutes is not enough to establish actual or constructive knowledge).

2. **Consent procured by fraud.** Courts recognize that, in a general way, consent procured by fraud is not valid. Do you see how the outcome in *Doe v. Johnson* could be characterized as consent procured by fraud? If induced by false information, consent may not be valid even if one voluntarily participates in the touching. *See Hackett v. Fulton County Sch. Dist.*, 238 F. Supp. 2d 1330 (N.D. Ga. 2002).

3. **Avoiding the effect of consent.** To avoid the effect of a manifested consent, the plaintiff's mistake must be "about the nature and quality of the invasion intended by the conduct." W. PROSSER & J. KEETON, PROSSER AND KEETON ON TORTS § 18 (5th ed. 1984). Eating a chocolate from a box of poisoned candy seems like a mistake about the nature and quality of the contact. Mistakes or misrepresentations about collateral matters such as price or timing do not nullify the consent. *See* 1 DOBBS, HAYDEN & BUBLICK, THE LAW OF TORTS § 111 (2d ed. 2011).

4. **Revocation of consent.** Subject only to the slightest qualification, the plaintiff can revoke consent at any time by communicating the revocation to the defendant. Thus a landowner who has consented to another person's presence on the land could order the person to leave; if the visitor does not leave, he becomes a trespasser. A person who consents to intimate contact with another can have a change of heart and revoke consent; if that is communicated to the other person, any further contact would become tortious. *See id.* § 108.

5. **Consent to crime.** When the plaintiff is injured during an illegal activity in which he has agreed to participate (such as an illegal boxing match), courts have struggled to find a consistent approach to the issue of consent. Some have held consent to a crime is invalid, so that the tort claim can proceed. Others have said that that the plaintiff's consent bars the tort claim. The Restatement's rule is that the plaintiff's consent is a bar just as in any other case. RESTATEMENT (SECOND) OF TORTS § 892C (1979). However, if the statute makes the conduct illegal in order to protect the plaintiff from her own consent, as might be the case with a statutory rape law for example, the plaintiff's consent should not bar her claim. Suppose a statute makes it unlawful to hire a child under 15 for work near industrial machinery. Should the child's consent be a bar? *See id*; 1 DOBBS, HAYDEN & BUBLICK, THE LAW OF TORTS § 116 (2d ed. 2011).

A Mini-Problem for Review

"On May 29, 2007, Mr. Christopherson [a supervisor at Prosper, Inc.] asked for volunteers for a new motivational exercise. He offered no explanation to his team members regarding the nature of the exercise. In his search for volunteers, Mr. Christopherson challenged the loyalty and determination of his team members. Mr. Hudgens volunteered to be a part of the exercise to prove his loyalty and determination. Mr. Christopherson then led his team members to the top of a hill near Prosper's office. Once on the hill, Mr. Christopherson ordered Mr. Hudgens to lie down, facing up, with his head pointed downhill. Mr. Christopherson ordered other team members to hold Mr. Hudgens down by his arms and legs. Mr. Christopherson then slowly poured water from a gallon jug over Mr. Hudgens's mouth and nose so that he could not breathe. Mr. Hudgens struggled and tried to escape but, at Mr. Christopherson's direction, the other team members held him down. After concluding the exercise, Mr. Christopherson instructed his team members that they should work as hard at making sales as Mr. Hudgens had worked at trying to breathe." *Hudgens v. Prosper, Inc.,* 243 P.3d 1275 (Utah 2010). Based on these facts, Mr. Hudgens filed a Complaint alleging a number of intentional torts. What intentional torts do you see? If the defendants argued that Mr. Hudgens consented to their conduct, how would you analyze that argument?

§ 3. PUBLIC AND PRIVATE NECESSITY

SUROCCO V. GEARY

3 Cal. 69 (1853)

MURRAY, CHIEF JUSTICE, delivered the opinion of the Court.

This was an action, commenced in the court below, to recover damages for blowing up and destroying the plaintiffs' house and property, during the fire of the 24th of December, 1849.

Geary, at that time Alcalde of San Francisco, justified, on the ground that he had the authority, by virtue of his office, to destroy said building, and also that it had been blown up by him to stop the progress of the conflagration then raging.

It was in proof, that the fire passed over and burned beyond the building of the plaintiffs', and that at the time said building was destroyed, they were engaged in removing their property, and could, had they not been prevented, have succeeded in removing more, if not all of their goods.

The cause was tried by the court sitting as a jury, and a verdict rendered for the plaintiffs, from which the defendant prosecutes this appeal under the Practice Act of 1850.

The only question for our consideration is, whether the person who tears down or destroys the house of another, in good faith, and under apparent necessity, during the time of a conflagration, for the purpose of saving the buildings adjacent, and stopping its progress, can be held personally liable in an action by the owner of the property destroyed. . . .

The right to destroy property, to prevent the spread of a conflagration, has been traced to the highest law of necessity, and the natural rights of man, independent of society or civil government. "It is referred by moralists and jurists to the same great principle which justifies the exclusive appropriation of a plank in a shipwreck, though the life of another be sacrificed; with the throwing overboard goods in a tempest, for the safety of a vessel; with the trespassing upon the lands of another, to escape death by an enemy. It rests upon the maxim, Necessitas inducit privilegium quod jura privata."

The common law adopts the principles of the natural law, and places the justification of an act otherwise tortious precisely on the same ground of necessity.

This principle has been familiarly recognized by the books from the time of the saltpetre case, and the instances of tearing down houses to prevent a conflagration, or to raise bulwarks for the defense of a city, are made use of as illustrations, rather than as abstract cases, in which its exercise is permitted. At such times, the individual rights of property give way to the higher laws of impending necessity.

A house on fire, or those in its immediate vicinity, which serve to communicate the flames, becomes a nuisance, which it is lawful to abate, and the private rights of the individual yield to the considerations of general convenience, and the interests of society. Were it otherwise, one stubborn person might involve a whole city in ruin, by refusing to allow the destruction of a building which would cut off the flames and check the progress of the fire, and that, too, when it was perfectly evident that his building must be consumed. . . .

The counsel for the respondent has asked, who is to judge of the necessity of the destruction of property?

This must, in some instances, be a difficult matter to determine. The necessity of blowing up a house may not exist, or be as apparent to the owner, whose judgment is clouded by interests, and the hope of saving his property, as to others. In all such cases the conduct of the individual must be regulated by his own judgment as to the exigencies of the case. If a building should be torn down without apparent or actual necessity, the parties concerned would undoubtedly be liable in an action of trespass. But in every case the necessity must be clearly shown. It is true, many cases of hardship may grow out of this rule, and property may often in such cases be destroyed, without necessity, by irresponsible persons, but this difficulty would not be obviated by making the parties responsible in every case, whether the necessity existed or not.

The legislature of the State possess the power to regulate this subject by providing the manner in which buildings may be destroyed, and the mode in which compensation shall be made; and it is to be hoped that something will be done to obviate the difficulty, and prevent the happening of such events as those supposed by the respondent's counsel.

In the absence of any legislation on the subject, we are compelled to fall back upon the rules of the common law.

The evidence in this case clearly establishes the fact, that the blowing up of the house was necessary, as it would have been consumed had it been left standing. The plaintiffs cannot recover for the value of the goods which they might have saved; they were as much subject to the necessities of the occasion as the house in which they were situate; and if in such cases a party was held liable, it would too frequently happen, that the delay caused by the removal of the goods would render the destruction of the house useless.

The court below clearly erred as to the law applicable to the facts of this case. The testimony will not warrant a verdict against the defendant.

Judgment reversed.

NOTES

1. **Public necessity: scope of the privilege.** The rule applied in *Surocco* is reflected in the Restatement Second of Torts § 196 (privileging interference with land) and § 263 (privileging interference with chattels). The privilege of public necessity protects against actual harms done, where public rather than merely private interests are involved, the defendant had a reasonable belief that action was needed, and the action he took was a reasonable response to the need. The privilege protects not only public officials but also private citizens who act in the public interest. *See* 1 DOBBS, HAYDEN & BUBLICK, THE LAW OF TORTS § 118 (2d ed. 2011). The "essence of the doctrine is that the government is acting under pressure of public necessity and to avert impending peril." The rule still applies today. *See Brewer v. State*, 341 P.3d 1107 (Alaska 2014) (burning plaintiff's vegetation to deprive advancing wildfires of fuel was justified by public necessity, barring tort claim as well as takings claim).

2. **Policy.** Does the public necessity privilege represent good policy? Does it make any difference in your assessment whether the defendant is a private actor as opposed to a government employee?

3. **Injustice to the property owner?** Even if the privilege serves a useful purpose in freeing the helpful citizen from liability, does it work an injustice in making the private property owner sacrifice his property to the public good?

4. **State takings clauses.** In part to address a perceived injustice to the property owner, some states have held that where the defendant is a "state

actor" who destroys property for the public good in an emergency, the state itself should compensate the property owner under the Takings Clause of the state constitution. These clauses generally provide that no private property shall be taken for public use without just compensation. *See, e.g., Wegner v. Milwaukee Mut. Ins. Co.*, 479 N.W.2d 38 (Minn. 1991) (when police used flash-bang grenades against suspected felons who had run into plaintiff's house, Minnesota's Takings Clause required payment; "At its most basic level, the issue is whether it is fair to allocate the entire risk of loss to an innocent homeowner for the good of the public.").

5. **What is a taking?** California itself has reaffirmed *Surocco* even where the defendant is a government actor, however, holding that the Takings Clause of its state constitution does not extend to police destruction or seizure of property, even if done to benefit the public. *Customer Co. v. City of Sacramento*, 895 P.2d 900 (Cal. 1995). Some other states have followed this analysis, holding that police destruction or seizure of property is not a constitutional "taking." *See, e.g., Eggleston v. Pierce Cty.*, 64 P.3d 618 (Wash. 2003); *Kelley v. Story Cty. Sheriff*, 611 N.W.2d 475 (Iowa 2000); *Sullivant v. City of Oklahoma City*, 940 P.2d 220 (Okla. 1997). Also, "it must be shown that there was an invasion of property rights that was intended or was the foreseeable result of authorized governmental action." *Henderson v. City of Columbus*, 827 N.W.2d 486 (Neb. 2013). Accordingly, a homeowner's house was not "taken or damaged for public use" when it was flooded by raw sewage during a rainstorm because there was no showing that a government actor knew of or could foresee the damage to private property.

6. **Insurance.** Might *Surocco* be justified today on the ground that fire insurance is commonly purchased by all landowners and that it is a cheap and efficient way of dealing with the loss by fire?

PLOOF V. PUTNAM, 71 A. 188 (Vt. 1908). The defendant owned an island in Lake Champlain. The plaintiff, with his wife and two children, were sailing a sloop on the lake when a violent tempest arose. To avoid destruction of the sloop and injury to himself and his family, the plaintiff moored the boat at the defendant's dock. The defendant, through his servant, unmoored the boat. The sloop and its contents were destroyed and the people in it injured. The plaintiff claimed that unmooring the sloop was a trespass to it and that the defendant had a duty to permit the sloop to remain moored there. *Held,* for the plaintiff. "There are many cases in the books which hold that necessity . . . will justify entries upon land and interferences with personal property that would otherwise have been trespasses. . . . If one have a way over the land of another for his beasts to pass, and the beasts, being properly driven, feed the grass by morsels in passing, or run out of the way and are promptly pursued and brought back, trespass will not lie. A traveler on a highway who finds it obstructed from a sudden and temporary cause may pass upon the adjoining land without

becoming a trespasser because of the necessity. An entry upon land to save goods which are in danger of being lost or destroyed by water or fire is not a trespass. . . . One may sacrifice the personal property of another to save his life or the lives of his fellows. . . . It is clear that an entry upon the land of another may be justified by necessity for mooring the sloop."

VINCENT V. LAKE ERIE TRANSPORTATION CO.
124 N.W. 221 (Minn. 1910)

O'BRIEN, J.

The steamship Reynolds, owned by the defendant, was for the purpose of discharging her cargo on November 27, 1905, moored to plaintiff's dock in Duluth. While the unloading of the boat was taking place a storm from the northeast developed, which at about 10 o'clock P.M., when the unloading was completed, had so grown in violence that the wind was then moving at 50 miles per hour and continued to increase during the night. There is some evidence that one, and perhaps two, boats were able to enter the harbor that night, but it is plain that navigation was practically suspended from the hour mentioned until the morning of the 29th when the storm abated, and during that time no master would have been justified in attempting to navigate his vessel, if he could avoid doing so. After the discharge of the cargo the Reynolds signaled for a tug to tow her from the dock, but none could be obtained because of the severity of the storm. If the lines holding the ship to the dock had been cast off, she would doubtless have drifted away; but, instead, the lines were kept fast, and as soon as one parted or chafed it was replaced, sometimes with a larger one. The vessel lay upon the outside of the dock, her bow to the east, the wind and waves striking her starboard quarter with such force that she was constantly being lifted and thrown against the dock, resulting in its damage as found by the jury, to the amount of $500.

We are satisfied that the character of the storm was such that it would have been highly imprudent for the master of the Reynolds to have attempted to leave the dock or to have permitted his vessel to drift away from it. . . . Nothing more was demanded of them than ordinary prudence and care, and the record in this case fully sustains the contention of the appellant that, in holding the vessel fast to the dock, those in charge of her exercised good judgment and prudent seamanship. . . .

The appellant contends by ample assignments of error that, because its conduct during the storm was rendered necessary by prudence and good seamanship under conditions over which it had no control, it cannot be held liable for any injury resulting to the property of others, and claims that the jury should have been so instructed. An analysis of the charge given by the trial court is not necessary, as in our opinion the only question for the jury was the amount of damages which the plaintiffs were entitled to recover, and no complaint is made upon that score.

The situation was one in which the ordinary rules regulating property rights were suspended by forces beyond human control, and if, without the direct intervention of some act by the one sought to be held liable the property of another was injured, such injury must be attributed to the act of God, and not to the wrongful act of the person sought to be charged. If during the storm the Reynolds had entered the harbor, and while there had become disabled and been thrown against the plaintiffs' dock, the plaintiffs could not have recovered. Again, if while attempting to hold fast to the dock the lines had parted, without any negligence, and the vessel carried against some other boat or dock in the harbor, there would be no liability upon her owner. But here those in charge of the vessel deliberately and by their direct efforts held her in such a position that the damage to the dock resulted, and, having thus preserved the ship at the expense of the dock, it seems to us that her owners are responsible to the dock owners to the extent of the injury inflicted. . . .

In Ploof v. Putnam, 71 Atl. 188, the Supreme Court of Vermont held that where, under stress of weather, a vessel was without permission moored to a private dock at an island in Lake Champlain owned by the defendant, the plaintiff was not guilty of trespass, and that the defendant was responsible in damages because his representative upon the island unmoored the vessel, permitting it to drift upon the shore, with resultant injuries to it. If, in that case, the vessel had been permitted to remain, and the dock had suffered an injury, we believe the shipowner would have been held liable for the injury done.

Theologians hold that a starving man may, without moral guilt, take what is necessary to sustain life; but it could hardly be said that the obligation would not be upon such person to pay the value of the property so taken when he became able to do so. And so public necessity, in times of war or peace, may require the taking of private property for public purposes; but under our system of jurisprudence compensation must be made.

Let us imagine in this case that for the better mooring of the vessel those in charge of her had appropriated a valuable cable lying upon the dock. No matter how justifiable such appropriation might have been, it would not be claimed that, because of the overwhelming necessity of the situation, the owner of the cable could not recover its value.

This is not a case where life or property was menaced by any object or thing belonging to the plaintiff, the destruction of which became necessary to prevent the threatened disaster. Nor is it a case where, because of the act of God, or unavoidable accident, the infliction of the injury was beyond the control of the defendant, but is one where the defendant prudently and

[Handwritten marginal notes, left margin:] Court explains i f D steamship had entered the harbor during the storm, became disabled and been thrown against the P dock, then the P could not have recovered however in this case steamship was deliberately held against the dock. D preserved its ship at the expense of P's dock. Therefore D is responsible for damages done

[Handwritten marginal notes, lower left:] Court explains / argues and gives holding

[Handwritten marginal notes, right:] Court cites Ploof v. Putnam and believe a different holding would have occured

[Handwritten marginal notes, center:] Court explain Theologians also talks about public necessity may require the taking of private property for public purposes, but under system compensation be may made

advisedly availed itself of the plaintiffs' property for the purpose of preserving its own more valuable property and the plaintiffs are entitled to compensation for the injury done.

Order affirmed.

LEWIS, J. I dissent. . . . In my judgment, if the boat was lawfully in position at the time the storm broke, and the master could not, in the exercise of due care, have left that position without subjecting his vessel to the hazards of the storm, then the damage to the dock, caused by the pounding of the boat, was the result of an inevitable accident. . . .

I am of the opinion that one who constructs a dock to the navigable line of waters, and enters into contractual relations with the owner of a vessel to moor at the same, takes the risk of damage to his dock by a boat caught there by a storm, which event could not have been avoided in the exercise of due care, and further, that the legal status of the parties in such a case is not changed by renewal of cables to keep the boat from being cast adrift at the mercy of the tempest.

NOTES

1. **Private necessity: scope of the privilege.** Can you glean the scope of the private necessity privilege from reading *Ploof* and *Vincent* together? How does the private necessity privilege differ from the public necessity privilege? What might justify the difference? *See* 1 DOBBS, HAYDEN & BUBLICK, THE LAW OF TORTS § 117 (2d ed. 2011).

2. **Contractual rights.** Presumably the shipowner and dock owner made some consensual arrangement about the use of the dock. If the shipowner had the right to continued use of the dock under that arrangement, can it be said that by renewing the lines he took any benefit he was not entitled to?

3. **An economic perspective.** Does it matter whether courts adopt a legal rule that requires a boat owner to pay for damage to the dock or a rule that does not require such payment? It might not matter to whether the parties achieve an efficient allocation of resources. In his 1960 article entitled *The Problem of Social Cost*, 3 J. OF LAW & ECON. 1, economist Ronald Coase explained why. Parties can bargain around any legal rule in order to reach an efficient allocation of resources. Imagine for example that the boat is worth $500. If it goes out in the storm its full value will be lost. If it stays tethered to the dock, it will cause $1000 of damage to the dock. Given those damage estimates, the efficient allocation of resources would be to forgo the value of the boat rather than cause greater injury to the dock. Of course, the parties will reach this efficient result—letting the boat go—if the boat owner has to pay for damage done to the dock. In that scenario, the owner would face the choice of incurring a $500 loss or a $1000 loss, and would let the boat go in order to incur the lesser loss. However, if the boat owner does not have to pay for the damage to the dock, might the owner chose a $1000 loss to the dock owner rather than a $500 cost of the boat owner's own? Perhaps not. Given the

opportunity to bargain, the dock owner could pay the boat owner an amount of money between $500 and $1000 to let the boat go and both parties would be better off. At times, however, the legal rule may indeed matter to whether the parties reach the efficient result. When barriers to bargaining are high, such as when significant transaction and information costs are present, the parties may not be able to bargain effectively. In addition, the legal rule may matter a great deal to the parties themselves. The distribution of legal entitlements will affect the distribution of wealth between them. Under the rule that requires the boat owner to pay for damage, the owner will have a $500 loss from letting the boat go. If the boat owner is not required to pay for damage, the boat owner will at worst have no loss, and at best will have a gain of $500.

4. **The role of fault.** Is *Vincent* contrary to *Van Camp v. McAfoos*, the child tricyclist case we saw in Chapter 1? After all, the court recognized that the captain was not at fault, yet imposed liability.

5. **Scope of private necessity.** For some purposes, "a trespasser is one 'who enters or remains upon land in the possession of another without a privilege to do so created by the possessor's consent or otherwise.' Thus a person entering pursuant to a lawful privilege is not a trespasser under D.C. law." Would the necessity privilege justify a person climbing over a fence to chase after his dog or would such a person be a trespasser without a privilege? *See Toomer v. William C. Smith & Co., Inc.*, 112 A.3d 324 (D.C. 2015).

6. **Necessity to take a life?** The driver of a school bus with twenty children on board is coming down a mountain road. On her left is a sheer precipice. On her right is solid rock. As the bus picks up speed, a car coming up the hill traveling very fast appears in the bus' lane. It is now clear that the driver must act. If she stays where she is, a collision will ensue. If she turns left, she will take the children over the cliff. She can turn right before gaining any more speed, but if she does so she will certainly strike two children waiting at the bus stop. This would kill the two children or seriously maim them, but it will probably save most of those on the bus. On the rationale of *Vincent* would the driver be liable for the deaths of the two children? Professor George Christie, in *The Defense of Necessity Considered from the Legal and Moral Points of View,* 48 DUKE L.J. 975 (1999), analyzes the positions of a number of philosophers. He himself thinks that an intentional killing to save a greater number of lives is not privileged.

REFERENCES: 1 DOBBS, HAYDEN & BUBLICK, THE LAW OF TORTS §§ 80–119 (2d ed. 2011); DOBBS, HAYDEN & BUBLICK, HORNBOOK ON TORTS §§ 7.1–7.21 (2d ed. 2016).

PART 3

THE PRIMA FACIE CASE
FOR NEGLIGENCE

• • •

CHAPTER 5

THE PRIMA FACIE CASE FOR NEGLIGENCE AND THE ELEMENT OF DUTY

• • •

§ 1. THEORY AND ELEMENTS OF NEGLIGENCE

A. THE FAULT BASIS OF LIABILITY

OLIVER WENDELL HOLMES, THE COMMON LAW
1881 Howe ed. 1963 pp. 76–78

The general principle of our law is that loss from accident must lie where it falls, and this principle is not affected by the fact that a human being is the instrument of misfortune. But relatively to a given human being anything is accident which he could not fairly have been expected to contemplate as possible, and therefore to avoid. . . .

A man need not, it is true, do this or that act,—the term act implies a choice,—but he must act somehow. Furthermore, the public generally profits by individual activity. As action cannot be avoided, and tends to the public good, there is obviously no policy in throwing the hazard of what is at once desirable and inevitable upon the actor.

The state might conceivably make itself a mutual insurance company against accidents, and distribute the burden of its citizens' mishaps among its members. There might be a pension for paralytics, and state aid for those who suffered in person or estate from tempest or wild beasts. . . . [T]he prevailing view is that its cumbrous and expensive machinery ought not to be set in motion unless some clear benefit is to be derived from disturbing the status quo. . . . Unless my act is of a nature to threaten others, unless under the circumstances a prudent man would have foreseen the possibility of harm, it is no more justifiable to make me indemnify my neighbor against the consequences, than to make me do the same thing if I had fallen upon him in a fit, or to compel me to insure him against lightning.

B. SOME INSTITUTIONS OF NEGLIGENCE PRACTICE

Intentional torts were defined in highly structured ways. In effect, the law of intentional torts prohibited specific acts like intentional touchings

91

or intentional confinement of another person. The tort broadly called negligence is not defined by naming specific forbidden acts. Instead, negligence may be any conduct that creates an unreasonable risk of harm to others. It is actionable as a tort when that risk comes to fruition in actual harm. Before we explore the detailed meanings of negligence, we must recognize several important legal institutions or problems that condition negligence law. These are in no sense merely a general background; they are practices we must have in mind when we try to understand what it really means to impose liability for negligence.

1. *Litigation finance—attorney's fees.* As we know from Chapter 1, each party must pay his or her own attorney. This has led to the contingent fee, under which the plaintiff may retain an attorney without payment of any fee unless the plaintiff wins the case. If the plaintiff wins, the attorney will share in the recovery, usually between 25% to 50%. In large time-consuming cases, large awards for pain and suffering or for punitive damages are required if an attorney is to take the case, for otherwise the attorney won't be paid enough to make the case economically feasible.

2. *Liability insurance.* Although liability insurance for automobiles may be compulsory, the policy limit—the sum available to pay for injuries—is likely to be too low to cover serious injury.

3. *The role of settlement.* The number of personal injury trials is small. However, the number of personal injuries is large. The volume of routine negligence claims in, say, auto accidents, is vast. Almost all injury claims are settled without trial. To come up with a reasonable estimate of a case's settlement value, lawyers for each side must determine what facts will be proved if the case goes to court and what legal rules will affect the outcome. Accordingly, lawyers must know the rules and also how they are likely to be applied in court. Although lawyers approach the cases as adversaries, they must make neutral, balanced judgments about how the case will appear to the judge and jury. The lawyer who relies on a rule that represents injustice or bad policy may find that the judge will reject the rule or that the jury will find a way not to apply it. Accordingly, lawyers, and students, must make careful evaluation of the rules announced in cases.

C. LEGAL ELEMENTS OF A NEGLIGENCE CLAIM

Drawing on the important considerations just discussed, courts have developed a general formula for the negligence claim. To receive compensation, the plaintiff must allege and prove facts establishing five elements:

(1) The defendant owed the plaintiff a legal duty;

(2) The defendant, by behaving negligently, breached that duty;

Negligence Elements

(3) The plaintiff suffered actual damage;

(4) The defendant's negligence was a factual cause of this damage; and

(5) The defendant's negligence was a "proximate cause" of this damage or, as is sometimes said, the damage is within the "scope of liability" of the defendant.

Different courts may state these required elements in slightly different ways, but the differences are matters of style, not substance. All courts require the plaintiff to sustain the burden of proving each of the five elements. All courts also agree that if the plaintiff fails to meet the burden of proving any one of them, the plaintiff cannot recover. In the following materials, we explore each of these elements in turn.

§ 2. THE GENERAL DUTY OF CARE: THE REASONABLE AND PRUDENT PERSON STANDARD

"Although it was not required in early English law, in order to establish a negligence cause of action today, the plaintiff must show that the defendant owes her a duty of care. 'A duty, in negligence cases, may be defined as an obligation, to which the law will give recognition and effect, to conform to a particular standard of conduct toward another.' . . . [D]uty is a question for the judge. . . . In general, when an actor's conduct, creates, maintains, or continues a risk of physical harm, he ordinarily has a duty of care. When such a duty is owed, the standard of care to be applied is ordinarily reasonable care under the circumstances." DOBBS, HAYDEN & BUBLICK, HORNBOOK ON TORTS § 10.1 (2d ed. 2016). [Under that general standard, an actor must exercise the care that would be exercised by a reasonable and prudent person under the same or similar circumstances to avoid or minimize risks of harm to others.]

This chapter begins with the ordinary situation in which an actor owes a duty of care and the standard is reasonable care. After we have reviewed this usual situation in which an actor owes a duty of reasonable care, we will see in later chapters that, in some contexts, actors may owe no duty at all. Also, courts sometimes modify the standard of care for particular contexts like medical negligence.

STEWART V. MOTTS
654 A.2d 535 (Pa. 1995)

MONTEMURO, JUSTICE. . . .

The sole issue presented before us is whether there exists a higher standard of "extraordinary care" for the use of dangerous instrumentalities over and above the standard of "reasonable care" such that the trial court erred for failing to give an instruction to the jury that the Appellee should have used a "high degree of care" in handling gasoline. Because we believe that there is but one standard of care, the standard of "reasonable care," we affirm.

Court explains they belief in one standard of care which is reasonable care

Facts of Case

The pertinent facts of this case are simple and were ably stated by the trial court:

On July 15, 1987, Plaintiff, Jonathon Stewart, stopped at Defendant, Martin Motts' auto repair shop and offered assistance to the Defendant in repairing an automobile fuel tank. In an effort to start and move the car with the gasoline tank unattached, the Plaintiff suggested and then proceeded to pour gasoline into the carburetor. The Defendant was to turn the ignition key at a given moment. While the exact sequence of events was contested, the tragic result was that the car backfired, caused an explosion and resulted in Plaintiff suffering severe burns to his upper body.

Steward argued in trial court that since gasoline is inflammability and a dangerous substance if not handled properly it deserved a high degree of care

[In Stewart's suit against Motts, the plaintiff asked the judge to instruct the jury in part "that gasoline due to its inflammability, is a very dangerous substance if not properly handled. . . . With an appreciation of such danger, and under conditions where its existence reasonably should have been known, there follows a high degree of care which circumscribes the conduct of everyone about the danger. . . ." The judge refused to so instruct and the jury returned a verdict for the defendant.]

Court reaffirms principle that one standard of care be applied to negligence acts involving dangerous instrumentality

We begin our discussion by reaffirming the principle that there is but one standard of care to be applied to negligence actions involving dangerous instrumentalities in this Commonwealth. This standard of care is "reasonable care" as well stated in the Restatement (Second) of Torts: "The care required is always reasonable care. The standard never varies, but the care which it is reasonable to require of the actor varies with the danger involved in his act and is proportionate to it. The greater the danger, the greater the care which must be exercised. . . ." Restatement (Second) of Torts § 298 comment b (1965). . . .

Trial court ruled in favor of defendant

Properly read, our cases involving dangerous agencies reaffirm these well accepted principles found in the Restatement. In *Konchar v. Cebular*, 333 Pa. 499, 3 A.2d 913 (1939) . . . we recognized that the question of the plaintiff's contributory negligence was to be determined using the reasonable care standard in light of the particular circumstances of the case. One such circumstance, we acknowledged, was that gasoline, a dangerous substance, was involved requiring that the reasonably prudent person exercise a higher degree of care under these circumstances. Taken in context, our statement that the plaintiff was under a "high duty of care" did nothing more than reaffirm the general principle that the care employed by a reasonable man must be proportionate to the danger of the activity. . . .

Citing Koncher v Cebular list court concluded that care employed by a reasonable man must be proportional to the danger of the activity

Our use of the language "higher degree of care" merely stated the common sense conclusion that the use of a dangerous agency would require the reasonably prudent person to exercise more care. . . .

In summation, this Commonwealth recognizes only one standard of care in negligence actions involving dangerous instrumentalities—the standard of reasonable care under the circumstances. It is well established by our case law that the reasonable man must exercise care in proportion to the danger involved in his act.

With these principles in mind we must next examine the jury instructions in this case. The trial judge explained to the jury that negligence is "the absence of ordinary care which a reasonably prudent person would exercise in the circumstances here presented." The trial judge further explained: "It is for you to determine how a reasonably prudent person would act in those circumstances. Ordinary care is the care a reasonably prudent person would use under the circumstances presented in this case. It is the duty of every person to use ordinary care not only for his own safety and the protection of his property, but also to avoid serious injury to others. What constitutes ordinary care varies according to the particular circumstances and conditions existing then and there. The amount of care required by law must be in keeping with the degree of danger involved. . . ."

We find that this charge, when read as a whole, adequately instructed the jury. The charge informed the jury that the proper standard of care was "reasonable" or "ordinary" care under the circumstances in accordance with the law of this Commonwealth. The charge properly instructed the jury that the level of care required changed with the circumstances. The charge also informed the jury that the level of care required increased proportionately with the level of danger in the activity. We find nothing in this charge that is confusing, misleading, or unclear. . . .

For the reasons set forth above, we affirm the order of the Superior Court.

NOTES

1. **The general standard of care.** *Stewart* applies the general standard of care for negligence cases. When a plaintiff sues a defendant on a negligence theory, the defendant is held to the standard of care that would be exercised by a reasonable person under the same or similar circumstances at the time of the alleged negligence. *See Mobile Gas Serv. Corp. v. Robinson,* 20 So. 3d 770 (Ala. 2009).

2. **Dangerous instrumentalities: The orthodox view.** *Stewart* also states the orthodox view for negligence cases involving the use of dangerous instrumentalities: (a) the standard of care remains the reasonable and prudent person standard, but (b) if the foreseeable danger is high, the reasonable

person will ordinarily exercise a greater degree of care than if the foreseeable danger is low. *E.g., Butler v. Acme Mkts., Inc.,* 426 A.2d 521 (N.J. Super. Ct. App. Div. 1981), *aff'd,* 445 A.2d 1141 (N.J. 1982). The *standard* thus remains the same whether danger is high or low. What changes with the danger is the *amount of care* that a reasonable person would take. *E.g., Purtle v. Shelton,* 474 S.W.2d 123 (Ark. 1971).

3. **Departures from the orthodox view.** Courts do not always observe the orthodox view; some have held instead that when the danger is greater, the standard itself is higher. *See Wood v. Groh,* 7 P.3d 1163 (Kan. 2000) (citing cases); 1 DOBBS, HAYDEN & BUBLICK, THE LAW OF TORTS § 141 (2d ed. 2011).

4. **Judge and jury.** Why does it matter whether the standard itself changes as the degree of foreseeable danger rises? What impact might an instruction based on such a conception have on the jury?

POSAS V. HORTON
228 P.3d 457 (Nev. 2010)

DOUGLAS, J. . . . :

Appellant Emilia Posas was driving in her car when a woman pushing a stroller began to cross the street in the middle of traffic, directly in front of Posas's car. Posas stopped suddenly to avoid hitting the jaywalking pedestrian. Respondent Nicole Horton was driving immediately behind Posas and hit the rear of Posas's car with the front-end of her car. . . . Horton was three to four feet behind Posas's vehicle right before the accident occurred, and she did not see the pedestrian cross in front of Posas. Horton testified, "yeah, obviously, I was following too close, I rearended her . . . you know, I made a mistake." . . . As a result of the accident, Posas filed a personal injury action against Horton. Despite Posas's objection during the settling of jury instructions, the jury was given a sudden-emergency instruction. The sudden-emergency instruction stated:

A person confronted with a sudden emergency which he does not create, who acts according to his best judgment or, because of insufficient time to form a judgment fails to act in the most judicious manner, is not guilty of negligence if he exercises the care of a reasonably prudent person in like circumstances.

The jury returned a verdict in favor of Horton, finding her free from liability for the accident. Posas moved for a new trial, which the district court denied. This appeal followed.

Posas argues that the district court erred in giving the sudden-emergency instruction to the jury. We agree. . . .

In order to be entitled to the sudden-emergency jury instruction, the proponent must show there is sufficient "evidence to support a finding that [the proponent] had been suddenly placed in a position of peril through no negligence of his or her own, and in meeting the emergency . . . acted as a reasonably prudent person would in the same or a similar situation. There must be evidence of a sudden and unforeseeable change in conditions to which a driver was forced to respond to avoid injury." In determining the standard of reasonable care, the Restatement (Second) of Torts further states, "[t]he fact that the actor is not negligent after the emergency has arisen does not preclude his liability for his tortious conduct which has produced the emergency." The Restatement (Third) of Torts: Liability for Physical and Emotional Harm § 9 (2010) also supports this principle. . . . The types of emergencies that courts have found to warrant a sudden-emergency instruction include a "dust cloud, a moving object, a sudden blocking of the road, the sudden swerving of another vehicle, blinding lights, a dense patch of fog," an unexpected brake failure, and a stopped vehicle without emergency flashers activated at night. . . .

Horton argues that she met the burden for the sudden-emergency instruction because the emergency was created by the pedestrian suddenly and unexpectedly crossing the street, that she did not cause the pedestrian to cross the street, and that Horton and Posas each acted as a reasonable person would have by braking to keep from hitting the pedestrian. However, Horton's own testimony belies that fact in light of her statement that she "was following too close." Thus, we conclude that Horton cannot appropriately claim that she faced a sudden emergency. She placed herself in a position of peril through her own negligence.

[As discussed in a prior case] certain so-called emergencies should

be anticipated, and the actor must be prepared to meet them when he engages in an activity in which they are likely to arise. Thus, under present day traffic conditions, any driver of an automobile must be prepared for the sudden appearance of obstacles and persons in the highway, and of other vehicles at intersections.

Id. (quoting W. Page Keeton, et al., *Prosser and Keeton on the Law of Torts* § 83 (5th ed.1984)). . . . The instruction tended to mislead or confuse the jury, and the error was prejudicial. . . . But for the error, as to the use of reasonable care by Horton, a different result may have been reached by the jury. . . . Accordingly, we reverse the judgment of the district court and remand for a new trial consistent with this opinion.

NOTES

1. **Relevance of emergency.** Is the *fact* of emergency irrelevant under the rule enunciated in *Posas*? If you represented a defendant in such a case, could you use that fact in determining what sum to offer in settlement, or in what to say to the jury in closing argument?

2. **Separate instructions.** Several courts have now said that the idea behind the emergency instruction is adequately covered by the instruction defining the reasonable care standard and that the separate emergency instruction should never be given. *See Lyons v. Midnight Sun Transp. Servs., Inc.,* 928 P.2d 1202 (Alaska 1996). Colorado recently joined the list of states that have abolished the sudden emergency instruction. *See Bedor v. Johnson,* 292 P.3d 924 (Colo. 2013). Nevertheless, some courts still feel these instructions need to be given to the jury. *See Hagenow v. American Family Mut. Ins. Co.,* 846 N.W.2d 373 (Iowa 2014).

3. **The Third Restatement.** The Restatement takes no position about whether an emergency instruction is appropriate, but it would take the fact of emergency into account. According to the Restatement: "If an actor is confronted with an unexpected emergency requiring rapid response, this is a circumstance to be taken into account in determining whether the actor's resulting conduct is that of the reasonably careful person." RESTATEMENT (THIRD) OF TORTS: LIABILITY FOR PHYSICAL AND EMOTIONAL HARM § 9 (2010). The fact of emergency is taken into account because it may indicate that "opportunities for deliberation have been limited by severe time pressure." *Id.* cmt. a. Yet if the emergency faced by the actor is due to the actor's own prior negligence, the defendant is liable for the plaintiff's harm notwithstanding the reasonableness of the defendant's later conduct. *Id.* cmt. d. If Horton had not been following Posas too closely, would the pedestrian's entry into the roadway count as a sudden emergency? Is it at all relevant that Horton did not in fact see the pedestrian? *See Tidd v. Kroshus,* 870 N.W.2d 181 (N.D. 2015) (bicyclist riding at night was struck by the car of the defendant, who testified that he had not seen the plaintiff prior to striking her).

4. **Definition of emergency.** What constitutes an "emergency" remains a relevant question in those states that allow emergency instructions in some cases. The usual definition is a sudden, unexpected and unforeseen happening or condition that calls for immediate action, and that was not created by the party asserting the emergency. *See, e.g., Herr v. Wheeler,* 634 S.E.2d 317 (Va. 2006). In *Lifson v. City of Syracuse,* 958 N.E.2d 72 (N.Y. 2011), the court concluded that sun glare that temporarily blinded the defendant motorist was not a "sudden and unexpected circumstance," and thus the trial court erred in giving an emergency instruction. On the other hand, in *Frazier v. Drake,* 357 P.3d 365 (Nev. Ct. App. 2015), the court found an emergency where a bee suddenly flew into a truck's cabin and landed on the driver's eye. The court in *Kelly v. Berg,* 870 N.W.2d 481 (Wis. Ct. App. 2015), said "one of the elements of the emergency doctrine is that the time in which action is required is short enough to preclude a deliberate and intelligent choice of action. . . . In other words, the person's reaction to the danger must be 'practically instinctive or intuitive.'" Under that reasoning, the court held that an emergency instruction was improper where the plaintiff ran outside to separate fighting dogs, because she "had time to contemplate her course of conduct before acting."

SHEPHERD V. GARDNER WHOLESALE, INC., 256 So. 2d 877 (Ala. 1972). Plaintiff Roxie Shepherd tripped over a raised concrete slab in the sidewalk in front of defendant's business. Shepherd suffered from cataracts, leaving her with 20/100 vision in one eye and 20/80 in the other. "[A] person with impaired vision is not required to see what a person with normal vision can see. Such would be impossible, and one is not guilty of negligence by using the public sidewalks with the physical inability to see what a person with normal vision can see. A person laboring under a physical disability such as defective vision is not required to exercise a higher degree of care to avoid injury than is required of a person under no disability. Ordinary care in the case of such a person is such care as an ordinarily prudent person with a like infirmity would have exercised under the same or similar circumstances."

[handwritten margin: facts of case]

[handwritten margin: physical disabled person not required to exercise a higher dgr of care then is reqmd of a person wuth no disbl.]

[handwritten left margin: Rule ←]

[handwritten: Ordinary care]

NOTES

1. **Role of physical impairments.** *Shepherd* reflects the rule on the role of physical impairments, disabilities, or limitations in setting the standard of care in negligence cases. The newest Restatement provides that "The conduct of an actor with physical disability is negligent only if it does not conform to that of a reasonably careful person with the same disability." RESTATEMENT (THIRD) OF TORTS: LIABILITY FOR PHYSICAL AND EMOTIONAL HARM § 11(a) (2010). What if the general rule were otherwise?

2. **Effect of the physical impairment rule on the plaintiff.** Is the rule an advantage for the physically disabled, or does the rule actually cut both ways? What if a person is blind, gets into a car and drives, and causes an accident because he cannot see. Posit that a sighted person would not have caused the accident at all. Does the physical impairment rule free the blind person from liability on those facts? What, exactly, is the standard of care on such facts? *See* RESTATEMENT (THIRD) OF TORTS: LIABILITY FOR PHYSICAL AND EMOTIONAL HARM § 11 cmt. b (2010); *cf. Roberts v. State,* 396 So. 2d 566 (La. Ct. App. 1981) (blind man knocked over the plaintiff in a crowded post office).

3. **Effect of the physical impairment rule on the defendant.** If the plaintiff is not negligent for failing to see an obstacle, is the defendant necessarily negligent for failing to correct it? What would happen if both the plaintiff and the defendant were not negligent? *See Bruns v. City of Centralia,* 21 N.E.3d 684 (Ill. 2014) (uneven sidewalk was an open and obvious danger that city had no duty to fix). In some cases, federal and state disability accommodation statutes may play a role in determining defendants' obligations. In other cases, as a matter of common law the defendant may be expected to take greater care in light of plaintiff's disability. For example, in *Green v. Box Butte Gen. Hosp.,* 818 N.W.2d 589 (Neb. 2012), hospital staff permitted a paraplegic patient to transfer himself from his wheelchair to shower chair, during which transfer patient fell to the floor, injuring his

[handwritten bottom: For people with disbility we use a more subjective standard of care ex a person with a disability needs to act as a reasonable]

shoulder. Whether the hospital's conduct breached a standard of care was a factual issue for the jury's consideration.

4. **Old age.** Cases hold that old age, as such, is not taken into account in setting the standard of care. What if old age produces particular physical disabilities, however, such as an inability to move quickly as a hazard approaches? Should that be taken into account?

5. **Exceptional physical ability.** Suppose, instead of having a physical infirmity, the actor has strength and agility not possessed by normal persons, or that the actor's reaction time is exceptionally good. How would you express the standard of care owed by such a person?

6. **Intoxication.** What is to be done about an intoxicated person? Suppose one is wildly intoxicated, but drives in a perfect way. Injury results, though the driving is flawless. Presumably the law should not attempt to judge the ultimate worth or character of persons, but should judge conduct instead. The general rule is that an intoxicated person owes the same care as a sober person, and that if his overt conduct would be negligence in a sober person, it is also negligence in a drunken one. What can be made of this? Can it be reconciled with the rule that one considers physical impairments as one of the circumstances? Is it possible that in the case of voluntary intoxication the risk is taken when intoxicants are consumed, rather than later when the defendant drives?

7. **Sudden incapacitation.** Courts have uniformly held that where a person's alleged negligence is caused by a sudden physical incapacitation that is not foreseeable, there should be no liability. The standard of care, of course, is that of a reasonable and prudent person under the same or similar circumstances. Thus, for example, if a reasonable and prudent person would have had no notice of the sudden seizure or heart attack, and that incapacitation caused the conduct that led to the plaintiff's injury, the defendant is not legally responsible. RESTATEMENT (THIRD) OF TORTS: LIABILITY FOR PHYSICAL AND EMOTIONAL HARM § 11 cmt. d (2010). Many courts place the burden of proving sudden incapacitation on the defendant. *See, e.g., Roman v. Estate of Gobbo*, 791 N.E.2d 422 (Ohio 2003) (driver of vehicle died from sudden heart attack and caused accident). What if a person has a serious medical condition and has been warned by doctors not to drive, but does so anyway, suffers a seizure, and causes an accident?

8. **Contributory negligence.** The focus of contributory negligence is often on the idea that the plaintiff should take reasonable care for herself, not on her failure to take care for others. The difference between plaintiff and defendant negligence is a slight one, and the standard of care is often the same, whether the risks were to self or others. RESTATEMENT (THIRD) OF TORTS: LIABILITY FOR PHYSICAL AND EMOTIONAL HARM § 3 cmt. a (2010); RESTATEMENT (THIRD) OF TORTS: APPORTIONMENT OF LIABILITY § 3 cmt. b (2000). Some thinkers say that the objective standard of reasonable care should not apply to unreasonable risks to self. Can you formulate an argument for or against this view?

CREASY V. RUSK

730 N.E.2d 659 (Ind. 2000)

SULLIVAN, JUSTICE. . . .

In July, 1992, Lloyd Rusk's wife admitted Rusk to the Brethren Healthcare Center ("BHC") because he suffered from memory loss and confusion and Rusk's wife was unable to care for him. Rusk's primary diagnosis was Alzheimer's disease. Over the course of three years at BHC, Rusk experienced periods of anxiousness, confusion, depression, disorientation, and agitation. Rusk often resisted when staff members attempted to remove him from prohibited areas of the facility. On several occasions, Rusk was belligerent with both staff and other residents. In particular, Rusk was often combative, agitated, and aggressive and would hit staff members when they tried to care for him. . . .

On May 16, 1995, Creasy and another certified nursing assistant, Linda Davis, were working through their routine of putting Rusk and other residents to bed. Creasy knew that Rusk had been "very agitated and combative that evening." By Creasy's account:

> [Davis] was helping me put Mr. Rusk to bed. She was holding his wrists to keep him from hitting us and I was trying to get his legs to put him to bed. He was hitting and kicking wildly. During this time, he kicked me several times in my left knee and hip area. My lower back popped and I yelled out with pain from my lower back and left knee.

. . . Rusk moved for summary judgment and the trial court granted his motion. Creasy appealed. The Court of Appeals reversed, holding "that a person's mental capacity, whether that person is a child or an adult, must be factored [into] the determination of whether a legal duty exists." . . .

[T]he generally accepted rule in jurisdictions other than Indiana is that mental disability does not excuse a person from liability for "conduct which does not conform to the standard of a reasonable man under like circumstances." Restatement (Second) of Torts § 283B; accord Restatement (Third) of Torts § 9(c) (Discussion Draft Apr. 5, 1999) ("Unless the actor is a child, the actor's mental or emotional disability is not considered in determining whether conduct is negligent."). People with mental disabilities are commonly held liable for their intentional and negligent torts. No allowance is made for lack of intelligence, ignorance, excitability, or proneness to accident. See Restatement (Second) of Torts § 283B cmt. c.

Legal scholars and authorities recognize that it is "impossible to ascribe either the volition implicit in an intentional tort, the departure from the standard of a 'reasonable' person which defines an act of ordinary negligence, or indeed any concept of 'fault' at all to one who . . . is by definition unable to control his [or her] own actions through any exercise of reason." Rather, the Restatement rule holding people with mental disabilities liable for their torts was founded upon public policy considerations.

The public policy reasons most often cited for holding individuals with mental disabilities to a standard of reasonable care in negligence claims include the following.

(1) Allocates losses between two innocent parties to the one who caused or occasioned the loss. . . . *(Compensation)*

(2) Provides incentive to those responsible for people with disabilities and interested in their estates to prevent harm and "restrain" those who are potentially dangerous. . . .

(3) Removes inducements for alleged tortfeasors to fake a mental disability in order to escape liability. . . .

(4) Avoids administrative problems involved in courts and juries attempting to identify and assess the significance of an actor's disability. As a practical matter, it is arguably too difficult to account for or draw any "satisfactory line between mental deficiency and those variations of temperament, intellect, and emotional balance."

(5) Forces persons with disabilities to pay for the damage they do if they "are to live in the world." A discussion draft for the Restatement (Third) of Torts rephrases this policy rationale and concludes: "[I]f a person is suffering from a mental disorder so serious as to make it likely that the person will engage in substandard conduct that threatens the safety of others, there can be doubts as to whether this person should be allowed to engage in the normal range of society's activities; given these doubts, there is nothing especially harsh in at least holding the person responsible for the harms the person may cause by substandard conduct." Restatement (Third) of Torts § 9 cmt. e (Discussion Draft April 5, 1999). . . .

Since the 1970s, Indiana law has strongly reflected policies to deinstitutionalize people with disabilities and integrate them into the least restrictive environment. National policy changes have led the way for some of Indiana's enactments in that several federal acts either guarantee the civil rights of people with disabilities or condition state aid upon state compliance with desegregation and integrationist practices. . . .

These legislative developments reflect . . . a determination that people with disabilities should be treated in the same way as non-disabled persons.

[T]he Restatement rule may very well have been grounded in a policy determination that persons with mental disabilities should be institutionalized or otherwise confined rather than "live in the world." It is clear from our recitation of state and federal legislative and regulatory developments that contemporary public policy has rejected institutionalization and confinement for a "strong professional consensus in favor of . . . community treatment . . . and integration into the least restrictive . . . environment." . . . We observe that it is a matter of some irony that public policies favoring the opposite ends—institutionalization and confinement on the one hand and community treatment and integration into the least restrictive environment on the other—should nevertheless yield the same common law rule: that the general duty of care imposed on adults with mental disabilities is the same as that for adults without mental disabilities.

. . . We hold that a person with mental disabilities is generally held to the same standard of care as that of a reasonable person under the same circumstances without regard to the alleged tortfeasor's capacity to control or understand the consequences of his or her actions.

[However, one employed to take care of a patient known to be combative because of Alzheimer's disease has no complaint for injuries sustained in doing so. As to such a caretaker the duty of care is a one-way street, from caretaker to patient, not the other way around. Hence Rusk is not liable on these facts.]

NOTES

1. **Other cases.** *Accord*, that a mentally disabled person, involuntarily hospitalized, does not owe a duty of care to his professional caregiver and hence is not liable for negligence or recklessness causing the caregiver harm, *Berberian v. Lynn,* 845 A.2d 122 (N.J. 2004). Cases that state a subjective standard for mentally deficient plaintiffs seem to be in reality cases based on the limited duty a confined disabled person owes to his caregiver. However, *Hofflander v. St. Catherine's Hosp., Inc.,* 664 N.W.2d 545 (Wis. 2003), clearly states a subjective standard for situations like the one in *Creasy v. Rusk.* On the court's analysis, would *Creasy* have come out differently if Rusk had injured a person who was in the hospital visiting another patient?

2. **"Defense" vs. "standard of care."** Sometimes insanity is discussed as a possible "defense," but it seems clear that the underlying issue is about the standard of care, not about defenses. The view of the Restatement (Third) of Torts § 11(c) (2010), the Restatement (Second) of Torts § 283B (1965), and the prevailing orthodoxy, is that neither insanity nor mental deficiency relieves the actor from liability, and that the actor's conduct must conform to the general standard of care of a reasonable person under similar external circumstances. Can the defendant meet that standard?

3. **Mental and psychological limitations.** Low intelligence and other mental or psychological limitations are treated the same way. Thomas is a sane man of low intelligence. He has never connected the danger of fire with his storage of rags, newspapers, and paint thinner in his garage. A fire originates in his garage and spreads to his neighbor's house. The jury will be

instructed that Thomas is held to the care of a reasonable and prudent person. He does not escape liability because he did "the best he could do," or because he behaved as well as others of similar intelligence would have. Why might the tort law hold him to an objective standard of reasonable care?

4.   **Considering rationales.** In its policy reasoning, the court in *Creasy* notes that the standard it adopts "[a]llocates losses between two innocent parties to the one who caused or occasioned the loss." Is this the typical rule in tort law? In the *Van Camp* case from Chapter 1? Are the rules of liability for insane and mentally deficient persons based upon justice? Deterrence? The *Creasy* court suggests that policies supporting the "opposite ends" of community treatment and institutionalization nevertheless lead to the same common law rule. Can that be right?

5.   **Consistency?** Are the rules for mental disability at odds with the rules for physical disability? Can you harmonize or justify the difference in the law's treatment of these two situations? What about a mental disability that clearly springs from a physical disability—such as mental retardation that results from cerebral palsy? Should that condition be taken into account in setting the standard of care? *See, e.g., Burch v. Am. Family Mut. Ins. Co.,* 543 N.W.2d 277 (Wis. 1996).

––––––––––––

HILL V. SPARKS, 546 S.W.2d 473 (Mo. Ct. App. 1976). Wayne Sparks was an operator of earth-moving machinery and had several seasons experience with a machine known as an earth scraper. At an exhibit of such machines he drove one, instructing his sister to stand on a ladder on the machine. It hit a mound of dirt and, because of its large rubber tires, bounced back. Sparks' sister was thrown forward in front of the left wheel and was run over before Sparks could stop the machine. She died almost instantly. This is an action for her death. "[Sparks], as an operator, with several seasons experience with earth scrapers, was familiar with the propensities of such machines. . . . He had heard decedent's husband, upon observing a boy riding on the scraper ladder during the demonstration, tell a Liberty Equipment employee to get the boy off the scraper because if he fell he would fall right under the wheel. Despite his knowledge and experience, appellant directed his sister to ride as a passenger on the ladder while he operated the machine. . . . 'The standard of the reasonable man requires only a minimum of attention, perception, memory, knowledge, intelligence, and judgment in order to recognize the existence of the risk. If the actor has in fact more than the minimum of these qualities, he is required to exercise the superior qualities that he has in a manner reasonable under the circumstances.' 2 Restatement of Torts (2d) § 289. . . . The evidence in this case presented an issue submissible to the jury of whether . . . appellant met the requisite standard of care."

NOTES

1.   **Special training.** A high school sports coach has received special courses dealing with injured students. Would the standard of care require the coach of a small high school team to use this special knowledge in deciding whether to keep an injured player in a football game? *See Cerny v. Cedar Bluffs Junior / Senior Pub. Sch.,* 628 N.W.2d 697 (Neb. 2001), *on appeal after remand,* 679 N.W.2d 198 (Neb. 2004); *cf. Dakter v. Cavallino,* 866 N.W.2d 656 (Wis. 2015) (driver of semi tractor-trailer had duty to exercise degree of care appropriate for his profession or trade).

2.   **Experts' knowledge of risk.** With babies, sudden infant death syndrome (SIDS) is a small risk. Allowing babies to sleep on their stomachs multiplies the risk—the risk is at least double, maybe as much as 12 times as great as the risk when babies sleep on their backs. If a baby dies from SIDS after the daycare center has placed her to sleep on her stomach, would the plaintiff need some kind of testimony to show that the daycare center should have known of the risk? What if the daycare center admits that it knew about a recommendation of the American Academy of Pediatrics against prone sleeping because of the risk of SIDS associated with it? *LePage v. Horne,* 809 A.2d 505 (Conn. 2002).

3.   **Expertise when the actor is not acting in her capacity as an expert.** A medical doctor's special training will certainly be taken into account where the doctor is a defendant in a medical malpractice case, a situation we address at length in Chapter 13. But what if a doctor is a plaintiff in a lawsuit, claiming an injury caused by another doctor's negligence in failing to diagnose the plaintiff's condition when the plaintiff was a patient? Should the plaintiff's special knowledge and training be taken into account in determining whether he was contributorily negligent in failing to tell the defendant doctor about all of his symptoms? *See Jackson v. Axelrad,* 221 S.W.3d 650 (Tex. 2007).

STEVENS V. VEENSTRA

573 N.W.2d 341 (Mich. Ct. App. 1998)

MURPHY, PRESIDING JUDGE. . . .

As a fourteen-year-old, defendant Aaron Veenstra took a driver's education course offered through the Calumet Public School system. Veenstra had skipped four grades in elementary school and graduated from high school early. He was taking driver's education so that he would have transportation to college. Before the driver's education course, Veenstra had never driven an automobile on a public road in a developed area. On the first day of the driving portion of the class, Veenstra stopped the automobile he was driving at an intersection. When the traffic cleared, Veenstra made a right turn. However, Veenstra turned too sharply and headed at plaintiff who was getting out of his parked automobile. Both Veenstra and the driving instructor attempted to turn Veenstra's automobile away from plaintiff. Veenstra testified that as he was heading for plaintiff, he may have hit the accelerator instead of the brake. As a result, Veenstra's automobile struck plaintiff.

At trial, over plaintiff's objection, the trial court gave the following instruction:

A minor is not held to the same standard of conduct as an adult. When I use the words "ordinary care" with respect to the minor, Aaron S. Veenstra, I mean that degree of care which a reasonably careful minor of age, mental capacity and experience of Aaron S. Veenstra would use under the circumstances which you find existed in this case. It is for you to decide what a reasonably careful minor would do or would not do under such circumstances.

Utilizing this instruction, the jury found that Veenstra was not negligent.

On appeal, plaintiff claims that the trial court's instruction was improper and mandates reversal. We agree. . . .

Generally, in the context of negligence actions, the capability of minors, seven years of age or older, is not determined on the basis of an adult standard of conduct, but rather is determined on the basis of how a minor of similar age, mental capacity, and experience would conduct himself. However, Michigan "has a longstanding policy of holding all drivers, even minors, to an adult standard of care." A minor who engages in an adult activity that is dangerous, e.g., driving an automobile, is charged with the same standard of conduct as an adult. . . .

Veenstra and the trial court consider this case to be distinguishable from prior cases holding that minors driving automobiles are held to an adult standard of conduct and call for an exception to that rule. . . . Veenstra defines the activity he was involved in as not simply driving an automobile, but driving an automobile as part of a driver's education course to satisfy the legislative requirements placed upon those under eighteen years of age seeking to obtain an operator's license, and claims that because he was engaged in an activity, which by definition is limited to minors, he was not engaged in an adult activity and should not be held to an adult standard of conduct. We disagree.

One rationale behind holding a minor driving an automobile to an adult standard of conduct is that, because of the frequency and sometimes catastrophic results of automobile accidents, it would be unfair to the public to permit a minor operating an automobile to observe any standard of care other than that expected of all others operating automobiles. It would seem illogical to think that the dangers associated with driving are lessened when the activity is undertaken by a minor with little or no experience. While we concede that Veenstra was attempting to satisfy requirements placed only upon minors, we do not think that changes the nature of, or danger associated with, driving an automobile. . . .

While the process of learning involves unique dangers, for which some allowance may be justified for beginners undertaking some activities, when the probability of, or potential harm associated with, a particular activity is great, anyone engaged in the activity must be held to a certain minimum level of competence, even though that level may lie beyond the capability of a beginner. See 2 Restatement Torts, 2d, § 299, comment d, pp. 71–72. In other words, some activities are so dangerous that the risk must be borne by the beginner rather than the innocent victims, and lack of competence is no excuse. We believe that driving an automobile is such an activity, and that anyone driving an automobile, regardless of age, must be held to the same standard of competence and conduct.

Reversed and remanded for a new trial. . . .

NOTES

1. **General rule for children.** *Stevens* discusses the general rule: a child accused of negligence is held to the standard of care of a reasonably careful child of the same age, intelligence, and experience. 1 DOBBS, HAYDEN & BUBLICK, THE LAW OF TORTS §§ 134–36 (2d ed. 2011). Is the ordinary child standard purely subjective?

2. **Applying the adult standard.** Courts have imposed the adult standard almost exclusively in cases of minors operating motorized vehicles. So a 13-year-old might be held to an adult standard when operating a snowmobile. *Robinson v. Lindsay,* 598 P.2d 392 (Wash. 1979). Similarly, a 12-year-old might be held to an adult standard while operating a motor boat, but only to a child standard while operating a bicycle. *Hudson v. Old Guard Ins. Co.,* 3 A.3d 246 (Del. 2010). What should be the standard when a 14-year-old allows an 11-year-old to operate a golf cart? *See Hudson-Connor v. Putney,* 86 P.3d 106 (Or. Ct. App. 2004). Meager authority has imposed the adult standard when a minor uses firearms. *See Goss v. Allen,* 360 A.2d 388 (N.J. 1976).

3. **Policies for the adult standard.** Should children be held only to the child standard when they are engaged in "carefree" activities appropriate to their development but to the adult standard when they engage in "inherently dangerous" or "adult" activities? Or should other factors enter into the equation as well? Suppose an adult rides on a snowmobile with an operator he knows to be 10 years of age. Would it be reasonable to demand and expect an adult standard of care of the child? RESTATEMENT (THIRD) OF TORTS: LIABILITY FOR PHYSICAL AND EMOTIONAL HARM § 10 cmt. f (2010). Should the result differ in a case of contributory negligence when the child's conduct poses risks to himself? *See Strait v. Crary,* 496 N.W.2d 634 (Wis. Ct. App. 1992).

4. **The rule of sevens.** A few courts still say that minors over 14 are presumed capable of negligence, those between seven and 14 are presumed incapable of it, and those below seven are incapable of negligence as a matter

of law. The rule of sevens is not so common now, but most states hold that children of very young years, three and under, are simply incapable of negligence. The Restatement (Third) of Torts § 10(b) provides that children under five are incapable of negligence.

5.   **Trial problems.** Even though Veenstra was driving a car, the trial court held that the adult standard did not apply. What made the lawyers try to distinguish this case and argue for application of a child standard here?

§ 3. NEGLIGENCE PER SE: USING SAFETY-RELATED RULES TO SPECIFY PARTICULAR TORT DUTIES

MARSHALL V. SOUTHERN RAILWAY CO., 62 S.E.2d 489 (N.C. 1950). Plaintiff was driving at night on a paved road about 30 feet wide. Defendant's railroad trestle above the road was supported by large timbers, which narrowed the road to about 15 feet under the trestle. As plaintiff approached this, a car came toward him with bright lights on and plaintiff ran into the trestle supports. Plaintiff sued defendant railway company for negligently placing and leaving the trestles where it did without lighting or signaling them. The trial judge sustained defendant's motion for nonsuit at the end of the plaintiff's evidence. *Held*, affirmed. "[I]t is manifest from the evidence that plaintiff failed to exercise due care at the time and under the circumstances of his injury. . . . It is a general rule of law, even in the absence of statutory requirement, that the operator of a motor vehicle must exercise ordinary care, that is, that degree of care which an ordinarily prudent person would exercise under similar circumstances. And in the exercise of such duty it is incumbent upon the operator of a motor vehicle to keep a reasonably careful lookout and to keep same under such control at night as to be able to stop within the range of his lights."

NOTE

Negligence as a matter of law and negligence per se. Is the court here saying that plaintiff was guilty of contributory negligence "as a matter of law," that is, that there is no room for reasonable jurors to differ about this conclusion? Or is it saying that there is a rule of law that one must be able to stop within the range of one's lights, whether or not a reasonable person would be able to do so? What's the difference?

CHAFFIN V. BRAME
64 S.E.2d 276 (N.C. 1951)

ERVIN, JUSTICE.

[Plaintiff was driving about 40 miles an hour at night on a paved highway 18 feet wide. A car approached driven by one Garland, who refused to dim his headlights. Plaintiff, blinded by the lights, ran into a truck left unlighted and blocking the entire right lane. Plaintiff sued the person responsible for the truck, who argued that the plaintiff was guilty of contributory negligence as a matter of law. The trial court, however, permitted the case to go to the jury, which returned a verdict for the plaintiff. To sustain his position, the defendant invokes the long line of cases beginning with Weston v. Southern R. Co., 194 N.C. 210, 139 S.E. 237, and ending with Marshall v. Southern R. Co., 233 N.C. 38, 62 S.E.2d 489, declaring either expressly or impliedly that "it is negligence as a matter of law to drive an automobile along a public highway in the dark at such a speed that it can not be stopped within the distance that objects can be seen ahead of it."

. . . "Few tasks in trial law are more troublesome than that of applying the rule suggested by the foregoing quotation to the facts in particular cases. The difficulty is much enhanced by a tendency of the bench and bar to regard it as a rule of thumb rather than as an effort to express in convenient formula for ready application to a recurring factual situation the basic principle that a person must exercise ordinary care to avoid injury when he undertakes to drive a motor vehicle upon a public highway at night. The rule was phrased to enforce the concept of the law that an injured person ought not to be permitted to shift from himself to another a loss resulting in part at least from his own refusal or failure to see that which is obvious. But it was not designed to require infallibility of the nocturnal motorist, or to preclude him from recovery of compensation for an injury occasioned by collision with an unlighted obstruction whose presence on the highway is not disclosed by his own headlights or by any other available lights. When all is said, each case must be decided according to its own peculiar state of facts. This is true because the true and ultimate test is this: What would a reasonably prudent person have done under the circumstances as they presented themselves to the plaintiff?"

It thus appears that the cases invoked by the defendant enunciate no mere shibboleth. They simply apply to the factual situations involved in them the fundamental truth that the law charges every person with the duty of exercising ordinary care for his own safety. . . .

When the plaintiff's evidence is taken in the light most favorable to him, it reasonably warrants these inferences: The plaintiff was keeping a proper lookout and driving at a reasonable speed as he traveled southward along Route 18. On being partially and temporarily blinded by the glaring lights of Garland's approaching automobile, the plaintiff reduced the speed of his car, and proceeded with extreme caution. The plaintiff exercised due care in adopting this course of action instead of bringing his car to a complete stop because he reasonably assumed that Garland would seasonably dim his headlights in obedience to the law, and thus restore to the plaintiff his full normal vision. The plaintiff had no reason whatever to anticipate or expect that the defendant's truck had been left standing on the traveled portion of the highway ahead of him without lights or warning signals until his car came within 30 feet of it. He did everything possible to avert the collision just as soon as the truck became visible.

This being true, we cannot hold that the plaintiff was guilty of contributory negligence as a matter of law....

There is in law no error.

NOTE

Judicial rules of conduct. Almost all rules of this kind have come to grief, or have caused it. Holmes once took the view that it was contributory negligence not to stop, look, and listen at a railroad crossing and that, if vision was impaired, one might be expected to get out of the car and walk to the edge of the track to assess the danger. *Baltimore & O.R. Co. v. Goodman*, 275 U.S. 66 (1927). Cardozo was later able gently to push this decision aside, pointing to some of the injustices that could result. "Illustrations such as these," he said, "bear witness to the need for caution in framing standards of behavior that amount to rules of law. The need is the more urgent when there is no background of experience out of which the standards have emerged. They are then, not the natural flowering of behavior in its customary forms, but rules artificially developed and imposed from without." *Pokora v. Wabash Ry.*, 292 U.S. 98 (1934).

MARTIN V. HERZOG, 126 N.E. 814 (N.Y. 1920). Defendant, driving at night, crossed over the center line on a curve and struck a buggy occupied by decedent, causing his death. In a wrongful death action the defendant contended that decedent was negligent in driving without lights. A statute provided in part: "Every vehicle on wheels whether stationary or in motion, while upon any public street ... shall have attached thereto a light or lights to be visible from the front and from the rear from one hour after sunset to one hour before sunrise. . . . A person violating the provisions of this section shall be guilty of a misdemeanor punishable by a fine not to exceed ten dollars." The trial judge charged the jury that decedent's violation of the statute could be considered as evidence of contributory negligence but not as negligence in itself. The jury found for the plaintiff. The Appellate Division reversed for new trial. In the Court of Appeals, by Cardozo, J., held, the Appellate Division is affirmed. "We think the unexcused omission of the statutory signals is more than some evidence of negligence. It is negligence in itself. . . . Yet the jurors were instructed in effect that they were at liberty in their discretion to treat the omission of lights either as innocent or as culpable. They were allowed to 'consider the default as lightly or gravely' as they would. They might as well have been told that they could use a like discretion in holding a master at fault for the omission of a safety appliance prescribed by positive law for the protection of a workman. Jurors have no dispensing power, by which they may relax the duty that one traveler on the highway owes under the statute to another."

NOTES

1.   **Negligence per se vs. statutes that create a private right of action.** Negligence per se is not applicable to all statutes. First, the doctrine applies only to statutes that declare conduct unlawful but are silent as to civil liability—statutes that either do not expressly provide for civil liability or which "cannot be readily interpreted as impliedly creating a private right of action." RESTATEMENT (THIRD) OF TORTS: LIABILITY FOR PHYSICAL AND EMOTIONAL HARM § 14 cmt. b & c (2010). Where a statute itself provides for civil liability, creating a private right of action, the court must simply apply it. For example, a statute could provide that the owner or keeper of a dog that damages the property or person of another must pay compensation to the person whose property or person is harmed. *See, e.g., Auster v. Norwalk United Methodist Church*, 943 A.2d 391 (Conn. 2008) (applying CONN. GEN. STAT. § 22–357). In such cases the court simply applies and enforces the statutory right.

2.   **Types of statutes covered by the negligence per se rule.** In a negligence per se case, the legislature has neither expressly nor impliedly provided for civil liability. For example, a statute might set a speed limit for vehicles on the highway, prescribing a criminal penalty for violation, but not mentioning anything at all about the liability of a violator to someone harmed by a crash caused by speeding. In that case, the negligence per se doctrine comes into play.

3.   **The rule's effect on the duty of care.** The position taken by Cardozo in *Martin v. Herzog* is the one followed by the Restatement and most courts, namely, that the unexcused violation of such statutes is, subject to some qualifications, "negligence per se." This means that violation of the statute—even though the statute itself does not say this—actually determines the actor's negligence. Said another way, when a court applies the negligence per se rule to a statute, the statute itself supplants the usual common law standard of care, and violation of the statute establishes the elements of duty and breach. *See* RESTATEMENT (THIRD) OF TORTS: LIABILITY FOR PHYSICAL AND EMOTIONAL HARM § 14 (2010). Why might courts, exercising their common law authority, treat an actor's violation of safety-related statutes as negligence per se? *See id.* § 14 cmt. c.

4.   **Jurisdictional variations.** Some states make violation of such a statute some *evidence of negligence* that may be considered by the jury, rather than regarding the statute as setting the standard of care. *See, e.g.*, WASH. REV. CODE § 5.40.050; *Brooks v. Lewin Realty III, Inc.*, 835 A.2d 616 (Md. 2003); *Kalata v. Anheuser-Busch Cos.*, 581 N.E.2d 656 (Ill. 1991). This puts the ultimate decision on the negligence issue with the jury. California's rule is

different still: Evidence Code § 669 says that when a statute applies and a person has violated it, the failure of that person to exercise due care is presumed. The burden is then placed upon the violator to rebut that presumption.

5.   **Statutory instruments covered by the rule.** Courts usually apply the negligence per se rule to violations of city ordinances and even to violations of administrative regulations as well as to state and federal statutes. *See Winger v. CM Holdings, L.L.C.*, 881 N.W.2d 433 (Iowa 2016) (breach of safety-related requirement, here a guardrail height rule, in a municipal ordinance is negligence per se). A few, however, hold that violation of an ordinance or administrative regulation is merely some evidence of negligence. *See Lang v. Holly Hill Motel, Inc.*, 909 N.E.2d 120 (Ohio 2009).

O'GUIN v. BINGHAM COUNTY

122 P.3d 308 (Idaho 2005)

TROUT, JUSTICE.

Frank and Leslie O'Guin, acting as individuals and as legal guardians of Frank O'Guin Jr. (the O'Guins), appeal the district court's grant of summary judgment in favor of Bingham County, Bingham County Commissioners and Bingham County Public Works, (collectively the County). Because the district court erred in its determinations regarding the negligence *per se* claim, we reverse the grant of summary judgment.

On July 7, 1999, Shaun and Alex O'Guin were killed while playing at the Bingham County landfill. Apparently, a section of the pit wall collapsed and crushed the children. Their older brother, Frank Jr., initially discovered their bodies at the bottom of the pit. Earlier that day, the children had been eating lunch at Ridgecrest Elementary School as part of a summer lunch program. As they started walking home, the children went through an unlocked gate at the back of the schoolyard and through a privately owned empty field. The empty field is situated between the landfill and the schoolyard. The border between the empty field and the landfill was unobstructed. At the time of the children's death, the landfill was open to the public one day a week. It was closed on the day the children were killed and no landfill employees were present on the site.

[The O'Guins sued the County for negligence, claiming among other things that the County was negligent *per se*, relying on Idaho statutes and federal regulations. The trial court granted the County's motion for summary judgment on the count of negligence per se, and the O'Guins appealed.]

Generally, the question of whether a duty exists is a question of law, over which we exercise free review. Negligence *per se,* which results from the violation of a specific requirement of law or ordinance, is a question of law, over which this Court exercises free review.

The dispute in this case focuses on the duty or standard of care the County owed to the O'Guin children. . . . In Idaho, it is well established that statutes and administrative regulations may define the applicable standard of care owed, and that violations of such statutes and regulations may constitute negligence *per se*. A court may adopt 'as the standard of conduct of a reasonable man the requirements of a legislative enactment or an administrative regulation. The effect of establishing negligence *per se* through violation of a statute is to conclusively establish the first two elements of a cause of action in negligence. Negligence *per se* lessens the plaintiff's burden only on the issue of the 'actor's departure from the standard of conduct required of a reasonable man.' " Thus, the elements of duty and breach are taken away from the jury.

In order to replace a common law duty of care with a duty of care from a statute or regulation, the following elements must be met: (1) the statute or regulation must clearly define the required standard of conduct; (2) the statute or regulation must have been intended to prevent the type of harm the defendant's act or omission caused; (3) the plaintiff must be a member of the class of persons the statute or regulation was designed to protect; and (4) the violation must have been the proximate cause of the injury.

As to the first element, the district court found, and we agree, that the statute and regulations in this case clearly define the County's standard of conduct. . . . These regulations require the County to fence or otherwise block access to the landfill when an attendant is not on duty. The Legislature has specifically declared it to be "unlawful" to fail to comply with the landfill rules. In this case, the record reveals that on July 7, 1999, some of the landfill boundaries were not fenced or blocked. There is also evidence that the landfill was closed and no attendant was on duty on July 7, 1999. Therefore, the district court was correct that the regulations clearly define the County's required standard of conduct, and the County failed to meet that standard.

The second element asks whether the death of the O'Guin children is the type of harm the statute and regulations were intended to prevent. Idaho Code Section 39–7401(2) states:

> [I]t is the intent of the legislature to establish a program of solid waste management which complies with 40 CFR 258 . . . to facilitate the development and operation of solid waste disposal sites, to effect timely and responsible completion of statutory duties and to ensure protection of human health and the environment, to protect the air, land and waters of the state of Idaho.

This section demonstrates the legislature's desire to ensure the "protection of human health" in the "development and operation of solid waste disposal sites." It also makes specific reference to 40 C.F.R. § 258. . . . Section 258.25

of the Code of Federal Regulations states "[o]wners or operators of all municipal solid waste landfill units must control public access . . . by using artificial barriers, natural barriers, or both, as appropriate to protect human health." . . . "[P]rotection of human health" . . . certainly includes possible injury or death to people on the facility grounds. Operators of a landfill have a duty not only to prevent illegal dumping and unauthorized vehicular traffic, but to control public access as well.

. . . These statutes and rules demonstrate that the Legislature intended to safeguard both human health and safety. The injury to the safety of the O'Guin children is the type of harm the Idaho statute and regulations were intended to prevent because the children's deaths relate directly to control of public access and protection of human health and safety.

As to the third element, the O'Guin children are members of the class of persons the regulations were designed to protect. The regulations state "[u]nauthorized vehicles and persons shall be prohibited access to the site." As trespassers, the O'Guin children were certainly "unauthorized persons" and the regulations do not differentiate between the unauthorized person who comes to the landfill to dump improper materials and the unauthorized person who comes to the landfill to play. Furthermore, the regulations require the landfill "be fenced or otherwise blocked to access when an attendant is not on duty." This regulation demonstrates the connection between the requirement that the landfill perimeter be fenced or blocked and the protection of persons whose access is unauthorized. Therefore, the regulations controlling access were designed to protect the human health and safety of the unauthorized person who comes to a landfill when an attendant is not on duty and the O'Guin children fit within that category.

Finally, as to the fourth element, there is at least a disputed issue of fact created by an affidavit in the record, as to whether the County's violation of the statute and regulations resulted in the O'Guin children's deaths.

After concluding the regulations established a duty and that the County had breached that duty, the district court held "the O'Guins' allegations of negligence *per se* do not change the duty owed by the County to trespassers." This was error. There was no need for the district court to look to the common law duty owed to trespassers once it determined the statutory duty applied. Liability may become established upon proof that the violation of the statute caused the injuries of the plaintiff and the plaintiff's subsequent damages. A statute that adequately defines the required standard of care "supplants the reasonable person standard encompassed in the concept of ordinary negligence." . . . .

. . . Standing alone, the regulations in this case are sufficient to satisfy the duty element for a negligence *per se* action. The O'Guins' use of statutory obligations to establish the County's duty under a negligence *per se* action replaces the common law duty of landowners to trespassers. . . . The district court's grant of summary judgment is vacated and the case remanded for further proceedings. . . .

JUSTICE EISMANN, Dissenting.

I cannot concur in the majority opinion because the regulations cited therein as supporting a claim of negligence *per se* were clearly not intended to prevent the type of harm involved in this case. . . .

The majority opinion relies upon IDAPA 58.01.06.005.02 and 40 C.F.R. 258.25 as providing the applicable standard of care. Neither of those regulations is intended to prevent trespassers from injuring themselves through an accident at a landfill. They are intended to prevent trespassers from dumping or salvaging materials that may be harmful to health or the environment. . . .

The concern is illegal dumping of wastes that are dangerous to human health and the environment. The word "health" is not normally construed to include freedom from accidents. Rather, it simply means "freedom from disease or abnormality." The majority can reach its conclusion only by redefining the word "health" to include "safety." Such redefinition is not supported either by Idaho law or by the federal regulations. . . .

The [federal] regulation only requires barriers to prevent "unauthorized vehicular traffic and illegal dumping of wastes." The required barriers need not be able to keep out trespassing pedestrians who may accidentally injure themselves at the landfill. . . . [T]he regulation was not intended to require municipal solid waste disposal facilities to fence out trespassing pedestrians. . . .

NOTES

1. **The class of persons and type of harm tests.** The class of persons and type of harm requirements are fairly uniform from state to state. *See* RESTATEMENT (THIRD) OF TORTS: LIABILITY FOR PHYSICAL AND EMOTIONAL HARM § 14 cmt. f & g (2010). As California's high court puts it, the negligence per se rule "arises from a tortfeasor's failure to exercise due care in violation of a statute designed to protect a class of persons, of which the injured party is a member, from the type of injury sustained." *Ramirez v. Nelson*, 188 P.3d 659 (Cal. 2008). *See* 1 DOBBS, HAYDEN & BUBLICK, THE LAW OF TORTS §§ 151–55 (2d ed. 2011).

2. **Judicial applications of the class of persons and type of harm tests.** As you might glean from the *O'Guin* case, there is a good deal of flexibility built in to the determination of whether the injured person is in the protected class and whether the type of harm that occurred is of the same type

that the statute was designed to protect against. How does the court in *O'Guin* determine who is in the protected class, and what types of harm the statute was designed to protect against? How do we know whether the majority or the dissent is correct about what the legislature intended?

3. **Judicial adoption of statutes and judicial discretion.** *Must* the court consider legislative purpose to protect a certain class of persons or to protect against a certain type of harm? Decisions regarding the proper civil standard of conduct rest with the courts. Thus, the courts must ultimately decide whether they will adopt a statutory standard to define the standard of reasonable persons in specific circumstances." *Rains v. Bend of the River*, 124 S.W.3d 580 (Tenn. Ct. App. 2003) (in an action brought by parents based on their 18-year-old son's suicide by firearm, refusing to adopt as negligence per se a statute that banned the sale of ammunition to minors); *see also Maurer v. Speedway, LLC*, 774 F.3d 1132 (7th Cir. 2014).

4. **Judicial ability to determine the scope of a statute's per se application.** Suppose a statute provides that heavy machinery used at construction sites must automatically make back-up noises when in reverse gear, and that the statute is for the protection of workers at the job site. If the machine in violation of the statute backs over an unsuspecting architecture student who is on the premises to be shown how a building is constructed, he may have no negligence per se claim. *Cf.* RESTATEMENT (SECOND) OF TORTS § 286 illus. 1 (1965). Yet the contractor violated the statute. It would have cost him no more to have complied with it for the purpose of protecting everyone than for the purpose of protecting workers on the job. Besides this, the legislature might have thought back-up beepers were needed "because of danger to workers," without really intending to exclude the possibility of saving other persons as well. These things might suggest that the class of person/class of risk rule should not be used to limit liability or that the courts should use very general classifications. *Scott v. Matlack, Inc.*, 39 P.3d 1160 (Colo. 2002).

5. **Statutes used as per se rules.** Varied statues have been given per se effect. *See Aleo v. SLB Toys USA, Inc.*, 995 N.E.2d 740 (Mass. 2013) (federal regulation governing swimming pool slides); *Kiriakos v. Phillips*, 139 A.3d 1006 (Md. 2016) (state regulation barring allowing an individual under 21 to possess or consume alcohol); *Howard v. Zimmer, Inc.*, 299 P.3d 463 (Okla. 2013) (federal regulation under the Medical Device Amendments to the FDCA); *Miss. Dep't of Transp. v. Nosef*, 110 So. 3d 317 (Miss. 2013) (specific law requiring warning signs to be placed around highway culverts).

6. **Statutes intended to protect the public at large.** One might think that if a court determines that the class protected by a statute is the public at large, the plaintiff will always fit within it. But many courts have held that a statute that does not create a duty to an identifiable class—a subset of the general public, in other words—cannot be given per se effect. *See, e.g., Pehle v. Farm Bureau Life Ins. Co.*, 397 F.3d 897 (10th Cir. 2005). *See also* 1 DOBBS, HAYDEN & BUBLICK, THE LAW OF TORTS § 153 (2d ed. 2011).

7. **The "defining the standard of conduct" requirement.** Why does the *O'Guin* court say that a statute cannot be given negligence per se effect unless it "clearly defines the required standard of conduct?" Could any statute be given per se effect if it did not?

8. **Establishing breach of the per se rule.** The *O'Guin* court says the effect of establishing negligence per se "is to conclusively establish the first two elements of a cause of action in negligence." According to the court, "the elements of duty and breach are taken away from the jury." Is that always true? What if the defendant claimed that the landfill boundaries actually had been fully fenced or blocked? Establishing negligence per se requires the plaintiff to prove that the statute to be applied was in fact violated. *Lindblom v. Sun Aviation, Inc.*, 862 N.W.2d 549 (S.D. 2015) (absent an admission of statutory violation, negligence per se is a question for finder of fact). How does the jury's role in determining breach differ when the defendant owes a statutory duty rather than only a duty of reasonable care?

9. **The "causation" requirement.** Many cases say that the negligence per se rule does not impose liability for violation of a statute unless violation is a "proximate" cause of the plaintiff's harm. At times courts use the term "proximate cause" to mean both factual (but-for) cause and scope of liability—concepts addressed in upcoming chapters. For example, what if a third child testified that he saw the O'Guin children enter the landfill by climbing over the fence in a place that was fenced in accordance with statute?

10. **Licensing statutes.** Should courts adopt licensing statutes as standards of care? Perhaps the most famous case on this topic is *Brown v. Shyne*, 151 N.E. 197 (N.Y. 1926). The plaintiff alleged that the defendant held himself out to practice medicine, that his treatments paralyzed her, and that he had no license to practice medicine. The New York Court of Appeals held that the plaintiff could not get to the jury on this allegation but would instead be required to allege and prove negligence by ordinary means. Might it matter whether a physician lacks a license because she has not yet fully satisfied the state's residency requirement or because she has no medical training? RESTATEMENT (THIRD) OF TORTS: LIABILITY FOR PHYSICAL AND EMOTIONAL HARM § 14 cmt. h (2010).

11. **Common law negligence.** What would happen if the majority in *O'Guin* had determined that negligence per se did not apply? Notice that the plaintiff can claim negligence on ordinary common law principles even if the statute has no effect. The standard of care landowners owe to trespassers may be lower than reasonable care in some cases, as we will see in Chapter 12. Indeed, the lower court in *O'Guin* determined that the common law standard of care the defendant landfill owed to the child trespassers was only a duty to refrain from willful and wanton acts, which had not been demonstrated. If the plaintiff is a trespasser who is not owed an ordinary duty of reasonable care under the common law, showing that negligence per se rules apply becomes particularly significant to the plaintiff. See *Blackburn Ltd. P'ship v. Paul*, 90 A.3d 464 (Md. 2014) (child trespasser fell into the swimming pool at an

apartment complex as a result of the defendant's failure to comply with a state regulation on barriers around pools).

GETCHELL V. LODGE

65 P.3d 50 (Alaska 2003)

FABE, CHIEF JUSTICE.

On the morning of January 16, 1998, Joyce Getchell and Barbara Lodge drove to work on the Kenai Spur Highway. Getchell headed south on the highway towards Kenai. Lodge headed north towards Nikiski. A thin layer of ice covered the unsanded road; the morning was dark. There was a dispute at trial about what happened next. However, because we draw all factual inferences in favor of the non-moving party when reviewing motions for JNOV and new trial, what follows is Lodge's account.

Because of the darkness, the icy road conditions, and the possibility of moose crossing the highway, Lodge was driving at about forty-five miles per hour, even though the speed limit was fifty-five. A moose emerged out of the darkness from Lodge's right and tried to cross the road as Lodge neared Mile 20 of the highway. Lodge hit her brakes as hard as she could. She testified that her car skidded immediately and began to rotate in a counterclockwise direction. Lodge lost control of her car as it continued to rotate and slide. Ultimately, the car crossed the center line of the road. The car finished rotating and came to a stop in the southbound lane. As Getchell headed south towards Mile 20, driving between forty-five and fifty-five miles per hour, she saw a car in her lane. Getchell hit the passenger side of Lodge's car. The impact injured Getchell's ankle, requiring surgery. . . .

Getchell brought a personal injury negligence action against Lodge. . . . Superior Court Judge Harold M. Brown conducted a three-day jury trial . . . . The jury found Lodge not negligent. . . .

Getchell argues that the trial court erred in denying her motions for JNOV and new trial, contending that reasonable jurors could have only concluded that Lodge acted negligently. Getchell structures her argument around the tort consequences of Lodge's alleged violation of two Alaska traffic regulations.[9] Getchell contends that because Lodge crossed the

---

[9]   . . . A plaintiff who establishes that a defendant violated a traffic regulation makes a prima facie case that the defendant acted negligently. The defendant then bears the burden to prove affirmatively that his violation was excused. . . . "Excuse" is a fluid concept. We have adopted the Restatement (Second) of Torts's position on excused violations of traffic regulations. Section 288(A) provides:

(1) An excused violation of a legislative enactment or an administrative regulation is not negligence.

(2) Unless the enactment or regulation is construed not to permit such excuse, its violation is excused when

(a) the violation is reasonable because of the actor's incapacity;

(b) he neither knows nor should know of the occasion for compliance;

center lane of traffic into Getchell's lane she violated 13 AAC 02.085 and 13 AAC 02.050. Because Lodge violated these traffic regulations, Getchell argues, the burden of proof shifted to Lodge to show by a preponderance of the evidence that her conduct was excused. . . .

Getchell is correct that Lodge can only claim excuse if she handled her moose-avoidance maneuver and the resulting skid in a non-negligent manner. . . .

Lodge testified that she slammed on her brakes to avoid a moose in her lane. According to Lodge, her brakes locked and she skidded into Getchell's lane. Reasonable jurors could have concluded that the presence of the moose in the road excused Lodge's skid into the oncoming lane of traffic. Skidding to avoid a moose is the type of excuse contemplated by § 288A of the Restatement (Second) of Torts . . . . Comment h of this section aptly describes this situation:

> *Emergency.* As in other cases of negligence (see § 296), the violation of an enactment or regulation will ordinarily be excused when the actor is confronted with an emergency which is not caused by his own misconduct.

It is plausible that the jury concluded that the moose created an emergency situation for Lodge and that they therefore excused the unfortunate consequences of her attempt to avoid the moose.

The jury also heard other evidence from which it could have reasonably concluded that Lodge was not negligent. Lodge points out that she had very little time to react after she saw the moose in the road. Lodge's accident reconstruction expert, James Stirling, expressed his opinion that Lodge had approximately "three-point-some seconds before" she would have collided with the moose. According to Stirling, Lodge's perception of the danger, before she took any evasive action, would have consumed one-and-a-quarter to one-and-a-half seconds. Thus, Lodge argues, she had one-and-a-half seconds at most to slow the car down and correct the slide. Stirling testified that "[g]iven the surface and how slick it was, and given the speed of 45 miles an hour, [Lodge's attempts to correct her car's rotation] would have had to have been almost instantaneous to stop. . . . I would think she would have to perform higher than the average driver to do it." Based upon this testimony, reasonable jurors could have concluded that "Lodge was unable after reasonable care to comply with [13 AAC 02.085 and 13 AAC 02.050]." . . . Because we find that there was evidence from which reasonable jurors could have differed in their judgment of the facts as to

---

(c) he is unable after reasonable diligence or care to comply;

(d) he is confronted by an emergency not due to his own misconduct;

(e) compliance would involve a greater risk of harm to the actor or to others.

RESTATEMENT (SECOND) OF TORTS § 288(A) (1965).

whether Lodge acted negligently, we <u>AFFIRM the trial court's denial of</u>
<u>Getchell's motions for JNOV and new trial</u>. . . .

NOTES

1.   **Excuses for a statutory violation.** In a number of cases, courts
that ordinarily recognize the per se rule have held that a statutory violation
was excused. This has been the holding, for example, where the statute
required good brakes, but the brakes suddenly failed without the driver's fault.

2.   **The Restatement list.** The Third Restatement has reworked and
clarified the list of excuses from the Second Restatement quoted in *Getchell*. It
now provides that a violation of a statute is "excused and not negligent" if
(a) the violation is <u>reasonable in light of</u> the actor's <u>childhood</u>, physical
disability, or physical <u>incapacitation;</u> (b) the actor exercises reasonable care in
attempting to comply with the statute; (c) the actor neither knows nor should
know of the factual circumstances that render the statute applicable; (d) the
actor's violation of the statute is due to the confusing way in which the
requirements of the statute are presented to the public; or (e) the actor's
compliance with the statute would involve a greater risk of physical harm to
the actor or to others than would noncompliance. RESTATEMENT (THIRD) OF
TORTS: LIABILITY FOR PHYSICAL AND EMOTIONAL HARM § 15 (2010).

3.   **Child's standard in negligence per se cases.** Which prevails
when a child violates a statute, the common law child standard of care or the
statutory standard? In other words, does the negligence per se rule apply to
children? In *Bauman v. Crawford*, 704 P.2d 1181 (Wash. 1985), the court said:
"We hold <u>that a minor's violation of a stat</u>ute does n<u>ot constitute pro</u>of of
<u>negligence per se,</u> but may, in proper cases, be introduced as evidence of a
<u>minor's negligence</u>." Why would holding children to the statutory standard be
such a bad idea, especially where they are engaged in childish activities like
walking across a street or riding a bicycle?

4.   **Non-excuses.** Is it a valid excuse for a person to say that he did not
agree with the statute's provisions? Or to argue that he was ignorant of the
law? Or what if the violator can prove that people customarily violate the
statutory provisions? No is the answer to all of these questions. *See*
RESTATEMENT (THIRD) OF TORTS: LIABILITY FOR PHYSICAL AND EMOTIONAL
HARM § 15 cmt. a (2010).

> REFERENCES: 1 DOBBS, HAYDEN & BUBLICK, THE LAW OF TORTS
> §§ 120–125 (negligence generally), §§ 126–137 (standards of care),
> §§ 141–144 (special dangers and emergencies) & §§ 145–158
> (negligence per se) (2d ed. 2011); DOBBS, HAYDEN & BUBLICK,
> HORNBOOK ON TORTS Ch. 9 (negligence generally), Ch. 10 (duty) &
> Ch. 11 (negligence per se) (2d ed. 2016).

CHAPTER 6

BREACH OF DUTY

■ ■ ■

§ 1. ASSESSING FORESEEABLE RISKS AND COSTS

Once the court determines that the defendant owed the plaintiff a duty, and what that duty was—usually the duty of reasonable care—the question for the jury is whether the defendant breached that duty by failing to exercise the requisite amount of care. The defendant who breaches the duty of care is said to be negligent.

Negligence is overt conduct that creates unreasonable risks that a reasonable person would avoid. The risk of harm is unreasonable when a reasonable and prudent person would foresee that harm might result *and would avoid conduct that creates the risk.* Conduct may include a failure to act if action is required, but a mere state of mind is not conduct. If the defendant daydreams but drives properly in all respects, he might be careless in the lay sense, but he is not legally negligent. As the Seventh Circuit succinctly stated in *Beck v. Dobrowski*, 559 F.3d 680, 682 (7th Cir. 2009): "Negligence is not a state of mind; it is a failure . . . to come up to the specified standard of care."

As the New Jersey Supreme Court has said, "[t]o act non-negligently is to take reasonable precautions to prevent the occurrence of foreseeable harm to others. What precautions are 'reasonable' depends upon the risk of harm involved and the practicability of preventing it." *Weinberg v. Dinger*, 524 A.2d 366 (N.J. 1987).

A. ACTS THAT CREATE RISK

Legal professionals think of intentional torts in contrast with negligence. However, an intentional *act* is not necessarily an intentional *tort*. For example, if you intentionally drive at a very high speed you may be taking an unreasonable risk; if you do so and collide with another car, you'd be negligent. What else would be necessary to show you were chargeable with an intentional tort rather than negligence?

———

PROBLEM

Brown v. Stiel

The Stiel Company, a construction contractor, decided to build a building for its own use. It provided an architect with the basic design elements, and plans were drawn which Stiel then followed in building. Stiel chose a design in which the major structural components were steel. It rejected a design based on poured concrete in favor of steel beams because the steel beam construction was, in the particular situation, much cheaper and quicker. However, as Stiel knew, the kind of steel beam construction proposed generally caused or was associated with accidents which caused death or serious injury. In fact, it was known that for a building the size of Stiel's, three workers or others would be killed or paralyzed or otherwise seriously injured. The concrete building also involved predictable injuries; but, for a building this size, the prediction was that only one person would be injured. Stiel nevertheless chose the riskier steel construction because of time and cost differences.

Resulting harm

There was a collapse of some steel beams and John White, an employee of Stiel who had done steel work for many years, fell to the ground and suffered a broken back and permanent paralysis from the neck down. The same collapse dropped a steel beam on Billy Brown, a delivery person for a nearby deli. Billy Brown was on the premises bringing an order for the supervising architect when the beam fell. Brown lost a leg as a result of the building's collapse.

NOTES

1. **Intentional acts and intentional harms.** Did Stiel Co. commit an intentional tort? Consider whether this case differs from a case in which someone throws a brick from the roof of a building into a crowd below.

2. **Injury as a cost of business.** Suppose a court holds that no intentional tort is shown in this problem. Even so, maybe Stiel ought to pay for the harm done as a matter of justice or social policy. If certain costs are more or less inevitable in a business, maybe those costs should be regarded as a cost that business should bear as a part of its overhead. If a construction company expects that its own construction vehicles will periodically collide and sustain damage, it will budget for this cost and charge sufficient amounts to cover this cost as well as all others. Should the same be done when it comes to human costs?

3. **Workers' compensation.** Workers' compensation statutes proceed upon the theory that work-connected injuries may generally be regarded as a part of the employer's cost of doing business—the human "breakage," analogous to broken plates in a restaurant. Since such losses are more or less inevitable in a statistical sense, the employer simply budgets for them— charging sufficiently for its work to cover the costs.

4. **Plaintiffs not covered by workers' compensation.** Is there any justification for holding Stiel liable to White for workers' compensation but not holding Stiel liable to Brown?

5. **A negligence action.** Assuming that Brown cannot recover workers' compensation from Stiel because he was not an employee, and that he cannot recover from the deli because the workers' compensation statute did not cover businesses with very few employees, would Brown nevertheless have an action under common law tort theory? Consider the introductory comments about negligence as well as the cases that follow.

B. FORESEEABILITY OF HARM AND QUESTIONS FOR THE JURY

PIPHER V. PARSELL
930 A.2d 890 (Del. 2007)

HOLLAND, JUSTICE.

The plaintiff-appellant, Kristyn Pipher ("Pipher"), appeals from the Superior Court's judgment as a matter of law in favor of the defendant-appellee, Johnathan Parsell ("Parsell"). Pipher argues that the Superior Court erred when it ruled that, as a matter of law, Parsell was not negligent. We agree and hold that the issue of Parsell's negligence should have been submitted to the jury. ———> Holding!

On March 20, 2002, around 6 p.m., Pipher, Parsell and Johnene Beisel ("Beisel"), also a defendant, were traveling south on Delaware Route 1 near Lewes, Delaware, in Parsell's pickup truck. All three were sitting on the front seat. Parsell was driving, Pipher was sitting in the middle, and Beisel was in the passenger seat next to the door. They were all sixteen-years-old at the time. ——> Minor doing adult activity

As they were traveling at 55 mph, Beisel unexpectedly "grabbed the steering wheel causing the truck to veer off onto the shoulder of the road." Parsell testified that Beisel's conduct caused him both shock and surprise. Although Beisel's conduct prompted him to be on his guard, Parsell further testified that he did not expect Beisel to grab the wheel again. Nevertheless, his recognition of how serious Beisel's conduct was shows he was aware that he now had someone in his car who had engaged in dangerous behavior.

Parsell testified that he did nothing in response to Beisel's initial action. Approximately thirty seconds later, Beisel again yanked the steering wheel, causing Parsell's truck to leave the roadway, slide down an embankment and strike a tree. Pipher was injured as a result of the collision.

Pipher's testimony at trial was for the most part consistent with Parsell's testimony. Pipher recalled that the three occupants in the vehicle were talking back and forth and that the mood was light as they drove south on Route 1. She also testified that after Beisel yanked the steering wheel for the first time, Parsell was able to regain control of the truck. According to Pipher, despite the dangerous nature of the conduct, Parsell and Beisel just laughed about it like it was a joke. Pipher testified she felt that Beisel grabbed the steering wheel a second time because Parsell "laughed it off" the first time.

At trial, Parsell acknowledged that he could have taken different steps to try to prevent Beisel from grabbing the steering wheel a second time. First, Parsell acknowledged, he could have admonished Beisel not to touch the steering wheel again. Second, he acknowledged that he could have pulled over to the side of the road and required Beisel to get into the back seat. Third, Parsell acknowledged that he could have warned Beisel that he would put her out of the vehicle.

The trial judge concluded that, as a matter of law, Parsell had no duty to do anything after Beisel yanked the wheel the first time because it would be reasonable for the driver to assume that it would not happen again. The trial judge also ruled that (1) there was no negligence in failing to discharge the dangerous passenger and (2) that failing to admonish the dangerous passenger was not negligence. . . .

A driver owes a duty of care to her or his passengers because it is foreseeable that they may be injured if, through inattention or otherwise, the driver involves the car she or he is operating in a collision. Almost forty-five years ago, this Court held that a minor who operates a motor vehicle on the highways of Delaware will be held to the same standard of care and "must accord his [or her] own passengers the same diligence and protection which is required of an adult motorist under similar circumstances." . . .

Pipher argues that after Beisel grabbed the steering wheel initially, Parsell was on notice that a dangerous situation could reoccur in the truck. Pipher further argues that once Parsell had notice of a possibly dangerous situation, he had a duty to exercise reasonable care to protect his passengers from that harm. Finally, Pipher concludes that Parsell was negligent when he kept driving without attempting to remove, or at least address, that risk. . . .

In general, where the actions of a passenger that cause an accident are not foreseeable, there is no negligence attributable to the driver. But, when actions of a passenger that interfere with the driver's safe operation of the motor vehicle are foreseeable, the failure to prevent such conduct may be a breach of the driver's duty to either other passengers or to the public. Under the circumstances of this case, a reasonable jury could find that

Parsell breached his duty to protect Pipher from Beisel by preventing Beisel from grabbing the steering wheel a second time.

The issue of Parsell's alleged breach of duty to Pipher, the foreseeability of Beisel's repeat conduct, and the proximate cause of Pipher's injuries were all factual determinations that should have been submitted to the jury. Accordingly, the judgment of the Superior Court, that was entered as a matter of law, is reversed. This matter is remanded for further proceedings in accordance with this opinion.

NOTES

1. **An alternate scenario.** Would the trial court have been correct in ruling that there was no breach of duty as a matter of law if Beisel had caused the accident the first time she grabbed the wheel? Why would that be a different case? *Cf. Brown v. Mobley,* 488 S.E.2d 710 (Ga. Ct. App. 1997) (no evidence that eventual conduct of intoxicated passenger should have been anticipated).

2. **Facts related to breach.** Given Beisel's prior conduct, should the breach issue have gone to a jury? What facts should a jury consider on remand? State the strongest arguments for both the plaintiff and the defendant on the breach issue.

3. **Foreseeability as a prerequisite for breach.** Foreseeability of some type of harm is central to the issue of whether a person's conduct breached the standard of reasonable care. An actor can be negligent only if his conduct created a foreseeable risk and the actor recognized, or a reasonable person would have recognized, that risk. *See Rallis v. Demoulas Super Mkts., Inc.,* 977 A.2d 527 (N.H. 2009); *Smith v. Finch,* 681 S.E.2d 147 (Ga. 2009) ("negligence may be established where it is shown that by exercise of reasonable care, the defendant might have foreseen that some injury would result from his act or omission, or that consequences of a generally injurious nature might have been expected").

4. **When harm is unforeseeable.** When a reasonable person in the defendant's circumstances would not foresee any danger, the defendant is "simply not negligent." *Allen v. Lockwood,* 156 So. 3d 650 (La. 2015) (unpaved grassy church parking area that had been used for decades without incident did not create an unreasonable risk of harm); *Wray v. Green,* 126 A.3d 476 (R.I. 2015) (no evidence of *breach* where the defendant was stopped behind the left-turning plaintiff and a third car shoved him into the plaintiff's car).

5. **Evaluating foreseeability.** If instead of distracting the driver from inside the car, the friend sends text messages from another location, is injury foreseeable? The New Jersey Superior Court in *Kubert v. Best,* 75 A.3d 1214 (N.J. Super. Ct. App. Div. 2013), was called on to decide "whether one who is texting from a location remote from the driver of a motor vehicle can be liable to persons injured because the driver was distracted by the text." The court noted "[i]t is foreseeable that a driver who is actually distracted by a text

message might cause an accident and serious injuries or death, but it is not generally foreseeable that every recipient of a text message who is driving will neglect his obligation to obey the law and will be distracted by the text." Consequently, the court held that "the sender of a text message can potentially be liable if an accident is caused by texting, but only if the sender knew or had special reason to know that the recipient would view the text while driving and thus be distracted." Whether or not you agree with the *Kubert* court's decision on foreseeability, you can also see why foreseeability of harm is one question in breach, but not the only one.

6. **The Third Restatement.** Under the Restatement (Third) of Torts, "the assessment of the foreseeability of a risk is no longer part of the duty analysis, but is to be considered when the [fact finder] decides if the defendant failed to exercise reasonable care." RESTATEMENT (THIRD) OF TORTS: LIABILITY FOR PHYSICAL AND EMOTIONAL HARM § 7 cmt. j (2010). This means that when there is some evidence that the risk was foreseeable the question is typically one for the jury to resolve in terms of breach. *See Brokaw v. Winfield-Mt. Union Cmty. Sch. Dist.*, 788 N.W.2d 386 (Iowa 2010) (because reasonable minds could disagree with respect to factual questions, issue of whether basketball coach should have foreseen that basketball player would strike opposing team player should be left to jury decision). The Third Restatement's conception that foreseeability should not be used in determining the existence of a duty continues to gain some adherents. *See, e.g., Rodriguez v. Del Sol Shopping Ctr. Assocs., L.P.*, 326 P.3d 465 (N.M. 2014). Why does it matter if a court addresses foreseeability in the element of breach or the element of duty?

LIMONES V. SCHOOL DISTRICT OF LEE COUNTY
161 So. 3d 384 (Fla. 2015)

LEWIS, J. . . .

At approximately 7:40 p.m. on November 13, 2008, fifteen-year-old Abel Limones, Jr., suddenly collapsed during a high school soccer game. . . . When Abel was unable to rise, Thomas Busatta, the coach for East Lee County High School, immediately ran onto the field to check his player. Abel tried to speak to Busatta, but within three minutes of the collapse, he appeared to stop breathing and lost consciousness. . . . Busatta, who was certified in the use of an automated external defibrillator (AED), testified that he yelled for an AED. The AED in the possession of Riverdale High School was actually at the game facility located at the end of the soccer field, but it was never brought on the field to Busatta to assist in reviving Abel. . . .

[R]esponders from the Emergency Medical Service (EMS) arrived and utilized a fully automatic AED on Abel and also administered several drugs in an attempt to restore his heartbeat. After application of shocks and drugs, emergency responders revived Abel, but not until approximately 8:06 p.m., which was twenty-six minutes after his initial collapse. Although

Abel survived, he suffered a severe brain injury due to a lack of oxygen over the time delay involved. As a result, he now remains in a nearly persistent vegetative state that will require full-time care for the remainder of his life.

[Limones' parents brought an action against the county school board for negligence, alleging that it breached a common law and statutory duty when it failed to apply an automated external defibrillator (AED) on Abel after his collapse. Florida statute requires all public schools in the Florida High School Athletic Association to have an operational AED on school property and to train "all employees or volunteers who are reasonably expected to use the device" in its application. The parents hired an expert who testified that the failure to use an AED earlier caused Abel's brain damage. The trial court entered summary judgment in favor of the school board.]

The Second District Court of Appeal determined that a clearly recognized common law duty existed. . . . [S]chool employees must reasonably supervise students during activities that are subject to the control of the school. However, the Second District incorrectly expanded Florida law and invaded the province of the jury when it further considered whether Respondent was required to make available, diagnose the need for, or use the AED on Abel. . . .

Respondent owed Abel a duty of supervision and to act with reasonable care under the circumstances; specifically, Respondent owed Abel a duty to take appropriate post-injury efforts to avoid or mitigate further aggravation of his injury. "Reasonable care under the circumstances" is a standard that may fluctuate with time, the student's age and activity, the extent of the injury, the available responder(s), and other facts. Advancements with technology and equipment available today, such as a portable AED, to treat an injury were most probably unavailable twenty years ago, and may be obsolete twenty years from now. We therefore leave it to the jury to determine, under the evidence presented, whether the particular actions of Respondent's employees satisfied or breached the duty of reasonable care owed.

For several reasons, we reject the decision of the Second District to narrowly frame the issue as whether Respondent had a specified duty to diagnose the need for or use an AED on Abel. First, as stated above, reasonable care under the circumstances is not and should not be a fixed concept. Such a narrow definition of duty, a purely legal question, slides too easily into breach, a factual matter for the jury. We reject the attempt below to specifically define each element in the scope of the duty as a matter of law, as this case attempted to remove all factual elements from the law and digitalize every aspect of human conduct. . . .

We hold that Respondent owed a common law duty to supervise Abel, and that once injured, Respondent owed a duty to take reasonable measures and come to his aid to prevent aggravation of his injury. It is a matter for the jury to determine under the evidence whether Respondent's actions breached that duty and resulted in the damage that Abel suffered. . . . We therefore quash the decision below and remand this case for trial.

NOTES

1.   **Duty to use an AED?** Why does the Florida Supreme Court think it's a problem for the lower courts to decide whether the school district had a duty to use an AED? What is the problem with describing the duty this way? How does this problem influence the procedural outcome in the trial court?

2.   **Judge vs. jury.** Courts sometimes talk about the standard of duty rather than simply leave it to the jury to assess breach of duty. *See Not Afraid v. State*, 352 P.3d 71 (Mont. 2015) (requiring plaintiff to establish the standard of care that would be exercised by a governmental entity in placing, installing, and maintaining concrete barriers on a roadway). Although the creation of specific duties seems an outdated way of taking cases from the jury, you can still find cases that take such an approach. The underlying problem is to allocate decision-making power between judge and jury. The jury is to decide pure facts (Was the stop light red?). It is also to make certain value judgments (Did the defendant's failure to stop amount to negligence?). It also determines credibility of witnesses, as we will see ahead.

3.   **Usurping the jury's role in breach.** Where a landowner or city fails to trim bushes, leaving an intersection obscured and leading to traffic accidents, courts have often said the defendant had no duty to trim the bushes. Such cases swipe any judgment about reasonable care from the jury. However, courts can also be vigilant about recognizing the boundaries of the judicial role, as was the court in *Limones*.

NOTE: ASSESSING THE LANGUAGE OF FORESEEABILITY AND RISK

Focus for a moment, not on the ideas, principles, or rules, but on the *language* courts often use to express themselves about negligence and how we must read and understand that language.

"Courts often use the term 'foreseeable' as a shorthand expression. They might say, for example, that a defendant is negligent if harm was foreseeable. Such statements should not ordinarily be taken in a literal way. Harm is a foreseeable consequence of almost all acts, but courts definitely do not mean that *all* acts are negligent. Courts are likely to use the term 'foreseeable' to mean that harm was not only foreseeable but also too likely to occur to justify risking it without added precautions. Similarly, courts sometimes speak about some harms as more foreseeable than others, which can be understood to mean that the risk or probability of harm is greater in some cases than in others. Along the same lines, when courts say that harm is unforeseeable, they may mean that although harm was actually foreseeable on the facts of the case, a reasonable person would not have taken action to prevent it because the risk of harm was low, and harm was so improbable that a reasonable person would not have taken safety precautions. Put differently, to say that harm was unforeseeable often seems to mean only that the foreseeable harm was not probable enough to require precaution, meaning ultimately that the defendant's conduct was not unreasonably risky." DAN B. DOBBS, THE LAW OF TORTS § 143 (2001); *see also* 1 DOBBS, HAYDEN & BUBLICK, THE LAW OF TORTS § 159 (2d ed. 2011).

Consider the court's language in *Romine v. Village of Irving*, 783 N.E.2d 1064 (Ill. App. Ct. 2003). Police officers ejected two unruly, intoxicated people from a fair, knowing that those people were from out of town. Once ejected, the intoxicated people drove their car negligently, causing injuries to the plaintiff. The plaintiff included the police officers in the suit for damages on the ground that the police officers should have arrested the intoxicated persons to prevent their dangerous driving. The court said that police officers could not foresee criminal acts in general and in particular drunken driving by intoxicated persons they ejected from a fair. Can either of these statements be taken literally? Surely police can foresee criminal activity in general—after all, they are hired to prevent it and to arrest its perpetrators. And intoxicated driving seems not only foreseeable but as the court itself said, all too common. So what might the court have been trying to say when it used the "foreseeability" locution?

C. UNSTRUCTURED WEIGHING OF RISKS AND COSTS

INDIANA CONSOLIDATED INSURANCE CO. v. MATHEW
402 N.E.2d 1000 (Ind. Ct. App. 1980)

HOFFMAN, JUDGE.

Appellant Indiana Consolidated Insurance Company seeks review of the finding that Robert D. Mathew (Mathew) did not act in a negligent manner so as to be liable for damages done to his brother's garage when a Toro riding lawnmower that Mathew was starting caught fire. Appellant insured the garage and premises under a homeowner's insurance policy and is pursuing this claim against Mathew by virtue of its subrogation rights.[1]

[T]he facts favorable to Mathew disclose that on May 1, 1976 Mathew's brother was out of town for the weekend. The two brothers lived across the

---

[1] A fire insurer or collision insurer who pays its insured's loss "stands in the shoes" of the insured for the purpose of suing any tortfeasor whose tortious acts caused the loss.—Eds.

street from each other and took turns mowing both lawns. In the late afternoon Mathew decided to mow both lawns and went to his brother's garage where a twelve horsepower Toro riding lawnmower was stored. The mower was approximately eight years old, was kept in good mechanical condition, and had required only minor tune-ups and belt replacements for the rotary mower assembly. Mathew pulled the mower away from the side wall of the garage and after checking the gas gauge filled the lawnmower approximately three-fourths full with gasoline using a funnel. He then went back across the street to his home for approximately twenty minutes. Upon returning to the garage Mathew started the lawnmower. However, he noticed a flame in the engine area under the hood and immediately shut the engine off. He opened the hood and saw a flame four to five inches tall under the gas tank. Using some clean towels Mathew tried to snuff out the flame but was unsuccessful. He could find no other means to extinguish the fire. The flames continued to grow and the machine began spewing gasoline, so he ran to his home to call the fire department. He returned to find the garage totally engulfed in flames.

At trial Mathew testified that he was afraid to try to push the flaming machine outside the garage for fear that the tank would explode in his face.

Indiana Consolidated brought this action against Mathew alleging that he breached a duty owed to his brother to exercise due care in starting the lawnmower and therefore stands liable for the damages resulting from his negligence. After a bench trial the court below entered the following finding, to-wit:

The Court having heretofore taken this matter under advisement and having considered the evidence introduced in the trial of this cause and being sufficiently advised, now enters Findings as follows: The Court now finds . . . that there is no evidence of negligence on the part of the defendant, Robert D. Mathew, and that the plaintiff should take nothing by its complaint.

IT IS THEREFORE ORDERED, ADJUDGED AND DECREED BY THE COURT that the plaintiff, Indiana Consolidated Insurance Company, take nothing by its complaint; and Judgment is entered for and on behalf of the defendant, Robert D. Mathew. Costs of this action are taxed to the plaintiff.

On appeal appellant contends that the judgment is contrary to law because Mathew was negligent in filling the gas tank, in starting the mower in an enclosed area, and in failing to push the flaming mower out of the garage. The standard by which Mathew's conduct is to be measured is whether he exercised the duty to use due care in operating the mower that an ordinary prudent man would exercise under the same or similar circumstances.

The record amply supports the finding that Mathew did not act in a negligent manner in filling the gas tank. He testified that he did so carefully, with the use of a funnel. He did not fill the tank full, and he was adamant in his belief that he did not spill any gasoline. He hypothesized that even had any gas been spilled it would have evaporated in the cool air during the twenty-minute period before he started the mower. Appellant is merely asking this Court to reweigh the evidence in regard to any gasoline spillage due to Mathew's admission on cross-examination that he could have spilled some fuel. The trier of fact resolved this issue in favor of Mathew, finding that he exercised due care in fueling the mower, and it must remain undisturbed upon appeal. [Appellant is again reminded that any conflicts in testimony when appeal from a negative judgment is taken must be resolved in favor of the appellee.]

Appellant's contention that Mathew should be held liable for the act of negligently starting the mower inside the garage is also without merit. It cannot seriously be contended that the evidence shows that Mathew acted other than a reasonably prudent man in pulling the mower out into an open area of the garage and starting it. The mower was a riding type that was of considerable weight and size. Garages are designed to permit the starting of motorized vehicles such as automobiles and are commonly used for such purpose. That this particular mower would catch fire at this particular time was not reasonably foreseeable. [As one is not required to anticipate that which is unlikely to happen, the trial court did not err in determining that Mathew was not negligent in starting the mower inside the garage.]

Appellant's further allegation that Mathew negligently failed to push the flaming mower out of the garage area is refuted by the evidence that the machine was spewing gasoline and that he was afraid for his safety should the tank explode. Mathew therefore chose to leave and summon help from the local fire department. [One who is confronted with a sudden emergency not of his own making is not chargeable with negligence if he acts according to his best judgment. The sudden emergency doctrine requires the person so confronted to do that which an ordinary prudent man would do under like circumstances.] Mathew's course of action can be deemed an exercise of ordinary prudence. The law values human life above property. Greater risk of one's person is justified to save life than is reasonable in protecting property. If Mathew had tried to push the riding mower ten feet into an open area the machine might have exploded and caused much graver damage to his person than was suffered by the destruction of the garage. [Contrary to appellant's position several jurisdictions have ruled that one may be deemed negligent in voluntarily risking life or serious injury for the purpose of saving mere property.] . .

The judgment is not contrary to law and is therefore affirmed.

NOTES

1.   **Factors for evaluating breach.** Which specific acts of the defendant's were alleged to have been negligent? What factors permitted the trial court to find that the defendant was not negligent?

2.   **Burden of alternative conduct.** How can you measure the costs or burdens of alternative conduct? For example, what if a child fell on wet grass while participating in a relay race at defendant's camp? *See Fintzi v. N.J. YMHA-YWHA,* 765 N.E.2d 288 (N.Y. 2001). Does it matter to the analysis that the alternative conduct proposed by the defendant imposes costs or burdens on third parties?

3.   **Analyzing breach.** A woman fell while taking off her shoes before going through airport security, and sued the Transportation Safety Administration (TSA) for negligence in not providing her a chair. The record showed that "of the thousands of passengers passing through the security screening measures at the airport prior to plaintiff's injury, no similar incidents had occurred." The trial court granted summary judgment for the defendant, holding that there was no breach of duty. In light of *Pipher* and *Indiana Consolidated,* how would you analyze this issue on appeal? *See Barnes v. United States*, 485 F.3d 341 (6th Cir. 2007).

STINNETT V. BUCHELE
598 S.W.2d 469 (Ky. Ct. App. 1980)

BREETZ, JUDGE.

This is a tort action filed by an employee against his employer for injuries sustained during the course and scope of his employment. The lower court granted summary judgment to the employer on the ground that there was no showing that the injury was caused by the negligence of the employer. We affirm. ——> holding

The accident which gave rise to this suit was also the subject of a workmen's compensation claim. The Workmen's Compensation Board denied benefits because the employee, being employed in agriculture, was exempt from the coverage of the Workmen's Compensation Act. We have today, by separate and non-published opinion, affirmed the board in that regard . . .

Earl S. Buchele is a practicing physician in Hardinsburg, Kentucky. He hired Alvin Stinnett as a farm laborer in January 1976. In September of that year Mr. Stinnett undertook to repair the roof on a barn located at one of Dr. Buchele's farms known as the Cloverport Farm. The repairs were to consist of nailing down the edges of the roof that had been loosened by the wind and painting the roof with a coating. Stinnett was severely injured when he fell from the roof while applying the coating with a paint roller.

Stinnett urges in his brief to this court that Dr. Buchele was negligent for failing to comply with occupational and health regulations and also for his failure to provide a safe place to work. Dr. Buchele denies both of those assertions, and, additionally, argues that Stinnett was contributorily negligent as a matter of law. We do not reach the issue of contributory negligence. . . .

Nor do we find any evidence to be submitted to the jury that Dr. Buchele was negligent in failing to provide Stinnett with a safe place to work. We agree with Stinnett when he states that Dr. Buchele had the obligation to furnish him:

> . . . a place reasonably safe having regard for the character of work and reasonably safe tools and appliances for doing the work. The measure of duty is to exercise ordinary or reasonable care to do so. The standard is the care exercised by prudent employers in similar circumstances.

We also agree with the sentence immediately preceding the quotation from that same opinion: "An employer's obligation to its employee is not the frequently impossible duty of furnishing absolutely safe instrumentalities or place to work."

Although we may consider that painting a barn roof is dangerous work, we cannot say that Dr. Buchele can be held liable for failing to provide a safe place to work solely because he asked Stinnett to work on the roof. We hold, therefore, that there was no showing of any negligence on the part of Dr. Buchele arising solely out of the fact that he had asked Stinnett to paint the barn roof.

Stinnett next argues . . . that a reasonable and prudent employer would have provided safety devices of some kind even though not required to by force of statute or regulation and that the question whether Dr. Buchele measured up to the standards of an ordinarily careful and prudent employer is one for the jury . . . The liability of the employer:

> . . . rests upon the assumption that the employer has a better and more comprehensive knowledge than the employees, and ceases to be applicable where the employees' means of knowledge of the dangers to be incurred is equal to that of the employer. 53 Am. Jur. 2d, Master and Servant, § 160.

Stinnett had been in the painting business with his brother-in-law for two years before he began working for Dr. Buchele. Although the record is not clear whether Stinnett, his brother-in-law or both did the painting, they did paint a church steeple and an undetermined number of barn roofs. On occasion safety belts and safety nets had been used while painting the barn roofs. Stinnett was injured on a Sunday. Dr. Buchele was not present and he did not know that Stinnett was going to work on the barn roof on that particular day. Dr. Buchele had, however, purchased the material that Stinnett was applying to the roof when he fell. [Stinnett did not ask Dr. Buchele to procure a safety net nor did he check to see if one was available. He admitted he could have used a safety rope around his waist but he did not think any were available] . . .

In short, <u>we find no evidence of negligence on the part of Dr. Buchele to submit to a jury.</u>

NOTES

1. **Workers' compensation exclusions.** Although workers' compensation statutes have been adopted everywhere, <u>they do not include all workers within their benefits.</u> Statutes may exclude agricultural employees, domestic employees, and casual employees, for example. One special case is that of the worker on interstate railroads. Under the Federal Employers Liability Act, 45 U.S.C.A. §§ 51 *et seq.*, called FELA, these workers have expanded tort rights, but no workers' compensation. [In general, workers not covered by compensation laws must, like Mr. Stinnett, seek recovery under the tort system]

2. **Social vs. individual responsibility for injuries.** Even if Dr. Buchele was not at fault and this was simply an accident, Mr. Stinnett was injured. Persons in this position may not be able to work at all and may have substantial medical needs. Apart from human sympathy, is there any reason to consider this as a social problem rather than as Mr. Stinnett's individual problem? If there are social problems represented in injury cases and society ought to respond in some fashion, does that indicate that Dr. Buchele as an individual ought to bear any of Mr. Stinnett's loss?

3. **Expecting the plaintiff to care for himself.** How did the court conclude that Dr. Buchele was not negligent? Was it unforeseeable that Stinnett might fall off the roof if he did not have safety equipment? Consider *Lowery v. Echostar Satellite Corp.*, 160 P.3d 959 (Okla. 2007). *In Lowery*, a customer of a satellite TV company was injured when she fell off the roof of her garage while attempting to repair her satellite dish. She claimed the company was negligent in exposing her to the risks of falling off the roof by refusing to repair the dish and instead insisting that she should make the minor repairs herself, even over her protestations that she was inexperienced and did not want to climb the roof. She was actually talking with the company's customer service department on her cordless phone when she fell. The court affirmed the trial court's grant of summary judgment for the company, concluding that there was no evidence that the company "was in a superior position to protect her," such as by knowing of some danger of harm beyond those normally presented by climbing up on any roof. The court said it was "beyond good sense" to hold otherwise. Consider how the courts in *Stinnett* or *Lowery* would have ruled if the plaintiff had suffered from serious dementia—was likely to forget where he or she was—and the defendant knew it. *See Daniels v. Senior Care, Inc.*, 21 S.W.3d 133 (Mo. Ct. App. 2000). Sometimes the question of what care

an employer can expect from an employee is a fact question. *See Stichen v. Talcott Props.*, 292 P.3d 458 (Mont. 2013) (issue of fact as to whether the landlord should have anticipated harm to a janitor working on the premises).

4.　**The obviousness of danger.** "[T]he obviousness of a risk may make the likelihood of its materializing so slight that there is no need to try to eliminate the risk." *Halek v. United States,* 178 F.3d 481 (7th Cir. 1999); *see also Pinson v. 45 Dev., LLC*, 758 F.3d 948 (8th Cir. 2014) (dangers of installing a sign above a storefront canopy were obvious, particularly when the injured person had over ten years' experience installing signs). Is that an explanation for the *Stinnett* holding? The *Lowery* court, *supra* Note 3, referred more than once in its discussion to "the obvious risks of climbing onto a rooftop." You may think this principle is sometimes misapplied. However, the principle itself might still be sound. That is, perhaps it is not unreasonable to fail to take action to lessen a risk to someone that is so patently obvious that the other person can be relied upon to avoid it on his own.

5.　**Expecting care by third persons.** In some cases a reasonable person may not breach a duty when the person reasonably relies on another to protect the plaintiff. If parents accompany a child to a backyard party and know of the swimming pool there, can the host reasonably think the risk of injury to the child is low in spite of the dangers of a pool? Why? *See Herron v. Hollis,* 546 S.E.2d 17 (Ga. Ct. App. 2001). What if the parents do not know the host has a pool that can be reached by a small child? *Cf. Perri v. Furama Restaurant, Inc.*, 781 N.E.2d 631 (Ill. App. Ct. 2002). Some courts reach their conclusions in terms of duty rather than breach. *See, e.g., Foss v. Kincade*, 766 N.W.2d 317 (Minn. 2009) (homeowner owed no duty to protect child in home who was under mother's supervision); *Lasley v. Hylton*, 764 S.E.2d 88 (Va. 2014) (host who let guest's two daughters, ages 8 and 12, drive his all-terrain vehicles (ATVs) owed no duty and breached no duty to a child guest when "a child's parent is present and supervising, and knows or should know of open and obvious risks associated with an activity," and the child participates in that activity "with the parent's permission"). Is it right to say that the defendants had no duty? Why might it matter if the issue is framed as one of duty rather than breach? Could both the defendant and the parent have breached a duty to the child?

BERNIER V. BOSTON EDISON CO.

403 N.E.2d 391 (Mass. 1980)

KAPLAN, JUSTICE.

About 2:30 p.m., May 24, 1972, the plaintiffs Arthur Bernier, Jr., and Patricia J. Kasputys, then eighteen and fifteen years old, were let out of school and, after going to Kasputys's house, sauntered to an ice cream parlor on Massachusetts Avenue in Lexington Center, one of the town's major shopping areas. A half hour later, Alice Ramsdell entered her 1968 Buick Skylark automobile parked, pointed east, on the south side of

not propul
performer or
crash unreasonable
risk of injury

Massachusetts Avenue (which here runs west-east), in the last metered space about fifteen to twenty feet short of where the avenue meets Muzzey Street, a one-way street beginning at the avenue and running south. No traffic signals were posted at the junction with Muzzey Street.

As Ramsdell started her car, she noted, checking her rear-view and side-view mirrors, that there was a car—later identified as a Cadillac convertible driven by John Boireau—some seventy-five feet behind her. She wanted to make a right turn on Muzzey Street. Just before pulling out, Ramsdell observed that the Cadillac was much closer to her than before. Boireau, too, wished to turn right onto Muzzey Street. As there were no cars ahead of her before the intersection, Ramsdell thought she could make the turn before the Cadillac interfered.

Accident

As Ramsdell was pulling left slightly away from the curb, Boireau passed her traveling (as he said) about five miles an hour. Whether Ramsdell's car then "bolted" out and struck Boireau's car as he was negotiating the right turn, or Boireau turned into Ramsdell's car as the two attempted to make the turn, was the subject of conflicting testimony. So, too, the estimates of Ramsdell's speed on impact with Boireau varied from five to thirty miles an hour. Both drivers said they recognized the trouble and braked, but not before a minor collision occurred some ten to fifteen feet into the Muzzey Street intersection, Boireau's right front fender being slightly dented by contact with Ramsdell's left front fender.

What might have been a commonplace collision turned into a complicated accident. On impact, Ramsdell, a woman of sixty-nine, hit her head against her steering wheel and suffered a bloody nose. She testified she "lost complete control of that car." Dazed, she unknowingly let her foot slip from the power brake to the gas pedal. In the result, after veering right around Boireau's car and perhaps slowing slightly, she accelerated across the remaining twenty feet of Muzzey Street, bounced to the south sidewalk, about nine feet wide, of Massachusetts Avenue, and moved about fifty-five feet down the sidewalk. On this passage the car scraped the front of a camera store, hit and levelled a parking meter, struck and damaged extensively the right rear section of a Chevrolet Chevelle automobile (the third parked car beyond Muzzey Street), knocked down an electric light pole owned by the defendant Boston Edison Company (Edison), and struck the plaintiffs who had left the ice cream parlor and were walking side by side west, into the face of the oncoming car. There was much confusion at trial whether, after hitting the meter and car, Ramsdell first hit the pole and then the plaintiffs, or first the plaintiffs and then the pole, but no one denied she hit all three. The car came to a stop two to three feet over the stump of the pole with its left wheels in the gutter and its right wheels on the sidewalk, and in contact with the Chevelle.

Ramsdell lost control + hit Ps

[handwritten top margin: duty < reasonable care under circumstances]

The electric light pole, when hit, fell away from Ramsdell's car toward the east, struck a Volkswagen automobile parked along Massachusetts Avenue (the fourth car from Muzzey Street), and came down across the legs of Bernier. Boireau was able with help to lift the pole off Bernier. Bernier's thighs and left shin bone were broken, the latter break causing a permanently shortened left leg; and he had other related injuries. *[margin: Pole fell on Bernier]* Kasputys lay within two feet of the pole further in from the curb than Bernier. There was no eyewitness testimony that she had been struck by the pole. She was unconscious and vomiting. She suffered a skull fracture on the right side of her head where pieces of metal and length of wire were found imbedded, and developed permanent pain in her left lower leg. *[margin: Kasputy's injuries]*

[Bernier and Kasputys sued Ramsdell, Boireau, and Edison. The claims against Edison alleged that it had negligently designed, selected, constructed and maintained the pole. The jury found against Ramsdell and Edison. Edison appeals.]

[T]he gravamen *[handwritten: → serious word of complaint or allegation]* of the plaintiffs' case, as it appeared at trial, was that Edison had failed through negligence to design a pole that was accommodated reasonably to foreseeable vehicular impacts so as to avoid pedestrian injuries, and that the continued use of the pole created an unreasonable risk of such injuries. *[margin: P contention / argument]*

As designer or codesigner of the pole and in control of its maintenance, Edison "must anticipate the environment in which its product will be used, and it must design against the reasonably foreseeable risk attending the product's use in that setting." Certainly the evidence showed that a risk of automobiles colliding with Edison poles—in particular No. 6 poles—was not only foreseeable but well known to the company. About 100 to 120 Edison poles a year were knocked down in such collisions in Edison's "Northeast Service Center" which included Lexington. . . . A so-called "knock down truck" worked steadily replacing downed poles in the district and installing new ones, and there were estimates by employees that in their years of field work they had replaced "thousands" of Edison poles. One employee said he had been personally involved in replacing at least a hundred poles of the type involved in the accident at bar. *[margin: Court argument; also that foreseeable to and well known to the company ex collision with edison pole]*

[margin left: Rule; Foreseeable risk by D]

As in the case of vehicles, design should take into account "foreseeable participation in collisions." And for the speeds to be encountered and consequences entailed in collisions, one analyzes the whole "setting." This was a busy shopping area with heavy pedestrian and vehicular traffic.

. . . Edison installed this No. 6 pole on February 3, 1949. It was of reinforced concrete, twenty-six feet nine inches in height, and ran from an eight inch base to a 5 3/8 inch top diameter. Four anchor bolts held it to a base that extended 4 2/3 feet below the surface. The pole was hollow, allowing for feeder wires to come from an underground cable up to the luminaire. Implanted in the concrete shaft were six vertical steel rods, each *[margin: description of pole]*

.375 (3/8) inch thick. Total weight of the pole and luminaire structure was 1,200 pounds.

What precautions were taken in the design to guard against the risk of pedestrian injury through collapse of a No. 6 pole upon impact by a vehicle? According to the evidence, the problem was not seriously adverted to. . . . Overall, the major considerations in Edison's design of poles (including their materials) seemed to be cost, adaptability to Edison's existing system of power supply and connecting apparatus, and capacity of Edison employees to install the poles safely.[4]

. . . To begin with, since injuries might be serious (as the present case indeed indicated), the likelihood of accidents need not be high to warrant careful consideration of safety features.

The plaintiffs' major witness concerning design safety was Howard Simpson, who had a doctorate in engineering and practiced as a consulting structural engineer. His qualifications as an expert on the strength of reinforced concrete were unchallenged. In his opinion, the concrete of the thickness specified for No. 6 poles lacked "ductility," the quality which would allow a pole, when struck by a car, to absorb part of the impact and bend without breaking. No. 6 would shatter when hit with sufficient force; indeed, one of the Edison supervisors testified about No. 6 that the concrete "all crumbles at the point of impact." As the exposed steel rods could not then support the weight of the pole, it would fall. As to the force sufficient to break No. 6 in this fashion, Simpson testified that the pole would succumb to a 1968 Buick Skylark with a passenger, spare tire, and full gas tank going as slowly as six m.p.h. A medium-sized truck weighing 10,000 pounds could level No. 6 when traveling at 1.5 m.p.h.

Simpson went on to say that the strength of the pole could have been substantially improved by using steel rods of larger diameter or by placing steel "hoops" or "spirals" perpendicular to those vertical rods. In his opinion the latter device would have enabled the pole to withstand the impact of the Buick at 11 m.p.h.—an important advance, as a car going 9 m.p.h. has an energy considerably greater than that at 6 m.p.h. Such hoops and spirals had been in use since the early 1900's in columns for buildings. Simpson calculated the cost per pole of the hoops at $5.75 and the spirals at $17.50.

We should add here that there was evidence from Edison employees of the existence of other pole-types, possibly of greater strength, that would at least have warranted comparison by Edison with the No. 6 pole in respect to safety values. Various metal poles (aluminum and steel) might

---

[4] It is fair to mention, however, that one engineer thought metal poles might have been passed over because they would tend to become electrified when downed and subject pedestrians to shock. Another thought pedestrian safety was adequately handled by having a reputable manufacturer fabricate the poles. There was some indication that Edison did not install so-called "breakaway" poles in areas such as Lexington Center because of danger to pedestrians.

have deserved such study. Edison's own No. 26, of prestressed concrete, designed in 1968, might have been an improvement. . . .

Edison argues that a finding of negligence here left it in the grip of a "polycentric" problem. If it chose to protect pedestrians by using stronger poles, motorists might be more seriously injured when they hit poles which did not break. If it chose to protect motorists, pedestrians would claim recovery when poles fell on them. No designer or owner, Edison added, is required to make or use a product wholly accident-free. There is some disingenuousness in this argument as the evidence shows Edison paid scant attention in the design of the No. 6 pole to the safety either of motorists or pedestrians. But we think there is nothing in the argument to relieve Edison of a duty to take precautions against knock-downs by cars, and it would seem reasonable for Edison to consider pedestrian safety with particular seriousness. Persons in a car are protected by a metal and glass shield sometimes three times as heavy as the pole's entire weight; pedestrians are exposed. Whether drivers are hurt any less by impact at similar speeds with poles that topple than with poles that bend rather than fall is unknown to us and apparently to Edison as well. To be sure, many more cars will hit poles than poles will hit pedestrians, but a six m.p.h. threshold for cars, and less for trucks, seems little protection indeed.

. . . Here the jury could rationally find negligence of design and maintenance. They could find that the vehicular speed at which No. 6 would topple was grievously low, creating an unacceptable risk of grave injury to persons at the scene (who in shopping areas such as Lexington Center might be numerous). The impact resistance of the pole could have been improved by relatively minor alterations available at the time and not inconveniencing Edison or the public, or possibly by the use of another type of pole with greater resistance. In balancing all the pertinent factors, the jury made a judgment as to the social acceptability of the design. . . .

Judgments affirmed.

NOTES

1. **Negligence factors.** What factors are important to the court's belief that negligence was proved?

2. **Building a case.** Lawyers must introduce evidence to build their case. What evidence did the plaintiffs supply to show that Edison could foresee cars colliding with the poles and the poles falling? That precautions existed? What evidence did Edison introduce to support the reasonableness of its conduct? What other evidence could it have offered?

3. **Unquantified risk and benefit.** Do you have a good idea just how risky it was to use these poles? How much benefit was there in using these poles? To whom did the benefit, if any, flow? Suppose 1,500 people a year are injured by falling poles. It would cost $3,000–$5,000 to replace each pole with

a breakaway pole that would greatly reduce, if not eliminate, these injuries. However, there are 88 million poles nationwide. Should it be left to a jury to decide in individual cases whether failure to furnish breakaway poles was negligent? Should precautions be required when they are inexpensive, like the hoops and spirals, but not otherwise?

4. **Social utility of the conduct.** What difference does it make to the negligence analysis if the defendant's conduct has social utility or value? In *Parsons v. Crown Disposal Co.*, 936 P.2d 70 (Cal. 1997), the plaintiff was thrown from the horse he was riding when the defendant's garbage truck, operating in a normal manner, startled the horse with loud noises. Affirming a summary judgment for the defendant, the court said that the main factor in the case is the social value of defendant's conduct. Because garbage collection activity is a vital public service and a matter of high social utility, the defendant is not negligent merely because he uses a machine that produces noises necessary to its regular operation, even though fright of horses might be foreseeable. *See also, e.g., Giant Food, Inc. v. Mitchell*, 640 A.2d 1134 (Md. 1994) (defendant's attempted "hot pursuit" recovery of stolen property did not expose other store customers to any unreasonable risk of harm; the "degree of risk of harm to invitees must be weighed against the privilege" to protect one's property); *Gooden v. City of Talladega*, 966 So. 2d 232 (Ala. 2007) (police officer not negligent for engaging in a high-speed chase where the speeding motorist posed "a clear and immediate threat to the safety of other motorists").

D. STRUCTURED WEIGHING OF RISKS AND UTILITY

UNITED STATES V. CARROLL TOWING CO.
159 F.2d 169 (2d Cir. 1947)

L. HAND, CIRCUIT JUDGE.

[Proceedings in admiralty involving several different entities interested in the collision and sinking of a barge, the Anna C. The Conners company owned the barge, which was loaded with flour. Grace Line employees, operating the Carroll Towing Company tug, negligently caused the Anna C to break adrift. She was carried by wind and tide against a tanker, whose propeller broke a hole in her bottom. Conners' bargee was not on board, and the damage was not reported to anyone. Had there been a bargee there, the Grace Line employees, who had pumps available, could have saved the Anna C; as it was, she careened, dumped her cargo of flour, and sank. The court first held that Grace Line and Carroll Towing were liable, and then considered whether the absence of a bargee on board the Anna C was negligence that reduced recovery to Conners.

It appears from the foregoing review that there is no general rule to determine when the absence of a bargee or other attendant will make the owner of the barge liable for injuries to other vessels if she breaks away from her moorings. . . . It becomes apparent why there can be no such general rule, when we consider the grounds for such a liability. Since there are occasions when every vessel will break from her moorings, and since, if she does, she becomes a menace to those about her; the owner's duty, as in other similar situations, to provide against resulting injuries is a function of three variables: (1) The probability that she will break away; (2) the gravity of the resulting injury, if she does; (3) the burden of adequate precautions. Possibly it serves to bring this notion into relief to state it in algebraic terms: if the probability be called P; the injury, L; and the burden, B; liability depends upon whether B is less than L multiplied by P: i.e., whether B < PL. Applied to the situation at bar, the likelihood that a barge will break from her fasts and the damage she will do, vary with the place and time; for example, if a storm threatens, the danger is greater; so it is, if she is in a crowded harbor where moored barges are constantly being shifted about. On the other hand, the barge must not be the bargee's prison, even though he lives aboard; he must go ashore at times. . . . In the case at bar the bargee left at five o'clock in the afternoon of January 3rd, and the flotilla broke away at about two o'clock in the afternoon of the following day, twenty-one hours afterwards. The bargee had been away all the time, and we hold that his fabricated story was affirmative evidence that he had no excuse for his absence. At the locus in quo—especially during the short January days and in the full tide of war activity—barges were being constantly "drilled" in and out. Certainly it was not beyond reasonable expectation that, with the inevitable haste and bustle, the work might not be done with adequate care. In such circumstances we hold—and it is all that we do hold—that it was a fair requirement that the Conners Company should have a bargee aboard (unless he had some excuse for his absence), during the working hours of daylight.

NOTES

1.   **Risk-utility.** As we have seen, many cases approve risk-utility balancing to determine negligence, although very often in a form less structured than the formula Judge Hand advanced. *See, e.g., Doe Parents No. 1 v. State, Dep't of Educ.,* 58 P.3d 545 (Haw. 2002); *see also* 1 DOBBS, HAYDEN & BUBLICK, THE LAW OF TORTS § 160 (2d ed. 2011).

2.   **Specific alternative conduct**. We have also seen in this chapter that the party asserting negligence first identifies some specific act of negligence, by pointing to what the defendant did or did not do and identifying some specific safer conduct that might have been pursued. If the alternative conduct was safer, the court will want to know how much safer and something about its costs. What was the specific alternative conduct Judge Hand was considering in *Carroll Towing*?

3.   **A hypothetical.** Suppose that, by not having a bargee on board at all times, the barge would break loose and cause damage to itself or others about once a year, and that the average damage would be $25,000. Suppose

also that the cost of keeping a bargee on board at all times to prevent this would be an average of $30,000 a year. Judge Hand seems to say this would be a case of no negligence, and Judge Posner says this is correct because the function of the fault system is to impose liability rules that will bring about "efficient" or cost-justified rules of safety. A rule that required the barge owner to spend $30,000 to save $25,000 would be inefficient and not cost-justified. *See* Richard A. Posner, *A Theory of Negligence*, 1 J. LEG. STUDIES 29, 32 (1972).

4.   **Probability and severity of harm.** Consider the hypothetical variation of *Carroll Towing* given in Note 3. Where does probability come in? The answer is that it is built into the "average." Suppose that the probability is that the barge without a full-time bargee will break loose once every *other* year with the damage of $25,000. The probability of harm is reduced, and this will be reflected in a new average—$12,500 instead of $25,000. Try working this out the other way—by supposing that the barge will break loose *twice* a year. Would it then be negligent not to have a full-time bargee? Might the same type of analysis work with respect to severity of harm? *See Smith v. Finch*, 681 S.E.2d 147 (Ga. 2009) (reasonable care "often requires the consideration of unlikely but serious consequences").

5.   **Risk-utility and physical injury.** In the light of this kind of thinking, reconsider the *Brown v. Stiel* problem. Does the *Carroll Towing* formula assist in structuring your analysis? Does the test's utility wane where the defendant's conduct risked physical injury or death rather than just property damage?

6.   **Duty and breach.** Judge Hand says in *Carroll Towing* that "the owner's duty . . . is a function of three variables. . . ." Does it seem to you that he is really assuming a *duty* of reasonable care and then addressing the question of *breach* of that duty? The Third Restatement says that the major factors in analyzing whether conduct is negligent are "the foreseeable likelihood that the person's conduct will result in harm, the foreseeable severity of any harm that may ensue, and the burden of precautions to eliminate or reduce the risk of harm." *See* RESTATEMENT (THIRD) OF TORTS: LIABILITY FOR PHYSICAL AND EMOTIONAL HARM § 3 (2010).

NOTE: APPLYING THE RISK-UTILITY FORMULA

1.   *Estimating risks.* Everything we do carries *some* risk. In applying the Hand formula, how do we know the degree of risk attributable to the defendant's activity? One answer might be that Hand was not proposing a formula into which actual numbers could be substituted for the "algebra." Instead, Hand might have been proposing only a model, an indication about the nature of the decision or estimate we need to make. Do the cases preceding *Carroll Towing* suggest that courts were estimating costs or benefits of the defendant's conduct compared to some supposedly safer alternative?

2. *Estimating costs or benefits.* How do you *know* how much a safety precaution would cost or how much the activity benefits people? Almost any activity has *some* benefit and almost any safety precaution has *some* costs, although one safety precaution—a warning of danger—is usually almost costless, so that under *Carroll Towing* a warning might be due even if the danger is small. *See* RESTATEMENT (THIRD) OF TORTS: LIABILITY FOR PHYSICAL AND EMOTIONAL HARM § 18 (2010). It is often much easier to reduce to numbers than are risks. That is so because many costs can be identified in dollar-numbers. Benefits can also be identified in dollar-numbers by asking about the earnings, savings, or increase in capital value effected by the activity.

3. *Judicial application of the BPL factors.* Applying a risk-utility test to a breach question when the plaintiff tripped over a deviation in the sidewalk, the court in *Chambers v. Vill. of Moreauville,* 85 So. 3d 593 (La. 2012), wrote: "a municipality . . . is only liable for conditions that create an unreasonable risk of harm. Here, the utility of the sidewalk is high. Additionally, it would be fiscally exorbitant to require municipalities to correct all sidewalk deviations of one-and-one-quarter to one-and-one-half inches. Further, the risk of harm created by the deviation is low; there has never been a reported complaint about the deviation in the approximately forty years it has been in existence, the area of the sidewalk is well traveled, the deviation is relatively small, and it developed due to natural causes. Additionally, the deviation was readily observable, and [the plaintiff] failed to exercise the requisite standard of care while traversing this particular area of the sidewalk. Accordingly, we find the condition does not present an unreasonable risk of harm."

4. *The forgotten gopher hole.* As you leave your house one morning, on the way to try a tort case, you observe that a burrowing animal has dug a hole in your yard, very close to the sidewalk. Recognizing that the hole is a risk to anyone who might step off the sidewalk, you make a mental note to fill the hole or barricade it as soon as you get home. But at the end of a long, hard day before a hostile jury, an irascible judge, and an unappreciative client, you have forgotten the hole. You plop in front of the television. In the meantime, a neighbor on his way to bring you a misdelivered copy of *Torts Illustrated* steps off the sidewalk in the dark, and breaks his ankle as he falls into the hole. Are you negligent? Does *Carroll Towing* help you decide? Might the risk-utility formula be more helpful for evaluating some types of negligence than others? *See* RESTATEMENT (SECOND) OF TORTS § 289 (1965) (memory of the reasonable person is required). Professor Latin points out that many routine cases involve nothing more than mistake and momentary inattention. Howard Latin, *"Good" Warnings, Bad Products, and Cognitive Limitations,* 41 U.C.L.A. L. REV. 1193 (1994).

5. *Variable probabilities and information costs.* Look back at *Indiana Consolidated Ins. Co. v. Mathew.* What if leaving the burning mower in the garage created a 90% probability of fire damage to the garage of about $10,000 and no more, but a 5% probability of fire totally destroying the house at a loss of $100,000, a 4% probability of a fire spread that would cause losses of more than a million dollars, and a 1% probability of no harm. Does it seem preposterous to say that the jury should somehow factor all this into its negligence decision? Suppose the homeowner does not know how to estimate those probabilities. Information about the existence and degree of risk is itself an item of cost.

NOTE: EVALUATING THE RISK-UTILITY ASSESSMENT

1. *What values?* What values or tort goals does the risk-utility assessment foster? Since everything we do carries some degree of risk, one argument for a risk-utility assessment is that it provides deterrence in the "right" amount. Relatedly, it maximizes community resources, for the community is richer if its members do not spend $10 to save someone else $5.

2. *Objections.* Although economically oriented lawyers often like the risk-utility formula as Hand expressed it in *Carroll Towing*, there has been a strong current of objection to it so far as it emphasizes wealth or money. One approach says that basic liberties—freedom of action and security— are primary and take precedence over considerations of wealth. Under this approach, security from harm would be weighed against freedom of action, one basic liberty against another, but losses of liberty would not be offset by increases in wealth. *See* Gregory C. Keating, *Reasonableness and Rationality in Negligence Theory,* 48 STAN. L. REV. 311, 383 (1996).

3. *Alternatives to the risk-utility formula?* If you reject a weighing of risks and utilities, costs and benefits, how could you judge whether the defendant is negligent? Consider: Juries could judge (1) intuitively that "it seems negligent"; (2) solely by statutory prescriptions such as speed limits; (3) by hard-and-fast rules developed by judicial prescriptions, like the rule that you are always negligent if you drive so that you cannot stop within the range of your vision; (4) by custom of the community or the business involved; (5) by a moral rule that imposes liability if the defendant did anything more risky than he would have done to prevent the same harm to himself or his own property. How does the *Carroll Towing* formula stack up among the alternatives? On the risk-utility balance generally, *see* 1 DOBBS, HAYDEN & BUBLICK, THE LAW OF TORTS §§ 160–62 (2d ed. 2011).

[handwritten: 14 & 149]

§ 2. ASSESSING RESPONSIBILITY WHEN MORE THAN ONE PERSON IS NEGLIGENT

[handwritten margin note: Comparative Neg applies only to P]

Many tort cases involve at least two tortfeasors who contribute to the harm done. To analyze and evaluate such cases properly, we need to understand as clearly as possible that [liability of one person does not necessarily exclude liability of another] Equally, we need to understand how responsibility is apportioned—that is, who will pay what for damages caused. We deal with more advanced issues about this topic later on. For now, we can set out the structure of apportionment you should have in mind as we begin to read negligence cases.

[handwritten margin note: If a∂ sues liability]

In considering the rules set out in this section, you might want to have in mind a case like *Bernier v. Boston Edison Co.*, covered in the last section.

(1) **Comparative fault.** If Mrs. Ramsdell had been injured and sued Boston Edison, the rules in most states would allow her to recover, but with her damages reduced in proportion to her fault. The plaintiff's recovery is not ordinarily reduced to reflect her fault when the defendant is guilty of an intentional tort, but recovery is nowadays generally reduced in negligence and strict liability cases. The idea is that each faulty party must bear his or her share of the losses. The defendant's liability is correspondingly reduced so that he pays less than all of the plaintiff's damages. In some cases, the plaintiff actually recovers nothing at all, even though the defendant is also negligent in a substantial way.

(2) **Apportionment among defendants.** What would happen in the suits by Bernier and Kasputys against Boston Edison and Ramsdell if those defendants were chargeable with 80% and 20% of the fault respectively? Since both are negligent, it looks as if both should share in payments to the plaintiff. Ideally, then, Boston Edison would pay 80% of the damages for Bernier's permanently shortened leg and Kasputys' permanent pain and other injuries. Correspondingly, Ramsdell would pay 20% of those damages. Tort law recognizes this ideal by adopting one of two systems to accomplish it. One of these systems, called the joint and several liability system, also tries to accommodate some other ideals.

(3) **Joint and several liability.** "Joint and several liability" sounds mysterious, but it means that the plaintiff can enforce her tort claim against either tortfeasor. She can actually obtain a judgment against both, but she cannot collect more than her full damages. Although it looks as if Kasputys had very substantial damages indeed, let's suppose for convenience that her damages came to $10,000. Under the rule of joint and several liability, the plaintiff might enforce that judgment entirely against either Boston Edison or against Ramsdell. But that is not the end of the story.

[handwritten margin note: - means P can enforce the claim against either tortfeasor]

(4) **Contribution.** If Boston Edison paid the entire judgment of $10,000, it would be paying more than its fair share of the damages relative to Ramsdell. Under the joint and several liability system, most states would allow Boston Edison to obtain *contribution* from Ramsdell so as to make its payment proportional to its fault. Under today's rules, if Ramsdell's fault were 20% of the whole and Boston Edison's fault were 80%, Boston Edison should recover contribution from Ramsdell equal to 20% of the damages, $2,000. What is the net cost to Boston Edison after recovery of contribution? Do the rules of joint and several liability plus the rules of contribution carry out the goals of tort law?

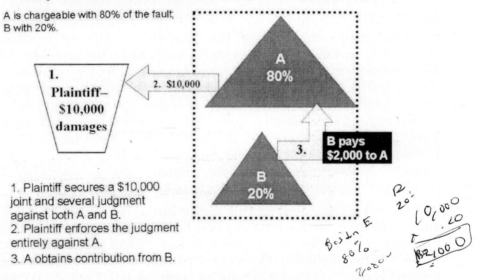

Example of Joint and Several Liability With Contribution

A is chargeable with 80% of the fault; B with 20%.

1. Plaintiff– $10,000 damages

2. $10,000

A 80%

B 20%

3. B pays $2,000 to A

1. Plaintiff secures a $10,000 joint and several judgment against both A and B.
2. Plaintiff enforces the judgment entirely against A.
3. A obtains contribution from B.

In the diagram, the plaintiff is not at fault and recovers all her losses resulting from the injury. Defendant A, although initially liable for all the losses, eventually recoups contribution from B. The net result is that A, who is chargeable with 80% of the fault, ultimately pays 80% of the plaintiff's damages, and B, with 20% of the fault, pays 20%. The principle applies, of course, without regard to the amount of the damages.

(5) **Insolvent or immune tortfeasors.** Suppose hypothetically that Mrs. Ramsdell had no insurance and no personal assets from which Kasputys could collect a judgment. Or suppose that Mrs. Ramsdell for some reason was immune to tort liability. (As bad as it sounds, it is true that some wrongdoers are free to commit torts without any liability.) On these suppositions, the joint and several liability rule means that the plaintiff would recover her damages from Boston Edison but that as a practical matter Boston Edison could not recover contribution, either because Mrs. Ramsdell had an immunity or because she had no assets with which to pay contribution. The joint and several liability system, then, in effect requires

the solvent tortfeasor, Boston Edison, to pick up and pay the insolvent, uninsured, or immune tortfeasor's share. In such a case, the law's ideal— payment proportioned to fault—is not achieved. What other important goal is being accommodated by the joint and several liability system?

(6) **Several liability and comparative fault apportionment among tortfeasors.** An alternative scheme of apportionment has been enacted in a substantial number of states. We'll call it several liability, proportionate share liability, or comparative fault liability. In the several or proportionate share systems, the trier of fact makes a comparative fault apportionment of liability. This several liability system differs from joint liability in that no tortfeasor is liable for more than his proportionate share. On our hypothetical assumptions about *Bernier*, the plaintiffs there would collect only 80% of their damages from Boston Edison in a several liability system, because Boston Edison's fault was only 80% of the whole set of faults. Thus contribution is not needed. The plaintiffs would have to take their chances on collecting the remaining 20% from Mrs. Ramsdell. If Mrs. Ramsdell for any reason could not pay, the plaintiffs would bear 20% of their own losses.

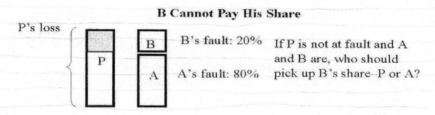

B Cannot Pay His Share

P's loss

B — B's fault: 20%

P

A — A's fault: 80%

If P is not at fault and A and B are, who should pick up B's share—P or A?

(7) **Evaluating the two systems for apportioning loss.** When tortfeasor A is fully insured and tortfeasor B has neither insurance nor assets, which system is more consistent with tort goals, the joint and several liability system or the comparative apportionment system?

(8) **Recapping.** This is a lot of specialized information to absorb at one time. Maybe the best recap is to try your hand at applying the rules for sharing damages liabilities. Suppose:

(a) Patricia, a single mother often up at night with her child, is sleepy while driving to work. Dunn, driving a truck, attempts to cross the street in front of Patricia. Patricia was probably slow in hitting her brakes. She broadsided Dunn's truck. Dunn wasn't injured but Patricia was. The jury finds that Dunn's fault was 90%, Patricia's 10%, and that her damages come to $10,000. What amount of money must Dunn (or his liability insurance company) pay under the rules followed in most states?

(b) Agatha and Bert are each driving a car. Both are negligent and they collide in a city intersection. The force of the collision causes Bert to lose control. Consequently, his car strikes a pedestrian, Paul. Paul's injury results in medical expense, loss of wages, and pain. The jury assesses his damages at $100,000 and finds that Agatha's negligence was 75% of the whole, while Bert's was only 25%. (i) In a joint and several liability system, suppose that both Agatha and Bert are insured for liability or otherwise able to pay, but Paul enforces the judgment solely against Bert. What does Bert pay and what contribution rights does he have? (ii) If Agatha is insolvent and uninsured, what is Bert's position in a joint and several liability system? (iii) In a several liability system with comparative fault apportionment?

(9) **Additional variations.** This section focuses on two main systems for apportioning loss—several liability and joint and several liability. In truth, states employ a number of additional variations. The Restatement (Third) of Torts lists three more typical ways in which states apportion liability. *See* RESTATEMENT (THIRD) OF TORTS: APPORTIONMENT OF LIABILITY §§ 18–21 (Tracks A-E) (2000). These approaches are: 1) *Type of damages.* Some jurisdictions retain joint and several liability, but only for certain elements of damage such as economic harm. Parties are severally liable for noneconomic harm. 2) *Threshold percentage.* Other jurisdictions retain joint and several liability only if the defendant's assigned percentage of responsibility exceeds a certain threshold percentage such as 50%. If the defendant is assigned a lesser percentage of responsibility, several liability would apply. 3) *Reapportionment of uncollectible shares.* Still other jurisdictions assign responsibility but then reallocate the losses if an allocated share of the damages cannot be collected. If the plaintiff is unable to collect one defendant's share of the judgment, that share is reallocated among the remaining parties in the same ratio as that of the percentage shares of fault assigned to them. *See* 1 DOBBS, HAYDEN & BUBLICK, THE LAW OF TORTS § 487 (2d ed. 2011). In example 8 (b) imagine that $50,0000 of plaintiff's damages are for economic losses and $50,000 for noneconomic losses. Also imagine that the fault of Agatha is 30%, the fault of Bert 40%, and the fault of Paul 30%. If Bert is insolvent, what amount would Agatha pay in a jurisdiction with (1) a type of damage system, (2) a threshold percentage system of 50%, or (3) a reapportionment system?

(10) **Bases of liability included in the apportionment.** Traditionally, comparative negligence compared the negligent conduct of one defendant with the negligent conduct of the plaintiff, and later, of other defendants. More recently, some jurisdictions have elected to compare negligence with strict liability, recklessness, and, in some circumstances, even intentional torts. With important limitations, particularly in the realm of intentional torts, the Third Restatement embraces such a view. *See* RESTATEMENT (THIRD) OF TORTS: APPORTIONMENT OF LIABILITY § 1 cmt. b (2000). Apportionment that involves different bases of liability raises a number of complicated issues which will be addressed in Chapter 25.

(11) **Parties included in the apportionment.** In a number of jurisdictions, a jury is asked to apportion the liability not just of plaintiffs and defendants who are parties in the case, but also of non-parties who are at fault. *See, e.g., Cramer v. Starr,* 375 P.3d 69 (Ariz. 2016). Suppose that the plaintiff sues another driver for a rear-end collision that caused her injury and required her to undergo a subsequent surgery. The driver defendant asks that responsibility be apportioned not only to the plaintiff and defendant, but also to the doctor who performed the plaintiff's spinal-fusion surgery after the accident. The jury apportions 20% of the responsibility for plaintiff's back injury to the negligent driver and 80% to the non-party surgeon. In a several liability jurisdiction, what would plaintiff recover? Is this a desirable result?

§ 3. PROVING AND EVALUATING CONDUCT

A. PROVING CONDUCT

SANTIAGO V. FIRST STUDENT, INC.

839 A.2d 550 (R.I. 2004)

PER CURIAM. . . .

[Defendant operates a school bus. Plaintiff alleged that in 1997, when she was in the eighth grade and being transported on one of defendant's buses, it collided with a car at an intersection the plaintiff cannot now identify. Defendant moved for summary judgment and "provided an affidavit prepared by its safety coordinator asserting that there were no company records confirming that an accident had even occurred" in November 1997.]

When plaintiff was deposed as part of pretrial discovery in this case, she testified that she could not remember the street or the neighborhood where the accident occurred. She also admitted that she "could [not] find [the] street today if [she] wanted to." The plaintiff did, however, offer a brief description of her recollection of the events. She remembered that the bus was driving on a one-way street approaching a stop sign. According to plaintiff, she saw the unidentified vehicle approaching the intersection, coming toward the bus from the right. She was then jerked forward when the bus driver applied the brakes and the bus collided with the unidentified vehicle. As a result of the collision, plaintiff says, the right side of her face hit the seat in front of her. Police did not respond to the accident and, consequently, there is no police report describing the incident.

Admitting that she did not see the collision occur, plaintiff was unable to offer any details about it. She was unable to say whether the unidentified car had a stop sign. She did not know whether the bus was damaged or the extent of the damage to the other vehicle, other than that its side mirror was knocked off. . . .

[The trial judge granted summary judgment for the defendant.]

Reviewing the evidence in the light most favorable to plaintiff, we must accept her assertion that she was injured in an accident. To assign negligence to defendant based on the evidence in the record, however, would impermissibly cross the line from reasonable inference and venture into the realm of rank speculation. The plaintiff admitted that she did not see how the collision occurred. Although she testified that a stop sign controlled the flow of traffic coming from the bus's direction, she does not allege that the bus driver failed to stop at the sign as directed. The plaintiff is unable to describe any actions on the part of the driver of the unidentified vehicle or unidentified bus driver relating to the accident. Indeed, there is no evidence of the interaction between the bus and the unidentified car, except that the two vehicles collided. Furthermore, plaintiff can provide no other witnesses capable of offering a meaningful description of the accident.

. . . The plaintiff attempts to justify a lack of evidence to support her case by pointing to the nature of the accident. . . . The fact that the plaintiff's case may be extremely difficult to prove, however, does not relieve her of the burden of presenting sufficient evidence to demonstrate the existence of a material question of fact. The plaintiff has not met that burden in this case and the defendant, therefore, is entitled to judgment as a matter of law.

[Affirmed.]

NOTES

1.   **Evidence of negligence.** Is there evidence sufficient to get the plaintiff to the jury on the issue of breach in the following cases?

a.   The defendant was driving on a street 30 feet wide in clear weather. No cars were parked on the side. He ran into a three-year-old child in the street. No one saw how the child got in the street and no one saw the impact itself. The plaintiff asserts a claim on behalf of the child. *Gift v. Palmer,* 141 A.2d 408 (Pa. 1958).

b.   The plaintiff claims that she slipped on a shiny floor. She did not testify "that her fall was occasioned by any foreign substance on the floor, or that polish or wax had been negligently applied to the floor by defendant." *Habershaw v. Michaels Stores, Inc.,* 42 A.3d 1273 (R.I. 2012).

c.   A bus driver, one Mr. Bumpass, hits the brakes as he approaches a stop sign. The plaintiff, a passenger on the bus, falls backward and breaks her leg. The plaintiff argues that the "jerk" caused by Bumpass's application of the brakes was of such extraordinary force that his negligence could be inferred. *Robinson v. Wash. Metro. Area Transit Auth.*, 774 F.3d 33 (D.C. Cir. 2014).

[handwritten: May not be sufficient if so — d their end of when happen? or circumstances evidence]

2. **Defendant's alternative conduct.** Could a reasonable person listen to the proof in the *Santiago, Gift, Habershaw*, and *Robinson* cases and state exactly how the defendant should have altered his conduct to make it safer?

[handwritten: Goes to "ordinary care" standard — may be required and may be negligent]

NOTE: CONFLICTING AND NON-CONFLICTING TESTIMONY

1. *Difficulty in obtaining accurate statements of facts.* Witnesses, parties and non-parties alike, frequently give contradictory versions of events. Sometimes they contradict themselves. Contradictions may occur even where all witnesses are honest, particularly in injury cases where events occur quickly and accompanied by stress. Memory is poor in those circumstances. *See* ELIZABETH LOFTUS, EYEWITNESS TESTIMONY (1979).

2. *How the law handles contradictory testimony.* When witnesses contradict each other, and even when one witness contradicts himself, the jury or other trier of fact determines which testimony to believe, basing judgment as best it can on the witnesses' demeanor, opportunity to observe, capacity for memory and other such factors. Credibility of witnesses is thus ordinarily a jury question.

3. *Uncontradicted evidence.* Even if the plaintiff puts on uncontradicted evidence in her own favor, the jury might disbelieve her witnesses and return a verdict for a defendant. In rare cases, courts hold that the plaintiff's uncontradicted evidence in a particular case is so overwhelming, consistent and clear, that a directed verdict for the plaintiff is permissible, even though the plaintiff has the burden of proof.

[handwritten: "Self-serving testimony can be disbelieved by jury"]

FORSYTH V. JOSEPH, 450 P.2d 627 (N.M. Ct. App. 1968). Decedent was an occupant of a car struck by the Villa truck. The trial court found Villa to be negligent, partly because of excessive speed. There was evidence that Villa skidded 129 feet before the impact. *Held*, affirmed. "The speed limit was 55 miles per hour. The court found he was exceeding this speed and was traveling at the rate of 55 miles per hour at the point of impact. These findings are supported by the evidence. Even Villa testified that his speed 'at the point of impact' was 55 miles per hour. In addition thereto, we have the skid marks to which reference is above made, the force of the impact which knocked the Joseph vehicle about 20 or 25 feet and spun it about 90 degrees, and the continued momentum of Villa's vehicle, which carried it through the fence and into the open field where it came to a rest."

NOTES

1. **Use of circumstantial evidence.** Circumstantial evidence—which is to say evidence of one fact that permits an inference of another fact—is often the most important evidence in tort cases. Although circumstantial evidence must be weighed case by case, in general it is entitled to as much weight as direct evidence. Almost all negligence cases involve at least some factual inferences. The inference may, of course, assist the defendant rather than the plaintiff. What inference would you draw if the proof showed defendant stopped his car in 33 feet?

2. **Circumstantial evidence and legal conclusions.** Ordinary circumstantial evidence is evidence of one fact that tends to establish some other fact. What if a man steps onto the roof of an elevator to effect a repair, suddenly utters, "S * * *," and disappears from view as the elevator door closes, followed by a loud "boom"? *See Walker v. Chi. Hous. Auth.*, 30 N.E.3d 539 (Ill. App. Ct. 2015) (the trier of fact may reasonably infer that he slipped on oil on the roof of the elevator and fell to his death, despite the fact that no one actually saw him fall).

3. **An alert.** Perhaps Villa did not literally mean he was traveling 55 at the point of impact. What else might he have meant? What is the responsibility of the lawyer about such a matter? Notice that Villa's admission was considered against him.

4. **Judge and jury.** Questions of fact and questions of credibility are for the jury to decide. What about *inferences* of fact, such as those involved in *Forsyth*? The answer is that the jury is also the decision maker as to inferences, provided there is room for reasonable persons to draw or reject those inferences.

5. **Evidence to assist in drawing inferences.** In many instances one might reject an inference of fact simply for lack of knowledge. Suppose the evidence is that the defendant left skid marks of 137 feet, and that his car was at a complete stop at the end of the marks. Do you know how fast he was going? What evidence could be introduced to assist a judge or jury in drawing an inference about speed?

NOTE: WITNESSES' OPINIONS AS THE FACTS AND FACTUAL INFERENCES

1. *Non-expert opinion.* Witnesses are not usually permitted to give opinions on "ultimate" issues that are reserved for jury decision in the case. For example, a witness would not be permitted to testify, "In my opinion, the defendant was negligent." The witness is required instead to state facts within his knowledge, for instance, "I saw the defendant run the red light." A few statements that might be classed as opinions are permitted, however, as a kind of shorthand or summing up of direct experience. An eyewitness

may be permitted to estimate speed, distance, or intoxication, for example. It would be difficult to express any more accurately the facts on which it is based, and juries are likely to understand that the impression or estimate is no more than that.

2. *Expert opinion.* Experts are usually allowed to give expert opinion or conclusions within the field of their expertise, provided the testimony is likely to be helpful to the jury on an issue in the case.

[handwritten: → Important → No infrastate to create expert testimony outside of litigation]

Expert opinion testimony raises serious issues. One very common problem is that experts often differ. One expert may testify that in her opinion the plaintiff suffers a serious paralysis that is irremediable, while another may testify that in his opinion the plaintiff is not injured at all or, if injured, will recover speedily. Juries have little basis for resolving such conflicts of opinion except on the basis of a feeling that one expert is more impressive than another—which perhaps suggests one of the reasons that courts are reluctant about opinion testimony in the first place.

A second problem with expert testimony is that the witness may not in fact be an expert at all with respect to his particular testimony; or that the expert may be an expert in some sense but still offer an opinion that is only speculation.

Another problem with expert testimony is that it may overwhelm the jury. Experts are often prestigious by reason of their professional status, and some are more or less professional witnesses whose presence and demeanor may be highly impressive. The seemingly independent status of the expert witness may suggest a disinterested appraisal, which may lend this testimony even more weight in the jury's mind, though in fact some experts become quite partisan.

NOTE

Should we be skeptical about our ability to resolve disputes by judging negligence? Chance plays a big role in determining whether you will recover if you are injured. There may be no witness to the event other than the defendant himself; the evidence may be conflicting; and witnesses on your side may be unappealing personalities and disliked by jurors, while witnesses on the other side may be pleasant and convincing.

PROBLEM

Kibler v. Maddux

You have been retained by the parents of Tommy Kibler, 4 years of age, to bring suit for Tommy's injuries. On January 6, Linda Rodriguez called Mrs. Kibler and invited Tommy to come play with her son, also 4, at her house. It was rainy and Mrs. Kibler dressed him in a slicker and took him to the Rodriguez home about 2:30. She asked Mrs. Rodriguez to call when she was ready for Tommy to come home, saying she would pick him up rather than let him cross the street alone. She had trained him to wait for her at the curb. About 4:00, Mrs. Rodriguez called and told Mrs. Kibler she would dress Tommy in his slicker and take him to the curb where Mrs. Kibler would meet him. It was anticipated that Mrs. Kibler would arrive slightly before or at the same time as Tommy, but she slipped and fell on her slippery sidewalk and walked rather slowly and painfully. Tommy arrived at the curb and waited for his mother, looking in the direction she was to come from.

In the meantime, Irene Maddux was proceeding north on Spruce Street driving her car. She arrived at the crest of a slope and at that point she could see Tommy standing at the curb in his yellow slicker about 400–500 yards away. She proceeded on towards that point, driving at 20 m.p.h. because of the rain, slippery roads, and gathering dusk. She watched Tommy constantly as she approached. When she reached a point she thinks was about 15 feet from Tommy, he suddenly ran out in front of her. It later became clear that he had waited somewhat longer for his mother than he expected to, and that when he saw her coming, he ran toward her. Maddux hit the brakes and also swerved to the right, but her left front fender struck Tommy and knocked him about 30 feet, causing some considerable injury.

Both sides have taken depositions and all the facts stated above are established. Defendant Maddux has moved for summary judgment on the basis of these admitted or established facts. How do you evaluate your case? What arguments can you make?

NOTES

1. **Determining negligence claims.** In many cases, as in *Kibler*, it is possible to point to more than one act or omission that might constitute negligence. On occasion, lawyers fail to perceive their best claims of negligence and argue only the most obvious. Suppose the trial judge decided to hold a brief oral argument on the defendant's motion for summary judgment, and you have an opportunity to state in what respects Ms. Maddux could be found negligent by the trier. Would your primary argument be that she was driving too fast considering the weather?

2. **Jury evaluation.** Courts are reluctant to decide negligence cases on summary judgment motions in some cases. Why is this? Juries are often called upon to decide not merely bare facts but also to make normative evaluations of the conduct involved. *See also Amos v. Lincoln Cty. Sch. Dist. No. 2*, 359 P.3d 954 (Wyo. 2015) (during a community basketball game at school, a lunchroom bench propped against the wall fell on a 5-year-old and killed him; the court reversed summary judgment for the defendant on the ground that "even where the material facts are undisputed, the question of whether a defendant breached its duty is generally one left to the finder of fact"). Of course, where facts are in dispute, summary judgement is also inappropriate. *See Johnson v.*

Wash. Gas Light Co., 109 A.3d 1118 (D.C. 2015) (fact question whether utility replaced access cover after maintenance or left utility hole uncovered).

B. EVALUATING CONDUCT THROUGH NOTICE AND OPPORTUNITY TO CURE

THOMA v. CRACKER BARREL OLD COUNTRY STORE, INC.

649 So. 2d 277 (Fla. Dist. Ct. App. 1995)

KAHN, JUDGE. . . .

After eating breakfast at the Cracker Barrel, Thoma took three or four steps away from her table when her left foot slid out from under her, causing her to fall. The fall occurred in a common aisle, near the passage from the kitchen to the restaurant. When Thoma got up, she noticed an area 1 foot by 2 feet containing drops of clear liquid. She claims to have slipped on this liquid. Thoma was in the restaurant about thirty minutes before her accident. During that time, she saw no one drop anything on the floor in the area where she fell. [In Thoma's suit against the restaurant, the trial court granted defendant's motion for summary judgment.]

Mr. Leonard McNeal was the only known witness to the fall. He arrived at breakfast about 15 minutes before the accident. His seat was some 12 to 15 feet away from where Thoma fell. McNeal described the area as "a normal area where waitresses would frequently go in and out (the kitchen) door." McNeal felt sure he saw waitresses carrying beverage pitchers in that area. He did not see any Cracker Barrel customers carrying drinks in the area, nor did he see anyone drop or spill anything.

Cracker Barrel's manager, Mr. Charlie Gray, inspected the area of the fall and saw no foreign substance whatever on the floor. According to Mr. Gray, the Cracker Barrel is not a buffet restaurant and he would not expect customers to get up and walk around with food or drinks.

To recover for injuries incurred in a slip and fall accident, the plaintiff must show that the premises owner either created a dangerous condition or had actual or constructive knowledge of a dangerous condition. Notice of a dangerous condition may be established by circumstantial evidence, such as evidence leading to an inference that a substance has been on the floor for a sufficient length of time such that in the exercise of reasonable care the condition should have become known to the premises owner. *[Black Letter Law!]*

We have recently reversed a defense summary judgment in a similar case, *Gonzalez v. Tallahassee Medical Center, Inc.*, 629 So. 2d 945 (Fla. 1st DCA 1993). In that case, Gonzalez slipped and fell on a liquid substance that looked like water, but could have been "syrup or Sprite." Her grandson testified that . . . the fall occurred near a soda drink dispenser set out for customer use and in an area where the cashier had a clear view. The grandson was in the cafeteria ten to fifteen minutes before the accident and did not hear or see anyone spill a liquid in the area of the fall. While we declined to speculate on what a jury might do with those facts, we held that inferences arose which "could establish the length of time the dangerous condition had been present on the floor, a critical element in proving that appellee, through the exercise of ordinary care, should have known of the condition."

In the present case, Thoma and McNeal took their breakfast at a location near where Thoma eventually fell. Despite their proximity, neither Thoma nor McNeal saw anyone drop or spill anything. The area of the fall was in clear view of Cracker Barrel employees, since they traversed it regularly on their way in and out of the kitchen. If a jury were to believe Thoma's description of the liquid as covering an area 1 foot by 2 feet, it might also be convinced that Cracker Barrel employees, in the exercise of due diligence, should have noticed the liquid before the accident. No one except Cracker Barrel employees were seen to carry food or beverage in the area of the fall, and the manager of the restaurant would not have expected customers to move around carrying food or drinks.

Cracker Barrel notes that "common sense" suggests "a plethora" of reasonable inferences other than the inferences urged by appellants. We certainly agree with this observation, but take issue with the suggestion that the existence of other possible inferences requires affirmance of the summary judgment in favor of Cracker Barrel. It will be for a jury to determine whether a preponderance of the evidence supports the inferences suggested by Thoma.

Reversed and Remanded.

NOTES

1. **Three common theories of liability.** Lawyers have developed several means of attempting to prove a defendant's negligence when the plaintiff slips on foreign substances in the defendant's place of business. The plaintiff can show negligence on the part of the defendant by proving either that: (a) the defendant created and failed to take reasonable actions to abate the hazard, as where a waiter spills sauce on the floor; (b) the defendant did not directly create the condition but discovered or should have discovered a condition created by others (often called "constructive notice") and failed to take reasonable steps to prevent injury from that condition; or (c) the defendant's mode or method of business operations made it foreseeable that others would create a dangerous condition, and the defendant failed to take reasonable measures to discover and remove it, as where a grocery's bean bin is constructed so that customers will regularly cause loose beans to fall on the floor, or where customers help themselves at a drink station. *See, e.g., Fisher v. Big Y Foods, Inc.*, 3 A.3d 919 (Conn. 2010); *cf. Parker v. Holiday Hosp. Franchising, Inc.*, 446 S.W.3d 341 (Tenn. 2014) (a property owner cannot be

held liable on a premises liability theory unless the plaintiff proved "the elements of a negligence claim, and in addition . . . either that the condition was caused or created by the [owner] or if the condition was created by someone other than the [owner], that the [owner] had actual or constructive notice that the condition existed prior to the accident"; hotel patron who sued the hotel for injuries suffered when a bench in a handicap-accessible shower collapsed had shown neither, so summary judgment for the defendant was appropriate).

2. **Evidence that the defendant should have discovered.** How do you prove that the defendant should have discovered a foreign substance spilled on the floor by a customer? The chief method approved by the courts is to show that the substance had been there for a relatively long time. The jury is then permitted to conclude that a reasonable person should have discovered and remedied it. When such proof is presented, courts may say that the defendant was on constructive notice of the danger, meaning only that he should have discovered it. Getting evidence of this kind may be difficult, and when the evidence shows instead that some hazard was only present for a brief period of time, the plaintiff will have failed to prove constructive notice. *Hartley v. Waldbaum, Inc.*, 893 N.Y.S.2d 272 (App. Div. 2010). Consequently, in *Wal-Mart Stores, Inc. v. Spates*, 186 S.W.3d 566 (Tex. 2006), evidence that an empty plastic six-pack ring was on the floor near a store employee for 30 to 45 seconds before plaintiff tripped on it was insufficient as a matter of law to prove constructive notice. Similarly, in *Antim v. Fred Meyer Stores, Inc.*, 251 P.3d 602 (Idaho Ct. App. 2011), summary judgment for the defendant store was appropriate when the customer slipped and fell on a folded mat where there was evidence that the mat had been flat 25 minutes before the plaintiff fell and no evidence showed how the mat became folded. Another method of showing constructive notice is to show prior accidents. *See Sullivan v. Abovenet Commc'ns*, 112 A.3d 347 (D.C. 2015) (evidence that a pedestrian had tripped on uneven surface surrounding manhole cover two weeks earlier raised fact issue as to whether the contractor had constructive notice of the defect).

3. **Evaluating reasonableness.** The main focus of this segment of the book is the evaluation of conduct. If we infer that loose green beans that fell out of the grocery store bin have been on the floor for an hour, we are left with the problem of evaluating the defendant's conduct. In some cases you might doubt whether courts or juries really have any way of saying that a reasonable and prudent store operator would have discovered a slippery substance on the floor within 15 minutes. On this issue consider: (a) The plaintiff can show the volume of customer traffic in the area where she fell. Would that be relevant to show that inspections by the storekeeper should have been more frequent? *See Jones v. Brookshire Grocery Co.*, 847 So. 2d 43 (La. Ct. App. 2003). (b) Can the risk-utility test be applied in evaluating the restaurant's conduct in *Thoma?* Could you evaluate the conduct as negligent or not by considering the consumer's reasonable expectations instead?

4. **Judicial help for the plaintiff.** Clearly slip-and-fall plaintiffs have serious proof problems. Some courts have developed corollary rules to help the plaintiff a little. In *Ortega v. Kmart Corp.*, 36 P.3d 11 (Cal. 2001), the court

suggested leeway for the plaintiff when it said: "Whether a dangerous condition has existed long enough for a reasonably prudent person to have discovered it is a question of fact for the jury, and the cases do not impose exact time limitations. Each accident must be viewed in light of its own unique circumstances." The Alaska high court has held that "factfinders can best ascertain whether the proprietor of a grocery store acted reasonably in maintaining the store's premises considering all of the circumstances," expressly making any of the three common theories described in Note 1 above a factor, but not a required element, in a plaintiff's case. *Edenshaw v. Safeway, Inc.*, 186 P.3d 568 (Alaska 2008). A few courts have shifted the burden of proof to the shopkeeper to exculpate itself once the plaintiff has shown a fall due to a foreign substance. *See, e.g., Lanier v. Wal-Mart Stores, Inc.*, 99 S.W.3d 431 (Ky. 2003).

§ 4. VIOLATION OF PRIVATE STANDARD OR COMMON CUSTOM

A. THE ACTOR'S OWN STANDARD

WAL-MART STORES, INC. V. WRIGHT, 774 N.E.2d 891 (Ind. 2002). A woman slipped on a puddle of water in the outdoor garden area of a Wal-Mart store. She sued for her injuries, alleging that Wal-Mart was negligent in the maintenance, care and inspection of the premises. The parties stipulated to the admission of a number of Wal-Mart's employee documents assembled as a "Store Manual." Several of the provisions detailed procedures for dealing with spills and other floor hazards. At the end of the trial, the plaintiff tendered a jury instruction that said: "You may consider the violation of any rules, policies, practices and procedures contained in these manuals and safety handbook along with all of the other evidence and the Court's instructions in deciding whether Wal-Mart was negligent. The violation of its rules, policies, practices and procedures are a proper item of evidence tending to show the degree of care recognized by Wal-Mart as ordinary care. . . ." The trial judge gave the instruction over Wal-Mart's objection. The jury found for the plaintiff, reducing her damages for her own comparative fault.

Held, the instruction was improper and the verdict must be reversed. "[Y]ou can set standards for yourself that exceed ordinary care and the fact that you've done that shouldn't be used, as this [instruction] says, as evidence tending to show the degree that you believe is ordinary." Wal-Mart's "rules and policies may exceed its view of what is required by ordinary care in a given situation. Rules and policies in the Manual may have been established for any number of reasons having nothing to do with safety and ordinary care, including a desire to appear more clean and neat to attract customers, or a concern that spills may contaminate merchandise. The law has long recognized that failure to follow a party's precautionary steps or procedures is not necessarily failure to exercise ordinary care. . . . 1 Dan B. Dobbs, The Law of Torts § 165 (2000). We think this rule is salutary because it encourages following the best practices without necessarily establishing them as a legal norm." The instruction is also erroneous for suggesting that jurors could apply "Wal-Mart's subjective view—as evidenced by the Manual—rather than an objective standard of ordinary care."

· Logistical concerns about closing of courts.
· Allows room for abuse w/o the severity of legal system

NOTES

1. **Private standards.** Why does the court believe that not giving internal safety rules the force of legal norms "encourages following the best practices"?

2. **Reasonable care and private standards.** Why not use a company's own standard to set the legal standard? In *Jenkins v. Jordan Valley Water Conservancy*, 321 P.3d 1049 (Utah 2013), the water conservancy's decision to replace a pipe could not be used to establish the standard of care for negligence purposes. The court wrote: "An internal determination that a pipeline should be replaced does not establish a tort law duty to do so. Internal decisions may be made for any number of reasons—convenience, caution, maximization of budget, mistake—having little to do with the standard of care. Thus, the resolution of this issue cannot be narrowly focused, as the court of appeals put it, on the decision to delay three years before replacing the pipeline. Instead, the critical issue is whether the applicable standard of care required the District to replace the pipeline near the Jenkins home. And we cannot see how the Jenkinses could show that it did without expert testimony."

internal safety rules do not establish a tort law duty to do so

3. **The Restatement view.** The Restatement takes a "flexible position" on the admissibility of evidence regarding the actor's departure from its own standard. RESTATEMENT (THIRD) OF TORTS: LIABILITY FOR PHYSICAL AND EMOTIONAL HARM § 13 cmt. f (2010). That practice may be relevant to foreseeability or risk, feasibility of precautions, or the plaintiff's reliance on a particular type of care. However, even when the evidence is admissible "it does not set a higher standard of care for the actor." *See Morgan v. Scott*, 291 S.W.3d 622 (Ky. 2009) (car dealership's internal rule requiring an employee to accompany a test driver did not create a duty of care to a third party injured by test driver); *Everitt v. Gen. Elec. Co.*, 979 A.2d 760 (N.H. 2009) (internal policy regarding procedures to be followed in dealing with impaired employees did not create duty to the public).

B. CUSTOM

DUNCAN V. CORBETTA, 577 N.Y.S.2d 129 (App. Div. 1991). "The plaintiff William C. Duncan was injured when he began to descend a wooden exterior stairway at the defendant's residence and the top step collapsed. The court erred by precluding the plaintiffs' expert from testifying that it was common practice to use pressure-treated lumber in the construction of

Facts

Court held

such stairways, even though the nonpressure-treated lumber used was permissible under the applicable building code. Proof of a general custom and usage is admissible because it tends to establish a standard by which ordinary care may be judged even where an ordinance prescribes certain minimum safety requirements which the custom exceeds. However, no significant prejudice resulted from the error. The plaintiffs failed to establish that the defendant had a role in the design or construction of the stairway." Judgment for defendant affirmed.

NOTES

1. **General rule.** Evidence that the defendant violated customary safety precautions of the relevant community is usually sufficient to get the plaintiff to the jury. The Third Restatement says that a person's "departure from the custom of the community, or of others in like circumstances, in a way that increases the risk" is evidence of that person's negligence "but does not require a finding of negligence." RESTATEMENT (THIRD) OF TORTS: LIABILITY FOR PHYSICAL AND EMOTIONAL HARM § 13(b) (2010).

2. **Customary statutory violations.** In *Duncan v. Corbetta*, the court was willing to say that a defendant who complied with all the safety requirements of a statute might still be negligent if he failed to follow a safety custom. What if a litigant who failed to comply with a statute or ordinance wants to introduce evidence that the law is customarily violated; that is, that custom tends to show that violation is reasonable conduct? Judges generally disfavor such a use of custom evidence. *See, e.g., Robinson v. District of Columbia*, 580 A.2d 1255 (D.C. 1990) (rejecting party's argument that it was reasonable to disobey traffic law by jaywalking outside the marked crosswalk, as allegedly shown by "common practice of pedestrians at the location of the accident").

3. **What custom proves.** Existence of a safety custom might conceivably prove a number of different things. It might, for example, prove that harm was foreseeable, which is to say that the activity was recognizably risky; it might prove that the defendant knew or should have known of the risk; and it might prove that the risk was an "unreasonable" one unless the customary precaution is taken, or at least that it was unreasonable in the opinion of the community in general.

4. **Custom other than safety custom.** What if the custom is well-established and even widespread, but there is no evidence whether the custom arose from safety considerations or from convenience? In *Levine v. Russell Blaine Co.*, 7 N.E.2d 673 (N.Y. 1937), the plaintiff injured her hand on a rough, bristly rope for which defendant was responsible. There was an infection and later the arm had to be amputated. The plaintiff sought to introduce evidence that by custom the rope supplied should have been a smooth one. The court said:

A smoother rope might have advantages other than greater safety. Its customary use might be due to these advantages, and might not show a general recognition that risk of injury would arise from use of a rougher rope. Proof of such custom or practice would then be insufficient, standing alone, to show negligence . . . but the chain of proof might, in this case, have been completed if evidence of customary use of a different rope had been supplemented by expert evidence explaining how and why one kind of rope may cause a foreseeable risk of injury which others customarily avoid.

5. **Safety manuals.** Could a plaintiff introduce into evidence safety manuals or codes promulgated by private or governmental organizations to show that the defendant, in failing to follow such manuals or codes, fell below the standard of reasonable care? Many courts have allowed such evidence. *See, e.g., McComish v. DeSoi*, 200 A.2d 116 (N.J. 1964) (holding that safety codes were admissible as evidence of what was customarily done, although they did not set the standard of care). Some safety codes prepared by trade associations or industry groups have been adopted by statute or ordinance. Many city ordinances, for example, adopt a building or electrical code prepared by industry. In such a case, the privately prepared safety code takes on the force of a statute or ordinance and is not only admissible but may set the standard of care.

THE T.J. HOOPER
60 F.2d 737 (2d Cir. 1932)

L. HAND, CIRCUIT JUDGE.

The barges No. 17 and No. 30, belonging to the Northern Barge Company, had lifted cargoes of coal at Norfolk, Virginia, for New York in March, 1928. They were towed by two tugs of the petitioner, the "Montrose" and the "Hooper," and were lost off the Jersey Coast on March tenth, in an easterly gale. The cargo owners sued the barges under the contracts of carriage; the owner of the barges sued the tugs under the towing contract, both for its own loss and as bailee of the cargoes; the owner of the tug filed a petition to limit its liability. All the suits were joined and heard together, and the judge found that all the vessels were unseaworthy; the tugs, because they did not carry radio receiving sets by which they could have seasonably got warnings of a change in the weather which should have caused them to seek shelter in the Delaware Breakwater en route. He therefore entered an interlocutory decree holding each tug and barge jointly liable to each cargo owner, and each tug for half damages for the loss of its barge. The petitioner appealed, and the barge owner appealed and filed assignments of error. . . .

[Radio broadcasts gave forecasts of coming heavy weather. Reasonable masters would have put in at a safe harbor had they received the broadcasts. The masters of these tugs did not receive the broadcasts] because their private radio receiving sets, which were on board, were not in working order. These belonged to them personally, and were partly a toy, partly a part of the equipment, but neither furnished by the owner, nor supervised by it. It is not fair to say that there was a general custom among coastwise carriers so to equip their tugs. One line alone did it; as for the rest, they relied upon their crews, so far as they can be said to have relied at all. An adequate receiving set suitable for a coastwise tug can now be got at small cost and is reasonably reliable if kept up; obviously it is a source of great protection to their tows. Twice every day they can receive these predictions, based upon the widest possible information, available to every vessel within two or three hundred miles and more. Such a set is the ears of the tug to catch the spoken word, just as the master's binoculars are her eyes to see a storm signal ashore. Whatever may be said as to other vessels, tugs towing heavy coal laden barges, strung out for half a mile, have little power to maneuver, and do not, as this case proves, expose themselves to weather which would not turn back stauncher craft. They can have at hand protection against dangers of which they can learn in no other way.

Is it then a final answer that the business had not yet generally adopted receiving sets? There are, no doubt, cases where courts seem to make the general practice of the calling the standard of proper diligence; we have indeed given some currency to the notion ourselves. Indeed in most cases reasonable prudence is in fact common prudence; but strictly it is never its measure; a whole calling may have unduly lagged in the adoption of new and available devices. It never may set its own tests, however persuasive be its usages. Courts must in the end say what is required; there are precautions so imperative that even their universal disregard will not excuse their omission. But here there was no custom at all as to receiving sets; some had them, some did not; the most that can be urged is that they had not yet become general. Certainly in such a case we need not pause; when some have thought a device necessary, at least we may say that they were right, and the others too slack. . . . [H]ad [the tugs] been properly equipped, they would have got the Arlington reports. The injury was a direct consequence of this unseaworthiness.

Decree affirmed.

NOTES

1. **The standard of the industry.** In Elkerson v. N. Jersey Blood Ctr., 776 A.2d 244 (N.J. Super. Ct. App. Div. 2001), a man died, allegedly as a result of receiving a transfusion of blood tainted with hepatitis. In the suit against the blood bank that had supplied the blood, the plaintiff's evidence showed that a better test was available to detect hepatitis. But evidence also showed that no blood banks used the better test. The trial judge instructed the jury that the defendant was to be judged by the standard practice of the blood banking

industry at the relevant time. So instructed, the jury found that the defendant was not negligent. If you represented the plaintiff, what proposition would you assert in your brief on appeal?

2. **Custom as evidence.** Earlier decisions sometimes held that (a) evidence of custom was wholly inadmissible; or (b) on the contrary, custom represented the sole standard of care. As *The T.J. Hooper* would suggest, these older rules are largely obsolete. *See* RESTATEMENT (THIRD) OF TORTS: LIABILITY FOR PHYSICAL AND EMOTIONAL HARM § 13(a) (2010) ("An actor's compliance with the custom of the community, or of others in like circumstances, is evidence that the actor's conduct is not negligent but does not preclude a finding of negligence.") *See also Mobile Gas Serv. Corp. v. Robinson,* 20 So. 3d 770 (Ala. 2009) (gas industry custom to disconnect service when it fed known hazardous appliances is not conclusive but may be considered by jury to determine whether defendant exercised reasonable care in violating the custom). However, some courts are still cautious about admitting custom evidence, lest the jury treat it as a standard of care. *See, e.g., Jones v. Jitney Jungle Stores of Am., Inc.,* 730 So. 2d 555 (Miss. 1998).

3. **Custom and reasonable care.** As Justice Holmes famously put it in *Tex. & P. Ry. v. Behymer,* 189 U.S. 468 (1903), "what usually is done may be evidence of what ought to be done, but what ought to be done is set by the standard of reasonable prudence, whether it is usually complied with or not." Why say that reasonable care trumps custom? Does that decision make sense in *T.J. Hooper*?

4. **Custom and the standard of care.** If you have reservations about the risk-utility rule of *Carroll Towing*, how about using custom as the standard of care and the test of negligence? Would this policy be wise at least in the case of sophisticated parties? *Rodi Yachts, Inc. v. Nat'l Marine, Inc.,* 984 F.2d 880 (7th Cir. 1993). Should the court in *T.J. Hooper* have let custom serve as a standard for those sophisticated parties?

§ 5. COMPLIANCE WITH STATUTE

As discussed in Chapter 5, statutes can sometimes define the duty of care. In these cases, violation of statutes can sometimes be determinative of an actor's negligence under the doctrine of negligence per se, and in other cases the statutory violation may provide evidence of negligence. Does an actor's compliance with statute preclude a finding of negligence?

MILLER V. WARREN, 390 S.E.2d 207 (W.Va. 1990). The plaintiffs awoke in their motel room to find it filled with smoke. They attempted to get out, but the door was too hot to touch. They suffered serious burns before they were rescued. In a suit against the motel, the plaintiffs asserted that the motel should have had smoke alarms in the rooms. The fire code did not require such alarms, however. The trial judge instructed the jury: "compliance with the fire codes under the law meets the standard of care and duty required of the defendant as it relates to the installation or lack of installation of safety devices unless other circumstances appear which would require additional care in order to comply with the requirements to use ordinary care in attendant circumstances." The jury, so instructed, found for the defendant. *Held*, reversed and remanded for new trial. "Failure to comply with a fire code or similar regulation constitutes prima facie negligence, if an injury proximately flows from the non-compliance and the injury is of the sort the regulation was intended to prevent. [But] [c]ompliance with a regulation does not constitute due care per se. Compliance with the appropriate regulations is competent evidence of due care, but not conclusive evidence of due care. If the defendants knew or should have known of some risk that would be prevented by reasonable measures not required by the regulation, they were negligent if they did not take such measures. It is settled law that a statute or regulation merely sets a floor of due care. Circumstances may require greater care, if a defendant knows or should know of other risks not contemplated by the regulation."

[handwritten margin note: Black Letter Law!]

NOTES

1. **The effect of statutory compliance.** Statutory requirements usually reflect a minimum standard of care, not a maximum obligation. Courts traditionally agree that compliance with statute or regulation is not a defense. Compliance with statute is some *evidence* of reasonable care, even though it is not conclusive. *See* RESTATEMENT (THIRD) OF TORTS: LIABILITY FOR PHYSICAL AND EMOTIONAL HARM § 16 (2010). Does this remind you of another negligence doctrine? Why wouldn't evidence of compliance with statute be dispositive on the issue of breach?

2. **Compliance and fault.** Evidence of compliance with statute typically suggests that a defendant was not negligent. *Jablonski v. Ford Motor Co.*, 955 N.E.2d 1138 (Ill. 2011) ("conformance to industry standards is relevant, but not dispositive on the issue of negligence," thus car company's compliance with statute in design of vehicle was probative but not dispositive on issue of negligence). That industry standards require less care than the plaintiff seeks "is but one piece of information" in a negligence analysis. In *McDermott v. State*, 113 A.3d 419 (Conn. 2015), although a bystander was standing more than two tree lengths from the tree being removed, which was the industry standard, the negligence action on behalf of the bystander who was killed by a flying log posed questions for the trier of fact.

3. **Concerns about compliance evidence**. As with custom, some courts are cautious about admitting evidence of compliance with statute, lest the jury treat it as a standard of care. In *Malcolm v. Evenflo Co.*, 217 P.3d 514 (Mont. 2009), a four-month-old boy suffered fatal brain injuries from a rollover accident. The court barred from jury consideration, as more prejudicial than probative, evidence that the defendant's child safety seat complied with minimum federal standards. However, that ruling concerned the plaintiff's

strict liability claim. Statutory compliance evidence was permitted with respect to the fault-based question of punitive damages.

§ 6. UNSPECIFIED NEGLIGENCE: RES IPSA LOQUITUR

[handwritten: " Thing that speaks for itself" ← ... RES IPSA LOQUITUR — occurrence of an accident implies negligence]

"Some circumstantial evidence is very strong, as when you find a trout in the milk." H.D. Thoreau, Journal, *November 11, 1850* (B. Torrey, ed. 1906).

A. ORIGINS AND BASIC FEATURES

BYRNE V. BOADLE
2 H. & C. 722, 159 Eng. Rep. 299 (Exch. 1863)

[Plaintiff gave evidence that he was walking in Scotland Road when he lost all recollection. Witnesses testified that a barrel of flour fell on him. The defendant's shop was adjacent and the barrel appeared to have fallen or to have been dropped from the shop. The trial judge "nonsuited" the plaintiff, taking the view that the plaintiff had put on no evidence of negligence. The plaintiff's attorney then sought review in a higher court by obtaining a "rule nisi to enter the verdict for the plaintiff. . . ." What follows includes a portion of the argument by Charles Russell for the defendant before Barons Channell, Bramwell, Pigott and Chief Baron Pollock of the Exchequer Court.]

Charles Russell now showed cause. First, there was no evidence to connect the defendant or his servants with the occurrence. . . . Surmise ought not to be substituted for strict proof when it is sought to fix a defendant with serious liability. The plaintiff should establish his case by affirmative evidence.

Secondly, assuming the facts to be brought home to the defendant or his servants, these facts do not disclose any evidence for the jury of negligence. The plaintiff was bound to give affirmative proof of negligence. But there was not a scintilla of evidence, unless the occurrence is of itself evidence of negligence. There was not even evidence that the barrel was being lowered by a jigger-hoist as alleged in the declaration. [Pollock, C.B. There are certain cases of which it may be said res ipsa loquitur, and this seems one of them. In some cases the Courts have held that the mere fact of the accident having occurred is evidence of negligence, as, for instance, in the case of railway collisions.] On examination of the authorities, that doctrine would seem to be confined to the case of a collision between two trains upon the same line, and both being the property and under the management of the same Company. Such was the case of Skinner v. The London, Brighton and South Coast Railway Company (5 Exch. 787), where the train in which the plaintiff was ran into another train which had stopped a short distance from a station, in consequence of a luggage train before it having broken down. In that case there must have been negligence, or the accident could not have happened. Other cases cited in the textbooks, in support of the doctrine of presumptive negligence, when examined, will be found not to do so. Amongst them is Carpue v. The London and Brighton Railway Company (5 Q.B. 747), but there, in addition to proof of the occurrence, the plaintiff gave affirmative evidence of negligence, by showing that the rails were somewhat deranged at the spot where the accident took place, and that the train was proceeding at a speed which, considering the state of the rails, was hazardous. . . . Later cases have qualified the doctrine of presumptive negligence. In Cotton v. Wood (8 C.B.N.S. 568), it was held that a Judge is not justified in leaving the case to the jury where the plaintiff's evidence is equally consistent with the absence as with the existence of negligence in the defendant. In Hammack v. White (11 C.B.N.S. 588, 594), Erle, J., said that he was of opinion "that the plaintiff in a case of this sort was not entitled to have the case left to the jury unless he gives some affirmative evidence that there has been negligence on the part of the defendant." [Pollock, C.B. If he meant that to apply to all cases, I must say, with great respect, that I entirely differ from him. He must refer to the mere nature of the accident in that particular case. Bramwell, B. No doubt, the presumption of negligence is not raised in every case of injury from accident, but in some it is. We must judge of the facts in a reasonable way; and regarding them in that light we know that these accidents do not take place without a cause, and in general that cause is negligence.] The law will not presume that a man is guilty of a wrong. It is consistent with the facts proved that the defendant's servants were using the utmost care and the best appliances to lower the barrel with safety. Then why should the fact that accidents, of this nature are sometimes caused by negligence raise any presumption against the defendant? There are many accidents from which no presumption of negligence can arise. [Bramwell, B. Looking at the matter in a reasonable way it comes to this—an injury is done to the plaintiff, who has no means of knowing whether it was the result of negligence; the defendant, who knows how it was caused, does not think fit to tell the jury.] Unless a plaintiff gives some evidence which ought to be submitted to the jury, the defendant is not bound to offer any defense. This plaintiff cannot, by a defective proof of his case, compel the defendant to give evidence in explanation. [Pollock, C.B. I have frequently observed that a defendant has a right to remain silent unless a prima facie case is established against him. But here the question is whether the plaintiff has not shewn such a case.] In a case of this nature, in which the sympathies of a jury are with the plaintiff, it would be dangerous to allow presumption to be substituted for affirmative proof of negligence.

Littler appeared to support the rule, but was not called upon to argue.

Pollock, C.B. We are all of opinion that the rule must be absolute to enter the verdict for the plaintiff. The learned counsel was quite right in saying that there are many accidents from which no presumption of negligence can arise, but I think it would be wrong to lay down as a rule that in no case can presumption of negligence arise from the fact of an accident. Suppose in this case the barrel had rolled out of the warehouse and fallen on the plaintiff, how could he possibly ascertain from what cause it occurred? It is the duty of persons who keep barrels in a warehouse to take care that they do not roll out, and I think that such a case would, beyond all doubt, afford prima facie evidence of negligence. A barrel could not roll out of a warehouse without some negligence, and to say that a plaintiff who is injured by it must call witnesses from the warehouse to prove negligence seems to me preposterous. [The other Barons concurred.]

NOTES

1. **The function of res ipsa loquitur.** Consider how res ipsa loquitur evidence differs from ordinary circumstantial evidence. Using *Byrne* as a model, can you state exactly what *Byrne* has permitted that has not been permitted in earlier decisions?

2. **Showing negligence.** The judges in *Byrne*, which is more or less the original res ipsa loquitur case, repeatedly referred to the common sense interpretation of the facts before them—the accident, they felt, "spoke for itself," and what it said was that the defendant must have been negligent.

3. **Specific requirements.** Modern courts have developed rules for the application of res ipsa loquitur. States differ as to their particular requirements. Traditionally, in order for res ipsa to apply, the plaintiff has to show three things: (1) the accident which produced a person's injury was one which ordinarily does not happen in the absence of negligence, (2) the instrumentality or agent which caused the accident was under the exclusive control of the defendant, and (3) the circumstances indicated that the untoward event was not caused or contributed to by any act or neglect on the part of the injured person. *See, e.g., Eaton v. Eaton,* 575 A.2d 858 (N.J. 1990). The Second Restatement refined this traditional test, providing that a plaintiff must prove: (1) the event is of a kind which ordinarily does not occur in the absence of negligence; (2) other responsible causes, including the conduct of the plaintiff and third persons, are sufficiently eliminated by the evidence; and (3) the indicated negligence is within the scope of the defendant's duty to the plaintiff. RESTATEMENT (SECOND) OF TORTS § 328D (1965). Are these requirements materially different from each other? The Third Restatement offers still another formulation—that negligence can be inferred when the accident causing harm is a type that "ordinarily happens as a result of the negligence of a class of actors of which the defendant is the relevant member." RESTATEMENT (THIRD) OF TORTS: LIABILITY FOR PHYSICAL AND EMOTIONAL HARM § 17 (2010). We should expect variation in local rules, but always

remember that a different articulation may be intended to express substantially the same ideas.

NOTE: PROCEDURAL INCIDENTS AND EFFECTS OF RES IPSA LOQUITUR

1. *Sufficiency of evidence issue.* The application of res ipsa loquitur means that, on the negligence issue, the plaintiff will survive a motion for summary judgment and get to the jury, which can then decide the case either way. Once the judge determines that reasonable people can conclude that negligence is probable, the jury is permitted to infer negligence but it is not required to do so. *Deuel v. Surgical Clinic, PLLC,* 2010 WL 3237297 (Tenn. Ct. App. 2010) (res ipsa loquitur "permits, but does not compel, a jury to infer negligence from the circumstances of an injury;" it allows an inference of negligence, but it does not alter the burden of proof or the standard of care).

2. *Instructing on res ipsa.* If the plaintiff has adduced evidence from which the jury could conclude that the elements of res ipsa loquitur are present, then trial judges commonly give a res ipsa loquitur instruction to the jury. The instruction "merely tells the jury that if they do find the existence of these elements then they may draw the inference of negligence," not that they must do so. *K-Mart Corp. v. Gipson,* 563 N.E.2d 667, 670 (Ind. Ct. App. 1990); *see also Banks v. Beckwith,* 762 N.W.2d 149, 153 (Iowa 2009) ("if reasonable minds might differ about whether the injury could result from surgery in the absence of negligence, the court should instruct on res ipsa").

3. *Permissible inference effect.* Most courts hold that res ipsa creates a permissible inference that the jury may draw if it sees fit, and further that res ipsa does not shift the burden of persuasion from the plaintiff. Thus even if the defendant introduces no evidence at all, the jury may reject the inference and bring in a verdict for the defendant. Juries do in fact sometimes decide for defendants on res ipsa loquitur claims. *See, e.g., Gubbins v. Hurson,* 987 A.2d 466 (D.C. 2010).

4. *Abnormally strong inferences of negligence.* To say that the inference of negligence is merely permitted, not required, is to say that the plaintiff who makes out a permissible inference case would not be entitled to summary judgment. But could there be cases so strong that the permissible inference becomes a mandatory inference so that the trial judge would grant summary judgment after all? In *Quinby v. Plumsteadville Family Practice, Inc.,* 907 A.2d 1061 (Pa. 2006), where a quadriplegic patient fell off an examination table at the doctor's office and subsequently died. The court found that no reasonable jury could believe

that this occurred for any reason other than the defendant's leaving the patient unattended and unrestrained. We see another example in *De Leon Lopez v. Corporacion Insular de Seguros*, 931 F.2d 116 (1st Cir. 1991), where two women gave birth to twins in the University Hospital at Puerto Rico Medical Center. The hospital somehow switched one twin from each set, so that each mother went home with two children, but only with one of her own. The mistake was discovered after a year and a half. The court thought that occasions for directing a verdict for the plaintiff were "hen's-teeth rare," but nevertheless affirmed such a ruling.

5.   *The presumption effect.* A small number of courts say that res ipsa loquitur is *not* merely a common sense assessment of evidence which permits an inference of fault, but that, instead, it creates a "presumption" of negligence. The term "presumption" can be used loosely or can have technical meanings, explored in evidence courses. Courts usually mean that once the presumption applies, the defendant has the burden of showing he is *not* negligent.

Sometimes courts describe the presumption as (a) shifting the *burden of persuasion* or (b) shifting the *burden of production* (meaning production of evidence), or the burden of going forward with evidence. *See* 1 DOBBS, HAYDEN & BUBLICK, THE LAW OF TORTS § 170 (2d ed. 2011) (describing presumptions and their effects). On the side of shifting the burden of production, rather than shifting the burden of persuasion, see *Chapman v. Harner*, 339 P.3d 519 (Colo. 2014). *Chapman* overruled earlier precedent and explained that res ipsa is like other rebuttable presumptions: once the defendant produces sufficient evidence, "the presumption is destroyed and only a permissible inference of negligence remains."

6.   *Rebuttal by defendant.* Suppose the defendant does in fact offer proof about his conduct. What does this do to the res ipsa loquitur inference? Can the plaintiff still get to the jury? Suppose in *Byrne* the defendant offers proof that a trucker unaffiliated with the defendant was loading the flour and negligently dropped it. Suppose instead that the defendant proved it did everything normally, exercised all precautions about the flour storage, and cannot understand why the injury took place? Would the results be different under these two versions of the defendant's proof? The defendant's rebuttal evidence might be disbelieved by the trier, so the judge cannot appropriately remove res ipsa loquitur from the case merely because the defendant has offered alternative explanations or other rebuttal evidence. *See McLaughlin Freight Lines, Inc. v. Gentrup*, 798 N.W.2d 386 (Neb. 2011) (although cattle owner testified that he secured and latched the gate to his cattle pen, when cattle had escaped and were on the highway where they caused an accident, a reasonable jury could determine that cattle do not escape a steel enclosure in the absence of negligence).

B. IS NEGLIGENCE MORE PROBABLE THAN NOT?

KOCH V. NORRIS PUBLIC POWER DISTRICT, 632 N.W.2d 391 (Neb. Ct. App. 2001). The defendant's high-voltage line broke and fell, starting a fire that did considerable damage to the plaintiff's property. The weather was sunny and dry, and winds at 40 mph were ordinary. There was some inconclusive evidence that the line might have been shot by a bullet, but other evidence suggests that a bullet did not cause the line to fall. *Held,* the plaintiff may rely on res ipsa loquitur. "[P]ower lines do not normally fall without fault on behalf of the company that maintains them and . . . res ipsa loquitur is applied in the absence of a substantial, significant, or probable explanation. . . . It seems clear that power lines should be built and maintained so they do not fall without the intervention of nature or a person and that therefore if a line falls without explanation, it must have been negligently constructed or maintained.'

COSGROVE V. COMMONWEALTH EDISON CO., 734 N.E.2d 155 (Ill. App. Ct. 2000). On a stormy night, the electric company's power lines were seen to be sparking in the alley behind the plaintiffs' house. At some point the power line was seen to fall. A few hours after the sparking was noticed, a fire occurred in the alley. Evidence indicated that a leak in a buried gas line was ignited by the sparks. The fire injured the plaintiffs. *Held*, the plaintiff cannot rely on res ipsa loquitur as to the electric company but can rely on it as to the gas company. "Other forces [besides negligence] may cause a downed power line, such as wind, lightning, storm, or an animal chewing through the wire." But a "ruptured gas line feeding a fire does not ordinarily occur in the absence of negligence. Gas mains are buried beyond the reach and interference of the general public, and the probability is great that breaks therein are occasioned by defects in the pipes or improper utilization thereof. In the ordinary course of events, gas explosions and fires do not occur; when one does occur, an inference of fault is justifiable. This inference may be explained or rebutted. However, even if the gas company is blameless, its superior knowledge of the facts at hand and its responsibility to the community create a duty to come forward and make an explanation."

NOTES

1. **Judging probabilities.** In determining the probabilities that the defendant was somehow negligent, judges draw on their common experience in life, rarely on actual data. The reasoning in *Koch* and *Cosgrove* is fairly typical. And once the trial judge believes jurors have the common life experience to make the judgment, the question will be passed to the jury for its verdict. On the jury's role in determining probabilities, see *MacClatchey v. HCA Health Servs. of Fla., Inc.,* 139 So. 3d 970 (Fla. Dist. Ct. App. 2014)

(whether a framed picture on the wall of a patient's hospital room would have fallen in the absence of the hospital's negligence was a question of fact for the jury; summary judgment for defendant reversed). Some courts seem to go beyond requiring a probability of negligence and require a certainty. *See Dickens v. Sahley Realty Co.*, 756 S.E.2d 484 (W. Va. 2014) (affirming summary judgment for the defendant in a res ipsa case: "The doctrine applies only in cases where defendant's negligence is the only inference that can reasonably and legitimately be drawn from the circumstances."). In some cases, judges believe juries lack sufficient knowledge or experience to conclude that negligence is more probable than not. *E.g., Scott v. James,* 731 A.2d 399 (D.C. 1999) (stressing jury's lack of knowledge of chemistry).

2. **Res ipsa and "ordinary accidents."** If res ipsa applies only when a permissible inference arises that the event would not ordinarily occur without negligence, does that mean that res ipsa is inapplicable to "ordinary accidents" that often occur without negligence? Some courts have said just that. *See, e.g., Linnear v. Centerpoint Energy Entex/Reliant Energy*, 966 So. 2d 36 (La. 2007).

WARREN V. JEFFRIES

139 S.E.2d 718 (N.C. 1965)

PER CURIAM.

Terry Lee Enoch, a six-year-old child, was injured when a wheel of defendant's Chevrolet automobile ran over his body, and from these injuries he died. Plaintiff instituted this action to recover for his alleged wrongful death. From judgment of involuntary nonsuit entered at the close of plaintiff's evidence, plaintiff appeals.

Plaintiff's evidence, taken as true for the purposes of this appeal, discloses these facts:

Defendant drove to Terry's home to see Terry's father and parked his car in the yard. Terry's father was not at home and defendant went in the house and waited for his return. The car was left standing on an incline. During the time there were in and around the house about a dozen children, including Terry; their ages ranged from 18 months to 20 years. The car remained parked for about an hour prior to the accident, and during this interval no one had gone to the car or touched it for any purpose. One of the children needed shoe polish and defendant gave Terry's mother the keys to his automobile so she could drive it to a store for the polish. She and five children, including Terry, started to the car. It was raining and Terry didn't want to wear his glasses; he gave them to his mother and she went back in the house to put them up. The five children (eldest, 20 years) got in the rear seat of the car; it was a 4-door sedan, and none of them got in the front seat. They did not touch any of the control mechanisms of the car. Terry was the last to get in and when he "closed the door something clicked in the front and ... the car started rolling" backwards in the direction of a large ditch. One of the older children opened the door and told the others to jump out. All jumped out, Terry first. When he jumped out he fell, and the front wheel ran over his chest.

The mother's graphic description of her son is so typical of an alert and active little boy that it is worthy of preservation. "He was full of fun at all times, he never was still unless he was asleep, he was either laughing or playing or doing something to let you know he was around. One thing I remember, the lady I worked for give (sic) him a little puppy and he was crazy about this little dog. . . ."

Plaintiff alleges defendant was negligent in that (1) he failed to set the hand brake, (2) failed to engage the transmission, and (3) neglected to maintain adequate brakes as required by G.S. § 20–124. There is no evidence as to the condition of the brakes, whether the hand brake had been set, or whether the car was in gear. Apparently the car was not examined after the accident. What caused it to make a "clicking" sound and begin rolling backwards is pure speculation. The doctrine of *res ipsa loquitur* is not applicable.

Affirmed.

NOTES

1. **Questioning *Warren*.** Testimony, which the jury could believe, excluded the possibility of tampering by the children. Why, then, isn't *Warren v. Jeffries* a res ipsa case like any other case of a car inexplicably going off the road? Is there an explanation for the accident that would *not* involve negligence of the defendant?

2. **Inferences from plaintiff's failure to offer available proof?** Would it have helped the plaintiff to put on evidence that the car was examined immediately after the accident by a qualified mechanic and that the examination revealed nothing throwing light on the occurrence? Did the court in effect draw an inference against the plaintiff for failure to introduce some such testimony? *See, e.g., DeBusscher v. Sam's East, Inc.*, 505 F.3d 475 (6th Cir. 2007) (portable basketball goal on display in store fell on the plaintiff; the fact that the defendant sent the goal to the claims department without checking the ballast level showed that "evidence of the true explanation for the accident was more readily accessible" to the defendant).

3. **Judge Posner's bus example.** Consider also *Howard v. Wal-Mart Stores, Inc.*, 160 F.3d 358 (7th Cir. 1998). In that case, Judge Posner discussed a hypothetical case in which the plaintiff was struck by a bus. At that location, 51% of all buses are owned by company A and 49% by company B. Does the plaintiff make out a case against A by showing these facts plus negligence and causation? "If the 51/49 statistic is the plaintiff's only evidence, and he does not show that it was infeasible for him to obtain any additional evidence, the

inference to be drawn is not that there is a 51 percent probability that it was a bus owned by A that hit the plaintiff. It is that the plaintiff either investigated and discovered that the bus was actually owned by B (and B might not have been negligent and so not liable even if a cause of the accident, or might be judgment-proof and so not worth suing), or that he simply has not bothered to conduct an investigation. If the first alternative is true, he should of course lose; and since it may be true, the probability that the plaintiff was hit by a bus owned by A is less than 51 percent and the plaintiff has failed to carry his burden of proof. If the second alternative is true—the plaintiff just hasn't conducted an investigation—he still should lose. A court shouldn't be required to expend its scarce resources of time and effort on a case until the plaintiff has conducted a sufficient investigation to make reasonably clear that an expenditure of public resources is likely to yield a significant social benefit. This principle is implicit in the law's decision to place the burden of producing evidence on the plaintiff rather than on the defendant.

4. **Inferences against a defendant for failing to explain?** In some cases, the defendant or his witnesses appear to have extensive knowledge of relevant facts, but never offer any testimony about them. Where a plaintiff apparently has access to evidence but fails to introduce it, an inference may arise that the absent evidence was unfavorable to the plaintiff. *See, e.g., District of Columbia v. Singleton,* 41 A.3d 717 (Md. 2012) (bus left the road and crashed into a tree on a dry sunny day; bus passengers, who were asleep at the time of collision, sought to apply res ipsa loquitur without calling at trial the bus driver or other known eyewitnesses to the accident, or introducing evidence of the police accident report). What inference arises from the fact that 99.95% of healthy dogs recover from surgery? *Milke v. Ratcliff Animal Hosp., Inc.,* 120 So. 3d 343 (La. Ct. App. 2013) (none; "the plaintiff declined a necropsy that might have revealed the cause of [a dog's] death").

5. **Specific evidence of negligence.** What if the plaintiff relies on res ipsa loquitur, but also produces specific evidence of the defendant's negligence? Under the traditional rule, still followed in some jurisdictions, the plaintiff is not permitted to do that. *See Gray v. BellSouth Telecomm., Inc.,* 11 So. 3d 1269, 1273 (Miss. Ct. App. 2009). The more modern approach does allow a plaintiff to put on proof of the defendant's particular negligent conduct while relying on res ipsa loquitur in the alternative—as long as the specific evidence does not provide a "complete explanation" of the accident. *Widmyer v. Southeast Skyways, Inc.,* 584 P.2d 1 (Alaska 1978) (allowing res ipsa in an air-crash case). Why would res ipsa loquitur not be needed, or allowed, when the plaintiff's evidence provides a complete explanation of what occurred?

C. ATTRIBUTING THE FAULT TO THE DEFENDANT RATHER THAN OTHERS

GILES V. CITY OF NEW HAVEN, 636 A.2d 1335 (Conn. 1994). Plaintiff, an elevator operator, sued Otis Elevator Company (defendant), for its negligent failure to inspect, maintain and repair an elevator compensation chain. On the date plaintiff sustained injuries, the elevator began to shudder and shake, and the compensation chain fell to the bottom of the elevator shaft with a loud crash. Fearing for her safety, the plaintiff reversed the direction of the elevator, directed it to the nearest floor, and jumped from the cab sustaining additional injuries. At the time the plaintiff suffered her injuries, the defendant had a long standing exclusive contract with the building owner to maintain and inspect the elevator and its component parts. The elevator was installed by the defendant approximately sixty-one years before the accident. The parties disputed whether the compensation chain had broken before plaintiff rapidly changed the direction of the elevator, or because plaintiff had done so. The Appellate Court concluded that the plaintiff had presented sufficient evidence to warrant presentation of the question of negligence under the doctrine of res ipsa loquitur to the jury. *Held*, affirmed. "The defendant challenges the application of the res ipsa loquitur doctrine to this case because in its view the plaintiff failed to demonstrate that the defendant had exclusive control over the elevator. Specifically, the defendant argues that because plaintiff operated the elevator and controlled its movement and its chain's sway, she could not benefit from the doctrine notwithstanding defendant's own duty to maintain and inspect the elevator and to warn of any dangerous propensity. We disagree. . . . [I]n describing the extent of the defendant's control of the use of the instrumentality [that caused the event], we have never held that any use whatsoever of the instrumentality by the plaintiff would automatically preclude application of res ipsa loquitur. So restrictive an interpretation would substantially undermine the efficacy of the doctrine. Rather, our previous discussions of use were meant to reflect the idea of management and control, factors that help to limit the application of the res ipsa loquitur doctrine to those situations in which the defendant's negligence was more probably than not the cause of the plaintiff's injuries. . . . The point of requiring control by the defendant is, as indicated by Prosser, to provide the basis for an inference that whatever negligence was involved may properly be charged to the defendant. . . . If the jury could reasonably find that defendant's control was sufficient to warrant an inference that the defendant was more likely responsible for the incident than someone else, even in the absence of proof of absolute exclusivity and control over the instrumentality by the defendant, the trial court must allow the jury to draw that inference. [In this case, the court concluded, that they could. Moreover, Connecticut's adoption of comparative negligence compels the conclusion that res ipsa can apply to a case even where the plaintiff's negligence contributed to the injury, as cases from at least seven other states have also held.] [T]he plaintiff was entitled to have a jury consider her claim that the defendant's negligence was the cause of her personal injuries.]

[handwritten margin note: Must permit jury to infer D's control]

NOTES

1. **Contemporary view of control rule.** *Giles* reflects a contemporary view of the control rule. "Control" is only one way of establishing the important point that the negligence was probably that of the defendant, not that of someone else. *Krinitt v. Idaho Dep't of Fish & Game*, 357 P.3d 850 (Idaho 2015). In *Krinitt*, a clipboard flew out of a 3-person helicopter and hit the tail rotor, causing the helicopter to crash. Evidence showed that that clipboard came out of the helicopter door where the Fish & Game employee was sitting. Res ipsa loquitur applied. The court wrote: "The evidence must afford a rational basis for concluding that the cause of the accident was probably such that defendant would be responsible for any negligence connected with it. That does not mean that the possibility of other causes must be altogether eliminated, but only that their likelihood must be so reduced that the greater probability lies at the defendant's door."

2. **Instrumentalities accessible to the public.** When, as in *Giles*, an instrumentality is more or less accessible to the public, numerous persons may have interfered with the instrumentality, so the defendant is not literally in exclusive control. In some cases, courts bar the claim. *Hagler v. Coastal Farms Holdings, Inc.*, 309 P.3d 1073 (Or. 2013); others do not. *See MacClatchey v. HCA Health Servs. of Fla., Inc.*, 139 So. 3d 970 (Fla. Dist. Ct. App. 2014) (framed picture fell from hospital wall; fact that room was open to many people did not bar the claim).

3. **Exploding-bottle cases.** Under a liberal formulation of the control requirement, the plaintiff might show that any fault was attributable to the defendant by excluding other causes. Suppose the plaintiff buys a soft drink from a grocery, takes it home, and suffers an injury when the bottle "explodes." The bottler obviously was not in control at the time of injury. Nor do we know when the negligence was likely to have occurred. The grocer or a customer might well have dropped the bottle, causing a chip for which the bottler is not responsible. In a leading case, *Escola v. Coca Cola Bottling Co.*, 150 P.2d 436 (Cal. 1944), the California Supreme Court held that the plaintiff could use res ipsa loquitur by showing that the defendant had control at the time of the probable negligence, and that this could be shown by excluding the negligence of others. Thus the plaintiff might show that the bottle had not been subjected to any unusual treatment in the grocery store, and on making such proof would be permitted to use res ipsa loquitur.

4. **Plaintiff's fault and defendant's breach.** Plaintiff's fault can blend with the issue of the defendant's breach. In *Winfrey v. GGP Ala Moana LLC*, 308 P.3d 891 (Haw. 2013), the pregnant plaintiff was on the roof of a shopping mall acting in an odd manner and saying unusual things (for example, that a baby was stuck in the exhaust duct). After refusing to get down from the roof and jumping onto the duct, she became stuck in it. Sometime after she was removed from the duct she died of hyperthermia and respiratory compromise. Because the death could have occurred without the mall owner's negligence, res ipsa loquitur did not apply. The facts in *Winfrey* suggest

plaintiff fault, but can you see why the comparative fault issue might not be reached? As in *Stinnett*, based on an expectation that the plaintiff could care for herself, the defendant might have breached no duty at all.

5. **Effect of comparative fault systems.** Some courts apparently assume that the plaintiff-fault rule was a rule of contributory negligence. These courts have concluded that, with the advent of comparative fault, under which any contributory negligence will reduce but not bar the plaintiff's claim, the plaintiff-fault limit on res ipsa should be abolished or modified. *E.g., Cox v. May Dep't Store Co.*, 903 P.2d 1119 (Ariz. Ct. App. 1995).

PROBLEM

Cashman v. Van Dyke

Darrick Van Dyke testified that he came home from work at 9:00 p.m. and his house was cold. He went downstairs and lit the furnace. He smelled no odor and noticed nothing unusual. He went to bed around 11:00 p.m. and awoke to an explosion with his house on fire. He was seriously injured by the fire and neighbor Marguerite Cashman's home next door burned down as well.

You represent Cashman. Do you have a res ipsa loquitur case against anyone? Must you do further investigation? What lines of investigation, if any, would you pursue?

REFERENCES: 1 DOBBS, HAYDEN & BUBLICK, THE LAW OF TORTS §§ 141–176 (2d ed. 2011); DOBBS, HAYDEN & BUBLICK, HORNBOOK ON TORTS §§ 12.1–13.7 (2d ed. 2016).

CHAPTER 7

ACTUAL HARM AND FACTUAL CAUSE

■ ■ ■

§ 1. ACTUAL HARM

The third element of a negligence prima facie case is that the plaintiff must suffer legally cognizable harm, frequently referred to as actual damages. The plaintiff who proves that the defendant's conduct was negligent, but fails to show that actual damages resulted from it, will lose the case.

RIGHT V. BREEN
890 A.2d 1287 (Conn. 2006)

KATZ, J.

In May, 2000, the plaintiff had stopped his automobile at a red traffic light when it was struck from behind by a vehicle driven by the defendant. There was minor damage to the plaintiff's vehicle, but no physical injuries were reported at the accident scene. Thereafter, the plaintiff brought this action, alleging that, as a result of the defendant's negligence, he had suffered bodily injury leading to both economic and noneconomic damages[1] . . .

[At trial, plaintiff presented evidence that his injuries resulted from the collision. The defendant, however, presented evidence that the injuries resulted from the plaintiff's five previous automobile accidents.] Using a verdict form provided by the plaintiff, the jury returned a verdict of zero economic damages and zero noneconomic damages. . . .

The plaintiff then filed motions to set aside the verdict and for additur, arguing that, under Connecticut case law, he was entitled to at least nominal damages because he had suffered a technical legal injury that admittedly had been caused by the defendant. The defendant objected to the motions, arguing that . . . although she had admitted to causing the collision, she had denied the causal relationship between the collision and the plaintiff's alleged injuries. The trial court granted the plaintiff's motions, setting aside the jury's verdict and awarding the plaintiff $1,

---

[1] Neither the plaintiff's complaint nor his amended complaint sought recovery for the damage done to his automobile.

177

based upon the abundant appellate case law cited. [The trial court also awarded plaintiff $467.10 in costs as the prevailing party.]

The defendant appealed from the judgment of the trial court. . . . [Although the Appellate Court described our prior precedents, which apparently required an award of nominal damages] as "inconsistent and troubling," it observed that it was not at liberty to overrule or discard [those] precedents and, accordingly, affirmed the trial court's judgment. . . . This certified appeal followed. . . . *→ Supreme Court*

The [defendant contends that, because causation and actual injury are essential elements of a negligence claim, a plaintiff's claim of negligence must fail entirely if he cannot establish these elements] . . .

Connecticut common law requires proof of actual damages to support a cause of action sounding in negligence. . . . [N]one of our cases has held that a plaintiff may prevail in a negligence action without alleging and proving actual damage. . . . [T]his was the rule at common law. . . . No contrary authority is cited and the common law rule, ancient as it may be, has been approved by contemporary commentators.

Unwillingness to break with precedent (Reasoning)

Although the rule making actual damage an element of a cause of action in negligence may have originated in the common law distinction between trespass and trespass on the case, we are not inclined to obliterate the distinction between intentional and unintentional conduct in terms of legal consequences which it serves to implement. Where the plaintiff's right has been intentionally invaded, its vindication in a court of law and the award of nominal and even exemplary damages serves the policy of deterrence in a real sense. It is difficult to imagine what purpose would be furthered by permitting anyone who is jostled in a crowd or otherwise suffers some unintended contact with his person or injury to his dignity to set in motion the judicial machinery necessary for a recovery of nominal damages. That judges and juries have more important business to occupy them is as true today as it was in ancient times when the rule originated. There is nothing arcane about the wisdom of not cluttering the courts with trivia. . . .

Public Policy considerations (Reasoning)

[C]onduct that is merely negligent, without proof of an actual injury, is not considered to be a significant interference with the public interest such that there is any right to complain of it, or to be free from it.

[The judgment of the Appellate Court is reversed and the case is remanded to that court with direction to reverse the judgment of the trial court . . . and to modify the order of costs accordingly.] ——→ *Holding!*

NOTES

1. **Nominal damages.** Nominal damages are damages in name only— usually one dollar or six cents. Remember that attorneys for plaintiffs are

normally paid only if they win and then by a percentage of the recovery. Would you take a case if your contingent fee could only amount to 40% of one dollar? In personal injury cases the market—that is, the attorney's financial incentives—will typically exclude nominal damages claims from the courts. The issue normally arises, then, because the plaintiff and her attorney hope to prove substantial damages but fail to convince judge or jury. In some cases that find no actual harm from a collision, the facts suggest plaintiff fraud. *See, e.g.,* *Reardon v. Larkin*, 3 A.3d 376 (Me. 2010) (plaintiff who claimed to have been hit by a UPS driver, and asked his doctor to change his medical records).

2. **Damages recoverable in a personal injury case.** Recall the elements of damages from Chapter 1—past and future medical expenses, loss of wages or earning capacity, pain and suffering (including emotional harm), and damages for any other specifically identifiable harm, such as special expenses necessary to travel for medical care. Punitive damages are generally *not* recoverable in a negligence case, because entitlement to such damages depends on proof of the defendant's bad state of mind, variously described as willful, wanton, reckless, or malicious.

3. **Physical harm.** In *Right*, plaintiff *alleged* a form of legally cognizable harm—physical injury to his body. He just failed to *prove* any such harm, which was fatal to his case. Clearly, as a categorical matter, proven physical harm satisfies the actual harm requirement of a negligence prima facie case. *See* DOBBS, HAYDEN & BUBLICK, HORNBOOK ON TORTS § 14.1 (2d ed. 2016). "Physical harm" can mean either the physical impairment of the human body, or of real property, or tangible personal property. RESTATEMENT (THIRD) OF TORTS: PHYSICAL AND EMOTIONAL HARM § 4 (2010). A comment to the Restatement explains that "any detrimental change in the physical condition of a person's body or property counts as harmful impairment; there is no requirement that the detriment be major." *Id.*, cmt. c. Whether a specific kind of injury constitutes cognizable harm is a question of law for the court; pure emotional harm, or pure economic harm, without any physical injury to person or property, may not be considered legally cognizable in a negligence action. Where legally cognizable harm is proved, measuring the damages caused by such harm is a question of fact for the jury.

§ 2. FACTUAL CAUSE

The fourth element of a negligence prima facie case is factual cause, also called actual cause or cause in fact. The plaintiff must prove not only that she suffered legally recognized harm, but that the harm was in fact caused by the defendant. Factual cause is a very simple concept in most cases, but may be complicated in others.

Rul 180 - 188

A. THE BUT-FOR TEST OF CAUSATION

HALE V. OSTROW
166 S.W.3d 713 (Tenn. 2005)

Rule of Law
A plaintiff must
show causation in
fact to succeed in
negligence claim
by proving that
harm would not
have occured but
for the d's
negligen

E. RILEY ANDERSON, J. . . .

On May 27, 1998, plaintiff Shirley Hale ("Ms. Hale") was walking home from a bus stop in Memphis, Tennessee. She had taken a different bus than usual and so was walking a route along a sidewalk that she did not normally travel. As she proceeded south on Mississippi Boulevard, a busy street, she noticed that the sidewalk ahead was blocked. Bushes protruding from 1073 Mississippi Boulevard had overgrown the sidewalk and had grown around a telephone pole located on the sidewalk, blocking Ms. Hale's way. Ms. Hale determined that she had to leave the sidewalk and enter the street in order to bypass the obstruction. She noticed that the sidewalk was "crumbled." As she left the sidewalk, but before she reached the bushes, Ms. Hale looked into the street to check for traffic. As she looked up, she tripped over a chunk of concrete and fell into the street. Ms. Hale's left hip was crushed in the fall, and she required extensive medical care.

Harm

The bushes that had overgrown the sidewalk were located in front of 1073 Mississippi Boulevard. That property, a vacant lot, was owned by the defendants Max Ostrow, Erwin Ostrow, and Rose Ostrow (collectively, "the Ostrows" or "defendants"). The crumbled sidewalk, and the spot where Ms. Hale actually fell, were located in front of 1063 Mississippi Boulevard. That property was not owned by the defendants.

Court is.
Appeals
affirm

Ms. Hale filed suit against the Ostrows [as well as the other property owner and the City of Memphis. The Ostrows moved for summary judgment on the ground that Ms. Hale's "injury was caused by the defective sidewalk, not by the overgrown bushes." The trial court granted summary judgment which the Court of Appeals affirmed.] ——> *Procedural Posture*

. . . As we often recite, a negligence claim requires proof of two types of causation: causation in fact and proximate cause. Causation in fact and proximate cause are distinct elements of negligence, and both must be proven by the plaintiff by a preponderance of the evidence. Cause in fact and proximate cause are ordinarily jury questions, unless the uncontroverted facts and inferences to be drawn from them make it so clear that all reasonable persons must agree on the proper outcome.

Questions
for the
jury

The defendant's conduct is the cause in fact of the plaintiff's injury if, as a factual matter, it directly contributed to the plaintiff's injury. In a case such as this one, we must ask whether the plaintiff's injury would have happened "but for" the defendants' act. If not, then the defendants' conduct is a cause in fact of the plaintiff's injury. It is not necessary that the defendants' act be the *sole* cause of the plaintiff's injury, only that it be *a cause*.

Viewing the facts in the light most favorable to Ms. Hale, there is a genuine issue of material fact as to whether the overgrown bushes on the Ostrows' property were a cause in fact of her injury. Ms. Hale stated in her deposition that the bushes had completely overgrown the sidewalk, that she determined that she could not bypass the bushes on the sidewalk, and that she therefore decided to leave the sidewalk and step into the street. As she did so, she looked up to check for traffic and tripped over the broken sidewalk. But for the bushes overgrowing the sidewalk, Ms. Hale would not have looked up to check for traffic, as she would not have needed to step into the street. Might she nevertheless have tripped over the concrete and suffered the same injury? Indeed she might have. Given that the evidence on summary judgment must be viewed in the light most favorable to the plaintiff, however, the issue of causation, as well as the allocation of comparative fault, are determinations of fact to be made by the jury. . . .

[W]e reverse the decisions of the trial court and the Court of Appeals granting summary judgment to the defendants.

SALINETRO V. NYSTROM
341 So. 2d 1059 (Fla. Dist. Ct. App. 1977)

[Anna Salinetro was in an auto accident and underwent a medical examination in connection with back injuries sustained. Dr. Nystrom took x-rays of her lower back and her abdominal areas.]

PER CURIAM.

Although unknown to her, Anna was approximately four-six weeks pregnant at the time; however, neither Dr. Nystrom nor his receptionist or his x-ray technician inquired whether or not she was pregnant or the date of her last menstrual period. Thereafter, upon suspecting she was pregnant, on December 12 Anna visited her gynecologist, Dr. Emilio Aldereguia, who, after running some tests, confirmed her pregnancy. In January Dr. Aldereguia learned that Dr. Nystrom had taken x-rays of Anna's pelvis and advised her to terminate her pregnancy because of possible damage to the fetus by the x-rays. Anna underwent a therapeutic abortion and the pathology report stated that the fetus was dead at the time of the abortion. Thereafter, Anna filed the instant lawsuit against Dr. Nystrom for medical malpractice. . . .

After the presentation of all the evidence on Anna's behalf, Dr. Nystrom moved for a directed verdict on the ground she failed to make a prima facie case of medical malpractice. The trial judge granted the motion and entered judgment for Dr. Nystrom. . . .

[Handwritten margin notes: "factual caus.io"; "using But-for-her-but for the bushes on sidewalk she would not have looked up to check for traffic or needed to step into the street"; "Court trying to assess whether reasonable minds can disagree over causation"; "No taking! mess"; "→ Harm"; "Counter-factual should the dr or receptionist ask if she was pregnant or had missed her last menstrual period. Not sued the although it is reasonable it (would say there been determinative"; "harm would not have occurred"; "but for Sam doctor she was not present"; "result she would have gone there she didn't know as"; "Plaintiff was able to show causation"]

"For the sake of argument"

"standard of care too evolved"

Doctors now ask more subjective questions that spark conversation

Assuming arguendo that Dr. Nystrom's conduct fell below the standard of care in failing to inquire of Anna whether she was pregnant or not on the date of her last menstrual period, this omission was not the cause of her injury. Anna herself testified that even if asked about being pregnant, she would have answered in the negative. Anna further testified to the effect that being a few days late with her menstrual period was not unusual and did not indicate to her that she may have been pregnant at the time she went to Dr. Nystrom; that six days prior thereto she had visited Dr. Aldereguia, and he had found no evidence that she was pregnant. We further note that simply because Anna was late with her menstrual period would not in and of itself mean that she was pregnant because further tests were required to ascertain whether she was pregnant. Thus, this point is without merit.

NOTES

1. **But-for as a hypothetical or counterfactual test.** "Determining causation always requires evaluation of hypothetical situations concerning what might have happened, but did not.... [T]he very idea of causation necessarily involves comparing historical events to a hypothetical alternative." *Viner v. Sweet*, 70 P.3d 1046, 1053 (Cal. 2003). The but-for rule thus requires the judge or jury to imagine an alternate scenario that never happened, that is, to imagine what *would* have happened without the defendant's negligence. Do you see any problems with this?

Key job of lawyer is too pick out best counterfactual

2. **Linking the negligent act to the harm.** Notice from the cases above that proving factual harm requires the plaintiff to identify exactly how the defendant's conduct was negligent. To count as a factual cause under the but-for test, the plaintiff must prove that her harm would not have occurred had the defendant not acted negligently. In other words, factual cause is not established if the plaintiff's harm would have occurred even if the defendant had acted non-negligently. *See Jordan v. Jordan*, 257 S.E.2d 761 (Va. 1979) (defendant backed out of the driveway without looking in her rearview mirror, however, her husband was squatting behind the rear bumper where he wouldn't have been seen even if she had looked); *Sweeney v. City of Bettendorf*, 762 N.W.2d 873 (Iowa 2009) (plaintiff alleged that defendant city was negligent in failing to provide adult supervision near children attending a minor league baseball game, resulting in a child being struck by a flying bat, but failed to prove that the child would not have been hit if the city had provided such supervision); *Aegis Ins. Services, Inc. v. 7 World Trade Co., L.P.*, 737 F.3d 166 (2d Cir. 2013) (plaintiffs alleged that defendants negligently designed and constructed a building that collapsed in the 9/11/01 New York City terrorist attack; summary judgment for defendant was proper on factual cause grounds because the building "would have collapsed regardless of any negligence" of defendants in designing and constructing the building).

3. **The alternate scenarios in *Hale* and *Salinetro*.** The *Hale* court raised some uncertainty about what the alternate scenario in that case might

have been. Perhaps Ms. Hale would have tripped over the concrete and suffered the same injury even without the bush that blocked the sidewalk. If so, what result on the issue of factual cause? The *Salinetro* court felt the causation issue did not warrant review by the jury. Could the plaintiff have asserted a different act of negligence that would lead to a different conclusion about but-for causation? To establish factual causation in *Salinetro*, would the plaintiff need to show only that the doctor's negligence caused her to get an x-ray while pregnant, or something more?

4.   **Framing the hypothetical.** The focus of the hypothetical is on the *happening* of the defendant's negligent act, not the *reasons* the act was negligent. In *Cabral v. Ralphs Grocery Co.*, 248 P.3d 1170 (Cal. 2011), the driver of a car died in a rear-end collision with a tractor-trailer parked on the side of the freeway. The defendant claimed that parking the rig on the side of the road could not be a factual cause of harm, "because the same collision would have occurred had Horn [the rig's driver] stopped for emergency rather than personal reasons." The court disagreed with defendant's analysis: "The negligent conduct plaintiff claimed caused her husband's death was Horn's stopping his tractor-trailer rig at the site. The counterfactual question relevant to but-for causation, therefore, is what would have happened if Horn had not stopped his tractor-trailer rig there, not what would have happened if Horn had had a better reason to stop. . . . [S]topping by the side of a freeway for an emergency might be just as dangerous to other motorists as stopping for a snack, but an emergency stop will not create liability because it is justified. While potential liability differs in the two situations (emergency and non-emergency), causation does not."

5.   **Factual and proximate cause terminology.** In *Hale,* the court discusses factual cause and, later in the opinion, proximate cause (called "scope of liability" in the Third Restatement and a growing number of modern cases). Many jurisdictions are careful to address the two concepts separately. *See, e.g., Bernie v. Catholic Diocese of Sioux Falls*, 821 N.W.2d 232 (S.D. 2012) ("In order to prevail in a suit based on negligence, a plaintiff must prove duty, breach of that duty, proximate and factual causation, and actual injury."). However, many other courts group the concepts of factual and proximate cause together under the single heading "proximate cause." *See, e.g., Michaels v. CH2M Hill, Inc.*, 257 P.3d 532 (Wash. 2011) ("Proximate cause can be divided into two elements: cause in fact and legal cause."). *Hale* noted that the appellate court had used the but-for concept of factual cause but the label "proximate cause." Confusion between the two concepts is distressingly common. Scope of liability (proximate cause) is explored in the next chapter.

6.   **Factual and proximate cause analysis.** Conceptually, factual cause is very different from proximate cause. Some thinking is that the factual cause issue is truly a factual issue in the sense that it does not entail policy decisions. Proximate cause, by contrast, is primarily a policy judgment about the scope of liability. In *June v. Union Carbide Corp.,* 577 F.3d 1234 (10th Cir. 2009), the court explained: "Ordinarily, a cause is a 'factual cause' only if it is a but-for cause, *see* [Restatement (Third) of Torts: Liability for Physical and

Emotional Harm] § 26, although there is a potential exception . . . when there are multiple causes, *see id.* § 27." In addition, "the harm must be among the 'harms that result from the risks that made the actor's conduct tortious.' *Id.* § 29. Traditionally, this second component has been referred to as 'proximate cause,' a term that has baffled law students (to say nothing of jurors, lawyers, and judges) for generations; but the Restatement (Third) has wisely redescribed the subject matter as 'scope of liability.' "

7. **Res ipsa loquitur and factual cause.** Does res ipsa loquitur always assist the plaintiff on causal as well as on negligence issues? Suppose a surgeon leaves sponges in the plaintiff's abdomen after an operation and this is regarded as a res ipsa loquitur case. This causes some harm, for which the surgeon would then be liable. But suppose the plaintiff claims the sponges caused stomach cancer. Will there be a causal issue that will require proof even though this is a res ipsa loquitur case?

B. MULTIPLE CAUSES AND APPORTIONMENT

NOTE: LIABILITY OF TWO OR MORE PERSONS

1. *Two persons causing separate or divisible injuries: causal apportionment.* Under the but-for rule, more than one actor's conduct can be causal. In some cases, tortfeasor A may cause a broken arm while tortfeasor B causes a broken leg. So far as the two injuries are separate, liability can be apportioned by causation. Each tortfeasor will be liable for the harms that tortfeasor caused and no more. This explains why evidence of a second accident caused by another person is admissible as relevant to factual causation. *See, e.g., JLG Trucking, LLC v. Garza*, 466 S.W.3d 157 (Tex. 2016).

2. *Two persons causing a single indivisible injury: fault apportionment.* In some injuries, however, both tortfeasors' conduct contributes to a single injury. Suppose A negligently runs into a horse and then negligently leaves the carcass on the highway where it might cause a second accident. B then negligently runs into the carcass, causing injury to his passenger, P. But-for A's negligence, the second collision would not have occurred, as there would have been no horse on the road. But-for B's negligence, the second collision would not have occurred because he would have stopped or taken evasive action to avoid hitting it. The negligent acts of both A and B are but-for causes of the plaintiff's single injury and both are subject to liability. *See Spann v. Shuqualak Lumber Co. Inc.*, 990 So.2d 186 (Miss. 2008) (lumber company's negligence in causing a dense fog of emissions, along with the negligence of other drivers, can be factual cause of collision). How do we assign liability for harm to the tortfeasors in these multiple defendant cases? The question is which fault-apportionment rule to use, joint and several liability with possible contribution, or proportionate fault liability. When contribution is based on the relative

fault of the tortfeasors, both these systems are forms of a fault-apportionment approach.

3. *Glancing back*. Before we go on, glance back at the two preceding paragraphs to see how simple they really are. If we can say that A caused only a broken arm and B only a broken leg, we can simply apportion liability to causes. A is liable only for the broken arm because he caused that harm and no other. But conversely, if an indivisible injury is caused in fact by two or more persons, we cannot apportion liability by causation. We must instead use some form of fault apportionment.

4. *Some defendants' conduct not a but-for cause of all injury*. Now suppose that C, a doctor, negligently makes both injuries worse, so that each break takes a week longer to heal than necessary. Can you work out (a) who is causally responsible for the broken arm and its delayed healing? (b) how joint and several liability would apply or not to the claims arising from the broken arm? Here is a start: A's negligence is a but-for cause of the broken arm. His negligence is likewise a but-for cause of the delayed healing, isn't it? *See, e.g., Cooper v. Thompson*, 353 P.3d 782 (Alaska 2015). The negligence of the doctor, C, is not a but-for cause of the broken arm but is a but-for cause of the added harm. How would joint and several liability work?

5. *Liability for aggravation of a preexisting injury*. If the tortfeasor aggravates the plaintiff's preexisting disability, the tortfeasor is ideally liable only for the aggravation—a causal apportionment. *Perius v. Nodak Mut. Ins. Co.*, 782 N.W.2d 355 (N.D. 2010) ("When a defendant's negligence aggravates a preexisting injury, the defendant must compensate the victim for the full extent of the aggravation but is not liable for the preexisting condition itself."). This apportionment should be done by the jury, which will often require expert medical testimony. *Harris v. ShopKo Stores, Inc.*, 308 P.3d 449 (Utah 2013). When the tortious harm caused by the defendant combines with the preexisting condition such that a causal apportionment is not possible, joint liability or several liability may apply. *See CSX Transp., Inc. v. Miller*, 46 So.3d 434 (Ala. 2010) (where jury was unable to apportion liability between aggravation of injury and preexisting injury, liability for entire injury was appropriate).

6. *Liability without but-for causation*. Under some circumstances a defendant is liable for harm to the plaintiff even though the defendant's negligent or illegal conduct was not a but-for cause of the harm. This is the case with *respondeat superior* liability: the telephone company is liable for its driver's on-the-job negligent driving that causes the plaintiff's injury. Such liability is not based upon the telephone company's negligence at all, but on the idea that, as a matter of policy, it should be liable for its employee's harmful torts. The same idea applies to partners in some circumstances, each being liable for the other's act. Analogously, those who

act in a conspiracy or "in concert" to cause harm are all liable for the harm caused, even though only one of the conspirators is a direct cause of harm. At least one person's conduct must be a but-for cause of harm in such cases. If he is, the others are liable because they are deemed responsible for his acts. These paragraphs show that the conduct of two or more persons can be but-for causes and thus liable in some degree for the same harm. (The amount of liability depends upon whether the state follows joint and several liability or proportionate-share liability.)

What is to be said about but-for cause if the independent acts of either A or B would be sufficient to cause the full harm even if the other had not acted at all?

C. PROBLEMS WITH THE BUT-FOR TEST

LANDERS V. EAST TEXAS SALT WATER DISPOSAL CO., 248 S.W.2d 731 (Tex. 1952). The plaintiff owned a small lake stocked with fish. He alleged that on or about April 1 the pipe lines of the East Texas Salt Water Disposal Company broke and some 10 to 15 thousand barrels of salt water flowed over his land and into the lake, killing the fish and damaging the land. He alleged that the other defendant, Sun Oil Company, on or about the same day, also caused large quantities of salt water and oil to flow into his lake, killing the fish. Plaintiff asserted that both defendants were negligent. The defendants did not act in concert, but rather each acted independently. Under existing case law, a defendant who acted independently of other tortfeasors would be liable only for the harms he himself caused. The fact that such a defendant could not identify which harms were caused by his tort and which were caused by the other tortfeasor does not make him jointly and severally liable. And since the harms he caused individually cannot be identified, he is not individually liable for those, thus escaping all liability.

— *Held*, the existing case law is overruled. "If such has been the law, from the standpoint of justice it should not have been; if it is the law now, it will not be hereafter. . . . Where the tortious acts of two or more wrongdoers join to produce an indivisible injury, that is, an injury which from its nature cannot be apportioned with reasonable certainty to the individual wrongdoers, all of the wrongdoers will be held jointly and severally liable for the entire damages and the injured party may proceed to judgment against any one separately or against all in one suit. . . . There is, of course, no joint liability for the loss of trees and grass killed by the salt water escaping from the pipe line owned by East Texas Salt Water Disposal Company before such water entered the lake. . . ."

NOTES

1. **The but-for test applied to *Landers*.** Apply the but-for test to *Landers*. How does that test work if you believe the two bodies of salt water entered the plaintiff's lake at the same time? But-for the salt water spilled by the Disposal Company, would the plaintiff have avoided harm? Must you conclude that neither defendant caused the plaintiff's harm?

2. **Causation and divisible injury.** How does the but-for test work if you believe that one body of salt water reached the lake first? If, as the court suggests, trees and grass on one side of the lake were damaged only by salt water from the Salt Water Disposal Company, would both parties have been an actual cause of that loss? Would liability for that damage be apportioned in a different way than would liability with respect to the fish?

3. **Causation and apportionment of indivisible injury.** There are at least two issues in *Landers*: whether each party's negligence can be said to have been a factual cause of the plaintiff's harm, and if so, for what portion of the damages each defendant should be liable. At the time *Landers* was decided, joint and several liability for an indivisible injury was the norm and thus the *Landers* case treats these two issues as one. In a jurisdiction that has several liability, would it be possible to say in a case like *Landers* that the negligence of both parties was a factual cause of the plaintiff's full harm but that each party would be severally liable for damages? *See Staab v. Diocese of St. Cloud*, 813 N.W.2d 68 (Minn. 2012) (both property owner and plaintiff's husband were negligent for injuries caused when plaintiff's nonmotorized wheelchair went over unmarked drop off and threw plaintiff on to pavement; jury found property owner 50% at fault and plaintiff's husband 50% at fault, and thus under state's several liability statute property owner owed 50% of the damages).

4. **"Duplicative" causation.** Professor Richard Wright works out a modified and more complicated version of the but-for rule. Applying his rule, he draws a distinction between "preempted cause" and "duplicative cause." If each of the two salt flows in Landers was sufficient to kill all of the fish and would have done so regardless of the other flow, the two flows are "duplicative" causes. Professor Wright thinks cause should be defined in such a way that we would recognize the defendant's salt flow as a cause even if some other flow would have killed the fish anyway, and applies the same idea to all duplicative cause cases. *See* Richard Wright, *Causation in Tort Law*, 73 CAL. L. REV. 1735 (1985). Wright recognizes, however, that a straight but-for rule would not get this result.

5. **"Preemptive" causation.** Professor Wright's "preempted cause" category is illustrated by a case in which one tortfeasor poisons the victim's tea. Just as the victim puts the tea to his lips, the other tortfeasor shoots him dead. Death would have followed from the poison even if the second tortfeasor had fired no shot at all, just as one salt flow would have killed the plaintiff's fish even if no other flow had existed. But the two cases are not alike under

Professor Wright's test. The victim died of a gunshot wound, not poison. The poisoner's conduct is not a cause.

6. **Negligent and non-negligent causes.** What should be the result in *Landers* if instead of two negligent causes sufficient to cause the full harm, one of the sufficient causes was negligent and another was not negligent? In *Anderson v. Minneapolis, St. Paul & Sault Ste. Marie Railway*, 179 N.W. 45 (Minn. 1920), plaintiff's property was burned by a fire. Plaintiff's proof tended to show that the fire was set by defendant's engine. Defendant, however, offered proof tending to show that there were other fires in the area that might have originated from other and perhaps non-negligent causes. The trial judge instructed in part: "If you find that other fires not set by one of the defendant's engines mingled with one that was set by one of the defendant's engines, there may be difficulty in determining whether you should find that the fire set by the engine was a material or substantial element in causing plaintiff's damage. If it was, the defendant is liable; otherwise, it is not. . . ." The jury, so charged, found for the plaintiff.

If but-for causation does not work in some kinds of cases, what test or tests might be better to achieve the goals of tort law?

D. ALTERNATIVES TO THE BUT-FOR TEST

LASLEY V. COMBINED TRANSPORT, INC., 261 P.3d 1215 (Or. 2011). Plaintiff, decedent's father, brought this case against defendants Combined Transport, Inc. (Combined Transport) and Judy Clemmer (Clemmer). On the day that decedent died, a truck owned and operated by Combined Transport lost part of its load of large panes of glass on the I–5 freeway. During the clean-up, traffic backed up and decedent was stopped. Clemmer drove into decedent's pickup, causing leaks in its fuel system. The ensuing fire killed decedent. . . . The jury rendered a verdict against both defendants, finding Combined Transport 22 percent at fault and Clemmer 78 percent at fault for plaintiff's damages. The Court of Appeals held that excluded evidence showing that Clemmer was intoxicated at the time of the collision was relevant to "whether Combined Transport's negligence was a substantial factor in causing decedent's death and. . . [how to] apportion fault between defendants. . . ."

Held, the evidence was relevant to apportionment, but not causation. "The parties [] agree that it is factual, not legal cause, at issue in this case. . . . Combined Transport acknowledges, correctly, that the "substantial factor" test is a test of factual cause. . . . Causation in Oregon law refers to causation in fact, that is to say, whether someone examining the event without regard to legal consequences would conclude that the allegedly faulty conduct or condition in fact played a role in its occurrence. . . . In this case, both the conduct of Clemmer and the conduct of Combined Transport were substantial factors in contributing to decedent's death. Clemmer admitted that her conduct in driving her car into decedent's pickup with such force that leaks in its fuel system caused the pickup to ignite was a substantial factor in causing decedent's death. The jury found that Combined Transport's conduct in spilling a load of glass panes on the freeway caused decedent to bring his pickup to a stop. Based on expert testimony that, had decedent been moving at or close to the speed limit when Clemmer hit him, the impact of the collision would not have been as great, decedent's truck would not have ignited, and decedent would not have died, the jury found that Combined Transport's conduct also was a substantial factor in causing decedent's death. The additional fact that Combined Transport sought to prove—that Clemmer was intoxicated at the time of the collision—could not make Clemmer's conduct any more significant or Combined Transport's conduct any less significant in that causation analysis. . . . Combined Transport contends that it was entitled to prove that, because Clemmer was intoxicated, she would have collided with decedent's pickup and killed him, even if he had not been stopped on the freeway. . . . Although Combined Transport's alternative argument may have merit in the abstract, it fails on the record before us." The intoxication evidence, though irrelevant to the issue of causation, is relevant to the issue of apportionment of fault.

NOTES

1. **"Substantial factor": broad use.** *Lasley* suggests that the substantial factor test is broadly used in Oregon. At times courts say that the substantial factor test applies whenever "multiple causes of injury are present." *See Palermo v. Port of New Orleans,* 951 So.2d 425 (La. Ct. App. 2007). Of course, this needn't be so. The but-for test works well in many multiple defendant cases, as in the case of tortious conduct by two actors, each of which is necessary to the harm that happened but neither of which is alone sufficient to produce it. An example would be the case of the dead horse negligently left in the road and the negligent driver who runs into it. Both of the defendants are but-for causes of the harm to the passenger who is injured in the resulting car accident. Would the but-for test have worked well in *Lasley* too?

2. **"Substantial factor" as the exception.** The substantial factor test is one way courts sometimes deal with the two-sufficient-cause cases. Some courts hold that the substantial factor test is reserved for cases like *Landers* and *Anderson* in which the conduct of each of two or more tortfeasors is sufficient to cause the entire harm. The but-for test applies in all other cases. *See Viner v. Sweet,* 70 P.3d 1046 (Cal. 2003); *Thomas v. McKeever's Enterprises Inc.,* 388 S.W.3d 206 (Mo. Ct. App. 2012) (but-for test for causation is applicable in all traditional tort cases except those involving two independent torts, either of which is sufficient in and of itself to cause the injury, *i.e.,* the "two fires" cases).

3. **The Third Restatement's formulation.** The substantial factor test was recommended by the First and Second Restatements of Torts, and is still

used by many courts. The Restatement Third rejects the substantial factor test, not only in the two-sufficient-cause cases, but altogether, finding it both "confusing" and "misused" by courts. RESTATEMENT (THIRD) OF TORTS: LIABILITY FOR PHYSICAL AND EMOTIONAL HARM § 26 cmt. j (2010). It instead provides that if tortious conduct of one tortfeasor, A, fails the but-for test only because there is another set of conduct also sufficient to cause the harm, then A's conduct is still a factual cause of that harm. *Id.* § 27. Would such a test have worked in *Landers* and *Anderson*?

4.   **Judicial concern.** A number of courts have expressed concern about the substantial factor test. In *John Crane, Inc. v. Jones*, 604 S.E.2d 822 (Ga. 2004), a case that sought recovery for a mill employee's exposure to asbestos, the Georgia Supreme Court wrote of "very real problems with applying a 'substantial factor' standard." According to the court, "In the analysis of a negligence action, the plaintiff must satisfy the elements of the tort, that is, the plaintiff must show a duty, a breach of that duty, causation, and damages. It would be a departure from the analysis to add the requirement that the causal connection must be substantial. Once the term 'substantial factor' is employed in the general negligence law vocabulary, there is the danger that it will be used not only to describe a general approach to the legal cause issue, but will turn into a separate and independent hurdle that the plaintiff will have to overcome in addition to the standard elements of a claim of negligence. So too, has there been great difficulty and disparity in the courts' definition of 'substantial factor.' " The but-for test may lead to more neutral, factual judgments about actual cause. Is substantial factor a test or measure of anything at all?

5.   **Trivial contributions.** The Third Restatement provides that "when an actor's negligent conduct constitutes only a trivial contribution to a causal set that is a factual cause of harm," the harm is not considered within the scope of liability. RESTATEMENT (THIRD) OF TORTS: LIABILITY FOR PHYSICAL AND EMOTIONAL HARM § 36 (2010). The example the Restatement provides is of a person exposed to asbestos for 40 years from one source and for a single day from another. Dean Prosser gave the illustration of a match thrown into a forest fire. These illustrations seem easy in the extreme. But what about exposure to one asbestos source for 40 years and to another for two years? Can you see why the Restatement now treats this issue as one of policy under scope of liability rather than as an issue of factual cause?

NOTE: INCREASED RISK SHOWING CAUSATION

Suppose the defendant negligently constructs stairs that are too steep and negligently fails to light them. The plaintiff falls down them in the dark and is injured. Can you say the condition of the premises was a cause of the plaintiff's harm? After all, the plaintiff might fall for many reasons. Many cases are like this, particularly when the defendant *fails* to provide a safety measure. The defendant negligently fails to have a lifeguard on duty at a motel. A child drowns. Would a lifeguard have saved the child? In many cases like this, courts permit juries to find that the defendant's negligent act or omission was a factual cause of the plaintiff's harm.

Can we say those cases represent a principle or rule that when the defendant negligently creates a risk of the very harm that befell the plaintiff, causation is established, or at least that an inference of causation is permitted? In *Zuchowicz v. United States,* 140 F.3d 381, 390–91 (2d Cir. 1998), Judge Calabresi, a most eminent torts scholar, referring to opinions of Cardozo and Traynor, said:

> [T]hey stated that: if (a) a negligent act was deemed wrongful *because* that act increased the chances that a particular type of accident would occur, and (b) a mishap of that very sort did happen, this was enough to support a finding by the trier of fact that the negligent behavior caused the harm. Where such a strong causal link exists, it is up to the negligent party to bring in evidence denying *but for* cause and suggesting that in the actual case the wrongful conduct had not been a substantial factor.

Judge Calabresi further refined this conception in *Gemmink v. Jay Peak Inc.,* 807 F.3d 46 (2d Cir. 2015) ("[T]he greater the risk that the defendant's conduct will result in the harm the plaintiff suffered, the more likely that a jury will be allowed to find that such conduct was the cause of that harm."), and *Estate of Gustafson ex rel. Reginella v. Target Corp.,* 819 F.3d 673 (2d Cir. 2016) (under New York law, where there is no "direct evidence of the likelihood of causation," the first question is whether the defendant's negligence "increase[d] the chances of plaintiff's injury, and by how much?").

In some toxic-tort cases, evidence of exposure has been used to create an inference of causation. *Rowhouses, Inc. v. Smith,* 133 A.3d 1054 (Md. 2016) (childhood exposure to lead-based paint in apartment unit). In *John Crane, Inc. v. Jones,* 604 S.E.2d 822 (Ga. 2004), in which the plaintiff contracted mesothelioma because of occupational exposure to asbestos dust, to show factual cause "plaintiff must identify the asbestos-containing product of a particular defendant and show that [he] worked in proximity to [use of that product]." Where the plaintiff cannot prove exposure to the defendant's particular asbestos-containing product, however, the case will be lost on factual cause grounds. *See Grant v. Foster Wheeler, LLC,* 140 A.3d 1242 (Me. 2016) (evidence "too speculative" to support a finding that the plaintiff encountered asbestos fibers from defendant's product while working as a ship-factory cleaner decades ago).

E. PROOF: WHAT HARM WAS CAUSED?

Liability for negligence attaches only when factual cause links the defendant's negligence to the plaintiff's injury. Consequently, how we define the harm to the plaintiff and the negligence of the defendant can be important parts of the causation question.

In *Dillon v. Twin State Gas & Electric Co.*, 163 A. 111 (N.H. 1932), the defendant's negligence in failing to insulate a wire caused a 14-year-old boy to be electrocuted just as he slipped off of a bridge and was about to fall into a river in which he would have been killed or seriously injured. Did the electrocution cause the loss of the boy's whole life, or simply the loss of a few additional minutes of it?

SUMMERS V. TICE

199 P.2d 1 (Cal. 1948)

CARTER, JUSTICE.

Each of the two defendants appeals from a judgment against them in an action for personal injuries. Pursuant to stipulation the appeals have been consolidated.

Plaintiff's action was against both defendants for an injury to his right eye and face as the result of being struck by bird shot discharged from a shotgun. The case was tried by the court without a jury and the court found that on November 20, 1945, plaintiff and the two defendants were hunting quail on the open range. Each of the defendants was armed with a 12 gauge shotgun loaded with shells containing 7 1/2 size shot.... The view of defendants with reference to plaintiff was unobstructed and they knew his location. Defendant Tice flushed a quail which rose in flight to a ten foot elevation and flew between plaintiff and defendants. Both defendants shot at the quail, shooting in plaintiff's direction. At that time defendants were 75 yards from plaintiff. One shot struck plaintiff in his eye and another in his upper lip. Finally it was found by the court that as the direct result of the shooting by defendants the shots struck plaintiff as above mentioned and that defendants were negligent in so shooting and plaintiff was not contributorily negligent....

The one shot that entered plaintiff's eye was the major factor in assessing damages and that shot could not have come from the gun of both defendants. It was from one or the other only.

It has been held that where a group of persons are on a hunting party, or otherwise engaged in the use of firearms, and two of them are negligent in firing in the direction of a third person who is injured thereby, both of those so firing are liable for the injury suffered by the third person, although the negligence of only one of them could have caused the injury. Both drivers have been held liable for the negligence of one where they engaged in a racing contest causing an injury to a third person. These cases speak of the action of defendants as being in concert as the ground of decision, yet it would seem they are straining that concept and the more reasonable basis appears in Oliver v. Miles, supra. There two persons were hunting together. Both shot at some partridges and in so doing shot across the highway injuring plaintiff who was traveling on it. The court stated they were acting in concert and thus both were liable. The court then stated: "We think that . . . each is liable for the resulting injury to the boy, although no one can say definitely who actually shot him. *To hold otherwise would be to exonerate both from liability, although each was negligent, and the injury resulted from such negligence.*" . . .

When we consider the relative position of the parties and the results that would flow if plaintiff was required to pin the injury on one of the defendants only, a requirement that the burden of proof on that subject be shifted to defendants becomes manifest. They are both wrongdoers negligent toward plaintiff. They brought about a situation where the negligence of one of them injured the plaintiff, hence it should rest with them each to absolve himself if he can. The injured party has been placed by defendants in the unfair position of pointing to which defendant caused the harm. If one can escape the other may also and plaintiff is remediless. Ordinarily defendants are in a far better position to offer evidence to determine what one caused the injury. . . .

Cases are cited for the proposition that where two or more tortfeasors acting independently of each other cause an injury to plaintiff, they are not joint tortfeasors and plaintiff must establish the portion of the damage caused by each, even though it is impossible to prove the portion of the injury caused by each. In view of the foregoing discussion it is apparent that defendants in cases like the present one may be treated as liable on the same basis as joint tortfeasors, and hence the last cited cases are distinguishable inasmuch as they involve independent tortfeasors.

In addition to that, however, it should be pointed out that the same reasons of policy and justice [which] shift the burden to each of defendants to absolve himself if he can—relieving the wronged person of the duty of apportioning the injury to a particular defendant—apply here where we are concerned with whether plaintiff is required to supply evidence for the apportionment of damages. If defendants are independent tortfeasors and thus each liable for the damage caused by him alone, and, at least, where the matter of apportionment is incapable of proof, the innocent wronged party should not be deprived of his right to redress. The wrongdoers should be left to work out between themselves any apportionment. Some of the cited cases refer to the difficulty of apportioning the burden of damages between the independent tortfeasors, and say that where factually a correct division cannot be made, the trier of fact may make it the best it can, which would be more or less a guess, stressing the factor that the wrongdoers are not in a position to complain of uncertainty. . . .

The judgment is Affirmed.

Holdings:— judgment of Lower Court was affirmed because D failed to meet their burden of proving who was responsible for P's injury; therefore because each acts and negligent each was responsible to P for damages from injuries sustained by P

NOTES

1. **The harm caused.** One negligent tortfeasor in *Summers* caused the harm to the plaintiff's eye. What harm did the other tortfeasor's negligence cause? In evidentiary terms, was the plaintiff worse off because there were two negligent defendants rather than one? In a recent hunting case, a hunter shot at a deer. Another member of his hunting party then shot in the same direction and injured a person from another group. Even though the first hunter's bullet did not hit the injured plaintiff, the court found that the first hunter also could be liable to the plaintiff if (1) his shooting was negligent and (2) it was reasonably foreseeable that shooting in that direction would encourage his companion to shoot that way negligently too. *See Hellums v. Raber,* 853 N.E.2d 143 (Ind. Ct. App. 2006).

2. **Alternative causation.** In the alternative-cause cases, both tortfeasors are negligent, but only one of them has caused the plaintiff's harm. The difficulty is that it is impossible to determine which one is the cause. The doctrine was originally rooted in joint and several liability, but has been adopted even in jurisdictions that have adopted several liability. *See Salica v. Tucson Heart Hosp.–Carondelet, L.L.C.,* 231 P.3d 946 (Ariz. Ct. App. 2010) (citing *Summers* with approval and holding that to avoid the " 'unfairness of denying the injured person redress simply because he cannot prove how much damage each [tortfeasor] did, when it is certain that between them they did all,' tortfeasors are left to apportion damages among themselves when causation is potentially indeterminable"). Indeed, the argument for allowing the alternative causation rule may be stronger when the effect of the rule is not to assign full liability to the negligent defendant but instead to allow the negligent defendant who potentially has a causal role to be counted as one defendant in the broader apportionment. 1 DOBBS, HAYDEN & BUBLICK, THE LAW OF TORTS § 193 (2d ed. 2011).

3. **Shifting the burden of proof on causation.** A and B, each acting negligently, separately cause injury to the plaintiff. As a practical matter, the plaintiff cannot show how much of the injury was caused by A and how much by B. Under traditional rules, A and B are jointly and severally liable. Does this work when a large number of defendants contribute to harm? Suppose the plaintiff was exposed at work to various identified products of 55 different defendants, that toxins from these products entered his body, and "that each toxin that entered his body was a substantial factor in bringing about, prolonging, or aggravating" cancer. Would such facts sufficiently show causation? *See Bockrath v. Aldrich Chem. Co., Inc.,* 980 P.2d 398 (Cal. 1999). If your answer is "yes," what exactly is left to be decided in the case, if anything?

4. **The Restatement view.** Under the RESTATEMENT (THIRD) OF TORTS: LIABILITY FOR PHYSICAL AND EMOTIONAL HARM § 28 (2010), "When the plaintiff sues all of multiple actors and proves that each engaged in tortious conduct that exposed the plaintiff to a risk of harm and that the tortious conduct of one or more of them caused the plaintiff's harm but the plaintiff cannot reasonably be expected to prove which actor caused the harm, the burden of proof, including both production and persuasion, on factual cause is shifted to the defendants."

5. **Harm by one of seven.** In *State v. CTL Distribution, Inc.,* 715 So.2d 262 (Fla. Dist. Ct. App. 1998), one or more truckers spilled a hazardous substance when making deliveries of that substance at a certain business. The state environmental agency sued the seven truckers who delivered the substance. It proved that one of them, CTL, had once spilled the substance and argued that *Summers v. Tice* would authorize liability for all seven. How would you rule on causation if you were the judge? Under the Restatement, might the case be different if the state could prove that all seven had spilled a hazardous substance, only one of which caused the harm?

MOHR V. GRANTHAM

262 P.3d 490 (Wash. 2011)

OWENS, J. . . .

[O]n the afternoon of August 31, 2004, Mrs. Mohr suffered a hypoglycemic event that caused her to run her car into a utility pole at approximately 45 m.p.h. She was taken by ambulance to the emergency room at Kadlec Medical Center (KMC). Having visible lacerations on her face from the car accident, Mrs. Mohr was given a neurological assessment upon arrival, at around 4:00 p.m., and a computerized tomography (CT) scan of her brain about an hour later. These tests were overseen or authorized by Dr. Dale Grantham, who was charged with Mrs. Mohr's care at KMC on August 31. The results were normal.

Following those neurological tests, however, Mrs. Mohr reported and was observed to have neurological symptoms, including being wobbly on her feet and having severe pain after being administered pain medication. Dr. Grantham informed one of Mrs. Mohr's physician sons, Dr. Brandt Mohr, by phone that he would carry out another neurological assessment before discharging her. He did not. Instead, he prescribed a narcotic, Darvocet, and sent Mrs. Mohr home with her husband. At that point, Mrs. Mohr could not walk herself to or from the car and had to be carried to bed by her husband when they arrived home. The Mohrs were not given discharge instructions that included specific information about head injuries.

Mrs. Mohr was again transported to KMC by ambulance just after 7:00 a.m. on September 1, 2004. . . . However, Dr. Dawson [the attending physician that morning] did not provide any anticoagulant or antithrombotic treatment or therapy. . . .

Before the transfer [to the intermediate care unit at 11:30 a.m.], Mrs. Mohr's two physician sons had arrived at KMC to be by her side. They tried to get both Dr. Dawson and then, after her transfer, Dr. Watson to order a CT angiogram. A CT angiogram was not done until 2:30 p.m., after the Mohr sons had Dr. Watson repeatedly paged. Then, although the results were available at 3:27 p.m., Dr. Watson was not located or informed until 4:50 p.m. that the CT angiogram showed a dissected carotid artery. He still did not order anyone to administer anticoagulant therapy, antiplatelet agents, or any other treatment. Dr. Watson had prescribed aspirin around 2:00 p.m. but did not order its immediate administration.

Mrs. Mohr's sons finally arranged a transfer and transport to Harborview Medical Center. . . . Only shortly before her transport at 6:00 p.m. on September 1, 2004, was Mrs. Mohr finally given aspirin, though it had to be administered in suppository form because, by then, she could no longer swallow.

Mrs. Mohr is now permanently brain damaged; a quarter to a third of her brain tissue was destroyed. In particular, the portions of her brain that were damaged are involved with motor control, sensation, and spatial reasoning.

Mrs. Mohr and her husband filed suit, claiming that Mrs. Mohr received negligent treatment, far below the recognized standard of care. They argue that the doctors' negligence substantially diminished her chance of recovery and that, with nonnegligent care, her disability could have been lessened or altogether avoided. The Mohrs' claim relies, at least in part, on a medical malpractice cause of action for the loss of a chance. In support of their claim, the Mohrs presented the family's testimony, including her two sons who are doctors, and the testimony of two other doctors, Kyra Becker and A. Basil Harris. The testimony included expert opinions that the treatment Mrs. Mohr received violated standards of care and that, had Mrs. Mohr received nonnegligent treatment at various points between August 31 and September 1, 2004, she would have had a 50 to 60 percent chance of a better outcome. The better outcome would have been no disability or, at least, significantly less disability.

On April 16, 2009, the Benton County Superior Court granted summary judgment for the defendants on the basis that the Mohrs did not show "but for" causation. . . . The Mohrs appealed, and the Court of Appeals certified the case for our review. . . .

In the medical malpractice context, is there a cause of action for a lost chance of a better outcome? . . .

Whether there is a cause of action for a lost chance of a better outcome in the medical malpractice context is a question of law, which we review de novo. . . .

[In our opinion in *Herskovits*, in which an allegedly negligent failure to diagnose lung cancer likely diminished the plaintiff's chance of long-term survival from 39 percent to 25 percent, we found that Herskovits's lost chance was actionable. In *Herskovits*,] the lead opinion, signed by two justices, and the concurring opinion, which garnered a plurality, agreed on the fundamental bases for recognizing a cause of action for the loss of a chance. The lead opinion explained:

> To decide otherwise would be a blanket release from liability for doctors and hospitals any time there was less than a 50 percent chance of survival, regardless of how flagrant the negligence.

The plurality similarly noted that traditional all-or-nothing causation in lost chance cases " 'subverts the deterrence objectives of tort law.' " Both opinions found that "the loss of a less than even chance is a loss worthy of redress." With emphasis, the lead opinion agreed, stating that " '[*n*]*o matter how small that chance may have been—and its magnitude cannot be ascertained—no one can say that the chance of prolonging one's life or decreasing suffering is valueless.*' "

> The lead and plurality opinions split over *how,* not whether, to recognize a cause of action. . . . [T]he lead opinion held that the appropriate framework for considering a lost chance claim was with a "substantial factor" theory of causation. . . .

The "substantial factor test" is an exception to the general rule of proving but for causation and requires that a plaintiff prove that the defendant's alleged act or omission was a substantial factor in causing the plaintiff's injury, even if the injury could have occurred anyway.

Rather than looking to the causation element, the plurality opinion in *Herskovits* focused instead on the nature of the injury. . . . The plurality found it more analytically sound to conceive of the injury as the lost chance. . . .

[T]he *Herskovits* majority's recognition of a cause of action in a survival action has remained intact since its adoption. . . . Washington courts have, however, generally declined to extend *Herskovits* to other negligence claims [including legal malpractice, contaminated food claims, and asbestos exposure]. Such limitation is common: "[T]he courts that have accepted lost opportunity as cognizable harm have almost universally limited its recognition to medical-malpractice cases." RESTATEMENT (THIRD) OF TORTS: LIABILITY FOR PHYSICAL AND EMOTIONAL HARM § 26 cmt. n at 356–57 (2010). . . . Since *Herskovits,* the majority of states that have considered the lost chance doctrine have adopted it, although with varying rationales. Several states have rejected the doctrine. . . .

We find no *persuasive* rationale to distinguish *Herskovits* from a medical malpractice claim where the facts involve a loss of chance of avoiding or minimizing permanent disability rather than death. . . . [T]he same underlying principles of deterring negligence and compensating for injury apply. . . .

Now nearly 30 years since *Herskovits* was decided, history assures us that *Herskovits* did not upend the world of torts in Washington, as demonstrated by the few cases relying on *Herskovits* that have been heard by Washington appellate courts.

We hold that *Herskovits* applies to lost chance claims where the ultimate harm is some serious injury short of death. We also formally adopt the reasoning of the *Herskovits* plurality. Under this formulation, a plaintiff bears the burden to prove duty, breach, and that such breach of duty proximately caused a loss of chance of a better outcome. This reasoning of the *Herskovits* plurality has largely withstood many of the concerns about the doctrine, particularly because it does not prescribe the specific manner of proving causation in lost chance cases. Rather, it relies on established tort theories of causation, without applying a particular causation test to *all* lost chance cases. Instead, the loss of a chance is the compensable injury. . . .

In *Herskovits,* both the lead and concurring opinions discussed limiting damages. This is a common approach in lost chance cases, responsive in part to the criticism of holding individuals or organizations liable on the basis of uncertain probabilities. RESTATEMENT (THIRD) OF TORTS: LIABILITY FOR PHYSICAL AND EMOTIONAL HARM § 26 cmt. n at 356 ("Rather than full damages for the adverse outcome, the plaintiff is only compensated for the lost opportunity. The lost opportunity may be thought of as the adverse outcome discounted by the difference between the ex ante probability of the outcome in light of the defendant's negligence and the probability of the outcome absent the defendant's negligence."). Treating the loss of a chance as the cognizable injury "permits plaintiffs to recover for the loss of an opportunity for a better outcome, an interest that we agree should be compensable, while providing for the proper valuation of such an interest." *Lord v. Lovett,* 146 N.H. 232, 236, 770 A.2d 1103 (2001). In particular, the *Herskovits* plurality adopted a proportional damages approach, holding that, if the loss was a 40 percent chance of survival, the plaintiff could recover only 40 percent of what would be compensable under the ultimate harm of death or disability (i.e., 40 percent of traditional tort recovery), such as lost earnings. This percentage of loss is a question of fact for the jury and will relate to the scientific measures available, likely as presented through experts. Where appropriate, it may otherwise be discounted for

[handwritten margin note: Don't collect for full damages for a substantial cause but should be compensated in proportion to the loss]

margins of error to further reflect the uncertainty of outcome even with a nonnegligent standard of care] . . .

Interpreting the facts in the light most favorable to the Mohrs, they have made a prima facie case under the lost chance doctrine. . . . [W]e reverse the order of summary judgment and remand to the trial court for further proceedings.

MADSEN, C.J. (dissenting). . . .

It is a fundamental principle that in a medical malpractice action the plaintiff must prove causation of the plaintiff's actual physical (or mental) injury before tort liability will be imposed. To avoid the difficulty posed by this requirement, the majority recognizes a cause of action for which the plaintiff does not have to prove that "but for" the physician's negligence, the injury would not have occurred. . . . The majority simply redefines the injury as the lost chance. With this semantic leap—essentially a fiction—the causation problem is fixed.

But in reality the problem remains. No matter how the lost chance cause of action is characterized, the plaintiff is freed of the requirement of proving causation because, no matter how the action is described, the end result is that liability is imposed based on *possibilities* and not on *probabilities*. . . .

As the [District Court of Alaska] in *Crosby* correctly responded, "[i]f a plaintiff's chance of recovery was reduced from 20 percent to 10 percent, then permitting recovery for that 10 percent loss enables a plaintiff to recover damages even when the plaintiff's actual physical injury was *not* more likely than not caused by a defendant's alleged negligence." . . .

The "deterrence" justification identified by the majority is in fact unrelated to preventing harm-causing negligence. As Benjamin Cardozo famously explained long ago, " 'negligence in the air' " is not actionable. Physicians, and indeed individuals involved in thousands of actions, are negligent every day without legal consequence because, despite the involvement or presence of others, their acts *do not actually cause harm* to the other persons.

The Texas Supreme Court aptly observed, when it "reject[ed] the notion that the enhanced deterrence of the loss of chance approach might be so valuable as to justify scrapping [the] traditional concepts of causation," that *"[i]f deterrence were the sole value to be served by tort law, we could dispense with the notion of causation altogether and award damages on the basis of negligence alone."* . . .

Moreover, the goal of compensation is not served, either, because there is no way to prove a physician's acts or omissions in fact caused the actual physical harm, rather than the actual harm resulting from the preexisting condition. . . .

The ramifications of the majority's opinion are unknown but potentially far-reaching. The majority opinion has the potential to alter health care in this state, as physicians would have to contemplate whether to provide an unprecedented level of care to avoid liability for even a slightly diminished *chance* of a better outcome. As noted, even a small percentage of chance can equal a substantial award. At the same time, it is no secret that health care insurance coverage is already strained, for those who even have such insurance, and adopting this doctrine cannot help but impact the nature and extent of insurance reimbursement for potential tests and treatments ordered as an eventual result of the majority's decision to expand liability to an unprecedented degree in this state.

All of these matters are public policy considerations for the legislature. . . .

NOTES

1.   **Choosing a rule.** The *Mohr* majority and dissent present three different approaches that a court might take in deciding lost opportunity claims. What are the two approaches addressed by the majority? What is the approach suggested by the dissent? These approaches were also discussed in *Lord v. Lovett*, 770 A.2d 1103 (N.H. 2001), a lost opportunity case cited by the *Mohr* court and involving negligent misdiagnosis of a spinal cord injury. What are the merits of the different approaches?

2.   **The traditional rule.** Remember that the plaintiff must prove each element of her case by a preponderance of the evidence. This means the "greater weight" of the evidence—more likely than not. Translated into numbers, the traditional rule would require plaintiff to persuade the trier that the probabilities are greater than 50% that each element is established. Some courts insist that this rule should then preclude recovery when a patient dies after a physician's misdiagnosis increases the patient's chance of death when the patient had only a 50–50 chance of living anyway. *E.g., Fennell v. Maryland Hosp. Ctr., Inc.*, 580 A.2d 206 (Md. 1990). In a few states, legislatures have selected the traditional rule, abrogating court decisions to the contrary. *See* MICH. COMP. LAWS § 600.2912a(2) ("In an action alleging medical malpractice, the plaintiff cannot recover for loss of an opportunity to survive or an opportunity to achieve a better result unless the opportunity was greater than 50%"); S.D. CODIFIED LAWS § 20–9–1.1.

3.   **Relaxed causation tests.** Some courts, either by their words or deeds, have relaxed the plaintiff's burden of proof of causation in cases when a physician causes the loss of a chance of 50% or less. The causation requirement is relaxed by permitting plaintiffs to submit their cases to the jury upon demonstrating that the increased risk created by defendant's negligence was a substantial factor or that the defendant's conduct "destroyed a substantial possibility" of achieving a more favorable outcome. In this group, courts permit juries to award full damages, as if the plaintiff had proved causation by a

[handwritten annotation:] Rule of Law

In Washington a P. asserting a clm for medical negligence may show in place of the "but for" causation requirement that the d's action was a substantial factor in causing the p's injury preponderance of the evidence. *See, e.g., Hamil v. Bashline*, 392 A.2d 1280 (Pa. 1978).

4. **Duty-to-try analysis.** A similar but more striking approach appeared in *Gardner v. National Bulk Carriers, Inc.*, 310 F.2d 284 (4th Cir. 1962). Gardner, a seaman on board a ship at sea, was called to stand watch at 11:30, but he could not be found. He had last been seen five or six hours earlier. The ship notified the Coast Guard but did not attempt to return to those areas of the sea where, at any time during the five hours, he might have fallen overboard. In a suit for Gardner's death, the defendant argued that factual cause had not been shown, since a search probably could not have found a man who had gone overboard hours earlier. But the Fourth Circuit held that the duty of the captain was to make every reasonable effort. "It was less than a duty to rescue him, but it was a positive duty to make a sincere attempt at rescue. . . . [C]ausation is proved if the master's omission destroys the reasonable possibility of rescue." The court apparently envisioned full liability for the seaman's death.

5. **Quantified value-of-the-chance approach.** Still another approach is to say that causal rules are not changed. Instead, the lost opportunity for a better outcome is *itself* the injury for which the negligently injured person may recover. *See Alexander v. Scheid*, 726 N.E.2d 272 (Ind. 2000) (in case involving delay in cancer diagnosis; "We think that loss of chance is better understood as a description of the injury. . . . If a plaintiff seeks recovery specifically for what the plaintiff alleges the doctor to have caused, i.e., a decrease in the patient's probability of recovery, rather than for the ultimate outcome, causation is no longer debatable. Rather, the problem becomes one of identification and valuation or quantification of that injury."). Under this approach, if the *chance* of survival was 40% and the defendant's negligence more likely than not eliminated that *chance*, then the defendant would be liable for the loss he has caused—the chance. In damages, this is presumably 40% of the damages for which the defendant would be liable if he caused death. A number of courts, as in *Mohr*, have favored this approach, which appears to be gaining some momentum. *See, e.g., Dickhoff ex rel. Dickhoff v. Green*, 836 N.W.2d 321 (Minn. 2013) ("[W]e agree with those courts that treat the reduction of a patient's chance of recovery or survival as a distinct injury.").

6. **What *must* be proved by a preponderance of the evidence under quantified approach.** Under the lost chance rule, are there some things that still *must* be proved by a preponderance of the evidence, that is, under a more-likely-than-not standard? *See Almonte v. Kurl*, 46 A.3d 1 (R.I. 2012) (although court might consider loss of chance under an appropriate factual scenario, plaintiff had not presented any expert testimony that emergency room doctor's negligence caused patient's suicide within 36 hours of discharge or caused a loss of a chance for a better outcome). What if the plaintiff proved that there was a 40% chance that the patient had a 30% chance? *See Alphonse v. Acadian Ambulance Servs., Inc.*, 844 So.2d 294 (La. Ct. App. 2003); *Alberts v. Schultz*, 975 P.2d 1279 (N.M. 1999). Some courts have

concluded, particularly in the loss of chance context, that the loss must be "substantial" before it is compensable. However, others have rejected this view. In *Alexander v. Schied,* 726 N.E.2d 272 (Ind. 2000), the court wrote, "Because we measure damages by probabilizing the injury, the likelihood that plaintiffs will bring claims for trivial reductions in chance of recovery seems small. If, in the future, we face a volume of insignificant claims, perhaps such a rule will become necessary. For now, we are content to rely on basic economics to deter resort to the courts to redress remote probabilities or insubstantial diminutions in the likelihood of recovery." What are the economics that would deter claims for trivial reductions?

7. **Reducing damages to reflect probability where causation is more likely than not.** "If the patient in our example was entitled to 25 percent of his full damages because he had only a 25 percent chance of survival, he should be entitled to 75 percent of his damages if he had a 75 percent chance of survival—not 100 percent of his damages on the theory that by establishing a 75 percent chance he proved injury by a preponderance of the evidence. He proves injury in both cases, but in both cases the injury is merely probabilistic and must be discounted accordingly." *Doll v. Brown,* 75 F.3d 1200, 1206 (7th Cir. 1996) (Posner, J.). *See also* John Makdisi, *Proportional Liability: A Comprehensive Rule to Apportion Tort Damages Based Probability*, 67 N.C. L. REV. 1063 (1989) (supporting general use of lost chance or probabilistic causation). How would this change the "normal" rules of causation? How would juries determine these percentages? Some courts have rejected the idea that a probabilistic approach should be used where the injury is more probable than not. *See Kivland v. Columbia Orthopaedic Group, LLP*, 331 S.W.3d 299 (Mo. 2011) (where the plaintiff can prove that it is more likely than not that the defendant's negligent medical care caused the patient's death, the recovery should be based on the state's wrongful death statute and "loss of chance" has no application at all).

8. **Judicial acceptance of loss of chance.** The value-of-the-chance theory has now gained substantial support, primarily as a result of a 1981 article, Joseph H. King, Jr., *Causation, Valuation and Chance in Personal Injury Torts*, 90 YALE L. J. 1353 (1981).

Evaluating the Approaches

9. **Deterrence.** Which rule (if any) seems to provide the most appropriate deterrence? Take a look at the hypothetical facts and table below.

Three Cancer Patients

Each patient has a 1/3 or 33.33% chance of survival if properly treated. The defendant negligently treats each one and all three die. In each case, damages for wrongful death would have been $100,000 if the negligence is treated as a cause of the harm. We cannot in fact know which one would have lived had proper treatment been provided, but the overwhelming likelihood is that one would have lived. An omniscient trier of fact would know which one (line four).

	Recovery	Total Liability
Traditional rule	$0.0	$0.0
Relaxed causation	$100,000 each	$300,000
Lost chance	$33,333.33 each	$100,000
Omniscient trier	$100,000 to one estate	$100,000

10. **Lost chance liability in other contexts?** " 'Loss of a chance' is a novel theory of causation commonly used by courts in the United States in medical misdiagnosis cases. Yet the theory has a vastly broader potential application than this. In fact, it could be applied in virtually every case of questionable causation." David A. Fischer, *Tort Recovery for Loss of a Chance,* 36 WAKE FOREST L. REV. 605 (2001). Should the doctrine apply outside medical malpractice cases? Professor Fischer explores the question and concludes that case-by-case policy analysis will be required. You might think that courts could appropriately limit the lost chance recovery to cases in which the defendant owed a duty to maximize the plaintiff's chances. That would certainly cover physicians who are hired for the very purpose of maximizing chances. Would the reasoning extend to other professionals like attorneys? So far, as mentioned in *Mohr,* courts have applied value of the chance reasoning mainly to physician-patient cases. *See Hardy v. Southwestern Bell Tel. Co.,* 910 P.2d 1024 (Okla. 1996) (refusing to extend loss-of-chance theory "beyond the established boundary of medical malpractice").

DILLON V. EVANSTON HOSPITAL, 771 N.E.2d 357 (Ill. 2002). A catheter was inserted into the plaintiff's body in the course of a medical procedure. As planned, it was removed, except that a portion broke off and remained in her body. Neither her doctor nor the hospital so advised her. Much later, she discovered that the remaining portion had worked its way in two pieces into her heart, one part floating freely in the heart, the other with its tip embedded in the wall of the right ventricle. In the plaintiff's suit against doctor and hospital, the jury found for the plaintiff and awarded damages for past and future pain and suffering and also damages for increased risk of future harm. *Held*, judgment for plaintiff on increased risk is permissible, but the case is reversed for more adequate instruction. "[T]heories of lost chance of recovery and increased risk of future injury have similar theoretical underpinnings." However, the trial judge's instruction on the increased risk damages requires reversal because it failed to require (a) evidence of increased risk of future harm and (b) damages proportioned to the probability that the risks of future harm would materialize.

NOTE

Present injury. In an Illinois case subsequent to *Dillon*, the defendant negligently caused a car accident with a pregnant woman. The woman required x-rays and medication which doctors told her could cause disabilities in the fetus. Because of these risks and risks to her own health from continuing the pregnancy—a pelvic bone fracture which could not be fixed during a pregnancy—she elected to terminate the pregnancy. The Illinois Supreme Court denied recovery under its wrongful death act on the ground that the fetus' increased risk of future harm was not a present injury for which the fetus could have brought an action for damages against the defendant. The court distinguished *Dillon* on the ground that the catheter embedded in plaintiff's heart was a present injury. *See Williams v. Manchester*, 888 N.E.2d 1 (Ill. 2008). If the woman would have continued the pregnancy absent the accident, wasn't the defendant's negligence a cause of the fetus' death?

AN END NOTE: LIABILITY WITHOUT CAUSATION?

From a moral or normative point of view, would it be wrong to hold a defendant liable when he has committed negligent acts but, fortuitously, has not caused harm? From the point of view of deterring unsafe conduct, would liability without causation be a good idea? *See* Margaret A. Berger, *Eliminating General Causation: Notes Towards a New Theory of Justice and Toxic Torts*, 97 COLUM. L. REV. 2117 (1997). Consider this possible rule for liability without proof of causation: The defendant is liable without proof that his conduct caused legal harm if, but only if

(1) the defendant has acted negligently; and

(2) the negligence created an identifiable risk; and

(3) the plaintiff was one of the persons subjected to that risk; and

(4) the plaintiff actually suffered harm of the kind risked by the defendant.

REFERENCES: DOBBS, HAYDEN & BUBLICK, HORNBOOK ON TORTS §§ 14.1–14.11 (2d ed. 2016); 1 DOBBS, HAYDEN & BUBLICK, THE LAW OF TORTS §§ 183–197 (2d ed. 2011); David W. Robertson, *The Common Sense of Cause in Fact*, 75 TEX. L. REV. 1765, 1780 (1997); Symposium, *Causation in the Law of Torts*, 63 CHI–KENT L. REV. 397 (1987).

CHAPTER 8

SCOPE OF LIABILITY (PROXIMATE CAUSE)

■ ■ ■

§ 1. THE PRINCIPLE: SCOPE OF RISK

The final element that a plaintiff must prove in a negligence case is that her harm fell within the scope of defendant's liability, in other words, that the harm resulted from the risks that made the defendant's conduct negligent in the first place. In more traditional language, the scope-of-liability concept has been termed "proximate cause" or "legal cause." This is an issue of fact for the jury. Scope-of-liability determinations involve case-specific inquiries into whether the defendant should be held legally responsible to the plaintiff. Even when the defendant was negligent and in fact caused the harm to the plaintiff, the defendant is not liable if the actual harm was not within the scope of the risk the defendant created.

Why would it be either just or good policy to hold that a defendant is not liable for harm he has, in fact, negligently caused? Suppose that the defendant is Dr. Dayden, a surgeon who performed a vasectomy operation upon Mr. Fallow some years ago. Because the vasectomy was negligently performed, Mr. Fallow sired a child, William. William, when he reached the age of six, set fire to the plaintiff's garage. The plaintiff has now sued William, Mr. Fallow, and Dr. Dayden. The plaintiff can show that Dr. Dayden negligently performed the vasectomy and that his negligence in fact was one of the causes of William's conception and birth. The plaintiff can also show that since his garage would not have been burned but for William's existence, Dr. Dayden's negligence in the vasectomy operation was a cause in fact of that harm.

Probably all lawyers would agree that the surgeon is not liable for the burning of the garage. The reasons for this outcome may be expressed in different ways. Many judicial opinions are likely to emphasize "causation," the attenuated causal link between the surgeon's negligence and the harm ultimately done by William. Yet while causation is often the conventional locution, the underlying idea seems to be more precise and more principled: Liability for negligence is liability for the unreasonable risks the defendant created, not for reasonable risks or for those that were unforeseeable. We don't think a vasectomy is negligently performed because it might cause a fire, so the fire loss was outside the risks that led us to think Dr. Dayden was negligent.

However judges express themselves on scope-of-liability issues, ask yourself in each case whether the reason for relieving the defendant of liability was merely one of practicality or policy. Or is the reason a moral one, grounded in justice, for limiting an actor's liability to harms that result from unreasonable risks?

THOMPSON V. KACZINSKI

774 N.W.2d 829 (Iowa 2009)

HECHT, JUSTICE.

James Kaczinski and Michelle Lockwood resided in rural Madison County, near Earlham, on property abutting a gravel road. During the late summer of 2006, they disassembled a trampoline and placed its component parts on their yard approximately thirty-eight feet from the road. Intending to dispose of them at a later time, Kaczinski and Lockwood did not secure the parts in place. A few weeks later, on the night of September 16 and morning of September 17, 2006, a severe thunderstorm moved through the Earlham area. Wind gusts from the storm displaced the top of the trampoline from the yard to the surface of the road.

Later that morning, while driving from one church to another where he served as a pastor, Charles Thompson approached the defendants' property. When he swerved to avoid the obstruction on the road, Thompson lost control of his vehicle. His car entered the ditch and rolled several times. Kaczinski and Lockwood were awakened by Thompson's screams at about 9:40 a.m., shortly after the accident. When they went outside to investigate, they discovered the top of their trampoline lying on the roadway. Lockwood dragged the object back into the yard while Kaczinski assisted Thompson.

Thompson and his wife filed suit, alleging Kaczinski and Lockwood breached statutory and common law duties by negligently allowing the trampoline to obstruct the roadway. Kaczinski and Lockwood moved for summary judgment, contending they owed no duty under the circumstances because the risk of the trampoline's displacement from their yard to the surface of the road was not foreseeable. The district court granted the motion, concluding Kaczinski and Lockwood breached no duty and the damages claimed by the plaintiffs were not proximately caused by the defendants' negligence. The Thompsons appealed. We transferred the case to the court of appeals, which affirmed the district court's ruling. We granted the Thompsons' application for further review. . . .

[Defendant had no statutory duty to avoid obstructing a highway right-of-way because that duty applied only to an intentional obstruction. However, defendants did owe a common law duty of reasonable care. We turn next to the issue of causation, raised by the district court.]

We have held causation has two components: cause in fact and legal cause. The decisions of this court have established it is the plaintiff's burden to prove both cause in fact and legal (proximate) cause. The latter component requires a policy determination of whether "the policy of the law must require the defendant to be *legally responsible* for the injury." . . .

"Tort law does not impose liability on an actor for all harm factually caused by the actor's tortious conduct." Restatement (Third) ch. 6 Special Note on Proximate Cause. . . . [T]he drafters of the Restatement (Third) have clarified the essential role of policy considerations in the determination of the scope of liability. "An actor's liability is limited to those physical harms that result from the risks that made the actor's conduct tortious." *Id.* § 29. This principle, referred to as the "risk standard," is intended to prevent the unjustified imposition of liability by "confining liability's scope to the reasons for holding the actor liable in the first place." As an example of the standard's application, the drafters provide an illustration of a hunter returning from the field and handing his loaded shotgun to a child as he enters the house. *Id.* cmt. *d,* illus. 3. The child drops the gun (an object assumed for the purposes of the illustration to be neither too heavy nor unwieldy for a child of that age and size to handle) which lands on her foot and breaks her toe. Applying the risk standard described above, the hunter would not be liable for the broken toe because the risk that made his action negligent was the risk that the child would shoot someone, not that she would drop the gun and sustain an injury to her foot.

The scope-of-liability issue is fact-intensive as it requires consideration of the risks that made the actor's conduct tortious and a determination of whether the harm at issue is a result of any of those risks. When, as in this case, the court considers in advance of trial whether

the plaintiff's harm is beyond the scope of liability as a matter of law, courts must initially consider all of the range of harms risked by the defendant's conduct that the jury *could* find as the basis for determining [the defendant's] conduct tortious. Then, the court can compare the plaintiff's harm with the range of harms risked by the defendant to determine whether a reasonable jury might find the former among the latter.

The drafters advance several advantages of limiting liability in this way. First, the application of the risk standard is comparatively simple. The standard "appeals to intuitive notions of fairness and proportionality by limiting liability to harms that result from risks created by the actor's wrongful conduct, but for no others." It also is flexible enough to "accommodate fairness concerns raised by the specific facts of a case."

Foreseeability has previously played an important role in our proximate cause determinations. . . . The drafters of the Restatement

(Third) explain that foreseeability is still relevant in scope-of-liability determinations. . . . Properly understood, both the risk standard and a foreseeability test exclude liability for harms that were sufficiently unforeseeable at the time of the actor's tortious conduct that they were not among the risks—potential harms—that made the actor negligent. . . .

Although the risk standard and the foreseeability test are comparable in negligence actions. . . [the Restatement drafters] explain that a foreseeability test "risks being misunderstood because of uncertainty about what must be foreseen, by whom, and at what time."

We find the drafters' clarification of scope of liability sound and are persuaded by their explanation of the advantages of applying the risk standard as articulated in the Restatement (Third), and, accordingly, adopt it.

Our next task, then, is to consider whether the district court erred in concluding the harm suffered by the Thompsons was, as a matter of law, outside the scope of the risk of Kaczinski and Lockwood's conduct. We conclude the question of whether a serious injury to a motorist was within the range of harms risked by disassembling the trampoline and leaving it untethered for a few weeks on the yard less than forty feet from the road is not so clear in this case as to justify the district court's resolution of the issue as a matter of law at the summary judgment stage. A reasonable fact finder could determine Kaczinski and Lockwood should have known high winds occasionally occur in Iowa in September and a strong gust of wind could displace the unsecured trampoline parts the short distance from the yard to the roadway and endanger motorists. Although they were in their home for several hours after the storm passed and approximately two-and-a-half hours after daybreak, Kaczinski and Lockwood did not discover their property on the nearby roadway, remove it, or warn approaching motorists of it. On this record, viewed in the light most favorable to the Thompsons, we conclude a reasonable fact finder could find the harm suffered by the Thompsons resulted from the risks that made the defendants' conduct negligent. Accordingly, the district court erred in deciding the scope-of-liability question as a matter of law in this case. . . . Accordingly, we reverse the district court's dismissal of this claim and remand this case for trial. . . .

NOTES

1. **Applying the risk rule.** "An actor's liability is limited to those physical harms that result from the risks that made the actor's conduct tortious." RESTATEMENT (THIRD) OF TORTS: LIABILITY FOR PHYSICAL AND EMOTIONAL HARM § 29 (2010). Look at the facts in *Thompson*. Some kind of risk or foreseeable harm makes the court think that the defendant might have been negligent. What kind of risks did the defendant's conduct create? Did the harm that transpired result from those risks?

2. **Formulations of the principle.** Take a few minutes to consider the idea that the harm that occurred to the plaintiff must be of the same general nature as the foreseeable risk created by the defendant's negligence. Evaluate the following as alternative statements of the idea. (1) Liability must be rejected unless a reasonable person would have reasonably foreseen and avoided harm of the same general kind actually suffered by the plaintiff. (2) The defendant who negligently creates a risk to the plaintiff is subject to liability when that risk or a similar one results in harm, but not when some entirely different risk eventuates in an entirely different harm. Is the example of a hunter who hands a gun to a young child who drops it on her toe helpful in illustrating the risk rule? What is the range of harms that made the hunter's conduct negligent in that situation?

3. **Foreseeability in scope of risk and in breach.** The *Thompson* court says that foreseeability plays an important role in scope of liability, but we previously saw that it played a role in breach as well. Is the concept of foreseeability completely redundant in the two settings? Some courts have said that in breach we are concerned with the broader question of whether the defendant's conduct foreseeably risks some type of harm to someone such that the conduct should have been avoided. In scope of liability we are concerned with whether the defendant's conduct foreseeably risked the type of harm that actually happened to the plaintiff in the case at hand. So the foreseeability inquiry is more focused and specific in the scope of liability context. *See, e.g., C.H. v. Los Lunas Schools Bd. of Educ.,* 852 F. Supp.2d 1344 (D.N.M. 2012).

4. **Two ways of stating the elements of the plaintiff's case.** We have been careful in this book to state the factual cause element separately from the scope-of-liability or proximate cause element. In *Thompson,* the court began by referring to "causation" in its two parts, but then carefully separated the distinct elements. Many courts merge the two concepts by saying that the term proximate cause includes both factual cause and foreseeability. *Sibbing v. Cave,* 922 N.E.2d 594 (Ind. 2010); *HMC Hotel Props. II Ltd. P'ship v. Keystone-Tex. Prop. Holding Corp.,* 439 S.W.3d 910 (Tex. 2014). Viewing proximate cause as a conglomeration of elements risks confusion: when a court speaks of "proximate cause," it may not be clear whether the court is referring to the factual cause component, or the scope of liability component. We aim to avoid this confusion by keeping the two elements separate.

5. **Applying the rule in *Thompson*.**

(a) In *Melchor v. Singh*, 935 N.Y.S.2d 106 (App. Div. 2011), a worker used his employer's ladder. The ladder had old, worn feet and the worker placed bricks under the feet to help stabilize it. He had asked his supervisor for sandbags or another worker to hold the ladder steady, but did not receive either to assist him. While he was working, the bottom of the ladder slid away from the building and he was injured. Do you think the defendant's negligence in providing a deficient ladder was a proximate cause of the plaintiff's injuries? What tests would you use to guide your analysis?

(b)   In *Medcalf v. Washington Heights Condominium Ass'n, Inc.*, 747 A.2d 532 (Conn. App. Ct. 2000), the plaintiff went to visit her friend Skiades. When plaintiff arrived she called on the intercom from outside the building to ask Skiades to buzz her in. Because the building's buzzer system was broken, Skiades walked downstairs to let plaintiff in. Before Skiades got to the front door, plaintiff was attacked. If the building was negligent in failing to maintain the telephone security intercom system, was the harm that occurred "of the same general nature as the foreseeable risk created by defendant's negligence?" What risks might you have foreseen from the broken intercom system? A similar case is *Benaquista v. Municipal Housing Authority*, 622 N.Y.S.2d 129 (App. Div. 1995), where the defendant failed to maintain an intercom and the apartment owner was injured walking downstairs to admit a visitor.

ABRAMS V. CITY OF CHICAGO, 811 N.E.2d 670 (Ill. 2004). The plaintiff, suing for herself and the estate of her deceased child, alleged that the defendant was negligent in failing to send an ambulance to take her to the hospital for delivery of the child when her contractions were 10 minutes apart. As a result of this failure, a friend took her in a car. The friend drove through a red light, horn sounding, and was struck by Gregory Jones, driving at 75 m.p.h. Jones had been drinking and using cocaine. The plaintiff was left in a coma for two weeks and her child died. The trial court granted summary judgment for the defendant on the ground that the defendant's failure to provide an ambulance was not a proximate cause of the injuries. The intermediate court reversed. On review, *held*, the intermediate court erred, and the trial court's grant of summary judgment is affirmed. "[W]e conclude as a matter of law that the City could *not* have reasonably anticipated that a refusal to send an ambulance when labor pains are 10 minutes apart would likely result in plaintiff's driver running a red light at the same time that a substance-impaired driver was speeding through the intersection on a suspended license. Millions of women in labor make it safely to the hospital each year by private transportation. . . . While all traffic accidents are to some extent remotely foreseeable, this is not the kind of harm that was sufficiently foreseeable. . . ."

NOTES

1.   **Step 1: identifying the risks that called for more care.** "I'd better send an ambulance to this caller; otherwise, she might use a private car which would be in a collision." Would a reasonable dispatcher ever think that? If your answer is no, maybe you've decided that the risks created by the failure to dispatch an ambulance did not include car collisions. In that case, the plaintiff's injury and the child's death would not be within the scope of the risk we would have in mind when we said the defendant was negligent, so the conclusion is, "not within the scope of liability."

2. **Answering the scope of liability question.** Could reasonable people differ on whether negligent failure to send an ambulance for a pregnant woman might easily result in speeding to the hospital because of the delay? If the answer to that question is "yes," then scope of liability would be a question for the judgment of the jury on the foreseeability issue.

3. **Examples.** Try the idea on some other facts.

(a)   Defendant negligently pollutes a bay with oil. One risk is that the oil will cling to docks and have to be cleaned off. Fire is not a foreseeable risk, however, because everyone involved reasonably believes that the oil cannot catch fire on the cold waters of the bay. Their belief, though reasonable, proved wrong and by a fluke, the oil caught fire and burned the plaintiff's docks. If the scope-of-risk rule enunciated and applied in *Medcalf* controls here, can the plaintiff recover? *Overseas Tankship (U.K.) Ltd. v. Mort's Dock & Eng'g Co. Ltd. (The Wagon Mound)*, [1961] A.C. 388 (Privy Council 1961).

(b)   In violation of hospital policy, a hospital released a patient without an escort after the patient had received sedating medication. The patient got into a pedestrian-automobile accident, and police were called. On his way to the scene of the accident, the police officer's cruiser was struck by another vehicle, permanently injuring the officer. The officer sued the hospital for its negligent release of the patient. Was the accident of the same general type that the hospital should have foreseen and taken reasonable measures to prevent? *Leavitt v. Brockton Hospital, Inc.*, 907 N.E.2d 213 (Mass. 2009).

4. **Policy or justice: the risk rule or directness.** Maybe the scope-of-risk rule as articulated in *Thompson* and *Abrams* is wrong. It sometimes relieves a faulty defendant at the expense of the innocent plaintiff, doesn't it? For this reason, older cases sometimes held that the defendant would be liable, even for unforeseeable harms, so long as they were "direct" and no new tort by someone else intervened. Directness language sometimes creeps into cases today. For example, in *Anderson v. Christopherson*, 816 N.W.2d 626 (Minn. 2012), plaintiff fell and suffered a broken hip when he tried to separate an attacking unleashed dog from his own dog. The court said that whether the attacking dog's conduct was a proximate cause of plaintiff's injury depended on whether the injury was "a direct and immediate result" of the dog's conduct. In a case like this, where the dog did not attack the plaintiff directly, there was a fact question as to whether plaintiff's "intervention into the fight was voluntary." If it was, proximate cause would not be established. Is such a doctrine preferable?

5. **Policy or justice: justification for the risk rule.** If the scope-of-risk rule is right, what exactly is its justification? Consider: (1) The rule is purely pragmatic. Liability must stop somewhere. The but-for causation test would leave people exposed to continuous liability as long as they lived. (2) The risk rule is just, or at least logical. If liability is imposed only for negligence and negligence creates only a risk of harm A, then liability should be limited to harm A. Any other result would be a species of strict liability, that is, liability

for harms as to which the defendant created no unreasonable risks. *See* 1 DOBBS, HAYDEN & BUBLICK, THE LAW OF TORTS § 199 (2d ed. 2011).

PALSGRAF V. LONG ISLAND RAILROAD CO.
162 N.E. 99 (N.Y. 1928)

CARDOZO, C.J.

Plaintiff was standing on a platform of defendant's railroad after buying a ticket to go to Rockaway Beach. A train stopped at the station, bound for another place. Two men ran forward to catch it. One of the men reached the platform of the car without mishap, though the train was already moving. The other man, carrying a package, jumped aboard the car, but seemed unsteady as if about to fall. A guard on the car, who had held the door open, reached forward to help him in, and another guard on the platform pushed him from behind. In this act, the package was dislodged, and fell upon the rails. It was a package of small size, about fifteen inches long, and was covered by a newspaper. In fact it contained fireworks, but there was nothing in its appearance to give notice of its contents. The fireworks when they fell exploded. The shock of the explosion threw down some scales at the other end of the platform many feet away. The scales struck the plaintiff, causing injuries for which she sues. [The case was submitted to a jury, which returned a verdict for the plaintiff. The Appellate Division affirmed the judgment for the plaintiff.]

The conduct of the defendant's guard, if a wrong in its relation to the holder of package, was not a wrong in its relation to the plaintiff, standing far away. Relatively to her it was not negligence at all. Nothing in the situation gave notice that the falling package had in it the potency of peril to persons thus removed. Negligence is not actionable unless it involves the invasion of a legally protected interest, the violation of a right. "Proof of negligence in the air, so to speak, will not do. . . . [n]egligence is the absence of care, according to the circumstances." The plaintiff, as she stood upon the platform of the station, might claim to be protected against intentional invasion of her bodily security. Such invasion is not charged. She might claim to be protected against unintentional invasion by conduct involving in the thought of reasonable men an unreasonable hazard that such invasion would ensue. These, from the point of view of the law, were the bounds of her immunity, with perhaps some rare exceptions. . . . If no hazard was apparent to the eye of ordinary vigilance, an act innocent and harmless, at least to outward seeming, with reference to her, did not take to itself the quality of a tort because it happened to be a wrong, though apparently not one involving the risk of bodily insecurity, with reference to some one else. . . .

The risk reasonably to be perceived defines the duty to be obeyed, and risk imports relation; it is risk to another or to others within the range of apprehension. This does not mean, of course, that one who launches a destructive force is always relieved of liability, if the force, though known to be destructive pursues an unexpected path. "It was not necessary that the defendant should have had notice of the particular method in which an accident would occur, if the possibility of an accident was clear to the ordinarily prudent eye." Some acts, such as shooting are so imminently dangerous to any one who may come within reach of the missile however unexpectedly, as to impose a duty of provision not far from that of an insurer. Even today, and much oftener in earlier stages of law, one acts sometimes at one's peril. Under this head, it may be, fall certain cases of what is known as transferred intent, an act willfully dangerous to A resulting by misadventure in injury to B. Talmage v. Smith, 101 Mich. 370, 374, 59 N.W. 656, 45 Am. St. Rep. 414. These cases aside, wrong is defined in terms of the natural or probable, at least when unintentional. The range of reasonable apprehension is at times a question for the court, and at times, if varying inferences are possible, a question for the jury. Here, by concession, there was nothing in the situation to suggest to the most cautious mind that the parcel wrapped in newspaper would spread wreckage through the station. If the guard had thrown it down knowingly and willfully, he would not have threatened the plaintiff's safety, so far as appearances could warn him. His conduct would not have involved, even then, an unreasonable probability of invasion of her bodily security. Liability can be no greater where the act is inadvertent. . . .

The law of causation, remote or proximate, is thus foreign to the case before us. The question of liability is always anterior to the question of the measure of the consequences that go with liability. If there is no tort to be redressed, there is no occasion to consider what damage might be recovered if there were a finding of a tort. We may assume, without deciding, that negligence, not at large or in the abstract, but in relation to the plaintiff, would entail liability for any and all consequences, however novel or extraordinary. There is room for argument that a distinction is to be drawn according to the diversity of interests invaded by the act, as where conduct negligent in that it threatens an insignificant invasion of an interest in property results in an unforeseeable invasion of an interest of another order, as, e.g., one of bodily security. Perhaps other distinctions may be necessary. We do not go into the question now. The consequences to be followed must first be rooted in a wrong.

The judgment of the Appellate Division and that of the Trial Term should be reversed, and the complaint dismissed, with costs in all courts.

ANDREWS, J. (dissenting.) . . .

[1: Duty runs to the world at large and
negligence toward one is negligence to all]

The result we shall reach depends upon our theory as to the nature of negligence. Is it a relative concept—the breach of some duty owing to a particular person or to particular persons? Or where there is an act which unreasonably threatens the safety of others, is the doer liable for all its proximate consequences, even where they result in injury to one who would generally be thought to be outside the radius of danger? This is not a mere dispute as to words. We might not believe that to the average mind the dropping of the bundle would seem to involve the probability of harm to the plaintiff standing many feet away whatever might be the case as to the owner or to one so near as to be likely to be struck by its fall. If, however, we adopt the second hypothesis, we have to inquire only as to the relation between cause and effect. We deal in terms of proximate cause, not of negligence. . . .

But we are told that "there is no negligence unless there is in the particular case a legal duty to take care, and this duty must be one which is owed to the plaintiff himself and not merely to others." Salmond Torts (6th Ed.) 24. This I think too narrow a conception. Where there is the unreasonable act, and some right that may be affected there is negligence whether damage does or does not result. That is immaterial. Should we drive down Broadway at a reckless speed, we are negligent whether we strike an approaching car or miss it by an inch. The act itself is wrongful. It is a wrong not only to those who happen to be within the radius of danger, but to all who might have been there—a wrong to the public at large. . . .

It may well be that there is no such thing as negligence in the abstract. "Proof of negligence in the air, so to speak, will not do." In an empty world negligence would not exist. It does involve a relationship between man and his fellows, but not merely a relationship between man and those whom he might reasonably expect his act would injure; rather, a relationship between him and those whom he does in fact injure. If his act has a tendency to harm some one, it harms him a mile away as surely as it does those on the scene. . . .

In the well-known Polemis Case, [1921] 3 K.B. 560, Scrutton, L.J., said that the dropping of a plank was negligent, for it might injure "workman or cargo or ship." Because of either possibility, the owner of the vessel was to be made good for his loss. The act being wrongful, the doer was liable for its proximate results.[1]. . .

---

[1]   The facts that made these statements significant were probably known to many of Judge Andrews' readers. Workers on deck negligently caused a wooden plank to fall into the hold, no doubt risking injury to workmen below, to goods, or even to the ship, but not foreseeably risking a fire. Nevertheless, the wood somehow sparked a fire that destroyed the ship and those responsible for the workmen's negligence were held liable for this startling result.—Eds.

The proposition is this: <u>Every one owes to the world at large the duty of refraining from those acts that may unreasonably threaten the safety of others</u>. Such an act occurs ... Unreasonable risk being taken, its consequences are not confined to those who might probably be hurt. . . .

[2: Liability is limited by proximate cause, not
by defining the scope of duty or negligence]

The right to recover damages rests on additional considerations. The plaintiff's rights must be injured, and this injury must be caused by the negligence. We build a dam, but are negligent as to its foundations. Breaking, it injures property down stream. We are not liable if all this happened because of some reason other than the insecure foundation. But, when injuries do result from our unlawful act, we are liable for the consequences. It does not matter that they are unusual, unexpected, unforeseen, and unforeseeable. But there is one limitation. The damages must be so connected with the negligence that the latter may be said to be the proximate cause of the former.

[3: Proximate cause is determined by several factors,
not by the scope of the defendant's negligence]

These two words have never been given an inclusive definition. What is a cause in a legal sense, still more what is a proximate cause, depend in each case upon many considerations, as does the existence of negligence itself. Any philosophical doctrine of causation does not help us. A boy throws a stone into a pond. The ripples spread. The water level rises. The history of that pond is altered to all eternity. It will be altered by other causes also. Yet it will be forever the resultant of all causes combined. Each one will have an influence. How great only omniscience can say. You may speak of a chain, or, if you please, a net. An analogy is of little aid. Each cause brings about future events. Without each the future would not be the same. Each is proximate in the sense it is essential. But that is not what we mean by the word. Nor on the other hand do we mean sole cause. There is no such thing.

Should analogy be thought helpful, however, I prefer that of a stream. The spring, starting on its journey, is joined by tributary after tributary. The river, reaching the ocean, comes from a hundred sources. No man may say whence any drop of water is derived. Yet for a time distinction may be possible. Into the clear creek, brown swamp water flows from the left. Later, from the right comes water stained by its clay bed. The three may remain for a space, sharply divided. But at last inevitably no trace of separation remains. They are so commingled that all distinction is lost.

As we have said, we cannot trace the effect of an act to the end, if end there is. Again, however, we may trace it part of the way. A murder at Serajevo may be the necessary antecedent to an assassination in London twenty years hence. An overturned lantern may burn all Chicago. We may follow the fire from the shed to the last building. We rightly say the fire started by the lantern caused its destruction.

A cause, but not the proximate cause. What we do mean by the word "proximate" is that, because of convenience, of public policy, of a rough sense of justice, the law arbitrarily declines to trace a series of events beyond a certain point. This is not logic. It is practical politics. Take our rule as to fires. Sparks from my burning haystack set on fire my house and my neighbor's. I may recover from a negligent railroad. He may not. Yet the wrongful act as directly harmed the one as the other. We may regret the line was drawn just where it was, but drawn somewhere it had to be. We said the act of the railroad was not the proximate cause of our neighbor's fire. Cause it surely was. The words we used were simply indicative of our notions of public policy. Other courts think differently. But somewhere they reach the point where they cannot say the stream comes from any one source. . . .

There are some hints that may help us. The proximate cause, involved as it may be with many other causes, must be, at the least, something without which the event would not happen. The court must ask itself whether there was a natural and continuous sequence between cause and effect. Was the one a substantial factor in producing the other? Was there a direct connection between them, without too many intervening causes? Is the effect of cause on result not too attenuated? Is the cause likely, in the usual judgment of mankind, to produce the result? Or, by the exercise of prudent foresight, could the result be foreseen? Is the result too remote from the cause, and here we consider remoteness in time and space. . . . Clearly we must so consider, for the greater the distance either in time or space, the more surely do other causes intervene to affect the result. When a lantern is overturned, the firing of a shed is a fairly direct consequence. Many things contribute to the spread of the conflagration—the force of the wind, the direction and width of streets, the character of intervening structures, other factors. We draw an uncertain and wavering line, but draw it we must as best we can. . . .

Once again, it is all a question of fair judgment, always keeping in mind the fact that we endeavor to make a rule in each case that will be practical and in keeping with the general understanding of mankind. . . .

In fairness he would make good every injury flowing from his negligence. Not because of tenderness toward him we say he need not answer for all that follows his wrong. We look back to the catastrophe, the fire kindled by the spark, or the explosion. We trace the consequences, not indefinitely, but to a certain point. And to aid us in fixing that point we ask what might ordinarily be expected to follow the fire or the explosion.

This last suggestion is the factor which must determine the case before us. The act upon which defendant's liability rests is knocking an apparently harmless package onto the platform. The act was negligent. For its proximate consequences the defendant is liable. If its contents were broken, to the owner; if it fell upon and crushed a passenger's foot, then to him; if it exploded and injured one in the immediate vicinity, to him also. . . . Mrs. Palsgraf was standing some distance away. How far cannot be told from the record—apparently 25 or 30 feet, perhaps less. Except for the explosion, she would not have been injured. We are told by the appellant in his brief, "It cannot be denied that the explosion was the direct cause of the plaintiff's injuries." So it was a substantial factor in producing the result—there was here a natural and continuous sequence—direct connection. The only intervening cause was that, instead of blowing her to the ground, the concussion smashed the weighing machine which in turn fell upon her. There was no remoteness in time, little in space. And surely, given such an explosion as here, it needed no great foresight to predict that the natural result would be to injure one on the platform at no greater distance from its scene than was the plaintiff. Just how no one might be able to predict. Whether by flying fragments, by broken glass, by wreckage of machines or structures no one could say. But injury in some form was most probable.

Under these circumstances I cannot say as a matter of law that the plaintiff's injuries were not the proximate result of the negligence. That is all we have before us. The court refused to so charge. No request was made to submit the matter to the jury as a question of fact, even would that have been proper upon the record before us.

NOTES

1. **Integrating *Palsgraf* and *Thompson*.** Reading *Palsgraf* and *Thompson* together, we can say that the defendant is liable only for harms within the scope of the risks he negligently created. More specifically, the defendant is liable only (a) for types of injuries foreseeably risked by his negligence and (b) to classes of persons foreseeably risked by his negligence. In other words, the defendant is not liable unless a reasonable person in defendant's circumstances should have foreseen that his conduct risked injuries of the same general type that occurred to a general class of persons within which the plaintiff is found.

2. **Was the defendant negligent?** Could Cardozo have just as easily said that the defendant was not negligent at all, towards anyone? If a reasonable person would foresee no harm to anyone as a result of his actions we do not need to reach the proximate cause issue. Why not?

3. **Foreseeable injury.** If some kind of harm could have been foreseen in *Palsgraf*, to what class of persons should the guard have foreseen injury? Was Mrs. Palsgraf within that class? Modern cases often free a defendant from liability where the plaintiff is not within a class foreseeably risked by the negligent conduct. *See, e.g., Mellon Mortgage Co. v. Holder*, 5 S.W.3d 654 (Tex. 1999) (woman raped in defendant Mellon's parking garage by a policeman who

had pulled her over several blocks away was "not a member of [a] class . . . that Mellon could have reasonably foreseen would be the victim of a criminal act in its garage"). However, the Restatement now suggests that no separate reference need be made to unforeseeable plaintiffs. Could you characterize the harm in *Palsgraf* as a different type of harm than that risked by the conductor's negligence? *See* RESTATEMENT (THIRD) OF TORTS: LIABILITY FOR PHYSICAL AND EMOTIONAL HARM § 29 cmt. n, illus. 9 (2010).

4. **Cardozo's duty/negligence locution compared to proximate cause language.** In *Palsgraf,* Cardozo seemed concerned with scope of risk but did not invoke the concept of proximate cause by that name. Instead, he concluded that "[r]elatively to her it was not negligence at all," because no harm to her was foreseeable. Although expressed in terms of duty or negligence, the rule is just like one that asserts the defendant's conduct is not a proximate cause when the defendant could not foresee harm to persons situated like the plaintiff. However, who decides duty and who decides proximate cause?

5. **Jury role.** Scope of risk is a matter that must necessarily be determined on the facts of each case. Consequently, when the question is about the scope of risk, the question is usually one for the jury so long as reasonable people could differ. *Rascher v. Friend*, 689 S.E.2d 661 (Va. 2010) ("[W]hether an act was a proximate cause of an event is best determined by a jury. This is so simply because the particular facts of each case are critical to that determination."). Why did Cardozo, then, refuse to permit a jury to decide foreseeability in *Palsgraf*?

6. **Andrews: rejecting the duty/negligence locution.** Judge Andrews, dissenting, tried to establish two points. First, he argued that a person who is negligent to *any* class of persons is negligent to everyone who is in fact injured. He rejected Cardozo's effort to deal with the issue as one of duty or negligence. Instead, for Andrews, the issue became one of proximate cause.

7. **Andrews: the limited role of foreseeability in proximate cause determinations.** Andrews' second point was that proximate cause was *not* a matter of foreseeability alone. For Andrews, proximate cause was a matter of a host of factors. Since it was not foreseeability alone that determined proximate cause for Andrews, he would not allow the railroad to escape liability for its supposed negligence merely because no reasonable person would expect the package to cause harm to someone a distance away.

8. **Adopting a scope of risk or foreseeability approach.** When courts are concerned with the scope-of-risk question, they have often adopted Andrews' proximate cause locution but Cardozo's foreseeability test. The result is that decisions on proximate cause today almost always emphasize foreseeability in some form as a limitation on liability. They are thus scope-of-risk cases. Only a few cases continue to reflect some affinity with Andrews' view that liability could be imposed for types of harm or to classes of person who were not reasonably foreseeable victims, and even these may find policy

reasons against liability beyond the scope of the risk in particular cases. *See Fandrey v. American Family Mut. Ins. Co.,* 680 N.W.2d 345 (Wis. 2004).

NOTE: THE RESCUE DOCTRINE

How does the risk rule work in this kind of case: Defendant negligently creates a risk to *A*. *B*, who was not subject to the risk or who escaped it, attempts to rescue *A* and is hurt in the process. Defendant, having created a risk to *A*, is liable to him. Is he also liable to *B*? *Palsgraf* might lead one to answer that he is not, or that the issue would turn on whether rescue would be foreseeable in the particular situation at the time defendant was guilty of negligence. Judge Cardozo's own answer, however, was otherwise.

In *Wagner v. International Railway*, 133 N.E. 437 (N.Y. 1921), the railway permitted passengers to stand in between the cars while the train was moving over a high trestle. One of them fell off into a gorge as the train rounded a curve. The plaintiff attempted to climb down to locate the victim, who was his cousin. In the course of this attempt, the plaintiff himself was injured. Cardozo, speaking in his Delphic manner, held that the railway was liable to the rescuer. "Danger invites rescue," he said, suggesting, perhaps, that rescue is foreseeable or is foreseeable as a matter of law. But he added a few sentences later: "The wrongdoer may not have foreseen the coming of a deliverer. He is accountable as if he had." The latter statement might be read as rejecting any criterion of foreseeability, or it might be read to mean only that a reasonable person would have foreseen rescue, whether the defendant subjectively foresaw it or not.

Whatever Cardozo meant, the cases have generally agreed that the rescuer can recover from the defendant whose negligence prompts the rescue if the rescuer had a reasonable belief that the victim was in peril. *See, e.g., Rasmussen v. State Farm Mut. Aut. Ins. Co.,* 770 N.W.2d 619 (Neb. 2009); *Clinkscales v. Nelson Securities, Inc.,* 697 N.W.2d 836 (Iowa 2005). The rule includes cases in which the defendant negligently injures or endangers himself and the plaintiff is injured in attempting a rescue. *See Sears v. Morrison,* 90 Cal. Rptr.2d 528 (Ct. App. 1999).

Try applying the rescue doctrine to these cases: (A) Dorothy Lambert was in an accident, allegedly caused by a tortfeasor's negligence. Her husband, over a block away in an office, heard of the accident; he rushed out to reach his wife, slipped on a patch of ice, and was injured. Is the tortfeasor liable to the husband as a rescuer? *Lambert v. Parrish*, 492 N.E.2d 289 (Ind. 1986). (B) Defendant ran over a small child. Police officers came to the scene. One gave aid to the child while the second helped in controlling a crowd and the child's hysterical parent. While so engaged, the second officer collapsed and suffered a fatal heart attack. Is the defendant liable to the officer's survivors or estate because the officer was a rescuer? *Snellenberger v. Rodriguez*, 760 S.W.2d 237 (Tex. 1988).

Should the rescue doctrine apply when the rescuer is attempting to save property rather than persons? In *Jacobson v. Ron*, 2009 WL 144992 (Tex. App. 2009), defendant purchased property from plaintiff's family trust and began demolishing the building before paying off the note. Plaintiff was injured while attempting to rescue the building and stop demolition. What result?

NOTE: VIOLATION OF STATUTE
AND "PROXIMATE CAUSE"

As we saw in Chapter 5, in most states, violation of a non-tort statute is "negligence per se," but this rule is conditioned upon a finding that the statute was designed to protect against the type of harm that occurred and the class of persons to which the plaintiff is a member.

A well-known and very clear example of this is *Larrimore v. American National Insurance Co.*, 89 P.2d 340 (Okla. 1939). A statute forbade laying out poisons. The defendant provided a rat poison to its tenant, a coffee shop. The coffee shop put the poison near the coffee burner. The plaintiff was injured when she lit the burner because the poison exploded due to its phosphorous content. The trial judge, as trier of fact, found for the defendant. The Supreme Court of Oklahoma affirmed, commenting:

> It is not enough for a plaintiff to show that the defendant neglected a duty imposed by statute. He must go further and show that his injury was caused by his exposure to a hazard from which it was the purpose of the statute to protect him. . . . Those only to whom [the statutory] duty is due and who have sustained injuries of the character its discharge was designed to prevent can maintain actions for its breach.

The court is stating the fundamental scope-of-risk rule as applied to a statutory liability, isn't it?

§ 2. ASSESSING THE SCOPE OF THE RISK

A. IS HARM OUTSIDE THE SCOPE OF THE RISK BECAUSE OF THE MANNER IN WHICH IT OCCURS?

HUGHES V. LORD ADVOCATE
[1963] A.C. 837 (H.L.)

[Post Office employees were working on an underground telephone cable in Edinburgh, Scotland. At 5:00 they took a tea break, leaving unguarded an open manhole, covered with a tent and surrounded by kerosene lanterns. Two boys, 8 and 10 years old, found the unguarded site, tied one of the lanterns to a rope they found, and descended into the manhole. They came back up without mishap, but once back on top, they knocked or dropped the lantern into the hole. The accepted reconstruction of what happened next was that the lantern broke and that, quite unforeseeably, some of the kerosene vaporized. This gaseous form of the kerosene came into contact with the flame of the lantern and there was a large explosion, followed by a raging fire. Hughes, the eight year old, fell into the manhole as a result of the explosion and suffered severe burns, some of them on his fingers as he tried to climb out by holding to the heated metal ladder. He brought an action against the Lord Advocate of Scotland, as representative of the Post Office. The courts of Scotland held in favor of the Lord Advocate on the grounds that though burns were foreseeable, the vaporization of the kerosene and the explosion were not.]

LORD REID. . . . I am satisfied that the Post Office workmen were in fault in leaving this open manhole unattended and it is clear that if they had done as they ought to have done this accident would not have happened. It cannot be said that they owed no duty to the appellant. But it has been held that the appellant cannot recover damages. . . .

[T]here could be a case where the intrusion of a new and unexpected factor could be regarded as the cause of the accident rather than the fault of the defender. But that is not this case. The cause of this accident was a known source of danger, the lamp, but it behaved in an unpredictable way. . . . This accident was caused by a known source of danger, but caused in a way which could not have been foreseen, and, in my judgment, that affords no defense. I would therefore allow the appeal.

LORD GUEST. . . . In dismissing the appellant's claim, the Lord Ordinary and the majority of the judges of the First Division reached the conclusion that the accident which happened was not reasonably foreseeable. . . . Concentration has been placed in the courts below on the explosion which, it was said, could not have been foreseen because it was caused in a unique fashion by the paraffin forming into vapour and being ignited by the naked flame of the wick. But this, in my opinion, is to concentrate on what is really a non-essential element. . . .

[B]ecause the explosion was the agent which caused the burning and was unforeseeable, therefore the accident, according to them, was not reasonably foreseeable. In my opinion, this reasoning is fallacious. An explosion is only one way in which burning can be caused. Burning can also be caused by the contact between liquid paraffin and a naked flame. In the one case paraffin vapour and in the other case liquid paraffin is ignited by fire. I cannot see that these are two different types of accident. They are both burning accidents and in both cases the injuries would be burning injuries. Upon this view the explosion was an immaterial event in the chain of causation. It was simply one way which burning might be caused by the potentially dangerous paraffin lamp. . . .

LORD PEARCE. . . . Did the explosion create an accident and damage of a different type from the misadventure and damage that could be foreseen? In my judgment it did not. The accident was but a variant of the foreseeable. . . . The resulting damage, though severe, was not greater than or different in kind from that which might have been produced had the lamp spilled and produced a more normal conflagration in the hold. I would therefore allow the appeal.

DOUGHTY V. TURNER MANUFACTURING CO., LTD., [1964] 1 Q.B. 518 (C.A. 1963). Defendant's manufacturing process involved use of two vats of molten liquid maintained at 800 degrees centigrade, into which metal parts were immersed. Covers made of asbestos and cement were set beside the vat, to be put on as needed to conserve heat. Such covers had been used in this process in England and in the United States for over 20 years. A worker knocked one of the covers into the molten liquid. The cover sank without causing a splash. After one or two minutes the molten liquid erupted and injured the plaintiff, who was standing nearby. Thereafter experiments indicated that a compound of asbestos and cement would undergo a chemical change when subjected to temperatures over 500 degrees centigrade, so that hydrogen and oxygen in the material would combine to form water. The water at this temperature would turn to steam and produce an explosion or eruption. The trial judge held in favor of the plaintiff, finding negligence on the part of the worker in knocking the cover into the vat. *Held*, appeal allowed, judgment for defendants.

LORD PEARCE: "The evidence showed that splashes caused by sudden immersion . . . were a foreseeable danger which should be carefully avoided. The falling cover might have ejected the liquid by a splash, and in the result it did eject the liquid, though in a more dramatic fashion." Therefore, the plaintiff's counsel argued, the accident was "merely a variant of foreseeable accidents by splashing. . . . [I]t would be quite unrealistic to describe this accident as a variant of the perils from splashing. The cause of the accident, to quote Lord Reid's words, was 'the intrusion of a new and unexpected factor.' There was an eruption due to chemical changes underneath the surface of the liquid as opposed to a splash caused by displacement from bodies falling on to its surface. In my judgment, the reasoning in Hughes v. Lord Advocate cannot be extended far enough to cover this case."

HARMON, L.J.: "In my opinion the damage here was of an entirely different kind from the foreseeable splash."

DIPLOCK, L.J.: "The first risk . . . is that if [the cover] is allowed to drop on to the hot liquid in the bath with sufficient momentum it may cause the liquid to splash on to persons. . . . The second risk is that if it becomes immersed in a liquid the temperature of which exceeds 500 degrees centigrade, it will disintegrate and cause an under-surface explosion which will eject the liquid. . . . There is no room today for mystique in the law of negligence. It is the application of common morality and common sense to the activities of the common man." The plaintiff's attorney relied on Hughes v. Lord Advocate where the plaintiff's burns were more serious than they would have been expected to be. "But they were the direct consequence of the defendant's breach of duty and of the same kind as could reasonably have been foreseen, although of unforeseen gravity. But in the present case the defendants' duty owed to the plaintiff in relation to the only foreseeable risk, that is of splashing, was to take reasonable care to avoid knocking the cover into the liquid or allowing it to slip in such a way as to cause a splash which would injure the plaintiff. Failure to avoid knocking it into the liquid . . . was of itself no breach of duty to the plaintiff."

NOTES

1.   **Manner of harm vs. type of injury.** There is obviously much room for judicial judgment in characterizing the risks that are foreseeable, but how do we explain *Doughty*? The court says it is applying the general principle expressed in *Hughes* that in order to hold a defendant liable, the precise manner of harm need not be foreseeable if the general type of harm was foreseeable. Is the type of harm that occurred in *Doughty* different from what was risked by the defendant's conduct?

2.   **Level of generality.** How foreseeable the harm is may depend on the level of generality with which it is described. If the type of harm risked in *Hughes* or *Doughty* was "a burn injury," isn't that the type of harm that occurred? If the type of harm is instead described very specifically, in *Doughty* for example, as "a burn injury due to a splash of hot liquid when the cover is knocked in and liquid is displaced," the type of harm risked might be different from that which occurred. What is the appropriate level of generality to use for characterizing the risk of harm? The Restatement (Third) of Torts leaves these

matters to factfinders' "judgment and common sense." RESTATEMENT (THIRD)
OF TORTS: LIABILITY FOR PHYSICAL AND EMOTIONAL HARM § 29 cmt. i (2010). Do
you think common sense would lead all factfinders to the same conclusion?
Does this make the lawyers' role more important?

B. IS HARM OUTSIDE THE SCOPE OF THE RISK BECAUSE ITS EXTENT IS UNFORESEEABLE?

HAMMERSTEIN V. JEAN DEVELOPMENT WEST, 907 P.2d 975 (Nev. 1995).
Plaintiff, about 70 years of age, was a guest at the defendant's hotel. As the
hotel knew, he was a diabetic. Walking up and down stairs was bad for
him, but there were no rooms on the ground floor and besides, there was
an elevator. In the early morning hours a fire alarm went off. Elevators
were locked and plaintiff had to walk down from the fourth floor. In doing
so he twisted his ankle. Much later, on returning to his room, he found a
blister on his foot. This eventually became a gangrenous infection probably
because of his diabetes, which interferes with circulation in the lower
extremities. There was in fact no fire and the fire alarm system had gone
off without a fire on numerous occasions but had never been corrected.
Held, summary judgment for the defendant was error. "It should have been
foreseeable to Nevada Landing that if its fire alarm system was
unreasonably faulty, harm to a certain type of plaintiff, i.e., one of its
guests, could result. Also, this particular variety of harm, injuring an ankle
or foot on the way down a stairwell, is a foreseeable variety of harm in this
circumstance. The extent of the infection on Hammerstein's leg may not
have been foreseeable, but the underlying injury should have been."

NOTES

1.   **The thin-skull rule.** The term "thin skull" or "eggshell skull" is
widely used in tort law in reference to some variant on the following facts.
Defendant negligently strikes the plaintiff. The blow is such that a normal
person would suffer only slight injury, such as a bruise. The plaintiff, however,
has an unusually thin skull, a fact the defendant does not know. As a result of
the minor blow, the plaintiff suffers terrible injuries. If the defendant is in fact
guilty of tort—that is, if he was negligent or guilty of intentional harm—then
the fact that the harm was much worse than anyone would have expected does
not limit his liability. This is the thin-skull rule. It is often generalized by
saying that the defendant "takes the plaintiff as he finds him;" that is, with
whatever extra damages the plaintiff might have because the plaintiff has a
"thin skull," or has diabetes, or is pregnant, or suffers hemophilia, or is
otherwise pre-disposed to suffer more. A leading case is *McCahill v. New York
Transportation Co.,* 94 N.E. 616 (N.Y. 1911). There the defendant ran into the
plaintiff, who suffered a broken thigh. In the hospital he began to suffer
delirium tremens, from which he died. This resulted only because of a preexisting alcoholic condition. The defendant took the plaintiff as he found him
and was held liable for his death.

2.   **Nuances.** The thin-skull rule does not make the tortfeasor liable for the pre-existing condition itself; rather, the rule calls for liability for any *aggravation* of that original condition that is caused by the defendant's negligence, even where that aggravation was unforeseeable. *See Harris v. ShopKo Stores, Inc.*, 308 P.3d 449 (Utah 2013). Nor do the thin-skull cases impose liability without fault. The defendant's act must have been one that would cause *some* harm to an ordinary person, or the defendant must have been at fault because he knew or should have known of the plaintiff's susceptible condition. The thin-skull rule merely holds that the defendant does not escape liability for the unforeseeable personal reactions of the plaintiff, once negligence or intentional fault is established.

3.   **A broader principle.** The thin-skull rule may reflect a broader principle, and indeed that is the way the court in *Hammerstein* articulated its holding: a defendant may be liable for the full extent of a plaintiff's harm, even where the extent of that harm was unforeseeable, where the other elements of a prima facie case are established. *See also* RESTATEMENT (THIRD) OF TORTS: LIABILITY FOR PHYSICAL AND EMOTIONAL HARM § 29 cmt. p & § 31 (2010).

§ 3. IS HARM OUTSIDE THE SCOPE OF RISK BECAUSE IT ALSO RESULTS FROM INTERVENING PERSONS OR FORCES?

NOTE: SCOPE OF RISK AND NATURAL AND CONTINUOUS SEQUENCE

Imagine this case: Tortfeasor A leaves an unlighted excavation in the sidewalk. Tortfeasor B negligently jostles the plaintiff, causing him to fall into the excavation.

> "The proximate cause of an injury is that which, in a natural and continuous sequence, unbroken by any efficient intervening cause, produces an injury, and without which the injury would not have occurred."

These words and others very similar have been used in literally hundreds of American cases. Many courts continue to define "proximate cause" in terms of a "natural and continuous sequence unbroken by any intervening cause." *See, e.g., McIlroy v. Gibson's Apple Orchard,* 43 A.3d 948 (Maine 2012); *Kellermann v. McDonough,* 684 S.E.2d 786 (Va. 2009). This language has done quite a bit to obscure issues and principles. For one thing, courts have recognized repeatedly, and we ourselves have seen, that there may be many tortfeasors who are all liable and thus all proximate causes. When judges speak of "the" proximate cause rather than "a" proximate cause, they may be pushing the jury to an unconscious bias against finding both tortfeasors liable. *See, e.g., Holmes v. Levine,* 639 S.E.2d 235 (Va. 2007) (holding that a jury instruction that the plaintiff had to prove that defendant's negligence was "*the* proximate cause of the death of [decedent]" was reversible error, where evidence supported that there could be other proximate causes of the death).

When tortfeasors act in sequence, the first tortfeasor often argues that the second tortfeasor's act is an "intervening cause" that "supersedes" his liability entirely. Courts often use metaphorical rather than principled language here: a superseding cause breaks the causal chain.

The emphasis on intervening causes and causal chains has obscured the more fundamental scope-of-risk principle: An intervening act of some second tortfeasor should relieve the first tortfeasor of liability only when the resulting harm is outside the scope of the risk negligently created by the first tortfeasor. An "intervening cause that lies within the scope of the foreseeable risk, or has a reasonable connection to it, is not a superseding cause." *Fancyboy v. Alaska Village Elec. Co-op., Inc.*, 984 P.2d 1128 (Alaska 1999). Further, "proximate cause requires only that the general kind of harm be foreseeable for an actor's conduct to be considered the proximate cause of plaintiff's injuries." *Winschel v. Brown*, 171 P.3d 142 (Alaska 2007) (reversing a summary judgment for defendant on superseding cause grounds).

A. INTENTIONAL OR CRIMINAL INTERVENING ACTS

MARCUS V. STAUBS
736 S.E.2d 360 (W.Va. 2012)

PER CURIAM: . . .

This case involves a single-car automobile accident which resulted in the death of 14-year-old Samantha Staubs (hereinafter "Samantha") and serious injury to her sister, 13-year-old Jessica Staubs (hereinafter "Jessica"). Both were passengers in a vehicle stolen and driven by 14-year-old Misty Johnson (hereinafter "Misty"), who was intoxicated. [The alcohol was obtained when 18-year-old defendant Jonathan "Ray" Marcus picked up some of the girls to take them to a party and on the way drove the group across the West Virginia/Virginia line to a convenience store. At the store, defendant's 26-year-old friend Steven Woodward went in alone and bought four, forty-ounce containers of "Hurricane" brand malt liquor. There was conflicting testimony about whether Marcus had asked Woodward to purchase alcohol for the girls and whether Marcus knew that alcohol was being purchased for that purpose. At the party the girls began drinking the alcohol. A parent came home and told the girls they could not stay the night. There was testimony that Samantha called Marcus for a ride, which he declined to provide.]

Finding no one available to pick them up, Misty and Samantha left [the] house stating they were going to steal a car. They returned minutes later with a truck they stole from neighbor Mack Jenkins and retrieved

Kelly and Jessica. Minutes later, with Misty at the wheel and Samantha an unsecured front passenger, the vehicle hit an embankment. Samantha was killed; Jessica sustained a head injury. . . .

Respondent Lori Ann Staubs filed suit as the mother and next friend of Jessica Staubs and as Administratrix of the Estate of Samantha Staubs against petitioner [Marcus] and others. Respondent alleged that petitioner and Woodward negligently "provided" alcohol to the minors. . . .

[Both parties] took the position that the material facts were undisputed. . . . [T]he trial court entered an order denying petitioner's motion for summary judgment and granting respondent [Staub's] cross-motion for summary judgment. . . . The trial court then made the following findings: (1) that petitioner had a duty to both plaintiffs to "obey the law," and that through his role in obtaining the alcohol, he had violated two statutes (2) that by virtue of his violation of these statutes, he was *prima facie* negligent; (3) that by refusing to pick the girls up later in the evening at their request, he was guilty of common law negligence; (4) that his negligence was a proximate cause of the accident; (5) that Misty's actions in stealing the vehicle, driving without a license, and driving intoxicated were not intervening causes . . . [and] as a result of the foregoing, petitioner was liable to respondent. It is from this finding that petitioner appeals. . . .

[The questions of negligence per se and common law breach are for the jury. We turn to the question of proximate cause.]

Petitioner [Marcus] argues that the illegal consumption of alcohol by the minors, the theft of the vehicle, and Misty's reckless operation of the vehicle without a license and while intoxicated, all constitute intervening causes. . . .

[Marcus] essentially argues that criminal acts are *per se* intervening causes. In support, petitioner cites to *Yourtee v. Hubbard,* 196 W. Va. 683, 690, 474 S.E.2d 613, 620 (1996), wherein the Court stated that "[g]enerally, a willful, malicious, or criminal act breaks the chain of causation." Once again, however, petitioner relies on a generality expressed in *dicta* in *Yourtee,* with little regard for the exception discussed therein . . . which states:

> A tortfeasor whose negligence is a substantial factor in bringing about injuries is not relieved from liability by the intervening acts of third persons if those acts were reasonably foreseeable by the original tortfeasor at the time of his negligent conduct.

[Marcus] nevertheless argues that the criminal acts in this case were not reasonably foreseeable by him and therefore, break the chain of causation. . . .

In the instant case, we find that it is properly within the province of the jury, under proper legal instruction, to determine the measure of petitioner's knowledge of and participation in the procurement of the alcohol, whether the alcohol was "furnished" to the minors, and then, if so, whether given the facts and circumstances leading up to those events, the subsequent acts of the minors and their friends were reasonably foreseeable to petitioner. Therefore, we find the trial court's award of summary judgment improperly invaded the province of the fact-finder in determining whether petitioner's alleged actions were the proximate cause of the accident at issue and whether the subsequent criminal actions constituted intervening causes and, as such, was error.

———————

COLLINS V. SCENIC HOMES, INC., 38 So.3d 28 (Ala. 2009). Scenic Homes constructed an apartment development. It is undisputed that it did not use a licensed architect to design the plan and to draft the building specifications. Discovery indicated that Scenic Homes did not comply with the applicable fire-safety codes. Inadequate fire-retardant building materials were used, the sprinkler system was inadequate, and the windows in the units were too small to provide a viable exit route for persons living in the apartment complex. Twenty years after the complex was built, a fire started there. April Collins died and several others were injured. After an investigation, Henry Rice was arrested for setting the fire, and he ultimately pleaded guilty to arson. The plaintiffs brought suit against Scenic Homes and Russell, the building owner. The trial court granted summary judgment based on the intervening criminal act. *Held*, summary judgment was improper. "The question is whether the injuries allegedly caused by the inability to escape from the fire were the foreseeable result of the alleged failure of Scenic Homes to build and Russell to maintain a reasonably safe building with regard to fire safety. Indeed, it is a foreseeable risk that a fire at an apartment complex, however started, will cause harm to the inhabitants of the complex if the premises owner fails to provide adequate fire-suppression safeguards and an adequate means of escape from the fire. . . . Because the evidence before us indicates that a genuine issue of material fact exists as to whether Scenic Homes constructed and Russell maintained and operated a reasonably safe apartment building with regard to fire safety, the summary judgment for Scenic Homes and Russell is reversed."

NOTES

1. **History of intervening criminal acts.** In *Watson v. Kentucky & Indiana Bridge & Railroad*, 126 S.W. 146 (Ky. 1910), defendant railroad negligently derailed a gasoline tank car and it sprung a leak. A man named Duerr threw a match into the area; an explosion resulted, causing the plaintiff injury. The court held that if Duerr acted "for the purpose of causing the explosion," the railroad would not be liable. The railroad "is not bound to anticipate the criminal acts of others by which damage is inflicted." A view

common in the 19th and early 20th centuries was that the deliberate infliction of harm by a "moral being," who was adequately informed, free to act, and able to choose, would "supersede" the negligence of the first actor. *See* H.L.A. HART & A.M. HONORE, CAUSATION IN THE LAW 129 (1962). Some modern courts continue to adhere to the view that an intervening criminal act is a superseding cause as a matter of law. *See, e.g., Mitchell Crane Services, Inc. v. Page*, 126 So.3d 29 (Miss. 2013).

2. **A modern view.** *Watson* was repudiated in *Britton v. Wooten*, 817 S.W.2d 443 (Ky. 1991), where the court said that if the defendant negligently created the increased risk of fire or its spread, the defendant could be held responsible. Today, most courts, in line with *Marcus* and *Collins*, say that criminal acts may be foreseeable, and so within the scope of the created risk.

3. **Framing the foreseeability question.** Look carefully at the way the foreseeability issue is phrased in *Marcus* and the way it is phrased in *Collins*. Do you see a difference? The Restatement Third section on "Intervening Acts and Superseding Causes" states that "When a force of nature or an independent act is also a factual cause of harm, an actor's liability is limited to those harms that result from the risks that made the actor's conduct tortious." RESTATEMENT (THIRD) OF TORTS: LIABILITY FOR PHYSICAL AND EMOTIONAL HARM § 34 (2010). Is that just the ordinary risk rule? Does it make a difference if the court asks if the injuries allegedly caused by the defendant were the foreseeable result of the defendant's alleged negligence or instead if the court asks if the intervening acts of the third persons were reasonably foreseeable by the defendant? How might the framing of that question matter in *Collins?*

4. **Foreseeability of intervening criminal acts.** Many courts focus on the foreseeability of the intervening criminal act itself. *See Wiener v. Southcoast Childcare Ctrs., Inc.,* 88 P.3d 517 (Cal. 2004); *King v. Anderson County,* 419 S.W.3d 232 (Tenn. 2013). Foreseeability in this context can involve fact questions, as in *Marcus.*

5. **Applying a risk rule.** A landlord leasing apartments failed to control access to the landlord's copy of keys. Someone used the landlord's keys to gain entrance to the plaintiff's apartment. The intruder raped the plaintiff. In the plaintiff's suit against the landlord, the defendant argued that the intruder was a superseding cause. The court said, "[t]he happening of the very event the likelihood of which makes the actor's conduct negligent and so subjects the actor to liability cannot relieve him from liability." *Tenney v. Atlantic Assocs.,* 594 N.W.2d 11 (Iowa 1999).

6. **The "very duty" rule.** The Restatement Third provides that "When an actor is found liable precisely because of the failure to adopt adequate precaution against the risk of harm of another's acts or omissions, or by an extraordinary force of nature, there is no scope-of-liability limitation on the actor's liability." RESTATEMENT (THIRD) OF TORTS: LIABILITY FOR PHYSICAL AND EMOTIONAL HARM § 34 cmt. d (2010). Try applying the logic: If the defendant airplane manufacturer negligently designs airplane cockpit doors so that

terrorists can take over and crash the plane, could the designer who is found to be negligent possibly claim that the terrorism was an unforeseeable and therefore superseding cause? *See In re Sept. 11 Litigation,* 280 F. Supp. 2d 279 (S.D.N.Y. 2003).

7.   **The role of time.** The negligence in *Collins* took place twenty years before the harm came about. Should that fact have barred the claim? In *Williams v. State,* 969 N.E.2d 197 (N.Y. 2012), a state office of mental health negligently allowed a committed patient, required to be under supervision at all times, to use a restroom out of sight. He escaped, which the office did not report to police. Two years later he attacked a woman, causing serious injuries to her leg. He had originally been committed for a documented history of violence towards women. The New York court felt the proximate cause analysis incorporated a "temporal dimension." No liability.

[handwritten: → There is a temporal dimension, does the court blend this with foreseeability?]

NOTE: SUICIDE

1.   *Traditional rule and exceptions.* What if the defendant's negligence allegedly causes another person to commit, or attempt, suicide? Most states continue to follow the traditional rule—an intentional suicide or suicide attempt is a superseding cause of plaintiff's harm, freeing the defendant from any liability for negligence, because it is unforeseeable as a matter of law. *See, e.g., Johnson v. Wal-Mart Stores, Inc.,* 588 F.3d 439 (7th Cir. 2009). Courts have recognized two main exceptions to this traditional rule: (1) where the defendant's tortious conduct induces a mental illness or an "uncontrollable impulse" in the plaintiff (or decedent) from which the suicide attempt (or suicide) results; and (2) where there is a special relationship between the two parties, that presumes or includes knowledge by the defendant of plaintiff's risk of committing suicide. *Johnstone v. City of Albuquerque,* 145 P.3d 76 (N.M. Ct. App. 2006).

2.   *A case-by-case foreseeability approach.* A smaller number of courts have rejected any categorical rule for suicides, instead adopting a foreseeability test that is applied on a case-by-case basis. Under this approach, a jury could find proximate cause where a defendant's negligence created a foreseeable risk of a suicide or suicide attempt. *See, e.g., Delaney v. Reynolds,* 825 S.E.2d 554 (Mass. App. Ct. 2005) (defendant stored his unlocked loaded gun in the house he shared with plaintiff, whom he knew to be a depressed substance abuser; jury could find that his negligence in storing his gun created a foreseeable risk of the plaintiff's suicide attempt).

3.   *Scope of duty and scope of risk.* Do the suicide cases turn as much on the scope of the defendant's duty to the plaintiff as on the scope of risks created? A doctor who cares for a suicidal patient may well owe a duty that encompasses protecting that patient from self-harm. *See, e.g., P.W. v. Children's Hosp. Colorado,* 364 P.3d 891 (Colo. 2016). Does that mean that

a doctor's negligence in treatment, followed by the patient's act of self-destruction, is a proximate cause of that harm? *See Komlodi v. Picciano*, 89 A.3d 1234 (N.J. 2014) (for the jury to determine whether patient's oral ingestion of a narcotic patch was reasonably foreseeable, given patient's known propensity to abuse alcohol and drugs); *Kivland v. Columbia Orthopaedic Group, LLP*, 331 S.W.3d 299 (Mo. 2011) (issue of fact whether plaintiff's husband's suicide was proximately caused by defendant surgeon's negligence that left him in a great deal of pain). What if the evidence shows that the patient would probably have committed suicide no matter what his doctor had done? *See Rodriguez-Escobar v. Goss*, 392 S.W.3d 109 (Tex. 2013).

B. NEGLIGENT INTERVENING ACTS

DERDIARIAN V. FELIX CONTRACTING CORP.

414 N.E.2d 666 (N.Y. 1980)

COOKE, CHIEF JUDGE.

[Defendant Felix Contracting Corp. was installing an underground gas main, and for this purpose had excavated most of the eastbound lane of traffic. Felix engaged Bayside Pipe Coaters to seal the mains. Bayside had a kettle of liquid enamel, boiling to 400 degrees at the job site. Derdiarian worked for Bayside and was in charge of the kettle. Against Derdiarian's wishes, Felix insisted that he set up the kettle on the west side of the excavation facing the oncoming, eastbound traffic. Felix protected against this oncoming traffic by a single wooden horse barricade and by use of a single flagman.

[James Dickens was driving eastbound on Oak Street when he suffered a seizure and lost consciousness. Dickens was under treatment for epilepsy and had neglected to take his medication at the proper time. His car crashed through a single wooden horse-type barricade and struck the plaintiff, throwing him into the air. He was "splattered over his face, head and body with 400 degree boiling hot liquid enamel from a kettle struck by the automobile.... Although plaintiff's body ignited into a fire ball, he miraculously survived the incident."

[The jury found in favor of the plaintiff against Dickens, Felix, and Consolidated Edison. The Appellate Division affirmed. Only the claim against Felix is involved here.]

To support his claim of an unsafe work site, plaintiff called as a witness Lawrence Lawton, an expert in traffic safety. According to Lawton, the usual and accepted method of safeguarding the workers is to erect a barrier around the excavation. Such a barrier, consisting of a truck, a piece of heavy equipment or a pile of dirt, would keep a car out of the excavation and protect workers from oncoming traffic. The expert testified that the barrier should cover the entire width of the excavation. He also stated that there should have been two flagmen present, rather than one, and that warning signs should have been posted advising motorists that there was only one lane of traffic and that there was a flagman ahead.

Following receipt of the evidence, the trial court charged the jury, among other things, that it could consider, as some evidence of negligence, the violation of a Mount Vernon ordinance. The ordinance imposed upon a construction "permittee" certain safety duties. Defendant Felix now argues that plaintiff was injured in a freakish accident, brought about solely by defendant Dickens' negligence, and therefore there was no causal link, as a matter of law, between Felix' breach of duty and plaintiff's injuries.

The concept of proximate cause, or more appropriately legal cause, has proven to be an elusive one, incapable of being precisely defined to cover all situations. This is, in part, because the concept stems from policy considerations that serve to place manageable limits upon the liability that flows from negligent conduct. Depending upon the nature of the case, a variety of factors may be relevant in assessing legal cause. Given the unique nature of the inquiry in each case, it is for the finder of fact to determine legal cause, once the court has been satisfied that a prima facie case has been established. To carry the burden of proving a prima facie case, the plaintiff must generally show that the defendant's negligence was "a substantial cause of the events which produced the injury." Plaintiff need not demonstrate, however, that the precise manner in which the accident happened, or the extent of injuries, was foreseeable (Restatement, Torts 2d, § 435, subd. 2).

Where the acts of a third person intervene between the defendant's conduct and the plaintiff's injury, the causal connection is not automatically severed. In such a case, liability turns upon whether the intervening act is a normal or foreseeable consequence of the situation created by the defendant's negligence. If the intervening act is extraordinary under the circumstances, not foreseeable in the normal course of events, or independent of or far removed from the defendant's conduct, it may well be a superseding act which breaks the causal nexus. Because questions concerning what is foreseeable and what is normal may be the subject of varying inferences, as is the question of negligence itself, these issues generally are for the fact finder to resolve.

There are certain instances, to be sure, where only one conclusion may be drawn from the established facts and where the question of legal cause may be decided as a matter of law. Those cases generally involve independent intervening acts which operate upon but do not flow from the original negligence. Thus, for instance, we have held that where an automobile lessor negligently supplies a car with a defective trunk lid, it is not liable to the lessee who, while stopped to repair the trunk, was injured by the negligent driving of a third party. (Ventricelli v. Kinney System Rent A Car), [45 N.Y.2d 950, 411 N.Y.S.2d 555, 383 N.E.2d 1149 (1978)]. Although the renter's negligence undoubtedly served to place the injured party at the site of the accident, the intervening act was divorced from and not the foreseeable risk associated with the original negligence. And the injuries were different in kind than those which would have normally been expected from a defective trunk. In short, the negligence of the renter merely furnished the occasion for an unrelated act to cause injuries not ordinarily anticipated.

By contrast, in the present case, we cannot say as a matter of law that defendant Dickens' negligence was a superseding cause which interrupted the link between Felix's negligence and plaintiff's injuries. From the evidence in the record, the jury could have found that Felix negligently failed to safeguard the excavation site. A prime hazard associated with such dereliction is the possibility that a driver will negligently enter the work site and cause injury to a worker. That the driver was negligent, or even reckless, does not insulate Felix from liability. Nor is it decisive that the driver lost control of the vehicle through a negligent failure to take medication, rather than a driving mistake. The precise manner of the event need not be anticipated. The finder of fact could have concluded that the foreseeable, normal and natural result of the risk created by Felix was the injury of a worker by a car entering the improperly protected work area. An intervening act may not serve as a superseding cause, and relieve an actor of responsibility, where the risk of the intervening act occurring is the very same risk which renders the actor negligent.

[Affirmed].

NOTES

1. **Does manner of harm *ever* matter?** Is *Derdiarian* consistent with the scope-of-risk principle? The defendant could foresee some kind of harm from a motor vehicle entering the excavation and that is what happened. The precise manner in which the injury came about, as we know from *Hughes,* does not necessarily matter. Think about whether the manner in which the injury came about ever matters to the analysis of reasonable foreseeability. Where the harm occurs in some bizarre, unforeseeable manner, is that irrelevant to judging whether the type of harm was foreseeable? Suppose on facts like *Derdiarian* the injury occurs because an airplane crashes into the excavation. Try working that out under a scope-of-risk analysis.

2. **Foreseeability of risk or result?** Many, many cases use foreseeability in some fashion when there are intervening causes, and like *Derdiarian,* often speak of foreseeability of the intervening cause itself rather than foreseeability of the general result. *See Puckett v. Mt. Carmel Reg'l Med. Ctr.,* 228 P.3d 1048 (Kan. 2010) ("If the intervening cause is foreseen or might have been foreseen by the first actor, his negligence may be considered the

proximate cause, notwithstanding the intervening cause."). *See also Summy v. City of Des Moines*, 708 N.W.2d 333 (Iowa 2006). Is this the risk rule coupled with a tendency to describe the risk by describing the mechanism that brings the risk about?

3. **Foreseeable negligence of others.** In *Eckroth v. Pennsylvania Elec. Inc.*, 12 A.3d 422 (Pa. 2010), defendant negligently turned off decedent's electricity for nonpayment of bills. Two days later, with the electricity still off, a resident left a lit candle in the bathroom overnight on a shelf where towels and toilet paper were located. During the night the candle fell, resulting in the death of four people. Could the defendant have foreseen the resident's conduct?

4. **Obviousness of the original risk.** Does it matter to the analysis if the risks created by the first negligent actor are (or should be) "obvious" to the second actor? Why might that matter? In *Latzel v. Bartek*, 846 N.W.2d 153 (Neb. 2014), a landowner negligently allowed corn to grow seven feet high, up to a ditch near a rural intersection. This obscured drivers' vision of the cross-road. Drivers of two cars crossed the blind intersection simultaneously, and in the ensuing crash a passenger was killed. In the passenger's estate's suit against the landowner, the trial court granted summary judgment on proximate cause grounds. *Held*, affirmed. "There was no evidence that the landowners could have reasonably foreseen the drivers' conduct. . . . [A]lthough the landowners anticipated speeding, they were not bound to anticipate that drivers would disregard the obvious danger of traversing a visually obstructed unmarked intersection without being able to see what they needed to see to do so safely." Should a jury decide whether this is a foreseeable risk created by allowing corn to grow up in such a way as to become a visual obstruction, or is it better policy to hold the drivers solely responsible as a matter of law?

5. **Scope of the original risk.** "[I]f the intervening act of the third person constitutes negligence, that negligence does not constitute a superseding cause if the actor at the time of his negligent conduct should have realized that a third person might so act. In fact, if the likelihood that a person may act in a particular manner is . . . one of the hazards which makes the actor negligent, such an act whether innocent, negligent, intentionally tortious or criminal does not prevent the actor from being liable for harm cause thereby." *Michaels v. CH2M Hill, Inc.*, 257 P.3d 532 (Wash. 2011). If it is negligent to leave your unlocked loaded gun in a shoebox on a closet shelf, is your child's act of taking the gun out, playing with it, and accidentally shooting his friend a superseding cause of that other child's death? *Adames v. Sheahan*, 909 N.E.2d 742 (Ill. 2009). Have we seen this rule before?

VENTRICELLI V. KINNEY SYSTEM RENT A CAR, INC.

383 N.E.2d 1149, *modified*, 386 N.E.2d 263 (N.Y. 1978)

[Defendant Kinney leased plaintiff a car with a defective trunk lid that did not close satisfactorily. Kinney unsuccessfully attempted a repair.

While the car was parked on Mott Street, the plaintiff and a passenger were attempting to slam the lid shut. One Maldonado was parked several car lengths behind the plaintiff. His car suddenly "jumped ahead" and ran into the plaintiff. The jury awarded plaintiff $550,000 for his injuries. The Appellate Division reversed and dismissed as to Kinney.]

MEMORANDUM.

Order of the Appellate Division affirmed, with costs. Proximate cause and foreseeability are relative terms, "nothing more than a convenient formula for disposing of the case" (Prosser, Law of Torts [4th ed.], § 43, p. 267). In writing of the "orbit of the duty," Chief Judge Cardozo said "[t]he range of reasonable apprehension is at times a question for the court, and at times, if varying inferences are possible, a question for the jury." (Palsgraf v. Long Is. R.R. Co., 248 N.Y. 339, 345, 162 N.E. 99, 101). So it is with proximate cause and foreseeability.

Although the negligence of the automobile renter, defendant Kinney, is manifest, and was, of course, a "cause" of the accident, it was not the proximate cause.] "What we do mean by the word 'proximate' is that, because of convenience, of public policy, of a rough sense of justice, the law arbitrarily declines to trace a series of events beyond a certain point." (Palsgraf v. Long Is. R.R. Co., 248 N.Y. 339, 352, 162 N.E. 99, 103, supra [Andrews, J., dissenting]). The immediately effective cause of plaintiff's injuries was the negligence of Maldonado, the driver of the second car, in striking plaintiff while he was standing behind his parked automobile. That Kinney's negligence in providing an automobile with a defective trunk lid would result in plaintiff's repeated attempts to close the lid was reasonably foreseeable. Not "foreseeable," however, was the collision between vehicles both parked for a brief interval before the accident. Plaintiff was standing in a relatively "safe" place, a parking space, not in an actively traveled lane. He might well have been there independent of any negligence of Kinney, as, for example, if he were loading or unloading the trunk. Under these circumstances, to hold the accident a foreseeable consequence of Kinney's negligence is to stretch the concept of foreseeability beyond acceptable limits (see Prosser, Law of Torts [4th ed.], pp. 267–270; Restatement, Torts 2d, § 435, subd. 2).

FUCHSBERG, JUDGE (dissenting). . . .

Ample was the proof that, to the knowledge of the rental company, the trunk door on the automobile it furnished to the plaintiff had a penchant for flying open so as to obstruct the operator's view while the vehicle was moving. Given these facts, it was not only foreseeable, but a most reasonable rather than a remote expectation, that a driver confronted by such an emergency would alight and promptly proceed to the rear of the car to attempt to secure the lid manually so that he might continue on his way without further danger to others and himself. The seemingly ineluctable consequence was to expose the driver to the danger of being struck by another vehicle while he was positioned behind the trunk. On these facts, it could readily be found, as the jury apparently did here, that the choice between the alternatives—the danger from the obstruction of the driver's view from the vehicle and the danger of being struck while engaged in the act of removing the danger—was thrust on the plaintiff by Kinney's negligence. Of course, whether, in making the choice he did, plaintiff himself was negligent similarly raised a factual issue within the province of the jury. . . .

Quote C. to jury

NOTES

1. **Compare to *Derdiarian*.** The plaintiff in *Ventricelli* is injured trying to minimize a risk created by the rental company. Why, then, can't the plaintiff win here? Is the intervening fault of Mr. Maldonado somehow less foreseeable than the intervening act of Mr. Dickens in the *Derdiarian* case? Is the fact that the plaintiff in *Ventricelli* was not left in a "position of danger" by the rental company's negligence a sufficient way to distinguish the case from *Derdiarian*? Is the "position of danger" analysis merely a variant of the scope-of-risk rule?

2. **A variation.** If the plaintiff had pulled over to the shoulder of the highway to fix the trunk and was hit by another car while there, should the case have come out differently?

MARSHALL V. NUGENT
222 F.2d 604 (1st Cir. 1955)

MAGRUDER, J.

[Plaintiff Marshall was a passenger in Harriman's car. There was ice and hard-packed snow on the highway. As Harriman topped a hill, he saw a truck coming toward him, partly in his lane. Harriman went off the road. The truck driver, Warren Prince, stopped to help pull Harriman's car back on the road. This effort partly blocked the road again, so the plaintiff walked toward the top of the hill to flag any approaching motorists. Before he could reach the top, Nugent drove over the hill, saw the Socony-Vacuum Oil Co. truck blocking the road, and attempted to avoid it. He skidded into the plaintiff, Marshall. Marshall sued both Nugent and the truck driver. The jury found against the truck driver, who appeals urging that he was not a proximate cause.]

Procedural Posture

To say that the situation created by the defendant's culpable acts constituted "merely a condition," not a cause of plaintiff's harm, is to indulge in mere verbiage, which does not solve the question at issue, but is simply a way of stating the conclusion, arrived at from other considerations, that the causal relation between the defendant's act and the plaintiff's injury is not strong enough to warrant holding the defendant legally responsible for the injury.

The adjective "proximate," as commonly used in this connection, is perhaps misleading, since to establish liability it is not necessarily true that the defendant's culpable act must be shown to have been the next or immediate cause of the plaintiff's injury. . . .

[S]peaking in general terms, the effort of the courts has been, in the development of this doctrine of proximate causation, to confine the liability of a negligent actor to those harmful consequences which result from the operation of the risk, or of a risk, the foreseeability of which rendered the defendant's conduct negligent.

Of course, putting the inquiry in these terms does not furnish a formula which automatically decides each of an infinite variety of cases. Flexibility is still preserved by the further need of defining the risk, or risks, either narrowly, or more broadly, as seems appropriate and just in the special type of case.

Regarding motor vehicle accidents in particular, one should contemplate a variety of risks which are created by negligent driving. There may be injuries resulting from a direct collision between the carelessly driven car and another vehicle. But such direct collision may be avoided, yet the plaintiff may fall and injure himself in frantically racing out of the way of the errant car. . . . Or the plaintiff may faint from intense excitement stimulated by the near collision, and in falling sustain a fractured skull. . . . This bundle of risks could be enlarged indefinitely with a little imagination. In a traffic mix-up due to negligence, before the disturbed waters have become placid and normal again, the unfolding of events between the culpable act and the plaintiff's eventual injury may be bizarre indeed; yet the defendant may be liable for the result. In such a situation, it would be impossible for a person in the defendant's position to predict in advance just how his negligent act would work out to another's injury. Yet this in itself is no bar to recovery.

When an issue of proximate cause arises in a borderline case, as not infrequently happens, we leave it to the jury with appropriate instructions. . . .

Exercising that judgment on the facts in the case at bar, we have to conclude that the district court committed no error in refusing to direct a verdict for the defendant Socony on the issue of proximate cause. . . .

Plaintiff Marshall was a passenger in the oncoming Chevrolet car, and thus was one of the persons whose bodily safety was primarily endangered by the negligence of Prince, as might have been found by the jury, in "cutting the corner" with the Socony truck in the circumstances above related. In that view, Prince's negligence constituted an irretrievable breach of duty to the plaintiff. Though this particular act of negligence was over and done with when the truck pulled up alongside of the stalled Chevrolet without having actually collided with it, still the consequences of such past negligence were in the bosom of time, as yet unrevealed.

If the Chevrolet had been pulled back onto the highway, and Harriman and Marshall, having got in it again, had resumed their journey and had had a collision with another car five miles down the road in which Marshall suffered bodily injuries, it could truly be said that such subsequent injury to Marshall was a consequence in fact of the earlier delay caused by the defendant's negligence, in the sense that but for such delay the Chevrolet car would not have been at the fatal intersection at the moment the other car ran into it. But on such assumed state of facts, the courts would no doubt conclude, "as a matter of law," that Prince's earlier negligence in cutting the corner was not the "proximate cause" of this later injury received by the plaintiff. That would be because the extra risks to which such negligence by Prince had subjected the passengers in the Chevrolet car were obviously entirely over; the situation had been stabilized and become normal, and, so far as one could foresee, whatever subsequent risks the Chevrolet might have to encounter in its resumed journey were simply the inseparable risks, no more and no less, that were incident to the Chevrolet's being out on the highway at all. But in the case at bar, the circumstances under which Marshall received the personal injuries complained of presented no such clear-cut situation. . . .

NOTES

1.   **Termination of risk.** A phrase once used was "termination of the risk." In *Pittsburg Reduction Co. v. Horton*, 113 S.W. 647 (Ark. 1908), a boy named Copple found explosive dynamite caps that the defendant had negligently left in a place where children could be expected to pick them up. Copple kept them at home and his mother knew of them. A week later he traded them to a 13-year-old boy, Jack Horton. Horton lost a hand while playing with them. The court thought that Mrs. Copple's knowing tolerance of the shells "broke the causal connection" and that the defendant which had negligently scattered them around for the children to find would not be liable. "Charlie Copple's parents having permitted him to retain possession of the caps, his further acts in regard to them must be attributable to their permission and were wholly independent of the original negligence of appellants." Commentators have suggested that this is an example of a "terminated risk." Defendant's conduct created a risk but the risk so created was no longer existent. How do you have to describe the risk if this view is taken? Is the termination of the risk idea consistent with the risk principle?

2.   **A recent case.** In *Baumann v. Zhukov*, 802 F.3d 950 (8th Cir. 2015), two truck drivers negligently crashed, blocking an interstate highway; the traffic backup was almost a mile long. Vehicles activated hazard lights, and police, fire and ambulance vehicles had overhead lights flashing. The Schmidts

were in a car at the back of the long line. Some forty minutes after the original accident, Slezak drove his tractor-trailer into the Schmidts' car at about 75 miles per hour, killing the entire family. In a suit by the Schmidts' estates against the two drivers who caused the original accident, the trial court granted summary judgment for the defense on the ground that the "unanticipated negligence of Slezak was an 'efficient intervening cause.' " The appeals court affirmed, pointing to the length of time between the two crashes and the "patently obvious hazard" that faced Slezak, concluding that "no reasonable jury could conclude otherwise." The dissenting judge argued that in this case, "where to draw the line on proximate cause is an issue for the finder of fact."

3. **Reaching apparent safety.** The termination of the risk idea emphasizes that the plaintiff had reached a position of "apparent safety." "Safety" was presumed in *Horton* because one could presumably believe that a mother, having actually discovered the caps, would confiscate them or otherwise provide for safety. But this was not because the defendant's fault had terminated; the defendant had no reason to think the caps had been put in the protective custody of the mother. But if *Horton* is wrong, liability must end somewhere. What would you suggest?

4. **Liability for subsequent medical negligence.** Defendant negligently injures Plaintiff, who is then taken to a hospital for treatment. Is the Defendant liable for any subsequent negligence in medical treatment? While you might see this as a "position of safety" for the plaintiff, virtually all courts agree that when a defendant causes harm to a person, that defendant will also be liable for any "enhanced harm" caused by the later negligent provision of aid, including negligent medical treatment. *See* RESTATEMENT (THIRD) OF TORTS: LIABILITY FOR PHYSICAL AND EMOTIONAL HARM § 35 (2010). Is this rule consistent with the more general scope-of-risk rule?

———————

PROBLEM

Wolfe v. Gramlich, Inc.

Your client, Gramlich Inc., is being sued by Louis Wolfe on a negligence theory. The following facts are not disputed. Gramlich, as part of its business, maintained a large tank for storing tar. It negligently allowed the tar to spill over, so that the tar flowed from its premises onto an area where plaintiff, a 9-year-old boy, and other children often played.

One day, plaintiff walked into the tar to such depth that his feet were covered up to his ankles. When he returned to his house, his parents saw the tar on his feet and began to remove it by taking the child into the middle of the back yard and using a solvent which is regarded as a safe product for removing tar from skin. While the parents were so engaged, a second child ran into their yard and unexpectedly exploded a cap from a cap-pistol which created a spark that ignited the fumes from the solvent and resulted in serious burns to plaintiff's legs.

Gramlich's general counsel believes that it might be able to move for summary judgment on the ground that even if its actions were negligent, Wolfe's injuries were not within the scope of liability. She has asked you, as outside counsel, to advise her on the motion's strengths and weaknesses.

NOTE: THE FUTURE OF SCOPE-OF-RISK ANALYSIS

Proximate cause rules arose before the full development of the joint and several liability system coupled with contribution. Those rules also arose before the development of comparative fault systems. As we will begin to see in the next chapter, comparative fault systems are capable of apportioning liability among many tortfeasors, imposing greater liability upon those who are more at fault. Scope of liability rules, on the other hand, are all-or-nothing. In the intervening cause situation, the first actor may escape liability altogether, while the second bears the whole burden. That is surely as appropriate as it ever was when it is clear that the second defendant created an entirely new and different risk. When the judge merely feels that the second actor is much more at fault, it may be that proximate cause/superseding cause analyses are counterproductive and that comparative fault rules, with each tortfeasor liable for some portion of the damages, may provide the best solution.

Several courts have now said that superseding cause analyses are to be abandoned as confusing and duplicating the basic foreseeability/scope-of-risk rules. *See Barry v. Quality Steel Prods., Inc.,* 820 A.2d 258 (Conn. 2003); *Control Techniques, Inc. v. Johnson,* 762 N.E.2d 104 (Ind. 2002). Do you regard this as a step toward resolving more cases by allocating liability according to fault rather than on an all-or-nothing basis?

REFERENCES: DOBBS, HAYDEN & BUBLICK, HORNBOOK ON TORTS §§ 15.1–15.21 (2d ed. 2016); 1 DOBBS, HAYDEN & BUBLICK, THE LAW OF TORTS §§ 198–217 (2d ed. 2011); JOSEPH A. PAGE, TORTS: PROXIMATE CAUSE (2002).

PART 4

DEFENSES TO THE NEGLIGENCE CASE

■ ■ ■

About Defenses

A plaintiff who proves every element of a prima facie case for negligence will survive a directed verdict and get her claim to the jury. Nevertheless, her recovery may be defeated or reduced if the defendant mounts a successful affirmative defense. The defendant has the burden of proving affirmative defenses. This chapter and the two that follow examine the major affirmative defenses. The defenses covered in the next three chapters are the traditional ones. Legislatures may create other defenses for particular cases.

Many other impediments to the plaintiff's recovery exist but are not necessarily affirmative defenses. Among these are rules that reduce or eliminate a defendant's duty of care and those that provide for complete immunity from tort liability. In addition, procedural impediments applied to particular claims like medical malpractice may vastly reduce the number of successful suits. Finally, among the partial defenses enacted by some legislatures are damages caps, limiting liability in particular cases. All of these appear in later chapters.

CHAPTER 9

FAULT OF THE PLAINTIFF

• • •

§ 1. CONTRIBUTORY NEGLIGENCE:
THE COMMON LAW RULE

BUTTERFIELD V. FORRESTER

11 East. 60, 103 Eng. Rep. 926 (1809)

This was an action on the case for obstructing a highway, by means of which obstruction the plaintiff, who was riding along the road, was thrown down with his horse, and injured, & c. At the trial before Bayley J. at Derby, it appeared that the defendant, for the purpose of making some repairs to his house, which was close by the road side at one end of the town, had put up a pole across this part of the road, a free passage being left by another branch or street in the same direction. That the plaintiff left a public house not far distant from the place in question at 8 o'clock in the evening in August, when they were just beginning to light candles, but while there was light enough left to discern the obstruction at 100 yards distance: and the witness, who proved this, said that if the plaintiff had not been riding very hard he might have observed and avoided it: the plaintiff however, who was riding violently, did not observe it, but rode against it, and fell with his horse and was much hurt in consequence of the accident; and there was no evidence of his being intoxicated at the time. On this evidence Bayley J. directed the jury, that if a person riding with reasonable and ordinary care could have seen and avoided the obstruction; and if they were satisfied that the plaintiff was riding along the street extremely hard, and without ordinary care, they should find a verdict for the defendant: which they accordingly did. [The plaintiff sought a "rule" which would have granted him a new trial.]

BAYLEY J. The plaintiff was proved to be riding as fast as his horse could go, and this was through the streets of Derby. If he had used ordinary care he must have seen the obstruction; so that the accident appeared to happen entirely from his own fault.

LORD ELLENBOROUGH C.J. A party is not to cast himself upon an obstruction which has been made by the fault of another, and avail himself of it, if he do not himself use common and ordinary caution to be in the right. In cases of persons riding upon what is considered to be the wrong

243

side of the road, that would not authorize another purposely to ride up against them. One person being in fault will not dispense with another's using ordinary care for himself. Two things must concur to support this action, an obstruction in the road by the fault of the defendant, and no want of ordinary care to avoid it on the part of the plaintiff. [The new trial was refused.]

NOTES

1. **Contributory negligence.** After *Butterfield v. Forrester*, the courts developed the rule of contributory negligence as a complete, all-or-nothing defense. Even relatively minor failure of the plaintiff to exercise ordinary care for her own safety would completely bar recovery. This remained true even if the defendant's negligence was extreme, so long as it fell short of a reckless or wanton act.

2. **Justifying *Butterfield*.** It is important, for reasons that will later become apparent, to identify the several grounds on which the result in *Butterfield v. Forrester* might be justified.

(a) *The fault principle.* If liability is to be based upon fault and the defendant fined because his fault causes harm, should the same fault principle compel the faulty plaintiff to lose his case entirely?

(b) *Proximate cause.* Could *Butterfield v. Forrester* be understood as applying some view of proximate cause in which the plaintiff is treated as a superseding cause? Test this idea. Imagine that a child, standing near the obstruction, had been injured when the horse fell. Would the defendant, if negligent, have been liable for that? —> Examining Causality

(c) *Negligence.* Granted that the defendant owed the plaintiff a duty of care, was that duty breached? Formulate an argument that the defendant's conduct was not negligent at all. Try to draw on specific cases or hypotheticals for a principle or general idea that furthers the defendant's argument. —> Defendant's actions indicate he took care to make sure others were safe

3. **Origin of the rule.** Why do you think the contributory negligence rule developed in such a stringent fashion? Rules often develop from social and economic needs or assumptions. But sometimes a rule develops from a conceptual failure, that is, because legal professionals are unable at the moment to put together a coherent or logical idea about what a rule ought to be. Does the contributory negligence rule reflect social or economic standards or merely a conceptual failure? —> Presenting formalist construction of fault allocation

4. **Avoiding the bar to recovery.** In several situations courts found reasons not to apply the contributory negligence defense. When an exception applied, the plaintiff made a full recovery in spite of her own fault. It was still an all-or-nothing system, but when an exception applied it was "all" rather than "nothing" for the plaintiff. We will look at these exceptions and how they fare under modern comparative negligence law in §§ 4–6 below.

§ 2. ADOPTING COMPARATIVE FAULT RULES

NEW YORK MCKINNEY'S CIV. PRAC. LAW § 1411

In any action to recover damages for personal injury, injury to property, or wrongful death, the culpable conduct attributable to the claimant or to the decedent, including contributory negligence or assumption of risk, shall not bar recovery, but the amount of damages otherwise recoverable shall be diminished in the proportion which the culpable conduct attributable to the claimant or decedent bears to the culpable conduct which caused the damages.

WISCONSIN STAT. ANN. § 895.045

Contributory negligence does not bar recovery in an action by any person or the person's legal representative to recover damages for negligence resulting in death or in injury to person or property, if that negligence was not greater than the negligence of the person against whom recovery is sought, but any damages allowed shall be diminished in the proportion to the amount of negligence attributed to the person recovering. . . .

NOTES

1. **Adoption of comparative fault rules.** The Federal Employers' Liability Act (FELA), 45 U.S.C. § 53, was promulgated in 1906 to facilitate claims against interstate railroads by workers injured on the job. It adopted a comparative negligence system as one of its major provisions. The plaintiff's negligence still reduces, but does not bar, a worker's recovery under this statute. *See CSX Transp., Inc. v. Begley,* 313 S.W.3d 52 (Ky. 2010). Another federal statute, the Jones Act, applied the FELA rules to seafaring workers. Only a handful of states adopted comparative fault systems until a wave of change occurred after the late 1960s. As of the early 21st century, only Alabama, North Carolina, Maryland, Virginia, and the District of Columbia have failed to adopt comparative fault rules. In those jurisdictions, the plaintiff's contributory fault remains a complete bar. *See Coleman v. Soccer Ass'n of Columbia,* 69 A.3d 1149 (Md. 2013) (court would not abrogate common law contributory negligence rule in light of legislative policy to retain the rule, evidenced by the failure of numerous bills that would have abolished or modified it).

2. **Terminology.** Although the New York and Wisconsin statutes are both comparative fault statutes, notice the terminology. Each notes that "contributory negligence" diminishes the plaintiff's proportion of damages. The term "contributory negligence" can still be properly used to describe the negligence of the plaintiff even when the effect of that negligence is no longer to bar the plaintiff's claim. But use of the term "contributory negligence" can be confusing because of its historic association with the older all-or-nothing effect. In court cases, judges may use the term contributory negligence to mean

fault of the plaintiff with or without the all-or-nothing effect. However, to be clear, in the notes we will use "contributory negligence" when we refer to the all-or-nothing effect and "comparative negligence" or "comparative fault" when we refer to proportionate liability. The term "comparative fault" is similar to the term "comparative negligence" but can sometimes be construed more broadly to include causes of action other than negligence.

3. **Pure vs. modified comparative fault.** The approach represented by the New York statute, *supra*, is called pure comparative fault. The approach represented by the Wisconsin statute is called modified comparative fault. Under modified comparative fault, a plaintiff who is assigned more than a 50% fault share recovers nothing whatever; the negligence of the plaintiff bars all recovery because her negligence is greater than the defendant's. *Lake v. D & L Langley Trucking, Inc.*, 233 P.3d 589 (Wyo. 2010).

4. **Jury role in attributing fault percentages.** How much fault is attributable to each party? If the evidence permits reasonable people to differ, this is a "fact" question, not a question of law. *Gonzalez v. Union Pac. R.R. Co.*, 872 N.W.2d 579, 587 (Neb. 2015) (it was for the trier of fact to determine whether the negligence of a child who crossed a train track equaled or exceeded that of Union Pacific, which failed to blow its horn at an obscured intersection); *Bitgood v. Greene*, 108 A.3d 1023 (R.I. 2015). Attribution of fault percentages is necessarily a rough approximation even though it is expressed in mathematical terms. The jury is usually told, in effect, to treat the total fault in the case as 100%, and to then find the percentage of fault attributable to each person.

5. **Applying the rules.** Suppose four cars, driven by P, B, C, and D all collide. P is guilty of 5% of the negligence, B 10%, C 40% and D 45%. P has damages of $100,000. What does P recover? — $95,000

6. **Information for the jury.** Should the jury be told how its comparative fault findings will impact an award of damages? In *Sollin v. Wangler*, 627 N.W.2d 159 (N.D. 2001), Dale Wangler, who was attempting to load a 1200-pound bale of straw into a grinder, dropped it on Richard Sollin, causing serious injuries. The jury assigned 50% of the fault to Sollin, the plaintiff, and 50% to Wangler, the defendant. It then awarded Sollin $100,000 in damages and Wangler $8,000. The trial judge did not answer the jury's question—"is the % of fault going to determine damage awards?" The North Dakota comparative fault statute barred plaintiffs from recovering if their fault was "as great as the combined fault of all other persons." The North Dakota Supreme Court rejected "the blindfold rule" and held that the jury should have been informed of the legal consequences of its verdict."

§ 3. APPLYING COMPARATIVE FAULT RULES

A. APPORTIONING FAULT

POHL V. COUNTY OF FURNAS
682 F.3d 745 (8th Cir. 2012)

MURPHY, CIRCUIT JUDGE. . . .

[Juston Pohl, a resident of Michigan, was returning to a friend's farmhouse. It was 9 p.m. Light snow was falling. Pohl mistakenly turned onto Drive 719 instead of Road 719.] Drive 719 is a gravel road that does not have a posted speed limit but is subject to a general statutory limit of 50 miles per hour. Unlike Road 719 which continues in a straight line . . . Drive 719 has a ninety degree curve one mile after its intersection with Highway 47. . . .

After turning onto Drive 719, Pohl accelerated to 63 mph, traveling with his high beam headlights on. When Pohl neared the warning sign, he braked too late to prevent the car from missing the curve and going off the road. The car hit an embankment, rolled, and came to rest upside down in a culvert. Pohl lost consciousness. When he came to, he realized he could not move his legs. Since he was unable to walk, he remained in the car all night hoping to be rescued. No help had arrived by daybreak, and Pohl managed to drag himself to a nearby farmhouse where the residents called an ambulance. It was later determined that he had a fracture and cord compression in his thoracic spine as well as frostbite in his feet. . . .

Pohl sued the county for common law negligence under the district court's diversity jurisdiction. He alleged that his injuries were the result of the county's negligent placement of the sign warning about the curve and its negligent failure to maintain it. . . .

At trial Pohl offered his own testimony and that of a traffic engineer and other lay witnesses. . . . Ronald Hensen, a traffic engineer, . . . testified that the sign did not comply with the standards set by the United States Department of Transportation's Manual on Uniform Traffic Control Devices (the Manual), which governs traffic control signs in Nebraska. The sign was deficient, he said, because it was heavily scratched and thus not retroreflective. . . . Hensen explained that because the sign lacked retroreflectivity, the 110 foot distance between the sign and the curve was not enough to provide drivers adequate notice of the curve ahead. He testified that a distance of at least 300 feet would have been needed to comply with the Manual and that "I don't know that I've ever seen in place a sign that defective." In discussing the accident, he explained that had Pohl been traveling at the speed limit of 50 mph, he would have entered the curve at a speed of 45 mph and would have still left the roadway.

The county's case consisted of two expert witnesses and hundreds of photographs of the accident scene. Gregory Vandenberg, a Nebraska state trooper who specializes in accident reconstruction, testified that following the crash he had analyzed data from the car's airbag control module which is also referred to as the black box. The black box records the vehicle's speed and braking pattern for the five seconds prior to deployment of the airbag. Based on these data he determined that the car had been traveling at 63 mph on Drive 719 and that Pohl had applied the brakes when he was closely aligned with the sign, slowing the car to 48 mph at the time it left the roadway. . . . If Pohl had been traveling at the speed limit and had braked when his car was aligned with the sign, the trooper's opinion was that the car would have slowed to a speed where Pohl could have safely negotiated the curve. He also explained that had Pohl been traveling at the speed limit but failed to steer, he would have left the roadway at 15 mph and had a less severe accident because the car likely would have stopped before colliding with the embankment. . . .

The district court found that the county was negligent because of the "combination of the sign's lack of retroreflectivity and its placement. . . . It further found that this negligence and Pohl's negligence in driving 13 miles over the speed limit were the proximate causes of his accident and injuries. In assessing the responsibility for the accident and Pohl's injuries the court allocated 60% of the negligence to the county and 40% to Pohl. The district court then calculated that Pohl was entitled to $678,606.14 in damages for medical expenses and pain and suffering, and awarded him $407,163.38 following a reduction for his comparative negligence.

[The county appeals. . . . Pohl cross appeals.] . .

When reviewing a district court's decision following a bench trial in a diversity action, "we look to state law for the standard of review on each issue." . . [Under Nebraska law, the question of whether a defendant is negligent by breaching a duty of care is a question of fact which is reviewed for clear error.] . . .

The [district court's] determination that the sign was not retroreflective was supported by Hensen's testimony that the sign was scratched and did not reflect adequate light to meet the Manual's requirement that a sign reflect "a large portion of the light coming from a point source to be returned directly back to a point near its origin." It was also supported by some of the nighttime flash photographs in evidence on which the warning sign for the curve was not visible, but a distant retroreflective sign was. . . .

Because the record supports the district court's findings that the sign was neither retroreflective nor adequately placed to warn nighttime drivers, the court did not err in finding the county negligent. . . .

The county also argues that Pohl cannot show proximate cause because his speeding was an efficient intervening cause. "[A]n efficient intervening cause is new and independent conduct of a third person, which itself is a proximate cause of the injury in question and breaks the causal connection between original conduct and the injury." Nebraska law makes clear however that an intervening cause cuts off a tortfeasor's liability only when it is not foreseeable. Testimony at trial indicated that traffic engineers assume that drivers will exceed the speed limit by 10 to 15 mph on a 50 mph road, and thus Pohl's travel 13 mph in excess of the speed limit was readily foreseeable.

We finally address the county's argument that . . . the district court erred by undervaluing Pohl's contributory negligence. Contributory negligence occurs where the plaintiff breaches a duty of care and his breach "concur[s] and cooperat[es]" with the defendant's negligence to form a proximate cause of the injury. Under Nebraska law, a plaintiff is barred from recovery if his negligence is equal to or greater than that of the defendant. Contributory negligence is an affirmative defense that must be proved by the party asserting it. Since the existence of such negligence is a question of fact, our review is again for clear error.

The county . . . contends that the trial court erred in its assessment of contributory negligence because it should have found that Pohl's contributory negligence in speeding exceeded the county's negligence, thus barring recovery. In support of this argument, it points to Vandenberg's testimony indicating that had Pohl been traveling at the speed limit, he would have been able to negotiate the curve successfully if he had braked when aligned with the sign. This testimony was contradicted, however, by Hensen's testimony that had Pohl been traveling at the speed limit, his speed at the curve would have still been too great to negotiate it successfully. Given this conflicting testimony, we cannot say that the district court clearly erred by not finding that Pohl's negligence exceeded that of the county. Cf. Anderson v. City of Bessemer, 470 U.S. 564, 574, 105 S. Ct. 1504, 84 L.Ed.2d 518 (1985) ("Where there are two permissible views of the evidence, the factfinder's choice between them cannot be clearly erroneous."). . . .

On cross appeal, Pohl . . . contends that the district court erred in finding that his injuries would have been less severe had he not been speeding. He essentially argues that because no evidence was introduced from a biomedical expert indicating how he would have suffered fewer injuries had he been traveling at a slower speed, the district court's finding of proximate cause was clearly erroneous. Pohl cites no authority indicating that such evidence is required where the record contains evidence that the accident would have been less severe had the plaintiff not been speeding. Vandenberg's testimony suggested that had Pohl been traveling at the speed limit when he braked and still gone off the road, he would have been traveling at only 15 mph on leaving the road as opposed to 48 mph. There would then have been a "less severe collision," and the car "likely . . . would have stopped short of the . . . embankment." Given this evidence, it was reasonable to find that the accident would have been less severe and Pohl would have sustained less serious injuries had he not been speeding. Accordingly, the district court did not clearly err by finding that his negligence at the time of the crash was a proximate cause of his injuries.

We finally address Pohl's contention that even if the district court's determinations regarding negligence and proximate cause were correct, it should have apportioned less negligence to Pohl. The apportionment of negligence "is solely a matter for the fact finder, and its action will not be disturbed on appeal if it is supported by credible evidence and bears a reasonable relationship to the respective elements of negligence proved at trial." *Tadros v. City of Omaha*, 269 Neb. 528, 694 N.W.2d 180, 187 (2005). As discussed above, the evidence supported the district court's finding that the negligence of both parties contributed to Pohl's injuries. Attributing 40% of the negligence to Pohl was reasonable considering the evidence that the accident would still have happened at a lower speed but with less severe injuries.

Accordingly, we affirm the judgment of the district court.

NOTES

1.   **Splitting.** Is this pretty much a modern day disposition of *Butterfield v. Forrester*? Does a 40%–60% split of the costs by the two negligent parties seem more just than an all-or-nothing outcome, or preferable from the point of view of deterrence and compensation? *See* Guido Calabresi & Jeffrey O. Cooper, *New Directions in Tort Law*, 30 VAL. U. L. REV. 859, 868 (1996) (noting modern tort law's rejection of all-or-nothing rules and trend toward splitting); Robert Cooter & Thomas Ulen, *An Economic Case for Comparative Negligence*, 61 N.Y.U. L. REV. 1067 (1996) ("[T]he rule of comparative negligence is more efficient than its alternatives when it is desirable to give moderate incentives for precaution to both parties rather than strong incentives to one party and weak incentives to the other. Such a situation occurs when the parties are symmetrically situated with respect to the ability of each to take precaution."). Traffic accidents are the quintessential case in which both parties may share responsibility if they fail to use reasonable care. *See Stephens v. CSX Transp., Inc.*, 781 S.E.2d 534 (S.C. 2015); *Samson v. Nahulu*, 363 P.3d 263 (Haw. 2015) (pedestrian's fault for walking outside crosswalk should be compared with driver's duty to exercise due care to avoid colliding with pedestrians).

2.   **Methods of comparing negligence.** What conduct was alleged to have been negligent on the part of the State? On the part of Pohl? If a reasonable factfinder, here the trial court judge, could find that both parties failed to use reasonable care, how should the parties' negligence be compared?

In *Purvis v. Grant Parish Sch. Bd.*, 144 So. 3d 922 (La. 2014), the court said that an allocation of fault to parties in negligence actions considers the following factors: (1) whether the conduct was inadvertent, or involved an awareness of the danger; (2) how great a risk was created by the conduct; (3) the significance of what was sought by the conduct; (4) the actors' capacities; and (5) any extenuating factors that might require the actor to proceed with haste. Should the factfinder give each party a *Carroll Towing* "score" measuring the extent of breach and then compare the scores?

In *Wassell v. Adams*, 865 F.2d 849 (7th Cir. 1989), Judge Posner suggested a different approach: "one way to make sense of comparative negligence is to assume that the required comparison is between the respective costs to the plaintiff and to the defendant of avoiding the injury." Suppose Pohl could have avoided the risk to himself by conduct that "costs" time or effort equivalent to one dollar and the county could have avoided the same risk to the plaintiff only by conduct that cost the equivalent of $99. Should the apportionment in that case be 99% and 1%? It might be easy to calculate the cost of replacing the defective sign in *Pohl*. Could the plaintiff's cost in time or effort to avoid the injury have been quantified in monetary terms as well?

3. **The process of comparing negligence.** In most cases the court does not discuss the method of comparing the parties' fault at all. Instead, as in *Pohl*, courts typically suggest that apportionment percentages are "a matter for the fact finder," and look to see whether the finding "is supported by credible evidence and bears a reasonable relationship to the respective elements of negligence proved at trial." *See Thompson v. Winn-Dixie*, 181 So. 2d 656 (La. 2015) (allocation of fault is a factual determination for the jury). Would evidence examined by the trial judge in *Pohl* also have been sufficient to support an apportionment of 30–70 or 70–30? Why not have an apportionment of 50–50?

4. **Avoiding the jury.** In particular cases, a court may conclude that reasonable people would necessarily find contributory negligence or that the plaintiff's comparative negligence is so great that as a matter of law a directed verdict or summary judgment for the defendant is appropriate. *E.g.*, *Phillips v. Fujitec Am., Inc.*, 3 A.3d 324 (D.C. 2010) (summary judgment on issue of contributory negligence when plaintiff who was stuck in an elevator tried to get out between floors although she was told she should stay put and that help was on the way). If on appeal, a court finds a "clearly wrong" apportionment of fault, it has been held that the appellate court should adjust the award, but only to the extent of lowering or raising it to the highest or lowest point which is reasonably within the trier of fact's discretion. *Johnson v. Morehouse Gen. Hosp.*, 63 So. 3d 87 (La. 2011) (adjusting fault among the parties). How might this result support judicial efficiency?

5. **The relationship between care by the parties.** At times, reasonable care by one party eliminates the need for care by the other. In a fraud and misrepresentation case against a lawyer, Judge Posner had this to say about fault of the plaintiff:

Due care is the care that is optimal given that the other party is exercising due care. It is not the higher level of care that would be optimal if potential tort victims were required to assume that the rest of the world was negligent. A pedestrian is not required to exercise a level of care (e.g., wearing a helmet or a shin guard) that would be optimal if there were no sanctions against reckless driving. Otherwise drivers would be encouraged to drive recklessly, and knowing this, pedestrians would be encouraged to wear helmets and shin guards. The result would be a shift from a superior method of accident avoidance (not driving recklessly) to an inferior one (pedestrian armor). . . . The law normally does not require duplicative precautions unless one is likely to fail or the consequences of failure . . . would be catastrophic.

Greycas, Inc. v. Proud, 826 F.2d 1560, 1566 (7th Cir. 1987). How does this kind of analysis work, if at all, in a case like *Pohl*?

6. **Comparative negligence vs. all-or-nothing results.** Despite evidence of its negligence, the county sought a completely favorable result based on two all-or-nothing arguments. Can you see them? Why were those arguments rejected?

7. **Harm to self and harm to others.** Should the plaintiff's fault be considered at all in a case in which that fault poses no risk to the defendant? The risks involved in a negligence action are often risks to others' safety. However, in comparative fault, the risks may be only to the plaintiff and not to others. Because of this difference in risk, some scholars have argued that the concepts of negligence and contributory negligence should be kept separate. Did Pohl's negligence risk harm to himself alone?

8. **Apportioning fault by an "equitable and just" approach.** Maine has a comparative negligence rule radically different from most. Instead of requiring the jury to reduce the plaintiff's damages in proportion to the plaintiff's relative fault, the statute requires the jury to make a reduction it considers to be equitable and just. Do you think the *Pohl* factfinder would have brought in a different verdict under the Maine statute?

B. APPORTIONING RESPONSIBILITY

RESTATEMENT (THIRD) OF TORTS: APPORTIONMENT OF LIABILITY
(2000)

§ 8. FACTORS FOR ASSIGNING SHARES OF RESPONSIBILITY

Factors for assigning percentages of responsibility to each person whose legal responsibility has been established include

(a) the nature of the person's risk-creating conduct, including any awareness or indifference with respect to the risks created by the conduct and any intent with respect to the harm created by the conduct; and

(b) the strength of the causal connection between the person's risk-creating conduct and the harm.

Comment: (c) . . . One or more of these factors may be relevant for assigning percentages of responsibility, even though they may not be a necessary element proving a particular claim or defense. However, these factors are irrelevant even to apportionment if there is no causal connection between the referenced conduct and the plaintiff's injuries. It should be noted that the mental-state factors in this Section may be considered for apportioning responsibility even if they are not themselves causally connected to the plaintiff's injury, as long as the risk-creating conduct to which they refer is causally connected to the injury.

NOTES

1. **The Restatement factors.** Is the Restatement correct in inviting the fact-finder to consider mental states of the parties and the strength of causal connections as well as the unjustified risks they created? Is this just an elaborate version of Maine's "equitable and just" apportionment?

2. **Apportioning responsibility outside negligence.** The Restatement provision contemplates a comparison beyond simply negligence-to-negligence, with its listing of "awareness or indifference" to risk and "intent with respect to harm" as factors in determining percentages. *See Berberich v. Jack*, 709 S.E.2d 607 (S.C. 2011) ("comparative negligence encompasses the comparison of ordinary negligence with heightened forms of misconduct such as recklessness, willfulness, and wantonness"). The *Berberich* court stopped short of permitting apportionment with intentional torts, although some courts not only allow but require this. *See Graves v. North Eastern Servs., Inc.*, 345 P.3d 619 (Utah 2015) (interpreting statutory definition of "fault" to include "intentionally tortious activity").

3. **Terminology.** Under the Restatement view, what would be the term used for the apportioned percentages—it wouldn't be percentages of "negligence" or "fault," would it? The term "comparative responsibility" is sometimes used for systems that include more than just negligence in the apportionment. Can you imagine why?

4. **Comparing fault and causation.** Think back to *Landers* from Chapter 7. In that case, salt water from an oil company and salt water from a disposal company killed the fish in the lake. Imagine that the oil company dumped twice as much salt water as the disposal company, and that the salt water was twice as concentrated, and therefore harmful. However, suppose also that an expert testified that it was somewhat more likely that the salt water from the disposal company reached the lake first. In addition, there was

testimony that the disposal company knew with substantial certainty that the salt water would enter the lake, while the oil company should have known of the unreasonable risk. Is the Restatement formula helpful here? The Restatement was careful to separate scope of liability from factual cause in most of its text. In § 8, however, isn't the term "causal connection" somewhat ambiguous?

§ 4. ALL-OR-NOTHING JUDGMENTS AFTER COMPARATIVE FAULT

1. **No plaintiff negligence**. Comparison of plaintiff and defendant fault is only at issue when both parties are negligent. If the plaintiff is not negligent, or if her negligence is not the factual or proximate cause of the harm, no comparison is necessary. *See Harmon v. Washburn,* 751 N.W.2d 297 (S.D. 2008) (as a matter of law, plaintiff was not negligent to pass another car on a bridge in a legal passing zone, such that trial court should not have permitted comparison); *RGR, LLC v. Settle,* 764 S.E.2d 8 (Va. 2014) (plaintiff not negligent as a matter of law where alleged alternative conduct—stopping on railroad tracks to look and listen for trains—would have placed him in even greater peril). Common features of the negligence analysis, such as the emergency doctrine, apply to the comparative negligence issue just as they do to the negligence question. *Henson v. Klein,* 319 S.W.3d 413 (Ky. 2010).

2. **Plaintiff negligence that is not the factual cause of injury**. Suppose the plaintiff is negligent because she is walking a dog she can't control. She then trips on the sidewalk. However, there is no evidence that she tripped on the sidewalk because she couldn't control the dog. Her negligence does not reduce her damages any more than it would make her liable for someone's injuries that were not caused by her negligence. *See Townsend v. Legere,* 688 A.2d 77 (N.H. 1997). *See also Pavlou v. City of New York,* 868 N.E.2d 186 (N.Y. 2007) (worker operated a crane with an excess load, but a crack in the crane made it unsafe to operate with any load).

3. **Plaintiff injury that is not within the scope of the risk created by the plaintiff's negligence.** It is also possible that the plaintiff's fault will be disregarded because the injury suffered was not within the risk created by that fault. Consider: a house guest negligently blunders onto a dark patio. He is negligent because he is unfamiliar with the place and he might easily trip or fall into the swimming pool. Instead he is struck by his host's runaway car which crashes through the back gate. *See* Dan B. Dobbs, *Accountability and Comparative Fault,* 47 LA. L. REV. (1987). *See also Estate of Moses ex rel. Moses v. Sw. Va. Transit Mgmt. Co.,* 643 S.E.2d 156 (Va. 2007) (reinstating a jury verdict for the plaintiff on the ground that it was within the province of the jury to decide whether the pedestrian's negligence—crossing in the middle of the street when the

street looked clear—was a proximate cause of the accident in which he was hit by a bus).

4. **No defendant negligence**. The same all-or-nothing result will obtain if the defendant is not negligent, or if the defendant's negligence is not the factual or proximate cause of the plaintiff's harm. When an element of the plaintiff's prima facie case against the defendant fails, comparative fault is irrelevant and the plaintiff recovers nothing.

5. **Sorting claims into all-or-nothing or comparative elements**. Under the old regime of contributory negligence, a court could say the plaintiff was at fault, or that the defendant's conduct was not a factual or legal cause of the plaintiff's harm, and the result would be the same whichever view the court took—no recovery for the plaintiff, as was the case in *Butterfield.* [With the adoption of comparative fault, you really need to know whether you are talking about plaintiff fault or defendant factual or proximate cause because the effects can now be quite different.]

6. **Reasonable care by the defendant in light of plaintiff fault?** What if the defendant doctor fails to diagnose a medical-expert patient who failed to give the doctor the information needed to make an accurate diagnosis? Is this a case of the plaintiff's comparative fault or a case of the defendant's non-negligence as in *Stinnett*? On similar facts, see *Juchniewcz v. Bridgeport Hosp.,* 914 A.2d 511 (Conn. 2007).

7. **Plaintiff's fault as a superseding cause of the harm**. Typically, when both plaintiff and defendant are at fault, the court will leave the apportionment of responsibility to the jury. [However, in some cases, courts disclaim plaintiff's recovery altogether on superseding cause grounds.] In *Exxon Co., U.S.A. v. Sofec, Inc.,* 517 U.S. 830 (1996), an Exxon tanker broke away from moorings owned by one defendant and operated by another. The captain managed to get the tanker safely past a number of perils nearby and safely out to sea. But once he reached safety, he neglected to get a fix on his position and he ran aground. The ship was substantially destroyed. Exxon claimed that the owner and operator of the moorings were responsible for the breakaway. The Court held that even if that were so, the captain's negligence in failing to fix his position once he had reached a position of relative safety was a superseding cause. So Exxon could recover nothing, even though admiralty law, which governed the case, uses pure comparative fault to divide damages.

8. **Causal apportionment of separate injuries**. Comparative fault reductions may also be inappropriate when the plaintiff and the defendant cause separate injuries which are capable of causal apportionment. Suppose the plaintiff negligently crashes her car into a tree, sustaining multiple injuries. Dr. Dann's negligent treatment causes paralysis of her legs, which appropriate medical treatment could have avoided. The physician in such a case is not liable for the initial injury itself, but may be

liable for enhancement of the plaintiff's injury—some or all of the damages for the plaintiff's leg paralysis.

9. **The mitigation of damages rule.** The avoidable consequences or mitigation of damages rule traditionally required the plaintiff to minimize her damages by reasonable efforts and expenses. As with other defenses, the burden is on the defendant to prove that the plaintiff failed to mitigate damages. *Tibbetts v. Dairyland Ins. Co.*, 999 A.2d 930 (Me. 2010); *Ramkumar v. Grand Style Transp. Enters., Inc.*, 998 N.E.2d 801 (N.Y. 2013) (plaintiff offered a reasonable explanation for the cessation of physical therapy when he stated in his deposition that his benefits were cut off five months previously). If a plaintiff whose foot was bruised by the defendant's negligence could avoid loss of the foot by taking antibiotics, she might be expected to do so. If she unreasonably refused and lost the foot as a result, she would not be allowed to recover for loss of the foot, although of course she would be permitted to recover for the bruise.

This is not a rule of comparative fault. Instead, it simply excluded all recovery for a particular item of harm when the court concluded either that the defendant was not a but-for cause of that harm or that the harm was outside the scope of the risk negligently created by the defendant because the plaintiff could have averted some of the damage. When the plaintiff failed to take the prescribed antibiotics, some courts might treat the loss of her foot as if it were caused entirely by the plaintiff's fault. Such courts would not compare fault of the plaintiff in failing to take antibiotics with fault of the defendant in causing the injury in the first place. Instead, they would simply exclude liability for loss of the foot. *See Langlois v. Town of Proctor*, 113 A.3d 44, 56 (Vt. 2014) (in this case, there are "no discrete damages allegedly attributable solely to plaintiff. Thus, we agree with the Town that the court should have instructed the jury on comparative negligence rather than on damages mitigation.").

Automatic exclusion of all recovery in the foot example looks like an attempt to make a causal apportionment. If so, it seems wrong, because the defendant in that case is clearly a but-for cause of the foot's loss and because the foot's loss also seems to be within the scope of the risk the defendant created. Perhaps with cases like this in mind, the Restatement specifically follows some statutes by converting avoidable consequences or minimizing damages cases to comparative fault cases. The plaintiff in the foot case would probably be at fault in failing to take prescribed antibiotics, and thus her fault would be compared with the defendant's fault. RESTATEMENT (THIRD) OF TORTS, APPORTIONMENT OF LIABILITY § 3 cmt. b (2000). *See also Oakly Enterprises, LLC v. NPI, LLC*, 354 P.3d 1073 (Alaska 2015) (distinguishing avoidable consequences from an apportionment of damages).

§ 5. ALLOCATING FULL RESPONSIBILITY TO THE DEFENDANT IN THE INTERESTS OF POLICY OR JUSTICE

BEXIGA V. HAVIR MANUFACTURING CORP., 290 A.2d 281 (N.J. 1972). Plaintiff John Bexiga, Jr., a minor, was operating a power punch press for his employer, Regina Corporation (Regina). John, Jr. was directed to place round metal discs, about three inches in diameter, one at a time, by hand, on top of the die. Once the disc was placed on the die, he would then depress the foot pedal activating the machine and causing the ram to descend and punch two holes in the disc. After this operation the ram would ascend and the equipment on the press would remove the metal disc. It was estimated by John, Jr. that one cycle as described above would take approximately 10 seconds and that he had completed about 270 cycles during the 40 minutes he operated the machine. In the accident, he noticed that a piece of metal wasn't in place so went back to correct it, but at the same time his foot depressed the pedal causing the ram to descend. His right hand was crushed by the ram of the machine, resulting in the loss of fingers and deformity of his hand. His father, John Bexiga, Sr., brought suit against Havir Manufacturing Corporation (Havir), the manufacturer of the machine. . . . A mechanical engineering expert testified the punch press amounted to a "booby trap" because there were no safety devices in its basic design. The machine did not have either a guardrail to prevent the operator's hands from entering the area between the ram and the die when the machine was activated, nor did it have a push-button device with the buttons so spaced as to require the operator to place both hands on them away from the die areas to set the machine in motion. *Held*, "[T]his case presents a situation where the interests of justice dictate that contributory negligence be unavailable as a defense to either the negligence or strict liability claims. The asserted negligence of plaintiff—placing his hand under the ram while at the same time depressing the foot pedal—was the very eventuality the safety devices were designed to guard against. It would be anomalous to hold that defendant has a duty to install safety devices but a breach of that duty results in no liability for the very injury the duty was meant to protect against."

NOTES

1. ***Bexiga* and comparative fault.** Should the principle in *Bexiga* apply after adoption of comparative fault? On the problem of allocating risks entirely to the defendant or the defendant's special duty to protect even a negligent plaintiff, see 1 DOBBS, HAYDEN & BUBLICK, THE LAW OF TORTS § 224 (2d ed. 2011). Although *Bexiga* found that the defendant's duty encompassed the plaintiff's negligence, it could be said in the alternative that the plaintiff was not negligent in light of his working conditions. *See Fernandes v. DAR Dev. Corp.*, 119 A.3d 878, 891 (2015) (worker's "behavior must be evaluated against

that of a reasonably prudent person in his exact circumstances, and that evaluation includes whether he had a meaningful choice in the manner in which he performed his assigned task").

2.   **Defendant's undertaking to protect the plaintiff.** In *McNamara v. Honeyman*, 546 N.E.2d 139 (Mass. 1989), decedent, who was mentally ill, hanged herself while confined in a state hospital. In a suit for her death, the trial judge rendered a judgment in favor of the plaintiffs against the Commonwealth. Although the court held that mentally ill people "can be comparatively negligent in some circumstances," it nevertheless held that "there can be no comparative negligence where the defendant's duty of care includes preventing the self-abusive or self-destructive acts that caused the injury."

3.   **Plaintiff negligence that occasioned the need for treatment.** What if a plaintiff's negligence occasions the need for defendant's services? In *Mercer v. Vanderbilt Univ.*, 134 S.W.3d 121 (Tenn. 2004), the plaintiff was driving with an estimated blood alcohol level of .20% when he caused a car accident. Several days later, to facilitate a CT scan, he was given a paralytic drug that made him temporarily ventilator dependent. Three portable oxygen tanks were attached to the ventilator. No one checked the ventilator, and the plaintiff stopped breathing. The patient was resuscitated after a code was called, but suffered severe and permanent brain damage. The trial court allowed the jury to compare plaintiff's and defendant's fault. The Tennessee Supreme Court held, however, that the plaintiff's antecedent negligence could not be considered. "[M]ost jurisdictions have held that a patient's negligence that provides only the occasion for medical treatment may not be compared to that of a negligent physician." Quoting another court for the rationale, the court stated, "It would be anomalous to posit, on the one hand, that a health care provider is required to meet a uniform standard of care in its delivery of medical services to all patients, but permit, on the other hand, the conclusion that, where a breach of that duty is established, no liability may exist if the patient's own pre-injury conduct caused the illness or injury which necessitated the medical care." The court agreed that "patients who may have negligently injured themselves are nevertheless entitled to subsequent non-negligent medical treatment and to an undiminished recovery if such subsequent non-negligent treatment is not afforded." *See also Harb v. City of Bakersfield*, 183 Cal. Rptr. 3d 59 (Ct. App. 2015) (in plaintiff's negligence action against city and ambulance company whose alleged delay in responding made consequences of stroke much worse, comparative fault could not apply to plaintiff's failure to take blood pressure medicine prior to stroke; comparative fault should apply only when the fault took place concurrently with or after delivery of care and treatment).

The Restatement approves of the result in cases like *Mercer* and *Harb,* but argues that the result cannot be explained on foreseeability/scope of risk grounds. RESTATEMENT (THIRD) OF TORTS: APPORTIONMENT OF LIABILITY § 7 cmt. m (2000). Can you see a basis for the Restatement's position?

4. **Statutes to protect vulnerable plaintiffs.** [Statutes sometimes impose a duty upon the defendant to protect plaintiffs who are vulnerable or disabled] Minor workers in dangerous occupations may be so protected by statutes. Similarly, a statute that requires school buses to remain stopped until school children have crossed the road is a recognition that the children may not exercise care to protect themselves when they cross. The school bus driver who violates such a statute may be denied the right to raise contributory negligence of the child as a defense. *See Van Gaasbeck v. Webatuck Cent. Sch. Dist. No. 1*, 234 N.E.2d 243 (N.Y. 1967). Would these be situations in which to impose a *Bexiga* duty upon the defendant?

5. **Other statutes.** Some statutes bar comparative fault claims even when plaintiffs can presumably care for themselves. With pervasive seatbelt use and many state statutes that now require it, failure to wear a seatbelt could count as comparative fault. *Barnes v. Paulin*, 900 N.Y.S.2d 886 (App. Div. 2010) (damages reduction based on seat belt nonuse); *Nabors Well Servs., Ltd. v. Romero*, 456 S.W.3d 553 (Tex. 2015) (evidence of use or non-use of seatbelts admissible for the purpose of allocating responsibility under statute, overruling prior precedent to the contrary). However, a large number of jurisdictions statutorily limit these comparative fault claims. Should they?

6. **Nonreciprocal risks and known disability.** One characteristic that unites many of these cases is that the defendant imposes a risk upon the plaintiff but the plaintiff's fault imposes no similar risk upon the defendant. In other words, the risks are not reciprocal or mutual. Contrast the ordinary automobile collision case in which each driver is acting negligently, thus creating risks to others as well as to self.

Maybe *Bexiga* and similar cases suggest that the plaintiff's vulnerability rightly plays a part in determining responsibility, but only in certain cases. The plaintiff's disability or vulnerability might be especially important if (1) the defendant knows of the plaintiff's disability which prevents or inhibits the plaintiff's care for himself; and (2) the plaintiff's risky conduct endangers himself but not others. Consider the following cases:

Case 1. A mentally disabled adult, Clay, works for a farmer, Johnson. Johnson took Clay in as a foster child, an arrangement made with the welfare department. Johnson put him to work with machinery on the farm, and explained his duties, but did not explain the dangers. Clay put his hand in a grinder and it was severely injured. A reasonable person would have perceived the risk and would not have put a hand in the grinder. Clay did not adequately perceive the risk because of his mental limitations. In Clay's suit against Johnson, the defense was contributory negligence.

Case 2. Kincheloe, a child of 12, is driving a car on a rural road. His neighbor, Davis, was driving in excess of the speed limit in the opposite direction, approaching Kincheloe. He recognized Kincheloe and knew he was inclined to take his father's car and pull dangerous stunts. Nevertheless, Davis did not slow down. Kincheloe pulled over in Davis' lane, and Davis was unable to avoid collision because of his speed. Both Davis and Kincheloe were injured.

In Kincheloe's claim against Davis, contributory negligence of Kincheloe was pleaded as a defense.

Case 3. Paulin, a mentally disabled adult, walked down a rural road in the pre-dawn hours. He walked on the right side and wore dark clothes. Dalrymple was driving in the same direction. As he neared Paulin, a car came from the opposite direction and Dalrymple dimmed his lights. He never saw Paulin until the last minute. He struck Paulin, who was seriously injured. Contributory negligence was the defense in Paulin's claim against Dalrymple.

Case 4. Perez and Dittman were both speeding as they traveled south on a public highway. Perez, who was 13, attempted to pass Dittman on a curve. At the same time Dittman lost control and began to skid over to his left. The two cars collided at this point. Each driver was injured. Contributory negligence is pleaded.

These examples might suggest that you agree with the principle in *Bexiga*, but might think that application of the principle to more concrete cases is debatable.

7. **Policy factors in allocation of risks to the defendant.** One article that examines cases in which courts bar plaintiff fault defenses after the shift from contributory negligence to comparative fault concludes that court-created limits are grounded in identifiable and consistent issues of principle or policy. The policies involved when judges limit comparative fault defenses include: plaintiff incapacity (plaintiff lacks total or partial capacity for self-care); structural safety (due to systemic differentials in knowledge, experience or control, the defendant can be expected to take better care of plaintiff's safety than can the plaintiff herself); role definition (defendant's obligation is to care for even a negligent plaintiff because of defendant's responsibilities as a professional rescuer); process values (litigating the comparative fault defense would harm litigants, create unmanageable litigation, or produce statements of relative fault where such statements are problematic); fundamental values (a determination of comparative fault would encroach on fundamental, sometimes constitutional values); and autonomy and self-risk (plaintiff's conduct risked only harm to self and as such receives more latitude for plaintiff choice). *See* Ellen M. Bublick, *Comparative Fault to the Limits,* 56 VAND. L. REV. 977 (2003). Are any of these policies at issue in the cases here?

CHRISTENSEN V. ROYAL SCHOOL DISTRICT NO. 160

124 P.3d 283 (Wash. 2005)

ALEXANDER, C.J. . . .

[Steven Diaz, a 26-year-old teacher engaged in sexual activity with his 13-year-old middle-school student Leslie Christensen. The sexual activity occurred in Diaz's classroom. Diaz claimed that Leslie voluntarily participated in the relationship.]

Leslie and her parents brought suit against Diaz, the Royal School District (the District), and Principal Andersen in federal district court. . . . In their complaint, they claimed that Diaz sexually abused Leslie. Damages were also sought against the District and Andersen based on the allegation that the District and its principal, Andersen, were negligent in hiring and supervising Diaz.

In a responsive pleading, the District and Andersen asserted an affirmative defense that Leslie's voluntary participation in the sexual relationship with Diaz constituted contributory fault . . . . Leslie moved for partial summary judgment on this issue, seeking to strike the affirmative defense. The trial court deferred ruling on the motion pending an answer from this court to the certified question [can contributory fault be assessed against a 13-year-old victim of sexual abuse for her participation in the relationship]. . . .

The existence of a legal duty is a question of law and "depends on mixed considerations of logic, common sense, justice, policy, and precedent."

The District and Andersen argue that contributory fault applies in this case because Leslie had a duty to protect herself against sexual abuse by an adult, a duty she allegedly ignored by voluntarily engaging in a sexual relationship with Diaz. . . .

The District and Andersen contend that contributory fault applies because "Washington has a long history of holding children responsible for their comparative negligence" and that Leslie had a duty to protect herself against sexual abuse but failed to do so. In support of this contention, they cite several cases where contributory fault has been applied against a child. Although the District and Andersen correctly pointed out that Washington does apply contributory fault and the duty of protecting oneself to children in some instances, the cases that they cite are not germane to our inquiry, as none involve sexual abuse. The act of sexual abuse is key here. As indicated above, our public policy is directed to protecting children from such abuse. . . .

[At issue in this case is the idea that a claim of contributory negligence is barred because the acts of sexual molestation were intentional, even though the contributory negligence defense itself is raised by a negligent rather than an intentional tortfeasor.]

Our conclusion that the defense of contributory negligence should not be available to the Royal School District and Principal Anderson is in accord with the established Washington rule that a school has a "special relationship" with the students in its custody and a duty to protect them "from reasonably anticipated dangers." The rationale for imposing this duty is on the placement of the student in the care of the school with the resulting loss of the student's ability to protect himself or herself. . . .

[handwritten margin note: long about the relation upon question, thereby thwarts the school's efforts to ascertain if P was being abused.]

[B]ecause we recognize the vulnerability of children in the school setting, we hold, as a matter of public policy, that children do not have a duty to protect themselves from sexual abuse by their teachers. Moreover, we conclude that contributory fault may not be assessed against a 13-year-old child based on the failure to protect herself from being sexually abused when the defendant or defendants stand in a special relationship to the child and have a duty to protect the child. *See* Ellen M. Bublick, *Comparative Fault to the Limits,* 56 VAND. L. REV. 977, 1004 (2003). Andersen and the District had a clear duty to protect students in their custody, and this duty encompassed the obligation to supervise and control Diaz. . . .

[The defendant alleged that when asked about the sexual relationship by the principal, Leslie did not disclose it.] We have not said in this opinion that the school district should be precluded from defending on the basis that it was not negligent. The fact that it may not, under Washington law, assert that the 13-year-old child was contributorily negligent should not bar it from claiming at trial that it was careful in hiring and supervising the child's teacher and, thus, was without negligence. If, indeed, the District was thwarted in its efforts to ascertain if Leslie Christensen was abused by her teacher, that fact would likely be relevant on the issue of its alleged negligence. . . .

[handwritten margin note: Holding supports goal of protecting children]

The child, in our view, lacks the capacity to consent to the sexual abuse and is under no duty to protect himself or herself from being abused. An opposite holding would, in our judgment, frustrate the overarching goals of prevention and deterrence of child sexual abuse. . . .

SANDERS, J., dissenting. . . .

[Washington law holds minors responsible for contributory negligence in many contexts.] The majority dismisses these cases because they do not involve sexual conduct. I fail to see why a minor can be contributorily negligent for driving a snowmobile but cannot be contributorily negligent in a negligence action relating to sexual misconduct. Generally contributory negligence is a question of fact for the jury.

[handwritten margin note: Yikes]

But under the majority's rule, a 15-year-old girl can seduce a male teacher, and then sue the school district for damages knowing she cannot be found contributorily negligent in the school district suit as a matter of law. . . . [T]his provides a powerful incentive to engage in sexual misconduct. We are deceiving ourselves if we think children are unable to understand the risks and potential rewards. Perhaps some are not, but that is why a jury determines this question as a matter of fact in each case. . . . I see no reason to deviate from our standard rule on contributory negligence for minors in negligence cases involving sexual activity.

The majority appeals to a school's duty to protect students. Well and good. However, merely because a school must protect the children in its care does not relieve the students of any personal responsibility for their own conduct. Children should not be allowed to take advantage of the school's duty by forcing it to pay damages for injuries invited by the student or injuries which the district could have prevented *but for* obstruction by the student. Such a rule is inequitable and excuses all manner of mischief. . . .

This school district *did* take steps to protect the female student. School officials met with the girl and her parents to determine if anything untoward was occurring with the teacher. The girl, however, allegedly lied about her involvement with the teacher, thwarting the school district's efforts to protect her. She may be below the age of consent, but not below the age of honesty. Yes, school districts must protect their students, but students must cooperate. If a student undermines school officials' actions to protect her, she must bear at least some of the fault for resulting injury. If the girl lied, this is contributory negligence on her part and a proper defense for the school district. . . .

[A separate dissent is omitted.]

NOTES

1. **The plaintiff's "no duty" expression.** The Restatement provides that, in light of principle or policy, plaintiffs, like defendants, might sometimes have "no duty" to act reasonably in self-protection. RESTATEMENT (THIRD) OF TORTS: APPORTIONMENT OF LIABILITY § 3 cmt. d (2000). If a plaintiff has no duty to protect herself by the use of reasonable care, she cannot be charged with comparative fault for failing to do so. The no duty language is misapplied in one respect, since "duty" refers to an obligation enforceable by suit. The point of using no duty language, however, is to draw attention to a parallel set of rules that relieve defendants of liability for negligent conduct. For instance, we will see in Chapter 12 that landowners frequently do not owe a duty of reasonable care to trespassers. That means the landowner is free to be negligent toward trespassers. The idea of a plaintiff no-duty rule is that the same approach should be taken to protect the interests of the plaintiff.

2. **No duty of a child to guard against sexual abuse by an adult.** What policy interests might be served by the Washington Supreme Court's plaintiff no-duty rule? Child sexual activity with an adult could be treated like any other potential comparative fault by a child. When immature plaintiffs are confronted with involvement in adult activity, might child safety be promoted by placing greater responsibility on the more mature and experienced party? *See Bjerke v. Johnson,* 742 N.W.2d 660 (Minn. 2007) ("Beyond the strong public interest in protecting children from sexual abuse, it seems to us unlikely that children can be expected to comprehend the multitude of long-term effects of sexual abuse by an adult."); *C.C.H. v. Philadelphia Phillies, Inc.,* 940 A.2d 336 (Pa. 2008) ("children as a class . . . due to their youth or inexperience, lack the judgment necessary to protect themselves from sexual aggressors"). Or as the

dissent argues, will a no-duty rule encourage young plaintiffs to engage in sexual misconduct? In some ways, the no-duty rule in *Christensen* parallels the doctrine that requires children to use extra care when engaged in adult activities that pose risk to others. When engaged in adult activities that risk the children's own safety, others may owe extra care to them. Ellen M. Bublick, *Comparative Fault to the Limits,* 56 VAND. L. REV. 977 (2003).

3. **Failure to disclose sexual contact.** The dissent makes much of a contested fact that the plaintiff, when asked by school officials if she was being sexually abused, did not reveal the truth. Would it be relevant, either to a no-duty rule or to a reasonable care analysis, if research shows that fewer than 50% of adolescents ever reveal sexual abuse to anyone at all, and that those who reveal abuse usually reveal it only to a best friend or parent? *See* R.J.R. Levesque, *Sex Differences in the Experience of Child Sexual Victimization,* 9 J. OF FAM. VIOLENCE 357–69 (1994).

4. **Effect of no-duty rules.** The *Christensen* court struck the defendant's comparative fault defense. As the court made clear, the plaintiff still may not win her claim. Why would the plaintiff want a situation in which she either recovers fully or not at all—are there process considerations? What if victim blame is associated with increased psychological difficulties such as post-traumatic stress disorder? *See* Bonnie L. Katz & Martha R. Burt, *Self Blame in Recovery from Rape,* in RAPE & SEXUAL ASSAULT II 162 (Ann Wolbert Burgess ed., 1988). Might an attorney for the child plaintiff ever want a court to permit a comparative negligence defense in a case like *Christensen* nevertheless?

5. **Plaintiff's rights.** Some of the discourse on this topic is framed in terms of the plaintiff's rights or entitlements. In a quite different context, in *LeRoy Fibre Co. v. Chicago, Milwaukee & St. Paul Ry. Co.,* 232 U.S. 340 (1914), the plaintiff owned land abutting the defendant's railroad. He stacked flax on the land for use in his manufacturing business. He alleged that the railroad negligently emitted sparks and coals that set fire to and destroyed the flax. The defendant argued that the plaintiff was contributorily negligent in stacking the combustible flax so near the railroad. The jury, charged on the contributory negligence defense, found for the defendant. The Supreme Court held that the contributory negligence defense presented no question for the jury. The Court held that a contrary decision casts upon the plaintiff a duty to use his property not only to avoid injury to another, but also "to use his own property that it may not be injured by the wrongs of another." However, the "legal conception of property is of rights." One way to look at this problem is to recognize that property law, emphasizing the owner's right to use property as she pleases, is sometimes at odds with negligence law, which emphasizes the safety of conduct and evaluates safety case-by-case after the event has occurred. Both approaches represent important values in our culture. How should we determine which prevails? *See* William Powers, Jr., *Border Wars,* 72 TEX. L. REV. 1209 (1994). *See also* RESTATEMENT (THIRD) OF TORTS: APPORTIONMENT OF LIABILITY § 3 cmt. d (2000).

6. **Rights or entitlements not based on rights to possession of tangible property.** The plaintiff may be entitled to use her property even if in doing so she is in danger of harm by the defendant's negligence. Similarly, the plaintiff might have entitlements not grounded in tangible property. She might be entitled to, say, use the public streets although they are dangerous or shop for groceries at night although rape or robbery is an ever-present possibility. If she had such an entitlement, then she could not be charged with comparative negligence merely because she shopped at night.

7. **Determining plaintiff entitlements.** How should courts decide what entitlements a plaintiff has beyond those arising from ownership of tangible property? Can we identify any principle? Consider *Brandon v. Cty. of Richardson,* 624 N.W.2d 604 (Neb. 2001), where a transgendered rape victim reported a rape to the sheriff, who also knew that the rapists were dangerous and might murder Brandon if there were no police protection. The sheriff did not protect Brandon and the rapists did in fact murder Brandon. Should the estate's recovery against the sheriff be reduced on the ground that the victim was negligent in reporting the rape after the rapists warned not to do so? Does Brandon have an entitlement to report crime to the police even if it is risky to do so?

Is a plaintiff guilty of comparative negligence for wearing expensive jewelry in a neighborhood that has a high crime rate? In *Isik Jewelry v. Mars Media, Inc.,* 418 F. Supp. 2d 112 (E.D.N.Y. 2005), the music artist Albert Johnson, known as "Prodigy," left a video shoot wearing jewelry valued at over $100,000. He was robbed at gunpoint as he walked across the street to get some water from a convenience store. In a bailment action, the court examined whether Johnson failed to use reasonable care. The court found that Johnson was not negligent as a matter of law. Could the conclusion be said to reflect an entitlement by the plaintiff?

What of a comparative fault instruction based on the argument that the plaintiffs were unreasonable in refusing to immediately give their money and possessions to the three assailants who broke into their room, rather than insisting that they did not have money? *See InTown Lessee Assocs., LLC v. Howard,* 67 So. 3d 711 (Miss. 2011) ("To penalize a crime victim for his failure to cooperate with his assailant would constitute a bizarre and perverse misapplication of the doctrine of comparative fault. The trial court did not abuse its discretion in denying InTown's request for a comparative negligence instruction.").

8. **Concern about assignments of relative fault.** Might a plaintiff have an entitlement even outside the context of crime or abuse? What of a comparative fault defense alleging that a plaintiff, hit by a defendant who ran a light, is negligent to some degree for going on green. Can you see why a court might suggest that the plaintiff with the right of way has an entitlement? *See Hayes v. Price,* 313 S.W.3d 645 (Mo. 2010) ("a driver is entitled to assume a car going in the opposite direction will yield the right of way to oncoming traffic before turning," reversing 20% assignment of fault to plaintiff). Or could a front

seat passenger in a car be said to have no duty to the passengers in the back? *See Siruta v. Siruta*, 348 P.3d 549 (Kan. 2015) ("if there is no duty, 'a person cannot be at fault and therefore cannot be made a party subject to having his negligence compared.'")

9. **Autonomy: motorcycle helmets and 5" heels.** Comparative fault claims often involve plaintiffs' risk of harm to self rather than others. Should greater latitude be given for conduct that risks harm only to the plaintiff? In *McKinley v. Casson*, 80 A.3d 618 (Del. 2013), the court held that failure to wear a motorcycle helmet may not be grounds for a comparative fault claim: "In Delaware, motorcyclists over 19 years of age may ride without wearing a helmet. Thus, by statute, an adult does not violate a duty to exercise reasonable care by failing to wear a helmet. There being no statutory requirement to wear a helmet, the remaining question is whether there is a common law duty. We are aware of none, and we follow the numerous other jurisdictions that have declined to adopt a common law duty to wear a helmet."

What if a plaintiff risks her safety by wearing 5" heels? In *Bongiorno v. Americorp, Inc.*, 159 So. 3d 1027 (Fla. Dist. Ct. App. 2015), a worker brought a tort action against a property owner after she slipped on the bathroom floor. At a bench trial, the court found that the defendant was negligent and assigned 50% comparative fault to the plaintiff for wearing 4–5" heels to work. The plaintiff argued that she was not negligent for wearing high heels to work. The appellate court agreed. "Americorp failed to sustain its burden of proving that Bongiorno created a foreseeable zone of risk by wearing high-heeled shoes to work and, therefore, the trial court erred in finding her comparatively negligent for her injuries." Isn't it foreseeable that people wearing 4–5" heels might fall? Could the court justify its decision on grounds of policy rather than foreseeability?

10. **Entitlements vs. case-by-case adjudication of plaintiff fault.** Do we need entitlements decided by a judge like those in *Mercer, Christensen, LeRoy Fibre*, or *Brandon*? Do you think it would suffice instead to judge comparative fault case-by-case in light of the plaintiff's rights and legitimate interests? For example, couldn't we rely upon juries to hold as a matter of ordinary analysis of comparative fault that a woman is definitely not guilty of comparative fault merely because she shops late at night? If you think juries might be unreliable when it comes to deciding issues of comparative fault, would you expect entitlements formulated by judges in advance to be more trustworthy?

§ 6. TRADITIONAL EXCEPTIONS TO THE CONTRIBUTORY NEGLIGENCE BAR

Cases that allocate full responsibility to the defendant even after a shift to comparative fault may draw on traditional exceptions to the contributory negligence bar. To what extent are these doctrines still necessary?

A. THE RESCUE DOCTRINE

"The rescue doctrine is a rule of law holding that one who sees a person in imminent danger caused by the negligence of another cannot be charged with contributory negligence" when the actor attempts a rescue, unless the rescuer acted recklessly. *Ouellette v. Carde*, 612 A.2d 687 (R.I. 1992). In *Ouellette*, the defendant was pinned in a closed garage under a car the defendant had been fixing. There was gasoline all over the floor. The defendant called a friend for help but when the friend activated the electric garage door opener to rescue him, the gas ignited and the rescuer was badly burned. The rescuer sued the defendant, who asked for a comparative negligence instruction. The trial court denied the instruction and the jury found for the plaintiff-rescuer without reduction in damages. The award was upheld on appeal under the rescue doctrine.

After the advent of comparative fault, some courts leave the allocation of fault between the defendant and the rescuer-plaintiff to the jury. *See Govich v. N. Am. Sys., Inc.*, 814 P.2d 94 (N.M. 1991).

B. LAST CLEAR CHANCE OR DISCOVERED PERIL

In the traditional system that barred all recovery for contributory negligence, courts allowed the negligent plaintiff a full recovery when the plaintiff was left in a helpless position by his own negligence and the defendant, who had the last clear chance to avoid injury, negligently inflicted it anyway. *See* RESTATEMENT (SECOND) OF TORTS §§ 479, 480 (1965).

The doctrine first appeared in *Davies v. Mann*, 10 M. & W. 546, 152 Eng. Rep. 588 (Exch. 1842). In that case, the plaintiff had left his donkey tied in the road eating grass. The defendant negligently drove a team and wagon down the hill and ran over the animal, which, being fettered, was unable to move. The court held that the plaintiff's contributory negligence was no defense. Baron Parke said that the plaintiff "is entitled to recover," stressing that if the rule were otherwise, "a man might justify the driving over goods left on a public highway, or even a man lying asleep there."

The last clear chance doctrine held that if the defendant discovered or should have discovered the plaintiff's peril, and could reasonably have avoided it, the plaintiff's earlier negligence would neither bar nor reduce the plaintiff's recovery. A slightly less generous version, called the discovered peril doctrine, applied these rules only if the defendant actually did discover the plaintiff's peril. The plaintiff could not invoke these doctrines unless the plaintiff was helpless; if he could extricate himself from danger at any time, the defendant did not have the last chance to avoid injury and the negligent plaintiff's claim would be barred entirely.

In states that have adopted comparative fault systems, the last clear chance and discovered peril doctrines have been discarded, mostly on the ground that they were attempts to aid the plaintiff in a harsh system and not needed once comparative fault rules apply.

Should the last clear chance doctrine be retained in a modified comparative fault system? Would the fact that the defendant had the last chance still be relevant in determining relative fault? On both points, see 1 DOBBS, HAYDEN & BUBLICK, THE LAW OF TORTS § 226 (2d ed. 2011).

C. DEFENDANT'S RECKLESS OR INTENTIONAL MISCONDUCT

Contributory negligence was historically no defense to an intentional tort. By extension of this idea, courts also held that contributory negligence was no defense to willful, wanton, or reckless torts, defined as involving "utter indifference to or conscious disregard for the safety of others." Such torts border on intentional wrongdoing because they involve a bad state of mind as well as risky conduct. Under this rule, the plaintiff charged with contributory negligence was allowed a full recovery against a reckless or wanton defendant.

Once comparative negligence rules are adopted, should courts discard the old rule and simply let the jury apportion fault between plaintiff and defendant, even when the defendant is guilty of reckless conduct? Should comparative negligence rules apply when the defendant is guilty of an intentional tort? Consider these cases:

Case 1. Defendant strikes the plaintiff. When sued, he argues that the plaintiff was guilty of negligence because she provoked the attack.

Case 2. A negligently provides B with keys to A's car, knowing that B is dangerous, in a rage at P, and might attack her. B intentionally runs down P. After P recovers fully against A, A seeks contribution from B.

On the first question, in *Ezzell v. Miranne,* 84 So. 3d 641 (La. Ct. App. 2011), the defendant punched the plaintiff in the face after the plaintiff called him an "A-----e" (as the court delicately put it). The trial court allowed the jury to reduce the plaintiff's recovery by 5 per cent. Held, based on a state statute, this was improper.

D. PLAINTIFF'S ILLEGAL ACTIVITY

DUGGER V. ARREDONDO
408 S.W.3d 825 (Tex. 2013)

GREEN, JUSTICE.

[Friends Geoffrey Dugger and Joel Martinez drank tequila, snorted lines of black-tar heroin, and smoked marijuana. Martinez fell asleep, made a choking sound, and subsequently began vomiting. Dugger delayed in calling 911. When he did, police arrived about five minutes later, and paramedics ten minutes after that. Dugger did not tell the police or paramedics that Martinez had ingested heroin, only that he had drunk tequila and smoked marijuana. The paramedics treated Martinez for alcohol poisoning, but could not save him. Martinez died less than two hours later. Martinez's mother, Mary Ann Arredondo, brought a wrongful death action against Dugger. Arredondo alleged that Duggar was negligent in delaying to call emergency services and in failing to advise paramedics who arrived on the scene that Martinez had used heroin. Dugger asserted an affirmative defense based on the common law unlawful acts doctrine, which completely barred a plaintiff from recovery if, at the time of injury, the plaintiff was engaged in an unlawful act that was "inextricably intertwined with the claim and the alleged damages would not have occurred but for the illegal act." The trial court granted Dugger's motion for summary judgment based on the unlawful acts doctrine. Martinez's mother appealed, arguing that section of the Civil Practice and Remedies Code, which allows for comparative fault, replaced the common law unlawful acts doctrine. The court of appeals reversed.]

We hold that the Legislature's adoption of the proportionate responsibility scheme in Chapter 33 of the Civil Practice and Remedies Code evidenced its clear intention that a plaintiff's illegal conduct not falling within a statutorily-recognized affirmative defense be apportioned rather than barring recovery completely . . .

More than 120 years ago, this Court recognized the common law unlawful acts doctrine as barring a plaintiff from recovering damages if it could be shown that, at the time of injury, the plaintiff was engaged in an illegal act that contributed to the injury. The doctrine originated with the principle of in pari delicto or "unclean hands" in the contract context, but was extended to tort causes of action. The doctrine is based on the public policy that wrongdoers should not be compensated for their immoral acts.

As early as 1888, we recognized that "no action will lie to recover a claim for damages, if to establish it the plaintiff requires aid from an illegal transaction, or is under the necessity of showing or in any manner depending upon an illegal act to which he is a party." Since then, "[c]ourts throughout Texas ... have used this rule, along with public policy principles, to prevent a plaintiff from recovering damages that arose out of his or her own illegal conduct." ...

[handwritten margin note: Disagreement about Unlawful Acts Doct.]

Recently, scholars and courts have disagreed over the viability of the unlawful acts doctrine in modern jurisprudence. The Restatement (Second) of Torts and respected legal scholars reject the principle that tortious or criminal conduct can completely bar recovery. Several courts and legislatures, on the other hand, have approved of the unlawful acts doctrine in statutes and case law.

Since Texas's shift to the proportionate responsibility scheme, ... most Texas courts have used a plaintiff's unlawful act to measure proportionate responsibility and reduce recovery, rather than completely bar the plaintiff from recovering damages. ...

[handwritten margin note: Social / Recovery Issues w/ Doctrine]

Dugger and the dissent argue that if we do not uphold the unlawful acts doctrine, it will be easier for criminals to bring suits and recover. On the other hand, Arredondo argues that recognizing the unlawful acts doctrine could lead to a slippery slope where it would be impossible for many people to access the judicial system and try their claims because they were engaged in an unlawful act while sustaining injuries. Additionally, the Texas Civil Rights Project, as amicus curiae, contends that a broad unlawful acts doctrine could allow people who commit serious tortious conduct against others to have civil immunity merely because the claimant was not in compliance with every law at the time of the tortious conduct. ...

We hold that the common law unlawful acts doctrine is not available as an affirmative defense in personal injury and wrongful death cases. Like other common law assumption-of-the-risk defenses, it was abrogated by Chapter 33's proportionate responsibility scheme. Unless the requirements of the affirmative defense in section 93.001 are satisfied [when assumption of the risk is recognized for "a felony, for which plaintiff has been finally convicted" or certain cases involving "committing or attempting to commit suicide"], a plaintiff's share of responsibility for his or her injuries should be compared against the defendant's. We therefore affirm the judgment of the court of appeals, which reversed the summary judgment and remanded the case to the trial court.

HECHT, J. (dissenting). ...

The Court seems to think that because Chapter 33 abrogated other common law doctrines that barred recovery based on the plaintiff's conduct, like assumption of the risk, imminent peril, and last clear chance, it also abrogated the unlawful acts doctrine. But comparative responsibility determines the amount of recovery based on an allocation of fault contributing to injury. The unlawful acts doctrine holds that the allocation should not be made because any recovery rewards criminal conduct. This case is a good example. Assuming, as we must, that Dugger should have called 9–1–1 a few minutes earlier and should have disclosed Martinez's ingestion of heroin, what is his percentage of responsibility? How much should Dugger pay Arredondo for not acting promptly and not being forthcoming when Martinez was prohibited by law from ingesting the drug that killed him? The point is not simply that the question is hard, though it is, and assigning it to a jury makes it no easier. The point is that to award any damages lessens the law's prohibition against the use of heroin.

Now, if a robber slips in a puddle on the bank floor and breaks his leg, he can sue the bank. A rapist who falls in a hole in the victim's backyard can sue for damages. Lest these examples be thought extreme or unlikely, consider this: can a teenager sue a boy who sold him fireworks from which he extracted gunpowder to make a pipe bomb that exploded in his hands? No, in New York, said the New York Court of Appeals in Barker v. Kallash. In Texas, after today, the answer is yes.

One criticism of the unlawful acts doctrine, a criticism with substance, is that it does not have sufficient limiting principles. The doctrine has proven especially difficult to apply against undocumented aliens[24]. . . . No one argues that a motorist broadsided by a drunk driver should be prohibited from recovering because he was driving five miles an hour over the speed limit. Nor should the doctrine be used to resurrect outlawry for undocumented aliens. It is true that in the nineteenth century, the doctrine was used to deny recovery to persons injured while violating Blue Laws.[1] But if we were to discard every claim and defense that has been misused, there would be nothing left of the law. Properly applied, the doctrine serves the valuable purpose of promoting compliance with the law and should be retained. . . .

NOTES

1.   **After comparative fault.** The bar on recovery of a plaintiff who was involved in illegal activity was created at a time when contributory negligence was an all-or-nothing rule. Should the illegal activity defense survive the transition to comparative apportionment? While *Dugger* would apportion fault, *Greenwald v. Van Handel*, 88 A.3d 467 (Conn. 2014), retained the bar. The

---

[24] Compare *Carcamo-Lopez v. Doe*, 865 F.Supp.2d 736, 766–767 (W.D.Tex.2011) (citing the court of appeals' opinion in the present case to conclude that Texas' unlawful acts doctrine does not bar suit by an undocumented alien accidentally struck by a border patrol vehicle while crouching in the dark in vegetation near the bank of the Rio Grande River), with *Rico v. Flores*, 481 F.3d 234, 243–244 (5th Cir.2007) (concluding that it was uncertain whether the Texas unlawful acts doctrine would bar suit for the wrongful death of undocumented aliens who died in a railcar while entering the country illegally against the person hired to help them or the railway), and *Fuentes v. Alecio*, Civil Action No. C–06–425, 2006 U.S. Dist. LEXIS 93013, 2006 WL 3813780 (S.D.Tex. Dec. 26, 2006) (dismissing action for the wrongful death of an undocumented alien who expired from heat exhaustion while entering the country illegally as barred by the unlawful acts doctrine).

[1]   Laws prohibiting certain activities, such as selling alcoholic beverages on Sundays.—Eds.

issue is both important and current. *See Rodriguez v. Williams*, 355 P.3d 25 (N.M. App. 2015) (plaintiff's own intoxication did not bar recovery in suit for injuries suffered in car accident, but must be taken into account in a comparative fault analysis); *Tug Valley Pharmacy, LLC v. All Plaintiffs Below in Mingo Cty.*, 773 S.E.2d 627 (W. Va. 2015) (rejecting complete bar rule); *Cahn v. Copac, Inc.*, 198 So. 3d 347 (Miss. Ct. App. 2015) (finding a conflict between Mississippi illegal conduct rule and comparative fault rule and encouraging the state supreme court to resolve the issue).

2. **Illegal activity.** Does any illegal activity whatsoever by the plaintiff bar a claim? In *Winschel v. Brown*, 171 P.3d 142 (Alaska 2007), the trial court granted summary judgment for defendant because the plaintiff was illegally riding his ATV on a bicycle path when he was injured. The Alaska Supreme Court disagreed. This illegal activity did not preclude recovery because the crime was not "serious." However, the crime could be given "significant weight" in fixing the percentage of comparative fault. Does it matter to the availability of the defense if the illegal activity is violating the state's Blue Laws, driving above the speed limit, entering the country illegally, engaging in prostitution, or using heroin? *See Barker v. Kallish*, 468 N.E.2d 39 (N.Y. 1984) (15-year-old making a pipe bomb from firecrackers sold by a 9-year-old); *Price v. Purdue Pharma Co.*, 920 So. 2d 479 (Miss. 2006) (defrauding various doctors to obtain Oxycontin). Should the matter be resolved by how wrongful the plaintiff's conduct was? How closely the unlawful conduct was related to the harm? How wrongful plaintiff's conduct was when compared to the defendant's conduct? Does that latter question have to be a jury issue?

3. **Statutory bar**. Statutes in some states bar plaintiffs from all recovery in tort cases if they have engaged in particular forms of misconduct relating to the claim. For example, New Jersey has a statute that bars an uninsured motorist from maintaining a personal injury action for damages suffered in an auto accident. The statute was applied in *Aronberg v. Tolbert*, 25 A.3d 1121 (N.J. 2011), to bar a mother's wrongful death action where her son was uninsured.

4. **Commentary.** Joseph H. King, Jr., *Outlaws and Outlier Doctrines: The Serious Misconduct Bar in Tort Law*, 43 WM. & MARY L. REV. 1011 (2002), attacks the serious-misconduct bar as a frustration of tort law goals and the comparative negligence structure, as a doctrine unpredictable and selective in application, and as an invitation to judges to apply the moral flavor of the month. Should plaintiffs guilty of serious misconduct be allowed to present their cases to the jury and see what percentages of responsibility juries assign?

REFERENCES: Contributory and comparative negligence generally: 1 DOBBS, HAYDEN & BUBLICK, THE LAW OF TORTS §§ 218–231 (2d ed. 2011); DOBBS, HAYDEN & BUBLICK, HORNBOOK ON TORTS, Ch. 16 (2d ed. 2016). Comparative Negligence: VICTOR SCHWARTZ, COMPARATIVE NEGLIGENCE (5th ed. 2010); HENRY WOODS & BETH DEERE, COMPARATIVE FAULT (3d ed. 1996 & 2012 Supp.).

CHAPTER 10

ASSUMPTION OF THE RISK

• • •

§ 1. CONTRACTUAL OR EXPRESS
ASSUMPTION OF THE RISK

STELLUTI V. CASAPENN ENTERPRISES, LLC, 1 A.3d 678 (N.J. 2010). On the day that she joined the Powerhouse gym, Gina Stelluti participated in a "spinning" class. She advised the instructor of her inexperience and the instructor helped her adjust the stationary spin bike. During the class, the handle bars dislodged from the bike, causing Stelluti to fall and suffer injuries. Expert testimony suggested that the locking pin on the bike's handlebars was difficult to engage and had not been fully engaged at the time of the accident. Stelluti sued the gym for negligence in failing to properly maintain and set up the bike and in failing to properly instruct her about to how to use it. The lower court granted summary judgment based on a waiver and release Stelluti had signed, which said that she expressly agreed to discharge all claims against the health club "from any and all claims or causes of action." The appellate division affirmed, except to the extent that the agreement purported to insulate the defendant from reckless acts.

On appeal to the New Jersey Supreme Court, *held*, affirmed. Exculpatory clauses have been historically disfavored and subject to close judicial scrutiny. Although the agreement is a take-it-or-leave-it standardized preprinted form, and therefore a contract of adhesion, it is nevertheless enforceable in this context because Stelluti was not in a position of unequal bargaining power. "Stelluti could have taken her business to another fitness club, could have found another means of exercise aside from joining a private gym, or could have thought about it and even sought advice before signing up and using the facility's equipment." Contracting parties have a long-standing liberty to bind themselves as they see fit. The agreement itself is clear about the waiver of legal rights. It expressly covers "the sudden and unforeseen malfunctioning of any equipment," and prominently disclaims liability for "negligence on the part of the Club, its agents and employees." Looking at the public interest in this context, "Assumption of risk associated with physical-exertion-involving discretionary activities is sensible and has been applied in many other settings." There remains a standard for protection of adults in the context of gyms, and "had Powerhouse's

273

management or employees been aware of a piece of defective exercise equipment and failed to remedy the condition or to warn adequately of the dangerous condition, or if it had dangerously or improperly maintained equipment, Powerhouse could not exculpate itself from such reckless or gross negligence. That showing was not made on this record."

TUNKL V. REGENTS OF UNIVERSITY OF CALIFORNIA, 383 P.2d 441 (Cal. 1963). Tunkl brought this action for injuries received allegedly as a result of the negligence of the hospital operated by defendant. Tunkl was admitted to the hospital on condition that he execute a release, absolving the defendants "from any and all liability for the negligent or wrongful acts or omissions of its employees. . . ." The validity of this release was submitted to the jury, which found it to be valid and the trial court entered judgment for the defendants. *Held*, reversed. "While obviously no public policy opposes private, voluntary transactions in which one party, for a consideration, agrees to shoulder a risk which the law would otherwise have placed upon the other party, the above circumstances pose a different situation. In this situation the releasing party does not really acquiesce voluntarily in the contractual shifting of the risk, nor can we be reasonably certain that he receives an adequate consideration for the transfer. Since the service is one which each member of the public, presently or potentially, may find essential to him, he faces, despite his economic inability to do so, the prospect of a compulsory assumption of the risk of another's negligence. . . . From the observance of simple standards of due care in the driving of a car to the performance of the high standards of hospital practice, the individual citizen must be completely dependent upon the responsibility of others. . . . We cannot lightly accept a sought immunity from careless failure to provide the hospital service upon which many must depend."

NOTES

1. **Reconciling *Stelluti* and *Tunkl*.** On the strength of *Stelluti*, would the New Jersey court reject California's *Tunkl* decision? Quite to the contrary; the New Jersey court quoted *Tunkl* with approval in its analysis. How can you reconcile the two cases?

2. **The Restatement view.** "In appropriate situations, the parties to a transaction should be able to agree which of them should bear the risk of injury, even when the injury is caused by a party's legally culpable conduct. That policy is not altered or undermined by the adoption of comparative responsibility. Consequently, a valid contractual limitation on liability, within its terms, creates an absolute bar to a plaintiff's recovery from the other party to the contract. A valid contractual limitation on liability does not provide an occasion for the factfinder to assign a percentage of responsibility to any party.

or other person. . . ." RESTATEMENT (THIRD) OF TORTS: APPORTIONMENT OF LIABILITY § 2 cmt. b (2000).

3. **Defining "appropriate situations."** [Pre-injury releases of ordinary negligence claims for adults in recreational activities are usually upheld, as long as the releases are conspicuous, clear and unambiguous] *See Pearce v. Utah Athletic Foundation*, 179 P.3d 760 (Utah 2008). In that setting, public policy is often no impediment to enforcing a release. *See Donahue v. Ledgends, Inc.*, 331 P.3d 342 (Alaska 2014) ("[R]ecreational releases for negligence are not void as a matter of public policy, because to hold otherwise would impose unreasonable burdens on businesses whose patrons want to engage in high-risk physical activities."). If waivers for recreational activities shield entities from "potentially crushing liability," *Bukowski v. Clarkson University,* 971 N.E.2d 849 (N.Y. 2012), could their *non*-enforcement have any positive effect?

4. **Consent.** The theory of assumption of the risk is that the plaintiff has voluntarily consented to a known risk. Is it fair to say Stelluti knew about the handlebar risk and voluntarily agreed to take it on? A vigorous dissent in *Stelluti* disagreed: "The Court says a health club patron has the *right* to contract not only for unsafe conditions at a health club, but also for careless conduct by its employees. . . . This court has recognized that sophisticated commercial entities, exercising equal bargaining power, are capable of protecting their own interests. . . . Never before in the modern era has this Court upheld an exculpatory clause in which a commercial enterprise protects itself against its own negligence, at the expense of a consumer, who had no bargaining power to alter the terms of the contract. . . . [Tort law is not just about compensating victims but about preventing accidents]. . . . The exculpatory clause in this case unfairly allocates the risk from the commercial operator, who is in the best position to remove and prevent the dangers on the premises, to the unwary patron [and thus] encourages lack of due care."[Should a court confine express assumption of the risk to negotiated transactions between sophisticated parties?] Could there be concern about exculpatory clauses even in that context?

MOORE V. HARTLEY MOTORS
36 P.3d 628 (Alaska 2001)

FABE, CHIEF JUSTICE. . . .

Gayle Moore and her husband bought a Suzuki four-wheel ATV in May 1993 from Suzuki, Arctic Cat Motor Sports. At the time of the sale, the salesperson offered the Moores a $50 rebate upon completion of an ATV rider safety class. On October 23, 1993, the Moores attended an ATV rider safety class held on the property of Hartley Motors, Inc. James Croak instructed the class using the curriculum of the ATV Safety Institute. Before starting instruction, Croak requested that all participants sign a consent form and release. Moore signed the consent form and release.

[During the class, Moore was thrown from her ATV when it struck a rock obscured by high grass.]

Moore brought suit in July 1995 against Hartley Motors, the dealer that sold the Moores their ATV, ATV Safety Institute, and Jim Croak. She alleged that the defendants negligently failed to provide a safe ATV rider training course and location, and negligently concealed the fact that the course was unsafe. . . . The superior court granted summary judgment to the defendants.

[The release was supported by consideration and that the exculpatory clause is not invalid based on public policy because the ATV riding course is not an essential service. However,] the trial court erred in failing to consider the scope of the release signed by Moore. Moore agreed to release the ATV Safety Institute and all other organizations and individuals affiliated with the ATV safety class from liability, loss, and damages "including but not limited to all bodily injuries and property damage arising out of participation in the ATV RiderCourse." But the release does not discuss or even mention liability for general negligence. Its opening sentences refer only to unavoidable and inherent risks of ATV riding, and nothing in its ensuing language suggests an intent to release ATVSI or Hartley Motors from liability for acts of negligence unrelated to those inherent risks. Based on this language, we conclude that Moore released ATVSI and Hartley Motors only from liability arising from the inherent risks of ATV riding and ordinary negligence associated with those inherent risks. As we noted in *Kissick v. Schmierer*, an exculpatory release can be enforced if "the intent to release a party from liability for future negligence" is "conspicuously and unequivocally expressed.". . .

Moore claims that she was injured when she fell off her ATV after riding over a rock obscured by tall grass. . . . The allegedly improper course layout may be actionable if the course posed a risk beyond ordinary negligence related to the inherent risks of off-road ATV riding assumed by the release. As we have explained in the context of skiing, "[i]f a given danger could be eliminated or mitigated through the exercise of reasonable care, it is not a necessary danger" and is therefore not an inherent risk of the sport. . . . If the course was designed or maintained in such a manner that it increased the likelihood of a rider encountering a hidden rock, then the course layout may have presented an unnecessary danger; holding an ATV safety class on an unnecessarily dangerous course is beyond the ordinary negligence released by the waiver. . . . Moreover, the fact that the course was geared towards novice ATV riders may also affect the level of care required of ATVSI and Hartley Motors to reduce unnecessary dangers and unreasonable risk.

. . . Here Moore presented facts that could support a finding that the ATV safety course was laid out in an unnecessarily dangerous manner that was not obvious to novice ATV riders and therefore not within the scope of the release. Thus, it was error to grant summary judgment.]

[Reversed and remanded.] *→ Holding*

NOTES

1. **Contractual limits.** An express assumption of risk is a contract, subject to ordinary contract rules of interpretation and enforcement. For example, a pre-injury release will not be upheld if it is unclear or ambiguous. *See, e.g., Sanislo v. Give Kids the World, Inc.*, 157 So.3d 256 (Fla. 2015); *Hillerson v. Bismarck Public Schools*, 840 N.W.2d 65 (N.D. 2013). And an exculpatory contract must meet "higher standards for clarity than other agreements." *Provoncha v. Vermont Motocross Ass'n*, 964 A.2d 1261 (Vt. 2009). Moreover, a waiver must be conspicuous, not buried in a mass of print or reduced to a miniscule font size. Even if a release passes these tests, the court must determine, as in *Moore,* whether the *scope* of the release covers the claim being asserted by the injured plaintiff. *See, e.g., Donahue v. Ledgends, Inc.*, 331 P.3d 342 (Alaska 2014) (release did cover the risk of defendant rock gym's negligent hiring and supervision of employees).

2. **Public policy limits.** Do the cases, taken together, sufficiently indicate when public policy would permit or reject contractual assumption of the risk? "Public policy" is often a case-specific inquiry. States continue to strike down pre-injury releases on a number of different "public policy" grounds. *See, e.g., Yang v. Voyagaire Houseboats, Inc.*, 701 N.W.2d 783 (Minn. 2005) (likening a houseboat rental company to an innkeeper providing a "public service," thus rendering release invalid); *Brown v. Soh*, 909 A.2d 43 (Conn. 2006) (exculpatory agreements in the employment context offend public policy). In addition, some statutes limit the ability of parties to limit liability by contract. *See Kawasaki Kisen Kaisha Ltd. v. Regal-Beloit Corp.*, 561 U.S. 89 (2010) (transit of goods by rail carrier).

3. **The *Tunkl* factors.** As in *Stelluti* and *Moore,* many, many courts look at public policy in light of the *Tunkl* factors. According to the *Tunkl* court, a transaction "in which exculpatory provisions will be held invalid" exhibits some or all of the following characteristics:

> It concerns a business of a type generally thought suitable for public regulation. The party seeking exculpation is engaged in performing a service of great importance to the public, which is often a matter of practical necessity for some members of the public. [The party holds himself out as willing to perform this service for any member of the public who seeks it.] . . . [As a result of the essential nature of the service, in the economic setting of the transaction, the party invoking exculpation possesses a decisive advantage of bargaining strength against any member of the public who seeks his services.] In exercising a superior bargaining power the party confronts the public with a standardized adhesion contract of exculpation, and makes no provision whereby a purchaser may pay

additional reasonable fees and obtain protection against negligence. Finally, as a result of the transaction, the person or property of the purchaser is placed under the control of the seller, subject to the risk of carelessness by the seller or his agents.]

The Restatement (Third) of Torts draws on these factors in devising its similar list. RESTATEMENT (THIRD) OF TORTS: APPORTIONMENT OF LIABILITY § 2 cmt. e (2000).

4. **Reckless or intentional torts.** As in *Stelluti*, most courts hold that a contractual assumption of the risk clause barring recovery for recklessly or intentionally caused injury would offend public policy. *See, e.g., City of Santa Barbara v. Superior Court*, 161 P.3d 1095 (Cal. 2007) (majority of states hold that public policy precludes enforcement of a release that would shelter aggravated misconduct). When the plaintiff fails to prove the defendant's recklessness, should a general clause purporting to waive "all liability" be enforceable to bar a negligence claim? *See Moore v. Waller*, 930 A.2d 176 (D.C. 2007).

5. **Parental waivers of child's claims.** In *Galloway v. State*, 790 N.W.2d 252 (Iowa 2010), a parent signed a release for her 14-year-old daughter to attend an educational field trip organized by Upward Bound, a youth outreach program organized by the University of Northern Iowa. On the field trip, the child was struck by a car as she attempted to cross the street. Because a child "may or may not have the knowledge and experience to assess and avoid risks of injury created by the activity," the court joined the majority of courts in deciding that a parent's pre-injury release of a child's rights is invalid. *See also Woodman v. Kera, LLC*, 785 N.W.2d 1 (Mich 2010) (pre-injury waiver of liability of commercial children's play facility unenforceable). A small number of courts have disagreed, and determine the validity of such waivers on a case-by-case basis. *See, e.g., BJ's Wholesale Club, Inc. v. Rosen*, 80 A.3d 345 (Md. 2013) (based on statutes and common law of the state, a parent has broad decision-making authority with respect to children; exculpatory clause signed by parent releasing membership store from liability to child for negligence in children's play area was enforceable where it did not represent "a transaction affecting the public interest").

§ 2. IMPLIED ASSUMPTION OF THE RISK

SIMMONS V. PORTER
312 P.3d 345 (Kan. 2013)

The opinion of the court was delivered by BILES, J.:

[Adam Simmons was working for the Porters, doing business as Porter Farms, as a farm truck and machinery mechanic. Simmons was removing a leaky fuel tank from a Ford pickup truck, and noticed that the tank was not secured with proper fastenings. When he attempted to loosen the tank, it fell to one side and doused him with gasoline. He quickly pushed himself out from under the truck, but when he did so he kicked a shop light, which broke and ignited the gasoline, burning him seriously.]

He sued his employer for negligently failing to provide him with a reasonably safe workplace. The district court denied his claim based on the common-law assumption of risk doctrine, which can bar recovery when an employee who knows of a dangerous situation voluntarily exposes himself or herself to that danger. The Court of Appeals affirmed based on existing precedent. . . .

The assumption of risk doctrine is a common-law affirmative defense to negligence. In Kansas, the doctrine's operation has been limited to cases involving employer-employee relationships when the injuries at issue were not subject to the Workers Compensation Act. . . . The doctrine is premised on a view that there is an express or implied agreement within the employer-employee relationship that an employee accepts the risk of known dangers to which the employee is exposed as a part of the work and takes responsibility for any resulting injury. . . . In other words, assumption of risk bars recovery when two conditions are present: (1) the employee knew and understood the risk being incurred; and (2) the choice to incur the risk was entirely free and voluntary.

Kansas courts discussed assumption of risk as early as 1898. But in those early cases it was viewed as a "species of contributory negligence." . . . Over time, however, this court recognized distinctions between the two doctrines. . . . Under comparative fault [as set forth in K.S.A. § 60–258a], a plaintiff may recover damages so long as the plaintiff's negligence is less than the collective causal negligence of the other parties to the occurrence; but those damages are diminished in proportion to the plaintiff's own negligence. . . . In adopting comparative fault, the legislature intended to impose individual liability for damages based on the proportionate fault of all parties to the occurrence giving rise to the injuries. . . . The comparative fault statute expressly abolished contributory negligence, but is silent regarding assumption of risk. The question before us is whether the legislature's adoption of comparative fault should abrogate the assumption of risk doctrine.] . . .

[W]e severely constricted the assumption of risk doctrine in *Smith v. Massey-Ferguson, Inc.,* 883 P.2d 1120 (Kan. 1994). In that case, a farm employee sued his employer, his supervisor, and a combine manufacturer after seriously injuring his hand in a combine's moving parts. There was conflicting evidence on whether the employee intentionally reached into the moving parts or whether he accidentally came into contact with them. . . . On appeal, the *Smith* court considered whether the district court should have decided as a matter of law whether assumption of risk barred recovery, rather than submitting the issue to the jury. After reviewing our caselaw, the *Smith* court defined its task as considering "whether the danger posed . . . was so obvious that Smith (or an ordinarily prudent person) must have known of it and whether he (or the ordinarily prudent person) must have appreciated the danger attending its use." The court held the evidence did not conclusively show the employee knew or ought to have known of the danger and its consequences, so the district court properly submitted the issue to the jury.

Smith's holding illustrates assumption of risk's more recent and limited utility as an employer's vehicle for securing a judgment as a matter of law. *Smith* essentially recognizes that determining when assumption of risk might apply as a matter of law actually requires the district court to analyze facts in the same way a jury would scrutinize them in assessing a plaintiff's comparative fault—a function that, if performed by the court, is inconsistent with our long-standing caselaw requiring such facts to be determined by a jury. . . . And *Smith* still understood that as a matter of tort law, an employer has a duty to provide a safe workplace and equipment.

[Many state high courts have abandoned] assumption of risk because of comparative fault's enactment in their states. We find the rationale in these cases compelling and are [now clearly convinced preserving assumption of risk as a complete bar to recovery is no longer sound and should be of no practical effect given the statutory scheme of comparative fault.] . . .

[Reversed and remanded.]

NOTES

1. **Traditional implied assumption of risk.** The traditional formulation of the implied assumption of risk defense was that a plaintiff's claim was completely barred when the plaintiff knew and understood the risk being incurred, and made a free and voluntary choice to incur it. Only a few states continue to follow such a broad all-or-nothing rule today. *See, e.g., S&S Oil, Inc. v. Jackson,* 53 A.3d 1125 (Md. 2012) (assumption of risk differs from contributory negligence and separate jury instruction was required in slip-and-fall case); *Rickey v. Boden,* 421 A.2d 539 (R.I. 1980) (barring negligence claim by elevator operator injured when she fell on a narrow stairway in defendant's building while walking to a coffee-break area).

2. **Is knowing risk-taking really "consent?"** [The traditional complete-bar rule seems to equate a voluntary encounter with known risk with consent to accept all risks of a defendant's negligence. Does that reasoning seem sound?] Prosser did not think so, and gave the example of a jaywalking plaintiff. [The jaywalker assuredly voluntarily confronts a known risk by crossing the road outside the crosswalk, but voluntary confrontation of the risk does not communicate any implied consent to release automobile drivers from a duty of ordinary care.] The jaywalker might be negligent, but that should not bar the claim entirely on "assumption of risk" grounds; liabilities should be

determined through application of the comparative fault rules. *See* 1 DOBBS, HAYDEN & BUBLICK, THE LAW OF TORTS § 236 (2d ed. 2011) (citing PROSSER & KEETON ON TORTS § 68, at 490 (5th ed. 1984)).

3. **Abolishing the implied assumption of risk defense.** Many courts have now abandoned the implied defense entirely, often on the ground that the traditional approach is simply inconsistent with comparative fault. The American Law Institute takes the same position, pointing out that if the plaintiff is reasonable in facing a risk, she is not negligent, but that when she unreasonably confronts a known risk, her negligence in doing so reduces her recovery of damages. RESTATEMENT (THIRD) OF TORTS: APPORTIONMENT OF LIABILITY § 3 cmt. c (2000). The Restatement's position is subject to two important explanations. First, if the defendant reasonably believes that the plaintiff has accepted the risk, the defendant may not be negligent (and thus not liable at all) in relying on the plaintiff to achieve safety. *See Stinnett,* Chapter 6. Second, as noted in § 1 of this chapter, the Restatement recognizes a complete defense based on *express* assumption of the risk.

4. **Effect of abolition.** What happens when the defense is abolished? "Cases formerly resolved under assumption of risk rationales can now be resolved by (1) applying the comparative fault rules, (2) holding that the defendant had no duty of care, or (3) holding that the defendant did not breach a duty. Which resolution is appropriate depends upon the facts of the case." 1 DOBBS, HAYDEN & BUBLICK, THE LAW OF TORTS § 237 (2d ed. 2011). Suppose plaintiff and defendant are rural neighbors, far from medical help. Plaintiff's spouse or partner is injured and needs immediate medical attention, but plaintiff's car is not available. Defendant's car could be used, but it is in a mechanical condition dangerous to the driver. Should defendant refuse permission to use the car? If he explains the risks and permits its use, but the car's bad condition causes an injury to the plaintiff, would the plaintiff be entitled to recover, with a reduction for comparative fault? Or would the plaintiff be denied all recovery on no-duty or no-breach grounds?

GREGORY V. COTT
331 P.3d 179 (Cal. 2014)

CORRIGAN, J. . . .

The relevant facts are undisputed. In 2005, defendant Bernard Cott contracted with a home health care agency to assist with his 85-year-old wife and codefendant Lorraine, who had long suffered from Alzheimer's disease. The agency assigned plaintiff Carolyn Gregory to work in the Cotts' home.

Gregory was trained to care for Alzheimer's patients, and had done so in other assignments. She knew they could be violent. Bernard told her Lorraine was combative and would bite, kick, scratch, and flail. Gregory's duties included supervising, bathing, dressing, and transporting Lorraine, as well as some housekeeping. In September 2008, Gregory was washing dishes while Lorraine sat at the kitchen table. Bernard was not at home. As Gregory was washing a large knife, Lorraine approached her from behind, bumped into her, and reached toward the sink. When Gregory attempted to restrain Lorraine, she dropped the knife, which struck her wrist. As a result, Gregory lost feeling in several fingers and experienced recurring pain.

Gregory has received workers' compensation. She also sued the Cotts for negligence and premises liability, with a claim against Lorraine for battery. The trial court granted a defense motion for summary judgment. A divided Court of Appeal affirmed, holding that Gregory's claims were barred by the primary assumption of risk doctrine. We affirm the judgment.

Since its reformulation in *Knight v. Jewett*, 834 P.2d 696 (Cal. 1992), California's assumption of risk doctrine has taken two quite different forms. Primary assumption of risk is a complete bar to recovery. It applies when, as a matter of law, the defendant owes no duty to guard against a particular risk of harm. Secondary assumption of risk applies when the defendant does owe a duty, but the plaintiff has knowingly encountered a risk of injury caused by the defendant's breach. Liability in such cases is adjudicated under the rules of comparative negligence.

[Here,] the Cotts rely on the primary assumption of risk doctrine, which operates as an exception to the general duty of care. Primary assumption of risk cases often involve recreational activity, but the doctrine also governs claims arising from inherent occupational hazards. . . . We have never held that the doctrine of assumption of risk relieves all persons of a duty of care to workers engaged in a hazardous occupation. However, the doctrine *does* apply in favor of those who hire workers to handle a dangerous situation, in both the public and the private sectors. Such a worker, as a matter of fairness, should not be heard to complain of the negligence that is the cause of his or her employment. In effect, we have said it is unfair to charge the defendant with a duty of care to prevent injury to the plaintiff arising from the very condition or hazard the defendant has contracted with the plaintiff to remedy or confront." This rule encourages the remediation of dangerous conditions, an important public policy. Those who hire workers to manage a hazardous situation are sheltered from liability for injuries that result from the risks that necessitated the employment. . . .

The case most closely on point here is *Herrle v. Estate of Marshall*, 45 Cal.App.4th 1761 (1996). . . . The plaintiff, a certified nurse's aide at a convalescent hospital, was struck and injured by an Alzheimer's patient while moving the patient from a chair to bed. The parties agreed that violent behavior is a common symptom of Alzheimer's disease. The hospital had many such patients, and the plaintiff was trained to work with them.

The Court of Appeal observed that the situation precisely matched the contours of primary assumption of risk, as outlined in *Knight:* " 'the nature of the activity' was the protection of the patient from doing harm to herself or others; 'the parties' relationship to the activity' was plaintiff's professional responsibility to provide this protection, [and] the 'particular risk of harm that caused the injury' was the very risk plaintiff and her employer were hired to prevent." . . .

As the *Herrle* court recognized, primary assumption of risk in its occupational aspect is readily applicable to the relationship between hired caregivers and Alzheimer's patients. It was stipulated in *Herrle* that violent behavior is a common symptom of the disease, and that proposition is well supported by medical texts, legal commentary, and the facts of reported cases. It follows that the risk of violent injury is inherent in the occupation of caring for Alzheimer's patients. While many such patients never become violent, it is equally true that not all fires injure firefighters, and not all dogs bite veterinarians. Nevertheless, because the *risk* of injury from those causes is inherent in the occupations of firefighters and veterinarians, it is settled that no duty is owed to protect them from the very dangers they are hired to confront. *Herrle's* conclusion that Alzheimer's patients owe no duty of care to protect hired caregivers from the risk of injury has found support, and no disagreement, in other jurisdictions. (See 1 Dobbs et al., The Law of Torts (2d ed. 2011) § 237, p. 854.) . . .

Gregory notes that she was not a certified health care professional, and asserts that Lorraine was not her "patient." She points out that unlike the plaintiff in *Herrle,* she was not caring for her client at the time of her injury, but instead was engaged in housekeeping. Accordingly, Gregory maintains that primary assumption of risk should not bar her suit, and her claims should instead be analyzed under the secondary assumption of risk doctrine. Secondary assumption of risk, however, is predicated on the existence of a duty. . . .

Gregory suggests she was as much a housekeeper as a caregiver, and emphasizes that she was injured while washing dishes, not directly attending to Lorraine. If Gregory had been retained as a housekeeper, primary assumption of risk would not bar her action because she would not have been hired to manage the risks posed by Lorraine's dementia. But Gregory worked for a home health care agency, not a housekeeping service. The circumstance that her duties included some housekeeping does not alter the central reason for her employment: Lorraine's inability to care for herself due to Alzheimer's disease. This fact establishes their relationship as caregiver and patient, and supports the application of primary assumption of risk. It is undisputed that Gregory's duties included constant supervision of Lorraine, to protect not only Lorraine but also Bernard and Gregory herself. . . .

In general, primary assumption of risk does not bar recovery when the defendant's actions have unreasonably *increased* the risks of injury beyond those inherent in the activity. If Bernard had done or failed to do something that elevated Gregory's risk of injury, this limitation on the doctrine would apply. But, having hired Gregory to care for Lorraine, Bernard owed Gregory no duty to protect her from the ordinary risks that arose in the course of that employment. . . .

Gregory also contends that intentional conduct does not come within the scope of primary assumption of risk, so that her battery claim against Lorraine should survive. Determining Lorraine's intent when Gregory was injured, or indeed the intentions of any late-stage Alzheimer's patient, is an uncertain enterprise. In any event, whether "intentional" or not, violent conduct by such patients is an inherent aspect of the caregiving function, and therefore within the scope of the assumed risk. (Cf. *Avila v. Citrus Community College Dist.*, 131 P.3d 383 (Cal. 2006) [being intentionally hit by pitch is inherent risk in baseball].) . . .

NOTES

1. **Primary and secondary implied assumption of the risk.** As you can see, not all states agree with the trend towards wholesale abolition of the implied assumption of risk defense. A number currently use the approach embodied in *Gregory*, and subdivide the traditional defense into two parts: "primary" (which equates to no duty, or no breach), and "secondary" (which equates to comparative fault). If "primary assumption of risk" is simply a synonym for "no duty" or "no breach of duty," then why is it viewed as an affirmative defense? And why adopt the label "secondary assumption of risk" if it is simply a species (or a veritable twin) of comparative fault?

2. **"Inherent" risks.** Was the California court correct in holding that the plaintiff impliedly agreed to accept the risks of being struck by the person in her care? Suppose the plaintiff, hired as a housekeeper, trips on stairs because the children of the house have left some items there. The plaintiff had picked up things off the stairs before, so she knew about that risk. In *Betts v. Crawford*, 965 P.2d 680 (Wyo. 1998), the court held that the employer had a duty to provide a safe place to work, and that implied assumption of risk had no role to play. Affirming a jury verdict for plaintiff, albeit one that reduced her recovery by 15% for her own fault, the court said, "there is no distinction between contributory negligence and assumption of risk when raised as a defense to an established breach of duty." Are *Betts* and *Gregory* distinguishable? Or do they simply expose that duty is a policy decision on which judges will differ?

3. **Judge and jury.** Most of the states that follow the "primary" and "secondary" approach to implied assumption of risk say that in determining whether primary assumption of risk should bar the claim, the court, and not the jury, should determine what risks are "inherent" in a particular activity.

[Handwritten margin notes at top: Given Idaho('s) case of comparative negligence statute / Idaho does not recognize assumption of risk as an affirmative standard]

See, e.g., *Turner v. Mandalay Sports Entertainment, LLC,* 180 P.3d 1172 (Nev. 2008) (on the ground that primary assumption of risk is a duty issue, thus solely for the court to decide). Yet what risks are "inherent" in an activity is quite fact-sensitive. Is the judge being asked to perform an essential jury function, then? Is this a problem? *See* Dilan A. Esper & Gregory C. Keating, *Putting "Duty" in Its Place: A Reply to Professors Goldberg and Zipursky,* 41 LOY. L. A. L. REV. 1225 (2008).

§ 3. SPORTS CASES

ROUNTREE V. BOISE BASEBALL, LLC

296 P.3d 373 (Idaho 2013)

J. JONES, JUSTICE. . . .

The facts of this case are largely undisputed. Rountree has been a Boise Hawks season ticket holder for over 20 years. On August 13, 2008, he took his wife and two grandchildren to a Boise Hawks game at Memorial Stadium in Garden City. Rountree concedes the stadium has "exceptionally extensive [mesh] netting" to protect spectators from errant foul balls. . . . Rountree's tickets were in the "Viper" section, which is protected by netting. The stadium also has an area known as the "Hawks Nest," which is a dining area along the third base line covered by both vertical and horizontal netting. Adjacent to the Hawks Nest, at the "very end of the third base line," is the "Executive Club." The Executive Club, while covered by horizontal netting, "is one of the only areas in the whole stadium not covered by vertical netting."

At some point during the game, Rountree and his family went to the Hawks Nest to eat. After eating, they went to the Executive Club. While in the Executive Club, Rountree started talking to someone and stopped paying attention to the game. Approximately ten minutes later, Rountree heard the roar of the crowd and turned his head back to the game. He was struck by a foul ball and, as a result, lost his eye. . . .

[Rountree sued several defendants for negligence.] Boise Baseball moved for summary judgment, arguing that the district court should adopt the Baseball Rule, which limits the duty of stadium operators to spectators hit by foul balls, and find that Boise Baseball complied with it. Alternatively, Boise Baseball argued that Rountree impliedly "consented to the risk of being hit by a foul ball." The district court denied the motion on both grounds [and Boise Baseball appealed]. . . .

DISCUSSION

[A. The Baseball Rule]

. . . The precise duty owed by stadium owners and operators to spectators struck by foul balls is a matter of first impression in Idaho. The majority of jurisdictions to consider the issue have limited this duty by adopting some variation of the Baseball Rule. Though many variations exist, the <u>most common formulation of the Baseball Rule is that stadium owners and operators must provide screened seats for as many spectators as may be reasonably expected to call for them on any ordinary occasion</u>. [The second-most common variation, applied in approximately nine jurisdictions, is quite similar: that stadium owners and operators have a duty to provide a choice between a screened-in and an open seat for spectators.] The rationale behind this is put bluntly by the [court in *Cincinnati Baseball Club Co. v. Eno*, 147 N.E. 86 (Ohio 1925)]: "it is common knowledge that in baseball games hard balls are thrown and batted with great swiftness" and "they are liable to be thrown or batted outside the lines of the diamond." The *Eno* Court therefore concluded that "<u>due care on the part on the management does not require all of the spectators to be screened in</u>; that the management performs its duty toward the spectators when it provides screened seats in the grand stand and <u>gives spectators the opportunity of occupying them</u>."

Despite the district court's conclusion that only the Legislature could adopt the Baseball Rule, it is also within this Court's power to do so. The Court has established duties of care where none previously existed. . . . However, even though the court may have the power to adopt a rule, such as the Baseball Rule, which limits the duty of a business owner, we decline to do so here. . . . Boise Baseball admits that at least for "seven seasons[, Mr. Rountree's] accident is the only time a spectator has suffered a 'major' injury because of a foul ball" at Memorial Stadium. The <u>rarity of these incidents weighs against crafting a special rule</u>. There is no history of accidents that we can look to, and draw from, to sensibly create a rule. Furthermore, Boise Baseball has not provided any broader statistical evidence regarding the prevalence of foul ball injuries in general, and—assuming they are so prevalent—how varying stadium designs might prevent them. Without this information, drawing lines as to where a stadium owner's duty begins, where netting should be placed, and so on, becomes guesswork. These kinds of questions are appropriate for the Legislature because it has the resources for the research, study and proper formulation of broad public policy. Declining to adopt the Baseball Rule leaves policy formulation to the deliberative body that is better positioned to consider the pros and cons of the issue. . . .

[B. Primary implied assumption of risk]

The district court addressed a related issue in its denial of Boise Baseball's motion for summary judgment—the current status of primary implied assumption of risk under Idaho law. . . . Generally speaking, the implied assumption of risk doctrine is divided into two subcategories: "primary" and "secondary." . . . Primary implied assumption of risk arises when the plaintiff impliedly assumes those risks that are *inherent* in a particular activity. In contrasting the two subcategories, some courts have held that primary implied assumption of the risk, because it is "treat[ed] as part of the initial duty analysis, rather than as an affirmative defense," is compatible with comparative negligence schemes.

Idaho uses a comparative negligence standard. I.C. § 6–801 ("Contributory negligence or comparative responsibility shall not bar recovery in an action by any person or his legal representative to recover damages for negligence. . . ."). This creates a logical inconsistency with assumption of risk, which by definition bars recovery based on comparative responsibility. Thus, this Court held in *Salinas v. Vierstra*, 695 P.2d 369 (Idaho 1985), that, "the use of assumption of risk as a defense shall have no legal effect in this state." [*Salinas* did not disturb the complete-bar rule for express assumption of risk, but suggested that the "assumption of risk" terminology should be dropped even in that context, "to avoid misunderstanding and confusion."]

. . . We reaffirm our holding in *Salinas:* the use of assumption of risk as a defense shall have no legal effect. Furthermore, we . . . hold that the general rule from *Salinas* applies to both primary and secondary assumption of the risk. Thus, primary implied assumption of the risk is not a valid defense. As this Court explained in *Salinas,* "Section 6–801's intent is clear: Contributory negligence is not to be a complete bar to recovery; instead, liability is to be apportioned between the parties based on the degree of fault for which each is responsible." Accordingly, the *Salinas* Court warned of the "gross legal inconsistency [of] prohibiting the use of contributory negligence as an absolute bar," while allowing "its effect to continue" through assumption of risk defenses. Because "[t]he types of issues raised by a plaintiff's non-express assumption of risk are readily handled by contributory negligence principles," we concluded that "issues should be discussed in terms of contributory negligence, not assumption of risk, and applied accordingly under our comparative negligence laws."

Based on this analysis, we are not persuaded that primary implied assumption of the risk should be treated any differently. Allowing assumption of risk as an absolute bar is inconsistent with our comparative negligence system, whether the risks are inherent in an activity, or not. Moreover, cases involving primary implied assumption of the risk are "readily handled" by comparative negligence principles; as in any case, fault will be assessed, and liability apportioned, based on the actions of the parties. Whether a party participated in something inherently dangerous will simply inform the comparison, rather than wholly preclude it. Here, whether watching baseball is inherently dangerous, and the degrees of fault to be apportioned to Rountree and Boise Baseball, are questions for the jury. Because comparative negligence can adroitly resolve these questions, there is no need for this Court to disturb its holding in *Salinas:*

assumption of the risk—whether primary or secondary—shall not act as a defense.

[Affirmed.]

NOTES

1.   **The Baseball Rule.** As the Idaho court in *Rountree* says, a large number of states have adopted some version of a limited-duty rule for stadium owners and operators; some have done so by legislation, others by judicial decision. Was the *Rountree* court correct in leaving it to legislative action in Idaho, or should it have adopted such a rule in this case?

2.   **Duty of care owed to sports spectators.** By declining to adopt a Baseball Rule, and by holding that primary assumption of risk should play no role in the analysis of the case, is the *Rountree* court simply deciding that the stadium owner/operator owed the plaintiff a duty of reasonable care? Do you see, then, how the case will proceed? How might the plaintiff show a breach of duty? And how might the defendant claim that the spectator was comparatively negligent?

COOMER v. KANSAS CITY ROYALS BASEBALL CORP.

437 S.W.3d 184 (Mo. 2014)

PAUL C. WILSON, JUDGE.

John Coomer claims he was injured when he was hit in the eye with a hotdog thrown by Sluggerrr, the Kansas City Royals mascot. [Evidence showed that every Royals home game since 2000 has featured a "Hotdog Launch" between innings, in which Sluggerrr stands on top of the visitor's dugout and either fires hotdogs into the crowd using an air gun, or tosses hotdogs by hand to fans seated nearby.] Coomer sued the Kansas City Royals Baseball Corporation, claiming the team is responsible for Sluggerrr's negligence and the damages it caused. A jury found in favor of the Royals, and Coomer appeals. Among the jury instructions was one asking the jury to decide whether the risk of being injured by Sluggerrr's hotdog toss is one of the inherent risks of watching a Royals home game that Coomer assumed merely by attending. Whether a particular risk is inherent in watching a sporting event is a question of law for the court, not a question of fact for the jury. . . .

It is safe to say that judicial analysis and application of assumption of the risk doctrine has not always achieved high marks for clarity and precision. Historically, courts often failed to draw or maintain important distinctions between this doctrine and defenses such as contributory negligence, which, though they may have seemed similar to assumption of the risk, were quite different. Simons, *Reflections on Assumption of Risk,* 50 UCLA L.Rev. 481, 486 (2002) ("*Reflections*"). Admittedly, those distinctions seldom made any difference as a practical matter because any of these often-overlapping defenses was sufficient to bar completely all recovery by the plaintiff. At least this was so before the advent of comparative fault. . . .

Comparative Fault Def.

The version of comparative fault adopted by this Court in *Gustafson v. Benda,* 661 S.W.2d 11 (Mo. Banc 1983), fundamentally altered this landscape. Section 1(a) of the Uniform Comparative Fault Act (the "UCFA") provides that "any contributory fault chargeable to the claimant diminishes proportionately the amount awarded as compensatory damages for an injury attributable to the claimant's contributory fault, but does not bar recovery." *Gustafson,* 661 S.W.2d at 18 (quoting from the UCFA). Section 1(b) of the UCFA defines "fault" for purposes of section 1(a) to include "unreasonable assumption of risk not constituting an enforceable express consent." *Id.* . . .

Accordingly, when the plaintiff is injured by the defendant's negligence, this Court holds that the adoption of comparative fault in *Gustafson* precludes any consideration of the plaintiff's conduct in assuming that risk (i.e., implied secondary assumption of the risk) except as a partial defense under a proper comparative fault instruction. Conversely, because the "express" and "implied primary" applications of assumption of the risk result in determinations that the defendant has no duty to protect the plaintiff, the form of comparative fault adopted in *Gustafson* does not preclude these applications as a complete—not merely a partial—bar to the plaintiff's recovery. . . .

[T]he proper application of implied primary assumption of the risk in this case—unaffected by *Gustafson*—is this: if Coomer was injured by a risk that is an inherent part of watching the Royals play baseball, the team had no duty to protect him and cannot be liable for his injuries. But, if Coomer's injury resulted from a risk that is not an inherent part of watching baseball in person—or if the negligence of the Royals altered or increased one of these inherent risks and caused Coomer's injury—the jury is entitled to hold the Royals liable for such negligence and, to the extent the reasonableness of Coomer's actions are in dispute, the jury must apportion fault between the parties using comparative fault principles. . . .

According to the Royals, the risk to a spectator of being injured by Sluggerrr's hotdog toss shares the same essential characteristics as the other risks that this Court (and many others) determined long ago were inherent in watching a baseball game in person, i.e., risks that a spectator will be injured by a flying ball or bat. The Court disagrees.

The rationale for barring recovery for injuries from risks that are inherent in watching a particular sport under implied primary assumption of the risk is that the defendant team owner cannot remove such risks without materially altering either the sport that the spectators come to see or the spectator's enjoyment of it. No such argument applies to Sluggerrr's hotdog toss. Millions of fans have watched the Royals (and its forebears in professional baseball) play the National Pastime for the better part of a century before Sluggerrr began tossing hotdogs, and millions more people watch professional baseball every year in stadiums all across this country without the benefit of such antics. . . .

Accordingly, the Court holds as a matter of law that the risk of injury from Sluggerrr's hotdog toss is not one of the risks inherent in watching the Royals play baseball that Coomer assumed merely by attending a game at Kauffman Stadium. This risk can be increased, decreased or eliminated altogether with no impact on the game or the spectators' enjoyment of it. As a result, Sluggerrr (and, therefore, the Royals) owe the fans a duty to use reasonable care in conducting the Hotdog Launch and can be held liable for damages caused by a breach of that duty. . . .

[T]his Court vacates the judgment and remands the case.

NOTES

1. **The trial court's jury instruction.** The *Coomer* court holds that giving the jury instruction on implied assumption of risk constituted prejudicial error. The instruction said this: "In your verdict you must not assess a percentage of fault to defendant if you believe: First, the risk of suffering an injury by being struck by a hotdog thrown in a manner in which Sluggerrr threw the hotdog that plaintiff alleges struck him was a risk inherent in attending a game at Royals' Stadium, and Second, plaintiff comprehended the actual risk, and Third, plaintiff intelligently accepted the risk." What did the Supreme Court say was wrong with that instruction, exactly?

2. **Spectators and primary assumption of risk.** Primary assumption of risk or limited-duty rules (such as the Baseball Rule discussed in *Rountree*) are often applied to bar claims by spectators injured by risks inherent in the game. Could the *concept* behind this approach be captured by saying that stadium owners and operators simply have no duty to protect spectators (who are, after all, business invitees) against the ordinary hazards of the sports activity, or, perhaps more accurately, to protect against whatever inherent risks remain after due care is exercised? *See Hurst v. East Coast Hockey League, Inc.*, 637 S.E.2d 560 (S.C. 2006). If so, then is the continued use of a "primary assumption of risk defense" still needed?

3. **Determining inherent risks.** How does a court determine which risks are inherent in an activity? What does the *Coomer* court say? Few would argue that the risk of being hit by a hockey puck at a hockey match, or by a foul ball at a baseball game, are not inherent risks. *See, e.g., Hurst v. East Coast Hockey League, Inc.*, 637 S.E.2d 560 (S.C. 2006); *Sciarrotta v. Global Spectrum*, 944 A.2d 630 (N.J. 2008). What about a spectator who is hit by a foul ball, but says he was distracted by the antics of the home team's costumed mascot? Is that distinguishable from the situation in *Coomer*? *Harting v.*

Dayton Dragons Professional Baseball Club, L.L.C., 870 N.E.2d 766 (Ohio Ct. App. 2007).

4. **Increasing inherent risks.** A spectator may recover if the defendant has *increased* the inherent risks of watching the sport. *See* DOBBS, HAYDEN & BUBLICK, HORNBOOK ON TORTS § 17.8, at 422 (2d ed. 2016). Was that the situation in *Coomer*?

_____

NOTE: SPORTS PARTICIPANTS

1. *General rules.* Participants in sports activities are governed by rules similar to those that apply to spectators. In the language of primary assumption of risk, sports participants impliedly assume the risk of the dangers inherent in the sport, and thus have no claims for negligence if injury results from those inherent risks. In the newer terminology, we might say that the defendant either owes no duty to reduce inherent risks, or does not breach a duty by failing to protect a participant from such risks. *See* 1 DOBBS, HAYDEN & BUBLICK, THE LAW OF TORTS § 240 (2d ed. 2011).

2. *Inherent risks.* It is probably safe to say that in general, participating in a sporting activity—skiing, or playing baseball, for example—exposes you to risks that go beyond those of mere spectating. In some settings, these inherent risks do not include the risks created by defendant's negligence. For example, for a skier, falling and being hurt is an inherent risk of the sport, but hitting a hidden bush left on the beginner's slope because of the operator's negligence is not. *See Sunday v. Stratton*, 390 A.2d 398 (Vt. 1978). In other settings, especially those involving competitive sports, one participant may well face the inherent risk that another participant will act negligently and cause harm—that is, the negligence of excited players is simply an inherent risk of the game. A co-participant's violation of the rules of the sport may even be an inherent risk, leaving the injured player without a negligence claim. *See, e.g., Turcotte v. Fell*, 502 N.E.2d 964 (N.Y. 1986) (professional jockey, injured by another jockey's illegal jostling); *Avila v. Citrus Community College Dist.*, 131 P.3d 383 (Cal. 2006) (batter in college baseball game injured by intentionally thrown "bean ball").

3. *Limited-duty rules.* A number of courts, and some legislatures, have adopted a limited duty of care in this setting, providing that co-participants owe only a duty to avoid intentionally or recklessly injuring each other. *See, e.g., Angland v. Mountain Creek Resort, Inc.*, 66 A.3d 1252 (N.J. 2013) (common-law recklessness standard applied to suit by a snowboarder against another snowboarder who collided with him); *Feld v. Borkowski*, 790 N.W.2d 72 (Iowa 2010) (recklessness standard applied to claim by first baseman hit by a bat that flew out of batter's hands); *Noffke*

v. Bakke, 760 N.W.2d 156 (Wis. 2009) (applying statute immunizing co-participants in "contact sports" from negligence claims); *Karas v. Strevell*, 884 N.E.2d 122 (Ill. 2008) (applying "willful or wanton" standard to amateur hockey); *Gauvin v. Clark*, 537 N.E.2d 94 (Mass. 1989) (recklessness standard applied to college ice hockey players). Should such a limited-duty rule be applied in a non-contact sport? *See Shin v. Ahn*, 165 P.3d 581 (Cal. 2007) (risk of a golfer being struck by a carelessly hit golf ball).

4. *Expectations of the parties*. Rather than distinguishing between inherent and non-inherent risks, does it make more sense to focus on the reasonable expectations of the parties? In a case involving a collision of skiers, allegedly the result of negligence, one court thought that the duty of care should turn on the parties' reasonable expectations. As to skiing, the court thought "skiers will expect that other skiers will follow the rules and generally accepted practices of the sport of skiing." *Jagger v. Mohawk Mountain Ski Area, Inc.*, 849 A.2d 813 (Conn. 2004). Sometimes courts focus on player expectations that conduct will be unsafe. In *Bukowski v. Clarkson University*, 971 N.E.2d 849 (N.Y. 2012), a college pitcher pitched to a live batter indoors without a protective L-screen in front of him, which all experienced players know is dangerous. Should the player's expectation that the situation is unsafe excuse the defendant University from its duty of reasonable care? Are the parties' reasonable expectations shaped by the legal rule? Is that also true of which risks are inherent?

> R<small>EFERENCES</small>: D<small>OBBS</small>, H<small>AYDEN</small> & B<small>UBLICK</small>, H<small>ORNBOOK ON</small> T<small>ORTS</small>
> §§ 17.1–17.8 (2d ed. 2016); 1 D<small>OBBS</small>, H<small>AYDEN</small> & B<small>UBLICK</small>, T<small>HE</small> L<small>AW</small>
> <small>OF</small> T<small>ORTS</small> §§ 232–240 (2d ed. 2011).

CHAPTER 11

DEFENSES NOT ON THE MERITS

• • •

§ 1. STATUTES OF LIMITATION AND REPOSE

Statutes of limitation are not peculiar to tort law. Almost every kind of claim must be brought within a period of time specified by statutes of limitation. If the claim is brought later, it is barred by the statute, even though it is otherwise a legitimate claim. The traditional statute of limitations serves at least two distinct purposes. One is to bar "stale" claims, the presentation of which might be unfair or costly because evidence is lost or subtly altered with time. A second is to permit both personal and business planning and to avoid the economic burden that would be involved if defendants and their insurance companies had to carry indefinitely a reserve for liability that might never be imposed. The time limit for tort claims may vary depending on the tort. The period is often short in cases of libel or slander, but in cases of personal injury the statute, in most instances, will allow the plaintiff two or three years in which to bring his action. Once the action is properly brought, the statute of limitations has no other function. It does not, for example, require *trial* by any certain time, only the commencement of the action.

The traditional analysis of statutes requires the action to be brought within the statutory period after the claim "accrues." When the claim accrues, starting the ticking of the limitations period clock, is often a contested issue. Statutes of repose, discussed at the end of this section, are similar, but serve some different purposes.

CRUMPTON V. HUMANA, INC.
661 P.2d 54 (N.M. 1983)

H. VERN PAYNE, C.J.

This is a frivolous appeal. We also note that there is a strong indication in the record that counsel for the appellant ineptly and perhaps negligently handled his client's case. Counsel for the appellant failed to file suit before the applicable statute of limitations had run. We are disappointed when members of our State Bar betray the trust and confidence of their clients by engaging in careless and unprofessional practice.

On February 8, 1979, Wanda Crumpton underwent surgery at Llano Estacado Medical Center in Hobbs. She alleged that she sustained injuries to her neck and legs when an attending nurse attempted to lower her hospital bed on February 11, 1979. Her suit was filed more than three years later on February 15, 1982. The trial court granted a motion for summary judgment on the ground that the suit was barred by the three-year statute of limitations.

Crumpton argues that her injury was not ascertainable until some time after the accident occurred. Further, she contends that the statute of limitations should have been tolled during the time the parties were negotiating.

These arguments are entirely without merit. In her deposition, Crumpton plainly testified that her injuries occurred on February 11, 1979. She also testified that she is still having problems in her shoulders, legs and sides which she attributed to the February 11, 1979 incident. Crumpton offers no evidence to contradict the fact that the alleged negligent act and injury occurred simultaneously on February 11, 1979. In our view, the fact that she had continuing treatments and hospitalizations after the injury does not necessarily make the date of the injury unascertainable.

. . . [T]he statute of limitations commences running from the date of injury or the date of the alleged malpractice.

Crumpton cites no authority for her argument that the statute of limitations should be tolled during the time when the parties were negotiating a settlement. The record indicates that defendants did not fraudulently lead Crumpton to believe that the case would be settled at some future date. In fact, the record indicates that in May 1981, defendants sent Crumpton a letter wherein defendants made a final offer for a compromise settlement of the case.

Accordingly, we affirm the trial court's grant of summary judgment against Crumpton. Because we determine this appeal to be frivolous and entirely without merit, costs and attorneys fees are to be borne by appellants.

NOTES

1. **Preventing legal malpractice.** Attorneys responsible for failure to file a meritorious suit (or a defense) in time are subject to liability to the client for malpractice. *See* KATHLEEN MARIE ERWINS & JASON T. VAIL, PROFILE OF LEGAL MALPRACTICE CLAIMS 2008–2011 (2012). What would you do to be sure you never filed a late claim, answer, or motion? Why might the attorney have delayed filing suit? Sometimes the client is late in consulting an attorney. Why might a client delay?

2. **Continuous treatment.** A growing number of states have adopted a special rule in medical malpractice cases that delays the start of the statute of limitations until the treatment for which the patient consulted the physician has been concluded. *See, e.g., Chalifoux v. Radiology Associates of Richmond, Inc.*, 708 S.E.2d 834 (Va. 2011); *Harrison v. Valentini*, 184 S.W.3d 521 (Ky. 2006). Suppose a radiologist reading an x-ray fails to detect cancer and reports a clean bill of health to the primary physician. Months later he reads a new x-ray but this time is not negligent. Does the second reading indicate continuous treatment so that the statute starts then? *Cf. Montgomery v. South County Radiologists, Inc.*, 49 S.W.3d 191 (Mo. 2001); *Hoe v. Saint Francis Medical Center*, 284 S.W.3d 738 (Mo. App. 2009) (doctor committed a single negligent act on which the statute of limitations had expired, treatment six years later for the same condition did not "revive" the claim).

A similar concept has been applied to legal malpractice claims, as well as in other contexts in which a plaintiff has been subjected to a series of wrongful acts by the defendant. *See, e.g., John Doe 1 v. Archdiocese of Milwaukee*, 734 N.W.2d 827 (Wis. 2007) (where child was abused over a long period of time, statute of limitations began to run at the time of the last incident of molestation); *Feltmeier v. Feltmeier*, 798 N.E.2d 75 (Ill. 2003) (husband's continued abuse of wife).

3. **Accrual of a claim.** The *Crumpton* court says the limitations period begins to run "from the date of injury or the date of the alleged malpractice." This reflects a traditional rule, still followed in some states, and in some particular contexts (especially medical malpractice), that the clock begins to run on a plaintiff's claim as soon as a suit could be brought, theoretically, even if the plaintiff was *unaware* of the negligent act, or even of the fact of injury. *See, e.g., Libby v. Eighth Jud. Dist. Ct.*, 325 P.3d 1276 (Nev. 2014) (applying statute that fixes "date of injury" as the accrual date for medical malpractice cases, barring plaintiff's claim despite her lack of awareness of the cause of her infection until much later); *Shearin v. Lloyd*, 98 S.E.2d 508 (N.C. 1957) (surgeon left a sponge in patient during operation; claim accrued on the date of the operation, even where plaintiff did not know about the sponge problem until much later). Such a result is obviously harsh, and beginning in the 1960s a number of states changed it, adopting instead the "discovery rule," ~~discussed below~~.

[handwritten margin note: Modern "discovery" Rule]

LINCOLN ELECTRIC CO. v. MCLEMORE, 54 So.3d 833 (Miss. 2010). Stanley McLemore worked as a welder for almost thirty years. In the course of his career, McLemore worked all over the country. In December 2001, McLemore experienced difficulty welding and developed slowness in his left hand and arm. McLemore went to a chiropractor, who sent him to a neurologist who told him he had Parkinsonism or Parkinsonian syndrome, and his condition could have been related to welding. McLemore visited an attorney's office. Subsequently, McLemore saw six doctors, one of whom, in

[handwritten margin note: P's cause of action accrues at point at which he discovered, or by reasonable diligence should have discovered th injury (not discovery of the injury and its cause)]

December 2002, advised McLemore to discontinue welding. [In 2005, Dr. Swash, McLemore's main expert witness at trial, diagnosed McLemore with manganism, an atypical Parkinsonism that is caused by exposure to manganese.] McLemore filed a complaint against the defendant manufacturers of welding rods on March 3, 2006. The trial court denied a summary judgment motion based on the statute of limitations, and the jury returned a verdict in favor of McLemore for $1,855,000. *Held,* reversed. "Pursuant to Mississippi Code Section 15–1–49(2), a plaintiff's cause of action accrues at the point at which he discovered, or by reasonable diligence should have discovered, the injury. Therefore, this Court must consider the application of the latent-injury/discovery rule and whether McLemore's statute of limitations began to run when either (1) he knew of his Parkinsonism, or (2) he knew of the diagnosis of manganism. . . [T]he plain language of Section 15–1–49 supports an interpretation 'that the cause of action accrued upon discovery of the injury, *not discovery of the injury and its cause.*'] . . McLemore knew of his injury on September 3, 2002. McLemore failed to file his cause of action within the applicable statute of limitations."

NOTES

1. **What counts as "discovery."** Exactly what "discovery" ought to count for purposes of the discovery rule? Statutes and case law create some divergence. Typically the statute of limitations will not begin to run until at least (1) all elements of the tort are present, and (2) the plaintiff discovers, or as a reasonable person should have discovered, that (a) she is injured and (b) the defendant had a causal role, or there was enough chance that the defendant was connected to the injury to require further investigation. 1 Dobbs, Hayden & Bublick, The Law of Torts § 243 (2d ed. 2011). Does the *Lincoln Electric* case seem to fit within that rule?

2. **Duty to investigate.** [Many courts applying a discovery rule stress that plaintiffs are under a duty to investigate once they have notice of certain facts.] *See, e.g., Lyas v. Forrest General Hosp.,* 177 So.3d 412 (Miss. 2015) ("To benefit from the discovery rule, a plaintiff must be reasonably diligent in investigating her injuries."); *Norgart v. Upjohn Co.,* 981 P.2d 79 (Cal. 1999) (discovery rule requires plaintiff to "seek to learn the facts necessary to bring the cause of action in the first place—he cannot wait for them to find him").

3. **Awareness of the defendant's negligence.** Some authority delays accrual until the plaintiff discovers, or should reasonably have discovered, evidence of the defendant's potential *negligence.* In *Walk v. Ring,* 44 P.3d 990 (Ariz. 2002), the plaintiff knew she suffered injury after dental work, but did not initially think the dentist was at fault. The court held that the claim accrued only when she discovered that other dentists thought he was at fault. Somewhat similarly, Connecticut has said that the statute runs from the time injury is or should have been discovered, but that "injury" means *actionable injury.* In turn, actionable injury means an injury caused by negligence. So the

statute would not commence to run until the plaintiff discovered or should have discovered all the elements of a cause of action, including *both* the defendant's negligence *and* the defendant's causal link to the injury, or at least reason to investigate those issues. *Lagassey v. State,* 846 A.2d 831 (Conn. 2004).

4. **The jury's role.** The discovery rule avoids the harsh result of the "date of injury" rule, but it substitutes a good deal of uncertainty, since discovery will depend on the individualized facts of each case. It also injects a normative issue—when plaintiff *should* have discovered the injury and its likely cause. As in *Lincoln Electric,* questions often arise about when the plaintiff discovered sufficient facts to start the limitations clock, or a reasonable person would have done so. These questions are for the jury, if reasonable people can differ. *See, e.g., Ridgway Lane & Associates, Inc. v. Watson,* 189 So.3d 626 (Miss. 2016) (fact issue about when plaintiff homeowner knew or should have known of his breathing problems, in action against defendants who failed to repair a ceiling leak that caused mold to grow inside his home). Does the individualized inquiry under the discovery rule undercut the purposes of having statutes of limitation in the first place?

5. **Identity of the defendant.** Courts have not agreed on whether the identity of the defendant must be known or reasonably knowable before a claim accrues. Compare *Harrington v. Costello,* 7 N.E.3d 449 (Mass. 2014) ("Knowledge of the responsible person's identity seems implicit in the requirement that a plaintiff know that the defendant's conduct caused him harm; without such knowledge, the plaintiff does not know whom to sue."), with *Fox v. Ethicon Endo-Surgery, Inc.,* 110 P.3d 914 (Cal. 2005) (that plaintiff neither knows nor suspects the identity of the defendant "does not delay accrual . . . because the identity of the defendant is not an element of a cause of action"). The rationale for the latter approach appears to be that a plaintiff who knows of the existence of a cause of action has time to discover the defendant's identity, often by filing a "Doe" complaint and using the tools of discovery to gain the required knowledge in order to serve the proper defendant. Where a tortfeasor intentionally conceals his identity from the plaintiff, however, he may be estopped from asserting the statute of limitations. *See Bernson v. Browning-Farris Indus.,* 873 P.2d 613 (Cal. 1994).

NOTE: LATENT POTENTIAL HARM

Partial Injury, Latent Potential

Accrual of a claim under the discovery rule is not delayed simply because the plaintiff does not know of the full extent of her injury or damages. *See, e.g., Podrygula v. Bray,* 856 N.W.2d 791 (N.D. 2014); *Larson & Larson, P.A. v. TSA Indus., Inc.,* 22 So.3d 36 (Fla. 2009). But suppose a tort occurs and the plaintiff knows it, yet the plaintiff believes damages may later become much worse than they are at present. While it is perfectly possible to claim and recover damages that will occur in the future, under traditional rules this can be done only if the proof shows that such damages will more likely than not occur. If the plaintiff sues now to stay within the statute of limitations, he will avoid that problem, but he will be limited to damages he can presently prove. The *res judicata* rules will prevent a second suit later on. If he waits to see whether damages will become much worse, he will eventually face the statute of limitations bar.

In *Hagerty v. L. & L. Marine Services, Inc.*, 788 F.2d 315 (5th Cir. 1986), Hagerty was drenched with dripolene, a carcinogen. He had some dizziness and leg cramps, and stinging in the extremities, all of which disappeared after showers. He undergoes regular medical checkups because of the cancer threat, but he does not presently have cancer and cancer is not "more likely than not." But his present fear of future cancer is real. Consider the options for the court:

(1) Adopt a view similar to that under the lost chance of recovery cases, Chapter 7. This would allow the plaintiff to recover now for any actual injury, plus all possible future injuries that might result from it, but future injuries would be reduced to reflect their probability. For example, if future cancer appearing in ten years is a 40% probability and would, if it occurs, impose damages of $100,000, the plaintiff would recover $40,000. This is the "enhanced-risk" or reduced-chance recovery.

(2) Reject the enhanced-risk recovery, allow present actual damages only, but with present damages, including the mental anguish or suffering resulting from the plaintiff's fear of future cancer.

(3) Reject the enhanced-risk and fear claims, allow the plaintiff to recover what he can prove in actual damages, and bar any future claims under *res judicata* rules.

(4) Reject enhanced-risk recovery, but allow present damages and leave open the possibility for a second suit if substantially different kinds of damage occur. This would allow recovery for cancer if it later develops.

The *Hagerty* court adopted the fourth option. This eliminates the dilemma created by the statute of limitations on the one hand and the *res judicata* rules on the other. A growing number of cases support allowing a second suit for damages if a different kind of injury occurs later, caused by the same exposure. The California Supreme Court adopted this approach in *Pooshs v. Philip Morris USA, Inc.*, 250 P.3d 181 (Cal. 2011). The court held that an earlier-discovered disease, COPD, does not trigger the statute of limitations on a suit based on a later-discovered separate latent disease, lung cancer, caused by the same tobacco use.

Exposure Without Symptoms

[Suppose the plaintiff is exposed to a toxin in sufficient quantities to raise the possibility of future harm that could occur in ten, twenty or thirty years.] But suppose also that the plaintiff has no present symptoms at all. You might think that in this kind of case there is no problem. There is no statute of limitations to confront because the plaintiff merely waits until injury occurs and then sues. [However, the plaintiff exposed to chemical poisons in her water or gases in the air she breathes may have two present "injuries" without symptoms.] First, the plaintiff may have fear of future harm and that fear may itself poison her life. Second, the plaintiff may have medical expense because continuous medical monitoring is important to minimize future harm by early detection) —> *courts acknowledges harms, that arise from likely physical future harm*

[Some decisions have treated the non-symptomatic exposure as a tort and have said, with *Hagerty*, that the plaintiff could recover now for the costs of medical monitoring and that an additional suit could be brought later if cancer or other serious disease actually occurs.] A landmark case is *Ayers v. Jackson Twp.*, 525 A.2d 287 (N.J. 1987). *See also Meyer ex rel. Coplin v. Fluor Corp.*, 220 S.W.3d 712 (Mo. 2007) (citing cases from a dozen other jurisdictions supporting such a theory). Other courts have rejected claims for medical monitoring damages in the absence of proven physical injury. *See, e.g., Paz v. Brush Engineered Materials, Inc.*, 949 So.2d 1 (Miss. 2007); *Henry v. Dow Chemical Co.*, 701 N.W.2d 684 (Mich. 2005).

Are you willing to say that any exposure, even though not accompanied by symptoms, is a tort for which damages can be recovered?

NOTE: TOLLING AND GRACE PERIODS

1. *The tolling concept.* The discovery rule is not the only avenue of relief for the late-suing plaintiff. Statutes of limitation may be tolled (a term of art, meaning *paused*) so that the clock is not running at all until some impediment to suing has been removed. This may occur before the limitations period ever begins, or after it has begun. For example, the statute of limitations may be tolled while the plaintiff is under a disability such as minority (that is, young age) or mental incompetence.

2. *Tolling for minority.* State laws generally toll the statute of limitations on a child's injury claim until the child has reached the age of majority, usually 18. Thus if the statutory period is two years and the injured child sued within two years after reaching the age of majority, the suit would be timely. Some state courts have held that legislation to the contrary violates their constitution. *See Kordus v. Montes*, 337 P.3d 1138 (Wyo. 2014); *Piselli v. 75th Street Med.*, 808 A.2d 508 (Md. 2002); *Sands ex rel. Sands v. Green*, 156 P.3d 1130 (Alaska 2007). Other courts have upheld

legislative restrictions on minority tolling against constitutional attack. *See, e.g., Christiansen v. Providence Health System of Oregon Corp.*, 184 P.3d 1121 (Or. 2008).

3. *Tolling for unsound mind.* Minority is a type of legal disability, but the law recognizes other types as well for tolling purposes. For purposes of commitment to an institution, an individual might be deemed of unsound mind if he is a danger to himself or others. In the statute of limitations context, however, unsound mind usually means that the individual is unable to manage his or her business affairs or estate, or to comprehend his or her legal rights or liabilities. *Ellis v. Estate of Ellis*, 169 P.3d 441 (Utah 2007); *Doe v. Roe*, 955 P.2d 951 (Ariz. 1998). Thus no matter what the psychological impediments to suit, the victim cannot have the benefits of tolling for unsound mind if he can manage his daily affairs by working, buying food, writing checks or the like. Whether the patient cannot manage day-to-day affairs such that tolling would apply is often a question of fact. In some jurisdictions, this issue may be resolved by the court in a pre-trial evidentiary hearing. *See Timothy G. v. State, Dept. of Health & Social Services*, 372 P.3d 235 (Alaska 2016).

4. *Other forms of tolling.* A statute of limitations also may be tolled for other reasons. For example, the statute of limitations may be tolled during the pendency of a suit seeking class action certification, or because the plaintiff is in prison or in the armed forces. *See* DOBBS, HAYDEN & BUBLICK, HORNBOOK ON TORTS § 18.6 (2d ed. 2016).

DASHA V. MAINE MEDICAL CENTER, 665 A.2d 993 (Me. 1995). [Defendant erroneously diagnosed the plaintiff as having a fatal brain tumor.] On that diagnosis, surgery plus radiation to the brain would prolong life for a short time and the plaintiff opted for that treatment. The treatment itself allegedly caused severe brain damage and the plaintiff became incompetent. [Two years after the misdiagnosis and treatments, another physician reviewed the diagnosis and discovered that it was erroneous. The plaintiff's original problem had been a relatively benign tumor not calling for such treatments.] His guardian sued, but by this time it was more than three years after the original misdiagnosis. Under Maine's legislation, the discovery rule did not apply because, by statute, it was unavailable in most medical malpractice cases. Nor did tolling for mental incapacity work because the plaintiff was mentally sound at the time of the misdiagnosis. The plaintiff argued that, nonetheless, the defendant should be equitably estopped from pleading the statute of limitations, since the defendant's own fault had caused the incapacity as well as the injury.

Held, no equitable estoppel applies. "[E]stoppel may be used to prevent the affirmative defense of the statute of limitations if the elements of estoppel are present. . . . The gist of an estoppel barring the defendant from

[handwritten margin notes: "Have to be mentally incapacitated at the time of injury (misdiagnosis)"]

[handwritten note: "Holding"]

invoking the defense of the statute of limitations is that the defendant has conducted himself in a manner which actually induces the plaintiff not to take timely legal action on a claim. The plaintiff thus relies to his detriment on the conduct of the defendant by failing to seek legal redress while the doors to the courthouse remain open to him."

"The stipulated facts of this case do not meet the elements of equitable estoppel. . . . MMC made no affirmative misrepresentation, as required to support the application of equitable estoppel. Although a claim of equitable estoppel can be supported by an act of negligence that is the equivalent of fraud, the misdiagnosis by MMC is not the equivalent of fraud sufficient to support the assertion of equitable estoppel. Dasha relied on the misdiagnosis to seek radiation treatments, but he did not rely on a representation of MMC to decide to forego seeking legal redress."

NOTES

1.   **Elements of equitable estoppel.** Was the estoppel decision in *Dasha* correct? Was the outcome of the case correct? "The elements of an equitable estoppel claim are (1) a delay in filing an action that is induced by the defendant; (2) the defendant misled the plaintiff; and (3) the plaintiff must have acted on the information in good faith to the extent that he failed to pursue his action in a timely manner." *Archuleta v. City of Rawlins*, 942 P.2d 404 (Wyo. 1997).

2.   **Force or threat.** If a defendant prevented suit by physical force or threats, he might be estopped from pleading the statute of limitations as a defense. *See John R. v. Oakland Unified School Dist.*, 769 P.2d 948 (Cal. 1989) (child molester); *Ortega v. Pajaro Valley Unified Sch. Dist.*, 75 Cal. Rptr.2d 777 (Ct. App. 1998) (same).

3.   **Fraudulent concealment.** A statute of limitations will be tolled if a defendant fraudulently conceals a cause of action from the plaintiff. This tolling may last until the plaintiff discovers, or should have discovered, either the fraudulent concealment itself, *see Gallant v. MacDowell*, 759 S.E.2d 818 (Ga. 2014), or the facts that establish a cause of action, *see Estate of Brice v. Toyota Motor Corp.*, 373 P.3d 977 (N.M. 2016) (outlining the elements of fraudulent concealment as follows: plaintiff must prove that (1) defendant knew of the alleged wrongful act and concealed it from plaintiff, or had material information that he failed to disclose, and (2) plaintiff did not know, or could not have known through reasonable diligence, of the cause of action within the statutory period). Many courts appear to require that the act of concealment be "active," such as by making an actual misrepresentation of fact as opposed to simply remaining silent, although that requirement is not imposed where the parties are in a fiduciary relationship the imposes a duty of disclosure. *Henderson Square Condominium Ass'n v. LAB Townhomes, LLC*, 46 N.E.3d 706 (Ill. 2015); *Anderson ex rel. Herren v. Iowa Dermatology Clinic, PLC*, 819 N.W.2d 408 (Iowa 2012).

4.   **Equitable tolling.** Courts have distinguished equitable estoppel, fraudulent concealment, and equitable tolling, on the ground that the first two involve some misconduct by the defendant while the latter does not. With equitable tolling, a court may decide to toll the statute "when a litigant has pursued his rights diligently but some extraordinary circumstance prevents him from bringing a timely action." *Lozano v. Montoya Alvarez*, 134 S.Ct. 1224 (2014). Does this give the court more flexibility than would a simple application of the discovery rule?

DURRE V. WILKINSON DEVELOPMENT, INC.
830 N.W.2d 72 (Neb. 2013)

WILKINS, J.:

On April 3, 2009, Durre and his wife were sitting in their pickup truck, which was parked at a gas station/fast-food restaurant in North Platte, Nebraska. About 1 p.m., the restaurant's sign fell onto the cab of the truck, injuring Durre and killing his wife.

The restaurant's sign and the pole structure to which the sign was attached were designed, built, and installed by Tri-City [Sign Company] employees. Tri-City obtained a building permit for the installation of the sign from the city of North Platte, designating 65 feet as the height of the sign. Installation of the sign was completed on or about May 15, 1999. There was no evidence that any of the defendants measured the height of the sign after its construction was completed. [The sign was, in fact, 75 feet high.] The sign collapsed as a result of the shearing of a section of the steel pole which held the sign. . . .

[On November 13, 2009, Durre sued Wilkinson Development, the owner of the restaurant's parking lot, for negligently maintaining the pole and sign. On March 10, 2011, Durre filed an amended complaint naming other defendants, including Tri-City, alleging that it negligently designed and constructed the pole and sign, and failed to warn of the sign's dangerous condition. In a second amended complaint, Durre alleged that Tri-City concealed the height of the sign from the public. The district court granted Tri-City's motion for summary judgment, concluding that Durre's actions were barred by the 10-year statute of repose in NEB. REV. ST. § 25–223. Durre appealed.]

The applicable statute, § 25–223, provides in part:

In no event may any action be commenced to recover damages for an alleged breach of warranty on improvements to real property or deficiency in the design, planning, supervision, or observation of construction, or construction of an improvement to real property more than ten years beyond the time of the act giving rise to the cause of action.

Durre has alleged a claim to recover for personal injury caused by Tri-City's negligence. He argues that § 25–223 does not apply to personal injuries resulting from an inherently dangerous condition or latent defect of the property caused by a contractor's negligence. We disagree.

Our resolution of this claim is controlled by our decision in *Williams v. Kingery Constr. Co.,* 404 N.W.2d 32 (Neb. 1987). Henry Williams, a school janitor, fell 30 feet backward inside a pipe chase. His fall was caused by a missing section of concrete wall and occurred more than 10 years after construction of the school was completed in 1968. Williams argued that § 25–223 applied only to causes of action for damage to property and not to actions for personal injury. We determined that § 25–223 applied to an action in tort for personal injuries caused by the negligent construction of a building. We held the 10-year period of repose began to run when construction of the building was completed. Thus, Williams' cause of action was time barred before it accrued. . . .

Durre's action against Wilkinson was filed in November 2009, which was more than 10 years after the May 1999 completion and installation of the sign. His action against Tri-City was not commenced until March 10, 2011. The 10-year statute of repose in § 25–223 barred Durre's claim for damages against Tri-City.

Durre argues that if § 25–223 applies to claims for personal injury, Tri-City's fraudulent concealment of the dangerous condition of the sign estopped it from asserting a statute of repose defense. . . . From our review of the pleadings and the evidence offered at the hearing on the motions for summary judgment, we conclude that Durre has failed to provide any evidence that created a material issue of fact whether Tri-City fraudulently concealed any material fact, either with the intention that Durre would act or refrain from acting, or which prevented Durre from timely filing his action against Tri-City. . . .

AFFIRMED.

NOTES

1. **Statutes of repose.** As the U.S. Supreme Court has explained, a statute of repose "puts an outer limit on the right to bring a civil action. That limit is measured not from the date on which the claim accrues but instead from the date of the last culpable act or omission of the defendant. . . . [T]he injury need not have occurred, much less have been discovered." *CTS Corp. v. Waldburger,* 134 S.Ct. 2175 (2014). A number of states have enacted statutes of this kind in the last several years, often aimed at protecting some special group, such as product manufacturers, doctors, architects, engineers, and construction contractors.

2. **Purpose and policy.** In *CTS v. Waldburger, supra* Note 1, the Court recognized that while "there is substantial overlap between the policies" of

statutes of limitation and statutes of repose, "each has a distinct purpose and each is targeted at a different actor." Statutes of limitation encourage plaintiffs to bring actions in a timely manner, as do statutes of repose. But statutes of repose "effect a legislative judgment that a defendant should be free from liability after the legislatively determined time." *Id.*

3. **Equitable tolling, the discovery rule, and fraudulent concealment.** Statutes of repose are not generally subject to equitable tolling, even in cases of extraordinary circumstances beyond the plaintiff's control. *Lozano v. Montoya Alvarez*, 134 S.Ct. 1224 (2014). The court in *Ambers-Phillips v. SSM DePaul Health Center*, 459 S.W.3d 901 (Mo. 2015), said that statutes of repose are "incompatible with equitable tolling." Why would that be?

What about the discovery rule? Can a plaintiff escape the statute of repose by proving that he neither knew nor should have known of the existence of facts that would allow a suit to be brought? Most courts have said no. *See, e.g., Ex parte Hodge*, 153 So.3d 734 (Ala. 2014); *Lamprey v. Britton Const., Inc.*, 37 A.3d 359, 365 (N.H. 2012).

Is fraudulent concealment different? The *Durre* court concludes that the plaintiff failed to prove any act of fraudulent concealment by Tri-City. If the plaintiff had made such proof, should *that* have tolled the statute of repose? Compare *Ingram v. Drouin*, 111 A.3d 1104 (N.H. 2015), with *Snyder v. Love*, 153 P.3d 571 (Mont. 2006).

4. **Constitutionality.** One line of attack on this sort of statute questions its constitutionality, usually on the basis of state constitutional provisions. Some courts have held such statutes unconstitutional, but others have upheld them. Much may depend on the exact wording of the particular state constitution. *See, e.g., Myers v. Crouse-Hinds Div. of Cooper Industries, Inc.*, 53 N.E.3d 1160 (Ind. 2016) (10-year statute of repose in Product Liability Act unconstitutional as applied, under the state constitution's Equal Privileges and Immunities Clause).

REFERENCES: DOBBS, HAYDEN & BUBLICK, HORNBOOK ON TORTS §§ 18.1.7 (2d ed. 2016); 1 DOBBS, HAYDEN & BUBLICK, THE LAW OF TORTS §§ 241–250 (2d ed. 2011).

§ 2. FEDERAL PREEMPTION

VREELAND V. FERRER
71 So.3d 70 (Fla. 2012)

LEWIS, J. . . .

Danny Ferrer entered into an agreement to lease an airplane from Aerolease of America, Inc. (Aerolease) for a period of one year. . . . [After takeoff,] the plane crashed. The pilot, Donald Palas, and his passenger, Jose Martinez, were killed in the crash. John Vreeland, in his capacity as administrator ad litem and personal representative of the Martinez estate, filed a wrongful death action against Aerolease. [Vreeland asserted a number of Florida state law tort claims, including a "dangerous instrumentality doctrine" claim that Aerolease, as owner of the aircraft, was liable and responsible for the negligence of the pilot in the operation and inspection of the aircraft.]

Aerolease moved for summary final judgment, contending that a provision of federal law, 49 U.S.C. § 44112 (1994), preempted Florida law. Section 44112, titled "Limitation of Liability," provides, in pertinent part:

> (b) Liability.—A lessor, owner, or secured party is liable for personal injury, death, or property loss or damage on land or water only when a civil aircraft, aircraft engine, or propeller is in the actual possession or control of the lessor, owner, or secured party, and the personal injury, death, or property loss or damage occurs because of—
>
> > (1) the aircraft, engine, or propeller; or
> >
> > (2) the flight of, or an object falling from, the aircraft, engine, or propeller.

[The trial court granted the motion.]

The dangerous instrumentality doctrine has been a part of Florida common law for almost one hundred years. In 1920, the Florida Supreme Court . . . articulated what is now known as the dangerous instrumentality doctrine and concluded that the doctrine is applicable to motor vehicles: . . .

> An automobile being a dangerous machine, its owner should be responsible for the manner in which it is used; and his liability should extend to its use by any one with his consent. He may not deliver it over to any one he pleases and not be responsible for the consequences.

In a subsequent decision, this Court held that an individual who rented vehicles as part of a business was responsible for the negligence of the driver who rented the vehicle. . . . Recently, the Fifth District Court of Appeal reiterated the concept and framework of the dangerous instrumentality doctrine and the purpose behind it:

> The doctrine imposes strict liability upon the owner of a motor vehicle by requiring that an owner who "gives authority to another to operate the owner's vehicle, by either express or implied consent, has a nondelegable obligation to ensure that the vehicle is operated safely." The doctrine is intended to foster greater financial responsibility to pay for injuries caused by motor vehicles because the owner is in the best position to ensure that there are adequate resources to pay for damages caused by its misuse. The doctrine also serves to deter vehicle owners from

entrusting their vehicles to drivers who are not responsible by making the owners strictly liable for any resulting loss. . . .

It was a federal court in 1951 that first applied Florida's dangerous instrumentality doctrine to aircraft. . . .

Our examination of these authorities and the reasoning underlying their pronouncements leave no room for doubt that, [ ] Florida law, by which we are here governed, . . . imposes liability upon the defendant for the acts and omissions of the pilot of its airplane which the jury was authorized to, and did, find constituted negligence. . . .

With regard to federal preemption, the United States Supreme Court has stated:

> Preemption may be either express or implied, and "is compelled whether Congress' command is explicitly stated in the statute's language or implicitly contained in its structure and purpose." . . We "begin with the language employed by Congress and the assumption that the ordinary meaning of that language accurately expresses the legislative purpose."
>
> Where a federal law does not expressly preempt state law, preemption may be inferred only where the scheme of federal regulation is sufficiently comprehensive to make reasonable the inference that Congress "left no room" for supplementary state regulation. Preemption of a whole field also will be inferred where the field is one in which "the federal interest is so dominant that the federal system will be assumed to preclude enforcement of state laws on the same subject."
>
> Even where Congress has not completely displaced state regulation in a specific area, state law is nullified to the extent that it actually conflicts with federal law. Such a conflict arises when "compliance with both federal and state regulations is a physical impossibility," or when state law "stands as an obstacle to the accomplishment and execution of the full purposes and objectives of Congress."

The United States Supreme Court has further explained that preemption is very carefully scrutinized when it touches upon areas traditionally governed by state law. . . . Tort law is one area that is clearly and traditionally regulated by the states. . .

At issue in this case is whether the federal law currently codified at 49 U.S.C. § 44112 preempts Florida state law with regard to the liability of aircraft owners under the dangerous instrumentality doctrine and, if it does, how broadly the scope of that preemption covers.

There is no express preemption language within [the federal statute.] Therefore, if Florida law with regard to aircraft owner/lessor liability is preempted by section 44112, that preemption can only be implied. . . To determine whether and to what extent section 44112 may impliedly preempt Florida law, it is necessary to review and understand the legislative history behind this provision. . . .

Every version of the owner/lessor liability federal statute since its enactment in 1948 has referenced injury, death, or property damage that has occurred on land or water, or on the surface of the earth. . . . The words "on land or water" or "on the surface of the earth" may be read to specify that the limitation on liability only applies to death, injury, or damage that is caused to people or property that are physically on the ground or in the water. Specifically, the limitation on liability would apply only to individuals and property that are underneath the aircraft during its flight, ascent, or descent. . . .

We conclude that by adopting a federal law that specifically referenced damages or injuries that occur on the surface of the earth, the 1948 Congress did not intend to preempt state law with regard to injuries to passengers or aircraft crew. . . .

Decisions with regard to how section 44112/1404 should be interpreted are varied. . . . [We agree with an interpretation adopted by a Michigan court that the federal statute shields a lessor of an airplane from tort liability for any injury or loss suffered "on the surface of the earth" but not for an injury that occurred "inside the aircraft."]

Florida's dangerous instrumentality doctrine imposes vicarious liability upon owners and lessors of aircraft, even where the aircraft is not within their immediate control or possession at the time of the loss. To the extent that the doctrine applies to injuries, damages, or deaths that occur on the surface of the earth, the doctrine conflicts with, and is therefore preempted by, section 44112. However, because the death of Martinez occurred while he was a passenger in a plane that crashed—not on the ground beneath the plane—the wrongful death action filed by Vreeland is not preempted by section 44112. Rather, Florida's dangerous instrumentality doctrine applies, and the Second District erroneously affirmed the summary final judgment entered by the trial court in favor of Aerolease on the basis of federal preemption. . . .

POLSTON, J., dissenting. . . .

I believe federal law preempts Florida's dangerous instrumentality doctrine here. . . . The majority's assertion that the federal statute does not apply because "Martinez was not 'on land or water' at the time of the crash—he was a passenger inside the aircraft" defies reality. Even though Martinez was in the aircraft when it hit land, his death occurred "on land," not in the aircraft prior to contact with land. The majority's view is inconsistent with the plain meaning of the statute, specifically the plain meaning of "on land."

NOTES

1.   **Supremacy of federal laws.** The Supremacy Clause of Article VI of the U.S. Constitution provides that the federal constitution and laws "shall be the supreme Law of the Land." Congress has the power to override state law as long as it acts within the limits of its own constitutional powers. According to the *Vreeland* court, under what circumstances might federal regulation preempt state tort law?

2.   **Scope of preemption.** If the intent to preempt state law is the "clear and manifest purpose of Congress" in enacting a particular law or regulation, *CSX Transportation, Inc. v. Easterwood*, 507 U.S. 658 (1993), then state laws that conflict with those federal provisions simply cannot be enforced. The effect is to displace tort law and leave the plaintiff without a remedy where the defendant has complied with federal regulations. Congress might preempt state tort law by (1) expressly doing so by statute; (2) occupying the field with heavy regulation so there is no room for state tort law; or (3) by passing laws that actually conflict with state law. A federal statute may be found to preempt some but not all of a plaintiff's state tort claims, or, as in *Vreeland*, to preempt claims by certain plaintiffs but not others.

3.   **A preemption example.** The federal government regulates many aspects of railroad operations. For example, federal regulations specify the kind of headlights required on railroad trains. The plaintiff is struck by a railroad train, the engine of which complies with these regulations. The plaintiff attempts to prove, in his state tort law suit, that better lights were available, that a prudent person would have used them on the engine, and that had they been used, the collision could have been avoided. If state tort law permitted this proof, would that be the same as "regulating" the railroad as to a federally-preempted matter? The court so held in *Marshall v. Burlington Northern, Inc.*, 720 F.2d 1149 (9th Cir. 1983), thus finding preemption.

REFERENCES: DOBBS, HAYDEN & BUBLICK, HORNBOOK ON TORTS § 18.8 (2d ed. 2016); 1 DOBBS, HAYDEN & BUBLICK, THE LAW OF TORTS § 250 (2d ed. 2011).

PART 5

LIMITING OR EXPANDING THE DUTY OF CARE ACCORDING TO CONTEXT OR RELATIONSHIP

■ ■ ■

"Duty" can be a confusing word in tort cases. Courts often use the term to describe a standard or measure of one's obligation. For instance, the normal duty is the duty to use the care of the reasonable, prudent person under the same or similar circumstances, but other standards or duties can be used. For example, in some cases the actor is under a strict duty to protect the plaintiff, meaning that he is liable even if he is not at fault. At the other end of the spectrum, there are cases in which the defendant owes no duty at all. In between there are several possible duties that demand more or less than ordinary care under the reasonable person standard. In many cases landowners owe people on the land only the duty to avoid willful or wanton injury. So the term duty usually refers to a *standard* or general principle that measures the defendant's obligations to the plaintiff. A *standard* can have general application beyond the facts of the particular case.

As already observed, however, courts sometimes use the term duty as a way of talking about what particular acts are required by the exercise of ordinary care. For instance, a court might say that defendant had "a duty to stop, look, and listen before crossing a railroad track." When a court uses the term duty in this way it is not setting a *standard* for cases generally; it is reaching a *conclusion* about the particular case or stating a very specific rule that cannot be generalized beyond the facts. You will see courts using the term duty in both ways. The aim of this Part, however, is to talk about duty in the first sense, as a standard. In this sense, duties (or standards) range from the very demanding to the very lenient.

CHAPTER 12

CARRIERS, HOST-DRIVERS AND LANDOWNERS

∎ ∎ ∎

§ 1. CARRIERS AND HOST-DRIVERS

DOSER V. INTERSTATE POWER CO., 173 N.W.2d 556 (Iowa 1970). Defendant's bus was involved in an automobile accident and a bus passenger was injured. The evidence was that the automobile turned left in front of the bus and the defendant argued that the plaintiff had not shown negligence. " 'carrier of passengers for hire must exercise more than ordinary diligence for their protection. Its duty stops just short of insuring their safety. It is bound to protect its passengers as far as human care and foresight will go and is liable for slight negligence.' . . . [T]he high degree of care must be exercised in *foreseeing*, as well as in *guarding against*, danger. Plaintiff made a prima facie case by showing she was injured while a passenger on the bus by a collision between the bus and the automobile. This cast upon defendants the burden to show their freedom from negligence in causing the collision. . . . Given the high degree of care demanded of common carriers and the factual situation presented, we hold the court was correct in submitting the various specifications of negligence to the jury."

NOTES

1. **The traditional common-carrier rule.** A common carrier is one who undertakes to transport all persons indiscriminately and is in the business of carrying passengers. 2 DOBBS, HAYDEN & BUBLICK, THE LAW OF TORTS § 263 (2d ed. 2011). Often the standard owed to passengers by such defendants is stated as "the highest degree of care," *see, e.g., Davis v. Dionne*, 26 A.3d 801 (Me. 2011); *Todd v. Mass Transit Admin.*, 816 A.2d 930 (Md. 2003), or "the utmost care," *see* CAL. CIV. CODE § 2100.

2. **Analysis of high degree of care.** How does the higher standard of care in *Doser* change the court's analysis? What is plaintiff's usual prima facie case and burden of proof with respect to negligence?

3. **Contemporary rejection of a heightened standard.** Many courts have now rejected the traditional higher standard of care in favor of the general negligence standard of reasonable care under the circumstances. For example, in *Nunez v. Professional Transit Management of Tucson*, 271 P.3d 1104 (Ariz.

2012), the court held that although common carriers have a special relationship with their passengers such that they owe a duty both to avoid creating dangers to passengers and to act affirmatively to aid passengers, this duty requires only the exercise of ordinary reasonable care. The court stressed the flexibility of the reasonable care standard and its ability to accommodate a wide range of situations involving risk. "[P]eople entrust their safety to others in many different contexts, such as undergoing surgery. In the medical context, however, the common law imposed upon the surgeon only the duty to act as a reasonable surgeon would under the circumstance." The court rejected the idea that a heightened degree of care made sense for this area of law alone, and addressed practical problems with applying the doctrine. *See also Bethel v. New York City Transit Auth.,* 703 N.E.2d 1214 (N.Y. 1998).

4. **The rationale for a higher standard.** Still, many states have retained a heightened standard for common carriers. What is the rationale for a higher duty? In *Speed Boat Leasing, Inc. v. Elmer,* 124 S.W.3d 210 (Tex. 2003), the court said, "The rationale for holding common carriers to a higher standard is that passengers should feel safe when traveling." Other courts have stressed that passengers on common carriers are being "passively carried or transported" and "surrender their freedom of movement and actions" to the carrier. *Nalwa v. Cedar Fair, L.P.,* 290 P.3d 1158 (Cal. 2012). Do these rationales really support a standard beyond reasonable care?

5. **Who is covered by a higher standard?** Many states that apply a heightened standard for common carriers see the category as "narrowly tailored" to include only those in the business of carrying "everyone who asks." *Chavez v. Cedar Fair, LP,* 450 S.W.3d 291 (Mo. 2014). This usually includes taxis, buses, railroads, airplanes, ferries, and other modes of commercial transportation. However, some courts have taken a more expansive view. *See, e.g., Gomez v. Superior Court,* 113 P.3d 41 (Cal. 2005) (amusement park ride); *Cash v. Otis Elevator Co.,* 684 P.2d 1041 (Mont. 1984) (elevator). State statutes may specify who fits within the category.

ALA. CODE § 32–1–2

The owner, operator or person responsible for the operation of a motor vehicle shall not be liable for loss or damage arising from injuries to or death of a guest while being transported without payment therefor in or upon said motor vehicle, resulting from the operation thereof, unless such injuries or death are caused by the willful or wanton misconduct of such operator, owner or person responsible for the operation of said motor vehicle.

NOTES

1. **Lower standards.** Some guest statutes state the standard as "gross negligence," others as "willful or wanton misconduct." There are variations of

these two basic forms. The willful, wanton standard may be construed to require not merely extremely negligent conduct, but also a bad state of mind. Litigation under guest statutes often examined whether a jury case had been made on the statutory gross negligence or willful misconduct standard.

2. **Who is a guest?** The guest statutes raised some less obvious issues, notably those associated with the question, "Who is a guest?" Problems arise if the "guest" is injured in entering or leaving the car, for example, and also if the "guest" is paying a part of the cost of travel, or is providing non-monetary assistance to the driver.

3. **Constitutionality of guest statutes.** Guest statutes were the product of a specific time, the late 1920s and the 1930s, and began to decline in the 1970s. In *Brown v. Merlo*, 506 P.2d 212 (Cal. 1973), the court held that the California guest statute was unconstitutional as a denial of equal protection under state law, partly because it treated guests and non-guests differently without any rational reason for doing so. The guest statute does not prevent collusion between host and guest because if they wish to collude they can testify that the passenger paid for the ride. The statute is not explicable as a means of encouraging hospitality because hospitality is extended to others who are not barred, and because in any event it is difficult to see why a "hospitable" host should be free to be negligent toward a guest. After *Brown* a good many other courts adopted similar reasoning under their own state constitutions. Legislatures too, repealed many guest statutes. In 1985, the Texas Supreme Court offered this count: "of the twenty-nine states which originally enacted guest statutes, only Texas and four other states still have such statutes." It then promptly reduced the number by holding the Texas statute unconstitutional. *Whitworth v. Bynum*, 699 S.W.2d 194 (Tex. 1985). Nebraska narrowly upheld its guest statute against constitutional attack by a 4–3 vote in *Le v. Lautrup*, 716 N.W.2d 713 (Neb. 2006).

4. **Limited duties—past and present.** The era of the guest statutes is largely over. Why bother to consider them? One reason is that guest statutes set up a limited legal duty that closely resembles some others we will see in this chapter. Consider as you proceed whether your evaluation of the guest statutes should reflect your evaluation of other limited duty cases. Consider also whether the constitutional considerations would be the same when we come to other cases of limited duties, starting with the landowners' rules.

§ 2. LANDOWNERS' DUTIES TO ENTRANTS

A. TRADITIONAL COMMON-LAW DUTIES

GLADON v. GREATER CLEVELAND REGIONAL TRANSIT AUTHORITY

662 N.E.2d 287 (Ohio 1996)

Greater Cleveland Regional Transit Authority ("RTA") appeals from a jury verdict awarding Robert M. Gladon $2,736,915.35 in damages arising from RTA's operation of a rapid transit train.

Gladon purchased a passenger ticket and boarded an RTA rapid transit train at Terminal Tower after attending a Cleveland Indians' night game with friends. During the baseball game, Gladon consumed about five 16-ounce beers. He left his friends at the stadium in search of a restroom, and ended up traveling alone on the RTA trains. [H]e mistakenly exited the train at the West 65th Street Station and, once on the platform, was chased and attacked by two unknown males. Gladon testified that he remembered being "rolled up in a ball" on the tracks but he could not recall if he had jumped onto the tracks or had been pushed onto the tracks. While there, however, he did recall being kicked in the head.

While Gladon lay on the tracks with his legs draped over the rail, an RTA rapid train approached the West 65th Street Station. Mary Bell, the train's operator, had the train in braking mode when she observed first a tennis shoe and then Gladon's leg on the tracks. The operator pulled the cinestar, or control handle, back and hit the "mushroom," or emergency brake. Unfortunately, the train struck Gladon causing him serious and permanent injuries.

Gladon sued RTA and the operator alleging negligence in the security of RTA's premises and in the operation of the train. Specifically, Gladon alleged that the operator was negligent by failing to bring the train to a stop "after the point she perceived or should have perceived the Plaintiff's peril prior to her striking the Plaintiff." The trial court granted RTA summary judgment as to the negligent security claim and the case proceeded to trial on the negligent operation claim.

The trial court overruled RTA's motion for a directed verdict at the close of Gladon's case-in-chief. The court instructed the jury that "as a matter of law that the only evidence produced by either side indicates that the plaintiff was an invitee." The court further informed the jury that "the driver of a rapid transit car with the right of way must use ordinary care. Therefore, to avoid colliding with a person found on the tracks, the defendant is required to use ordinary care to discover and to avoid danger." . . .

COOK, JUSTICE. . . .

In Ohio, the status of the person who enters upon the land of another (i.e., trespasser, licensee, or invitee) continues to define the scope of the legal duty that the landowner owes the entrant. Invitees are persons who rightfully come upon the premises of another by invitation, express or implied, for some purpose which is beneficial to the owner.

The status of an invitee is not absolute but is limited by the landowner's invitation. "The visitor has the status of an invitee only while he is on part of the land to which his invitation extends—or in other words, the part of the land upon which the possessor gives him reason to believe that his presence is desired for the purpose for which he has come. If the invitee goes outside of the area of his invitation, he becomes a trespasser or a licensee, depending upon whether he goes there without the consent of the possessor, or with such consent."

. . . RTA's invitation to Gladon to use their premises did not extend to the area on or near the tracks. In fact, Gladon acknowledged that RTA did not permit the public in the area on or near the tracks. . . .

Gladon contends that he retained his invitee status because there was no evidence that he "intentionally or purposely entered" upon the track area. According to the Restatement, "so far as the liability of the possessor of the land to the intruder is concerned, however, the possessor's duty, and liability, will be the same regardless of the manner of entry, so long as the entry itself is not privileged."

In determining whether the person is a trespasser within the meaning of this section the question whether his entry has been intentional, negligent or purely accidental is not material, except as it may bear on the existence of a privilege. . . .

The illustration employed by the Restatement to explain the duties owed to a trespasser is remarkably similar to Gladon's situation. "Without any negligence on his part A, standing on the platform of a subway station of the X Company, slips and falls onto the tracks. While there he is run over by the train of X Company, and injured. A is a trespasser, and the liability to him is determined by the rules stated in sections 333 and 336, notwithstanding the accidental character of his intrusion."

Furthermore, whether Gladon was privileged to enter the tracks is immaterial. A person privileged to enter the land is owed the same duties as a licensee. Because the duties owed to a licensee and trespasser are the same, whether Gladon was privileged to enter the land does not change the standard of care RTA owed to him.

. . . Because Gladon then became either a licensee or a trespasser for purposes of determining the duty RTA owed to him, the trial court erred in instructing the jury that he was an invitee as a matter of law.

[A] landowner owes no duty to a licensee or trespasser except to refrain from willful, wanton or reckless conduct which is likely to injure him. Furthermore, a railroad owes no duty to anticipate or prevent the presence of licensees or trespassers.

When a trespasser or licensee is discovered in a position of peril, a landowner is required to use ordinary care to avoid injuring him. The duty to exercise ordinary care arises after the landowner "knows, or from facts within his knowledge should know or believe," that a trespasser or licensee is on the land.

Having instructed the jury as a matter of law that Gladon was an invitee, the trial court assigned RTA a duty of ordinary care "to discover and to avoid danger." These instructions erred in two respects. First, the instructions imposed upon RTA a duty to use ordinary care to discover Gladon's presence. To the contrary, RTA was under no duty to anticipate trespassers and could only be liable for injuries resulting from willful or wanton conduct. Second, the instructions imposed upon RTA a duty to use ordinary care to avoid injuring Gladon prior to the operator's discovery of him. Rather, RTA's duty to use ordinary care to avoid injuring Gladon did not arise until RTA knew or should have known that Gladon was on the tracks. Whether the operator knew or should have known a person was on the tracks upon observing the tennis shoe remains a question for the jury.

Given that the instructions were erroneous and prejudicial, we reverse the judgment of the court of appeals and remand this cause for a new trial.

RTA owed Gladon no duty except to avoid injuring him by willful or wanton conduct prior to discovering Gladon on the tracks. Willful conduct "'involves an intent, purpose or design to injure.'" Wanton conduct involves the failure to exercise "'any care whatsoever toward those to whom he owes a duty of care, and his failure occurs under the circumstances in which there is great probability that harm will result.'"

At trial, Gladon produced evidence that the tracks were wet when the operator traveled eastbound toward the West 65th Street platform. The testimony of the operator indicates that she had the train in braking mode as she traveled through a dark area near the platform with her high beams on at an estimated 20 m.p.h. Generally, the speed limit in that area is 25 m.p.h., but when a train is going to pass rather than stop at a platform, the permitted speed is 5 m.p.h.

Gladon also presented RTA regulations which require operators to operate the trains on sight, within the range of vision, at all times, and to anticipate changes in the range of vision. . . .

Viewing these facts in the light most favorable to Gladon, we find that in this trial reasonable minds could have reached different conclusions regarding whether the speed of the train at the time the operator

CARRIERS, HOST-DRIVERS
CH. 12   AND LANDOWNERS   317

approached the West 65th platform meets the wanton standard in light of the operator's duty to adjust the train's speed to her range of vision and to the known track conditions. Therefore, the trial court did not err in overruling RTA's motions for a directed verdict or judgment notwithstanding the verdict.

RTA owed Gladon a duty to use reasonable care to avoid injuring Gladon after the operator discovered Gladon on the tracks. Here, again, the RTA contends that Gladon failed to produce evidence of a breach of that duty.

Viewing these facts presented in this trial in the light most favorable to Gladon, reasonable minds could have reached different conclusions as to whether the operator exercised ordinary care. First, the point at which this duty arose remains a question for the jury. Reasonable minds could have reached different conclusions regarding whether the operator should have known a person was on the tracks when she saw the tennis shoes. Second, when the operator did realize a person was on the tracks, she was not sure whether she pulled the cinestar all the way back to the maximum braking mode before she hit the "mushroom" when she observed Gladon's legs on the tracks. Furthermore, the operator testified that she was not sure whether she hit the "mushroom" before or after the train struck Gladon. . . .

Judgment reversed and cause remanded. [Dissenting and concurring opinions are omitted.]

NOTES

1. **The traditional classifications.** About half of the states continue to follow the traditional common-law rules when an entrant sues the landowner or occupier (which includes a renter or anyone who is on the land acting on the possessor's behalf) for injuries suffered on the land. This traditional scheme classifies entrants as trespassers, licensees, or invitees. A *trespasser* is any person who has no legal right to be on another's land and enters the land without the landowner's consent. An *invitee* is any person on the premises (1) at least in part for the pecuniary benefit of the landowner (a "business invitee") or (2) who is on premises held open to the general public (a "public invitee"). A *licensee* is someone who is on the land with permission, but with a limited license to be there; it is not inaccurate to say that a licensee is someone who is neither a trespasser nor an invitee.

2. **Social guests.** Notice that the traditional definition of invitee would exclude social guests in a home. Indeed, social guests are considered licensees in the traditional view, because they are not present for the pecuniary benefit of the landowner. Some states have now broadened the definition of invitee to include social guests. *See Burrell v. Meads,* 569 N.E.2d 637 (Ind. 1991). Is that a good idea?

3. **Classifying entrants.** Often the classification of the plaintiff can raise a fact question for the jury. And often the answer to that question is outcome-determinative; where a lesser duty is owed, a mere negligence claim will fail. Perhaps the hardest cases are those where the plaintiff is either an invitee or a licensee. What's the status category of a person visiting a patient in his hospital room? *Shelton v. Kentucky Easter Seals Soc., Inc.*, 413 S.W.3d 901 (Ky. 2013). How about a plaintiff who tripped on steps as she was going to a free religious course at a church of which she was not a member? Would it matter that the stated reason the church was offering classes was "to increase participation and expand its congregation?" *Turner v. Cathedral Ministries*, 27 N.E.3d 586 (Ohio App. 2015). How about a grandmother who babysits for her grandchild without pay at her child's home? *Reicheneker v. Reicheneker*, 651 N.W.2d 224 (Neb. 2002).

4. **Changing categories.** Can a person who enters the land with clear invitee status become a trespasser on the same property? What if a shopper in a department store goes into a closed door marked "Employees Only" and is injured when he trips over a box. Does *Gladon* provide guidance?

In a recent case, plaintiff was a guest in the defendant's hotel/casino complex. Instead of taking the "skyway bridge" between the two buildings, he took a "shortcut" down a steep hill between the hotel building and the casino building, and tripped and broke his leg on a retaining wall. To get to the grassy area in which he was injured, the plaintiff had to step through a line of shrubbery, but the area "was not clearly demarcated as private and off limits." Was he a business invitee at the time of injury, or a trespasser? *Ragonese v. Racing Corp. of West Virginia*, 769 S.E.2d 495 (W.Va. 2015).

5. **Duty owed to invitees.** Landowners and occupiers owe a duty of reasonable care to invitees. There are many specific common-law rules about what this entails. All such rules are merely specific applications of the general duty of care that we explored earlier in the course.

6. **Duty owed to trespassers and licensees.** (a) As *Gladon* indicates, under the traditional view, landowners do not owe a duty of reasonable care to either trespassers or licensees. Instead, the landowner owes only the duty to avoid intentional, wanton, or willful injury. *See* DOBBS, HAYDEN & BUBLICK, HORNBOOK ON TORTS §§ 20.2 & 20.5 (2d ed. 2016). That statement, however, is usually applied only when the landowner has not discovered or received notice of imminent danger to the entrant. (The Restatement Second uses the term "has reason to know," meaning that the defendant is aware of some specific fact, like the shoe on the track in *Gladon*, which directly shows the danger. The "should have known" language of reasonable care would not suffice.)

(b) If the landowner discovers both the presence of the entrant *and* the fact that he is about to encounter a danger, the situation is different. In that case, some courts might say that the landowner who fails to act reasonably in the face of this known danger to an entrant (by trying to warn him, for example), is then guilty of willful or wanton misconduct. Others might say with the *Gladon* court that in such a situation the landowner owes a duty of reasonable care (which may be expressed more specifically as a duty to warn him of the danger). The two ways of addressing this situation thus appear to come down to the same bottom-line, with liability in either case for failing to act with reasonable care in light of the known situation.

(c) Some courts impose a duty of care upon landowners who have not discovered the actual presence of a trespasser, provided the landowner knows trespassers frequently use a limited area. *See, e.g., Humphrey v. Glenn*, 167 S.W.3d 680 (Mo. 2005).

(d) The Restatement (Third) of Torts § 52 provides that a land possessor owes a "flagrant trespasser" only the duty not to act in an "intentional, willful or wanton manner." But to flagrant trespassers "who reasonably appear to be imperiled and helpless or unable to protect themselves," the duty is one of reasonable care. Besides the protection of the limited duty, a landowner may enjoy a privilege—a privilege to use reasonable force to expel the trespasser, for example, or to defend his property.

(e) Perhaps not surprisingly, courts can at times be unsympathetic to flagrant trespassers. One court found that even ignoring known imminent danger to the imperiled trespasser did not rise to the level of wanton, willful or reckless behavior. *See Estate of Cilley v. Lane*, 985 A.2d 481 (Me. 2009) (homeowner who asked former boyfriend to leave did not breach any duty to him when she failed to contact emergency assistance after he shot himself on her property and lay dying from his wounds).

7. **Conditions vs. activities.** Even in a state that follows the traditional classification scheme, a landowner will often be held to a duty of reasonable care in carrying out affirmative acts such as driving on his private roads, once he knows a trespasser is present. In the case of licensees, the landowner is said to owe a duty of reasonable care to all licensees in carrying out activities on the land. *Janis v. Nash Finch Co.*, 780 N.W.2d 497 (S.D. 2010) (duty to warn of concealed, dangerous conditions known to the landowner and to use ordinary care in active operations on the property). Thus the willful-wanton rule protecting landowners is mainly addressed to *conditions* on the land, such as a dangerous non-obvious excavation, a dangerous electrical connection, a hidden step, or a rotten railing that may give way. Not all courts draw the distinction between conditions and activities with any meaningful degree of precision, however. Does the *Gladon* court do so?

NOTE: CHILD TRESPASSERS

1. *General rule.* Courts have developed something of a special rule for young children who are injured while trespassing: a landowner owes a duty of reasonable care to a trespassing child if a reasonable landowner would know or foresee that (1) there is a dangerous condition on his land, (2) children are likely to trespass on his land, and (3) because of their youth

and inexperience, such children will face an unreasonable risk of serious injury] *See* DOBBS, HAYDEN & BUBLICK, HORNBOOK ON TORTS § 20.8 (2d ed. 2016).

2. *History.* The earliest cases were ones in which young children were lured to the land by some condition that was quite dangerous but particularly attractive to children, given their natural curiosity. In a leading case, a seven-year-old played on a revolving railroad turntable, a heavy piece of machinery used to rotate railroad engines. His leg was severed when he was caught in the turntable. The railroad argued that it owed no duty to the child because he was a trespasser. The court treated him as an invitee, based on the idea that he was "induced" onto the land to play on the turntable because of the "natural instincts" of children and the inherent attractiveness of the machinery. *Keffe v. Milwaukee & St. Paul Railway*, 21 Minn. 297 (1875). Courts began to call this child trespasser rule the "turntable doctrine," or the "attractive nuisance doctrine."

3. *Scope.* The child trespasser rule may be largely an application of ordinary negligence law. The idea is that young children "are entitled to a degree of care proportioned to their inability to foresee and avoid the perils that they may encounter." *Bennett v. Stanley*, 748 N.E.2d 41 (Ohio 2001) (adopting the rule from Restatement (Second) of Torts § 339 (1965)). But the duty is only one of reasonable care, and the landowner "does not automatically become liable for any injury a child trespasser may suffer on that land." *Id.* Further, modern cases say that the child need not be injured by the very temptation that caused the injury. *See, e.g., Henson ex rel. Hunt v. Intern. Paper Co.*, 650 S.E.2d 74 (Ind. 2007).

4. *Tender years.* The child trespasser rule applies only to children who, because of their "tender years," are foreseeably unlikely to appreciate dangers and to avoid them. *See, e.g., Burton v. State*, 80 A.3d 856 (R.I. 2013) ("It strains credulity to think that plaintiff, a seventeen-year-old who was about to complete his G.E.D., did not realize the risk involved in climbing a pipe to an upper-story window and entering a dark, abandoned building."). Thus the "attractive nuisance" doctrine applies mainly to children of grade school age or younger, and only rarely to teenagers.

5. *Identifying "attractive nuisances."* Some courts have said that "common hazards," such as fire and pools of water, cannot be considered attractive nuisances and the trespassing child who drowns in a stock pond is entitled to no protection from the landowner. The better explanation for many of these cases may be that there is a duty of care owed, but that given the importance of stock ponds and the difficulty of fencing them, the duty is not breached, which is to say the defendant is not negligent. This explanation is supported by the fact that even in states that announce a "common hazard" rule, recovery is sometimes allowed for swimming pool deaths and for injuries by hidden burning embers. Can a defendant's dog

be an attractive nuisance? *Clea v. Odom*, 714 S.E.2d 542 (S.C. 2011) (no, not a condition on land).

B. MODIFYING THE TRADITIONAL COMMON-LAW DUTIES OWED TO ENTRANTS

ROWLAND V. CHRISTIAN
443 P.2d 561 (Cal. 1968)

PETERS, JUSTICE.

[Plaintiff was a social guest in Miss Christian's apartment. The porcelain handle of a bathroom faucet broke in his hand and severed tendons and nerves. Miss Christian had known the handle was cracked and had in fact reported it to her lessors, but, though she knew plaintiff was going to the bathroom, she gave him no warning. These facts were established by affidavit and the trial judge gave summary judgment for the defendant.]

Section 1714 of the Civil Code provides: "Everyone is responsible, not only for the result of his willful acts, but also for an injury occasioned to another by his want of ordinary care or skill in the management of his property or person, except so far as the latter has, willfully or by want of ordinary care, brought the injury upon himself." . .." This code section, which has been unchanged in our law since 1872, states a civil law and not a common law principle. . . .

One of the areas where this court and other courts have departed from the fundamental concept that a man is liable for injuries caused by his carelessness is with regard to the liability of a possessor of land for injuries to persons who have entered upon that land. It has been suggested that the special rules regarding liability of the possessor of land are due to historical considerations stemming from the high place which land has traditionally held in English and American thought, the dominance and prestige of the landowning class in England during the formative period of the rules governing the possessor's liability, and the heritage of feudalism.

The departure from the fundamental rule of liability for negligence has been accomplished by classifying the plaintiff either as a trespasser, licensee, or invitee and then adopting special rules as to the duty owed by the possessor to each of the classifications. . . .

[The trespasser-licensee-invitee rules have created complexity and confusion.] Complexity can be borne and confusion remedied where the underlying principles governing liability are based upon proper considerations. Whatever may have been the historical justifications for the common law distinctions, it is clear that those distinctions are not justified in the light of our modern society and the complexity and confusion which has arisen is not due to difficulty in applying the original common law rules—they are all too easy to apply in their original formulation—but is due to the attempts to apply just rules in our modern society within the ancient terminology.

Without attempting to labor all of the rules relating to the possessor's liability, it is apparent that the classifications of trespasser, licensee, and invitee, the immunities from liability predicated upon those circumstances, and the exceptions to those immunities, often do not reflect the major factors which should determine whether immunity should be conferred upon the possessor of land. Some of those factors, including the closeness of the connection between the injury and the defendant's conduct, the moral blame attached to the defendant's conduct, the policy of preventing future harm, and the prevalence and availability of insurance bear little, if any relationship to the classification of trespasser, licensee and invitee and the existing rules conferring immunity.

Although in general there may be a relationship between the remaining factors and the classifications of trespasser, licensee, and invitee, there are many cases in which no such relationship may exist. Thus, although the foreseeability of harm to an invitee would ordinarily seem greater than the foreseeability of harm to a trespasser, in a particular case the opposite may be true. The same may be said of the issue of certainty of injury. The burden to the defendant and consequences to the community of imposing a duty to exercise care with resulting liability for breach may often be greater with respect to trespassers than with respect to invitees, but it by no means follows that this is true in every case. In many situations, the burden will be the same, i.e., the conduct necessary upon the defendant's part to meet the burden of exercising due care as to the invitees will also meet his burden with respect to licensees and trespassers. The last of the major factors, the cost of insurance, will, of course, vary depending upon the rules of liability adopted, but there is no persuasive evidence that applying ordinary principles of negligence law to the land occupier's liability will materially reduce the prevalence of insurance due to increased cost or even substantially increase the cost. . . .

[A man's life or limb does not become less worthy of protection by the law nor a loss less worthy of compensation under the law because he has come upon the land of another without permission or with permission but without a business purpose.]Reasonable people do not ordinarily vary their conduct depending upon such matters, and to focus upon the status of the injured party as a trespasser, licensee or invitee in order to determine the question whether the landowner has a duty of care, is contrary to our modern social mores and humanitarian values. The common law rules obscure rather than illuminate the proper consideration which should govern determination of the question of duty. . . .

It may be noted that by carving further exceptions out of the traditional rules relating to the liability to licensees or social guests, other jurisdictions reach the same result. . . .

The Judgment is Reversed.

TRAYNOR, C. J., and TOBRINER, MOSK and SULLIVAN, J. J., concur.

BURKE, Justice (dissenting).

I dissent. In determining the liability of the occupier or owner of land for injuries, the distinctions between trespassers, licensees and invitees have been developed and applied by the courts over a period of many years. They supply a reasonable and workable approach to the problems involved, and one which provides the degree of stability and predictability so highly prized in law. The unfortunate alternative, it appears to me, is the route taken by the majority in their opinion in this case; that such issues are to be decided on a case by case basis under the application of the basic law of negligence, bereft of the guiding principles and precedent which the law has heretofore attached by virtue of the relationship of the parties to one another.

Liability for negligence turns upon whether a duty of care is owed, and if so, the extent thereof. Who can doubt that the corner grocery, the large department store, or the financial institution owes a greater duty of care to one whom it has invited to enter its premises as a prospective customer of its wares or services than it owes to a trespasser seeking to enter after the close of business hours and for a nonbusiness or even an antagonistic purpose? I do not think it unreasonable or unfair that a social guest (classified by the law as a licensee, as was plaintiff here) should be obliged to take the premises in the same condition as his host finds them or permits them to be. Surely a homeowner should not be obliged to hover over his guests with warnings of possible dangers to be found in the condition of the home (e.g., waxed floors, slipping rugs, toys in unexpected places, etc., etc.). . . .

McCOMB, J., concurs.

NOTES

1. **Guest statutes connection?** *Rowland* was the first decision to abolish the categories and substitute the general duty of reasonable care. California was also the first state to hold guest statutes unconstitutional. *Brown v. Merlo*, 506 P.2d 212 (Cal. 1973). Is there any logical relation between the two decisions?

2. **Abolition of entrant-status categories.** After *Rowland*, some expected a tidal wave of decisions abolishing the traditional common-law entrant categories, but the complete-abolition trend rather quickly "lost its steam." *Baldwin v. Mosley*, 748 146 (Ark. 1988). Fewer than ten states now say

a duty of reasonable care is owed to every entrant on land. In many of those states, the duty of general care has been applied to child trespassers as well, thus eliminating those special rules. *See, e.g., Morse v. Goduti,* 777 A.2d 292 (N.H. 2001).

3. **Retaining categories, but extending reasonable-care duty to licensees.** A larger number of states (approaching 20) have retained the invitee-licensee-trespasser categories, but extend a duty of reasonable care to both invitees and licensees. This, rather than the move towards complete abolition of categories, appears to be the most current trend. *See, e.g., Koenig v. Koenig,* 766 N.W.2d 635 (Iowa 2009); *Saltsman v. Sharp,* 803 N.W.2d 553 (N.D. 2011); *Demag v. Better Power Equipment,* 102 A.3d 1101 (Vt. 2014). These states retain the limited-duty-to-trespassers rules even though they have dropped the licensee-invitee distinction. *See Bennett v. Napolitano,* 746 A.2d 138 (R.I. 2000) (citizen in park after it was closed for the night was a trespasser to whom reasonable care was not owed).

4. **Further nuances.** The Restatement Third takes the position that all entrants, whether invitees, licensees or trespassers, are owed a duty of reasonable care. However, landowners owe "flagrant trespassers" only a duty not to intentionally, willfully or wantonly injure them. RESTATEMENT (THIRD) OF TORTS: LIABILITY FOR PHYSICAL AND EMOTIONAL HARM § 52 (2010). Similarly, the California legislature enacted a statute which excludes from the ordinary duty of reasonable care those trespassers who are injured "during the course of, or after the commission of, any felonies [specified in the statute]." CAL. CIV. CODE § 847 (2012).

SCURTI V. CITY OF NEW YORK, 354 N.E.2d 794 (N.Y. 1976). A 14-year-old boy was electrocuted in a railroad yard after crawling through a hole in the fence. There was evidence that the fence was part of a city park and the city and others were joined as defendants. New York had previously abolished the trespasser-licensee-invitee distinctions and had adopted the standard of reasonable care for all entrants.

"Under the standard of reasonable care . . . the factors which sustained the landowner's immunity and inspired the exceptions under prior law will no longer be considered decisive. But, as indicated, most of them have some probative value. . . . The fact that the injury occurred on the defendant's property is certainly a relevant circumstance in assessing the reasonableness of defendant's conduct. The defendant has a right to use his property and to develop it for his profit and enjoyment. That often means that he must conduct dangerous activities or permit dangerous instruments and conditions to exist on the premises. However under those circumstances he must take reasonable measures to prevent injury to those whose presence on the property can reasonably be foreseen. Whether the threat is posed by a dangerous condition or a dangerous activity is of little significance in itself. It may have some bearing on the effort required to prevent the injury, but that depends on the facts of the particular case. In this connection it is important to note that the elimination of the immunity conferred by prior law should not pose an unreasonable burden on the use of the property since all that is now required is the exercise of reasonable care under the circumstances. The defendant can always show that it would have been unduly burdensome to have done more. . . . The fact that the plaintiff entered without permission is also a relevant circumstance. It may well demonstrate that the plaintiff's presence was not foreseeable at the time and place of the injury. . . . This does not mean that every case involving injury on private property raises a factual question for the jury's consideration. In any negligence case the court must always determine as a threshold matter whether the facts will support an inference of negligence. . . . However, in this particular case the question of reasonableness of the parties' conduct cannot be resolved as a matter of law."

NOTES

1. **The negligence standard.** When the categories have been abolished, the landowner is still not liable unless he is negligent. *E.g., Senkus v. Moore,* 535 S.E.2d 724 (W.Va. 2000). Do you believe there are any situations that cannot be justly resolved by applying the prudent person standard? Can you give an example?

2. **Status category as one factor.** How would you characterize what the *Scurti* court is doing with the plaintiff's trespasser status? What do you think of its reasoning? In *Louis v. Louis,* 636 N.W.2d 314 (Minn. 2001), the court said that after the abolition of the common-law distinctions, an entrant's status as an invitee or a licensee was no longer controlling, but that it remained "one element among many to be considered in assessing the landowner's duty to use reasonable care for the safety of persons invited on the premises." Do you agree with that approach?

C. OPEN AND OBVIOUS HAZARDS

KENTUCKY RIVER MEDICAL CENTER V. MCINTOSH
319 S.W.3d 385 (Ky. 2010)

NOBLE, J. . . .

On May 27, 2004, McIntosh, a trained and licensed paramedic, was transporting a critically ill patient to the Hospital. She and two Emergency Medical Technicians (EMTs) arrived at the ambulance dock, and began guiding the patient to the emergency room entrance.

Immediately outside the emergency room entrance there is a flat surface which is eleven feet wide to allow stretchers to be wheeled directly from the ambulance dock into the emergency room. This flat area rises on both sides to form a curb. This curb is unmarked and unprotected. Essentially, the area looks like a wide curb ramp used for wheelchair access, except that the "ramp" part is flat rather than at an incline.

McIntosh had helped transport about 400 patients to this emergency room entrance before, and she had always navigated past the protruding curb without incident. However, this time she tripped and fell over it, suffering a fractured hip and sprained wrist. McIntosh sued the Hospital, arguing that the curb was an unreasonably dangerous condition which caused her injuries.

McIntosh's Duty

While moving towards the entrance, McIntosh's attention was not focused on the curb; rather, she remained focused on attending to the critically ill patient. She testified that when transporting patients from the ambulance dock to the emergency room doors, it is the duty of a paramedic to remain focused on the patient's health and to make sure his intravenous lines do not get caught in the wheels of the stretcher, among other things. (In contrast, EMTs have the duty to physically push the patient from the ambulance to the doors.) One of the patient's family members testified that McIntosh was completely focused on the patient as he was pushed to the entrance.

Tripping hazard near ER is rare

In addition, evidence was introduced showing that having such a tripping hazard at an emergency room entrance is very rare, if not unique in Breathitt County and the counties adjoining it. In particular, McIntosh testified that she transports patients to several nearby hospitals and that none of them have any uneven surface between the ambulance dock and the doors. An EMT working for McIntosh also testified that among the eight to ten other entrances he had used, the Hospital was the only one that had a ledge or curb near the emergency room entrance. . . .

Hospital's MSJ denied

The Hospital moved the trial court for summary judgment, claiming that the open and obvious doctrine barred McIntosh's recovery as a matter of law. After considering the parties' briefs, the trial court summarily denied this motion.

Ultimately, the jury found the Hospital liable. It awarded McIntosh $40,409.70 for medical expenses, $65,000 for impairment of her earning capacity, and $50,000 for pain and suffering, for a total of $155,409.70. . . . The Hospital appealed to the Court of Appeals, which affirmed because "the Hospital could reasonably expect that a paramedic treating a critically-ill patient could be distracted, could forget (if she had ever observed it) that the curb was uneven, and could fail to protect herself against it." This Court granted discretionary review to determine whether the open and obvious doctrine should have completely barred McIntosh's cause of action. . . .

As a general rule, land possessors owe a duty to invitees to discover unreasonably dangerous conditions on the land and to either correct them or warn of them. However, the open and obvious doctrine states that land possessors cannot be held liable to invitees who are injured by open and obvious dangers. . . . [Defendant contends that open and obvious danger is a matter of duty; plaintiff responds that the existence of an open and obvious danger goes to the factual issue of fault].

Which of these two views is correct is not clear from the history of the doctrine because it arose in the era of contributory negligence. Under contributory negligence, any negligence on the part of the plaintiff completely barred recovery. Thus, it was irrelevant whether an open and obvious danger "excused a land possessor's duty to an invitee, or simply insulated the possessor from liability" by virtue of the plaintiff's contributory negligence in avoiding his own injury. "In either event, the injured invitee could not recover. . . ."

Dangerous Conditions vs. Open + Obvious

However, almost all states now have comparative fault—including Kentucky. Under comparative fault, whether the doctrine concerns duty or fault becomes very important. If duty is not excused by a known or obvious danger, the injured invitee might recover, albeit in a diminished amount, [by virtue of his own comparative fault]. In contrast, if the invitee's voluntary encounter with a known or obvious danger were deemed to excuse the land owner's duty, then there would be no negligence to compare—and, therefore, no recovery. This <u>distinction is the principal issue of this case</u>.

Landowner's duty to open + obvious dangers under comparative fault

Our sister states do not unanimously agree about the correct answer. However, "[t]he manifest trend of the courts in this country is away from the traditional rule absolving, ipso facto, owners and occupiers of land from liability for injuries resulting from known or obvious conditions." Instead, these courts allow the jury to evaluate the comparative fault of the parties, typical in modern negligence cases.

[The courts following this trend typically adopt the position of the Restatement (Second) of Torts with respect to open and obvious conditions, which states:

> A possessor of land is <u>not liable</u> to his invitees for physical harm caused to them by any activity or condition on the land whose danger is known or obvious to them, <u>unless the possessor should anticipate the harm</u> despite such knowledge or obviousness. Restatement (Second) of Torts § 343A(1) (1965). . . .]

The current, tentative draft of the Restatement (Third) takes a position consistent with the Restatement (Second), except that it "amplifie[s]" duties on land possessors in certain situations. See Restatement (Third) of Torts: Liab. Physical Harm § 51 cmt. k (T.D. No. 6, 2009). . . .

[T]his Court concludes that the modern trend, as embodied in the Restatement (Second) of Torts, is the better position. . . .

Rule

[handwritten: Relevant factors in considering whether open obvious]

Whether the danger was known and appreciated by the plaintiff, whether the risk was obvious to a person exercising reasonable perception, intelligence, and judgment, and whether there was some other reason for the defendant to foresee the harm, are all relevant considerations that provide more balance and insight to the analysis than merely labeling a particular risk "open and obvious." In sum, the[analysis recognizes that a risk of harm may be foreseeable and unreasonable, thereby imposing a duty on the defendant, despite its potentially open and obvious nature]. . . .

[handwritten: Landowner still liable if he has reasonable to anticipate distraction]

For many open and obvious dangers, the land possessor would have no reason to anticipate the harm, and so he would not be liable. However, sometimes "the possessor has reason to expect that the invitee's attention may be distracted, so that he will not discover what is obvious, or will forget what he has discovered, or fail to protect himself against it."[In these situations, the injury is still foreseeable, and so liability should still be imposed]. . .

Further, the modern approach is more consistent with Kentucky's rule of comparative fault.[By concluding that a danger was open and obvious, we can conclude that the invitee was negligent for falling victim to it, unless for some reason "to a reasonable man in his position the advantages of [encountering the danger] would outweigh the apparent risk] But this does not necessarily mean that the land possessor was not also negligent for failing to fix an unreasonable danger in the first place. Under our rule of comparative fault, the defendant should be held responsible for his own negligence, if any. . . .

The incompatibility between the open and obvious doctrine as an absolute, automatic bar to recovery and comparative fault is great. So great, in fact, that a few states have held that their comparative negligence statutes abolished the open and obvious doctrine outright. The incompatibility between the traditional open and obvious rule and comparative fault . . . should be resolved in favor of comparative fault.

This makes good policy sense. As the Supreme Court of Mississippi aptly stated:

> This Court should discourage unreasonably dangerous conditions rather than fostering them in their obvious forms. It is anomalous to find that a defendant has a duty to provide reasonably safe premises and at the same time deny a plaintiff recovery from a breach of that same duty. The party in the best position to eliminate a dangerous condition should be burdened with that responsibility. If a dangerous condition is obvious to the plaintiff, then surely it is obvious to the defendant as well. The defendant, accordingly, should alleviate the danger. . . .

[If the land possessor can foresee the injury, but nevertheless fails to take reasonable precautions to prevent the injury, he can be held liable.]. .

A land possessor's duties are not based only on his superior knowledge. These duties are also based on the land possessor's unique position as the only person who can fix the dangers. . . .

Turning to this case, this Court concludes that the Hospital owed a duty to McIntosh. . . . The Hospital had good reason to expect that a paramedic, such as McIntosh, would be distracted as she approached the emergency room entrance. . . . Thus, even though the curb may have been open and noticeable to some extent, in this case "the possessor has reason to expect that the invitee's attention may be distracted" from it. . . .

Conclusion
✱ Hospital liable

[Paramedics] are required to think and act quickly in the most time-sensitive and stressful of circumstances. It is likely that in such a situation, a paramedic such as McIntosh may forget that this particular entrance has a unique danger that she must avoid. . . . [T]he extent to which her absentmindedness comes into play should bear only on her comparative fault rather than as an absolute bar to her recovery.

It is important to stress the context in which McIntosh sustained her injury: she was rushing a critically ill patient into a hospital, in an effort to save his life. Even if we assume that she was neither distracted nor forgetful about the curb, we would still have to conclude that the benefits of her rushing to the door (at the risk of tripping over the curb) outweighed the costs of her failing to do so (at the risk of the patient's condition worsening, perhaps to the point of death, on the Hospital doorstep). . . .

In the present case, the Hospital owed a duty to McIntosh, given that her injury was foreseeable. McIntosh, in turn, had a duty to act reasonably to ensure her own safety, heightened by her familiarity with the location and the arguably open and obvious nature of the danger. Thus, there were genuine issues of material fact that were properly submitted to the jury. . . .

SCHRODER, J., dissenting:

Because I believe the open and obvious doctrine concerns a question of duty, I respectfully dissent. The other hospitals McIntosh served had no curbs to trip over. Appellants had a curb, which contained no building code or OSHA violations, and was open and obvious. It appears the Appellants are being held liable for a breach of a duty: a duty to build its emergency entrance like other hospitals in an undefined area. Until this decision, there was no such duty. Until today, a landowner or possessor of land could not be held liable to invitees who were injured by open and obvious dangers. Now, even though the alleged danger is open and obvious (like snow or ice on a sidewalk), if the possessor can anticipate the harm to an invitee, the possessor has a duty to fix the condition, or to somehow give additional warnings. In this case, to avoid future liability, the hospital will need to build the same type of entrance ramp as some unknown group of hospitals. This is an unwise and unnecessary change in the law in the Commonwealth.

NOTES

1. **"Open and obvious" defined.** A "condition is *obvious* when, objectively, 'both the condition and the risk are apparent to and would be recognized by a reasonable man, in the position of the visitor, exercising ordinary perception, intelligence and judgment.'" *Dick's Sporting Goods, Inc. v. Webb*, 413 S.W.3d 891 (Ky. 2013) (quoting Restatement (Second) of Torts § 343A(1) cmt. b (1965), holding that a wet tile that appeared dry was not an open and obvious hazard; a reasonable person may not have noticed the moisture "because of the inherent difficulty of detecting moisture on a tile floor"). Should swimmers in an apparently placid city park pond recognize the hazard presented by an unseen, dangerous hydroelectric current? *Volpe v. City of Lexington*, 708 S.E.2d 824 (Va. 2011).

2. **The no-duty rule.** At one time, courts routinely held that the landowner was not liable even to an invitee for injuries which were caused by an open and obvious danger. Some courts still say this. *See, e.g., General Motors Corp. v. Hill,* 752 So.2d 1186 (Ala. 1999) (parked 25-foot flatbed trailer, even if obscured by darkness, was an open and obvious danger to independent contractor driving a buggy around facility at night to fill vending machines). The idea is frequently expressed by saying the landowner simply owes no duty to protect an entrant from obvious dangers, *see Roy v. State*, 139 A.3d 480 (R.I. 2016) (diving into man-made pond), often because an obvious danger does not create an unreasonable danger in the first place, *see Bufkin v. Felipe's Louisiana, LLC*, 171 So.3d 851 (La. 2014) (pedestrian crossing street next to defendant contractor's dumpster, which obscured his vision, was struck by oncoming bicyclist; no duty to warn of a clearly visible obstruction).

3. **Obvious dangers and foreseeable risk.** Under the Restatement Second approach adopted by the *Kentucky River* court, when can we conclude that the defendant should have foreseen a plaintiff's encounter with an admittedly open and obvious hazard? Remember that most states adopting this view leave the issue to the jury, if reasonable people could differ. *See, e.g., Wotzka v. Minndakota Ltd. Parnership*, 831 N.W.2d 722 (N.D. 2013) (plaintiff slipped and fell when getting out of shower in defendant's hotel, where shower was not equipped with a non-skid strip, a bathmat, or a handrail). The cases addressing this issue tend to fall into two general groups. Can you see common themes in each of these categories?

Group 1: A landowner is constructing his own house and has not yet put a railing on a second-floor balcony. A painter (an invitee) accidentally steps off the balcony while stepping back to better see the area he has just painted. *Hale v. Beckstead*, 116 P.3d 263 (Utah 2005). Or suppose a customer trips over a pallet in the aisle of a drug store. *Gilmore v. Walgreen Co.*, 759 N.W.2d 433 (Minn. Ct. App. 2009).

Group 2: An employee of a catering company reported for a catering job at a Mercedes dealership. She could see that ice covered the entire area, and made it inside without slipping. But she slipped and fell soon thereafter, as she was walking from the building to her car to get her cell phone so she could contact her absent supervisor. Is her encounter with the ice foreseeable? *Wood v. Mercedes-Benz of Oklahoma City*, 336 P.3d 457 (Okla. 2014). Or suppose a utility customer must cross an obvious patch of ice to pay her utility bill. Unless she does so immediately, power will be cut off in her home in the dead of winter. If the utility is negligent in failing to sand the ice, is it foreseeable that someone exercising her right to enter will be injured?

4. **Open and obvious danger and comparative negligence.** A number of courts, as in *Kentucky River*, see the blanket rule against liability for open and obvious dangers as one that resurrects the all-or-nothing character of contributory negligence or implied assumption of the risk. *See, e.g., Hersh v. E-T Enterprises, Ltd. Parnership*, 752 S.E.2d 336 (W.Va. 2013) (abolishing "open and obvious doctrine" on that basis), *superseded by statute*, W. VA. ANN. CODE § 55–7–28 (2015) (expressly reversing *Hersh* and reinstating no-duty rule for open and obvious hazards).

5. **Duty to warn vs. duty to remedy the hazard.** In those states that look to whether the foreseeability of the plaintiff's encounter with an obvious hazard creates a duty of care, it may well matter whether the plaintiff argues that the defendant was under a duty to *warn* or a duty to *remedy. See, e.g., Dos Santos v. Coleta,* 987 N.E.2d 1187 (Mass. 2013) (no duty to warn of an obvious hazard, but duty to remedy the danger presented by a trampoline set up next to a shallow wading pool on defendant's property); *Roy v. State*, 139 A.3d 480 (R.I. 2016) (no duty to warn of the danger of diving into a shallow pond).

6. **Abandoning open and obvious danger.** In light of the tension between comparative fault and open and obvious danger, some courts have not only limited the open and obvious danger doctrine, but have abolished it altogether. *Shelton v. Kentucky Easter Seals Soc., Inc.*, 413 S.W.3d 901 (Ky. 2013); *Steigman v. Outrigger Enterprises, Inc.*, 267 P.3d 1238 (Haw. 2011). Is the "open and obvious" character of the mechanism of plaintiff's injury thus irrelevant? The *Shelton* court said abolishing the no-duty rule "should not be viewed as a major change in our law. The questions are not changing, their locations are." What do you think the court meant by that?

7. **The Restatement Third.** According to the Restatement Third, "Known or obvious dangers pose a reduced risk compared to comparable latent danger because those exposed can take precautions to protect themselves. Nevertheless, in some circumstances a residual risk will remain. . . . Land possessors have a duty of reasonable care with regard to those residual risks." RESTATEMENT (THIRD) OF TORTS: LIABILITY FOR PHYSICAL AND EMOTIONAL HARM § 51 cmt. k (2010). Is this similar to the Second Restatement standard? Was there residual risk in *Kentucky River*?

8. **Barring recovery.** When the plaintiff's fault is great, courts may be particularly inclined to use open and obvious danger as an absolute bar to recovery. In *O'Sullivan v. Shaw*, 726 N.E.2d 951 (Mass. 2000), the plaintiff was injured when he dived into the shallow end of an unmarked swimming pool while attempting to clear the shallow end and emerge at the deep end. The court held that the open and obvious danger doctrine barred his recovery. In a

case like *O'Sullivan,* would there be a way to bar the claim without the use of open and obvious danger?

D. RECREATIONAL-USE STATUTES

1. *Introduction.* Most states have now passed statutes dealing with "recreational users" on private land and waters. While they vary in their details, the gist of these statutes is to retain the landowners' special immunities as to any non-paying recreational user. The Michigan statute, for example, imposes liability only for "gross negligence or willful and wanton misconduct of the owner, tenant or lessee." It applies to "a person who is on the lands of another without paying . . . a valuable consideration for the purpose of fishing, hunting, trapping, camping, hiking, sightseeing, motorcycling, snowmobiling, or any other outdoor recreational use, with or without permission." MICH. COMP. L. ANN. § 324.73301.

California's recreational-use statute provides:

> An owner of any estate in real property . . . owes no duty of care to keep the premises safe for entry or use by others for any recreational purpose or to give any warning of hazardous conditions, uses of, structures, or activities on such premises to persons entering for such purpose, except as provided in this section.

CAL. CIV. CODE § 846. A duty of due care is owed under this section to those who have paid to enter and also those who are "expressly invited rather than merely permitted." Otherwise liability is only for "willful or malicious failure to guard or warn against a dangerous condition, use, structure or activity." Recreational purpose is defined to include many of the activities mentioned in the Michigan statute and others, such as sport parachuting, spelunking, and even "viewing or enjoying historical, natural, archaeological, natural, or scientific sites."

2. *Theory and coverage.* Although the motives for the statutes were undoubtedly associated with a desire to protect private landowners from suits and judgments, the *theory* erected for these statutes was that they were being enacted to limit liability in order to encourage landowners to make land available for recreation in a world becoming increasingly crowded.

Most courts have held that the recreational use statutes do not abrogate a landowner's duty of care to private guests, as opposed to members of the general public who are on the land for recreational purposes. *Estate of Gordon-Couture v. Brown,* 876 A.2d 196 (N.H. 2005) (guest of landowner drowned at private birthday party). Similarly, when a landowner accepts a fee for the plaintiff's use of the land, recreational statutes generally do not provide any protection to the landowner. *See Coleman v. Oregon Parks and Recreation Dept.,* 217 P.3d 651 (Or. 2009) (even when state did not charge a fee to campers who entered park, state's imposition of fees to use particular facilities removed the immunity).

3. *Effect of the statutes.* By lowering the standard of care, recreational-use statutes prevent liability when a defendant's failure to use reasonable care has caused injury, at times deadly injury. *See, e.g., Coan v. New Hampshire Dep't of Envtl. Servs.,* 8 A.3d 109 (N.H. 2010) (barring recovery by parents of boys who died swimming in defendant's lake, even where defendants knew of particular dangers created by nearby dam; statute required "intentionally caused injury or damage"). However, in some cases liability has been found despite the high standard required by the recreational-use statutes. *See Berman v. Sitrin,* 991 A.2d 1038 (R.I. 2010) (willful and malicious failure in case in which tourist was severely injured when a public walkway along an oceanside cliff crumbled and there had been multiple previous incidents of death and grievous injury along that walkway).

4. *Constitutionality.* Could recreational-use statutes be upheld in states that have already ruled guest statutes to be unconstitutional? Remember that one reason given for automobile guest statutes was that they would encourage hospitality. That sounds a great deal like the encouragement supposedly offered by recreational-use statutes. We have seen that the California court found the guest statute to be unconstitutional and that the hospitality purpose did not save it, since not all non-paying persons were treated alike. Interestingly enough, recreational-use statutes have been upheld against constitutional attack. *E.g., Olson v. Bismarck Parks and Recreation Dist.,* 642 N.W.2d 864 (N.D. 2002).

5. *Interpreting the statutes.* Many statutes leave much to be interpreted and fail to provide solutions for some obvious problems. Court interpretations of similar statutes are often quite diverse. Issues may arise, for example, because of where the injury occurred. *See, e.g., Liberty v. State, Dept. of Transp.,* 148 P.3d 909 (Or. 2006) (statute held not to apply to property owners who permitted members of the public to use their property as a means of access to another property that was used for a recreational purpose). At other times the interpretive difficulty relates to what the plaintiff was doing at the time of the injury, that is, whether the use was truly "recreational." *See, e.g., Lawson v. City of Diboll,* 472 S.W.3d 667 (Tex. 2015) (spectating at softball game in park was not "recreation" under statute); *Sallee v. Stewart,* 827 N.W.2d 128 (Iowa 2013) (chaperone was injured when she fell through hole in barn's hayloft while accompanying students on field trip to dairy farm; any activities in the hayloft did not constitute recreational uses under statute).

6. *Conditions vs. activities.* Some jurisdictions interpret recreational use statutes to protect against negligence liability for conditions on the

land, but not against liability for active negligence on the property. *See Combs v. Ohio Dept. of Natural Resources, Div. of Parks & Recreation*, 55 N.E.3d 1073 (Ohio 2016) (negligent operation of a boom mower); *Klein v. United States*, 235 P.3d 42 (Cal. 2010) (negligent driving of a vehicle).

§ 3. LANDLORDS' DUTY TO TENANTS

1. *The traditional view: lease as conveyance.* The traditional view is that a lease is a conveyance of land. The lessee is the "owner" of the land in question for the period of the lease, and the lessor has no more responsibility for the upkeep of the land than any other person who conveys land. Consequently, he is not liable to the lessee for injuries resulting from conditions on the land. A corollary rule is that the landlord owes no more to the tenant's guests than he owes to the tenant himself. Note that even under the traditional rule, a landlord might be liable on a contract theory for failure to repair defects, or on a tort theory for such things as failing to repair latent defects the landlord knows about, or doing repairs negligently.

2. *Changing concepts of leases.* Several modern decisions have departed from the traditional rules by imposing upon the landlord the duty to exercise ordinary care to the tenant or those on the premises by virtue of the tenant's rights. For example, where a tenant's infant fell into a bathtub containing scalding hot water, there was a fact issue with respect to whether the landlord and building management company negligently failed to maintain the apartment's hot water system in reasonably safe condition. *Simmons ex rel. Simmons v. Sacchetti*, 934 N.E.2d 877 (N.Y. 2010). If the landlord's duty was merely to warn of a danger rather than repair it, the tenants may be barred from recovery by something like the "open and obvious" rule. *See White v. Many Rivers West Ltd. Partnership*, 797 N.W.2d 739 (Minn. Ct. App. 2011) (landlord had no duty to enhance window screens to prevent a child from falling, and no duty to repair screens to a more secure strength than law would otherwise impose, where tenants were fully aware of the hazards the screens presented and had been warned about those dangers by the landlord).

3. *The Restatement rule.* The Restatement Third provides that lessors have a duty of reasonable care for (a) the portions of the leased premises over which the lessor retains control, (b) conduct of the lessor creating risks to others, and (c) disclosure of certain dangerous conditions. A landlord also has a duty based on applicable statutes, contractual or voluntary undertakings, and compliance with an implied warranty of habitability. RESTATEMENT (THIRD) OF TORTS: LIABILITY FOR PHYSICAL AND EMOTIONAL HARMS § 53 (2010). Some states abrogate the common law rule only for residential leases, *Lucier v. Impact Recreation, Ltd.*, 864 A.2d 635 (R.I. 2005), while others extend obligations to commercial landlords as well. *See Bishop v. TES Realty Trust*, 942 N.E.2d 173 (Mass. 2011).

4. *Statutory duties of landlords.* Many statutes now set standards or impose liability for specific defects, such as the knowing use of lead-based paint that poisons a tenant's child, *see Gore v. People's Savings Bank,* 665 A.2d 1341 (Conn. 1995), or a failure to disclose lead-based paint the lessor should have discovered on reasonable inspection, *Benik v. Hatcher,* 750 A.2d 10 (Md. 2000). Some state statutes require landlords to keep common areas in safe condition, and may be given negligence per se effect. *See, e.g., Mann v. Northgate Investors, L.L.C.,* 5 N.E.3d 594 (Ohio 2014).

§ 4. THE FIREFIGHTER'S RULE

MINNICH V. MED-WASTE, INC.
564 S.E.2d 98 (S.C. 2002)

JUSTICE PLEICONES.

[A federal District Court certified a question to the Supreme Court of South Carolina, asking whether the firefighter's rule barred a claim for injury to emergency professionals.] The District Court made the following factual findings:

Jeffrey Minnich ("Plaintiff") was employed by the Medical University of South Carolina ("MUSC") as a public safety officer. While working in this capacity, Plaintiff assisted in loading medical waste from the premises of MUSC onto a tractor-trailer truck owned by Defendant Med-Waste, Inc. Plaintiff noticed the unoccupied truck begin to roll forward, toward a public street. Plaintiff ran to the truck, jumped inside, and stopped the truck.

Plaintiff alleges he suffered serious injuries, proximately caused by the acts or omissions of the defendants' employees, for which he seeks to recover damages. The defendants assert that Plaintiff's claims are barred by the firefighter's rule. The firefighter's rule is a common law doctrine that precludes a firefighter (and certain other public employees, including police officers) from recovering against a defendant whose negligence caused the firefighter's on-the-job injury. . . .

Finding no definitive answer to the certified question in the case law of this state, we examine the various rationales advanced in support of the rule, and its applications and limitations in other states.

The common law firefighter's rule originated in the case of *Gibson v. Leonard,* 143 Ill. 182, 32 N.E. 182 (Ill.1892). There, the Illinois Supreme Court held that a firefighter who entered private property in the performance of his job duties was a licensee, and as such, the property owner owed the firefighter a duty only to "refrain from willful or affirmative acts which are injurious." Practically, this meant that a firefighter, injured while fighting a blaze on private property, could not recover tort damages from the property owner whose ordinary negligence caused the fire.

A number of courts reason that police officers and firefighters, aware of the risks inherent in their chosen profession, have assumed those risks. As such, the firefighter or police officer should not be allowed to recover when injured as a result of confronting these known and accepted risks.

A third rationale advanced is public policy. . . . First, injuries to firemen and policemen are compensable through workers' compensation. It follows that liability for their on-the-job injuries is properly borne by the public rather than by individual property owners. Second, firemen and policemen, unlike invitees or licensees, enter at unforeseeable times and at areas not open to the public. In such situations, it is not reasonable to require the level of care that is owed to invitees or licensees.

Still other courts reason that the public fisc pays to train firefighters and police officers on the ways to confront dangerous situations, and compensates them for doing so. If these public employees were permitted to bring suit against the taxpayers whose negligence proximately caused injury, the negligent taxpayer would incur multiple penalties in exchange for the protection provided by firefighters and police officers.

Not only have courts been unable to agree on a consistent rationale for the rule, they have not been able to agree on the proper parameters for the rule. A number of courts which recognize the firefighter's rule as a viable defense to negligence claims allow recovery for willful and wanton conduct resulting in injury. As one court observed, "a tortfeasor who acts willfully and wantonly is so culpable that the fireman's rule ought not to preclude the injured officer from suing the egregiously culpable wrongdoer." *Miller v. Inglis*, 223 Mich.App. 159, 567 N.W.2d 253 (1997).

Courts have allowed police officers and firefighters to recover for injuries resulting from an act of negligence unrelated to the specific reason for which the officer or firefighter was originally summoned. As stated by the Supreme Court of New Jersey:

> The core of the "fireman's rule" is that a citizen's ordinary negligence that occasioned the presence of the public safety officer shall not give rise to liability in damages for the injuries sustained by the officer in the course of the response to duty. . . The corollary of the rule is that independent and intervening negligent acts that injure the safety officer on duty are not insulated. . . .

More recently, a number of state legislatures have acted to limit or abolish the firefighter's rule. For instance . . . the Virginia legislature passed a statute providing that:

> An owner or occupant of real property containing premises normally open to the public shall, with respect to such premises, owe to firefighters . . . and law-enforcement officers who in the performance of their duties come upon that portion of the

premises normally open to the public the duty to maintain the same in a reasonably safe condition or to warn of dangers thereon of which he knows or has reason to know, whether or not such premises are at the time open to the public.

An owner or occupant of real property containing premises not normally open to the public shall, with respect to such premises, owe the same duty to firefighters . . . and law-enforcement officers who he knows or has reason to know are upon, about to come upon or imminently likely to come upon that portion of the premises not normally open to the public. . . .

Va.Code Ann. § 8.01–226 (Michie 2001). [The court also discussed statutes from California, Florida, Minnesota, New Jersey, New York and Nevada, some of which effectively abolished the rule altogether.]

. . . [T]hose jurisdictions which have adopted the firefighter's rule offer no uniform justification therefor, nor do they agree on a consistent application of the rule. The legislatures in many jurisdictions which adhere to the rule have found it necessary to modify or abolish the rule. The rule is riddled with exceptions, and criticism of the rule abounds.

Against this backdrop, we answer the certified question in the negative. South Carolina has never recognized the firefighter's rule, and we find it is not part of this state's common law. In our view, the tort law of this state adequately addresses negligence claims brought against non-employer tortfeasors arising out of injuries incurred by firefighters and police officers during the discharge of their duties. We are not persuaded by any of the various rationales advanced by those courts that recognize the firefighter's rule. The more sound public policy—and the one we adopt—is to decline to promulgate a rule singling out police officers and firefighters for discriminatory treatment.

CERTIFIED QUESTION ANSWERED.

NOTES

1.   **The firefighter's rule.** As *Minnich* indicates, the states disagree on the merits of the firefighter's rule. Some legislatures have abolished the rule. *Lazenby v. Mark's Const., Inc.*, 236 Ill.2d 83, 923 N.E.2d 735 (Ill. 2010); *Rowe v. Mazel Thirty, LLC*, 34 A.2d 1248 (N.J. 2012). Most states continue to apply the rule in some form, and some have adopted or reaffirmed it recently. *Higgins v. Rhode Island Hosp.*, 35 A.3d 919 (R.I. 2012); *Fordham v. Oldroyd*, 171 P.3d 411 (Utah 2007); *Espinoza v. Schulenburg*, 129 P.3d 937 (Ariz. 2006). In a number of states, the rule is applied as modified by legislation. New York courts apply the firefighter's rule, as limited by statute, to actions against a "police officer's or firefighter's employer or co-employee." *Wadler v. City of New York*, 14 N.Y.3d 192, 925 N.E.2d 875 (2010) (barring claim brought by police officer who was injured when the car he was driving was thrust four feet into

the air after a retractable, concrete security barrier at police headquarters' parking lot entrance was accidentally raised while he was driving across it). Most states continue to hold that a firefighter who is injured in fighting a fire has no claim against the negligent fire-setter.

2. **Assumed risk/no duty.** In those states which still adhere to the firefighter's rule, the exclusion of firefighters from the negligence system is often explained by saying that the firefighter assumed the risk. This could hardly be assumed risk in the sense of contributory fault; it is not negligent to fight fires in a professional way. So the firefighter's rule, though explained in terms of assumed risk, is merely another way of saying "it is appropriate to find that the defendant owes no duty of care." *Neighbarger v. Irwin Industries, Inc.,* 882 P.2d 347 (Cal. 1994).

3. **No duty/public policy.** "No duty" in turn reflects judicial notions of appropriate policy. The *Minnich* court finds the policy rationales for the firefighter's rule unconvincing. Other courts have reached the opposite conclusion. In *Babes Showclub, Jaba, Inc. v. Lair,* 918 N.E.2d 308 (Ind. 2009), a case in which a police officer was attacked by an unruly underage patron after responding to a bar's complaint about that patron, the Indiana Supreme Court wrote: "Many emergencies are caused by the negligence of some party. The public employs firefighters, police officers, and others to respond to emergencies, and these responders knowingly combat the effects of others' negligence." *See also Moody v. Delta W., Inc.,* 38 P.3d 1139 (Alaska 2002) ("The Firefighter's Rule reflects sound public policy."). What do you think?

4. **Expansions.** The earliest cases applying the firefighter's rule were anchored in premises liability law, and applied only to firefighters in suits against landowners and occupiers. But in many states it has been vastly expanded. First, the rule has been applied beyond its original landowner moorings, applying when the injury occurs outside the defendant's land and even where the defendant is not a landowner at all. *See, e.g., White v. State,* 19 A.3d 369 (Md. 2011) (firefighter's rule barred police officer's claim against the state for the negligence of a police dispatcher in reporting a shoplifting incident as an armed robbery, causing the officer to engage in a high-speed chase during which he was injured). Likewise, in most states the rule is no longer limited to firefighters; it has been applied to police officers, EMTs, and even lifeguards. Perhaps the operative category is not firefighters but publicly-employed professional risk-takers or public safety officers.

5. **Scope of risks covered by the rule.** Many courts (and a number of statutes) say that the firefighter's rule prohibits recovery by the professional rescuer for injuries from "the negligently created risk that was the very reason for his presence on the scene." *White v. State,* 19 A.3d 369 (Md. 2011). Other courts do not circumscribe the risks as narrowly, and have protected defendants from negligence suits where the rescuer was harmed by risks that are inherent, or reasonably foreseeable, in the situation the rescuer was compelled to confront. See, e.g., *Ellinwood v. Cohen,* 87 A.3d 1054 (R.I. 2014).

Whether a court takes a broader or narrower view of the covered risks may well be outcome-determinative. For example, if a police officer pulls over a car to make a traffic stop, and is then hit by a second, negligently driven vehicle, is the officer's negligence claim against the second driver barred by the rule? Compare *Ellinwood, supra* (broader approach: risk of being hit by second automobile was one that officer would foreseeably encounter, so rule applies), with *Harris-Fields v. Syze,* 600 N.W.2d 611 (Mich. 1999) (narrower approach: act of second driver was not what brought officer to the scene, so rule does not apply). *See also, e.g., Lee v. Luigi, Inc.,* 696 A.2d 1371 (D.C. 1997) (broader approach: risk of slipping on oil while investigating a burglary was covered by rule); *Lipson v. Superior Court of Orange County,* 644 P.2d 822 (Cal. 1982) (narrower approach: rule did not bar negligence claim for injuries caused by explosion of a gasoline tank on the premises, when firefighter was summoned to fight an electrical fire).

6.   **Other wrongdoing not covered by the rule.** (1) Most courts hold that the firefighter's rule does not foreclose suit against an intentional or willful wrongdoer. *Baldonado v. El Paso Natural Gas Co.,* 176 P.3d 277 (N.M. 2008). (2) At least in some jurisdictions, it does not foreclose suit for injuries arising from violation of a fire-safety statute or ordinance. *See, e.g., Mullen v. Zoebe, Inc.,* 654 N.E.2d 90 (N.Y. 1995).

7.   **Private rescuers.** The firefighter's rule has no application to private individuals who may undertake assistance at a fire. On the contrary, private persons are considered heroic and it is said under one branch of the "rescue doctrine" that it is not contributory negligence or assumed risk to render assistance in a physical emergency. "The extent of the risk which the volunteer is justified in assuming under the circumstances increases in proportion to the imminence of the danger. . . ." *Moravec v. Moravec,* 343 N.W.2d 762 (Neb. 1984) (plaintiff injured in fighting a fire could recover from homeowner who negligently set it). Some courts have said expressly that the firefighter's rule is an exception to the rescue doctrine.

PROBLEMS

Christie v. Embry Corp.

Christie, a girl of 11 years, entered a garbage dump maintained by the Embry Corporation on its own land. She was looking for any kind of old toys or comic books. Walking on what appeared to be a solid surface, she suddenly sank through and was burned on hot embers below. In her action against Embry Corp., she proved that in past times Embry had had to call the fire department to put out fires that spontaneously flared in the dump. She also proved that other children often went there looking for comics and toys, that there was no fence, and that there were many houses nearby. This was all the proof. *Can she get to the jury?*

Paget v. Owen

Paget asked Owen for permission to enter Owen's large farm to fish in one of the ponds. Owen agreed to this. Owen believed from the location involved, that Paget intended to take the north road on Owen's property. The north road had been undermined by flooding of a creek, though Owen did not know this. The south road had also been undermined by flooding of a different creek, and Owen was well aware of this. Paget drove into the farm land to fish the next day. Although the road appeared to be safe, it caved in where it had been undermined by the flooding. Paget's car overturned and he was injured. *Did Owen breach any duty? Does it matter which road Paget took?*

REFERENCES: DOBBS, HAYDEN & BUBLICK, HORNBOOK ON TORTS §§ 19.1–.3 (common carriers), §§ 20.1–.15 (landowners), and §§ 24.1–.4 (firefighter's rule) (2d ed. 2016); 2 DOBBS, HAYDEN & BUBLICK, THE LAW OF TORTS §§ 271–79 (landowners) and §§ 362–65 (firefighter's rule) (2d ed. 2011); GLEN WEISSENBERGER & BARBARA MCFARLAND, THE LAW OF PREMISES LIABILITY (4th ed. 2010).

CHAPTER 13

DUTIES OF HEALTH-CARE PROVIDERS

• • •

§ 1. THE STANDARD OF CARE IN MEDICAL MALPRACTICE ACTIONS

Medical malpractice suits are negligence suits, meaning that the plaintiff must prove duty and breach, actual harm, factual cause, and "proximate" cause. *See, e.g., Glenn v. Peoples*, 185 So.3d 981 (Miss. 2015). But there are some special rules for medical malpractice cases, deriving in part from the professional setting of the doctor-patient relationship.

With some exceptions, a medical doctor owes a duty of care only to patients, and only a patient can bring a medical malpractice suit. *See* DOBBS, HAYDEN & BUBLICK, HORNBOOK ON TORTS § 21.3 (2d ed. 2016). When a patient sues his or her doctor, there is no doubt that a duty of care is owed; the doctor's acceptance of the patient represents an undertaking of care by the doctor. *See, e.g., Cromer v. Children's Hosp. Med. Ctr.*, 29 N.E.3d 921 (Ohio 2015). In a patient vs. doctor suit, it is also beyond argument that on the scope of liability issue, the patient is a "foreseeable plaintiff."

But what standard of care applies? And how does a plaintiff prove the standard, and that it was breached, and that the doctor's negligence was a factual cause of the harm? Those questions may be analyzed differently than they would be in most negligence cases.

WALSKI V. TIESENGA
381 N.E.2d 279 (Ill. 1978)

KLUCZYNSKI, JUSTICE.

[Defendants operated to remove plaintiff's thyroid. A well-recognized risk of a thyroidectomy is that the recurrent laryngeal nerves, which run through the thyroid, may be damaged, with resulting loss of voice. One solution to the problem is to locate the nerves and segregate them before removal of the thyroid. In this case, however, there was a great deal of scar tissue present as a result of earlier operations and treatments and the defendants, instead of locating the nerve, made a wide cut so as to avoid the area where the nerve was thought to be. In fact they cut the nerve and

Procedural Posture

plaintiff's vocal chords are paralyzed. The trial court directed a verdict for the defendants and the intermediate appellate court affirmed.]

Dr. David M. Berger testified as an expert witness on plaintiff's behalf. . . His direct testimony concerning acceptable procedures for thyroid surgery was that "in my feeling the standards by which I feel are acceptable practice, one must identify and preserve the recurrent laryngeal nerves on all occasions." On cross-examination Dr. Berger testified that there are always options available in surgery but that in his own mind it was not a proper option to skirt the left recurrent laryngeal nerve. He stated he could not testify generally but only "on the basis of my own opinion as to what I consider a proper option." When asked on cross-examination if there existed a contemporary school of surgeons that will skirt the nerve when they encounter a host of adhesions, Dr. Berger responded that "in the institutions in which I trained that is not the teaching. And I can't speak for other institutions or other areas of training. I can only speak for my own." Defense counsel read a quotation to Dr. Berger from a medical textbook which indicated that there existed a certain amount of controversy in the medical community concerning deliberate exposure of the laryngeal nerve. The quotation concluded with the remark that the situation remained one in which each surgeon will find the approach which suits him best. Dr. Berger indicated that he did not fully agree with that statement, but indicated the decision whether or not to expose the nerve depends on the surgeon and the technique and care he uses. Dr. Berger stated that "[e]verybody who is a certified surgeon doesn't use the same methods, obviously."

One element of a cause of action for medical malpractice is proof of the standard of care by which the defendant physician's conduct is to be measured. . . . [T]he appellate decisions in this State have held that the plaintiff in a medical malpractice action generally must establish the standard of care through expert testimony. The plaintiff must then prove that, judged in the light of these standards, the doctor was unskillful or negligent and that his want of skill or care caused the injury to the plaintiff. Generally, expert testimony is needed to support a charge of malpractice because jurors are not skilled in the practice of medicine and would find it difficult without the help of medical evidence to determine any lack of necessary scientific skill on the part of the physician. However, in those situations where the physician's conduct is so grossly negligent or the treatment so common that a layman could readily appraise it, the appellate decisions indicate that no expert testimony is necessary. . . . A requirement that the standard of care be established through expert testimony except where the common knowledge of laymen is sufficient to recognize or infer negligence is broadly recognized throughout the country. . . .

Assist: No jury in a field they have little knowledge in

Plaintiff here had the burden of establishing that the defendant doctors were guilty of malpractice. She failed, however, to introduce evidence of the standard of care to which the defendants were bound to adhere. Plaintiff's expert, Dr. Berger, testified only concerning his own personal preference for isolating the laryngeal nerve under the facts presented to him in the hypothetical question. He at no time testified that there was a generally accepted medical standard of care or skill which required the identification of the laryngeal nerve under the circumstances. . . .

The appellate courts have held that the testimony of the defendant doctor may be sufficient to establish the standard of care, but it is apparent that the defendants' testimony here did not indicate a standard at variance with their actual conduct. Dr. Tiesenga testified that because of prior surgery on and treatment of plaintiff's thyroid, it would have been unwise to attempt to isolate her laryngeal nerve. The better practice, according to Dr. Tiesenga's testimony, was to skirt the area where the nerve might possibly be. Dr. Walsh concurred. When confronted with a statement from a recognized treatise that the first step in performing a thyroidectomy is to expose and identify the recurrent laryngeal nerve, Dr. Tiesenga agreed with the statement only as a general proposition. He testified that where there has been prior surgery and treatment, it is not always good practice to follow the procedure indicated in the treatise. . . .

It is insufficient for plaintiff to establish a prima facie case merely to present testimony of another physician that he would have acted differently from the defendant, since medicine is not an exact science. It is rather a profession which involves the exercise of individual judgment within the framework of established procedures. Differences in opinion are consistent with the exercise of due care. . . .

For the above reasons the judgment of the appellate court is affirmed.

NOTES

1. **The traditional medical standard.** The medical standard of care discussed in the malpractice opinions seldom sounds like a "standard" comparable to the standard of the reasonable and prudent person. The term "standard" suggests a measure or benchmark of some generality. The "medical standard," however, almost always reflects particular customs or procedures used under very particular circumstances, like the "wide-cut" procedure in *Walski*. In other words, the medical "standard" is understood as a rule for the very circumstances involved in the plaintiff's case. *See, e.g., Mody v. Center for Women's Health, P.C.*, 998 A.2d 327 (D.C. 2010) (standard of care required surgeon to reexamine patient's uterine wall after certain medical procedures, but only if perforations were suspected).

2. **Determining the standard.** "The standard of care is determined by the care customarily provided by other physicians, it need not be scientifically tested or proven effective: what the average qualified physician would do in a particular situation *is the standard of care*." *Palandjian v. Foster*, 842 N.E.2d

916 (Mass. 2006) (appropriate question was whether other doctors would have ordered an endoscopy for the patient given the patient's family history of gastric cancer, not whether the patient's risk of gastric cancer was in fact increased). The standard is not what the doctor *himself* would do. *See Murray v. UNMC Physicians,* 806 N.W.2d 118 (Neb. 2011). Nor is it necessarily enough to show that the care used was not good care. *Braswell v. Stinnett,* 99 So.3d 175 (Miss. 2012) ("Dentists are not required to do what is generally done, or what the average dentist would do. And our law certainly does not require dentists to conform to a vague, subjective standard such as good dental practice. Instead, our law requires a plaintiff to establish—through a qualified expert—what is required of a minimally competent dentist.").

3. **Jury instructions.** If the proof is sufficient to get the plaintiff to the jury, the instructions must reflect the medical, not the ordinary care, standard. Instructions often state that the physician must possess the learning, skill and ability of other physicians, must exercise reasonable care in the use of this knowledge and skill and must use his or her best judgment in the care of the patient.

Trial judges sometimes tell the jury that the physician is not liable for an honest mistake or bona fide error in judgment, that the physician is not expected to be infallible, or that he does not guarantee results. These instructions have come under attack by plaintiffs' lawyers as unduly emphasizing the defendant's side of the case, and as misleading to the jury. The "honest mistake" and "error in judgment" instructions have been disapproved in a number of cases. *See Passarello v. Grumbine,* 87 A.3d 285 (Pa. 2014) (such instructions should not be given at all, because they pose substantial risks of confusing juries on the standard of care); *Nestorowich v. Ricotta,* 767 N.E.2d 125 (N.Y. 2002) (error in judgment instruction proper only when physician is choosing among medically acceptable procedures); *McKinnis v. Women & Infants Hosp. of R.I.,* 749 A.2d 574 (R.I. 2000) (vacating judgment where jury instruction came "too close to implying that 'good faith judgment' or 'good faith error' constitutes a complete defense to a claim of medical malpractice," when such terms "have no place in jury instructions").

4. **Expert medical testimony.** In general, expert testimony is required whenever the issue presented is beyond the comprehension of a lay jury, and such testimony will assist the jury in understanding the deciding the issue. The medical standard of care is a classic example, given its very nature. If the plaintiff fails to adduce expert testimony on the medical standard of care, or if the testimony is inadequate to show the standard, the judge will direct a verdict for the defendant. *See, e.g., Toogood v. Rogal,* 824 A.2d 1140 (Pa. 2003). Whether the particular doctor's conduct fell below the standard is also a matter that generally requires expert testimony, *see Love v. Walker,* 423 S.W.3d 751 (Ky. 2014), although not where the doctor's negligence would be obvious to a lay person, *see Ex parte HealthSouth Corp.,* 851 So.2d 33 (Ala. 2002) (giving examples: leaving a sponge in after an operation, operating on the wrong leg, or ignoring a call for assistance). And expert testimony may be needed to prove that the doctor's negligence factually caused the plaintiff's harm—for example,

without an expert's input, how would a lay jury be able to determine whether a doctor's failure to notice an abnormal electrocardiogram more likely than not caused a patient's heart attack? *Rodriguez v. Clark*, 926 A.2d 736 (Md. 2007).

When expert testimony is required, not just any testimony will do. In *Daubert v. Merrell Dow Pharmaceuticals, Inc.*, 509 U.S. 579 (1993), the Supreme Court requires federal trial courts to review expert testimony for reliability. *See also* FED. R. EVID. 702. Many states have followed suit. Admissibility of expert testimony has become a critical issue in many negligence cases.

5.   **More than one medical "standard" or practice.** Suppose that most doctors in the relevant medical community believe that human bite wounds should not be closed with stitches, but that some disagree and believe that the wound should be stitched and treated with antibiotics. A patient suffers serious infection when his doctor closes the wound. What is the relevant medical standard? "Where competent medical authority is divided, a physician will not be held responsible if in the exercise of his judgment he followed a course of treatment advocated by a considerable number of recognized and respected professionals in his given area of expertise." *Sinclair v. Block*, 633 A.2d 1137 (Pa. 1993). What if the defendant says his practices represent a medical standard or school of thought even though no one else in the profession agrees? *See Yates v. University of W.Va. Bd. of Trustees*, 549 S.E.2d 681 (W.Va. 2001).

6.   **Rejecting *T.J. Hooper*.** Medical standards are not to be found in an authoritative book. For the most part, the medical standard of care is the practice of the relevant medical community. Does the medical standard rule reject the rule about custom in *T.J. Hooper*?

7.   **Rejecting reasonable care.** Medical standards will often reflect reasonable care. Notice that under the reasonable person standard, a professional practitioner would be obliged to exercise all the skill and knowledge he actually has, even if that is more skill or knowledge than other people have. So the medical care standard is not different from the reasonable person standard in this respect.

But the medical standard might require *less* care than the reasonable person standard. To see why, suppose Dr. Berger had testified that, as a matter of scientific fact, the risk of severing the nerve is doubled when the wide-cut procedure is used as compared to the nerve identification procedure and that there are no corresponding advantages to the wide-cut procedure. That testimony seems to be important under a *Carroll Towing* or reasonable care standard because it shows an increase of risk. But it does not seem relevant at all, much less determinative, under the medical standard, because it does not address what doctors actually do.

Is it fair to say that a customary standard can also require *more* care than the reasonable person standard in some instances? What result if the medical standard of care is to perform a procedure despite a lack of scientific evidence suggesting that the procedure is generally beneficial? *See Palandjian v. Foster*, 842 N.E.2d 916 (Mass. 2006).

8. **Accepting reasonable care standards**. A few decisions have indicated that in extreme cases, the reasonable person standard might be used. *See United Blood Serv's, Div. of Blood Sys., Inc. v. Quintana*, 827 P.2d 509 (Colo. 1992); *Helling v. Carey*, 519 P.2d 981 (Wash. 1974) (cheap, efficient test for glaucoma should be given with ophthalmic exam even if that was not the practice of the medical community). Professor Peters' study concludes that 12 cases have shifted to the reasonable care standard and that a number of others have implicitly done so. *See* Philip G. Peters, Jr., *The Quiet Demise of Deference to Custom: Malpractice Law at the Millennium*, 57 WASH. & LEE L. REV. 163 (2000). Logically, the shift implies that testimony about medical custom would no longer be necessary. Some cases like *Helling v. Carey*, in this note, are in accord with that, but it remains to be seen whether all those courts adopting reasonable care will go that far against long-standing tradition.

9. **Non-medical negligence of health-care providers.** Suppose that you, as a hospital patient, slip and fall because the hospital left a slippery substance on the floor. Would you be required to prove the standard of care for hospitals by expert testimony? *See Self v. Executive Comm. of Ga. Baptist Convention*, 266 S.E.2d 168 (Ga. 1980) (not a claim of medical malpractice, no requirement of expert testimony); *see also Sullo v. Greenberg*, 68 A.3d 404 (R.I. 2013) (doctor owed no "medical" duty of care to patient with respect to her fall on the entrance ramp to his office). Do you need expert testimony in this case: a doctor knows a patient is dangerous but fails to warn his coworkers? *Powell v. Catholic Med. Ctr.*, 749 A.2d 301 (N.H. 2000). If a court sees the plaintiff's claim as one for "ordinary" negligence as opposed to medical malpractice, not only will the plaintiff not need to adduce medical expert testimony—the point made in these notes—but the plaintiff will not have to comply with whatever special rules the jurisdiction has adopted for medical malpractice cases—a point made in § 4B of this chapter.

10. **Apology.** The defendant might conceivably admit before trial that he violated the appropriate standard of care. If he does so, evidence of this admission can be introduced to show the standard and its breach. Suppose the defendant, after an operation turns out badly, says "I made a mistake, that should not have happened." Would that suffice to show the standard? *Fossett v. Board of Regents of Univ. of Neb.*, 605 N.W.2d 465 (Neb. 2000). Some state statutes permit physicians to apologize to patients for mistakes without risk that the apology will be used in court. *See* Marilyn Wei, *Doctors, Apologies, and the Law: An Analysis and Critique of Apology Laws*, 40 J. HEALTH L. 107 (2007) (listing a dozen such laws). Is this a help to injured patients? To doctors? Compare Aaron Lazare, *The Healing Forces of Apology in Medical Practice and Beyond*, 57 DEPAUL L. REV. 251 (2008), with Lee Taft, *Apology Subverted: The Commodification of Apology*, 109 YALE. L. J. 1135 (2000). Is it preferable if the apology is accompanied by some form of compensation? Some states have adopted "Disclosure and offer" programs—institutional programs in which clinicians disclose unanticipated outcomes to patients and apologize,

sometimes followed by a modest compensation offer. Michelle M. Mello & Allen Kachalia, *Evaluation of Options for Medical Malpractice System Reform: A Report to the Medicare Payment Advisory Commission* 2, 36–42 (2010).

VERGARA V. DOAN
593 N.E.2d 185 (Ind. 1992)

SHEPARD, CHIEF JUSTICE.

Javier Vergara was born on May 31, 1979, at the Adams Memorial Hospital in Decatur, Indiana. His parents, Jose and Concepcion, claimed that negligence on the part of Dr. John Doan during Javier's delivery caused him severe and permanent injuries. A jury returned a verdict for Dr. Doan and the plaintiffs appealed. The Court of Appeals affirmed. Plaintiffs seek transfer, asking us to abandon Indiana's modified locality rule. We grant transfer to examine the standard of care appropriate for medical malpractice cases.

In most negligence cases, the defendant's conduct is tested against the hypothetical reasonable and prudent person acting under the same or similar circumstances. In medical malpractice cases, however, Indiana has applied a more specific articulation of this standard. It has become known as the modified locality rule: "The standard of care . . . is that degree of care, skill, and proficiency which is commonly exercised by ordinarily careful, skillful, and prudent [physicians], at the time of the operation and in similar localities." Appellants have urged us to abandon this standard, arguing that the reasons for the modified locality rule are no longer applicable in today's society. We agree.

The modified locality rule is a less stringent version of the strict locality rule, which measured the defendant's conduct against that of other doctors in the same community. When the strict locality rule originated in the late 19th century, there was great disparity between the medical opportunities, equipment, facilities, and training in rural and urban communities. Travel and communication between rural and urban communities were difficult. The locality rule was intended to prevent the inequity that would result from holding rural doctors to the same standards as doctors in large cities.

With advances in communication, travel, and medical education, the disparity between rural and urban health care diminished and justification for the locality rule waned. The strict locality rule also had two major drawbacks, especially as applied to smaller communities. First, there was a scarcity of local doctors to serve as expert witnesses against other local doctors. Second, there was the possibility that practices among a small group of doctors would establish a local standard of care below that which the law required. In response to these changes and criticisms, many courts adopted a modified locality rule, expanding the area of comparison to similar localities. . . .

Use of a modified locality rule has not quelled the criticism. Many of the common criticisms seem valid. The modified locality rule still permits a lower standard of care to be exercised in smaller communities because other similar communities are likely to have the same care. We also spend time and money on the difficulty of defining what is a similar community. The rule also seems inconsistent with the reality of modern medical practice. The disparity between small town and urban medicine continues to lessen with advances in communication, transportation, and education. In addition, widespread insurance coverage has provided patients with more choice of doctors and hospitals by reducing the financial constraints on the consumer in selecting caregivers. . . . Many states describe the care a physician owes without emphasizing the locality of practice. Today we join these states and adopt the following: a physician must exercise that degree of care, skill, and proficiency exercised by reasonably careful, skillful, and prudent practitioners in the same class to which he belongs, acting under the same or similar circumstances. Rather than focusing on different standards for different communities, this standard uses locality as but one of the factors to be considered in determining whether the doctor acted reasonably. Other relevant considerations would include advances in the profession, availability of facilities, and whether the doctor is a specialist or general practitioner.

. . . Plaintiff was permitted to present his expert witness, Dr. Harlan Giles, even though he was from Pittsburgh, Pennsylvania (not Decatur or a similar locality). Dr. Giles testified regarding his experience and knowledge of the standard of care in communities similar to Decatur and in hospitals similar in size to Adams County Memorial Hospital. He testified that in his opinion, considering all the factors incident to the pregnancy and birth of Javier Vergara, the standard of care required Dr. Doan to have delivered the baby by cesarean section. He stated that this opinion was based on the standard of care as it existed in 1979 in Decatur or similar communities. He also testified that the failure to have either an anesthesiologist or a qualified nurse anesthetist present at the delivery was a breach of the national standard of care for hospitals the size of Adams County Memorial and smaller. Evidently the jury disagreed with Dr. Giles and found Dr. Doan's conduct reasonable under the circumstances.

We regard our new formulation of a doctor's duty as a relatively modest alteration of existing law. It is unlikely to have changed the way this case was tried. We are satisfied that an instruction without the locality language would not lead a new jury to a different conclusion.

Therefore, we hold that giving instruction 23 was harmless and does not require reversal.

NOTES

1. **The local medical standard and problems of testimony.** Adoption of a local standard means that only a local physician, or one who knows what the local standard is, can testify against the defendant-doctor. *See, e.g., Mattox v. Life Care Centers of America, Inc.,* 337 P.3d 627 (Idaho 2014). What problems does this raise for the plaintiff? In *Robinson v. LeCorps,* 83 S.W.3d 718 (Tenn. 2002), the defendant practiced in Nashville, Tennessee, and the plaintiff's expert was from Johnson City, Tennessee. The expert testified that the defendant violated the national standard, and that the national standard was "the same as the recognized standard of acceptable professional practice as it would be in Nashville, Tennessee." The court, bound by a statutory locality rule, affirmed a dismissal of the claim because the testimony did not meet that rule. A statement that the standard "would be" the same was not good enough, perhaps meaning that the testimony should have been "is the same." *See also Shipley v. Williams,* 350 S.W.3d 527 (Tenn. 2011) ("a medical expert must demonstrate a modicum of familiarity" with the community in which a defendant practices by knowing statistical information about the community's size and practices, speaking with other local medical providers, or visiting the community); *Navo v. Bingham Memorial Hosp.,* 373 P.3d 681 (Idaho 2016) (no abuse of discretion to exclude testimony of out-of-locality expert who failed to establish he had "actual knowledge of what the standard of care is in Blackfoot as it existed" at the time of the alleged malpractice, where the local standard "had not been replaced by a national or statewide standard of care with which [the expert] was familiar").

2. **A national medical standard.** It is sometimes argued that adoption of a standard like *Vergara's* would be unfair to doctors in small towns, who might not have the latest equipment. Would a national medical standard be likely to require a small-town doctor to own CT scan technology? What about the reasonable person standard? In *Hall v. Hilbun,* 466 So.2d 856 (Miss. 1985), the Mississippi Court adopted a national standard which governs the physician's care and skill, but not the particular resources available to that physician. If you were a small-town doctor without equipment, what would you do about a patient who needed a CT scan?

3. **The standard for specialists.** The medical profession is organized to a large extent around recognized specialties, such as orthopedics, internal medicine, and obstetrics. Medical specialization usually entails several years of study following medical school and success in an examination administered by the "board" which certifies specialists. Specialists are held to the standard of their specialties; thus an orthopedic surgeon is held to a higher standard in setting a fracture than is a family practitioner. It is often assumed or held that the relevant medical community for them is the community of specialists, not a geographical community. *Wall v. Stout,* 311 S.E.2d 571 (N.C. 1984). States have disagreed on whether an expert witness can testify against a doctor who is a specialist in a different field. A number of state statutes now require that the only experts who can competently testify are those who actually practice within the same specialty, while some states more liberally permit an expert

to testify if she establishes her knowledge of the standards of the defendant's specialty. *See* DOBBS, HAYDEN & BUBLICK, HORNBOOK ON TORTS § 21.8 (2d ed. 2016).

NOTE: OTHER MEDICAL PROFESSIONALS

1. *Nurses.* Courts now seem to assume that nurses are held to the standard of nurses in a similar practice. *Massey v. Mercy Med. Ctr. Redding*, 103 Cal. Rptr.3d 209 (Ct. App. 2009) (standard of care for nurses is "the level of skill, knowledge and care that a reasonably careful nurse would use in similar circumstances").

2. *Pharmacists.* The rule in most states is that pharmacists owe their clients no duty to warn of side effects, that the physician has prescribed an excessive dosage, or that a drug is contraindicated, even though the patient may be seriously injured if the prescription is filled. *See, e.g., Kowalski v. Rose Drugs of Dardanelle, Inc.*, 378 S.W.3d 109 (Ark. 2011) (only the doctor has a duty to warn). In these jurisdictions, the pharmacist is liable only if he voluntarily undertakes to give appropriate warnings and negligently fails to do so. *Cottam v. CVS Pharmacy,* 764 N.E.2d 814 (Mass. 2002).

However, states continue to disagree about this issue and some courts have held that a pharmacist owes a duty to warn when serious contraindications are present or the drugs prescribed carry inherent risk. *See Klasch v. Walgreen Co.,* 264 P.3d 1155 (Nev. 2011) (when pharmacist knows that a particular customer has an allergy to a prescribed drug, the pharmacist has a duty either to warn the customer or to notify the prescribing doctor).

3. *Hospitals.* The present view seems to be that, in performing their own duties, hospitals owe a duty of reasonable care under national standards fixed by the Joint Commission on Accreditation of Hospitals. *See* 2 DOBBS, HAYDEN & BUBLICK, THE LAW OF TORTS § 316 (2d ed. 2011). Hospitals can be subject to liability if they fail to provide appropriate facilities, equipment, and staff support. *See Staley v. Northern Utah Healthcare Corp.*, 230 P.3d 1007 (Utah 2010) (upholding an order requiring hospital to make discovery of redacted records of patients as part of the evidence to support a claim of damaging understaffing).

HIRPA V. IHC HOSPITALS, INC., 948 P.2d 785 (Utah 1997). A patient in active labor at a hospital became unresponsive and her hands began to spasm. Her physician broadcast a "Code Blue" over the hospital intercom. Dr. Daines responded, entering the delivery room and taking over.

Seventeen minutes later, the patient was dead. The surviving spouse sued Daines and others involved in a federal court. Daines moved for summary judgment. He invoked a statute covering medical providers: "No person licensed under this chapter . . . who in good faith renders emergency care at the scene of the emergency, shall be liable for any civil damages as a result of any acts or omissions by such person in rendering the emergency care." The federal court certified questions to the state court. One question asked whether the statute applied. *Held*, the statute applies. This was an emergency. The statute is intended to encourage aid without fear of liability, so the location of the emergency in a hospital instead of a roadside is irrelevant, so long as the physician had no preexisting duty to aid. It has no application, however, when the physician already had a duty to aid the patient, for in that case he needs no encouragement. Whether the doctor was under a preexisting duty to the patient could depend upon the doctor-patient relationship, his contractual duty to respond, hospital rules or other factors.

NOTES

1. **Good Samaritan statutes.** The type of statute applied in *Hirpa* is called a Good Samaritan statute, after the Biblical story of the Samaritan who assists a man who had been attacked by robbers and left for dead on the road, after other passers-by had done nothing. Luke 10:25–37. All states have some form of a Good Samaritan statute, but the scope of immunity granted by such statutes varies from state to state. As the court wrote in *Velazquez v. Jiminez*, 798 A.2d 51 (N.J. 2002), "The country's Good Samaritan statutes broadly can be classified as falling into one of three categories: those that expressly exclude hospital care; those that expressly include hospital care; and those, like New Jersey's, that contain no explicit provision one way or the other." The *Velazquez* court said that its statute was designed "to encourage the rendering of medical care to those who would not otherwise receive it, by physicians who come upon such patients by chance, without the benefit of the expertise, assistance, equipment or sanitation that is available in a hospital or medical setting." Thus it did not extend immunity to physicians in the hospital setting. According to the court, in the hospital context "physicians' contracts, hospital protocols, ethical rules, regulatory standards and physicians' personal relationships" make it unlikely that, without immunity, physicians would stand by and allow patients to die. The court believed that the roadside accident is the kind of case for which the immunity is designed. Was there ever any need for immunity in such a case or would ordinary negligence rules protect the physician unless the physician imposes unreasonable risks even in the light of the emergency?

2. **Liability for gross negligence.** The Utah statute applied in *Hirpa* provides for complete immunity. A milder version of the Good Samaritan statute leaves open the possibility of liability for gross negligence, or for wanton conduct or intentional wrongdoing. *See, e.g.,* N.C. GEN STAT. § 20–166(d) (applying to any person, not merely to health care providers); ARIZ. REV.

STAT. § 32–1471 (gross negligence standard applies to licensed health care providers who act in an emergency, or any person who gratuitously offers help at the scene of an emergency). "Gross negligence" has been defined as "the absence of even slight diligence." *See Abdel-Samed v. Dailey*, 755 S.E.2d 805 (Ga. 2014) (fact issue whether actions taken by hospital emergency room staff in delaying treatment for plaintiff's hand injury constituted gross negligence).

3.   **Special emergency-care statutes.** Some states have other special statutes protecting physicians who act in an emergency. See, e.g., GA. CODE ANN. § 51–1–29.5 (applicable to emergency medical care provided in a hospital emergency department, requiring proof of gross negligence by clear and convincing evidence); ARIZ. REV. STAT. §§ 12–563 & 573 (allowing negligence claim in connection with medical care during labor and delivery, but requiring proof by clear and convincing evidence). A major study of preventable medical errors found that "High error rates with serious consequences are most likely to occur in intensive care units, operating rooms, and emergency departments." INSTITUTE OF MEDICINE, TO ERR IS HUMAN: BUILDING A SAFER HEALTHY SYSTEM (2000). Does that fact make legislation protecting doctors more necessary, or more troubling?

REFERENCES: DOBBS, HAYDEN & BUBLICK, HORNBOOK ON TORTS §§ 21.1–21.8 (medical malpractice duty) & 21.13 (Good Samaritan statutes) (2d ed. 2016); 2 DOBBS, HAYDEN & BUBLICK, THE LAW OF TORTS §§ 292–304 (2d ed. 2011).

§ 2. INFORMED CONSENT

HARNISH V. CHILDREN'S HOSPITAL MEDICAL CENTER
439 N.E.2d 240 (Mass. 1982)

O'CONNOR, JUSTICE.

The plaintiff underwent an operation to remove a tumor in her neck. During the procedure, her hypoglossal nerve was severed, allegedly resulting in a permanent and almost total loss of tongue function.

The plaintiff's complaint charges the defendant physicians and hospital with misrepresentation and negligence in failing to inform her before surgery of the risk of loss of tongue function. The complaint alleges that the purpose of the operation was cosmetic, that the loss of tongue function was a material and foreseeable risk of the operation, and that, had the plaintiff been informed of this risk, she would not have consented to the operation. There is no claim that the operation was negligently performed.

[A medical malpractice tribunal, which functions to screen malpractice claims against physicians, held that the plaintiff's proof was inadequate and on this basis the trial judge dismissed the action.]

... "There is implicit recognition in the law of the Commonwealth, as elsewhere, that a person has a strong interest in being free from nonconsensual invasion of his bodily integrity.... In short, the law recognizes the individual interest in preserving 'the inviolability of his person.' One means by which the law has developed in a manner consistent with the protection of this interest is through the development of the doctrine of informed consent." "[I]t is the prerogative of the patient, not the physician, to determine ... the direction in which ... his interest lie." Every competent adult has a right "to forego treatment, or even cure, if it entails what for him are intolerable consequences or risks however unwise his sense of value may be in the eyes of the medical profession. Knowing exercise of this right requires knowledge of the available options and the risks attendant on each. We hold, therefore, that a physician's failure to divulge in a reasonable manner to a competent adult patient sufficient information to enable the patient to make an informed judgment whether to give or withhold consent to a medical or surgical procedure constitutes professional misconduct and comes within the ambit of G.L. c. 231, § 60B.

... Communication of scientific information by the trained physician to the untrained patient may be difficult. The remotely possible risks of a proposed treatment may be almost without limit. The patient's right to know must be harmonized with the recognition that an undue burden should not be placed on the physician. These interests are accommodated by the rule that we adopt today, that a physician owes to his patient the duty to disclose in a reasonable manner all significant medical information that the physician possesses or reasonably should possess that is material to an intelligent decision by the patient whether to undergo a proposed procedure. The information a physician reasonably should possess is that information possessed by the average qualified physician or, in the case of a specialty, by the average qualified physician practicing that specialty. What the physician should know involves professional expertise and can ordinarily be proved only through the testimony of experts. However, the extent to which he must share that information with his patient depends upon what information he should reasonably recognize is material to the plaintiff's decision. "Materiality may be said to be the significance a reasonable person, in what the physician knows or should know is his patient's position, would attach to the disclosed risk or risks in deciding whether to submit or not to submit to surgery or treatment." The materiality determination is one that lay persons are qualified to make without the aid of an expert. Appropriate information may include the nature of the patient's condition, the nature and probability of risks involved, the benefits to be reasonably expected, the inability of the physician to predict results, if that is the situation, the irreversibility of the procedure, if that be the case, the likely result of no treatment, and the available alternatives, including their risks and benefits. The obligation to give adequate information does not require the disclosure of all risks of a proposed therapy, or of information the physician reasonably believes the patient already has, such as the risks, like infection, inherent in any operation.

Many jurisdictions have adopted the rule that a physician must disclose to his patient only such information as is customarily disclosed in similar circumstances. We think that the better is the one we adopt today. The customary practice standard overlooks the purpose of requiring disclosure, which is protection of the patient's right to decide for himself.

We recognize that despite the importance of the patient's right to know, there may be situations that call for a privilege of nondisclosure. For instance, sound medical judgment might indicate that disclosure would complicate the patient's medical condition or render him unfit for treatment. Where that it is so, the cases have generally held that the physician is armed with a privilege to keep the information from the patient. . . . The physician's privilege to withhold information for therapeutic reasons must be carefully circumscribed, however, for otherwise it might devour the disclosure rule itself. "The privilege does not accept the paternalistic notion that the physician may remain silent simply because divulgence might prompt the patient to forego therapy the physician feels the patient really needs" (footnotes omitted). *Canterbury v. Spence*, supra at 789. A full discussion of the privilege is neither required nor attempted here, because the burden of proving it must rest with the physician, and thus the question of privilege is inappropriate to the directed verdict standard. . . .

We turn to the question of causation. "An unrevealed risk that should have been made known must materialize, for otherwise the omission, however unpardonable, is legally without consequence." Whether the alleged undisclosed risk materialized is a medical question appropriate to the tribunal's inquiry. At trial, the plaintiff must also show that had the proper information been provided neither he nor a reasonable person in similar circumstances would have undergone the procedure. Such proof, not relating to medical questions, is not appropriate to the tribunal's inquiry.

[The court found that one of the defendants was only an assistant in the operation and had no duty to give the plaintiff information, and that the hospital itself was not liable.]

The judgment as to the defendants Muliken and Holmes is reversed. The judgment as to defendants Gilman and Children's Hospital Medical Center is affirmed.

So Ordered.

WOOLLEY V. HENDERSON, 418 A.2d 1123 (Me. 1980). Defendant operated on the plaintiff's back but because of an abnormality in the spine, he got the wrong interspace between the vertebrae. He also inadvertently tore part of the tissue encasing the spinal cord, which resulted in a number of medical problems for the plaintiff. A tear of this kind is a normal risk of this procedure, but the doctor had not informed the plaintiff. The trial court instructed the jury that the plaintiff was entitled only to disclosures of risks that would be made by a reasonable medical practitioner. The jury found in favor of the defendant. *Held,* affirmed. [The standard of disclosure is that of the reasonable medical practitioner and this will ordinarily require expert medical testimony.] This rule is justified (1) because this is professional malpractice and the professional standard must be used, (2) because there might be therapeutic reasons for withholding information, and (3) because since the plaintiff must produce medical testimony on other issues, this will add very little burden. The plaintiff in informed consent cases must also prove causation by the objective test, that is, that a reasonable person would have refused the treatment had full information been given, and that the plaintiff herself would have refused it.

NOTES

1. **Negligence vs. battery theory.** Courts recognize a medical battery claim against a doctor who operates when the plaintiff has not consented at all to that procedure. *See Shuler v. Garrett,* 743 F.3d 170 (6th Cir. 2014) (applying Tenn. law; patient was injected with drug over her objections). Some courts also treat cases of consent without appropriate information as battery cases. *See Montgomery v. Bazaz-Sehgal,* 798 A.2d 742 (Pa. 2002). The usual approach, however, is to treat informed consent claims under negligence, not battery rules. *See White v. Beeks,* 469 S.W.3d 517 (Tenn. 2015) (reciting history of informed consent); *Mole v. Jutton,* 846 A.2d 1035 (Md. 2004) (collecting cases).

2. **Practical consequences of the theory.** Use of a negligence approach is important for a number of reasons. The defendant doctor's liability insurance might not cover battery, an intentional tort. Also, negligence rules might make the doctor's duty to disclose depend upon the disclosure the medical community would make, which might require expert testimony. Many courts, like the *Woolley* court, have so held. Further, an informed consent claim may be subject to special statutory limits or conditions for recovery. *See Felton v. Lovett,* 388 S.W.3d 656 (Tex. 2012).

3. **Professional standard or the "patient rule"?** Beginning in the early 1970s, a series of major decisions retained the negligence theory of informed consent but rejected the requirement of proof from the medical community. These cases held that the standard was "materiality" of the information. In the absence of statutory directive otherwise, most of the recent major decisions have taken this view. *See, e.g., Cuc Thi Ngo v. Queen's Medical Center,* 358 P.3d 26 (Haw. 2015) (once patient adduces expert testimony to

show that a risk was material, whether the physician was required to supply that information to the patient is for the jury, applying a patient-oriented standard, and no expert is needed to answer that question). However, some courts still endorse a reasonable doctor standard. *See Orphan v. Pilnik*, 940 N.E.2d 555 (N.Y. 2010). How different is a standard that requires disclosure of information that would be material to the patient's treatment decision versus information that a reasonable doctor would provide? In *Marsingill v. O'Malley*, 128 P.3d 151 (Alaska 2006), the court thought these two standards were basically indistinguishable. *See also Spar v. Cha*, 907 N.E.2d 974 (Ind. 2009) ("A physician must disclose the facts and risks of a treatment which a reasonably prudent physician would be expected to disclose under like circumstances, and which a reasonable person would want to know.").

4. **Causation.** Should it matter if the patient consented to prior similar surgeries, which may indicate that she did not consent because of lack of knowledge of the associated risks? *Spar v. Cha,* 907 N.E.2d 974 (Ind. 2009). Most courts have required proof of factual cause. *See White v. Lembach*, 959 N.E.2d 1033 (Ohio 2011). In addition, they have required an "objective" test of causation. This means that the plaintiff cannot recover merely by showing that she herself would have refused the injury-causing operation had she been fully informed. She will have to go further and show that a reasonable person would also have refused it. Is this requirement because the courts are reluctant to permit a jury to believe the plaintiff's testimony on this point? If so, what about the usual rule that the jury is the sole judge of credibility? Or is the "objective" test of causation intended to limit protection to reasonable patients? Is that what autonomy is about—matching other people's expectations of reasonableness? Several courts have sought a compromise, saying that the issue is to be judged by the reasonable person standard in the light of the plaintiff's personal fears and religious beliefs. *Ashe v. Radiation Oncology Assocs.,* 9 S.W.3d 119 (Tenn. 1999).

5. **Incompetent patients and life-saving treatment.** The informed consent rules imply that the patient may refuse treatment. May a physician treat a competent patient over her objection if the treatment is required to save her life? *Shine v. Vega*, 709 N.E.2d 58 (Mass. 1999) (no); *Harvey v. Strickland*, 566 S.E.2d 529 (S.C. 2002) (no). Note that the duty of obtaining informed consent may well include a duty to tell a patient of the dangers of refusing a medical test; the doctor should not assume that a patient appreciates the risks of such a decision, especially where the test is largely risk-free and the consequences of refusal potentially fatal. *Truman v. Thomas*, 611 P.2d 902 (Cal. 1980) (doctor advised patient to have a pap smear, but failed to inform her of the risks of refusing the test). When a patient is incompetent, a court must make a substituted judgment determination—determine as best it can what choice that individual, if competent, would make with respect to medical procedures. *In re A.C.*, 573 A.2d 1235 (D.C. 1990).

WLOSINSKI V. COHN, 713 N.W.2d 16 (Mich. Ct. App. 2005). Michael Wrobel suffered kidney failure during his senior year in high school. After researching various medical facilities and their kidney transplant success rates, Michael and his family selected William Beaumont Hospital for treatment. In pre-operative consultations, Dr. Steven Cohn allegedly represented his kidney transplant success rate as "good." The plaintiff, Michael's mother, donated a kidney in an effort to save her son, and Dr. Cohn performed the transplant surgery. Michael experienced severe post-operative complications, resulting in the removal of his new kidney, which ultimately led to his death. Plaintiff's expert inferred medical incompetence by testifying that five out of seven kidney transplants that Dr. Cohn had performed in the months leading up to Michael's surgery had failed. The plaintiff contends that Dr. Cohn owed a duty to Michael to disclose his failure rate before obtaining consent to the procedure. *Held*, "The doctrine of informed consent requires a physician to warn a patient of the risks and consequences of a medical procedure. By itself, Dr. Cohn's success rate was not a risk related to the medical procedure. . . . [W]e simply hold that defendants, as a matter of law, did not have a duty to disclose Dr. Cohn's statistical history of transplant failures to obtain the decedent's informed consent."

NOTES

1. **Physician success rates.** Suppose a surgeon has little experience with the proposed brain surgery or a record of bad results. Must he inform his patient? *Johnson v. Kokemoor*, 545 N.W.2d 495 (Wis. 1996), held that the patient was entitled to information from her surgeon that more experienced brain surgeons were available and had substantially better success rates than inexperienced surgeons. Can the *Wlosinski* court's holding be justified on the ground that a reasonable patient would not have cared about the five out of seven failure rate, or is there some other issue at work? If doctors must disclose success rates, will doctors fudge their records? Reject high-risk patients to establish a better set of statistics? Even if doctors need not disclose information, can they lie about it? In *Willis v. Bender*, 596 F.3d 1244 (10th Cir. 2010), the court said that an informed consent claim is stated when a physician lies to a patient "in direct response to a patient's questions . . . in the course of obtaining the patient's consent and the [patient's] questions seek concrete verifiable facts . . . as to the quality of his performance or abilities."

2. **Procedure success rates.** What if the procedure itself is generally unsuccessful? *See Williamson v. Amrani*, 152 P.3d 60 (Kan. 2007) (expert testimony was necessary to determine whether the lack-of-success rate of recommended back surgery was something a reasonable medical practitioner would have disclosed to the patient).

3. **Jury decisions.** Whether information would be material to an intelligent decision by the patient is usually a jury question. Would a doctor be required to disclose to the patient that he might minimize the risk of an AIDS

infection from a blood transfusion by donating his own blood in advance of the operation? *See Doe v. Johnston*, 476 N.W.2d 28 (Iowa 1991). Suppose the doctor for an 81-year-old woman with a broken hip thinks surgery with screws to hold it together is a bad idea because of her age. He never informs her that without surgery she will probably never walk again. He prescribes bed rest only and in fact she is never able to walk thereafter. Did the doctor breach a duty of providing information? *Matthies v. Mastromonaco*, 733 A.2d 456 (N.J. 1999).

4. **Physician experience.** What if the surgeon merely represents that he has extensive experience in performing a highly risky operation when in fact he has much more limited experience? *See Howard v. University of Med. & Dentistry of N.J.*, 800 A.2d 73 (N.J. 2002). Some states apply to physicians state consumer protection acts which forbid unfair and deceptive practices.

REFERENCES: DOBBS, HAYDEN & BUBLICK, HORNBOOK ON TORTS §§ 21.9–21.12 (2d ed. 2016); 2 DOBBS, HAYDEN & BUBLICK, THE LAW OF TORTS §§ 307–311 (2d ed. 2011).

§ 3. STATUTORY REFORMS

A. THE MEDICAL MALPRACTICE "CRISIS"

The Institute of Medicine (IOM), in a respected and comprehensive study of medical errors, estimated that at least 44,000 and perhaps as many as 98,000 people die each year in hospitals as a result of preventable medical errors. The IOM concluded that more people die from medical errors than from motor vehicle accidents, breast cancer or AIDS. Common errors include adverse drug events, wrong-site surgery, and mistaken patient identities. To illustrate these problems, the study mentioned a patient who died of a chemotherapy overdose, another who had the wrong leg amputated, and another, a child, who died during minor surgery because of a drug mix-up. The IOM estimated the total cost of preventable medical errors (including the expense of additional care necessitated by the errors, lost income and household productivity, and disability) at between $17 billion and $29 billion per year. According to the IOM, the know-how already exists to prevent many of these mistakes. Consequently, it set a strategy to significantly reduce these errors. *See* INSTITUTE OF MEDICINE, TO ERR IS HUMAN: BUILDING A SAFER HEALTHY SYSTEM (2000). In a follow-up article, *Five Years After To Err is Human: What Have We Learned?*, the authors noted that there have been some narrow improvements in safety, but the progress is marginal and has not impacted the national statistics.

Despite the large number of medical errors, there has been a public outcry against medical malpractice litigation. Medical costs have increased enormously in the last generation. The cost of insurance for doctors has also increased. In some instances and in some years it has been difficult for doctors to procure liability insurance. *Five Years After To Err is Human* suggested insurance policies typically do not subsidize newer, safer equipment. However, if insurance is already unaffordable for some, will anyone be willing to pay the extra cost to reduce medical errors?

On the increased insurance costs, some people have pointed the finger at lawyers: costs go up and insurance becomes expensive or impossible to get because greedy lawyers bring too many malpractice suits (and courts permit judgments against doctors). This kind of talk can be misleading for several reasons:

(1)   Existing empirical evidence does not support claims that medical malpractice payouts are increasing significantly, let alone increasing at a staggering rate. For example, several studies looked at all settled and litigated medical malpractice claims in Texas during a time of "crisis." Although insurance premium costs had gone up dramatically during the time period, the costs of paid and settled malpractice claims remained largely stable. Bernard Black, Charles Silver, David A. Hyman & William M. Sage, *Stability, Not Crisis: Medical Malpractice Claims Outcomes in Texas, 1998–2002*, 2 J. EMPIRICAL LEGAL STUD. 207, 210 (2005). Moreover, headlines about large jury awards may be misleading because the vast majority of verdicts are not paid at their full value. In Texas, 75% of plaintiffs who received jury awards over $25,000 received payouts of less than their full award, with mean reductions of 29%. As the value of the award increased, so did the percentage reduction. For plaintiffs whose award was valued at over 2.5 million dollars, 98% received a reduced award with an average cut of 56%. *See* David A. Hyman, et al., *Do Defendants Pay What Juries Award? Post-Verdict Haircuts in Texas Medical Malpractice Cases, 1988–2003*, 4 J. EMPIRICAL. LEG. STUD. 3 (2007). Insurance policy limits act as an effective cap on recovery. In a study of 9,389 closed claims, 98.5% were resolved with payments at or below policy limits. In the few instances in which doctors did draw on their own assets, their personal contributions were relatively small, with only 10 of those contributions exceeding $300,000. For more comprehensive analysis, *see* Kathryn Zeiler, et al., *Physicians' Insurance Limits and Malpractice Payments: Evidence from Texas Closed Claims, 1990–2003*, 36 J. LEGAL STUD. 9 (2007).

(2)   The concern that doctors are particularly vulnerable defendants has not been borne out by empirical data. At least in some locales, plaintiffs prevail against medical doctors in only about one in five claims submitted to a jury. *See* Deborah Jones Merritt & Kathryn Ann Barry, *Is the Tort System in Crisis? New Empirical Evidence,* 60 OHIO ST. L.J. 315, 358 (1999). Also, a study of medical malpractice claims suggests that weak claims are not being paid. A study of over 1400 closed claims concluded that medical errors in fact existed in about 60% of the claims. Most of the claims that did *not* involve medical error by the investigators were *not* paid. David M. Studdert, et al., *Claims, Errors, and Compensation Payments in Medical Malpractice Litigation,* 354 NEW ENG. J. MED. 2024 (2006). Reviewing a large number of studies, one scholar concluded, "Plaintiffs who

received substandard care generally obtained compensation; plaintiffs who received proper care generally did not; and plaintiffs whose care quality was uncertain wound up in between." *See* David A. Hyman & Charles Silver, *Medical Malpractice Litigation and Tort Reform: It's the Incentives Stupid*, 59 VAND. L. REV. 1085, 1097 (2006).

(3)   As to increases in insurance costs, this has been partly a result of investment cycles. Insurers invest premium monies until they are needed to make payouts under the policy. These investments produce large incomes that help make the payments required by the policy. When investment income is down, premium income must go up if the insurer is to pay. So to some extent, the insurer and the insured are subject to the fluctuations of the market, and increased costs to the doctors reflect this as well as other factors. But premium increases were less than the increase of doctors' incomes. *See* 1 BARRY R. FURROW, THOMAS L. GREANEY, SANDRA H. JOHNSON, TIMOTHY S. JOST & ROBERT L. SCHWARTZ, HEALTH LAW § 6–20 (2d ed. 2000).

(4)   Costs of medical treatment have gone up for a number of reasons not associated with lawsuits. These include the costs of new equipment, buildings, and increased technology and an increase in the pool of elderly. In addition, an increase in the pool of patients who do not pay for services may add to costs, which must be borne by other patients or public funds.

B. LEGISLATIVE RESPONSES

The medical profession had sought favorable legislation before the insurance crisis—the Good Samaritan statutes, for example—but the insurance problem prompted even more demands for special rules. In at least two different crises, many states passed statutes attempting to relieve the insurance problem for health care providers, either directly or indirectly. Indirectly, some provisions attempt to facilitate insurance coverage. The exact package of provisions directly impacting tort law varies from state to state, but most states have adopted one or more of the kinds of provisions listed below.

(1) *Substantive Changes:*

(a) The plaintiff must prove actual negligence, or, more explicitly, res ipsa loquitur may not be used against a health care provider, or may not be used in traditional cases. In *Larsen v. Zarrett,* 498 N.W.2d 191 (N.D. 1993), the court interpreted a statute to forbid the use of res ipsa loquitur against a surgeon in a case in which the plaintiff awoke from an operation with an injury to a separate, previously healthy, portion of her body.

(b)   The standard of care must be local or statewide, not national.

(c)   Statutes of repose and statutes of limitation have an absolute outside limit even when the patient cannot discover the negligence for many years.

(d)   No malpractice claim may be based on a contract unless the contract is in writing.

(e)   Informed consent claims are limited or discouraged.

(2)   *Remedial Changes:*

(a)   State statutes limit damages and many include absolute caps on noneconomic damages or total recovery.

(b)   Joint and several liability is limited.

(c)   Amounts received from other collateral sources such as health and disability insurance may be deducted from the defendant's award.

(d)   Periodic payment plans are provided for large damage awards.

(e)   Limits on the attorney's fees that can be collected in a successful suit.

(3)   *Procedural Changes:*

(a)   Statutes strictly limit experts who can testify.

(b)   The plaintiff is required to get a certificate of merit—an affidavit at the beginning of the suit certifying that a qualified medical expert believes there are reasonable grounds for the suit.

(c)   Statutes of limitation are shortened and statutes of repose are initiated.

(d)   Plaintiff is required to submit her claims to pretrial arbitration or screening panels before suing.

(e)   Contracts between patient and medical provider may be permitted to require arbitration in lieu of tort claims.

(f)   Plaintiff must give notice of intent to sue and then cannot bring suit for a waiting period after that, with complex effects on the statute of limitations.

A particularly thoughtful article discussing some of these reforms is Michelle M. Mello & Allen Kachalia, *Evaluation of Options for Medical Malpractice System Reform: A Report to the Medicare Payment Advisory Commission* (2010). The article also outlines more "innovative reforms" which have not necessarily been adopted yet by any state. These reforms include a schedule of noneconomic damages, health courts, disclosure-and-offer programs, safe harbors for adherence to evidence-based practice guidelines, subsidized, conditional reinsurance, and enterprise medical liability.

What injuries fall under the statutes? Not all claims that occur in a health care setting are medical malpractice claims that garner the special statutory protections. A failure of a hospital's life support systems resulting from a power outage in the aftermath of Hurricane Katrina was not a medical malpractice claim, and thus not subject to the statutory restrictions. *LaCoste v. Pendleton Methodist Hosp., LLC*, 966 So.2d 519 (La. 2007). Nor was a lab's wrongful disclosure of plaintiff's HIV test results. *Doe 163 v. Quest Diagnostics, Inc.*, 395 S.W.3d 8 (Mo. 2013). Nor was a failure to protect the patient from fire. *Cf. Taylor v. Vencor*, Inc., 525 S.E.2d 201 (N.C. 2000).

Determining whether a particular claim falls within special statutes depends upon the wording of the statute and the court's own conception of policy. In *Rome v. Flower Memorial Hospital*, 635 N.E.2d 1239 (Ohio 1994), the court found injuries covered by the medical malpractice statute when the plaintiff, allegedly improperly secured to a tilting radiology table, slipped off and injured her head when the table was tipped up. This was medical malpractice because it was "ancillary" to an X-ray procedure that was medical in nature. The same result obtained in *Marks v. St. Luke's Episcopal Hosp.*, 319 S.W.3d 658 (Tex. 2010). In that case, plaintiff was injured after falling from his hospital bed after its footboard allegedly collapsed when he stepped on it. On review, the Texas Supreme Court held plaintiff's suit was properly labeled as a health care liability claim because the bed can be considered "medical equipment" and thus is "an integral and inseparable part of the health care services provided." And in *Dupuy v. NMC Operating Co.*, 187 So.3d 436 (La. 2016), a patient's claim that the hospital failed to maintain and service equipment used to sterilize surgical instruments was held to fall within the special statutes because it was "treatment related." Thus plaintiff was required to present his claims to a medical review panel before filing suit.

C. STATE CONSTITUTIONAL CHALLENGES TO STATUTORY REFORM

Plaintiffs can challenge medical malpractice statutes, like other tort reform legislation, under state constitutional guarantees. Statutes impeding medical malpractice claims have been challenged under state constitutional "open access to courts" provisions. In *Zeier v. Zimmer, Inc.*, 152 P.3d 861 (Okla. 2006), the Oklahoma Supreme Court examined a state statute which required plaintiffs filing medical malpractice actions to file a certificate of merit—an affidavit attesting that a qualified expert had been consulted and had issued an opinion sufficient to deem the claim meritorious. The court held that the affidavit requirement, which front-loaded litigation costs and disproportionately reduced claims by low-income litigants, was a monetary barrier to suit that violated state constitutional guarantees of open access to the courts. The affidavit requirement also violated the state constitutional prohibition against special laws. In this case the unlawful differential treatment was between victims alleging negligence generally and victims alleging medical negligence. The Oklahoma legislature amended the law, but it was struck down as unconstitutional again, on the same grounds, in *Wall v. Marouk*, 302 P.3d 775 (Okla. 2013). *See also Poutman v. Wenatchee Valley Medical Center, P.S.*, 216 P.3d 374 (Wash. 2009) (striking down on constitutional grounds a statutory requirement that a patient obtain a certificate of merit from a panel before filing suit).

Under another state constitutional clause, the "right to a remedy" clause, the Oregon Supreme Court struck down a statutory cap on damage awards. In *Clarke v. Oregon Health Sciences University*, 175 P.3d 418 (Or. 2007), the plaintiff, a minor patient who was deprived of oxygen after heart surgery, challenged two statutes that together greatly diminished her recovery. One statute capped recovery from a public entity and the other required substitution of the public entity, not its employees, as the sole defendant. Estimates of the economic damages for plaintiff's lifetime exceeded $12 million. Yet under the statutes, the maximum award available was $200,000. The court held that the statute confining claims against the public entity to $200,000 was constitutional with respect to the public entity, which would have been entitled to sovereign immunity at common law. However, the elimination of a cause of action against public employees or agents violates the remedy clause because the substituted remedy against the public body "is an emasculated version of the remedy that was available at common law."

However, some courts have been more cautious about striking down state statutes. For example, in *Miller v. Johnson,* 289 P.3d 1098 (Kan. 2012), a case in which doctors had removed the patient's left ovary instead of the right, the court held that a noneconomic damages cap of $250,000 in malpractice cases was reasonably necessary. In another case, *Ledbetter v. Hunter,* 842 N.E.2d 810 (Ind. 2006), the plaintiff raised a statutory challenge under the state constitution's privileges and immunities clause. Under this provision, the state legislature could not "grant to any citizen, or class of citizens, privileges or immunities, which, upon the same terms, shall not equally belong to all citizens." The statute challenged in *Ledbetter* required minors injured by medical malpractice before age six to file suit within two years of an injury or by their eighth birthday at the latest. Plaintiff contended that the legislation unconstitutionally subjected to differential treatment two classes of minors—those injured by medical negligence and those injured by other types of negligence.

However, the *Ledbetter* court held that the differentiation could be justified based on the legislature's rationale for the legislation—that it *could* prevent a reduction in health care services. This rationale was valid even though "neither the insurance carriers nor the health care associations could produce a single document showing that a change in the disability provision for minors in medical malpractice cases would have any adverse effect on the cost of insurance, the availability of health care services, or the ability to defend malpractice claims." The court left the matter to the legislature, suggesting that the lack of evidence "may well provide powerful support for legislative reconsideration of the challenged minor limitation period." *But cf. Schroeder v. Weighall*, 316 P.3d 482 (Wash. 2014) (striking down statute eliminating general tolling of minor's claims in medical malpractice cases, on the ground that it violated state constitutional prohibition against special privileges and immunities; defendant's assertion that medical malpractice claims by minors raised malpractice insurance rates was "speculative," and thus not a reasonable ground to support the statute).

CHAPTER 14

FAMILY MEMBERS AND CHARITIES

■ ■ ■

NOTE: IMMUNITIES

Landowners and health-care professionals—the types of defendants encountered in Chapters 12 and 13—usually obtain special protections from liability because courts limit the duties they owe to something less than the duty of reasonable care. Defendants such as family members, charities, and governmental entities—those we see in the next two chapters—are granted similar protections, but the locution is slightly different. Here courts say that these defendants are *immune from* tort suits or tort liability. The difference between a no-duty rule and an immunity rule, if a difference exists at all, is minuscule. The immunity rules are quite similar to the limited-duty rules, except that they tended in their original form to be absolute and without exception.

---

§ 1. FAMILY MEMBERS

A. THE TRADITIONAL FAMILY IMMUNITIES

Spouses. The common law took the view that upon marriage the wife lost her legal identity, which was merged with that of the husband. The logical result of this conception was, of course, that the spouses could not sue each other. *See* Carl W. Tobias, *Interspousal Tort Immunity in America*, 23 GA. L. REV. 359 (1989) (giving complete history of immunity).

Parent and child. There was no such conceptual reason to bar suits between parents and children. The parent-child immunity was introduced rather casually in *Hewellette v. George*, 9 So. 885 (Miss. 1891), with the unadorned argument that family harmony would not permit such actions. "[S]o long as the parent is under obligation to care for, guide, and control, and the child is under reciprocal obligation to aid and comfort and obey, no such action as this can be maintained." Other states followed this decision and it became mainstream law.

Scope and exceptions. (1) *Property interests.* Children were allowed, however, to sue parents to protect property, and after the Married Women's

Property Acts spouses were also allowed to sue for such property torts as conversion.

(2) *Relationship terminated.* The parental immunity terminated when the child reached the age of majority, or when the child was emancipated (that is, recognized as self-supporting, or married). Some states have held that the parent-child relationship might also be terminated when the parent dies—with the result that the parent's estate could be sued though the parent could not be.

(3) *Intentional torts.* Even in states that held a spouse or parents immune from negligent torts, liability was often imposed for intentional torts; this remains the rule in a number immunity-retaining states today. This means that the key issue in such states may be whether the parent acted intentionally, or perhaps willfully or with malice; if he did not, then the parent-child immunity applies. *See Needham v. Price*, 780 S.E.2d 549 (N.C. 2015).

(4) *Family injury from violation of duty owed to larger class.* Nor did the immunity apply where family members were involved only fortuitously in an injury-causing event; that is, the injury and the family relationship in no way intersected. For example, if a teenage daughter negligently drives a car and strikes a pedestrian in the cross-walk, the fact that he turns out to be her father would not bar recovery. *Schenk v. Schenk*, 241 N.E.2d 12 (Ill. App. Ct. 1968). Put differently, the immunity may be limited to cases in which the parental conduct involves discretion in discipline or supervision, and does not apply to ordinary negligent accidents. *See Cates v. Cates,* 619 N.E.2d 715 (Ill. 1993).

Rationale. Two reasons predominate as justifications for the family immunities: (1) To permit suits between family members would be to encourage fraud and collusion; and (2) to permit suits of this kind would be to interfere with the family, and disrupt family harmony or unity.

Can these reasons be fleshed out? If liability insurance covers the defendant spouse, there is, no doubt, a tendency of the insured spouse, with the approval of the other, to assert fault. What may be an ordinary home accident, with no witnesses, may become a case of "negligence" quite readily. And even if it is negligence, there is the probability that both spouses will share in some sense in the recovery. This obviously does not square with ordinary notions of accountability, because the faulty party, far from paying, would share in payment by his insurer.

In the case of parent-child actions, there was obviously some notion at one time that these would interfere with "discipline," and that if the child could sue, the parent's appropriate authority would be disrupted by judicial interference. This argument perhaps has little appeal today, especially if, as is often the case, the parent encourages the child's tort action in order to tap insurance funds. If there is no insurance, the danger is not fraud but misallocation of family funds. If a child recovers $100,000 from a parent, the parent may be unable to meet other obligations within the family, so that one child may enjoy relative riches while others are unable to receive any of the ordinary benefits of childhood. As these comments suggest, the two arguments of fraud and harmony can be expanded quite a bit. Is further elaboration of these arguments possible? When the arguments are fully developed, do you find them convincing?

Rejection of the immunities. By the end of the 1970s a majority of courts had abolished the spousal immunity, though sometimes only as to motor vehicle collisions. *See, e.g., Ellis v. Estate of Ellis,* 169 P.3d 441 (Utah 2007) (holding that Married Women's Act abrogates immunity for all claims); *Waite v. Waite,* 618 So.2d 1360 (Fla. 1993) (complete abrogation of immunity).

Parents and children. The courts have been a bit slower in abolishing the parent-child immunity, but it appears that a majority have now done so. Some states have abolished the immunity only for special groups of cases, such as those arising out of intentional torts, sexual abuse, motor vehicle accidents, or the conduct of a family business. *E.g., Henderson v. Woolley,* 644 A.2d 1303 (Conn. 1994) (immunity does not bar child's claim for sexual abuse).

Siblings. Generally, state courts have rejected immunity in the context of lawsuits between siblings. In *Lickteig v. Kolar,* 782 N.W.2d 810 (Minn. 2010), a sister sued her brother for sexual abuse that occurred while both were minors. The Minnesota Supreme Court examined the many state cases that follow the general rule that "intrafamilial immunity does not apply to suits between siblings." The court then followed that rule— permitting the sister, an adult at the time of the action, to sue.

B. THE CONTOURS OF PARENTAL IMMUNITY

NEEL V. SEWELL

834 F. Supp. 2d 648 (E.D. Mich. 2011)

ROSEN, CHIEF JUDGE.

On March 8, 2009, Plaintiff Brandon Neel, along with his father, Defendant David Edward Evans, and his aunt, Tina McLean, was helping his step-grandmother, Defendant Beverly Sewell, clean out her house in Monroe County, Michigan. To dispose of excess garbage that had accumulated during this process, a fire was started in the backyard. While Plaintiff was placing crushed plastic milk jugs on the fire, a bag containing an aerosol can exploded in the fire. Plaintiff, who was 17 years old at the time, sustained severe burns to his face and arms, and received treatment at the University of Michigan Hospital. . . . Plaintiff seeks to recover from his father, Defendant Evans, under the theory that his father negligently supervised him by failing to institute and maintain adequate standards for the safe disposal of flammable materials, and by failing to warn and instruct him regarding appropriate procedures to ensure his safety as he assisted in the disposal of hazardous materials. . . .

[Defendant Evans moved for summary judgment.] As the sole argument advanced in the present motion, Defendant Evans contends that, as Plaintiff's father, he is immune from liability under Michigan law for the claims of negligent supervision asserted against him. . . .

The Michigan courts . . . recogniz[e] as a general matter that parents do not enjoy across-the-board immunity from suits brought against them by their minor children. Most notably, in the seminal case of *Plumley v. Klein*, the Michigan Supreme Court abrogated the common-law doctrine of parental immunity, holding that "[a] child may maintain a lawsuit against his parent for injuries suffered as a result of the alleged ordinary negligence of the parent." The court then adopted two exceptions to this rule, however, stating that the Michigan courts would continue to recognize parental immunity "(1) where the alleged negligent act involves an exercise of reasonable parental authority over the child; and (2) where the alleged negligent act involves an exercise of reasonable parental discretion with respect to the provision of food, clothing, housing, medical and dental services, and other care." Whether conduct falls within one of these two *Plumley* exceptions where parental immunity remains available is a question of law for the court.

In his present motion, Defendant Evans appeals exclusively to the first of these two exceptions. . . . This first *Plumley* exception has been the subject of a number of decisions by the Michigan Court of Appeals. In *Paige v. Bing Construction Co.,* a two-year-old child died as a result of falling into a hole made by the defendant, Bing Construction. The defendant construction company brought a third-party complaint against the child's parents for negligent supervision, but the Court of Appeals upheld the trial court's dismissal of this third-party complaint. In so ruling, the court . . . concluded that this exception "does apply so as to bar a claim of negligent parental supervision," reasoning that the "parental authority" referred to in *Plumley* extends beyond discipline and "includes the providing of instruction and education so that a child may be aware of dangers to his or her well being. . . ."

Any remaining uncertainty as to the proper scope of the first *Plumley* exception was resolved in the most recent Michigan Court of Appeals decision on this subject, *Mickel v. Wilson*. In *Mickel*, the defendant father was attending a party with his three-year-old daughter, Jordyn, when she drowned in an inland lake. At the time of Jordyn's drowning, the father had left the beach area to use the restroom without specifically asking anyone to watch his daughter, believing that she was not left unattended because several other adults remained in the area. In addition, while the father was aware that Jordyn could not swim without a life preserver and the host of the party announced that life preservers were available, the father did not make his daughter wear one. Against this backdrop, the court found it undisputed that the plaintiff's claims rested upon the theory that the defendant father had "failed to properly supervise Jordyn." Accordingly, the Court of Appeals affirmed the trial court's dismissal of the claims against the father on grounds of parental immunity. . . .

Returning to the present case . . . [i]t is clear that [plaintiff's] allegations are intended to support a theory of negligent parental supervision. The conduct that the complaint identifies as negligent is a father's conduct in failing to properly watch over, warn, and instruct his minor son as he engaged in the hazardous activity of burning trash in a fire. The present facts, therefore, are precisely analogous to the man-made hole in Paige . . . and the drowning in *Mickel*. . . . As uniformly established through the above-cited rulings of the Michigan courts, such claims of negligent supervision are properly viewed as involving the "exercise of reasonable parental authority over [a] child," and thus are barred by parental immunity. . . .

[T]o the extent Plaintiff suggests that the particular conduct engaged in by his father cannot qualify as the exercise of "reasonable parental authority.". . . Michigan courts have emphasized that the [first exception] "requires a determination, not of the reasonableness of defendant's conduct, but rather of the scope of 'reasonable parental authority.'". . . [B]ecause the Court has determined that the type of conduct allegedly engaged in by Defendant Evans qualifies as the "exercise of reasonable parental authority," . . . there is no need to inquire whether this conduct was reasonable. . . .

For the reasons set forth above . . . IT IS HEREBY ORDERED that Defendant David Edward Evans' March 30, 2011 motion for summary judgment is GRANTED.

COMMERCE BANK V. AUGSBURGER, 680 N.E.2d 822 (Ill. App. Ct. 1997). The Illinois Department of Children and Family Services arranged for placement of a three-year-old with foster parents, the defendants here. The defendants allegedly confined the child "in an enclosed space described as the 'upper half of a divided shelf of a wooden cabinet inside a bedroom closet at [their] home with the door closed' and did not supervise or monitor her; as a result, she died of asphyxia and hyperthermia." *Held,* dismissal affirmed. The plaintiff did not allege an intentional tort. Illinois has limited the immunity to cases of parental discretion but "parental discretion in the provision of care includes maintenance of the family home, medical treatment, and supervision of the child." The defendant's conduct, though severe, was the very kind to be protected under this standard.

NOTES

1.   **Parental authority and discretion.** Many states follow the limited-immunity formula applied in *Neel* and *Augsburger*. The rule, which originated in *Goller v. White*, 122 N.W.2d 193 (Wis. 1963), effectively bars most children's claims of negligent parental supervision. The Restatement Second of Torts § 895F approved of this rule but phrased it in terms of a parental privilege for exercising discipline and parental discretion. Are you happy with the application of the formula in *Neel?* In *Augsburger?*

2.   **Limits on parental authority?** If the purpose of the parental authority and discretionary immunity is to "remove as a matter of policy or prudence, certain parenting decisions from the judicially created regulatory regime that is the negligence tort," what result when the parent's alleged negligence is the failure to provide a residential smoke detector required by city ordinance? *See Sepaugh v. LaGrone*, 300 S.W.3d 328 (Tex. App. 2009).

3.   **The reasonable person standard.** Some states have questioned whether a limited-immunity rule is ultimately akin to a full immunity rule. As the Arizona Supreme Court wrote, "Almost everything a parent does in relation to his child involves 'care, custody, and control.'" Those states have also questioned the wisdom of parental immunity, noting the "paradox of parental immunity can be seen if we assume that a neighbor child from across the street was a guest and was injured at the same time and under the same circumstances as [the parent's own child]." In one case due care would have been owed and in the other it would not. Accordingly, a few courts have said that parents may be liable to children under a reasonable person (or "reasonable parent") standard. *See Broadbent v. Broadbent,* 907 P.2d 43 (Ariz. 1995); *Anderson v. Stream*, 295 N.W.2d 595 (Minn. 1980). Under this standard, the test of the reasonableness of the parent's conduct is "what would an ordinarily reasonable and prudent parent have done in similar circumstances?" *Gibson v. Gibson*, 479 P.2d 648 (Cal. 1971). Does this demand too much of parents, or fail to recognize their important role in making decisions about care of children?

4.   **Immunity in negligent-supervision cases.** Other courts have moved in the opposite direction, holding parents owe no legally enforceable duty to supervise their children. As New York's court explained, "Each child is different, as is each parent; as to the former, some are to be pampered while some thrive on independence; as to the latter, some trust in their children to use care, others are very cautious. Considering the different economic, educational, cultural, ethnic and religious backgrounds which must prevail, there are so many combinations and permutations of parent-child relationships that may result that the search for a standard would necessarily be in vain—and properly so. . . . [P]arents have always had the right to determine how much independence, supervision and control a child should

have, and to best judge the character and extent of development of their child." *Holodook v. Spencer*, 350 N.Y.S.2d 199 (App. Div. 1973), *quoted with approval on appeal*, 324 N.E.2d 338 (N.Y. 1974). *See also Shoemake v. Fogel, Ltd.*, 826 S.W.2d 933 (Tex. 1992). Thus in *Holodook* there was no liability when a parent failed to control a small child who ran into the street and was struck by a car. New York has at times carried the "inadequate supervision" category to great lengths. In *Nolechek v. Gesuale*, 385 N.E.2d 1268 (N.Y. 1978), the court held that when a father provided a motorcycle to his teenage son, who was blind in one eye and had impaired vision in the other, it was only a case of "parental supervision," in the same way that decision to monitor a child's play is.

HOPPE V. HOPPE, 724 N.Y.S.2d 65 (App. Div. 2001). "The infant plaintiff was entrusted by his father, the defendant herein, with a hammer and a container of nails which contained an 'explosive nail gun cartridge.' He was injured when he struck the cartridge with the hammer, causing the cartridge to explode. [T]he Supreme Court correctly denied his motion for summary judgment dismissing the complaint. While a child may not sue a parent for negligent supervision, the infant plaintiff possesses a cognizable claim that his injuries were proximately caused by the defendant's alleged breach of a duty of care owed to the world at large, one that exists outside of, and apart from, a family relationship. 'The duty not to negligently maintain explosives is a duty owed to all and is not simply a duty emanating from the parent-child relationship.'"

NOTES

1.   **Applications.** A father, knowing his child cannot swim, leaves him alone in the swimming pool. The child is found at the bottom of the pool and rescued, but he suffers brain damage from lack of oxygen. In a suit by the child's guardian against the father, what results (a) under a limited-immunity formula as in *Neel*; (b) under a reasonable-parent standard; or (c) under New York's rule? Which rule is preferable?

2.   **Asserting parental immunity against other parties.** Although the issue of parental immunity is often raised in a direct suit in which the child sues the parent, the issue of immunity can also arise in suits in which the child sues another defendant and that defendant seeks to apportion fault to the parent, or seeks contribution from the parent, based on negligent supervision of the child. *See, e.g., Landis v. Hearthmark, LLC*, 750 S.E.2d 280 (W.Va. 2013) (parental immunity held to preclude defendants from asserting contribution claim against parents, but not to preclude their naming of parents as third-party defendants for fault allocation, where young child was burned while attempting to start a fire in the fireplace using fire starter gel left within reach of the child).

3.   **Foster parents, step-parents, and those standing *in loco parentis*.** Notice that the defendants in *Augsburger* were foster parents.

Courts are somewhat divided as to whether foster parents are entitled to parental immunity. Some courts have given step-parents the same immunity as parents. Still others suggest that anyone who stands *in loco parentis* (in the parent's shoes) should share the parental immunity. *See, e.g., Smith v. Smith*, 922 So.2d 94 (Ala. 2005) (saying that a non-parent stands in such a role when he or she "assumes the obligations incident to parental status" and "voluntarily performs the parental duties to generally provide for the child"). Are such extensions in line with the policies behind the parental immunity in the first place?

4. **Parent-child relationship.** If parental immunity is granted because of the special relationship between parent and child, should the immunity disappear in situations in which the parent-child relationship is minimal? In *Greenwood v. Anderson*, 324 S.W.3d 324 (Ark. 2009), the grandparents of a deceased five-year-old brought a negligence action against the child's father, who had been the driver in the automobile accident that killed the child. Because the suit was not based on the parent's intentional tort, Arkansas' parental immunity rules barred suit. The grandparents argued that Michael's father was a parent "in only the loosest sense" because he "failed to provide significant financial support to the child" and "spent little of his available time with the child." The court determined that the parental immunity defense did not depend on a significant relationship between parent and child and that inquiries into particular parent-child relationships would be a "highly subjective and ultimately undesirable" approach. Do categorical determinations promote administrative ease? Fairness in individual cases? Both?

§ 2. CHARITIES

Traditional rule. Beginning in the mid-nineteenth century, in response to an English decision, most American states adopted the view that charities were not liable in tort. This included virtually all "non-profit" organizations, such as hospitals, the Boy Scouts, the YWCA and many others; hospitals were by far the most important. The idea initially was that tort liability would divert trust funds from their intended charitable purpose.

Exceptions. This rule followed a development that is by now familiar. First a number of exceptions were developed, with varying emphasis and acceptance in each state:

(1) The charity was not exempt from liability as to non-trust funds. Charities would be liable to the extent that insurance or other free funds were available to pay the judgment.

(2) Some jurisdictions had phrased the rule by saying that the charity would not be liable for the negligence of its servants. Thus the hospital would not be liable for the negligence of the orderly who left a slippery substance on the floor. However, the view was developed that the charity

could somehow act "itself" rather than through agents or servants if it acted through its top administrators. In this view, if the hospital administrator had been negligent in hiring a dangerous orderly who was likely to and did attack patients, the hospital would not enjoy an immunity. This is sometimes called "administrative negligence."

(3)   The charity could not claim the immunity against those who paid for its services. So, for example, a hospital could not claim an immunity as to a paying patient, but could as to a "charity" patient. This was often expressed as a rule that beneficiaries of the charity's work were barred by the immunity, but others were not.

(4)   The charity could not claim an immunity as to its collateral commercial activities. Thus the YMCA ski trip, for which fees were charged, would not be protected by an immunity.

(5)   Intentional or "reckless" torts were not protected by the immunity in some states.

General abolition of immunity, with some dissenters. The Restatement (Second) of Torts § 895E (1979), states the rule that there is no charitable immunity, and most states have abolished it entirely, some by statute and some by judicial decision. However, some states retain the immunity, causing litigation over exceptions or over factors in a complicated analysis to determine whether the immunity applies in a particular case. *See, e.g., Byrd Theatre Foundation v. Barnett*, 754 S.E.2d 299 (Va. 2014); *O'Connell v. State*, 795 A.2d 857 (N.J. 2002); *George v. Jefferson Hosp. Ass'n*, 987 S.W.2d 710 (Ark. 1999). A few states have retained the charitable immunity for negligent torts, but not for intentional torts or willful or wanton acts. *See, e.g., Picher v. Roman Catholic Bishop of Portland,* 974 A.2d 286 (Maine 2009).

Hospitals. The statutes of some states abolish the immunity only as to particular charities such as hospitals. But given the modern functioning of hospitals, which may offer various services to the community beyond the mere provision of medical care, questions may arise whether the hospital should be granted absolute immunity retained for institutions organized for *charitable or educational* services, despite a statute allowing for limited liability for institutions organized for *hospital* services. *See, e.g., Kuchera v. Jersey Shore Family Health Center,* 111 A.3d 84 (N.J. 2015) (hospital not absolutely immune in suit by plaintiff who slipped and fell while attending a free eye screening; the purpose of the institution, not the use to which the facility is put to any given day, is determinative).

Damages caps. Other statutes abolish charitable immunity but cap damages in cases in which the tort involved activities in furtherance of charitable purposes. *See, e.g.,* MASS. GEN. LAWS ANN. 231 § 85K ($20,000 cap). Does that kind of statute raise concerns? *See English v. New England Medical Center, Inc.,* 541 N.E.2d 329 (Mass. 1989).

Individuals engaged in charitable activities. The traditional charitable immunity protected the charity itself in its form as a trust or corporation, but did not protect individuals who were engaged in its activities. A number of contemporary statutes provide some kind of limitation on the duty of various individuals associated with charities or even with individual charitable acts; the medical Good Samaritan statutes (Chapter 13) may be seen as an example. Some others are quite specific in identifying the specially privileged or protected group. For example, volunteers in various community sports programs may be singled out for protection.

Broader yet, some states have enacted statutes protecting all volunteers who assist non-profit corporations. *See, e.g., Ex parte Dixon Mills Volunteer Fire Dept., Inc.*, 181 So.3d 325 (Ala. 2015) (applying Volunteer Service Act; assistant fire chief of volunteer fire department was immune from negligence suit and was not liable where he did not act willfully or wantonly in causing a traffic accident). A federal statute provides absolute immunity for volunteers who work for non-profit corporations, then recognizes some exceptions. *See* 42 U.S.C.A. § 14503(a)(3). An interesting twist on this statute is that it protects volunteers working for any non-profit organization that escapes income taxes under the Internal Revenue Code, 26 U.S.C.A. § 501(c). That includes a number of organizations you might not think of as charities, such as the Chamber of Commerce.

REFERENCES: DOBBS, HAYDEN & BUBLICK, HORNBOOK ON TORTS §§ 23.1–23.2 (family members) & §§ 23.3–23.4 (charities) (2d ed. 2016); 2 DOBBS, HAYDEN & BUBLICK, THE LAW OF TORTS §§ 357–359 (family immunities); §§ 360–361 (charitable immunity) (2d ed. 2010).

CHAPTER 15

GOVERNMENTAL ENTITIES, OFFICERS AND EMPLOYEES

■ ■ ■

§ 1. TRADITIONAL IMMUNITIES AND THEIR PASSING: AN OVERVIEW

1. *Governmental tort immunity.* The English common law said "The King can do no wrong," an ambiguous statement that ultimately was taken to mean that one could not sue government in tort. This idea was carried over to America and perpetuated even after the American Revolution, with the result that the federal government and the states were immune from tort actions. This immunity extends to all their agencies unless statutes provide otherwise. In addition to this general "sovereign immunity" of the federal and state governments, the Eleventh Amendment of the United States Constitution has been construed to immunize states from being sued in federal court.

2. *Taking of property.* One important qualification to the governmental immunity is that under the Due Process clauses of the Fifth and Fourteenth Amendments of the United States Constitution, neither state nor federal governments may "take" private property for public purposes without just compensation.

3. *Tribal sovereign immunity.* "Indian tribes are domestic dependent nations that exercise sovereign authority over their members and territories. Suits against Indian tribes are thus barred by sovereign immunity absent a clear waiver by the tribe or congressional abrogation." *Okla. Tax Comm'n v. Citizen Band Potawatomi Indian Tribe of Oklahoma*, 498 U.S. 505 (1991); *see also Kiowa Tribe of Oklahoma v. Mfg. Techs., Inc.*, 523 U.S. 751 (1998) ("As a matter of federal law, an Indian tribe is subject to suit only where Congress has authorized the suit or the tribe has waived its immunity."). The lower courts have applied sovereign immunity to bar almost all tort claims against Indian tribes. *See, e.g., Furry v. Miccosukee Tribe of Indians of Florida*, 685 F.3d 1224 (11th Cir. 2012) (barring tort claim against tribe that owned and operated gambling and resort facility and allegedly, in violation of state liquor laws, knowingly sold excessive amounts of alcohol to a woman who died in an auto accident after leaving the facility).

4. *Municipal immunity*. Municipalities and other local entities are not "sovereigns." Rather, they are corporations chartered by the sovereign. They were traditionally accorded immunity nonetheless, but over the years, courts freely created various exceptions. Municipalities were and are of course liable for takings of property. But additionally, courts made them liable for nuisances such as unsanitary garbage dumps, and for torts committed in the course of proprietary activities, as distinct from governmental activities. For example, a city might be liable for negligence in the operation of a city-owned electrical company. Cities were also held liable in many states for negligent failure to maintain streets properly. Most states have now substantially limited municipal liability by statute.

5. *State government immunity*. New York State waived its sovereign immunity in 1929. Most states lagged behind for many years, but in the 1960s and 1970s, a number state courts and legislatures moved to limit or abolish state government immunity. Today most states have enacted broad waivers of immunity by statute, although many have retained some significant areas of immunity.

6. *Federal government immunity*. The federal government's immunity from tort suit eventually became a nuisance to the Congress because citizens who were denied access to courts often sought a recovery from their Congressperson via a "private bill" awarding compensation. Such bills consumed a good deal of Congressional time. To minimize time loss, Congress finally passed the Federal Tort Claims Act (FTCA) in 1946, in effect turning over many such claims to the judicial process. As we will see in the next section, the FTCA waived the federal government's immunity from tort suits, but did not do so completely.

§ 2. THE FEDERAL TORT CLAIMS ACT

A. THE GENERAL STRUCTURE OF THE FTCA

UNITED STATES V. OLSON
546 U.S. 43 (2005)

JUSTICE BREYER delivered the opinion of the Court.

The Federal Tort Claims Act (FTCA or Act) authorizes private tort actions against the United States "under circumstances where the United States, if a private person, would be liable to the claimant in accordance with the law of the place where the act or omission occurred." 28 U.S.C. § 1346(b)(1). We here interpret these words to mean what they say, [a]nd we reverse a line of Ninth Circuit precedent permitting courts in certain circumstances to base a waiver simply upon a finding that local law would make a "state or municipal entity" liable.

In this case, two injured mine workers (and a spouse) have sued the United States claiming that the negligence of federal mine inspectors helped bring about a serious accident at an Arizona mine. The Federal District Court dismissed the lawsuit in part upon the ground that their allegations were insufficient to show that Arizona law would impose liability upon a private person in similar circumstances. The Ninth Circuit, in a brief *per curiam* opinion, reversed this determination. It reasoned from two premises. First, where "unique governmental functions" are at issue, the Act waives sovereign immunity if "a state or municipal entity would be [subject to liability] under the law [. . .] where the activity occurred." Second, federal mine inspections being regulatory in nature are such "unique governmental functions," since "there is no private-sector analogue for mine inspections." The Circuit then held that Arizona law would make "state or municipal entities" liable in the circumstances alleged; hence the FTCA waives the United States' sovereign immunity. We disagree with both of the Ninth Circuit's legal premises.

The first premise is too broad, for it reads into the Act something that is not there. The Act says that it waives sovereign immunity "under circumstances where the United States, if a *private person*," not "the United States, if a state or municipal entity," would be liable. Our cases have consistently adhered to this "private person" standard. In *Indian Towing Co. v. United States*, 350 U.S. 61, 64 (1955), this Court rejected the Government's contention that there was "no liability for negligent performance of 'uniquely governmental functions.' " It held that the Act requires a court to look to the state-law liability of private entities, not to that of public entities, when assessing the Government's liability under the FTCA "in the performance of activities which private persons do not perform." . .

The Ninth Circuit's second premise rests upon a reading of the Act that is too narrow. The Act makes the United States liable "in the same manner and to the same extent as a private individual under *like circumstances*." 28 U.S.C. § 2674 (emphasis added). As this Court said in *Indian Towing*, the words "like circumstances" do not restrict a court's inquiry to the *same circumstances,* but require it to look further afield. The Court there considered a claim that the Coast Guard, responsible for operating a lighthouse, had failed "to check" the light's "battery and sun relay system," had failed "to make a proper examination" of outside "connections," had "fail[ed] to check the light" on a regular basis, and had failed to "repair the light or give warning that the light was not operating." These allegations, the Court held, were analogous to allegations of negligence by a private person "who undertakes to warn the public of danger and thereby induces reliance." It is "hornbook tort law," the Court added, that such a person "must perform his 'good Samaritan' task in a careful manner."

The Government in effect concedes that similar "good Samaritan" analogies exist for the conduct at issue here. It says that "there are private persons in 'like circumstances' " to federal mine inspectors, namely "private persons who conduct safety inspections." Reply Brief for United States 3. . . . [As we said in *Indian Towing*,] private individuals, who do not operate lighthouses, nonetheless may create a relationship with third parties that is similar to the relationship between a lighthouse operator and a ship dependent on the lighthouse's beacon. The Ninth Circuit should have looked for a similar analogy in this case.

Despite the Government's concession that a private person analogy exists in this case, the parties disagree about precisely which Arizona tort law doctrine applies here. We remand the case so that the lower courts can decide this matter in the first instance. The judgment of the Ninth Circuit is vacated, and the case is remanded for proceedings consistent with this opinion.

NOTES

1.   **Some key conditions of the waiver**. The FTCA is a broad waiver of sovereign immunity, but the statute itself contains a number of conditions. For example, before filing a suit in court the plaintiff must submit the claim to the government agency involved; suit is not permitted until the agency has refused payment or has delayed over six months in making a decision on it. Courts lack jurisdiction over suits filed prematurely. *See, e.g., Turner v. United States*, 514 F.3d 1194 (11th Cir. 2008). The statute also specifies that cases may be brought only in federal court, not state court. Neither side may have a jury; all FTCA trials are bench trials.

2.   **Governing law.** Although FTCA claims against the government must be brought in federal court, the substantive law that governs claims under the FTCA is *not* federal law. Instead, the FTCA itself requires the court to follow the law of the state in which the alleged tort occurred. 28 U.S.C.A. § 1346(b)(1). As you can see from *Olson*, this means that the outcome of a particular FTCA case may vary depending on the state in which the tort occurred. *See, e.g., Nelson v. United States*, 827 F.3d 927 (10th Cir. 2016) (U.S. immune from suit by bicyclist who fell into sinkhole, where Colorado Recreational Use Act would provide an immunity if a private person were sued for the same conduct).

3.   **Analogous private liability.** *Olson* clarifies that courts must look for analogies to private-person liability as a starting point in FTCA cases. The inquiry has two components. First, the plaintiff's cause of action against the government must be comparable to a cause of action against a private citizen that is recognized in the state in which the tort occurred. If there is no comparable cause of action, then the government cannot be liable under the FTCA. *See, e.g., McGowan v. United States*, 825 F.3d 118 (2d Cir. 2016) (under New York law, private citizens could not be held liable for the kind of wrongful

confinement alleged by plaintiff; "[p]rivate persons cannot establish facilities to detain other persons"). Second, even where there *is* a private analog, if a private person would not be liable under state law for engaging in the analogous activity, then the government is not liable, either. *See, e.g., In re FEMA Trailer Formaldehyde Products Liability Litigation (Mississippi Plaintiffs)*, 668 F.3d 281 (5th Cir. 2012) (because state statutes abrogate the liability of a private person who allows his property to be used without compensation in a natural disaster, the government's provision of trailers to hurricane victims is also immunized under the FTCA).

4. **Specific statutory exceptions for particular activities**. The statute itself lays out a number of specific instances in which the government is not liable, that is, in which the immunity is retained. One set of exceptions retains the immunity for specific governmental activities (combatant activities of the military and delivery of mail, for example) and for all claims arising in foreign countries. These exceptions have typically been read broadly, in favor of immunity. *See, e.g., Sosa v. Alvarez-Machain*, 542 U.S. 692 (2004) (holding that the "foreign country" exception bars all claims against the federal government based on any injury suffered in a foreign country, no matter where the alleged tortious act or omission giving rise to that injury occurred).

5. **Specific statutory exceptions for particular torts**. Another set of provisions in the statute retains the government's immunity for a number of specific torts, mostly those of a dignitary or economic kind. These include those "arising out of" assault, battery, false imprisonment, malicious prosecution, abuse of process, libel, slander, misrepresentation and interference with contract.

The immunity for assault, battery, and the like is not without its limits. First, the phrase "arising out of" is open to judicial interpretation, and may be interpreted narrowly in some cases. *See, e.g., Limone v. United States*, 579 F.3d 79 (1st Cir. 2009) (allowing intentional infliction of emotional distress claim even where government contended that it arose out of a malicious prosecution). Second, under the FTCA itself, the government may be liable for the assault, battery, or false imprisonment if it is committed by "investigative or law enforcement officers." Finally, if an *off-duty* employee commits a battery, the government might be liable for its negligence in fostering the risk.

6. **Judicially created exceptions.** The Court has construed the FTCA to permit liability of the government only for the negligent or other "wrongful" acts of government employees. Strict liability, even when a private individual would be strictly liable, is not permitted. *See Laird v. Nelms*, 406 U.S. 797 (1972). However, Congress can still appropriate funds directly to compensate for harm without fault. *See Land v. United States*, 29 Fed. Cl. 744 (Cl. Ct. 1993). Another judge-made exception, the so-called *Feres* doctrine, which bars active military personnel from suing the government for injuries suffered "incident to service," is considered in Part C below.

B. DISCRETIONARY IMMUNITY

WHISNANT V. UNITED STATES
400 F.3d 1177 (9th Cir. 2005)

BETTY B. FLETCHER, CIRCUIT JUDGE.

[Plaintiff-appellant Lorrin Whisnant worked for a company that provided seafood to the commissary on a Naval base. The commissary is operated by a government agency, DeCA. DeCA regulations require periodic safety inspections, but DeCA employees are allowed to decide how and when to conduct such inspections. The base contracts out maintenance work to Johnson Controls. Johnson Controls inspections showed in June, 1997, that mold had accumulated in the meat department of the commissary. Over the next three years, several employees and customers became ill. Tests conducted in October 2000 proved that toxic molds were present, and government closed the meat department shortly thereafter.]

As a result of his exposure to the mold prior to the closure of the meat department, Whisnant contracted pneumonia, and experienced headaches, swollen glands, sore throat, persistent cough, and other health problems. [He sued the government under the FTCA for damages for its negligence in allowing workers and customers to come into contact with the mold despite known health hazards.] The government moved to dismiss . . . on the ground that Whisnant's suit was barred by the discretionary function exception to the FTCA, 28 U.S.C. § 2680(a) (providing that the FTCA shall not apply to "[a]ny claim . . . based upon the exercise or performance or the failure to exercise or perform a discretionary function or duty on the part of a federal agency or an employee of the Government, whether or not the discretion involved be abused"). The district court granted the motion to dismiss. . . .

As the district court correctly noted, the Supreme Court has prescribed a two-part test for determining the applicability of the discretionary function exception. *See United States v. Gaubert,* 499 U.S. 315, 322–25 (1991); *Berkovitz v. United States,* 486 U.S. 531, 536–37 (1988). Courts are to ask first whether the challenged action was a discretionary one—i.e., whether it was governed by a mandatory statute, policy, or regulation. If the action is not discretionary, it cannot be shielded under the discretionary function exception. Second, courts ask whether the challenged action is of the type Congress meant to protect—i.e., whether the action involves a decision susceptible to social, economic, or political policy analysis. It is the government's burden to demonstrate the applicability of the discretionary function exception.

Application of the first prong is straightforward in Whisnant's case. No statute, policy, or regulation prescribed the specific manner in which the commissary was to be inspected or a specific course of conduct for addressing mold. The parties are in agreement on this point.

The dispute in this case concerns the application of the second *Gaubert/Berkovitz* prong. We have recently remarked upon the difficulty of charting a clear path through the weaving lines of precedent regarding what decisions are susceptible to social, economic, or political policy analysis. Government actions can be classified along a spectrum, ranging from those "totally divorced from the sphere of policy analysis," such as driving a car, to those "fully grounded in regulatory policy," such as the regulation and oversight of a bank. But determining the appropriate place on the spectrum for any given government action can be a challenge.

We begin by noting the lines of analysis that are foreclosed. Specifically, the Supreme Court has rejected two categorical approaches to this area of law. First, the applicability of the exception does not depend on whether the relevant decision was made by an individual at the "operational" or "planning" level. Second, actions that are regulatory or "uniquely governmental" in nature are not automatically covered by the exception by virtue of that designation.

A review of circuit precedent reveals two trends in the law that bear particularly on Whisnant's case. First, a dominant theme in our case law is the need to distinguish between design and implementation: we have generally held that the *design* of a course of governmental action is shielded by the discretionary function exception, whereas the *implementation* of that course of action is not. Second, and relatedly, matters of scientific and professional judgment—particularly judgments concerning safety—are rarely considered to be susceptible to social, economic, or political policy.

Thus, for example, in a suit alleging government negligence in the design and maintenance of a national park road, we held that designing the road without guardrails was a choice grounded in policy considerations and was therefore shielded under the discretionary function exception, but maintaining the road was a safety responsibility not susceptible to policy analysis. Similarly, in a suit alleging government negligence in the design and construction of an irrigation canal, we held that the decision not to line the canal with concrete was susceptible to policy analysis, but the failure to remove unsuitable materials during construction was not. . . . And in an action for the death of a prospective logger "trying out" for a job with a government contractor at a logging site under the management of a government agency, we held that while the government's authorization of the contract was protected under the discretionary function exception, the government's failure to monitor and ensure safety at the work site was not. . . .

Under these principles, Whisnant's suit is not barred by the discretionary function exception. Whisnant does not allege that the government was negligent in designing its safety inspection procedures; rather, he charges that the government was negligent in following through on those procedures to safeguard the health of employees and customers of the Bangor commissary. Like the government's duties to maintain its roads in safe condition, to ensure the use of suitable materials in its building projects, and to monitor the safety of its logging sites, the government's duty to maintain its grocery store as a safe and healthy environment for employees and customers is not a policy choice of the type the discretionary function exception shields. Cleaning up mold involves professional and scientific judgment, not decisions of social, economic, or political policy. Indeed, the crux of our holdings on this issue is that a failure to adhere to accepted professional standards is not susceptible to a policy analysis. Because removing an obvious health hazard is a matter of safety and not policy, the government's alleged failure to control the accumulation of toxic mold in the Bangor commissary cannot be protected under the discretionary function exception.

The government argues that implementation of the DeCA regulations regarding health and safety required employees "to balance the agency's goal of occupational safety against such resource constraints as costs and funding." In addressing government negligence in the implementation of safety precautions, we have several times rejected this precise argument. . . . [I]n *O'Toole v. United States,* we held that the discretionary function exception did not apply to a claim for private property damage resulting from the government's failure to maintain an irrigation ditch on its own property. . . . [W]e explained:

> The danger that the discretionary function exception will swallow the FTCA is especially great where the government takes on the role of a private landowner. Every slip and fall, every failure to warn, *every inspection and maintenance decision* can be couched in terms of policy choices based on allocation of limited resources. . . . Were we to view inadequate funding alone as sufficient to garner the protection of the discretionary function exception, we would read the rule too narrowly and the exception too broadly.

Like the plaintiffs in *O'Toole,* Whisnant is alleging that government negligence in the maintenance of its own property caused his injuries. Following *O'Toole,* then, we decline to permit the government to use the mere presence of budgetary concerns to shield allegedly negligent conduct from suit under the FTCA. To hold otherwise would permit the discretionary function exception to all but swallow the Federal Tort Claims Act. . . .

[T]he question of *how* the government is alleged to have been negligent is critical. If Whisnant were claiming that the government was negligent in electing to employ contractors rather than doing the work itself, or in designing its safety regulations, then his claim would most likely be barred; instead, he is claiming that the government negligently ignored health hazards that were called to its attention, and so his claim is not barred. Because it failed to recognize the import of this distinction, the district court mischaracterized Whisnant's allegations and thereby erred in dismissing his action.

While the government has discretion to decide how to carry out its responsibility to maintain safe and healthy premises, it does not have discretion to abdicate its responsibility in this regard. When it does so, the discretionary function exception cannot shield the government from FTCA liability for its negligent conduct. . . .

In this case, Whisnant has alleged negligence in the implementation, rather than the design, of government safety regulations, and the governmental decisions Whisnant claims were negligent concerned *Conclusion* technical and professional judgments about safety rather than broad questions of social, economic, or political policy. Therefore, the discretionary function exception to the FTCA does not bar Whisnant's suit.

We reverse the district court's dismissal of the action and remand for further proceedings consistent with this opinion.

NOTES

1. **Purposes of the discretionary immunity.** Why did Congress retain federal immunity for discretionary functions? In *United States v. Varig Airlines*, 467 U.S. 797 (1984), the Court explained that the discretionary immunity "marks the boundary between Congress' willingness to impose tort liability on the United States and its desire to protect certain governmental activities from exposure to suit by private individuals." Discretionary immunity is designed "to prevent judicial 'second-guessing' of legislative and administrative decisions grounded in social, economic, and political policy through the medium of an action in tort." Other courts have said that the immunity's purpose is in "keeping the judiciary out of the business of reviewing policy judgments by government employees." *Shuler v. United States*, 531 F.3d 930 (D.C. Cir. 2008). Why prevent the judiciary from passing on the legality of the policy-based actions of the other branches of government?

2. **Planning-level vs. operational-level decisions.** Federal courts once routinely drew immunity lines according to whether government decisions were made at the "planning level," in which case they immune, or at the "operational level," in which case they were not. But in *United States v. Gaubert*, 499 U.S. 315 (1991), the Court said, "It is the nature of the conduct, rather than the status of the actor, that governs whether the discretionary function exception applies in a given case." Thus a low-level government employee might select a course of action that would be considered discretionary, or a higher-level official might merely implement a policy, which

would not be immunized from liability. But where higher-ups are exercising "judgment," the discretionary function immunity is likely to be found.

3. **Property maintenance.** Decisions about routine property maintenance, even if they involve some element of choice, are usually not susceptible to policy analysis. *See, e.g., Gibson v. United States*, 809 F.3d 807 (5th Cir. 2016); *Young v. United States*, 769 F.3d 1047 (9th Cir. 2014). But does this mean that the government's failure to maintain property or buildings would never be protected by discretionary immunity? In *Terbush v. United States*, 516 F.3d 1125 (9th Cir. 2008), the court agreed that "matters of routine maintenance are not protected . . . because they generally do not involve policy-weighing decisions or actions." But the court added that "sometimes 'maintenance' is far from routine and may involve considerable discretion that invokes policy judgment." Especially where maintenance decisions require a federal agency "to prioritize among its repairs," or choose between maintenance and doing something else entirely, such decisions may implicate policy concerns. *Id.*

4. **Funding decisions.** Is it relevant to a determination of the scope of discretionary immunity that a challenged governmental decision was based partially on fiscal concerns? Does the *Whisnant* court say it is not? *Cf. Merando v. United States*, 517 F.3d 160 (3d Cir. 2008) (suit against government for failing to find and remove a dead tree that fell on plaintiffs in national park). Judge Posner, in *Collins v. United States*, 564 F.3d 833 (7th Cir. 2009), said that the "prioritization of demands for government money is quintessentially a discretionary function." Does that cut too broadly?

5. **Where the government makes no conscious decision.** In some cases, the government pursues a course of action without having made any conscious decision, either about policy or anything else. If the decision being challenged in the tort case was not actually grounded in policy considerations, but is merely *susceptible* to policy analysis, is that enough to satisfy the discretionary-function test? The Court in *Gaubert, supra* Note 2, said this: "The focus of the inquiry is not on the agent's subjective intent in exercising the discretion conferred by statute or regulation, but on the nature of the actions taken and on whether they are susceptible to policy analysis." Based on this language, many courts have held that whether government employees actually took policy objectives into account is irrelevant; to invoke the discretionary immunity, the government needs only to point to some support in the record that the decisions they made *could have been* subjected to a policy analysis. *See, e.g., Chadd v. United States*, 794 F.3d 1104 (9th Cir. 2015) (decision not to destroy a hostile mountain goat in Olympic National Park was susceptible to policy analysis); *Mahon v. United States*, 742 F.3d 11 (1st Cir. 2014) (decision whether to alter height of railing on second story of Commandant's house at Navy Yard was discretionary; the question is whether the exercise or non-exercise of discretion was "actually or potentially" affected by policy-related judgments). Is the "susceptible to policy analysis" approach too protective of the government? A dissenting judge in *Chadd, supra*, criticized the approach

as "bad law"; a concurring judge felt bound by precedent, but complained that the Circuit's interpretation of the approach "has gone off the rails."

NOTE: GOVERNMENT CONTRACTORS

1. *Suit against the government.* The FTCA expressly retains the government's immunity for claims arising out of the acts or omissions of private independent contractors working pursuant to government contracts. *See, e.g., Carroll v. United States,* 661 F.3d 87 (1st Cir. 2011) (FTCA immunizes government from liability for alleged negligence of a childcare facility on property owned by government, and of a landscaping business hired by the government to maintain that property). As you can see from *Whisnant,* however, the government is not immune *simply because* it contracted with a private party to perform some task; in *Whisnant,* the government hired the plaintiff's company to provide services but itself retained responsibility for implementing and enforcing certain safety measures. The key, then, is often whether the government exerts significant supervision over the contractor's day-to-day operations; if not, then the government may not be held responsible for the independent contractor's negligence. *See United States v. Orleans,* 425 U.S. 807 (1976).

2. *Suit against the contractor.* Whether the government contractor itself can assert the governmental immunity to escape liability is an entirely separate question. This is often called the "government contractor defense." In *Yearsley v. W.A. Ross Constr. Co.,* 309 U.S. 18 (1940), the Court held that when "authority to carry out the project was validly conferred" by the government, "there is no liability on the part of the contractor for executing its will." That is, where the government has contracted with a private person or entity to perform some task, and the contractor performs that task in conformity with the terms of the contract, the contractor cannot be liable at all. *See, e.g., Ackerson v. Bean Dredging LLC,* 589 F.3d 196 (5th Cir. 2009) (government contracted with defendants to dredge the Mississippi River; contractors immune).

Contractors have also been held to share the government's immunity for injuries arising out of combat activities, where the contractor has been "integrated" into those activities and is supervised by military commanders. *See, e.g., Saleh v. Titan Corp.,* 580 F.3d 1 (D.C. Cir. 2009) (contractors that provided interrogators to the military were immune from suit by Iraqi prisoners who claimed to have been tortured); *In re KBR, Inc., Burn Pit Litigation,* 744 F.3d 326 (4th Cir. 2014) (vacating trial court's grant of contractors' motion to dismiss, holding triable issues remained on whether contractors hired to provide waste disposal and water treatment services at military bases in Iraq and Afghanistan were integrated into the military chain of command).

LOGE V. UNITED STATES, 662 F.2d 1268 (8th Cir. 1981). A federal agency licensed a drug company to manufacture a live-virus oral polio vaccine. A risk of such vaccines is that either a recipient or a person who comes in contact with "shed" virus could develop polio. Recognizing that risk, the agency promulgated regulations pertaining to the safety and potency of these strains, and required drug manufacturers to prove their product's conformity to these regulations before getting a license to manufacture. Mrs. Loge was exposed to the virus and rendered a paraplegic after a doctor inoculated her infant son. She filed an FTCA action alleging that the government was negligent (1) in not requiring the drug manufacturer to comply with the government's own regulations and (2) in licensing at all, or in licensing without additional safety regulations.

Held, the first set of allegations state a claim under applicable state law and are not barred by the discretionary function immunity. The government "has no discretion to disregard the mandatory regulatory commands pertaining to criteria a vaccine must meet before licensing its manufacture or releasing a particular lot of vaccine for distribution to the public." However, "[i]nsofar as the Loges' amended complaint alleged that the government was negligent in promulgating or failing to promulgate regulations that would ensure the safety of live, oral poliovirus vaccines and properly protect susceptible persons such as Mrs. Loge, the district court correctly found that such actions by the government were discretionary functions and therefore immune from suit under FTCA."

NOTES

1. **Immunity for legislative inaction.** If a court could impose liability when Congress fails to enact safety legislation, courts, not elected members of the political branch, would have ultimate legislative control. Why would this be a problem?

2. **Violating mandatory regulations.** *Loge* says that the discretionary immunity does not extend to the violation of a "mandatory regulation." Do you see why that is so? *See Myers v. United States*, 652 F.3d 1021 (9th Cir. 2011).

3. **Violating nonmandatory regulations.** If a regulation exists and imposes duties, is it enough for the plaintiff to claim that the government official breached those duties? The focus is on whether the duties imposed are truly mandatory. If a regulation itself allows discretion in how it is to be complied with, then the government is likely entitled to assert the discretionary immunity even in the face of a regulation. *See, e.g., Spotts v. United States*, 613 F.3d 559 (5th Cir. 2010) (prison official's decision not to evacuate federal prisoners during and after a hurricane was protected by discretionary immunity; Bureau of Prisons standards and regulations

allegedly violated were not mandatory); *Indemnity Ins. Co. v. United States*, 569 F.3d 175 (4th Cir. 2009) (immunizing Coast Guard's alleged violations of provisions in Marine Safety Manual); *A. O. Smith Corp. v. United States*, 774 F.3d 359 (6th Cir. 2014) (immunizing Army Corps of Engineers decisions on how to deal with thousand-year flood event in Tennessee). Indeed, the existence of a law, regulation, or policy that allows a government employee the discretion to decide how to act creates a strong presumption that the challenged conduct qualifies as a discretionary function. *See In re Katrina Canal Breaches Litigation*, 696 F.3d 436 (5th Cir. 2012); *Mahon v. United States,* 742 F.3d 11 (1st Cir. 2014).

4. **A case example.** A camper falls off an unmarked and unfenced cliff in a campground on government property managed by the Army Corps of Engineers. A federal regulation requires the government to manage its resources so as to "provide the public with safe and healthful recreational opportunities." The Army Corps' written safety plan for the area includes an instruction that "dangerous terrain conditions, such as drop-offs, etc., will be properly marked or fenced." What is the relevance of the safety plan and regulation, and on what basis could the government be held liable in such a case? *Navarette v. United States*, 500 F.3d 914 (9th Cir. 2007).

C. THE *FERES* DOCTRINE

PURCELL V. UNITED STATES
656 F.3d 463 (7th Cir. 2011)

FLAUM, CIRCUIT JUDGE.

Christopher Lee Purcell ("Purcell") committed suicide in his barracks at the Brunswick Naval Air Station, where he was serving on active duty in the Navy. Navy and Department of Defense ("DOD") personnel were called to the scene after being informed that Purcell planned to kill himself. They arrived at his residence before he attempted suicide, but did not find the gun they were told he had. Later, they permitted Purcell to go to the bathroom accompanied by his friend. Upon entering, he pulled a gun from his waistband and committed suicide by shooting himself in the chest.

After attempting unsuccessfully to recover for Purcell's death from the Navy through administrative procedures, his family sought relief in federal court on a wrongful death claim under the Federal Tort Claims Act ("FTCA"). [The family's complaint alleged "that the United States failed to calm Purcell, to search him in accordance with Navy regulations, to maintain proper custody of him after removing his handcuffs, and to transport him to the Brunswick Naval Air Station security precinct in accordance with the Air Station's standard operating procedures." The complaint also alleged "that the responding officers irritated Purcell with profane, derogatory, and threatening comments that were contrary to standard operating procedures."] The district court found the case barred by the *Feres* doctrine, which provides that "the Government is not liable under the [FTCA] for injuries to servicemen where the injuries arise out of or are in the course of activity incident to service." . . .

Feres
Doctrine ✓

The FTCA provides that "[t]he United States shall be liable, respecting the provisions of this title relating to tort claims, in the same manner and to the same extent as a private individual under like circumstances." Excepted from this waiver of sovereign immunity, however, are claims "arising out of the combatant activities of the military or naval forces, or the Coast Guard, during time of war." 28 U.S.C. § 2680(j). In *Feres v. United States,* 340 U.S. 135 (1950), the Supreme Court further held that "the Government is not liable under the [FTCA] for injuries to servicemen where the injuries arise out of or are in the course of activity incident to service."

The *Feres* doctrine, while currently viable, is certainly not without controversy. It has been interpreted increasingly broadly over time, and has also been widely criticized. In *United States v. Johnson,* 481 U.S. 681 (1987), in a dissent signed by three other Justices, Justice Scalia wrote that "*Feres* was wrongly decided and heartily deserves the widespread, almost universal criticism it has received." But the majority in *Johnson* reaffirmed *Feres*, and the Court has not squarely addressed the doctrine since then. *Feres* thus remains the law until Congress or the Supreme Court decides otherwise.

When the Court reaffirmed *Feres*, it discussed three rationales that support the doctrine: (1) the need to protect the distinctively federal relationship between the government and the armed forces, which could be adversely affected by applying differing tort laws; (2) the existence of statutory compensatory schemes; and (3) the need to avoid interference with military discipline and effectiveness. . . . "The dispositive inquiry [is] whether the service-member stand[s] in the type of relationship to the military at the time of his or her injury that the occurrences causing the injury arose out of activity incident to military service." *Smith v. United States*, 196 F.3d 774 (7th Cir. 1999).

Applying that test, we conclude that the district court correctly dismissed Michael Purcell's suit based on *Feres*. At the time he committed suicide, which occurred in his on-base residential building, Purcell was on active duty; living in the barracks on a military base, experiencing, according to Michael Purcell, various social and emotional problems that developed shortly after he enlisted; and deliberately avoiding Navy and DOD personnel sent to Purcell's barracks to help him, whom Michael Purcell claims failed to follow their own military regulations, and some of whom, he explains, faced courts-martial and were punished via an extrajudicial proceeding for failing to adequately search and supervise Purcell. Together, these facts demonstrate that Purcell stood "in the type of relationship to the military at the time of his . . . injury that the occurrences causing the injury arose out of activity incident to military service," and thus that *Feres* bars his suit. . . .

Michael Purcell's counsel ably, although ultimately unpersuasively, opposes applying *Feres*. Primarily, he argues that Purcell's death had nothing to do with his military status, and that the military connections to the case are irrelevant because Purcell was effectively acting as and treated like a civilian during the relevant events. We disagree. As explained above, *Feres* is read broadly, and Michael Purcell cannot avoid its reach on the facts of this case. Michael Purcell also points out that neither Purcell nor his estate have received benefits related to his suicide. But that alone does not warrant reversal in this case. *See Maas v. United States,* 94 F.3d 291, 295 (7th Cir.1996) ("[T]his and other courts have applied *Feres* to bar claims that are incident to service even if a serviceman is not entitled to military benefits relating to those claims.").

Like many courts and commentators, we recognize the challenges presented by the *Feres* doctrine. In light of its enormous breadth, however, we AFFIRM the judgment of the district court.

NOTES

1. **Broad constructions of *Feres*.** As the *Purcell* court says, the *Feres* doctrine has been broadly construed to bar claims by active military personnel. *See, e.g., Kitowski v. United States,* 931 F.2d 1526 (11th Cir. 1991) (military trainer brutally held a recruit under water until he died); *United States v. Stanley,* 483 U.S. 669 (1987) (government conducted LSD experiments upon serviceman without informing him of risks; held to be "incident to service"). It also applies to bar claims brought for violation of Constitutional rights rather than for violation of state tort law. *Chappell v. Wallace,* 462 U.S. 296 (1983).

2. **"Incident to service."** *Feres* formally covers only those injuries that are "incident to service," seemingly on the assumption that the policy reasons advanced for rejecting liability more or less automatically apply when injury is incident to service and do not apply otherwise. *See Taber v. Maine,* 67 F.3d 1029 (2d Cir. 1995). Exactly what "incident to service" means is not clear. For example, sometimes a service member injured while on furlough will be found to have not been injured incident to service, *see, e.g., Schoenfeld v. Quamme,* 492 F.3d 1016 (9th Cir. 2007), whereas sometimes a soldier injured on furlough will be barred by *Feres* on exactly that ground, *see United States v. Shearer,* 473 U.S. 52 (1985). A soldier injured while on leave but still on active duty, however, is usually injured incident to service. *See, e.g., McConnell v. United States,* 478 F.2d 1092 (9th Cir. 2007) (*Feres* barred claim for death of Air Force pilot killed while waterskiing on Air Force base). Perhaps our best overall doctrinal summary is that *Feres* will not protect the government "if government negligence occurs when the plaintiff has no active connection with the military," with the caveat that "courts have usually interpreted 'incident

to service' quite broadly." 2 DOBBS, HAYDEN & BUBLICK, THE LAW OF TORTS § 338 (2d ed. 2011).

3. **The breadth of the "military discipline" rationale.** The term "military discipline" has been also given an extremely broad reading in *Feres* doctrine cases. In *United States v. Johnson*, 481 U.S. 681 (1987), a Coast Guard pilot, flying under the control of a civilian FAA controller, was killed in a crash. The surviving spouse asserted that the FAA was negligent in causing the death. The Court applied the *Feres* immunity, partly because "a suit based upon service-related activity necessarily implicates the military judgment and decisions" and "military discipline involves not only obedience to orders, but more generally duty and loyalty to one's service and to one's country. Suits brought by service members against the Government for service-related injuries could undermine the commitment essential to effective service and thus have the potential to disrupt military discipline in the broadest sense of the word."

4. **Criticisms of *Feres*.** The *Purcell* court notes that the *Feres* doctrine has been criticized, most famously in Justice Scalia's dissent in *Johnson*, *supra* Note 3. More recently, Justice Thomas, dissenting from the Court's denial of certiorari in *Lanus v. United States*, 133 S.Ct. 2731 (2013), expressed his agreement with Justice Scalia's view. *Feres* should be "reconsidered," he wrote, because it lacks support in the text of the FTCA and "has the unfortunate consequence of depriving servicemen of any remedy when they are injured by the negligence of the Government or its employees." Does the *Feres* doctrine reflect good public policy?

5. **Spouses and children.** *Feres* does not usually bar a recovery by a spouse or child of a person in the armed forces if the spouse or child is directly injured. Common examples of recovery by spouses or children are those involving medical malpractice in military hospitals. But even in this setting, *Feres* may bar the claim if the family member's injury had its "genesis" in an incident-to-service injury to the service person. *Ritchie v. United States*, 733 F.3d 871 (9th Cir. 2013). For example, where a newborn suffered brain injuries from lack of oxygen during childbirth, which was caused by an allegedly negligent administration of medication to her mother, an active-duty Air Force officer, the child's injury had its genesis in the mother's injury, which was "incident to service," thus barring the child's claim under *Feres*. *Ortiz v. United States*, 786 F.3d 817 (10th Cir. 2015).

§ 3. STATE AND MUNICIPAL GOVERNMENT IMMUNITY UNDER STATE LAW

In our system of government, the states are sovereigns, too, subject only to the limitations of the United States Constitution. At one time the states claimed sovereign immunity on the same basis as did the federal government. Most states now have now enacted tort claims statutes that provide for at least a partial waiver of sovereign immunity. As a matter of structure, most states follow the federal model (often copying from the FTCA) and waive the tort immunity generally, retaining it in particular, specified situations. A smaller, but still significant number work in reverse, retaining the immunity generally but abolishing it in particular, specified situations. Both kinds of statutes do retain substantial blocks of immunity for the states. A small number retain virtually complete immunity. Most states have special procedural rules and remedial restrictions on tort claims against the state. *See* 2 DOBBS, HAYDEN & BUBLICK, THE LAW OF TORTS § 342 (2d ed. 2011).

Municipalities within the states are sometimes covered under state tort claims statutes, so that municipal immunity parallels state government immunity. Other states have separate immunity rules for municipalities.

While generalization is difficult, a number of important issues recur in tort litigation against state and local entities under state law. Some of these issues parallel those faced in FTCA actions against the federal government; others are more or less unique to the non-federal setting—in part because of the different functions for which different levels of government are typically responsible.

RISS V. CITY OF NEW YORK
240 N.E.2d 860 (N.Y. 1968)

[Linda Riss was terrorized for months by a rejected suitor, Burton Pugach. He threatened to kill or maim her if she did not yield to him. She repeatedly sought protection from law enforcement officers. Eventually she became engaged to another man. At a party celebrating the event, she received a phone call warning her that it was her "last chance." She again called police, but nothing seems to have been done. The next day Pugach carried out his threat by having a person hired for the purpose to throw lye in Linda's face. She was blinded in one eye, lost a good portion of her vision in the other and suffered permanent scarring of her face. This is her action against the City of New York for failure to provide police protection. The trial court dismissed the complaint at the end of all the evidence and the Appellate Division affirmed.]

BREITEL, JUDGE.

This appeal presents, in a very sympathetic framework, the issue of the liability of a municipality for failure to provide special protection to a member of the public who was repeatedly threatened with personal harm and eventually suffered dire personal injuries for lack of such protection. . . .

It is necessary immediately to distinguish those liabilities attendant upon governmental activities which have displaced or supplemented

[handwritten margin note: Non-feasance / Police or third party did not create the risk]

[handwritten note at bottom: Analogous to police private security]

traditionally private enterprises, such as are involved in the operation of rapid transit systems, hospitals, and places of public assembly. Once sovereign immunity was abolished by statute the extension of liability on ordinary principles of tort law logically followed. To be equally distinguished are certain activities of government which provide services and facilities for the use of the public, such as highways, public buildings and the like, in the performance of which the municipality or the State may be liable under ordinary principles of tort law. The ground for liability is the provision of the services or facilities for the direct use of members of the public. In contrast, this case involves the provision of a governmental service to protect the public generally from external hazards and particularly to control the activities of criminal wrongdoers.

The amount of protection that may be provided is limited by the resources of the community and by a considered legislative-executive decision as to how those resources may be deployed. For the courts to proclaim a new and general duty of protection in the law of tort, even to those who may be the particular seekers of protection based on specific hazards, could and would inevitably determine how the limited police resources of the community should be allocated and without predictable limits. This is quite different from the predictable allocation of resources and liabilities when public hospitals, rapid transit systems, or even highways are provided.

Before such extension of responsibilities should be dictated by the indirect imposition of tort liabilities, there should be a legislative determination that that should be the scope of public responsibility.

It is notable that the removal of sovereign immunity for tort liability was accomplished after legislative enactment and not by any judicial arrogation of power. It is equally notable that for many years, since as far back as 1909, in this State, there was by statute municipal liability for losses sustained as a result of riot. Yet even this class of liability has for some years been suspended by legislative action, a factor of considerable significance. When one considers the greatly increased amount of crime committed throughout the cities, but especially in certain portions of them, with a repetitive and predictable pattern, it is easy to see the consequences of fixing municipal liability upon a showing of probable need for and request for protection. To be sure these are grave problems at the present time, exciting high priority activity on the part of the national, State and local governments, to which the answers are neither simple, known, or presently within reasonable controls. To foist a presumed cure for these problems by judicial innovation of a new kind of liability in tort would be foolhardy indeed and an assumption of judicial wisdom and power not possessed by the courts.

Nor is the analysis progressed by the analogy to compensation for losses sustained. It is instructive that the Crime Victims Compensation and "Good Samaritan" statutes, compensating limited classes of victims of crime, were enacted only after the most careful study of conditions and the impact of such a scheme upon governmental operations and the public fisc. And then the limitations were particular and narrow.

For all of these reasons, there is no warrant in judicial tradition or in the proper allocation of the powers of government for the courts, in the absence of legislation, to carve out an area of tort liability for police protection to members of the public. Quite distinguishable, of course, is the situation where the police authorities undertake responsibilities to particular members of the public and expose them, without adequate protection, to the risks which then materialize into actual losses (Schuster v. City of New York, 5 N.Y.2d 75,180 N.Y.S.2d 265,154 N.E.2d 534).

Accordingly, the order of the Appellate Division affirming the judgment of dismissal should be affirmed.

DE LONG v. COUNTY OF ERIE, 457 N.E.2d 717 (N.Y. 1983). At 9:29 Mrs. De Long called the 911 emergency number covering all cities and towns in Erie County, New York. She reported that someone was attempting to break in and gave her address. The "complaint writer" assured her someone would come right away. Since her own local police station in the town of Kenmore was only a block and a half away, assistance might have been readily available except for the fact that the complaint writer sent officers to an address in Buffalo instead of Kenmore. When the officers found "no such address," the complaint writer dropped the call as a "fake." In the meantime the burglar gained entrance and at 9:42 Mrs. De Long was seen running from the house bleeding. She collapsed and died of stab wounds. A jury found for the plaintiff in a wrongful death action. Held, affirmed. Where police refuse assistance, there is an issue of how to allocate public resources and it should be left to the executive and legislative branches. But in this case "the decision had been made by the municipalities to provide a special emergency service." . . ." There is, as defendants argue, a "familiar rule," that public entities are not liable for "negligence in the performance of a governmental function, including police and fire protection, unless a special relationship existed between the municipality and the injured party . . ." But here there is a special relationship between the city and the caller. The "victim's plea for assistance was not refused." The special relationship between the defendants and the caller required the defendants "to exercise ordinary care in the performance of a duty it has voluntarily assumed."

NOTES

1.   **Policy concerns over resource allocation.** In considering *Riss*, remember that New York had earlier abolished the state's sovereign immunity. Judge Breitel was obviously concerned about allocation of public resources by way of tort judgments. But *any* tort judgment against the city would allocate resources, including a judgment based on a city bus driver's negligence. Does the distinction between tort suits against the police department and those against the bus authority hold up?

2.   **Relevance of why assistance was refused.** Judge Breitel did not really say why the police in *Riss* refused assistance. He seemed to assume, however, that there was a professional reason bearing on resource allocation. Suppose that was not the case; suppose the police simply did not follow sound procedure, or made a clerical mistake and failed to record Miss Riss' call. Would the result be different?

3.   **Special relationships and reliance.** More recent cases from New York are clear in requiring that a plaintiff must show four things to establish that "special relationship" that would give rise to a duty on the part of a municipality to protect an individual plaintiff: (1) promises or actions that represent an assumption of an affirmative duty to act on the plaintiff's behalf; (2) knowledge by the municipality's agents "that inaction could lead to harm; (3) some form of direct contact between the municipality's agents and the injured party; and (4) that party's justifiable reliance on the municipality's affirmative undertaking." *Valdez v. City of New York*, 960 N.E.2d 356 (N.Y. 2011) (quoting *Cuffy v. City of New York*, 505 N.E.2d 937 (N.Y. 1987)).

New York courts have explained that the fourth requirement—justifiable reliance—is " 'critical' because it provides the essential causative link between the 'special duty' assumed by the municipality and the alleged injury." *Id*. In *Valdez*, the plaintiff claimed that she called the police and told them that her former boyfriend, Perez, had threatened to kill her, and that she was assured by the police that they would arrest him "immediately." After staying in her apartment for many hours, plaintiff left and was shot by Perez. The court held that it was not reasonable for the plaintiff to conclude that "she could relax her vigilance" based simply on a police promise that they were going to arrest Perez. Because she failed to prove justifiable reliance, the police owed her no duty of care. *See also McLean v. City of New York*, 905 N.E.2d 1167 (N.Y. 2009) (contact between city and plaintiff did not constitute any "promise" at all; therefore no special relationship arose and no duty was owed).

4.   **Duty of care and immunity.** Notice that the question of whether the plaintiff can prove a duty of care is distinct from the issue of whether the defendant can assert an immunity, such as discretionary immunity. *See, e.g., Coley v. City of Hartford*, 95 A.3d 480 (Conn. 2014) (police officer's decision not to remain at scene of domestic discord was discretionary). Can *DeLong* be seen as resting not on a "special relationship," but rather on the fact that no professional judgment at all was involved, only an operational mistake?

5. **Resource allocation, redux.** Does a "resource allocation" rationale for retaining immunity sweep too broadly? In *Zelig v. County of Los Angeles*, 45 P.3d 1171 (Cal. 2002), the court held that the county was not liable to the estate of a woman who was killed by her husband in the county courthouse despite the county's knowledge that she was coming to court, that her husband had threatened her, and that he was under a court order not to bring guns into her presence. The court stressed that its holding, whether "expressed as a limitation on duty or as a form of governmental immunity," rested on the notion that "the level of police protection is an allocative question best left to the political branches." In *Barillari v. City of Milwaukee*, 533 N.W.2d 759 (Wis.1995), the city was held immune from liability for the killing of a woman by her estranged boyfriend even though he had earlier sexually assaulted her and police had promised to protect her and to arrest him at a specific time when he was expected to come to her house. They failed to arrest him and did not tell her that he was still at large. Days later he murdered her and killed himself. The police "decisions" were discretionary, said the court: "The nature of law enforcement requires moment-to-moment decision making and crises management, which, in turn, requires that the police department have the latitude to decide how to best utilize law enforcement resources."

HARRY STOLLER AND CO. v. CITY OF LOWELL
587 N.E.2d 780 (Mass. 1992)

[The plaintiff's five brick buildings were destroyed by a fire which started on the sixth floor of one of them. A sprinkler system was in place and had been tested two days earlier. Firefighters, in violation of accepted practice, chose not to use it, fighting the fire with hoses instead. All five buildings and their contents were destroyed. After a jury awarded the plaintiff $785,000, the trial judge granted judgment NOV for the defendant under the state's statutory discretionary immunity. *Held*, reversed.]

WILKINS, J.

This court has declined to apply the discretionary function exception to a variety of governmental acts. A police officer deciding whether to remove from the roadways a motorist, known to be intoxicated, is not making a policy or planning judgment. A physician employed by a city is not engaged in a discretionary function, within the meaning of § 10(b), in her treatment of a patient in a hospital emergency room. . . . The failure to provide sufficient information to enable a person to protect his property against the conduct of a client of the Department of Mental Health does not involve the exercise of choice regarding public policy and planning but rather the carrying out of previously established policies or plans. . . .

There are aspects of firefighting that can have an obvious planning or policy basis. The number and location of fire stations, the amount of equipment to purchase, the size of the fire department, the number and location of hydrants, and the quantity of the water supply involve policy considerations, especially the allocation of financial resources. In certain situations, firefighting involves determinations of what property to attempt to save because the resources available to combat a conflagration are or seem to be insufficient to save all threatened property. In such cases, policy determinations might be involved, and application of the discretionary function exception would be required.

The case before us is different. The negligent conduct that caused the fire to engulf all the plaintiff's buildings was not founded on planning or policy considerations. [The question whether to put higher water pressure in the sprinkler systems involved no policy choice or planning decision. There was a dispute on the evidence whether it was negligent to fail to fight the fire through the buildings' sprinkler systems.] The firefighters may have thought that they had a discretionary choice whether to pour water on the buildings through hoses or to put water inside the buildings through their sprinkler systems. They certainly had discretion in the sense that no statute, regulation, or established municipal practice required the firefighters to use the sprinklers (or, for that matter, to use hoses exclusively). But whatever discretion they had was not based on a policy or planning judgment. The jury decided that, in exercising their discretion not to use the buildings' sprinkler systems, the Lowell firefighters were negligent because they failed to conform to generally accepted firefighting practices. When the firefighters exercised that discretion, policy and planning considerations were not involved. Therefore, the discretionary function exception does not shield the city from liability. . . .

NOTES

1.   **Suing police and fire departments.** As you can see from all of the cases in this section, courts are reluctant to second-guess fire and police departments in their decisions not to act. Some state statutes contain explicit provisions immunizing police and fire departments from suits alleging a failure to provide, or the method of providing, protection. *See, e.g.*, KAN. STAT. ANN. 2015 Supp. § 75–6104(n); MISS. CODE ANN. § 11–46–9(1)(c) (unless employee acted in "reckless disregard" of a person's safety). In line with *Riss*, New York has held that the fire department's failure to enforce a fire safety rule was not actionable on behalf of someone who suffered a fire loss that could have been avoided, and this was true even though the city had actual notice of the danger. *Motyka v. City of Amsterdam*, 204 N.E.2d 635 (N.Y. 1965). How then can we explain *Harry Stoller and Co.*? A few courts have imposed liability for failure to provide enforcement of fire safety laws. *Adams v. State*, 555 P.2d 235 (Alaska 1976). And statutes may impose a duty to enforce criminal law for the protection of potential victims, such as those subject to domestic violence. *See Roy v. City of Everett*, 823 P.2d 1084 (Wash. 1992).

2.   **Discretionary immunity.** Many state statutes contain discretionary immunity provisions, although state-court interpretations are not always identical those seen in the FTCA case law. For example, some states

require that the government must in fact make a policy decision for the immunity to attach; it is not enough that a challenged decision be merely "susceptible" to policy analysis. *See, e.g., Veolia Water Indianapolis, LLC v. National Trust Ins. Co.,* 3 N.E.3d 1 (Ind. 2014). A number of states draw a distinction between "discretionary" and "ministerial" acts, saying that immunity attaches to the former but not the latter, *Commonwealth v. Sexton,* 256 S.W.3d 29 (Ky. 2008) (immunity for failure to inspect and remove a dead tree), or between "planning" and "operational" decisions, with immunity for only the first, not the second, *Schroeder v. St. Louis County,* 708 N.W.2d 497 (Minn. 2006) (immunity for "planning-level" decision to permit gravel road graters to operate against traffic).

As with the FTCA, state-law discretionary immunity will shield many defendants from liability. The reported cases are many, and varied. Governments have been protected by this immunity for conduct ranging from the administration of security at the World Trade Center, *In re World Trade Center Bombing Litigation,* 957 N.E.2d 733 (N.Y. 2011), to the conduct of a child-abuse investigation, *Georgia Dept. of Human Services v. Spruill,* 751 S.E.2d 315 (Ga. 2013), to a decision not to install seatbelts in an inmate transport van, *Maryea v. Velardi,* 135 A.3d 121 (N.H. 2016).

3. **Suits over defects in government property.** A number of state statutes allow governmental entities to be sued when harm results from a defect in government property. For example, state and local governments are often under a duty to maintain roadways in a safe condition, a duty that may extend "beyond the asphalt" to adjacent roadside vegetation, *Wuthrich v. King County,* 366 P.3d 926 (Wash. 2016), a culvert under the road, *Barneck v. Utah Dept. of Transp.,* 353 P.3d 140 (Utah 2015), and the median strip, *Cordova v. City of Los Angeles,* 353 P.3d 773 (Cal. 2015). But the government may be immune if the claim is that the roadway or intersection was negligently designed. *See, e.g., Hampton v. County of San Diego,* 362 P.3d 417 (Cal. 2015) (applying statutory "design immunity"). What if the government becomes aware of a design feature that has created a dangerous condition? Should the state retain its "design" immunity, or at that point is the allegedly negligent conduct about something other than the design? Compare *Martinez v. New Mexico Dept. of Transp.,* 296 P.3d 468 (N.M. 2013), with *Turner v. State,* 375 P.3d 508 (Or. 2016). Statutes and regulations often specify that governments remain potentially liable for defects in sidewalks and public buildings. Some states retain immunity where injuries were caused by natural conditions on unimproved property. *See, e.g., Burnett v. State Dept. of Natural Resources,* 346 P.3d 1005 (Colo. 2015).

4. **Traffic lights and signage.** The defective-property basis for government liability often extends to negligently maintained traffic lights and signage. The government will face liability for failure to correct the problem where that failure is a cause of harm. Would you expect liability, though, where the suit alleged a negligent failure to install a traffic signal at an intersection? *See Risner v. Ohio Dept. of Transp.,* 46 N.E.3d 687 (Ohio 2015). Or if the claim was negligent placement of a warning sign at an intersection? *Truman v.*

Griese, 762 N.W.2d 75 (S.D. 2009). Or if the claim was about the location of a bus stop? *Bonanno v. Centr. Contra Costa Transit Auth.*, 65 P.3d 807 (Cal. 2003).

NOTE: THE PUBLIC DUTY DOCTRINE

1. *Scope.* The public duty doctrine is formally different from discretionary immunity. The public duty doctrine holds that public entities and officers are not liable to individuals for failure to carry out a duty, even a statutory duty, owed to the public at large rather than to particular individuals or groups. *See, e.g., Estate of McFarlin v. State,* 881 N.W.2d 51 (Iowa 2016). For example, some courts hold that a public entity is not liable for a police officer's failure to arrest a drunk driver who, left free, drunkenly injures or kills others. *Ezell v. Cockrell,* 902 S.W.2d 394 (Tenn. 1995). Perhaps the most important effect of the doctrine is that statutes commanding action by public entities or officers are frequently construed to impose public duties only, so that no private person can recover for a public officer's failure to enforce the statute.

2. *Special relationships and non-action.* The public duty doctrine can differ from the discretionary immunity not only in adopting the language of duty but also in recognizing that the duty may be narrowed and liability imposed if the officer or entity takes affirmative action that endangers the plaintiff or if the duty becomes individualized because of a special relationship with the plaintiff. *See, e.g., Eklund v. Trost*, 151 P.3d 870 (Mont. 2006) (special duty owed to pedestrian injured in high-speed chase). Thus an officer is not liable for failure to arrest a drunk, but that officer is liable if he himself causes injury by driving negligently. *See Hetzel v. United States,* 43 F.3d 1500 (D.C. Cir. 1995). This is essentially a specific application of rules about non-action. *See* Chapter 16. A number of courts have held that the public duty doctrine does not shield a defendant from liability where the public entity's agent has acted affirmatively, or has made a promise upon which the plaintiff justifiably relied. *See, e.g., Estate of Graves v. City of Circleville*, 922 N.E.2d 201 (Ohio 2010); *Kent v. City of Columbia Falls*, 350 P.3d 9 (Mont. 2015); *Cope v. Utah Valley State College*, 342 P.3d 243 (Utah 2014).

3. *Statutes creating special duties.* In addition, a statute might create a special duty to a particular group rather than to the public at large. In that case, the court may conclude that the statutory duty is not merely a duty owed to the public at large. For example, a statute creating a specific duty to protect victims of domestic violence may be construed to impose a duty to a special group, so that a failure to provide the protection required will be actionable. *See Washburn v. City of Federal Way*, 310 Wash.2d 732 (Wash. 2013).

4.   *Overlaps with discretionary immunity.* In spite of what has been said above, a number of courts have verbally identified the public duty doctrine with discretionary immunity. For instance, Rhode Island expresses the doctrine in terms of discretionary immunity by saying that it "shields the state and its political subdivisions from tort liability arising out of discretionary governmental actions that by their nature are not ordinarily performed by private persons."

5.   *Abolition of the doctrine.* The public duty doctrine is a common-law rule of long standing. *See South v. Maryland*, 59 U.S. 396 (1855). While most states continue to follow the rule, a growing number have abolished it, either by court decision or by legislation. *See Coleman v. East Joliet Fire Protection Dist.*, 46 N.E.3d 741 (Ill. 2016) ("[T]he underlying purposes of the public duty rule are better served by application of traditional tort principles and the immunity afforded by statutes than by a rule that precludes a finding of a duty on the basis of the defendant's status as a public entity."). Does the public-duty doctrine add anything to a normal duty analysis, or to immunity statutes, or is it "obsolete," as the *Coleman* court concluded?

§ 4. IMMUNITIES OF PUBLIC OFFICERS AND EMPLOYEES

SAMA V. HANNIGAN
669 F.3d 585 (5th Cir. 2012)

OWEN, CIRCUIT JUDGE:

[While in state prison, 36-year-old Carrie Rahat Sama was diagnosed with cervical cancer. She had previously had her right ovary removed. She was referred to doctors at the University of Texas Medical Branch for treatment. Dr. Edward Hannigan was her primary doctor. All of the consulting physicians agreed that a radical hysterectomy was warranted, although Sama told them that she wanted them to save her left ovary if possible. Immediately prior to the operation, her doctors told her that the likelihood of preserving the left ovary was low, but that the decision would be made during surgery. Dr. Michelle Benoit performed the surgery, assisted by Dr. Hannigan. Once surgery had commenced, the doctors determined that the left ovary was both "grossly abnormal" and "non-functional" and it would be in Sama's best interests to remove it, and did so. After surgery, Sama sued several of her doctors and state officials under § 1983 for violating her Eighth and Fourteenth Amendment rights. She did not dispute that she consented to a radical hysterectomy, but alleged that the removal of her ovary without her consent violated her right to refuse unwanted medical treatment and that the defendants were deliberately indifferent to her serious medical needs. Drs. Hannigan and Benoit moved for summary judgment on qualified immunity grounds. The trial court granted the motion, and this appeal followed.]

Procedural Posture

... Qualified immunity generally shields government officials performing discretionary functions, such as the administration of medical care, from liability for civil damages insofar as their conduct does not violate clearly established statutory or constitutional rights of which a reasonable person would have known. Once raised, the burden shifts to the plaintiff, who may rebut entitlement to immunity by demonstrating that "the official's allegedly wrongful conduct violated clearly established law." *Kovacic v. Villarreal*, 628 F.3d 209 (5th Cir. 2010).

For a right to be clearly established, "[t]he contours of the right must be sufficiently clear that a reasonable official would understand that what he is doing violates that right." *Anderson v. Creighton*, 483 U.S. 635 (1987). "[P]re-existing law must dictate, that is, truly compel (not just suggest or allow or raise a question about), the conclusion for every like-situated, reasonable government agent that what [the] defendant is doing violates federal law *in the circumstances*." *Pasco v. Knoblauch*, 566 F.3d 572 (5th Cir. 2009).

In their motion for summary judgment, Hannigan and Benoit argued they were entitled to qualified immunity from all of Sama's claims. . . . Exercising our discretion under *Pearson v. Callahan,* 555 U.S. 223 (2009), we may analyze and resolve this issue under the "clearly established" prong of the qualified immunity test. . . . [I]n *Cruzan v. Dir., Mo. Dep't of Health*, 497 U.S. 261 (1990), the Supreme Court addressed the scope of a person's liberty interest in refusing unwanted treatment. The Court explained, "[D]etermining that a person has a 'liberty interest' under the Due Process Clause [in refusing unwanted treatment] does not end the inquiry; 'whether respondent's constitutional rights have been violated must be determined by balancing his liberty interests against the relevant state interests.'" In the prison context, such countervailing state interests include providing appropriate, necessary medical treatment to inmates as well as prison safety and security.

[We accept as true Sama's assertions that she told her doctors she would not consent to the removal of her ovary, and that she refused to initial the portion of the consent form that explained the risks associated with ovarian surgery. However, Sama consented to the radical hysterectomy and never withdrew that consent even after being advised that her ovary might have to be removed.] We therefore are presented with a situation in which an inmate-patient has consented to a procedure while maintaining that she did not and would not consent to a necessary part of that procedure. Sama has not established that the completion of the radical hysterectomy under such circumstances violated clearly established law. The right to refuse medical treatment is not unqualified. The lines separating when a state actor may and may not constitutionally administer unwanted medical treatment are far from clear.

We also note that, as a factual matter, her alleged nonconsent to the removal of her ovary was qualified by her purpose for withholding consent, which was to attempt to harvest eggs at some point in the future; it was not a binary "yes" or "no." When, during surgery, the physicians observed the scar tissue, cysts, and abnormality of Sama's ovary, they relied on their medical judgment to conclude that the ovary was nonfunctional. . . . The physicians did nothing to foreclose Sama's ability to have a biological child: Sama's pre-existing condition prevented her from having a biological child. The reason that Sama gave for her desire to retain her ovary no longer obtained. The physicians' removal of Sama's ovary was arguably within her grant of consent in light of this circumstance. At the least, this leaves the general principle that an inmate may refuse medical treatment sufficiently uncertain in application to trigger qualified immunity. . . .

In light of all of these circumstances, we cannot say that the law is, or was at the time of the defendants' conduct, clearly established such that a reasonable official in Benoit's and Hannigan's position would understand that their conduct violated Sama's Fourteenth Amendment due process rights. Sama had the burden to negate qualified immunity. Accepting her assertions as true, and considering the other undisputed facts in the record before us, Sama has not cited, and we have not located, a Supreme Court or circuit court decision holding that a violation occurred under similar circumstances. . . .

In sum, the law governing Fourteenth Amendment claims involving unwanted medical treatment in the prison context is far from certain. Given the dearth of case law and the existence of at least some case law supporting the position that Hannigan's and Benoit's conduct was not contrary to clearly established law, Sama has failed to rebut the defendants' entitlement to qualified immunity on her Fourteenth Amendment claim, and summary judgment was appropriate.

For the foregoing reasons, the district court's judgment is AFFIRMED.

NOTES

1. **Qualified immunity: procedure.** The qualified immunity applied in *Sama* decides the outcome of many federal civil rights cases brought against state or local executive officers. It is "an immunity from suit rather than a mere defense to liability," and therefore an immediate appeal may be taken from a trial court's denial of a claim of qualified immunity. *Mitchell v. Forsyth*, 472 U.S. 511 (1985). Under *Pearson v. Callahan*, 555 U.S. 223 (2009), the court can rule on the two-part test of immunity in any order it wishes; since that decision, many cases are decided on the "clearly established" prong of that test without addressing the first prong at all. This may be because it is an easier question

for a court to answer, or because of the desire to avoid constitutional decision-making whenever possible. *See James v. City of Boise*, 376 P.3d 33 (Idaho 2016). Once the officer asserts the qualified privilege as an affirmative defense, the burden is on the plaintiff to prove it does *not* apply—that is, it is the plaintiff who must show that (1) the defendant deprived him of a constitutional right, and (2) the right was clearly established at the time of the violation. *See, e.g., Gradisher v. United States*, 794 F.3d 574 (6th Cir. 2015).

2.   **Qualified immunity: an objective test.** The qualified immunity test is objective rather than subjective. This means that an officer is protected from being sued where he or she "reasonably believes that his or her conduct complies with the law." *Pearson v. Callahan*, 555 U.S. 223 (2009); *see also Brosseau v. Haugen*, 543 U.S. 194 (2004) (qualified immunity protects an officer when he or she "makes a decision that, even if constitutionally deficient, reasonably misapprehends the law governing the circumstances"). But it also means the officer can be held liable in spite of his personal good faith if a reasonable officer would have known that the plaintiff's constitutional rights were impaired by the officer's action. *Harlow v. Fitzgerald*, 457 U.S. 800 (1982).

3.   **Qualified immunity: what "clearly established" means.** As *Sama* makes clear, the officer is immune from suit if the constitutional right at issue was not "clearly established" at the time of the allegedly wrongful act. As the Court has explained, "The contours of the right must be sufficiently clear that a reasonable official would understand what he is doing violates that right." *Anderson v. Creighton*, 483 U.S. 635 (1987). Further, the Court has repeatedly cautioned that courts should not define "clearly established right at a high level of generality. The dispositive question is whether the violative nature of particular conduct is clearly established." *Mullinix v. Luna*, 136 S.Ct. 305 (2015).

4.   **Suits under state law.** What if a state or local executive branch officer is sued under state law? Under the common law, state or local officers did not share the sovereign immunity of the states themselves. If their conduct is characterized by the court as ministerial, something about which they have no choice or discretion, they may be held liable for torts. If their acts are characterized as discretionary, they are usually protected by a *state-law* qualified immunity, that is, by an immunity destructible by improper purpose or "malice." *See, e.g., Rice v. Collins Communication, Inc.*, 236 P.3d 1009 (Wyo. 2010); *Baptie v. Bruno*, 88 A.3d 1212 (Vt. 2013). These tests leave much room for litigation.

NOTE: ABSOLUTE IMMUNITIES

1.   *Absolute immunity for judicial and legislative officers.* Judicial and legislative officers are traditionally given absolute immunity under the common law, so long as they are acting with jurisdiction and in their judicial or legislative capacity. The rule applies both to state and federal

officers. Thus both state and federal judges are absolutely immune in their judicial work. The immunity also applies whether the claim is based on ordinary state tort law or on federal civil rights claims.

2. *Quasi-judicial immunity.* This absolute immunity may extend to people who are not actually "officers," but this extension is not absolute. In *Butz v. Economou,* 438 U.S. 478 (1978), the Court listed three factors that could support extending absolute judicial immunity to non-judicial officers: (1) whether the official in question performed functions sufficiently comparable to those of officials who have traditionally been afforded absolute immunity at common law; (2) whether the likelihood of harassment or intimidation by personal liability was sufficiently great to interfere with the official's performance of his or her duties; and (3) whether procedural safeguards exist in the system that would adequately protect against unconstitutional conduct by the officer. The core question in extending immunity to non-judicial officers may be whether the person is functioning as an "arm of the court." *State v. Second Judicial District Court, County of Washoe,* 55 P.3d 420 (Nev. 2002).

NOTE: FEDERAL EXECUTIVE BRANCH OFFICERS

1. *Suits under federal law.* Section 1983 has no application to federal officers unless they happen to be acting under color of *state* law. There is no statute comparable to § 1983 granting a claim against federal officers acting under color of *federal* law. However, in *Bivens v. Six Unknown Named Agents of Federal Bureau of Narcotics,* 403 U.S. 388 (1971), the Court held that federal officers could be sued for constitutional violations directly under the Constitution. There is no general absolute immunity in such cases, but the same qualified immunity that we saw applied in *Sama* applies in a *Bivens* case. *See, e.g., Turkmen v. Hasty,* 789 F.3d 218 (2d Cir. 2015). That means that a federal executive branch officer cannot be sued under *Bivens* unless his actions violate the plaintiff's clearly established constitutional rights. *Ashcroft v. Iqbal,* 556 U.S. 662 (2009). Particular statutes may immunize federal officers from *Bivens* suits. *See, e.g., Hui v. Castaneda,* 559 U.S. 799 (2010).

2. *Suits under state law.* Where the federal officer is sued under *state* law, older authority afforded an absolute immunity for discretionary decisions, an immunity not destroyed by malice or improper purpose. This was true not only with judicial officers acting within their jurisdiction and with members of Congress doing legislative business, but also with executive officers acting within the "outer perimeter" of the scope of their duties. *Barr v. Matteo,* 360 U.S. 564 (1959). This may still be the law. The clearest case for the plaintiff against a federal officer is therefore the claim

that he violated the federal Constitution rather than state law. This would invoke the rules stated in the above paragraph.

3. *The FTCA immunity.* If a plaintiff claims that the federal officer was negligent in a case where no discretion is involved, the officer is given an immunity by the Federal Tort Claims Act (FTCA), leaving the plaintiff's sole claim against the government as an entity. The FTCA, pursuant to an amendment known as the Westfall Act, now explicitly provides that when the plaintiff sues a federal employee, the Attorney General may certify that the acts of the employee were within the scope of his federal employment. When such a certificate is presented to the court, the court must dismiss the suit against the allegedly negligent employee. The plaintiff may proceed against the United States alone, subject to all the limitations of the FTCA. *Osborn v. Haley*, 549 U.S. 225 (2007).

§ 5. STATE AND MUNICIPAL LIABILITY UNDER § 1983

Although state and municipal immunities have been widely abrogated or limited, considerable immunity remains, as the cases in preceding sections show. These immunities lead plaintiffs to assert federal civil rights claims against states and municipalities in hopes of avoiding any immunity.

State liability under § 1983. The Eleventh Amendment, as construed, provides that citizens cannot subject states to federal court suits against their will. In addition, the Supreme Court has held that states are not "persons" who can be sued under § 1983. *Will v. Mich. Dep't of State Police*, 491 U.S. 58 (1989). Although state officers may be sued for acts done in the course of their official duties, a judgment against the officer cannot serve as a basis for reaching the state's funds. *See Hafer v. Melo*, 502 U.S. 21 (1991).

Liability of municipalities under § 1983. It is now settled that municipalities are "persons" who may be liable under § 1983. There are two peculiarities about this, however. First, the municipality is liable only if the right is violated because of some "policy" or custom of the municipality. *Monell v. Dep't of Social Services*, 436 U.S. 658 (1978). It is not liable, in other words, for the casual derelictions of the police officer on the beat, but is liable for denial of a due process hearing to accused employees. Second, the municipality, unlike the officer, is not entitled to a good faith defense. *Owen v. City of Independence*, 445 U.S. 622 (1980).

REFERENCES: DOBBS, HAYDEN & BUBLICK, HORNBOOK ON TORTS §§ 22.1–22.16 (2d ed. 2016); 2 DOBBS, HAYDEN & BUBLICK, THE LAW OF TORTS §§ 334–356 (2d ed. 2011); LESTER S. JAYSON & ROBERT C. LONGSTRETH, HANDLING FEDERAL TORT CLAIMS: ADMINISTRATIVE AND JUDICIAL REMEDIES (2005).

PART 6

LIMITING THE DUTY OF CARE BASED ON RELATIONSHIPS OR THEIR ABSENCE

● ● ●

CHAPTER 16

NONFEASANCE

■ ■ ■

§ 1. THE MISFEASANCE-NONFEASANCE DISTINCTION

Dawson was standing at the window of his third-floor apartment when he saw a woman on the sidewalk below. The woman later proved to be Mrs. Perrera. A man approached her, took out a knife, and appeared to demand her purse. She resisted somewhat, and the man grabbed the purse. Dawson's telephone was within reach but he did not use it. The man did not depart after taking the woman's purse, but began some kind of verbal altercation. She tried to run, but he grabbed her and began to beat her. Dawson continued to watch as he beat her to death, perhaps as long as ten minutes. This is a wrongful death action brought by Perrera's family against Dawson. The allegation is that he could have prevented her death without danger to himself by calling 911. Taking this allegation to be true, the trial judge upheld Dawson's motion to dismiss the claim. We must affirm.

Dawson has no duty

The "case" above is fictional but true to life and to legal traditions. Under the general common law rule, one person owes another no duty to take active or affirmative steps for the other's protection. A defendant is generally subject to liability for misfeasance (negligence in doing something active)—but not for nonfeasance (doing nothing). *See Miglino v. Bally Total Fitness of Greater N.Y.*, 985 N.E.2d 128 (N.Y. 2013) (statute that requires health clubs to have at least one defibrillator and one certified operator on the premises did not create a duty on the part of the clubs to actually use the defibrillator). The Third Restatement captures this idea by saying that an actor who has not created a risk of harm to another has no duty of care to the other unless one of a listed number of affirmative duties applies; the listed duties are in essence exceptions to a no-duty rule. RESTATEMENT (THIRD) OF TORTS: LIABILITY FOR PHYSICAL AND EMOTIONAL HARM § 37 (2012). We see many of these exceptions in § 2 of this chapter.

Does the traditional misfeasance-nonfeasance distinction make sense? How can we even tell whether a case involves one or the other? *Newton v. Ellis*, 5 El. & Bl. 115, 119 Eng. Rep. 424 (K.B. 1855), is perhaps the classic case attempting to draw this distinction. The Local Board of Health contracted with Ellis to dig certain wells in the road. Ellis did so, leaving unlighted excavations at night. Newton's carriage was drawn into the unlighted hole and he was injured. Newton sued the contractor, Ellis, who argued this was "nonfeasance" and thus no duty was owed. Lord Campbell reasoned, "The action is brought for an improper mode of performing the work. How can that be called a nonfeasance? It is doing unlawfully what might be done lawfully: digging improperly without taking the proper steps for protecting from injury. . . . Cases where the action has been for a mere nonfeasance are inapplicable: the action here is for doing what was positively wrong." This reasoning can apply in many situations. Suppose the defendant drives a car. When a bicycle appears in front of him he does nothing. In particular, he does not move his foot to the brake pedal. As a result he strikes the cyclist. Is this nonfeasance? Can we really set a standard for determining what is and what is not mere inaction?

ESTATE OF CILLEY V. LANE, 985 A.2d 481 (Me. 2009). [Jennifer Lane broke off a romantic relationship with Joshua Cilley. Cilley visited Lane's trailer but Lane asked Cilley to leave. Cilley got a rifle. Lane herself left. She immediately heard a loud pop. She saw Cilley fall to the floor, and heard him say, "it was an accident." Lane did not see any blood, and "did not investigate or attempt to assess whether Cilley was injured." She went to another friend's trailer and told two friends that "Cilley had pretended to shoot himself inside her trailer." The friends investigated, found Cilley in peril, and summoned help. Cilley died as a result of a single gunshot wound to his abdomen. According to the physician who treated him, Cilley could have been resuscitated if he had arrived at the hospital five to ten minutes earlier. Cilley's Estate sued Lane, who moved for summary judgment on the Estate's claim of negligent failure to assist. The trial court granted Lane's motion, and the Estate appealed.]

Maine law does not impose a general obligation to protect others from harm not created by the actor. The fact that the actor realizes or should realize that action on his part is necessary for another's aid or protection does not of itself impose upon him a duty to take such action. . . . [T]he Estate asserts that Lane owed Cilley a duty because she was a social host and he was her guest. . . . Drawing the most favorable inference to the Estate, as we must, this fact still clearly shows that Cilley was no longer welcome in Lane's home. A licensee who is asked to leave and refuses becomes a trespasser. . . . Because Cilley was a trespasser at the time of the incident, Lane's only duty to him was to refrain from wanton, willful, or reckless behavior. . . . Lane's failure to contact emergency assistance for Cilley immediately after she heard the pop does not rise to the level of wanton, willful, or reckless behavior because Lane did not create the danger to Cilley, nor commit any act that led to his initial injury. . . .

[W]e are hesitant to create a duty that would impose liability for the failure to act, or nonfeasance. . . . One of the primary reasons for limiting duties in cases of nonfeasance is the potential for boundless liability. . . . We adhere to our established precedent and conclude that absent a special relationship or conduct that has endangered another, a person owes no duty to call aid for an injured person. . . . Judgment affirmed.

NOTES

1. **Rationales for the rule.** What are the rationales behind the nonfeasance rule? In *Stockberger v. United States*, 332 F.3d 479 (7th Cir. 2003), Judge Posner said this:

> Various rationales have been offered for the seemingly hardhearted common law rule: people should not count on nonprofessionals for rescue; the circle of potentially liable nonrescuers would be difficult to draw (suppose a person is drowning and no one on the crowded beach makes an effort to save him—should all be liable?); altruism makes the problem a small one and liability might actually reduce the number of altruistic responses by depriving people of credit for altruism (how would they prove they hadn't acted under threat of legal liability?); people would be deterred by threat of liability from putting themselves in a position where they might be called upon to attempt a rescue, especially since a failed rescue might under settled common law principles give rise to liability, on the theory that a clumsy rescue attempt may have interfered with a competent rescue by someone else.

Are there further rationales that support the rule?

2. **The *Yania* case.** In *Yania v. Bigan*, 155 A.2d 343 (Pa. 1959), Bigan was a strip-miner who had created large trenches on his property, one of which was filled with water 8 to 10 feet deep, with side walls 16 to 18 feet high. Yania, who operated another coal strip-mine, came onto Bigan's property to discuss a business matter. Bigan asked Yania to help him to start a pump to remove the water in the trench. Yania then jumped into the water and drowned. Bigan did not assist him. Yania's widow sued Bigan, claiming that he had "by the employment of cajolery and inveiglement" convinced Yania to jump, and then had a duty to rescue him. Affirming the trial court's grant of Bigan's motion to dismiss, the Pennsylvania Supreme Court said this: "The mere fact that Bigan saw Yania in a position of peril in the water imposed upon him no legal, although a moral, obligation or duty to go to his rescue unless Bigan was legally responsible, in whole or in part, for placing Yania in the perilous position. . . . The complaint does not aver any facts which impose upon Bigan legal responsibility for placing Yania in the dangerous position in the water and, absent such legal responsibility, the law imposes on Bigan no duty of rescue." Is *Yania* an easier case for the imposition of a duty to rescue than *Cilley*?

3. **The *Rocha* case.** In *Rocha v. Faltys*, 69 S.W.3d 315 (Tex. App. 2002), Rocha attended a party at his college fraternity house at which beer was available. At 2:45 a.m., Rocha and a fraternity brother, Faltys, accompanied by three female students, went to a local swimming spot on a river. Rocha and Faltys climbed to the top of a cliff overlooking the river. Faltys dove in and (according to the plaintiffs) encouraged Rocha to do the same even though Rocha could not swim. Rocha dove in and drowned despite the efforts of Faltys and the others to save him. Rocha's parents sued Faltys and others for negligence. Affirming a summary judgment for Faltys, the court cited the basic nonfeasance rule and held that Faltys owed Rocha no duty. What about the argument that by taking Rocha to the top of the cliff and encouraging him to jump in, Faltys assumed a duty of care? The court rejected that argument, noting the "basic principle of legal responsibility that individuals should be responsible for their own actions and should not be liable for others' independent misconduct." Simply taking an "adult man" to the top of a cliff does not create a dangerous situation giving rise to a duty, and "[n]one of the parties have identified any Texas case suggesting that an adult encouraging another adult to engage in a dangerous activity can give rise to a legal duty."

4. **Bad Samaritan statutes.** The *Cilley* opinion noted that some states have enacted statutes that impose criminal or civil liability for failure to rescue. VT. STAT .ANN. tit. 12, § 519. Should more states adopt a statute requiring reasonable assistance to a person known to be in "grave physical peril"? Would a statute have made a difference in the actual situations of *Cilley*, *Yania*, or *Rocha*?

5. **Duties to trespassers.** The Third Restatement places a possessor of land under "a duty to flagrant trespassers to exercise reasonable care if the trespasser reasonably appears to be imperiled and (1) helpless or (2) unable to protect him- or herself." RESTATEMENT (THIRD) OF TORTS: LIABILITY FOR PHYSICAL AND EMOTIONAL HARM § 52(b) (2012). Even earlier rules provide that when a trespasser or licensee is discovered in a position of peril, a landowner is required to use ordinary care to avoid injuring him. If the court had followed either of these rules, would the whole case have come out differently?

B.R. V. WEST

275 P.3d 228 (Utah 2012)

LEE, J.

David Ragsdale received medical treatment in 2007 from Trina West, a nurse practitioner at Pioneer Comprehensive Medical Clinic in Draper, Utah. Nurse West prescribed Ragsdale at least six medications, including Concerta, Valium, Doxepin, Paxil, pregnenolone, and testosterone. In January 2008, with all of these drugs in his system, Mr. Ragsdale shot and killed his wife, Kristy Ragsdale. Mr. Ragsdale subsequently pled guilty to aggravated murder.

The Ragsdales' young children, who were left parentless, filed suit through their conservator against Nurse West, her consulting physician Dr. Hugo Rodier, and the medical clinic. Plaintiffs alleged negligence in the prescription of the medications that caused Mr. Ragsdale's violent outburst and his wife's death. . . .

The district court granted the [defendants' motion to dismiss], concluding that West owed no duty of care to the plaintiffs because "no patient-health care provider relationship existed, at the time of the underlying events, between the plaintiffs . . . and the defendants." . . . Plaintiffs filed this appeal, contending that the district court incorrectly concluded that defendants did not owe a duty of care to the nonpatient plaintiffs. We agree and reverse.

As every first-year law student learns, duty is one of four essential elements of a cause of action in tort. In negligence cases, a duty is "an obligation, to which the law will give recognition and effect, to conform to a particular standard of conduct toward another." The question in this case is whether healthcare providers have a legal obligation to nonpatients to exercise reasonable care in prescribing medications that pose a risk of injury to third parties. Our cases have identified several factors relevant to determining whether a defendant owes a duty to a plaintiff, including: (1) whether the defendant's allegedly tortious conduct consists of an affirmative act or merely an omission, (2) the legal relationship of the parties; (3) the foreseeability or likelihood of injury; (4) "public policy as to which party can best bear the loss occasioned by the injury"; and (5) "other general policy considerations." Not every factor is created equal, however. . . .

A central point of the parties' disagreement in this case is whether a healthcare provider's duty requires the existence of a "special legal relationship." Defendants contend that healthcare providers owe no duty to a nonpatient who has been injured by a patient unless the patient has a special relationship with the provider—such as where the provider has custody or control of the patient, or where the provider is on notice that the patient is uniquely dangerous to specified third parties. Plaintiffs, for their part, insist that a special relationship is required "only where a claim is based on an omission or a failure to act." According to plaintiffs, the "most critical fact in this case is that Defendants' negligence consists of affirmative conduct," because affirmative acts are typically associated with a duty of care.

We side with the plaintiffs. The long-recognized distinction between acts and omissions—or misfeasance and nonfeasance—makes a critical difference and is perhaps the most fundamental factor courts consider when evaluating duty. Acts of misfeasance, or "active misconduct working positive injury to others," typically carry a duty of care. Nonfeasance "passive inaction, a failure to take positive steps to benefit others, or to protect them from harm not created by any wrongful act of the defendant"—by contrast, generally implicates a duty only in cases of special legal relationships. . . .

Special relationships "arise when one assumes responsibility for another's safety or deprives another of his or her normal opportunities for self-protection." *Webb*, 125 P.3d 906 (Utah 2005). Traditional examples include "common carrier to its passenger, innkeeper and guest, landowner and invitees to his land, and one who takes custody of another." *Id.* (citing RESTATEMENT (SECOND) OF TORTS § 314A (1965)).

We previously clarified the relationship between the nonfeasance and special-relationship factors. . . . [W]e explained:

> [T]he distinction between acts and omissions is central to assessing whether a duty is owed [to] a plaintiff. In almost every instance, an act carries with it a potential duty and resulting legal accountability for that act. By contrast, an omission or failure to act can generally give rise to liability only in the presence of some external circumstance—a special relationship.

A special legal relationship between the parties thus acts as a duty-enhancing, "plus" factor. Even in nonfeasance cases, where a bystander typically would owe no duty to prevent harm, a special legal relationship gives rise to such a duty. . . .

The district court cited *Joseph v. McCann*, 147 P.3d 547 (Utah 2006), in support of its conclusion that a physician-patient relationship is a prerequisite to a negligence claim against a physician. But . . . *Joseph* held that a physician did not owe a duty to a non-patient police officer when the physician was hired by the city to evaluate the officer's fitness for employment. . . . [T]he physician never *treated* the officer, but instead conducted a psychiatric evaluation on behalf of the employer. . . . That does not mean that the physician lacked a duty to avoid affirmatively causing physical injury to the officer. If the physician in *Joseph* had used a scalpel instead of a tongue depressor to facilitate a throat examination, presumably the duty would be as obvious as the ensuing injuries.

Plaintiffs' allegations of duty thus steer clear of the problems identified in our nonfeasance cases and in the court of appeals' decision in *Joseph*. This is not a case in which the healthcare provider is charged with failing to restrain Ragsdale or with failing to warn his family about his unstable condition. Rather, plaintiffs allege that defendants' affirmative acts of prescribing medication caused David Ragsdale to have a violent outburst and take his wife's life. And unlike in *Joseph*, plaintiffs are not purporting to step into the shoes of the party who retained the physician's services. Their claim is not a derivative one for harm to their father, but a personal one for their own injuries.

Handwritten margin note: Special relationships don't factor into this — unless of evidence of affirmative conduct

[For these reasons, a special relationship or physician-patient relationship need not underlie the defendants' duty to the plaintiffs in this case.] And as we explain below, the other duty factors do not justify eliminating defendants' duty to exercise care when engaging in the affirmative act of prescribing medication. . . .

As a general rule, we all have a duty to exercise care when engaging in affirmative conduct that creates a risk of physical harm to others.[11] There are exceptions to the rule, however, in categories of cases implicating unique policy concerns that justify eliminating the duty of care for a class of defendants.[12] The remaining duty factors aid us in determining whether to carve out an exception to the general rule. . . .

Our most basic concern with the parties' arguments is the failure to address duty at a categorical level. *Handwritten: Lack of applicability* Plaintiffs assert (without citation) that we have "repeatedly held that whether a duty exists must be decided on a case-by-case basis." They further claim that this court has "long emphasized that duty determinations should be fact specific." This is not a proper approach to the duty analysis. . . . Duty determinations should be articulated in "relatively clear, categorical, bright-line rules of law applicable to a general class of cases." . . . The [appropriate foreseeability question for duty analysis is whether a category of cases includes individual cases in which the likelihood of some type of harm is sufficiently high that a reasonable person could anticipate a general risk of injury to others.] So stated, this factor weighs in favor of upholding a duty in this case. The relevant category of cases consists of healthcare providers negligently prescribing medications to patients who then injure third parties. And the foreseeability question is whether there are circumstances within that category in which a healthcare provider could foresee injury. We think so.

Pharmaceuticals span a scale of foreseeable risk, with innocuous drugs at the unforeseeable end and powerful narcotics at the other. Some negligent prescription cases may very well involve little foreseeable risk of injury: Imagine a patient that has a rare violent reaction to ibuprofen. Yet other cases may involve highly foreseeable risks, as where a physician

---

[11] RESTATEMENT (THIRD) OF TORTS: LIABILITY FOR PHYSICAL & EMOTIONAL HARM § 7(a) ("An actor ordinarily has a duty to exercise reasonable care when the actor's conduct creates a risk of physical harm."); *id.* § 7 cmt. a ("[A]ctors engaging in conduct that creates risks to others have a duty to exercise reasonable care to avoid causing physical harm."); RESTATEMENT (SECOND) OF TORTS § 302 cmt. a ("In general, anyone who does an affirmative act is under a duty to others to exercise the care of a reasonable man to protect them against an unreasonable risk of harm to them arising out of the act. The duties of one who merely omits to act are more restricted, and in general are confined to situations where there is a special relation between the actor and the other which gives rise to the duty."). . . .

[12] RESTATEMENT (THIRD) OF TORTS: LIABILITY FOR PHYSICAL & EMOTIONAL HARM § 7(b) ("In exceptional cases, when an articulated countervailing principle or policy warrants denying or limiting liability in a particular class of cases, a court may decide that the defendant has no duty or that the ordinary duty of reasonable care requires modification."). . . .

mistakenly prescribes a high dose of a potent narcotic to an active airline pilot instead of the mild antibiotic the pilot needed. Because the class of cases includes some in which a risk of injury to third parties is reasonably foreseeable (as even defendants concede), the foreseeability factor weighs in favor of imposing a duty on healthcare providers to exercise care in prescribing medications so as to refrain from affirmatively causing injury to nonpatients. Whether in a particular case a prescription creates a risk of sufficient foreseeability that the physician should have exercised greater care to guard against injury is a question of breach. And whether the precise causal mechanism of a plaintiff's injuries was a foreseeable result of a defendant's prescriptions is a question of proximate cause. . . .

Finally, defendants offer a series of general policy arguments against the imposition of a duty on physicians to nonpatients. We find these policy concerns insufficient to sustain a categorical decision to withdraw a duty of care across the broad range of negligent prescription cases. . . . [For instance, defendants'] concerns about the impacts of a duty on malpractice insurance and healthcare costs falter. . . . The supposed effects on insurance premiums and patient costs are speculative, as neither defendants nor their amici have presented any evidence showing that insurance costs are lower in states that do not impose this type of duty on healthcare providers. And in any event, the alternative suggested by defendants is to impose these costs on injured parties and permit negligent physicians to remain unaccountable. It seems more reasonable to require physicians and their insurers to account for the consequences of physicians' careless acts than to foist that cost solely on the injured. . . .

Healthcare providers perform a societal function of undoubted social utility. But they are not entitled to an elevated status in tort law that would categorically immunize them from liability when their negligent prescriptions cause physical injury to nonpatients. We uphold a duty of healthcare providers to nonpatients in the affirmative act of prescribing medication and reverse the district court's conclusion to the contrary.

NOTES

1.   **Misfeasance.** In *B.R. v. West*, the Utah Supreme Court draws a line between misfeasance and nonfeasance. In misfeasance, the actor's affirmative act itself creates the duty, absent some policy reasons warranting an exception. In nonfeasance, there is no duty unless some additional factors such as a special relationship are present. What was the *B.R.* defendants' affirmative act that would count as misfeasance?

2.   **Creating a risk.** The Court also cites the Third Restatement's recent guidance. Under the Restatement language quoted in the case footnotes, when a defendant "creates a risk of physical harm," the defendant ordinarily has a duty to exercise reasonable care, absent exceptional policy reason that warrant an exception. RESTATEMENT (THIRD) OF TORTS: LIABILITY FOR PHYSICAL AND

EMOTIONAL HARM § 7 (2010). When a defendant "does not create a risk of physical harm," the default rule is no duty. Id. at § 37 (2012). In some cases, risk creation seems an obvious conclusion, as in the court's illustration of a doctor who uses a scalpel instead of a tongue depressor for a throat exam. In *B.R.*, is it clear that the nurse created a risk of physical harm? What concepts could you use to guide the analysis? Would misfeasance and nonfeasance help?

3. **Policy analysis.** Courts spend a lot of time and thought working through policy issues that support (or don't support) recognition of a duty or no-duty rule. One recent thoughtful example is the California Supreme Court's decision in *Kesner v. Superior Court*, 384 P.3d 283 (Cal. 2016). In that case, plaintiffs developed mesothelioma from exposure to asbestos brought home on their relatives' work clothes. The California Supreme Court recognized that "the general duty to take ordinary care in the conduct of one's activities" applies to the use of asbestos on an owner's premises or in an employer's manufacturing processes, and examined "whether a categorical exception to that general rule should be made" for take-home asbestos exposure cases. After examining many policies, the Court found that the employers created a risk. Specifically, "[a]n employee's role as a vector in bringing asbestos fibers into his or her home is derived from the employer's or property owner's failure to control or limit exposure in the workplace."

4. **Duty and the negligence case.** Does the fact that the plaintiff has established duty mean that he will prevail in a negligence case?

§ 2. EXCEPTIONS TO THE NO-DUTY-TO-ACT RULE

The nonfeasance rule has deep roots in Anglo-American jurisprudence, but has come under withering criticism for many decades. Many European countries impose an affirmative duty to rescue, often making a failure to rescue a criminal offense. *See* JULIE A. DAVIES & PAUL T. HAYDEN, GLOBAL ISSUES IN TORT LAW 120–29 (2008). A comment in the Second Restatement of Torts remarked that American decisions upholding the nonliability of those who declined an easy chance to rescue another from drowning "have been condemned by legal writers as revolting to any moral sense, but thus far they remain the law." RESTATEMENT (SECOND) OF TORTS § 314 cmt. c (1965).

Not surprisingly, then, courts have developed a number of exceptions to the no-duty rule. Some of these seem less like "exceptions" and more like situations where there has been an affirmative act and not nonfeasance in the first place. First, if a person knows or has reason to know that his conduct, whether tortious or innocent, has caused harm to another person, he then has a duty to render assistance to prevent further harm. *See South v. Nat'l R.R. Passenger Corp.*, 290 N.W.2d 819 (N.D. 1980) (without fault, train struck plaintiff; train personnel then had duty to assist reasonably). Second, if a person has created a continuing risk of harm, even innocently, a duty arises to employ reasonable care to prevent or minimize that risk

from coming to fruition.] RESTATEMENT (THIRD) OF TORTS: LIABILITY FOR
PHYSICAL AND EMOTIONAL HARM § 39 (2012). For example, in *Pacht v.
Morris*, 489 P.2d 29 (Ariz. 1971), the defendant innocently collided with a
horse on the highway, killing it. If he did not exercise reasonable care to
remove the horse or to provide some kind of effective warning, he would be
subject to liability if a second driver was injured by hitting the horse or in
trying to avoid hitting it.

[Another exception may be found if a statute or ordinance requires a
person to act affirmatively for the protection of another.] RESTATEMENT
(THIRD) OF TORTS: LIABILITY FOR PHYSICAL AND EMOTIONAL HARM § 38
(2012). We consider other exceptions in the materials that follow.

WAKULICH V. MRAZ
751 N.E.2d 1 (Ill. App. Ct. 2001)

JUSTICE MCBRIDE delivered the opinion of the court. . . .

[Suit for the death of 16-year-old Elizabeth Wakulich. The plaintiff
alleged that Michael and Brian Mraz, then 21 and 18 years old, provided a
quart of Goldschlager alcohol and offered Elizabeth money as a prize if she
could drink the entire bottle without losing consciousness or vomiting.
Dennis Mraz, the father of the young men, was allegedly in the house and
should have known these events.]

In the early morning hours of June 16, decedent, after drinking the
Goldschlager, lost consciousness. According to the complaint, Michael and
Brian then placed her in the downstairs family room, where they observed
her vomiting profusely and making "gurgling" sounds. They later checked
on her again, at which time they removed her vomit-saturated blouse and
placed a pillow under her head to prevent aspiration. [According to the
complaint, Michael and Brian did not seek medical attention for decedent
and actually prevented others present in the home from calling 911 or
seeking other medical intervention] Later in the morning, Dennis ordered
Michael and Brian to remove decedent from the home. They then took her
to a friend's home. Later, decedent was taken to a hospital where she was
pronounced dead.

[The complaint was dismissed for failure to state a cause of action on
the ground that Illinois case law eliminated any liability of social hosts for
providing alcohol. On appeal the plaintiff argues first that her allegations
that her daughter felt compelled to "fit in" with the social host's older sons,
and that they offered her money to drink a quart bottle of alcohol, state a
claim for negligence against the social host and her sons. We reject that
argument.]

Plaintiff next maintains that [she has pleaded sufficient facts to
establish a cause of action based upon defendants' failure to exercise due

care in voluntarily undertaking to care for plaintiff's decedent after she became unconscious] We agree.

"One who voluntarily undertakes to render services to another is liable for bodily harm caused by his failure to perform such services with due care or with such competence and skill as he possesses." . . .

Here, plaintiff has alleged that Michael and Brian voluntarily undertook affirmative steps to care for decedent and did so in a negligent manner. . . .

The viability of the voluntary undertaking counts . . . is not dependent on a duty created through the defendants' provision of alcohol to decedent but, rather, on the defendants having voluntarily undertaken to care for decedent after she became unconscious and having allegedly failed to exercise due care in the performance of that undertaking]. . . .

Defendants maintain that none of their alleged acts indicate a voluntary assumption of any responsibility for decedent's health or well-being. We disagree. Specifically, it was alleged that after decedent became unconscious, Michael and Brian carried her downstairs, placed her on a couch, observed her vomiting profusely and making gurgling noises, checked on her later, changed her vomit-saturated shirt, and placed a pillow underneath her head to prevent aspiration. The actions of Michael and Brian . . . clearly demonstrated an undertaking concerning decedent's well-being. . . . We find therefore, that plaintiff has sufficiently pled that defendants [Michael and Brian voluntarily assumed a duty to care for decedent]

Defendants maintain that they were not negligent in discharging any responsibility they did undertake, that a finding that there was a duty in this case creates uncertainty as to how that duty may be adequately discharged, and that decedent's death was not the proximate result of any voluntary undertaking on their part. We are confident that a jury or other trier of fact is capable of determining whether defendants, having voluntarily undertaken to care for the decedent after she became unconscious and began to vomit and gurgle, performed that undertaking with due care. We also find that the complaint alleges various acts, including allegations that defendants Michael and Brian prevented other individuals from calling for emergency medical intervention, from which a jury could find the defendants acted negligently in discharging their voluntarily assumed duty, proximately leading to decedent's death]

[The trial court erred in dismissing the counts based on voluntary undertaking.]

NOTES

1.   **Beginning to assist.** The Third Restatement recognizes that an actor who undertakes to render services to another, when the actor knows or should know that those services will reduce the risk of harm to the other, has a duty to use reasonable care in rendering those services if the failure to exercise care would increase the risk of harm beyond what would have existed without the undertaking; or if the other person relies on the actor's using reasonable care in the undertaking. RESTATEMENT (THIRD) OF TORTS: LIABILITY FOR PHYSICAL AND EMOTIONAL HARM § 42 (2012).

2.   **Making matters worse.** Where the defendant discontinues aid, the Third Restatement § 44(b) imposes liability if the defendant, by acting unreasonably, has left the victim in a "worse position than existed before" the defendant took charge. *See, e.g., Mita v. Guardsmark, LLC*, 328 P.3d 962 (Wash. Ct. App. 2014). Could it be said that Elizabeth Wakulich would have been better off if the men had not put a pillow under her head?

3.   **Duty to take charge reasonably.** Section 44(a) of the Third Restatement says that when a person voluntarily takes charge of an imperiled and helpless person, he has assumed a duty to take charge in a reasonable manner. Does that also explain the reasoning in *Wakulich*?

4.   **Special relationship.** The *B.R.* court talks about special relationships that can create a duty to act in nonfeasance cases. Section 40 of the Third Restatement recognizes seven kinds of formal relationships that place a defendant under a duty of reasonable care for the plaintiff's safety, including reasonable affirmative efforts to rescue. The relationships are those of (1) a common carrier with its passengers; (2) an innkeeper with its guests; (3) a business or possessor of land that holds its land open to the public with those lawfully on the land; (4) an employer with its employees, who while at work are either in imminent danger or are injured or ill and thereby rendered helpless; (5) a school with its students; (6) a landlord with its tenants; and (7) a custodian with those in custody, if the custodian "has a superior ability to protect" the plaintiff. The Third Restatement explicitly states that the list is not exclusive. Where the plaintiff and defendant are in a special relationship, the defendant will have a duty of reasonable care whether or not the defendant had anything to do with creating or increasing the risk of harm to the plaintiff. RESTATEMENT (THIRD) OF TORTS: LIABILITY FOR PHYSICAL AND EMOTIONAL HARM § 40 cmt. c (2012).

5.   **Other relationships.** What other preexisting relationships might generate a duty to act affirmatively when one party is in danger? What if two people are unmarried, but both parents of a particular child? *See* MERLE H. WEINER, A PARENT-PARTNER STATUS FOR AMERICAN FAMILY LAW (2015) (arguing for this category to be recognized as a special-relationship in a range of contexts, including tort law). What if two friends are "companions on a social venture"? *See Farwell v. Keaton*, 240 N.W.2d 217 (Mich. 1976).

PODIAS V. MAIRS

926 A.2d 859 (N.J. Super. Ct. App. Div. 2007)

PARRILLO, J.A.D.

. . . In the evening of September 27, 2002 and early morning hours of September 28, eighteen-year old Michael Mairs was drinking beer at the home of a friend Thomas Chomko. He eventually left with two other friends, defendants Swanson and Newell, both also eighteen years of age, to return to Monmouth University where all three were students. Mairs was driving. Swanson was in the front passenger seat and Newell was seated in the rear of the vehicle where he apparently fell asleep. It was raining and the road was wet.

At approximately 2:00 a.m., while traveling southbound in the center lane of the Garden State Parkway, Mairs lost control of the car, struck a motorcycle driven by Antonios Podias, and went over the guardrail. All three exited the vehicle and "huddled" around the car. Swanson saw Podias lying in the roadway and because he saw no movement and heard no sound, told Mairs and Newell that he thought Mairs had killed the cyclist. At that time, there were no other cars on the road, or witnesses for that matter.

Even though all three had cell phones, no one called for assistance. Instead they argued about whether the car had collided with the motorcycle. And, within minutes of the accident, Mairs called his girlfriend on Newell's cell phone since his was lost when he got out of the car. Swanson also used his cell phone, placing seventeen calls in the next one-and-one-half hours. Twenty-six additional calls were made from Newell's cell phone in the two-and-one-half hours after the accident, the first just three minutes post-accident and to Matawan, where Chomko resides. None of these, however, were emergency assistance calls. [As Swanson later explained: "I didn't feel responsible to call the police." And Newell just "didn't want to get in trouble."]

After about five or ten minutes, the trio all decided to get back in the car and leave the scene. Swanson directed, "we have to get to an exit." Upon their return to the car, Swanson instructed Mairs "not to bring up his name or involve him in what occurred" and "don't get us [Swanson and Newell] involved, we weren't there." The three then drove south on the parkway for a short distance until Mairs' car broke down. Mairs pulled over and waited in the bushes for his girlfriend to arrive, while Swanson and Newell ran off into the woods, where Newell eventually lost sight of Swanson. Before they deserted him, Swanson again reminded Mairs that "there was no need to get [Swanson and Newell] in trouble. . ." Mairs thought Swanson was "just scared" and that both defendants were concerned about Mairs "drinking and driving." Meanwhile, a motor vehicle operated by Patricia Uribe ran over Podias, who died as a result of injuries sustained in these accidents. . . . [The Administratrix of Podias' estate sued Mairs, Swanson and Newell. [Plaintiff appeals from the trial court's grant of summary judgment in favor of Swanson and Newell.] ----> Procedural Posture

Ordinarily, mere presence at the commission of the wrong, or failure to object to it, is not enough to charge one with responsibility inasmuch as there is no duty to take affirmative steps to interfere. Because of this reluctance to countenance "inaction" as a basis of liability, the common law "has persistently refused to impose on a stranger the moral obligation of common humanity to go to the aid of another human being who is in danger, even if the other is in danger of losing his life." . . .

Of course, exceptions are as longstanding as the rule. [Even those under no pre-existing duty may be liable if they voluntarily begin to assist and do so negligently.] . . . Over the years, liability for inaction has been gradually extended still further to a limited group of relations, in which custom, public sentiment, and views of social policy have led courts to find a duty of affirmative action. Thus, a duty to render assistance may either be "contractual, relational or transactional." In New Jersey, courts have recognized that the existence of a relationship between the victim and one in a position to provide aid may create a duty to render assistance. . . .

To establish liability, however, such relationships need not be limited to those where a pre-existing duty exists, or involving economic ties, or dependent on the actor's status as, for instance, a landowner or business owner. Rather, it [may only be necessary "to find some definite relation between the parties [ ] of such a character that social policy justifies the imposition of a duty to act." [Keeton, et al, *Prosser and Keeton on Torts* § 56 at 374 (5th ed.)]. . . .

So too, even though the defendant may be under no obligation to render assistance himself, he is at least required to take reasonable care that he does not prevent others from giving it. In other words, there may be liability for interfering with the plaintiff's opportunity of obtaining assistance. And even where the original danger was created by innocent conduct, involving no fault on the part of the defendant, there may be a duty to make a reasonable effort to give assistance and avoid further harm where the prior innocent conduct has created an unreasonable risk of harm to the plaintiff. Indeed, one commentator has suggested that "the mere knowledge of serious peril, threatening death or great bodily harm to another, which an identified defendant might avoid with little inconvenience, creates a sufficient relation to impose a duty of action." *Prosser, supra,* § 56 at 377.

Actually, the extension of liability based on these and other "relational" features mirrors evolving notions of duty, which are no longer tethered to rigid formalisms or static historical classifications. This progression is not surprising. The assessment of duty necessarily includes an examination of the relationships between and among the parties. The fundamental question is whether the plaintiff's interests are entitled to legal protection against the defendant's conduct. In this regard, the determination of the existence of duty is ultimately a question of fairness and public policy, which in turn draws upon notions of fairness, common sense, and morality. . . .

[W]e are satisfied that the summary judgment record admits of sufficient facts from which a reasonable jury could find defendants breached a duty which proximately caused the victim's death. In the first place, the risk of harm, even death, to the injured victim lying helpless in the middle of a roadway, from the failure of defendants to summon help or take other precautionary measures was readily and clearly foreseeable. Not only were defendants aware of the risk of harm created by their own inaction, but were in a unique position to know of the risk of harm posed by Mairs' own omission in that regard, as well as Mairs' earlier precipatory conduct in driving after having consumed alcohol. Even absent any encouragement on their part, defendants had special reason to know that Mairs would not himself summon help, but instead illegally depart the scene of a hit-and-run accident, *N.J.S.A.* 39:4–129; *see also N.J.S.A.* 39:4–130, either intentionally or because of an inability to fulfill a duty directly owed the victim, thereby further endangering the decedent's safety.

Juxtaposed against the obvious foreseeability of harm is the relative ease with which it could have been prevented. All three individuals had cell phones and in fact used them immediately before and after the accident for their own purposes, rather than to call for emergency assistance for another in need. The ultimate consequence wrought by the harm in this case—death—came at the expense of failing to take simple precautions at little if any cost or inconvenience to defendants. Indeed, in contrast to Mairs' questionable ability to appreciate the seriousness of the situation, defendants appeared lucid enough to comprehend the severity of the risk and sufficiently in control to help avoid further harm to the victim. In other words, defendants had both the opportunity and ability to help prevent an obviously foreseeable risk of severe and potentially fatal consequence.

In our view, given the circumstances, the imposition of a duty upon defendants does not offend notions of fairness and common decency and is in accord with public policy, [which] encourages gratuitous assistance by those who have no legal obligation to render it. Simply and obviously, defendants here were far more than innocent bystanders or strangers to the event. On the contrary, the instrumentality of injury in this case was operated for a common purpose and the mutual benefit of defendants, and driven by someone they knew to be exhibiting signs of intoxication. Although Mairs clearly created the initial risk, at the very least the evidence reasonably suggests defendants acquiesced in the conditions that may have helped create it and subsequently in those conditions that further endangered the victim's safety. Defendants therefore bear some relationship not only to the primary wrongdoer but to the incident itself. It is this nexus which distinguishes this case from those defined by mere presence on the scene without more, and therefore implicates policy considerations simply not pertinent to the latter.

Even assuming no independent duty to take affirmative action, at the very least defendants were obligated, in our view, not to prevent Mairs from exercising his direct duty of care. . . . [A]t the very least defendants collaborated in, verbally supported, or approved his decision to leave the scene, and at most actively convinced Mairs to flee as a means of not getting caught. . . . The entire aftermath of the incident betrays an orchestrated scheme among the three to avoid detection not only by taking no action to prevent further harm to the victim, but by affirmatively abandoning the scene, practically guaranteeing his death. . . .

We formulate today no rule of general application since the question of duty remains one of judicial balancing of the mix of factors peculiar to each case. We also stress the narrowness of the issue before us. . . . It is the degree of defendants' involvement, coupled with the serious peril threatening imminent death to another that might have been avoided with little effort and inconvenience, suggested by the evidence, that in our view creates a sufficient relation to impose a duty of action. Of course, it still remains a question of fact whether the primary wrongdoer was able to exercise reasonable care to summon emergency assistance or was prevented from doing so by defendants; whether, on the other hand, defendants knew or had reason to know that Mairs was unable or unwilling to do so, and thereafter were in a position to have influenced the outcome; whether the decision to abandon the victim was otherwise Mairs' alone or the result of encouragement, cooperation or interference from defendants; and finally, if the latter, whether the assistance was substantial enough to support a finding of liability. The facts here are certainly not such that all reasonable persons must draw the same conclusion. We cannot say that upon any version of the facts there is no duty.

Reversed and remanded.

NOTES

1. **Examining the disclaimer.** Why did the court insist it was "formulating no rule of general application?" Did it not articulate a rule about when a duty to assist will arise that could be applied in other cases?

2. **Moral vs. legal duties.** Compare *Farwell*, on the one hand, to *Estate of Cilley* and *Yania* on the other. Does one set of judges seem to regard the moral/legal dichotomy differently than the other set of judges?

REFERENCES: 2 DOBBS, HAYDEN & BUBLICK, THE LAW OF TORTS §§ 405–412 (2d ed. 2011); DOBBS, HAYDEN & BUBLICK, HORNBOOK ON TORTS Ch. 25 (2016).

CHAPTER 17

CONTRACT AND DUTY

∎ ∎ ∎

In many instances, particularly in the case of contracts related to physical safety, a contract or undertaking itself creates, modifies, or limits a tort duty. For example, I might have no duty whatsoever to feed your dogs while you are away, and my failure to do so would ordinarily be nonfeasance. However, suppose I agree to come to your house to feed your dogs every day while you are gone, but I fail to do so despite your reliance on me. When you return to find your dog has died of starvation, I might not only be liable for breach of contract, but also for tortious misfeasance in light of my bargained-for undertaking. See RESTATEMENT (THIRD) OF TORTS: LIABILITY FOR PHYSICAL AND EMOTIONAL HARM § 42 illus. 3 (2010).

Saying that a contract, undertaking, or relationship may create tort duties means that liability will be determined under the rules of tort law and that tort damages will be appropriate if the plaintiff prevails. These damages can include recovery for emotional distress as well as punitive damages.

§ 1. MISFEASANCE IN THE PERFORMANCE OF A CONTRACT AND LIABILITY FOR PHYSICAL HARM

AFFILIATED FM INS. CO. v. LTK CONSULTING SERVS., INC.
243 P.3d 521 (Wash. 2010)

FAIRHURST, J. . . .

The Seattle Monorail is the elevated transportation system that connects Seattle Center with downtown Seattle, Washington. One day in May 2004, after leaving the Seattle Center Station with a load of passengers, the monorail blue train caught fire. The fire started beneath the floor of the passenger compartment of the train's front two cars, but the fire soon pierced the floor and engulfed the seating in both front passenger cars. Smoke from the fire spread to all four blue train cars. On the other monorail track, the red train stopped alongside the blue train, helping passengers escape. The red train was damaged by smoke. The cause of the fire was later found to be electrical: a shaft in the monorail's blue train motor had disintegrated, colliding with an electrically charged collector shoe.

Ten years before the fire, in 1994, the city of Seattle (City) entered a monorail concession agreement with SMS. The agreement granted rights to SMS related to the operation of the monorail:

> The City hereby grants to [SMS] . . . the concession right and privilege to maintain and exclusively operate the Monorail System including the facilities, personal property and equipment, together with the right to use and occupy the areas, described in this section, all subject to the conditions and requirements set forth in this Agreement.

The agreement permitted SMS to run concession stands and required SMS to collect fares according to an agreed schedule. In exchange for these rights, SMS promised to pay "concession fees and charges" to the City.

The agreement allocated responsibility among SMS and the City for maintaining the monorail. . . . The agreement required SMS to grant the City "access to the Monorail System at all reasonable times to inspect the same and to make any repair, improvement, alteration or addition thereto of any property owned by or under control of the City. . . ."

The agreement also required SMS to carry an insurance "policy for fire and extended coverage, upset, collision and overturn, vandalism, malicious mischief, and other perils commonly included in the special coverage form," with the City designated as the loss payee. . . .

The City contracted with LTK in 1999 "to examine the Monorail system and recommend repairs." LTK completed its contractual obligations by 2002. The agreement between the parties is not before us, but we understand that SMS was not a party to the contract.

SMS and the City amended their agreement after the fire to allocate the costs and responsibilities for repairing the fire and smoke damage to the monorail. SMS's insurer, AFM, paid $3,267,861 to SMS and was subrogated to SMS's rights against LTK. Asserting those rights now, AFM seeks to recover damages from LTK for SMS's losses.

AFM brought suit against LTK . . . claiming that LTK was negligent "in changing the electrical ground system for the Blue and Red Trains." . . .

LTK . . . moved for summary judgment. LTK denied that it suggested changes to the trains' grounding system or that these changes were implemented, but for purposes of argument on summary judgment, assumes [that the cause of the fire was the train's faulty grounding system, the design of which LTK had suggested]. However, LTK argued that SMS's losses were purely economic and that it was not liable in tort for economic losses. . . . The losses were purely economic, in LTK's view, because. . . SMS did not have a property interest in the Seattle Monorail. The district court granted LTK's motion for summary judgment. . . . AFM appealed to the

United States Court of Appeals for the Ninth Circuit, which certified [a question for review].

["The question presented is whether SMS, which does not own the Seattle Monorail, can bring a tort action against LTK . . . , an engineering firm that worked on monorail maintenance before the fire, for negligently causing the fire." The federal district court had concluded that SMS's injury was "outside the bounds of tort recovery" because it was an economic loss for which recovery was barred under the "economic loss rule." However, "the "economic loss rule," which is "a doctrine that has attempted to describe the dividing line between the law of torts and the law of contracts," should not be treated as a bright-line "rule of general application" that holds that "any time there is an economic loss, there can never be recovery in tort." First, the definitions of economic injuries are broad and malleable. Second, "[e]conomic losses are sometimes recoverable in tort, even if they arise from contractual relationships."]

In a case like this one, where a court applying Washington law is called to "distinguish between claims where a plaintiff is limited to contract remedies and cases where recovery in tort may be available," the court's task is not to superficially classify the plaintiff's injury as economic or noneconomic. Rather, the court must apply the principle of Washington law that is best termed the independent duty doctrine. Under this doctrine, "[a]n injury is remediable in tort if it traces back to the breach of a tort duty arising independently of the terms of the contract." Using "ordinary tort principles," the court decides as a matter of law whether the defendant was under an independent tort duty. . . . The duty of care question implicates three main issues—"its existence, its measure, and its scope." DAN B. DOBBS, THE LAW OF TORTS § 226, at 578 (2000). So the duty question breaks down into three inquiries: Does an obligation exist? What is the measure of care required? To whom and with respect to what risks is the obligation owed?

To decide if the law imposes a duty of care, and to determine the duty's measure and scope, we weigh "considerations of 'logic, common sense, justice, policy, and precedent.' " "The concept of duty is a reflection of all those considerations of public policy which lead the law to conclude that a 'plaintiff's interests are entitled to legal protection against the defendant's conduct.' " Using our judgment, we balance the interests at stake. . . .

LTK seems to put at issue every aspect of its tort duty—the existence, measure, and scope. LTK argues, "LTK's duty of care was created by its contract with the City, and that contract created no independent duty to avoid SMS' or AFM's economic loss."

A.　Does an engineering firm undertaking engineering services assume a tort law duty of reasonable care independent of its contractual obligations?

At issue first is the existence of a duty of care independent of LTK's contract with the City. Viewed within the framework of our duty analysis, the question is this: Do the duty considerations dictate that engineers who provide services be required by law to use reasonable care? An initial policy consideration is the usefulness of private ordering. We assume private parties can best order their own relationships by contract. The law of contracts is designed to protect contracting parties' expectation interests and to provide incentives for "parties to negotiate toward the risk distribution that is desired or customary." In contrast, "tort law is a superfluous and inapt tool for resolving purely commercial disputes." If aggrieved parties to a contract could bring tort claims whenever a contract dispute arose, "certainty and predictability in allocating risk would decrease and impede future business activity." . . .

But this case reminds us that a fire can ignite as a result of an engineer's work, imperiling people and property. An interest we must consider is the safety of persons and property from physical injury, an interest that the law of torts protects vigorously. See DOBBS, supra, § 1, at 3 ("Legal rules give the greatest protection to physical security of persons and property."). The record before us does not indicate whether any passengers on the monorail were injured or if the fire caused damage to property beyond the Seattle Monorail. But the parties agree that the fire caused damage to the monorail trains themselves. And, in Washington, it is common knowledge that the monorail trains carry thousands of people every year between Seattle Center and downtown Seattle. A fire on these trains is a severe safety risk, highlighting the interest in safety that is at stake when engineers do their work.

Imposing a duty of care on engineers could be an effective way to guard against unreasonable curtailments of the safety interest in freedom from physical injuries. Because engineers occupy a position of control, they are in the best position to prevent harm caused by their work. Tort liability would force negligent engineers to internalize the costs of their unreasonable conduct, making them more likely to take due care. Further, engineers have ample training, education, and experience, and can use their professional judgment about the design needs of a particular project. By deterring unreasonable behavior before it occurs and placing responsibility in the hands of the persons who can best mitigate the risks, a duty of reasonable care could reduce the overall social costs.

We recognize that some economic considerations militate in favor of holding that an engineer in LTK's shoes is not under a duty of care. Engineers provide socially beneficial services. If tort claims against them were to be layered on top of the breach of contract suits that they already face, the costs of engineering services would likely increase. Although engineers could probably mitigate their risk exposure with malpractice insurance, they might pass along the increased costs of doing business to their clients. And the liability for some accidents could prove so costly that engineering companies go out of business. Society as a whole could incur more costs and could have fewer engineers willing to take on the risks of liability.

On balance, however, we think engineers who undertake engineering services in this state are under a duty of reasonable care. The interest in safety is significant. . . . Although we have not held so specifically until now, we think engineers' common law duty of care has long been acknowledged in this state. For example, in Seattle Western Industries, Inc. v. David A. Mowat Co., 110 Wash.2d 1, 10, 750 P.2d 245 (1988), implicitly recognizing the duty exists, we held that the scope of the "engineer's common law duty of care" is not necessarily always limited to the engineer's contractual obligations. . . . Nationally, it is the same. See, e.g., JAY M. FEINMAN, PROFESSIONAL LIABILITY TO THIRD PARTIES § 11.3.1, at 228 (2000) ("Most courts have extended liability to architects and engineers by applying the ordinary law of negligence").

We are aware of the economic drawbacks of the dangers of creating "liability in an indeterminate amount for an indeterminate time to an indeterminate class." Still, we think economic concerns about liability run amok are overstated and can be addressed through conventional concepts of the measure and scope of a duty of care.

B.   What is the measure of an engineer's duty of care?

A duty of care is necessarily limited to the level of care that is reasonable in the particular circumstances. . . . [T]he measure of reasonable care for an engineer undertaking engineering services is the degree of care, skill, and learning expected of a reasonably prudent engineer in the state of Washington acting in the same or similar circumstances. . . .

C.   Does the scope of an engineering firm's duty of care encompass companies in SMS's position and the class of harms like the ones suffered by SMS?

By scope, we mean that a duty of care encompasses classes of harm and classes of persons. See DOBBS, supra, § 182, at 450 ("[D]uty rules are classically categorical and abstract; they cover a class or category of cases."). A duty's scope involves a question of law. This is necessarily a judgment built on the duty considerations. . . .

1.   *Does an engineer's duty of care extend to the class of harm suffered by SMS?*

[T]he question here is whether an engineer's duty of care extends to safety risks of physical damage to the property on which the engineer works. We hold it does. As we have already observed, the harm in this case exemplifies the safety-insurance concerns that are at the foundation of tort law. A fire broke out suddenly on the Seattle Monorail's blue train, endangering people and causing extensive physical damage to property. Given the safety interest that justifies imposing a duty of care on engineers, LTK was obligated to act as a reasonably prudent engineer would with respect to safety risks of physical damage.

When a defendant is under a duty of care with respect to certain risks of harm and admits breach, as LTK assumes here, "the connection between the breach and the plaintiff's injury becomes a factual question of proximate cause." . . .

2. *Does an engineer's duty of care extend to the persons who have a property interest to use and occupy the property?*

A duty's scope can be limited to designated classes of persons. The issue is whether a duty of care respecting damage to property extends only to the persons who hold an ownership interest in that property. LTK argues that regardless of whether SMS's property interest can be classified as a lease, a license, or some other property interest, only the owner of property can sue in tort for damage to the property. . . .

We reject LTK's argument and hold that the scope of an engineer's duty of care extends to the persons who hold a legally protected interest in the damaged property. . . . [M]ore than one person can "own" or "hold" an interest in property. . . . [SMS's rights are] property interests in using and possessing the Seattle Monorail, and thus SMS was within the scope of LTK's duty of care. . . . Standing in SMS's shoes, AFM may claim the damages necessary to return SMS as nearly as possible to the position it would have been in, and any claimed damages for SMS's lost profits might be recoverable as damages consequential to LTK's negligence. . . .

[W]e hold that SMS may sue LTK for negligence. LTK, by undertaking engineering services, assumed a duty of reasonable care. This obligation required LTK to use reasonable care, as we have defined it, with respect to risks of physical damage to the monorail. SMS enjoyed legally protected interests in the monorail, and LTK's duty encompassed these interests. By subrogation to SMS's rights, AFM may pursue a claim for negligence against LTK. . . .

NOTES

1. **Independent tort duty.** When a tort suit is brought against a party to a contract, a number of courts, as in *Affiliated*, ask whether the alleged injury arises from a tort duty independent of the terms of the contract. *See, e.g., David v. Hett*, 270 P.3d 1102 (Kan. 2011); *Chapman Custom Homes, Inc. v. Dallas Plumbing Co.*, 445 S.W.3d 716 (Tex. 2014) (plumber allegedly failed to install a hot water heater properly, resulting in water damage to a residence; plumber's duty not to damage the house was independent of any obligation undertaken in the contract, and "the harm suffered is not merely the economic

loss of a contractual benefit"). *Could* a tort duty be fully independent of the contract? If LTK had not contracted to recommend repairs to the monorail system, could it nevertheless be held to account for failures of the system? Perhaps the *Affiliated* court's analysis is more instructive than this language. How did the court determine whether LTK owed a tort duty?

2. **The Restatement view.** The Restatement (Third) of Torts avoids the independent duty language. The default presumption of a duty of reasonable care applies when the defendant has created a risk. RESTATEMENT (THIRD) OF TORTS: LIABILITY FOR PHYSICAL AND EMOTIONAL HARM § 7 (2010). If he hasn't, the default rule is that the defendant has no duty of care. *Id.* § 37. Applying an older standard, at times cases ask whether the defendant "launched an instrument of harm." *In re Lake George Tort Claims*, 461 F. App'x 39, 40 (2d Cir. 2012) (boat canopy, which later collapsed).

3. **Risk creation.** Why should creating a risk of physical harm matter to the existence of a duty? Why does the court think engineers in *Affiliated* are in the best position to prevent harm? Can you tell when a defendant has actually created a risk?

4. **Scope of duty and disclaimers.** Many cases in which contracting parties create risks of physical harm look just like cases in which non-contracting parties create risks of physical harm. However, in the contractual cases, courts often ask not only whether a duty exists but also what is the scope of that duty. What if the contract between the city and LTK specifically "disclaims any and all liability for negligent work on the monorail system"? *See Severn Peanut Co., Inc. v. Indus. Fumigant Co.*, 807 F.3d 88 (4th Cir. 2015) (holding that plaintiff could not bring a negligence claim against the fumigation company whose alleged negligence caused a fire in plaintiff's peanut storage dome because their contract expressly excluded liability for consequential damages). In the LTK hypothetical, would the contract's disclaimer bar suit against LTK by the city? By an injured passenger on the train? What about SMS, which was not a party to the contract with LTK?

5. **The economic loss rule.** The district court barred the claim based on the "economic loss rule," a doctrine that frequently pops up when both tort and contract claims exist. *See S K Peightal Eng'rs, LTD v. Mid Valley Real Estate Solutions V, LLC*, 342 P.3d 868, 872 (Colo. 2015) ("The economic loss rule was adopted 'to maintain the boundary between contract law and tort law' "). Courts have many different iterations of this rule or rules. According to Professor Dobbs, "Two distinct rules tend to limit recovery of economic loss: (1) Subject to qualifications, one not in a special or contractual relationship owes no duty of care to protect strangers against stand-alone economic harm; and (2) again subject to qualifications, those in a special relationship arising out of contract or undertaking may not owe a duty of care to each other; rather, each party is limited to the contract. . . ." Dan B. Dobbs, *An Introduction to Non-Statutory Economic Loss Claims*, 48 ARIZ. L. REV. 713 (2006). Because the fire caused physical damage to property in which SMS had a property interest,

rules about economic loss would seem not to apply. As the court notes, even in cases involving economic loss, recovery is permitted in some circumstances.

6. **Applying economic loss rules.** What if, because of the monorail fire, a businessperson was late to a meeting and therefore lost a lucrative contract. Would the engineering firm be liable for *that* harm? In *Southwestern Bell Tel. Co. v. DeLanney*, 809 S.W.2d 493 (Tex. 1991), the court rejected tort liability where a telephone company failed to fulfill a contract to publish a Yellow Pages ad. "If the defendant's conduct—such as negligently burning down a house—would give rise to liability independent of the fact that a contract exists between the parties, the plaintiff's claim may also sound in tort. Conversely, if the defendant's conduct—such as failing to publish an advertisement—would give rise to liability only because it breaches the parties' agreement, the plaintiff's claim ordinarily sounds only in contract." Why not say there is a tort duty for negligent breach of the Yellow Pages contract?

7. **Subrogation.** Subrogation is a fancy word more simply expressed by the court's phrase about AFM "standing in SMS's shoes." Black's Law Dictionary defines subrogation as "[t]he substitution of one party for another whose debt the party pays, entitling the paying party to rights, remedies, or securities that would otherwise belong to the debtor." BLACK'S LAW DICTIONARY (10th ed. 2014). The gist of the idea is that because the insurer, AFM, paid the claim owed by SMS, it also has the same rights that belonged to SMS.

§ 2. NONFEASANCE IN THE PERFORMANCE OF A CONTRACT AND LIABILITY FOR PHYSICAL HARM

What if the defendant does not create a risk of physical harm to the plaintiff's property but instead agrees to render services that should reduce the plaintiff's risk of physical harm yet fails to follow through?

LANGLOIS v. TOWN OF PROCTOR
113 A.3d 44 (Vt. 2014)

DOOLEY, J.

This is an unusual dispute that arose from the failure of plaintiff Kathleen Langlois, owner of a building with commercial space on the first floor and an apartment on the second floor, to pay her water bill for the property to defendant Town of Proctor, and from the Town's alleged failure to turn the water off pursuant to the parties' agreement. Plaintiff alleged, in pertinent part, that she arranged with a representative of the Town that it would disconnect the water service so she would not incur further water expenses, but that the Town failed to do so. She further alleged that in reliance on the Town's promised undertaking she discontinued heating the building, causing the pipes containing water to freeze and split under the first floor of the building, which, in turn, flooded the first floor and basement, causing extensive damage to the building. The jury found the Town negligent and awarded plaintiff damages of $64,918.44. We reverse and remand because of the trial court's failure to instruct on comparative negligence, but affirm in all other respects. . . .

The main count involved in this appeal alleged that the Town was negligent for failure to turn off the water and that its negligence was the proximate cause of plaintiff's damages. Another count alleged that the parties had a contract with respect to the supply of water and that the Town breached the contract by sending a false notice that it had disconnected the water and by failing to remediate its inaction once it was discovered. . . .

[On the claims for negligence and breach of contract, the trial court] concluded:

> Plaintiff's claims are rooted in the Town's ordinance governing the relationship between the Town as water supplier and Plaintiff as ratepayer. The ordinance describes itself as "a contract between each ratepayer and the Town." This contractual relationship contained in the ordinance, coupled with Town's alleged misrepresentations in informing Plaintiff that her water had in fact been disconnected when it had not, provides a sufficient legal basis for Plaintiff's claims. . . .

The case was then tried before a jury, which rendered a verdict for plaintiff. . . . [T]he jury found that there was a contract between plaintiff and the Town "regarding the turning off of her water service," . . . [and] that the Town was negligent, that its negligence was a proximate cause of harm to plaintiff, and that plaintiff's damages were $64,918.44.

On appeal, the Town argues that it had no tort duty to properly turn off plaintiff's water service. . . .

Duty

We begin with the question of duty. As we held recently, . . . an action for negligence fails in the absence of a duty of care. Whether a duty was present, as well as the scope of any duty, is primarily a question of law. The Town argues that it had no duty to turn off the water, or to turn the service off in a particular way, for nonpayment of water charges. It further argues that the tort duty plaintiff asserted arose out of the contractual relationship between plaintiff and the Town, but that plaintiff's assertion is invalid because a tort duty must arise independent of any contractual obligations.

In response, plaintiff argues that the Town's tort duty arose from its undertaking to disconnect the water service and plaintiff's reliance upon that undertaking. She bases this argument on the Restatement (Second) of Torts § 323 (1965). . . . Section 323 provides:

... One who undertakes, gratuitously or for consideration, to render services to another which he should recognize as necessary for the protection of the other's person or things, is subject to liability to the other for physical harm resulting from his failure to exercise reasonable care to perform his undertaking, if

> (a) his failure to exercise such care increases the risk of such harm, or

> (b) the harm is suffered because of the other's reliance upon the undertaking. . . .

Without saying so directly, the Town challenges the application of § 323 by claiming that its underlying obligation is contractual. The Town relies on a sentence from *Springfield Hydroelectric Co. v. Copp,* in which this Court stated that a tort duty of care must be " 'independent of any contractual obligations.' " . . . The Town argues that there is no recognizable tort duty because plaintiff is basing the Town's duty on the breach of a contract to turn off the water. . . .

We conclude that the Town reads too much into *Springfield Hydroelectric.* The issue in that case was whether the plaintiff could obtain a tort recovery for purely economic losses in the absence of physical damage. . . . We did not hold that the duty on which plaintiff relies for a tort action can never be contractual.

In fact, many of our duty cases are based on undertakings involving contractually assumed duties. For example, in *Perry v. Green Mountain Mall,* the defendant had a contract with a mall owner to maintain the parking lot and roads around the mall. The plaintiff was an employee of a mall store who was injured when her car skidded on ice in the parking lot, and she sued defendant for negligent failure to remove the ice. We found that the plaintiff's complaint alleged a duty recognized under § 324A of the Restatement. Neither § 323 nor § 324A suggest that the duty stemming from the undertaking cannot be contractually based. Both apply to an undertaking "for consideration," which is one way to describe a contract. . . .

The evidence in this case was sufficient for a factfinder to find that the elements of § 323 were established. Plaintiff testified that the agent of the Town responsible for utility disconnections promised to disconnect the water service to the building. The Town's witnesses established that a Town worker went to the site in May 2009 and believed he had turned off the water at the "curbstop," a valve in the right of way. Thus, there was adequate evidence of an undertaking, whether gratuitous or contractual. . . .

Further, there was evidence that Town workers were aware of the consequences if water was not disconnected and went into an unheated building. In fact, there was testimony that this had happened to another customer about a year before the events of this case. Thus, there was evidence that Town workers recognized that turning off the water was necessary to protect plaintiff's property. Finally, plaintiff testified that she relied upon the Town employee's promise to have the water disconnected when she discontinued heat to the building, meeting the requirement of § 323(b).

[Although the Town had a duty to turn off plaintiff's water due to her reliance on the Town's promise to do so, the trial court's refusal to instruct the jury on comparative negligence constitutes reversible error. Accordingly, the case is reversed and remanded for a new trial.]

NOTES

1. **Gratuitously or for consideration.** Recall *Wakulich* from Chapter 16. There, the court found that the defendants had voluntarily undertaken to care for the plaintiff's decedent after she drank a quart of Goldschlager and became unconscious. The *Langlois* court says that the Restatement recognizes undertakings that arise "gratuitously or for consideration," and that therefore a contract itself may form the basis for the undertaking.

2. **The nature of the contract.** The jury in *Langlois* had found a contract based on the language of the ordinance and the statement by the Town's representative that the water would be turned off. Do you think that courts are more likely to find a tort duty arising from an undertaking when the contract is an informal one, as in *Langlois*, in contrast with a formal written agreement?

3. **Judge and jury.** The *Langlois* court says that "[w]hether a duty was present, as well as the scope of any duty, is primarily a question of law." Why, then, does the court rely on the jury's findings to uphold the conclusion that the Town had a duty to Langlois?

4. **Hypothetical.** What if the Town's employee sent to turn off Langlois' water had broken the pipe while turning the water off? Would the Town be liable for the damage caused by the broken pipe? Would the basis for the duty be different from what it would be here?

In *Affiliated FM Ins. Co. v. LTK,* what if LTK was hired to investigate whether the monorail's grounding system needed repairs but failed to notice an important safety issue? Would that situation produce the same result as in *Langlois*? In *LeBlanc v. Logan Hilton Joint Venture*, 974 N.E.2d 34 (2012), the Massachusetts Supreme Court held that the defendant architects could be liable for negligence in the inspection of electrical equipment that later caused electrocution. Although the contract limited the team to the design and regular inspection of the equipment, and imposed no duty to act, there was a professional duty of care to the third person electrician, sounding in tort, when the team failed to report problems.

5.   **Contracts to provide security.** Peter enters into a contract with a security company for a portable call button for his mother. When his mother pushes the button, however, the company directs emergency services to the wrong address, and due to the delay Peter's mother dies. Should Peter have a negligence claim against the security company? *See Spengler v. ADT Sec. Servs., Inc.,* 505 F.3d 456 (6th Cir. 2007) ("ADT's obligation to promptly and correctly dispatch EMS emanated only from the contract, not Michigan common law, and thus no tort claim is available."). There are other cases to the same effect. *See Abacus Fed. Sav. Bank v. ADT Sec. Servs., Inc.,* 967 N.E.2d 666, 670 (N.Y. 2012) (ADT not liable under tort theory for failure to monitor alarm system on bank vault, despite potential gross negligence); *Valenzuela v. ADT Sec. Servs., Inc.,* 475 F. App'x 115, 117 (9th Cir. 2012) (ADT's legal obligation to provide service arose solely from its contractual relationship with jewelers, not from any independent duty and therefore even gross negligence claim was inappropriate). Are these cases correctly decided? *See* 2 DOBBS, HAYDEN & BUBLICK, THE LAW OF TORTS § 412 (2d ed. 2011).

6.   **The Restatement Third: services designed to reduce risk of physical harm.** The Third Restatement's view is that an actor who undertakes to render services to another, when the actor knows or should know that the services will reduce the risk of physical harm to the other, owes a duty of reasonable care in carrying out that undertaking if (a) the failure to exercise care increases the risk of harm beyond that which would have existed without the undertaking, or (b) the other person relies on the undertaking. RESTATEMENT (THIRD) OF TORTS: LIABILITY FOR PHYSICAL AND EMOTIONAL HARM § 42 (2012). How might the Third Restatement provision have helped the plaintiffs in the ADT cases in the prior note?

§ 3. SCOPE OF DUTY BASED ON UNDERTAKING

DIAZ V. PHOENIX LUBRICATION SERVICE, INC.

230 P.3d 718 (Ariz. Ct. App. 2010)

GEMMILL, JUDGE.

On October 30, 2004, Plaintiff Joseph Bryant Diaz ("Bryant") took the Volvo owned by his parents . . . to a Jiffy Lube for an oil change. The oil change service purchased by Bryant included, among other things, a check of the Volvo's tire pressure. Jiffy Lube does not sell or replace tires, but does offer a separate tire rotation service and inspection for an additional fee. Bryant, however, purchased only the oil change service and does not recall asking Jiffy Lube to perform any work on the Volvo's tires or to inspect the condition of the tires.

A few weeks later, on November 21, 2004, Bryant was driving the Volvo. . . . It had been raining and Bryant lost control of the Volvo as it traveled over a wet portion of the road. The car traveled off the road and rolled over. As a result, Bryant suffered serious injuries, including paralysis. Plaintiffs assert that the worn condition of the tread on the inside portion of the Volvo's rear tires "caused or contributed to the underlying accident." . . .

[Plaintiffs filed suit against numerous defendants including Ford Motor Company, Volvo Car Corporation, Discount Tire Company and others. Specifically, Plaintiffs alleged that the Volvo had been taken to Discount Tire in July 2004 to have its rear tires replaced. According to Plaintiffs, Discount Tire did not properly inspect the rear tires to determine the existence of wear patterns that are symptomatic of suspension and alignment problems, which problems led to the subsequent dangerous wear patterns on the rear tires. Plaintiffs also sued Volvo North Scottsdale, which serviced the Volvo on September 29, 2004, and November 5, 2004, for negligently failing to inspect the Volvo's tires. Volvo North Scottsdale named Jiffy Lube as a non-party at fault, after which Plaintiffs amended their complaint to add Jiffy Lube as a defendant. Plaintiffs claim Jiffy Lube was negligent because the service it performed should have included an examination of the tires and notification of the tire wear.]

All of the Defendants except Jiffy Lube were eventually dismissed from the action. In July 2008, Jiffy Lube filed a motion for summary judgment asserting that it did not owe Plaintiffs a duty to inspect the inside tread of the Volvo's tires. [Defendant's motion for summary judgment was granted.] Plaintiffs timely appeal. . . .

The primary issue on appeal is whether Jiffy Lube owed a legal duty to Plaintiffs in regard to the allegedly worn tires. We conclude . . . that Jiffy Lube did not owe Plaintiffs a legal duty that would permit a recovery in this case. . . .

The existence of a duty is a question of law that we review de novo. . . . [T]he Arizona Supreme Court consider[s] two factors in evaluating the existence of a duty: (1) the relationship between the parties and (2) public policy considerations. The court explained that "[d]uties of care may arise from special relationships based on contract, family relations, or conduct undertaken by the defendant." In addition, the common law provides various categorical relationships that can give rise to a duty. . . . Public policy, the other factor used to determine the existence of a duty, may be found in state statutory laws and the common law. . . .

In this case, the relationship between the parties did not create a duty on the part of Jiffy Lube to inspect the tires. . . . [W]e disagree with Plaintiffs that their contractual relationship with Jiffy Lube extended to a safety inspection of the Volvo's tires such that Jiffy Lube owed a duty of reasonable care to inspect the tires. The oil change agreement between Jiffy Lube and Plaintiffs included only a check of the air pressure in the Volvo's tires, not an overall tire inspection.

Our supreme court has recently emphasized, in different contexts, the importance of the contracts between parties in determining the boundaries of potential liability. Similarly, the scope of Jiffy Lube's contractual undertaking significantly influences the determination of whether a duty existed to inspect the tires. On this record, Jiffy Lube did not undertake to inspect the degree and pattern of tire wear. . . .

Plaintiffs . . . point to the opinion of this court in *Reader v. Gen. Motors Corp.*, 13 Ariz. App. 207, 475 P.2d 497 (1970), *vacated on other grounds*, 107 Ariz. 149, 483 P.2d 1388 (1971), to support their argument that Jiffy Lube's duty to inspect the Volvo's tires arose from the contractual relationship between the parties. . . . *Reader* taken as a whole works against Plaintiffs' argument. . . . *Reader* stated that the principles set forth in *Glisson v. Colonial Buick Inc.*, 156 So. 2d 271 (La. Ct. App. 1963) and the Restatement (Second) of Torts § 403 (1965) were not inconsistent with its holding. In *Glisson*, the Louisiana Court of Appeals agreed with the trial court's observation that "[w]hen a mechanic contracts to repair a defect in an automobile he does not impliedly contract to inspect and repair the neighboring parts." Similarly, the Restatement (Second) of Torts § 403 notes that a "contractor who fails to exercise reasonable care to inform his employer of a dangerous condition, which he is not employed to repair, but which he discovers in the course of making the repairs agreed upon . . . may not be subject to the liability stated in this section." These principles, gleaned from authorities cited in *Reader,* support the conclusion that Jiffy Lube did not owe Plaintiffs a legal duty to inspect the tires because Jiffy Lube did not undertake to do so. . . .

Plaintiffs also assert that public policy warrants a conclusion that Jiffy Lube owed Plaintiffs a duty of care to perform a safety inspection of the tires. . . . [The Arizona Supreme Court recognized in a previous case] that . . . "[a]n actor ordinarily has a duty to exercise reasonable care when the actor's conduct creates a risk of physical harm." Because we do not perceive that Jiffy Lube's actions *created the risk* resulting from the allegedly worn tires, we conclude that . . . the proposed Restatement [does not support] the existence of a duty on the part of Jiffy Lube to inspect the tires for safety. . . .

[W]e derive guidance from the proposed Restatement regarding the importance of the scope of the undertaking by the defendant and the distinction between creating a risk and failing to discover a risk. In contrast to § 7 of the proposed Restatement, § 37 . . . provides that "[a]n actor whose conduct has not created a risk of physical harm to another has no duty of care to the other unless a court determines that one of the affirmative duties in §§ 38–44 is applicable." . . .

Illustration 4 in comment g to § 42 of the Restatement underscores that courts should usually limit the existence of a duty to the scope of the actual undertaking:

> Lindsay hires Margaret to fix a leaking plumbing fixture in a second-floor apartment. Margaret repairs the leak in a nonnegligent manner. After completing the repairs, Margaret realizes that water that had leaked earlier from the fixture continued to leak from the apartment onto an adjacent alley. When returning home that evening, Lindsay slips and falls on ice that had formed in the alley from the water that continued to leak. Lindsay sues Margaret claiming that she had a duty of reasonable care with regard to the water that leaked out of the fixture. *The risks posed by the water that had previously escaped from the fixture are beyond the scope of Margaret's undertaking to repair the fixture as a matter of law, and Margaret is not subject to liability for Lindsay's harm.* (Emphasis added.)

Applying these principles to the instant case, we conclude that public policy does not support the imposition of a duty on the part of Jiffy Lube . . . there is no duty based upon Jiffy Lube's limited undertaking. Similar to the illustration found in § 42 of the proposed Restatement, the risk posed by the Volvo's worn tires was beyond the scope of Jiffy Lube's undertaking, which involved merely checking each tire's air pressure, adjusting the pressure as necessary, and performing other non-tire-related services.

Finally, we address Plaintiffs' argument that a duty arose in this case "because the standard in the industry called for service [and] maintenance businesses like Jiffy Lube to inspect all visible vehicle components for hazards during the performance of their service work." The existence of a duty is a threshold legal question that must be determined by the court. Standard industry practice addresses primarily whether there has been a breach of duty. If Jiffy Lube did not owe Plaintiffs a duty to inspect the tires for dangerous wear, the standard of care and the potential breach thereof are irrelevant. . . .

Accordingly, we affirm the summary judgment entered by the trial court in favor of Jiffy Lube.

NOTES

1. **Risk creation.** What if, while checking the tire pressure, the mechanic in *Diaz* had carelessly nicked the tire with a sharp instrument, contributing to the tire's dangerous condition? Does the *Diaz* court suggest that would be the same case?

2. **Alternative protections.** The Restatement (Third) of Torts says that reliance is a specific manner of increasing the harm. A person who relies on the defendant's performance of a contract may decline "to pursue

alternative means for protection." For example, in the case in which a neighbor agrees to make daily visits to care for a pet while the owner is away, a duty of care is owed because the pet owner relies on the neighbor's promise. Why would reliance make the neighbor's agreement not just a valid contract, but also a valid basis for imposing a tort duty?

3. **Defining the scope of the undertaking.** *Diaz* employs the Restatement rule both to define when an undertaking to make something safer creates a duty and to limit the scope of the duty to the scope of the actual undertaking. *See also Hill v. Superior Prop. Mgmt. Servs., Inc.*, 321 P.3d 1054 (Utah 2013) (maintenance company under contract to mow lawn not liable to resident who tripped over an exposed tree root in a grassy area because maintenance company's duty "was limited to the extent of its undertaking"). Is the scope of the duty always defined by the written terms of the contract? The *Diaz* plaintiffs alleged that the industry custom during an oil change and tire pressure check was to check the tires for wear. What if the plaintiff had gone further and provided testimony that he relied on the fact that Jiffy Lube followed that custom and would have paid for an additional service or taken the car elsewhere if he had believed the defendant was not going to check the tires?

4. **Known risk.** If the facts showed that the mechanic in *Diaz* actually saw the problem, and realized the tread was too worn, but decided not to comment about it, would that be the same case? Is this the no-duty-to-act rule? *See Hill v. Sears, Roebuck & Co.*, 822 N.W.2d 190 (Mich. 2012) (electrical appliance installers had no duty to report an uncapped gas line; beyond the scope of contract for the installation of the appliances).

5. **Limited contracts.** Might a contractual undertaking simply expire with the contract? *See Folsom v. Burger King*, 958 P.2d 301 (Wash. 1998) (security company owed no duty to workers who pushed the still-working alarm during a robbery but were ignored because defendant was not under a contractual obligation to respond and their failure to remove the alarm did not represent a voluntary assumption of a duty). What if a defendant had only volunteered to drive his drunken friend for most of the night and then drop him off at his car—limited agreement defining the scope of the obligation? *See Gushlaw v. Milner*, 42 A.3d 1245, 1260 (R.I. 2012).

§ 4. PROMISES TO THIRD PERSONS

PALKA V. SERVICEMASTER MANAGEMENT SERVICES CORP., 634 N.E.2d 189 (N.Y. 1994). Palka was a nurse employed by Ellis Hospital. Ellis had contracted with Servicemaster to manage maintenance operations at the hospital. Before that, the hospital had conducted its own safety inspections of such things as fans mounted on walls. After Servicemaster took over, the hospital left all such programs to Servicemaster. Servicemaster did not exercise reasonable care with respect to wall-mounted fans and one of them fell on the plaintiff. She sued Servicemaster. *Held:* (1) safety of such items as wall-mounted fans was within the scope of the contract obligation; and

(2) Servicemaster was under a duty to the plaintiff, a non-contracting party. Palka "proved not only that Servicemaster undertook to provide a service to Ellis Hospital and did so negligently, but also that its conduct in undertaking that particular service placed Palka in an unreasonably risky setting greater than that, had Servicemaster never ventured into its hospital servicing role at all." "[U]nlike our decisions in Moch Co. v. Rensselaer Water Co. and Strauss v. Belle Realty Co., the instant case presents this array of factors: reasonably interconnected and anticipated relationships; particularity of assumed responsibility under the contract and evidence adduced at trial; displacement and substitution of a particular safety function designed to protect persons like this plaintiff; and a set of reasonable expectations of all the parties. These factors, taken together, support imposition of liability against this defendant in favor of this plaintiff."

NOTES

1.   **Duty to third persons.** The Restatement provides that an actor who undertakes to render services he knows or should know reduce the risk of harm to which a third person is exposed, has a duty of reasonable care if (a) the failure to exercise care increases the risk of harm beyond that which would have existed without the undertaking, (b) the actor has undertaken to perform a duty owed by another to a third person, or (c) the person to whom services are provided, the third person or another person relies on the undertaking. RESTATEMENT (THIRD) OF TORTS: LIABILITY FOR PHYSICAL AND EMOTIONAL HARM § 43 (2012). *See Landon v. Kroll Lab. Specialists, Inc.*, 999 N.E.2d 1121 (N.Y. 2013) (lab owed a duty of reasonable care to a probationer with respect to drug testing and reporting; "the release of a false positive report will have profound, potentially life-altering, consequences for a test subject. In particular, here, plaintiff faced the loss of freedom associated with serving an extended period of probation.").

2.   **Increased risk over what?** Did Servicemaster's failure to exercise reasonable care truly increase the risk of harm beyond that which would have existed without its undertaking? How would you prove that Palka would have been at less risk if Servicemaster had never ventured into its hospital servicing role? *See Herrington v. Gaulden*, 751 S.E.2d 813 (Ga. 2013) (medical director of hospital emergency department not liable on undertaking theory where he did nothing to escalate risk to patient; liability does not attach for failing to decrease risk of harm); *MacGregor v. Walker*, 322 P.3d 706 (Utah 2014) (no duty to aid victims of sexual abuse was triggered by defendant's creation of a professionally staffed help line where that undertaking did not increase risk of harm and plaintiff did not rely on the undertaking).

3.   **Baselines.** In *Paz v. State of California*, 994 P.2d 975 (Cal. 2000), a developer delayed in installing traffic signals which led to an accident. The court rejected the negligent undertaking theory on the ground that the delayed installation of the traffic signals was not an increased risk. Instead,

"defendants simply did not succeed in completing—before plaintiff's collision—a project that might have reduced the preexisting hazard at the intersection." To which baseline risk should the defendant's conduct be compared—the level of risk at the intersection before installation of the signal or the level of risk at the intersection if the sign had been installed on time? Could you say that the developer created a risk of harm when he failed to promptly address the situation he had been hired to fix? What if he had delayed for years beyond the agreed date for signal installation—is there ever a point at which he would have created a risk? Is this just another instance of nonfeasance-misfeasance reasoning?

§ 5. ACTION AS A PROMISE OR UNDERTAKING

FLORENCE V. GOLDBERG
375 N.E.2d 763 (N.Y. 1978)

JASEN, JUDGE.

[A mother took her 6-year-old child to school each day for two weeks, during which time the city police had stationed a guard at a street crossing. The mother, having observed this protection, ceased to take the child to school. On the day in question the crossing guard regularly assigned there called in sick. Departmental regulations called for sending a substitute if possible and, if not, to cover the most dangerous crossings. No substitute was sent and the principal of the school was not notified. The child was struck at the unguarded crossing and suffered severe brain damage. The plaintiffs recovered against the city and those responsible for operation of the car. The city appeals.]

[A] municipality cannot be held liable for failure to furnish adequate police protection. This duty, like the duty to provide protection against fire, flows only to the general public. (Riss v. City of New York, 22 N.Y. 2d 579, 583, 293 N.Y.S.2d 897, 899, 240 N.E.2d 860, 861. . . .)

[T]here is little question that the police department voluntarily assumed a particular duty to supervise school crossings. . . .

Significantly, the duty assumed by the police department was a limited one: a duty intended to benefit a special class of persons—viz., children crossing designated intersections while traveling to and from school at scheduled times. Thus, the duty assumed constituted more than a general duty to provide police protection to the public at large. Having witnessed the regular performance of this special duty for a two-week period, the plaintiff infant's mother relied upon its continued performance. To borrow once more from Chief Judge Cardozo, "[i]f conduct has gone forward to such a state that inaction would commonly result, not negatively merely in withholding a benefit, but positively or actively in working an injury, there exists a relation out of which arises a duty to go forward."

(Moch Co. v. Rensselaer Water Co., 247 N.Y. at p. 167,159 N.E. at p. 898, supra). Application of this principle to the present case leads unmistakably to the conclusion that the police department, having assumed a duty to a special class of persons, and having gone forward with performance of that duty in the past, had an obligation to continue its performance. Had the police department not assumed a duty to supervise school crossings, plaintiff infant's mother would not have permitted her child to travel to and from school alone. The department's failure to perform this duty placed the infant plaintiff in greater danger than he would have been had the duty not been assumed, since the infant's mother would not have had reason to rely on the protection afforded her child and would have been required, in her absence, to arrange for someone to accompany her child to and from school.

[There was also proof that the city was negligent in failing to provide a guard.]

The order of the Appellate Division should be affirmed, with costs.

NOTES

1.   **Action as undertaking.** The issue in many cases is whether the defendant's conduct counted as an undertaking at all. In *Florence*, is it clear that the city's actions counted as undertakings because they seemed to promise continued protection for the children?

Although action may sometimes invite reliance, reliance may not be reasonable at times when the party undertaking the service explicitly warned that reliance was inappropriate. Thus where a repairman attempted to repair a car's parking brake but instructed the car owner that he was unable to do so, the repair shop had satisfied its duty not to induce reasonable reliance. It could not be held liable to employee injured when the truck rolled backwards and injured him. *Lindsey v. E & E Auto. & Tire Serv., Inc.*, 241 P.3d 880 (Alaska 2010).

2.   **Promise as undertaking.** What if the parent of a 14-year-old girl, who plans to sleep over at a friend's house, says to the friend's parent that "his daughter was not to be in a car with any young, male drivers . . . no boys with cars," and the friend's parent agrees that she will not allow the girls to ride in a car driven by an inexperienced young male. Hours later, the parent permits just that, with tragic consequences—wildly reckless driving, an accident and the death of the first girl. Was the friend's parent's promise enough to create an undertaking? *See Kellermann v. McDonough*, 684 S.E.2d 786 (Va. 2009).

3.   **Why is undertaking relevant?** Turn to a different problem with "undertakings." The idea that "undertaking" may create a duty that did not otherwise exist is generally recognized but profoundly uncertain. First consider why an undertaking might be relevant to the question of the defendant's duty. Would it show: (a) a special relationship, established by the undertaking itself; (b) affirmative action, not mere nonfeasance; (c) the

equivalent of a promise from which a tort duty might arise if there is consideration or reliance? *See, e.g., State Auto Ins. Cos. v. B.N.C.*, 702 N.W.2d 379 (S.D. 2005) (discussing duty of care owed by daughter who undertook to watch her father's home while he was on vacation).

4. **Reliance and discriminatory enforcement.** If *Florence* requires reliance in order to justify recovery, is that desirable? What about a child whose parents never knew of the presence of a guard? Or a child both of whose parents knew there was no guard but neither of whom could take the child to school because they both worked? Is there anything wrong with permitting a recovery for the Florence boy but not for the child of non-relying parents?

5. **Scope of duty imposed by undertaking.** "The scope of any duty assumed depends upon the nature of the undertaking." *Delgado v. Trax Bar & Grill*, 113 P.3d 1159 (Cal. 2005). What is undertaken when a mother, seeing the crossing guards in the afternoon, assumes that the school has undertaken to provide crossing safety before and after school and thus allows her child to walk to school unaccompanied the next morning. There are no crossing guards and the child is struck in a crosswalk by a motorist. The school has never provided guards in the morning. Did it (a) undertake to provide crossing safety and do it negligently? or (b) undertake to provide afternoon guards only? *Jefferson Cnty. Sch. Dist. R-1 v. Gilbert,* 725 P.2d 774 (Colo. 1986).

REFERENCE: 2 DOBBS, HAYDEN & BUBLICK, THE LAW OF TORTS §§ 410–12 (2d ed. 2011); DOBBS, HAYDEN & BUBLICK, HORNBOOK ON TORTS §§ 25.6–25.7 (2d ed. 2016).

CHAPTER 18

THE DUTY TO PROTECT FROM THIRD PERSONS

• • •

§ 1. DEFENDANT'S RELATIONSHIP WITH THE PLAINTIFF

ISEBERG V. GROSS
879 N.E.2d 278 (Ill. 2007)

JUSTICE BURKE delivered the judgment of the court, with opinion:

In this interlocutory appeal, plaintiffs, Mitchell Iseberg (Iseberg) and his wife, Carol, seek reversal of the order dismissing with prejudice count I of their third amended complaint, brought against defendants, Sheldon Gross (Gross) and Henry Frank (Frank). In count I, plaintiffs alleged that Gross and Frank were negligent because they failed to warn Iseberg that a former mutual business partner, Edward Slavin (Slavin), had made threats against Iseberg's life. Slavin later acted on his threats and shot Iseberg, rendering him a paraplegic . . .

[Slavin and Gross started a business in 1995 under the name Vernonshire Auto Laundry Group, Inc. (VAL). Shortly afterward, Gross contacted Iseberg, a lawyer and real estate broker, who was in the process of acquiring land to develop into a strip mall. Frank and Iseberg formed a corporation, LFD, in order to complete that transaction. In 1996, VAL and LFD formed a partnership, with each company contributing funds to purchase the land. The purchase was made and title to the land was placed in a land trust, with VAL and LFD each owning 50%. A dispute arose among the partners and the partnership was dissolved, leaving VAL with sole ownership of the property. Much time passed and because the property did not sell, Slavin lost his entire investment. Plaintiffs alleged that Slavin became mentally unbalanced and that he focused his anger on Iseberg. Slavin told Gross several times that he wanted to harm Iseberg, once saying that he wanted to kill Iseberg and then commit suicide. Gross told Frank about these threats, but neither of them told Iseberg. In early 2000, Slavin rang the doorbell at Iseberg's home and shot him four times when he answered the door.]

. . . Because of the procedural posture of this case, the only issue before us is [whether a legal duty existed] . . . What we must decide is [whether Iseberg and defendants stood in such a relationship to one another that the law imposed on defendants an obligation of reasonable conduct for the benefit of Iseberg] Under common law, the universally accepted rule, articulated in section 314 of the Restatement (Second) of Torts, and long adhered to by this court, is that a private person has no duty to act affirmatively to protect another from criminal attack by a third person absent a "special relationship" between the parties. Historically, there have been four "special relationships" which this and other courts have recognized, namely, common carrier-passenger, innkeeper-guest, business invitor-invitee, and voluntary custodian-protectee. [When one of these special relationships exists between the parties and an unreasonable risk of physical harm arises within the scope of that relationship, an obligation may be imposed on the one to exercise reasonable care to protect the other from such risk, if the risk is reasonably foreseeable, or to render first aid when it is known that such aid is needed.] The existence of one of these four "special relationships" has typically been the basis for imposing an affirmative duty to act where one would not ordinarily exist.

In the case at bar, plaintiffs do not allege that one of the above-listed "special relationships" existed. . . . Instead, plaintiffs ask us to find, as did the dissenting appellate justice, that the facts alleged in the third amended complaint, viewed in a light most favorable to them, are sufficient to bring this case within an exception to the no-affirmative-duty rule. [Specifically, plaintiffs argue (1) that a duty to warn Iseberg of Slavin's threats arose because at the time of the shooting Iseberg was an agent of both Gross and Frank, and alternatively (2) that the court should abandon the requirement of a "special relationship."]

[On the agency argument, courts have found that a principal may have a duty to warn an agent if the principal knows of "an unreasonable risk involved in the employment, if the principal should realize that it exists and that the agent is likely not to become aware of it, thereby suffering harm." Here, however, the allegations in the complaint fail to establish the existence of a principal-agent relationship between defendants and Iseberg at the time of Iseberg's injury. Further, the complaint fails to allege that the risk of harm to Iseberg arose "from the particular nature" of the alleged agency relationship.]

[Plaintiffs also] contend that our recent case law demonstrates that the "special relationship" doctrine has been eroded in this state and that "the evolution of our case law has clearly been away from the formulaic application of the special relationship doctrine." Plaintiffs argue that the "special relationship" doctrine, in particular, and the no-duty rule, in general, are "antiquated" and out of step with contemporary societal morals. Thus, according to plaintiffs, the existence of an affirmative duty to warn or protect, particularly in situations where the parties are not strangers, should be a policy determination, made on a case-by-case basis, upon consideration of factors commonly used to determine the existence of a duty in ordinary negligence situations, *i.e.,* the reasonable foreseeability of the injury; the likelihood of the injury; the magnitude of the burden of guarding against the injury; and the consequences of placing that burden on the defendants. Plaintiffs urge us to abandon the "special relationship" framework for determining whether to impose an affirmative duty to protect against third-party attacks and to find a duty in the case at bar by applying the above four-factor negligence test. . . .

[Cases cited by plaintiffs are easily distinguishable.] Further, we can find no case in which this court has recognized an affirmative duty, based upon consideration of the four factors cited by plaintiffs, in the absence of a special relationship. Rather, the special relationship doctrine has been cited by this court in a number of recent cases, indicating our continued adherence to its general principles. . . .

Plaintiffs' only remaining argument for abandoning the "special relationship" doctrine is that the doctrine and the no-duty rule, in general, are antiquated and out of step with today's morality. While it is true that the no-duty rule has suffered criticism from a number of legal scholars, criticism of the rule is not new. Legal pundits have assailed the rule, citing its lack of social conscience, for as long as it has existed. . . . Contrary to plaintiffs' assertions, the no-affirmative-duty rule, as a common law tort principle, has been retained in every jurisdiction. . . . Thus, given the wide acceptance of the no-duty rule and the "special relationship" doctrine, it cannot be said that they are "antiquated" or "outmoded." . . . In *Rhodes,* we said, "the impracticality of imposing a legal duty to rescue between parties who stand in no special relationship to each other would leave us hesitant to do so." That statement is no less true today.

. . . The no-affirmative-duty rule and the "special relationship" doctrine stand as the law of this state. Accordingly, [an affirmative duty to warn or protect against the criminal conduct of a third party may be imposed on one for the benefit of another only if there exists a special relationship between them] In the case at bar, no such relationship existed between the defendants and Iseberg. Nor was it shown that a principal-agent relationship existed between the parties which gave rise to a duty to warn. . . . For these reasons, we affirm the judgment of the appellate court.

NOTES

1. **Special relationships.** The Restatement Second's list of special relationships has been widely applied, as the *Iseberg* court noted.

The Restatement Third's § 40 broadens the list to include employer-employee, school-student, and landlord-tenant, and changes the "business invitor-invitee" item to "a business or other possessor of land that holds its premises open to the public with those who are lawfully on the premises." Is this still too narrow? In *Grimes v. Kennedy Krieger Institute, Inc.*, 782 A.2d 807 (Md. 2001), the court recognized that a special relationship and concomitant tort duties might arise form a contract between the parties, from statute regulating their dealings, from the superior knowledge of one of them, and even, perhaps, from international law (the Nuremberg Code). In any event, special relationships are determined by the courts from the facts, not necessarily from a preconceived list.

2. **Why such a requirement?** Do you think the plaintiffs in *Iseberg* were correct in their argument that any "special relationship" requirement could be abandoned in favor of utilizing a more general test of duty, at least where the parties are not complete strangers? If that test were applied to the *Iseberg* facts, how would it work?

3. **Necessary, but not sufficient?** Is it enough to trigger a duty that the plaintiff and defendant are in a special relationship, or is more required? *See, e.g., Com. v. Peterson*, 749 S.E.2d 307 (Va. 2013) (assuming that a special relationship existed between state and students at Virginia Tech, state owed no duty to warn students about a possible shooter on campus where the danger was neither known nor foreseeable); *but see Rodriguez v. Del Sol Shopping Center Associates, L.P.*, 326 P.3d 465 (N.M. 2014) (business invitees were owed duty of reasonable care because of special relationship; foreseeability of harm goes to breach of duty, not to existence of duty itself).

4. **Employers and employees.** The *Iseberg* court rejected the plaintiffs "agency" argument on the complaint's factual allegations. Does an employer owe a duty of reasonable care to protect its employees from third parties? The Restatement Third adds employer-employee as a special relationship, as noted in Note 1, *supra*. The Restatement Second's § 314B recognizes such a duty, but only if the employee "comes into a position of imminent danger" and the employer knows it. *Accord, Dupont v. Aavid Thermal Tech., Inc.*, 798 A.2d 587 (N.H. 2002). A further requirement is that the risks of harm by a third person must arise within the scope of the employment relationship itself. *See* RESTATEMENT (SECOND) OF TORTS § 314A (1965); RESTATEMENT (SECOND) OF AGENCY §§ 471 & 521(1) (1958).

5. **Duty to protect plaintiffs against negligent acts by third parties.** We focus in this section of the book mainly on whether a duty exists to protect a plaintiff from a criminal act by a third person. The special relationship rules apply much the same way, however, even in cases where the plaintiff alleges that the defendant failed to protect her from the *negligence* of a third party. *See, e.g., Marshall v. Burger King Corp.*, 856 N.E.2d 1048 (Ill. 2006). Both the Second and Third Restatements are in accord. *See* RESTATEMENT (SECOND) OF TORTS §§ 314A & 344 (1965); RESTATEMENT (THIRD) OF TORTS: LIABILITY FOR PHYSICAL AND EMOTIONAL HARM §§ 19 (2010) & 40 (2012).

6. **Nonfeasance.** Is a special relationship required only where the plaintiff alleges that the defendant failed to act, or does it apply even when the defendant has acted and created a risk of harm? *See, e.g., Kellermann v. McDonough*, 684 S.E.2d 786 (Va. 2009) (defendant agreed to take charge of 14-year-old who was a friend of defendant's child, and promised to keep her from riding in a car with inexperienced drivers, but later allowed child to ride with a 17-year-old boy with a reputation for recklessness, with predictable results).

POSECAI V. WAL-MART STORES, INC.
752 So. 2d 762 (La. 1999)

MARCUS, JUSTICE. . . .

[On July 20, 1995, Mrs. Posecai shopped at Sam's Club, then returned to her car in Sam's parking lot. It was not dark, but a man hiding under her car grabbed her ankle and pointed a gun at her. He robbed her of jewels worth about $19,000 and released her. Mrs. Posecai sued Sam's, claiming it was negligent in failing to provide security guards in the parking lot. The courts below assessed almost $30,000 in damages against Sam's. Evidence showed that Sam's was adjacent to but was not in a high-crime area. From 1989 to 1995, there were three robberies on Sam's premises. But during the same period, there were 83 predatory offenses at 13 businesses in the same block as Sam's.]

A threshold issue in any negligence action is whether the defendant owed the plaintiff a duty. Whether a duty is owed is a question of law. In deciding whether to impose a duty in a particular case, the court must make a policy decision in light of the unique facts and circumstances presented. The court may consider various moral, social, and economic factors, including the fairness of imposing liability; the economic impact on the defendant and on similarly situated parties; the need for an incentive to prevent future harm; the nature of defendant's activity; the potential for an unmanageable flow of litigation; the historical development of precedent; and the direction in which society and its institutions are evolving. . . .

Other jurisdictions have resolved the foreseeability issue in a variety of ways, but four basic approaches have emerged. The first approach, although somewhat outdated, is known as the specific harm rule. According to this rule, a landowner does not owe a duty to protect patrons from the violent acts of third parties unless he is aware of specific, imminent harm about to befall them. Courts have generally agreed that this rule is too restrictive in limiting the duty of protection that business owners owe their invitees.

More recently, some courts have adopted a prior similar incidents test. Under this test, foreseeability is established by evidence of previous crimes on or near the premises. The idea is that a past history of criminal conduct will put the landowner on notice of a future risk. Therefore, courts consider the nature and extent of the previous crimes, as well as their recency, frequency, and similarity to the crime in question. This approach can lead to arbitrary results because it is applied with different standards regarding the number of previous crimes and the degree of similarity required to give rise to a duty.

The third and most common approach used in other jurisdictions is known as the totality of the circumstances test. This test takes additional factors into account, such as the nature, condition, and location of the land, as well as any other relevant factual circumstances bearing on foreseeability. As the Indiana Supreme Court explained, "[a] substantial factor in the determination of duty is the number, nature, and location of prior similar incidents, but the lack of prior similar incidents will not preclude a claim where the landowner knew or should have known that the criminal act was foreseeable." The application of this test often focuses on the level of crime in the surrounding area and courts that apply this test are more willing to see property crimes or minor offenses as precursors to more violent crimes. In general, the totality of the circumstances test tends to place a greater duty on business owners to foresee the risk of criminal attacks on their property and has been criticized "as being too broad a standard, effectively imposing an unqualified duty to protect customers in areas experiencing any significant level of criminal activity."

The final standard that has been used to determine foreseeability is a balancing test, an approach which has been adopted in California and Tennessee. This approach was originally formulated by the California Supreme Court in Ann M. v. Pacific Plaza Shopping Center in response to the perceived unfairness of the totality test. The balancing test seeks to address the interests of both business proprietors and their customers by balancing the foreseeability of harm against the burden of imposing a duty to protect against the criminal acts of third persons. The Tennessee Supreme Court formulated the test as follows: "In determining the duty that exists, the foreseeability of harm and the gravity of harm must be balanced against the commensurate burden imposed on the business to protect against that harm. In cases in which there is a high degree of foreseeability of harm and the probable harm is great, the burden imposed upon defendant may be substantial. Alternatively, in cases in which a lesser degree of foreseeability is present or the potential harm is slight, less onerous burdens may be imposed." Under this test, the high degree of foreseeability necessary to impose a duty to provide security, will rarely, if ever, be proven in the absence of prior similar incidents of crime on the property.

We agree that a balancing test is the best method for determining when business owners owe a duty to provide security for their patrons. The

THE DUTY TO PROTECT FROM

economic and social impact of requiring businesses to provide security on their premises is an important factor. Security is a significant monetary expense for any business and further increases the cost of doing business in high crime areas that are already economically depressed. Moreover, businesses are generally not responsible for the endemic crime that plagues our communities, a societal problem that even our law enforcement and other government agencies have been unable to solve. At the same time, business owners are in the best position to appreciate the crime risks that are posed on their premises and to take reasonable precautions to counteract those risks.

. . . The greater the foreseeability and gravity of the harm, the greater the duty of care that will be imposed on the business. A very high degree of foreseeability is required to give rise to a duty to post security guards, but a lower degree of foreseeability may support a duty to implement lesser security measures such as using surveillance cameras, installing improved lighting or fencing, or trimming shrubbery. . . .

In the instant case, there were only three predatory offenses on Sam's premises in the six and a half years prior to the robbery of Mrs. Posecai. The first of these offenses occurred well after store hours, at almost one o'clock in the morning. . . . Two years later, an employee of the store was attacked in the parking lot and her purse was taken, apparently by her husband. . . . It is also relevant that Sam's only operates during daylight hours and must provide an accessible parking lot to the multitude of customers that shop at its store each year. . . .

We conclude that Sam's did not possess the requisite degree of foreseeability for the imposition of a duty to provide security patrols in its parking lot. No Duty

NOTES

1. **Applying *Posecai*.** How does the balancing test in *Posecai* work in these cases: (a) The plaintiff is attacked in a mall parking lot and claims the mall owners should have provided better lighting; (b) The plaintiff is attacked in a mall which had security guards but scheduled the guards' rounds negligently so they were not covering the attack area appropriately; (c) The plaintiff leases space in an underground parking garage. She is sexually attacked at her car. The garage's surveillance cameras do not work; some of the lights are out; the place is deteriorating; there is a smell of urine. No crimes of personal violence have been committed in the garage though plenty of other crimes have been committed nearby. *Sharon P. v. Arman,* 989 P.2d 121 (Cal. 1999).

2. **Business creating or enhancing risks.** Suppose a business creates or enhances risks that third persons will attack customers. Should that trigger a duty? *Cf. Brown v. Delta Tau Delta,* 118 A.3d 789 (Me. 2015) (national fraternity had duty to exercise reasonable care for the safety of local chapter's

invitees, including plaintiff, who was sexually assaulted by a fraternity member, where national fraternity "had effectively handed over a residential building to a group of college students" and was aware of alcohol abuse in frat house). What if a business maintains a large, unguarded parking garage? In *Stewart v. Federated Department Stores, Inc.*, 662 A.2d 753 (Conn. 1995), the court imposed liability on a retail store for the murder of a customer in the store's parking garage. The court thought that the unguarded garage, constantly filled with customers laden with packages, was an "invitation" to violence. What if the business is merely located in a remote setting and stays open late? Might that make a violent attack actionable?

3.   **Imminent harm known.** Early cases involved landowners who were present when their invitees were subjected to some imminent threat of harm from others. *See, e.g., Greco v. Sumner Tavern, Inc.*, 128 N.E.2d 788 (Mass. 1955) (tavern owner liable for attack by man had been drinking in the defendant's tavern all day and causing "trouble" beforehand).

4.   **Prior similar incidents approach.** Gradually, a number of courts began to impose liability when attacks by third persons were foreseeable and the business failed to take reasonable steps to protect those on its premises. The usual basis for finding foreseeability in these cases is that there were previous crimes on the premises or nearby. *See, e.g., Nallan v. Helmsley-Spear, Inc.*, 407 N.E.2d 451 (N.Y. 1980). Predictably, what looks like a simple matter of evidence about foreseeability became something of a rule of law for some judges, so that if no similar incidents had occurred on or near the premises, crime was deemed unforeseeable and the business would not be under any duty to take reasonable steps to protect its visitors. *See, e.g., McKown v. Simon Property Group, Inc.*, 344 P.3d 661 (Wash. 2015). You can expect litigation over what counts as a similar incident. *See, e.g., Jenkins v. C.R.E.S. Management, L.L.C.*, 811 F.3d 753 (5th Cir. 2016) (applying Texas law, error for trial judge to exclude evidence of prior residential burglaries on the premises in case brought by plaintiff who was shot in her apartment) *Sturbridge Partners, Ltd. v. Walker*, 482 S.E.2d 339 (Ga. 1997) (knowledge of burglaries might mean that rape is foreseeable); *L.A.C. v. Ward Parkway Shopping Center Co.*, 75 S.W.3d 247 (Mo. 2002) ("Foreseeability does not require identical crimes in identical locations. Violent crimes against women, particularly, serve sufficient notice to reasonable individuals that other violent crimes, including sexual assault or rape of women, may occur.").

5.   **Totality of circumstances approach.** Many courts in answering the duty question now treat the foreseeability issue more holistically. *See, e.g., Bray v. St. John Health System, Inc.*, 187 P.3d 721 (Okla. 2008); *Monk v. Temple George Associates, LLC*, 869 A.2d 179 (Conn. 2005). As *Posecai* explains, this so-called "totality of circumstances" approach takes into account a number of factors, including the existence of prior criminal acts, but the existence of prior crimes is not determinative. *See, e.g., Clohesy v. Food Circus Supermarkets, Inc.*, 694 A.2d 1017 (N.J.1997) ("Generally, our tort law . . . does not require the first victim to lose while subsequent victims are permitted to at least submit their cases to a jury.").

6. **Balancing approach.** The balancing test is attracting more adherents. *See, e.g., Collum v. McCool*, 432 S.W.3d 829 (Tenn. 2013); *Bass v. Gopal, Inc.*, 716 S.E.2d 910 (S.C. 2011). It is not always favorable to plaintiffs, because under this approach the defendant may have no duty to deal with even foreseeable harm. The idea got its impetus from *Ann M. v. Pacific Plaza Shopping Center*, 863 P.2d 207 (Cal. 1993). In that case, the plaintiff, working in a store at a strip mall, was accosted by a man in her place of work, held at knife point, and raped. She sued the mall, claiming it should have had security guards. The court said: "Foreseeability, when analyzed to determine the existence or scope of a duty, is a question of law to be decided by the court. . . . [T]he social costs of imposing a duty on landowners to hire private police forces are also not insignificant. For these reasons, we conclude that a high degree of foreseeability is required in order to find that the scope of a landlord's duty of care includes the hiring of security guards." Given this test, the court held that the shopping mall was not liable in that case for failing to have security guards. *See also Wiener v. Southcoast Childcare Centers, Inc.*, 88 P.3d 517 (Cal. 2004) (utilizing balancing test, holding no duty on the part of a day care center to guard against a criminal act by man who intentionally drove his car through a fence at the center; the driver's "brutal criminal attack was unforeseeable").

7. **Duty vs. breach.** As summarized by the Tennessee court, the balancing test works this way: "In determining the duty that exists, the foreseeability of harm and the gravity of harm must be balanced against the commensurate burden imposed on the business to protect against that harm." *McClung v. Delta Square Ltd. P'ship*, 937 S.W.2d 891 (Tenn. 1996). This sounds like the risk-utility balance for determining negligence, doesn't it?

Does it matter that many courts have used this balancing test in determining *duty* rather than *breach* of duty? In *Staples v. CBL & Associates, Inc.*, 15 S.W.3d 83 (Tenn. 2000), Justice Holder argued in a concurring opinion that unless the question was so clear that reasonable people could not differ, the balancing should be done by the jury as part of its decision on the negligence issue, not by judges. *See also A.W. v. Lancaster County Sch. Dist. 0001*, 784 N.W.2d 907 (Neb. 2010) (foreseeability is a fact question for the jury on the breach issue, and is not part of a duty analysis); *Gipson v. Kasey*, 150 P.3d 228 (Ariz. 2007) (foreseeability is a fact issue for the jury on the breach and causation elements; "foreseeability is not a factor to be considered by courts when making determinations of duty"); *Rodriguez v. Del Sol Shopping Center Associates, L.P.*, 326 P.3d 465 (N.M. 2014) (foreseeability is a fact issue for the jury to consider on breach and proximate cause; "courts must articulate specific policy reasons, unrelated to foreseeability considerations, when deciding whether a defendant does or does not have a duty or that an existing duty should be limited").

8. **The Restatement Third on foreseeability.** The Restatement Third observes in a comment that judicial use of foreseeability in duty determinations "occurs more frequently and aggressively in cases involving an affirmative duty than in other cases," and that this tendency is "even more pronounced in cases in which the alleged duty involves protecting the plaintiff

from third parties, especially the criminal acts of third persons." RESTATEMENT
(THIRD) OF TORTS: LIABILITY FOR PHYSICAL AND EMOTIONAL HARM § 37, cmt. f
(2010). The comment goes on to opine that this approach—which may involve
the formulation of the kinds of tests the court discussed in *Posecai*—
"constitutes an incursion on the role of the jury as factfinder." Do you agree
with this critical assessment?

MARQUAY V. ENO, 662 A.2d 272 (N.H. 1995). Three female students in the
school district brought separate suits in federal court against the district
and individual employees, alleging that teachers or a sports coach had
assaulted, exploited, harassed or sexually abused them and that other
district employees, including teachers, superintendents, principals and
secretaries were or should have been aware of the misconduct. The federal
court certified a number of questions to the Supreme Court of New
Hampshire. Held, supervisory school employees, standing in as proxies for
parents where school attendance is compulsory, owe a duty to report sexual
abuse of students carried out by other school personnel. The duty flows
from compulsory school attendance, which impairs the parental and self-
protection of the students and, in the case of a supervisory employee of the
district, from the employee's relationship with the student. In the case of
those who can hire and fire, it flows also from the relationship with the
abuser. Liability for failure to report may be imposed, provided that
reporting would have prevented subsequent abuse.

NOTES

1.   **Liability of the abusers.** In *Marquay,* the plaintiffs claimed at-
school sexual abuse by employees of the school. The actual abusers are no
doubt liable.

2.   **Vicarious liability.** Employers (including school districts) are
normally liable for the torts of their employees, provided the torts are
committed within the scope of their employment. Thus a school district could
be vicariously liable for the negligence of school personnel in negligently hiring,
retaining or supervising teachers and counselors who abuse students. *C.A. v.
William S. Hart Union High Sch. Dist.*, 270 P.3d 699 (Cal. 2012). Vicarious
liability for the acts of the abuser, at least where that employee is acting for
purely personal reasons, may be doubtful, however. *See* Chapter 22.

3.   **Primary liability of schools.** When the school officials know or
should know of abuse or harassment by teachers or coaches, the officials seem
to be in violation of their duty of care if they do nothing about the abuse.
Marquay seems to support that rule. In addition, the United States Supreme
Court has held that a student states a civil rights claim if school officials do
nothing about sexual harassment by a sports coach. *Franklin v. Gwinnett
County Public Schools,* 503 U.S. 60 (1992). *See also Gebser v. Lago Vista Indep.*

Sch. Dist., 524 U.S. 274 (1998) (setting forth requirements for claim based on teacher's sexual harassment of student).

4. **Immunity of teachers.** The federal Coverdell Teacher Protection Act of 2001, 20 U.S.C.A. § 6736, immunizes teachers and administrators from liability for "harm caused by an act or omission of the teacher on behalf of the school," but applies only to states that accept federal funds for particular programs, and states are allowed to opt out of its provisions. State statutes may also immunize public-school teachers from liability for acts or omissions relating to supervision, care or discipline of students. *See, e.g.,* VA. CODE ANN. § 8.01–220.1:2. This immunity may not extend, however, to administrators. *See Burns v. Gagnon*, 727 S.E.2d 634 (Va. 2012) (vice principal not protected by statute).

WARD V. INISHMAAN ASSOCS. LTD. PARTNERSHIP
931 A.2d 1235 (N.H. 2007)

BRODERICK, C.J. . . .

[On July 12, 2002, Merry Sommers attacked Kristin Ward outside Ward's apartment, stabbing her several times. Sommers and Ward were neighbors in a 329-unit mixed income housing complex owned by Inishmaan Associates and managed by JCM Management Co. Friction between Sommers and Ward had begun in 1999. Sommers frequently made offensive verbal comments to Ward, persistently banged on a common wall that separated their two apartments, and made numerous and unsubstantiated complaints about Ward to the management. In March 2002, Sommers pushed the plaintiff's car door into her while the plaintiff was in the process of removing her son from his car seat. Ward complained to the police and regularly registered her complaints about Sommers' behavior with JCM personnel. After the stabbing incident, Sommers was arrested and charged with attempted murder. Ward sued Inishmaan and JCM for her injuries, alleging that they failed to protect her from Sommers' purported criminal assault. Sommers died before being brought to trial on the criminal charges.]

Following a three-day trial, the jury returned a verdict in favor of the plaintiff. . . . At the close of the plaintiff's case and again at the end of all the evidence, the trial court denied the defendants' motion for directed verdict. The defendants argue that that ruling was erroneous because the plaintiff's evidence failed to establish any of the special circumstances required by law to impose liability on a landlord for criminal assault by a third person . . .

This case is governed by our decision in Walls v. Oxford Management Co., 633 A.2d 103 (N.H. 1993). In that case we were presented with the question whether New Hampshire law imposes a duty on landlords to provide security to protect tenants from the criminal attacks of third

[handwritten margin note: Almost seems like the court was trying to find a way to uphold their verdict]

[handwritten margin note: as plaintiff]

persons. We recognized that the issues raised by that question "place[d] the court at the confluence of two seemingly contradictory principles of law. . . . On one hand lies the accepted maxim that all persons, including landlords, have a duty to exercise reasonable care not to subject others to an unreasonable risk of harm. On the other hand, a competing rule holds that private persons have no general duty to protect others from the criminal acts of third persons."

At the outset, we agreed with numerous courts that have held that, "as a general principle, landlords have no duty to protect tenants from criminal attack." As we noted, "there is much to be gained from efforts at curtailing criminal activity. Yet, we will not place on landlords the burden of insuring their tenants against harm from criminal attacks." We then further considered whether any of the exceptions to the general rule against holding individuals liable for the criminal attacks of others could apply to the landlord-tenant relationship . . .

[O]f four possible exceptions [recognized in the case law] to the general rule that landlords have no duty to protect tenants from criminal attack, we accepted two and rejected the others. Thus, under the holding in *Walls,* such a duty may arise "when a landlord has created, or is responsible for, a known defective condition on a premises that foreseeably enhance[s] the risk of criminal attack." In addition, a landlord who undertakes to provide security has a duty to act with reasonable care. "Where, however, a landlord has made no affirmative attempt to provide security, and is not responsible for a physical defect that enhances the risk of crime, we will not find such a duty. We reject liability based solely on the landlord-tenant relationship or on a doctrine of overriding foreseeability."

. . . Of the two possible exceptions in which a landlord may have a duty to protect tenants from criminal attack, neither one is present in this case. The plaintiff's evidence failed to establish that the defendants created or were responsible for a physical defect on the premises that foreseeably enhanced the risk of criminal attack. Nor did the plaintiff's evidence establish that the defendants undertook to provide security against criminal attacks. Therefore, we hold that the trial court's denial of the defendants' motion for a directed verdict constituted an unsustainable exercise of discretion, and we reverse that ruling. → Holding

[handwritten margin note: Whatever is the complaint for?]

. . . Because we hold that there was no duty as a matter of law, and that the trial court erred in denying the defendants' motions for a directed verdict and summary judgment, the case should not have been submitted to the jury. Accordingly, we vacate the jury's verdict and award and remand this case to the trial court for entry of judgment in favor of the defendants.

NOTES

1. **Affirmative duties of landlords.** Landlords clearly owe a number of duties to tenants. Many courts have held that a landlord owes a duty of reasonable care to tenants with respect to common areas under the landlord's control, although not all have done so. *See* RESTATEMENT (THIRD) OF TORTS: LIABILITY FOR PHYSICAL AND EMOTIONAL HARM § 40, cmt. m (2010). With respect to a duty to protect tenants from criminal attacks by others, many courts are in accord with *Ward* that the landlord-tenant relationship alone does not trigger that duty, *see, e.g., Funchess v. Cecil Newman Corp.*, 632 N.W.2d 666 (Minn. 2001), although some disagree, *see Peterson v. Kings Gate Partners-Omaha I, L.P.*, 861 N.W.2d 444 (Neb. 2015) (landlord-tenant relationship alone triggered duty of reasonable care; whether that duty was breached is a question of fact). Which approach is preferable?

2. **Landlord's provision of security standards.** Might a landlord assume a duty to protect tenants from third party attacks by beginning to provide security? The *Ward* court suggested that such a duty might be assumed by conduct. But the court in *Funchess*, supra Note 1, rejected such a rule, while recognizing that the states are divided on the issue: "We are not inclined to establish a rule that would discourage landlords from improving security. Transforming a landlord's gratuitous provision of security measures into a duty to maintain those measures and subjecting the landlord to liability for all harm occasioned by a failure to maintain that security would tend to discourage landlords from instituting security measures for fear of being held liable for the actions of a criminal."

In a leading case, *Kline v. 1500 Mass. Ave. Apartment Corp.*, 439 F.2d 477 (D.C. Cir. 1970), the plaintiff leased one of 585 apartments in the defendant's building. At that time, there were several forms of protection against intrusion, including a doorman. Seven years later, there was no doorman and other forms of protection had also been withdrawn, although assaults, larcenies and robberies against tenants in the common hallways had increased. Plaintiff was attacked and injured by an intruder in the hallway. The court held that the landlord was under a duty to protect tenants against attacks by third persons. Among other things, the court emphasized (a) the control of the landlord over common passageways and the tenant's lack of power to control them or to protect themselves there; (b) the special character of the modern urban multiple-unit lease; and (c) the notice of the landlord that the tenants were being subjected to crimes against their persons. The court added: "[T]he applicable standard of care in providing protection for the tenant is that standard which this landlord himself was employing . . . when the appellant became a resident. . . ." The court said that the precise protections need not be kept, but that the same relative degree of security had to be maintained.

3. **Physical defects on the premises increasing the risk.** Many courts have agreed that a landlord owes a duty to maintain the physical premises so as not to increase the risk of third-party attacks on tenants. Poor

lighting and non-working locks are common problems. *See, e.g., Hemmings v. Pelham Wood Ltd. Liability Partnership*, 826 A.2d 443 (Md. 2003).

4. **Tenant-on-tenant violence.** Why did it not matter to the duty analysis in *Ward* that the assailant was also a tenant in the defendants' apartment complex? What if the landlord knows that one tenant, especially a roommate of another tenant, has shown violent tendencies in the past and has threatened previous roommates—does that create a duty to warn? *See Galanis v. CMA Management Co.*, 175 So.3d 1213 (Miss. 2015). Should a landlord owe a duty to protect one tenant from another, even if the landlord does not owe a duty to protect a tenant from a stranger? *See* 2 DOBBS, HAYDEN & BUBLICK, THE LAW OF TORTS § 417 (2d ed. 2011); *see also* § 2 below.

5. **Allocation of responsibility.** Suppose a landlord negligently creates or enhances a risk that someone will criminally attack the plaintiff. Someone does attack the plaintiff but he cannot be found or has no funds. Recall that in states that have abolished joint and several liability, the rule is that each tortfeasor is liable only for his own proportionate fault share. What do you think the landlord's share would be as compared to the rapist? Should several liability states return to the joint and several liability rule for this kind of case? This point is considered in more detail in Chapter 25, but you may wish to have the problem in mind as you review the preceding cases and examine those that follow.

§ 2. DEFENDANT'S RELATIONSHIP WITH DANGEROUS PERSONS

DUDLEY V. OFFENDER AID & RESTORATION OF RICHMOND, INC., 401 S.E.2d 878 (Va. 1991). Spencer was a convicted felon with a long, active career in crime. In prison he engaged in vicious beatings of new inmates and set fires; psychologists warned that he was a potential security problem. Because of his violence and for other reasons, he was not eligible to serve any part of his term in a halfway house. Nevertheless, he was permitted to live in one, operated by a private organization. He repeatedly violated rules there, including rules about prompt return from outside work. Security was "practically nonexistent" and Spencer was permitted to leave without much control. He was unaccounted for at 7:00 p.m. During that night he broke into an apartment nearby, bound Davis, beat and raped her, then strangled her to death. In an action against the operator of the halfway house, the trial court sustained the defendant's demurrer.

Held, reversed and remanded. Under the general rule one owes no duty to control the conduct of a third person for the benefit of the plaintiff. However, if the defendant is in a special relationship to either the plaintiff or the third person, the defendant is under a duty of care. The halfway house, upon receiving Spencer, became a custodian in charge. The defendant's duty ran not only to victims that might be identified in advance but to all those who are "directly and foreseeably exposed to risk of bodily harm" from the defendant's negligence. The decedent was within the area of danger.

Foreseeability

NOTES

1. **Duty of custodians.** Most states impose a duty of reasonable care on custodians of dangerous individuals to prevent those individuals from harming members of the public. *See Scott v. Universal Sales, Inc.*, 356 P.3d 1172 (Utah 2015) (adopting § 319 of the Second Restatement of Torts); *see also* RESTATEMENT (THIRD) OF TORTS: LIABILITY FOR PHYSICAL AND EMOTIONAL HARM § 41 (2012). Is there a relationship between custody and foreseeability of harm? The *Scott* court said that custody provides the custodian "with a wealth of information about the inmates' physical and mental capacities to which no one else has comparable access." The court also stressed that the custodial relationship "involves the legal authority to control the person's movement and interactions with the public." Why would "control" matter in imposing a duty of care?

2. **Awareness of a threat to a specific individual.** A few states require, in order to impose a duty, that the custodian be aware of threats to a specific victim or to a group of which the victim is a member. The vast majority, however, do not. Does it make sense to limit a custodian's duty in this manner, or do other elements of the negligence case more appropriately apply?

3. **Custody and "control."** Prisons and hospitals are clearly covered by the custodian rules. But is strict "custody" required to invoke the duty of care imposed in *Dudley*? In *Scott, supra* Note 1, the plaintiff's attacker was an inmate with a long record and violent tendencies who had been placed in a "jail industries" work-release program in the community from which inmates could easily escape. The defendant argued that the custodian's duty should not attach, because there was no "actual, physical control over the individual." The Utah court said that accepting the argument "would create perverse incentives," and that focusing instead on "legal control . . . properly encourages all custodians to be careful about which individuals they expose to the general public through rehabilitative programs." Thus it was not necessary for the imposition of a duty that the defendant had the attacker under its "direct supervision" when he escaped.

4. **A duty to control tenants?** A landlord leases an apartment to a man who, after moving in, sometimes fires a gun from the back yard. The landlord does nothing about it. Subsequently the tenant kills a 10-year-old girl, who, while standing in her own yard, was struck by a bullet fired from the apartment building's yard. Did the landlord owe the victim a duty? In *Rosales v. Stewart*, 169 Cal. Rptr. 660 (Ct. App. 1980), the court said where the lessor has control over a danger from the tenant, he is under a duty of care, though he is not liable if there is no control. "In effect . . . the landlord is under a duty to third persons to do all that he legally can to get rid of a dangerous condition *on the leased premises*, even if it means getting rid of the tenant."

What about the decision to rent to a dangerous person in the first place? For example, what if a landlord suspects that a prospective tenant is a gang member? Should there be a duty not to rent to that person? *See Casteneda v. Olsher*, 162 P.3d 610 (Cal. 2007).

Or suppose a prospective tenant tells a prospective landlord that he has a vicious dog. Should the landlord refuse to lease the premises to him? *Strunk v. Zoltanski*, 468 N.E.2d 13 (N.Y. 1984), holds that the landlord is under a duty to take reasonable precautions to protect others from injury by the dog. But what if the court decides that the landlord lacks the ability to control the dog? *See Fields v. Hayden*, 81 A.3d 367 (Me. 2013) (no duty); *Smaxwell v. Bayard*, 682 N.W.2d 923 (Wis. 2004) (landlords owe duty to protect from a tenant's dogs only where the landlord was also the owner or keeper of the dog); *contra*, *Tracey v. Solesky*, 50 A.3d 1075 (Md. 2012) (landlord with knowledge that a tenant harbored a pit bull was strictly liable for injuries caused by the dog).

5.   **A duty to control a spouse or family members?** Consider: A wife knows her husband has a history of sexual misconduct with young children and might invite neighborhood girls to go swimming in the family pool while she is away. Has she any duty to warn anyone? What if she told neighbors it would be safe for the girls to swim? On similar facts, *see Pamela L. v. Farmer*, 169 Cal. Rptr. 282 (Ct. App. 1980). Compare *J.S. v. R.T.H.*, 714 A.2d 924 (N.J. 1998) (duty of care exists) with *D.W. v. Bliss*, 112 P.3d 232 (Kan. 2005) (no duty).

NOTE: A DUTY TO CONTROL CHILDREN?

1.   *Basic limits.* Remember that parents are not vicariously liable for a child's torts merely on the basis of the parental relationship. That is not to say, however, that parents may not be liable if they themselves are at fault. But in many states this potential liability has rather strict limits. A number of states have simply not recognized a cause of action for negligent supervision of a child. *See Beddingfield v. Linam*, 127 So.3d 1178 (Ala. 2013). Even in those states that recognize potential parental liability, parents are not liable for failure to control a child merely because the child is known to be rough. Instead, parents are liable only for failing to control some specific dangerous habit of a child of which the parent knows or should know in the exercise of reasonable care. *See Sinsel v. Olsen*, 777 N.W.2d 54 (Neb. 2009) (child threw fireworks into a crowd, no parental liability).

2.   *Children known to be violent.* In *Dinsmore-Poff v. Alvord*, 972 P.2d 978 (Alaska 1999), plaintiffs' decedent was murdered by defendants' 17-year-old son. The son had a long history of emotional disturbance and violence. In fact, he had been arrested once for shooting a boy. The parents did not impose curfews or search his belongings. The son used a gun to kill

his victim. The court absolved the parents. It said: "plaintiff must show more than a parent's general notice of a child's dangerous propensity. A plaintiff must show that the parent had reason to know with some specificity of a present opportunity and need to restrain the child to prevent some imminently foreseeable harm."

Williamson v. Daniels, 748 So. 2d 754 (Miss. 1999), absolved the mother of a 15-year-old boy who shot the plaintiff in the chest. Since the mother was not aware of this specific kind of misconduct in the past, she was not responsible. The court thought liability "would pose the risk of transforming parents from care givers and disciplinarians into the jailors and insurers of their minor children," and that "this is a role most parents are ill equipped to take on."

In one astonishing case the "child"—a teenager with a history of aggressive, anti-social behavior—began beating a woman with a hammer. He demanded she remove her clothes. A daughter ran for the phone; he began beating her with a hammer, then began to saw off an ear of his original victim. His parents were well aware of a long history of serious behavior. Psychiatrists had recommended that the boy be treated. The parents were not liable. Apparently the theory was that they could not have foreseen the particular type of violence. *Parsons v. Smithey*, 504 P.2d 1272 (Ariz.1973).

What if the parent or the parent's domestic partner knows that a ten-year-old child has a propensity for sexually abusing younger females and knows also that a four-year-old girl is playing in the home? *Gritzner v. Michael R.*, 611 N.W.2d 906 (Wis. 2000).

3. *Control.* Some courts stress a parent's inability to control their children's behavior as a reason not to impose a duty of reasonable care. This may be simply because the child is older. *See, e.g., Grover v. Stechel*, 45 P.3d 80 (N.M. Ct. App. 2002) (mother's only "control" over adult son who stabbed the plaintiff was financial); *Moore v. Crumpton*, 295 S.E.2d 436 (N.C. 1982) ("The opportunity to control a young man of [17 years] obviously is not as great as with a younger child."). A non-custodial parent may also lack the ability to control. *See K.H. v. J.R.*, 826 A.2d 863 (Pa. 2003) (child shot another with a BB gun given to him by non-custodial parent).

NOTE: A DUTY TO CONTROL EMPLOYEES

1. *Scope of duty.* Employers are generally vicariously liable for the torts of their employees committed within the scope of employment. *See* Chapter 22. But an employer may also owe a duty of reasonable care to protect others from intentional harm by employees, even where the employee acts outside the scope of employment. *See* RESTATEMENT

(SECOND) OF TORTS § 317 (1965) (special relationship between employer and employee places the employer under such a duty, if the employee is either on the employer's premises or is using the employer's chattel); RESTATEMENT (THIRD) OF TORTS: LIABILITY FOR PHYSICAL AND EMOTIONAL HARM § 41 (2012) (such a duty is imposed "when the employment facilitates the employee's causing harm" to another person).

2. *Negligent hiring or retention.* Many courts recognize that an employer may be directly liable for negligently hiring or retaining a dangerous person who later harms the plaintiff. *See, e.g., Spencer v. Health Force, Inc.*, 107 P.3d 504 (N.M. 2005); *Munroe v. Universal Health Serv., Inc.*, 596 S.E.2d 604 (Ga. 2004). Liability often turns on whether the employer knew or should have known that the employee's conduct would subject others to an unreasonable risk of harm. *See Cannizaro v. Marinyak*, 93 A.3d 584 (Conn. 2014).

3. *Negligent supervision or training.* Negligent supervision or training of an employee may also lead to liability. *See, e.g., Graves v. North Eastern Services, Inc.*, 345 P.3d 619 (Utah 2015) (provider of services to the disabled owed duty to supervise employee who sexually assaulted a child on the premises); *Doe v. Hartford Roman Catholic Diocesan Corp.*, 119 A.3d 462 (Conn. 2015) (diocese liable for negligent supervision of priest who sexually abused victim over many years; diocese knew that priest's prior acts of sexual molestation were tied to his alcoholism but did not take reasonable actions to monitor his alcohol problem). The duty of reasonable care may require the employer to conduct an investigation of an employee where there have been complaints about him. *See, e.g., Hall v. City of Newport*, 138 A.3d 814 (R.I. 2016) (family claimed bus driver harassed them).

TARASOFF V. REGENTS OF UNIVERSITY OF CALIFORNIA
551 P.2d 334 (Cal. 1976)

TOBRINER, JUSTICE.

On October 27, 1969, Prosenjit Poddar killed Tatiana Tarasoff. Plaintiffs, Tatiana's parents, allege that two months earlier Poddar confided his intention to kill Tatiana to Dr. Lawrence Moore, a psychologist employed by the Cowell Memorial Hospital at the University of California at Berkeley. They allege that on Moore's request, the campus police briefly detained Poddar, but released him when he appeared rational. They further claim that Dr. Harvey Powelson, Moore's superior, then directed that no further action be taken to detain Poddar. No one warned plaintiffs of Tatiana's peril.

Concluding that these facts set forth causes of action against neither therapists and police involved, nor against the Regents of the University of California as their employer, the superior court sustained defendant's demurrers to plaintiffs' second amended complaints without leave to amend. This appeal ensued.

[Margin note: Procedural Posture]

Plaintiffs' complaints predicate liability on two grounds: defendants' failure to warn plaintiffs of the impending danger and their failure to bring about Poddar's confinement. . . . Defendants, in turn, assert that they owed no duty of reasonable care to Tatiana and that they are immune from suit. . . .

In analyzing this issue, we bear in mind that legal duties are not discoverable facts of nature, but merely conclusory expressions that, in cases of a particular type, liability should be imposed for damage done. As stated in Dillon v. Legg (1968) 68 Cal. 2d 728, 734, 69 Cal. Rptr. 72, 76, 441 P.2d 912, 916: "The assertion that liability must . . . be denied because defendant bears no 'duty' to plaintiff 'begs the essential question whether the plaintiff's interests are entitled to legal protection against the defendant's conduct. . . . [Duty] is not sacrosanct in itself, but only an expression of the sum total of those considerations of policy which lead the law to say that the particular plaintiff is entitled to protection.' (Prosser, Law of Torts [3d ed. 1964] at pp. 332–333.)"

[Margin note: Matter of law "formalism"]

In the landmark case of Rowland v. Christian (1968) 69 Cal. 2d 108, 70 Cal. Rptr. 97, 443 P.2d 561, Justice Peters recognized that liability should be imposed "for an injury occasioned to another by his want of ordinary care or skill" as expressed in Section 1714 of the Civil Code. Thus, Justice Peters, quoting from Heaven v. Pender (1883) 11 Q.B.D. 503, 509 stated: " 'whenever one person is by circumstances placed in such a position with regard to another . . . that if he did not use ordinary care and skill in his own conduct . . . he would cause danger of injury to the person or property of the other, a duty arises to use ordinary care and skill to avoid such danger.' "

We depart from "this fundamental principle" only upon the "balancing of a number of considerations"; major ones "are the foreseeability of harm to the plaintiff, the degree of certainty that the plaintiff suffered injury, the closeness of the connection between the defendant's conduct and the injury suffered, the moral blame attached to the defendant's conduct, the policy of preventing future harm, the extent of the burden to the defendant and consequences to the community of imposing a duty to exercise care with resulting liability for breach, and the availability, cost and prevalence of insurance for the risk involved."

The most important of these considerations in establishing duty is foreseeability. As a general principle, a "defendant owes a duty of care to all persons who are foreseeably endangered by his conduct, with respect to all risks which make the conduct unreasonably dangerous." As we shall explain, however, when the avoidance of foreseeable harm requires a defendant to control the conduct of another person, or to warn of such conduct, the common law has traditionally imposed liability only if the defendant bears some special relationship to the dangerous person or to the potential victim. Since the relationship between a therapist and his patient satisfies this requirement, we need not here decide whether foreseeability alone is sufficient to create a duty to exercise reasonable care to protect a potential victim of another's conduct. . . .

Although plaintiffs' pleadings assert no special relation between Tatiana and defendant therapists, they establish as between Poddar and defendant therapists the special relation that arises between a patient and his doctor or psychotherapist. Such a relationship may support affirmative duties for the benefit of third persons. Thus, for example, a hospital must exercise reasonable care to control the behavior of a patient which may endanger other persons. A doctor must also warn a patient if the patient's condition of medication renders certain conduct, such as driving a car, dangerous to others. . . .

Defendants contend, however, that imposition of a duty to exercise reasonable care to protect third persons is unworkable because therapists cannot accurately predict whether or not a patient will resort to violence. In support of the argument amicus representing the American Psychiatric Association and other professional societies cites numerous articles which indicate that therapists, in the present state of the art, are unable reliably to predict violent acts; their forecasts, amicus claims, tend consistently to overpredict violence, and indeed are more often wrong than right. Since predictions of violence are often erroneous, amicus concludes, the courts should not render rulings that predicate the liability of therapists upon the validity of such predictions. . . .

We recognize the difficulty that a therapist encounters in attempting to forecast whether a patient presents a serious danger of violence. Obviously we do not require that the therapist in making that determination, render a perfect performance; the therapist need only exercise "that reasonable degree of skill, knowledge, and care ordinarily possessed and exercised by members of [that professional specialty] under similar circumstances." Within the broad range of reasonable practice and treatment in which professional opinion and judgment may differ, the therapist is free to exercise his or her own best judgment without liability; proof, aided by hindsight, that he or she judged wrongly is insufficient to establish negligence. . . .

Amicus contends, however, that even when a therapist does in fact predict that a patient poses a serious danger of violence to others, the therapist should be absolved of any responsibility for failing to act to

[margin handwritten note: Asking therapists to do too much]

protect the potential victim. In our view, however, once a therapist does in fact determine, or under applicable professional standards reasonably should have determined, that a patient poses a serious danger of violence to others, he bears a duty to exercise reasonable care to protect the foreseeable victim of that danger. While the discharge of this duty of due care will necessarily vary with the facts of each case, in each instance the adequacy of the therapist's conduct must be measured against the traditional negligence standard of the rendition of reasonable care under the circumstances. As explained in Fleming and Maximov, The Patient or His Victim: The Therapist's Dilemma (1974), 62 CAL. L. REV. 1025, 1067: ". . . The ultimate question of resolving the tension between the conflicting interest of patient and potential victim is one of social policy, not professional expertise. . . In sum, the therapist owes a legal duty not only to his patient, but also to his patient's would-be victim and is subject in both respects to scrutiny by judge and jury." . . .

The risk that unnecessary warnings may be given is a reasonable price to pay for the lives of possible victims that may be saved. We would hesitate to hold that the therapist who is aware that his patient expects to attempt to assassinate the President of the United States would not be obligated to warn the authorities because the therapist cannot predict with accuracy that his patient will commit the crime.

Defendants further argue that free and open communication is essential to psychotherapy; that "Unless a patient . . . is assured that . . . information [revealed by him] can and will be held in utmost confidence, he will be reluctant to make the full disclosure upon which diagnosis and treatment . . . depends." The giving of a warning, defendants contend, constitutes a breach of trust which entails the revelation of confidential communications.

We recognize the public interest in supporting effective treatment of mental illness and in protecting the rights of patients to privacy, and the consequent public importance of safeguarding the confidential character of psychotherapeutic communication. Against this interest, however, we must weigh the public interest in safety from violent assault. The Legislature has undertaken the difficult task of balancing the countervailing concerns. In Evidence Code section 1014, it established a broad rule of privilege to protect confidential communications between patient and psychotherapist. In Evidence Code section 1024, the Legislature created a specific and limited exception to the psychotherapist-patient privilege: "There is no privilege . . . if the psychotherapist has reasonable cause to believe that the patient is in such mental or emotional condition as to be dangerous to himself or to the person or property of

"Property elevated to a pretty paramount concern"

another and that disclosure of the communication is necessary to prevent the threatened danger."[13]

We realize that the open and confidential character of psychotherapeutic dialogue encourages patients to express threats of violence, few of which are ever executed. Certainly a therapist should not be encouraged routinely to reveal such threats; such disclosures could seriously disrupt the patient's relationship with his therapist and with the persons threatened. To the contrary, the therapist's obligations to his patient require that he not disclose a confidence unless such disclosure is necessary to avert danger to others, and even then that he do so discreetly, and in a fashion that would preserve the privacy of his patient to the fullest extent compatible with the prevention of the threatened danger. (See Fleming & Maximov, *The Patient or His Victim: The Therapist's Dilemma* (1974), 62 CAL. L. REV. 1025, 1065–1066.)

The revelation of a communication under the above circumstances is not a breach of trust or a violation of professional ethics; as stated in the Principles of Medical Ethics of the American Medical Association (1957), section 9: "A physician may not reveal the confidence entrusted to him in the course of medical attendance . . . *unless he is required to do so by law or unless it becomes necessary in order to protect the welfare of the individual or of the community.*" (Emphasis added.) We conclude that the public policy favoring protection of the confidential character of patient-psychotherapist communications must yield to the extent to which disclosure is essential to avert danger to others. The protective privilege ends where the public peril begins.

Our current crowded and computerized society compels the interdependence of its members. In this risk-infested society we can hardly tolerate the future exposure to danger that would result from a concealed knowledge of the therapist that his patient was lethal. If the exercise of reasonable care to protect the threatened victim requires the therapist to warn the endangered party or those who can reasonably be expected to notify him, we see no sufficient societal interest that would protect and justify concealment. The containment of such risks lies in the public interest. For the foregoing reasons, we find that plaintiffs' complaints can be amended to state a cause of action against defendants Moore, Powelson,

---

[13] Fleming and Maximov note that "White [section 1024] supports the therapist's less controversial *right* to make a disclosure, it admittedly does not impose on him a *duty* to do so. But the argument does not have to be pressed that far. For if it is once conceded . . . that a duty in favor of the patient's foreseeable victims would accord with general principles of tort liability, we need no longer look to the statute for a source of duty. It is sufficient if the statute can be relied upon . . . for the purposes of countering the claim that the needs of confidentiality are paramount and must therefore defeat any such hypothetical duty. In this more modest perspective, the Evidence Code's 'dangerous patient' exception may be invoked with some confidence as a clear expression of legislative policy concerning the balance between the confidentiality values of the patient and the safety values of his foreseeable victim." (Emphasis in original.) Fleming & Maximov, *The Patient or His Victim: The Therapist's Dilemma* (1974), 62 CAL. L. REV. 1025, 1063.

Gold, and Yandell and against the Regents as their employer, for breach of a duty to exercise reasonable care to protect Tatiana. . . .

Turning now to the police defendants, we conclude that they do not have any such special relationship to either Tatiana or to Poddar sufficient to impose upon such defendants a duty to warn respecting Poddar's violent intentions. Plaintiffs suggest no theory, and plead no facts that give rise to any duty to warn on the part of the police defendants absent such a special relationship. . . .

[Dissenting opinions omitted.]

NOTES

1. **Scope.** Consider whether, given a *Tarasoff* duty, therapists will be liable in every case in which a patient causes harm after making a threat. On what facts would a therapist be counted as reasonably prudent even if he fails to warn after a threat is made?

2. ***Tarasoff* and *Thompson*.** Four years after issuing *Tarasoff*, the California Court decided *Thompson v. County of Alameda*, 614 P.2d 728 (Cal. 1980). In that case, the court refused to impose liability upon a county which had released a dangerous criminal who was threatening to kill some unnamed child. When released on furlough, he did in fact kill a 5-year-old child. Can *Thompson* and *Tarasoff* be squared? The *Thompson* court suggested a possibility: "In those instances in which the released offender poses a predictable threat of harm to a named or readily identifiable victim . . . a releasing agent may well be liable for failure to warn such persons." *See also State Dep't of Corrections v. Cowles*, 151 P.3d 353 (Alaska 2006) (state owed duty to exercise care in supervising parolees only where officials knew or should know that the parolee posed a danger to a particular person or identifiable group of persons); *Osborn v. Mason County*, 134 P.3d 197 (Wash. 2006) (citing *Thompson*, holding county owed no duty to warn of sex offender's presence where victim was "unforeseeable"). Does this reasoning suggest that if Poddar had shown a clear and strong probability that he would kill a number of small children, or old women, the psychiatrist would not owe any duty to later victims? Is the *Thompson* reasoning sound? The Wisconsin Court thought there was "no legitimate policy" for the *Thompson* limitation on the duty of care, *Schuster v. Altenberg*, 424 N.W.2d 159 (Wis. 1988), and most jurisdictions have rejected it, at least in its narrowest form. *See Scott v. Universal Sales, Inc.*, 356 P.3d 1172 (Utah 2015) (reversing its own prior precedent that required an "identifiable victim," and collecting cases).

3. **Accepting the *Tarasoff* duty.** The Restatement Third recognizes the special relationship of "mental health professional with patients" as one giving rise to a duty of reasonable care to act for the protection of others. RESTATEMENT (THIRD) OF TORTS: LIABILITY FOR PHYSICAL AND EMOTIONAL HARM § 41 (2012). Many states have adopted some sort of *Tarasoff* duty by statute. In addition, the vast majority of courts that have considered the issue

have accepted such a duty. *See Kuligoski v. Brattleboro Retreat*, ___ A.3d ___, 2016 VT 54A, 2016 WL 5793088 (Vt. 2016) (extensively reviewing *Tarasoff's* acceptance in other states, including variations).

4. **Rejecting or modifying *Tarasoff*.** A few courts have rejected *Tarasoff. See, e.g., Tedrick v. Community Resource Center, Inc.*, 920 N.E.2d 220 (Ill. 2009) (largely on the ground that a mental health provider owes no duty to a non-patient); *Nasser v. Parker*, 455 S.E.2d 502 (Va. 1995). A duty to warn may be created, however, by a promise made to the victim. *See* 2 DOBBS, HAYDEN & BUBLICK, THE LAW OF TORTS § 423 (2d ed. 2011). Some courts have rejected a duty when the patient is not in the mental health provider's "custody" (as Poddar was not in *Tarasoff*). *See, e.g., Adams v. Board of Sedgwick County Com'rs*, 214 P.3d 1173 (Kan. 2009); *Santana v. Rainbow Cleaners*, 969 A.2d 653 (R.I. 2009).

BRIGANCE V. VELVET DOVE RESTAURANT, INC.
725 P.2d 300 (Okla. 1986)

HODGES, JUDGE.

[The defendant, the Velvet Dove Restaurant, served alcohol to a group of minors, including one Jeff Johnson. Defendant's employees knew Jeff Johnson drove the group to the restaurant. The plaintiffs alleged that alcohol served by the defendant caused Johnson to become intoxicated or increased his earlier intoxication and that this in turn caused a one-car accident in which the plaintiff Shawn was injured. The trial court dismissed the claim.]

At common law a tavern owner who furnishes alcoholic beverages to another is not civilly liable for a third person's injuries that are caused by the acts of an intoxicated patron. Such rule is principally based upon concepts of causation that, as a matter of law, it is not the sale of liquor by the tavern owner, but the voluntary consumption by the intoxicated person, which is the proximate cause of resulting injuries, so that the tavern owner is therefore not liable for negligence in selling the liquor.

In recent years, many states have retreated from the common law rule of nonliability for a liquor vendor regarding it as antiquated and illogical. Several states with dram shop laws have also recognized a new common law right of action against a vendor of liquor. Many of the jurisdictions which now recognize a civil right of action do so on the theory enunciated in Rappaport v. Nichols, 31 N.J. 188, 156 A.2d 1 (1959):

> "When alcoholic beverages are sold by a tavern keeper to a minor or to an intoxicated person, the unreasonable risk of harm . . . to members of the traveling public may readily be recognized and foreseen; this is particularly evident in current times when traveling by car to and from the tavern is so commonplace and accidents resulting from drinking are so frequent."

As shown by the modern trend, the old common law rule of nonliability has been changed by judicial opinion: "Inherent in the common law is a dynamic principle which allows it to grow and to tailor itself to meet changing needs. . . ."

. . . The development of the law of torts is peculiarly a function of the judiciary. Because duty and liability are matters of public policy they are subject to the changing attitudes and needs of society. . . .

Appellees assert that we are not free to change the common law because the Legislature has expressly spoken in this area by its 1959 repeal of Oklahoma's dram shop act and its failure to reenact such provision since that time. We are not persuaded by this argument. The dram shop act was not selectively repealed for it was repealed when intoxicants were legalized in 1959. Because the Legislature has failed to act to impose civil liability, for reasons unknown, does not unequivocally demonstrate legislative intent. To hold otherwise, would be indulging in a type of psychoanalysis of the Legislature. We simply cannot conclude that statutory silence is here indicative of legislative intent to bar the cause of action before us.

We also cannot accede to the view urged by appellees that this area of law is better dealt with by the Legislature. We find that on the basis of the clear trend in this area we are free to establish a civil cause of action by an injured third person against a commercial vendor of liquor for on the premises consumption. In rendering the opinion of Vanderpool v. State, 672 P.2d 1153, 1157 (Okla.1983), which modified the common law doctrine of governmental immunity, this Court stated in response to the oft-expressed view that if the doctrine is to be abrogated such should be done by the Legislature and not the courts of this State: "But having come to the conclusions that the judicially recognized doctrine of governmental immunity in its present state under the case law is no longer supportable in reason, justice or in light of the overwhelming trend against its recognition, our duty is clear. Where the reason for the rule no longer exists, that alone should toll its death knell."

We believe the application of the old common law rule of a tavern owner's nonliability in today's automotive society is unrealistic, inconsistent with modern tort theories and is a complete anachronism within today's society.

The automobile is a constant reminder of a changed and changing America. It has made a tremendous impact on every segment of society, including the field of jurisprudence. In the "horse and buggy" days the common law may not have been significantly affected by the sale of liquor to an intoxicated person. The common law of nonliability was satisfactory. With today's car of steel and speed it becomes a lethal weapon in the hands of a drunken imbiber. The frequency of accidents involving drunk drivers are commonplace. Its affliction of bodily injury to an unsuspecting public is also of common knowledge. Under such circumstances we are compelled to widen the scope of the common law.

We, thus, hold that one who sells intoxicating beverages for on the premises consumption has a duty to exercise reasonable care not to sell liquor to a noticeably intoxicated person. It is not unreasonable to expect a commercial vendor who sells alcoholic beverages for on the premises consumption to a person he knows or should know from the circumstances is already intoxicated, to foresee the unreasonable risk of harm to others who may be injured by such person's impaired ability to operate an automobile.

. . . A commercial vendor for on the premises consumption is under a common law duty to exercise ordinary care under the circumstances. We reach our conclusion in accordance with other courts finding a common law duty, relying on the general rule expressed in Restatement (Second) of Torts § 308 (1965):

> "It is negligence to permit a third person to use a thing or to engage in an activity which is under the control of the actor, if the actor knows or should know that such person intends or is likely to use the thing or to conduct himself in the activity in such a manner as to create an unreasonable risk of harm to others."

And, Restatement (Second) of Torts § 390 (1965):

> "One who supplies . . . a chattel for the use of another whom the supplier knows or has reason to know to be likely because of his youth, inexperience or otherwise to use it in a manner involving unreasonable risk of physical harm to himself and others . . . is subject to liability for physical harm resulting to them."

Even if a commercial vendor for on the premises consumption is found to have breached its duty, a plaintiff must still show the illegal sale of alcohol led to the impairment of the ability of the driver which was the proximate cause of the injury and there was a causal connection between the sale and a foreseeable ensuing injury. . . .

. . . Ordinarily the question of causation in a negligent tort case is one of fact for the jury and becomes one of law only when there is no evidence from which the jury could reasonably find a causal nexus between the negligent act and the resulting injuries. . . .

In adopting a new rule of liability which creates a civil cause of action, we specifically hold that the law hereby established will be applied prospectively to all causes of action occurring from and after the date the mandate issues herein [except that the rule of liability also applies to the parties in this case. Reversed and remanded.] ——> Holding!

NOTES

1. **The traditional approach to alcohol-sales cases.** Courts traditionally denied the kind of liability imposed in *Brigance* on the ground that the alcohol provider was not a proximate cause of harm done by the drinker. Some courts or legislatures still reject liability even for providing alcohol to minors or intoxicated persons. *See, e.g. Warr v. JMGM Group, LLC*, 70 A.3d 347 (Md. 2013).

2. **Rulings as a matter of law.** Scope of liability (proximate cause) is usually decided case by case, often by the jury but in any event on the facts peculiar to the case. In the older alcohol-provider cases, however, judges often made a rule of law for all cases: the provider's fault was *never* a proximate cause. Would it make more sense to say that this was a no-duty rule? Are there any policy bases for exculpating the seller of alcohol? What if the server cannot be sure whether a customer is intoxicated?

3. **Reversing the common-law rule.** The *Brigance* case is one of many that have reversed the traditional rules, and have imposed a common-law duty on the part of a licensed seller of alcohol to use reasonable care. Liability is often imposed when the defendant negligently sells alcohol to a minor or an intoxicated person who, as a result, injures the plaintiff. *See* DOBBS, HAYDEN & BUBLICK, HORNBOOK ON TORTS § 26.12 (2d ed. 2016). Statutes often determine who is liable, and under what circumstances; they sometimes provide an exclusive remedy, sometimes not. *See* NOTE: DRAM SHOP STATUTES, below.

4. **Fixing responsibility.** The common law has expressed in many ways a strong belief that each individual should be responsible for his or her own actions. Not only does this imply, for some judges, that one is not responsible for the acts of others, but it implies that responsibility should not be shared. Thus courts had some difficulty in imposing joint and several liability upon multiple wrongdoers. If the last actor was an intentional wrongdoer, the feeling at one time apparently was that he and only he should be liable. To impose joint liability would lighten his burden and thus diminish his accountability. What arguments can you mount against this kind of outlook? Relatedly, you'll want to remember why the plaintiff is suing the alcohol provider.

5. **Suits by the drinker.** In a state that allows for some alcohol-provider liability, does the provider owe a duty of care to the drinker himself, or only to third persons who may be injured? Some courts have said the duty runs to the drinker as well as to others. *See, e.g., Mann v. Shusteric Enterp., Inc.*, 683 N.W.2d 573 (Mich. 2004). However, most appear to hold that the adult drinker is responsible for his own injury and the provider owes him nothing. *See, e.g., Rodriguez v. Primadonna Co.*, 216 P.3d 793 (Nev. 2009); *Bridges v. Park Place Entn't*, 860 So. 2d 811 (Miss. 2003). If a duty of care is owed to the drinker himself, why is this not a *Bexiga* situation?

6. **Liability of social hosts: basic rules.** Not surprisingly, some courts willing to impose liability upon sellers of alcohol are not willing to impose liability upon social hosts who provide alcohol with the same results. *Reynolds v. Hicks*, 951 P.2d 761 (Wash.1998). Nevertheless, a growing number of courts have approved of such liability, especially where the host has knowingly provided alcohol to minors. *See, e.g., Nichols v. Progressive Northern Ins. Co.*, 746 N.W.2d 220 (Wis. 2008); *Marcum v. Bowden*, 643 S.E.2d 85 (S.C. 2007); *Martin v. Marciano*, 871 A.2d 911 (R.I. 2005) (underage drinker who was served alcohol at high school graduation party). Some states allow social host liability, but require a showing of recklessness rather than negligence in serving alcohol. *See, e.g., Hickingbotham v. Burke*, 662 A.2d 297 (N.H.1995); *Delfino v. Griffo*, 257 P.3d 917 (N.M. 2011) (applying statute). Oregon allows for social host liability, but only where the plaintiff proves by clear and convincing evidence that the social host served a visibly intoxicated guest. *See Deckard v. Bunch*, 370 P.3d 478 (Or. 2016) (construing OR. REV. STAT. § 471.565). Other statutes may make it illegal for an adult to allow underage persons to consume alcohol on the adult's property. In *Kiriakos v. Phillips*, 139 A.3d 1006 (Md. 2016), the court held that such a statute supported the imposition of a tort duty on social hosts in two consolidated cases, one brought by the mother of a minor who died in an auto accident after leaving a party, and the other by a pedestrian struck by a car driven by an intoxicated minor after leaving a party.

7. **Liability of social hosts: extensions.** California maintains an immunity for social hosts who merely furnish or give drinks away. But by statute, a person not licensed to sell alcohol who sells to an obviously intoxicated minor loses that immunity and can be liable in tort. Suppose a social host charges a fee to enter a party, and payment of that fee entitles guests to drink the provided alcoholic beverages. Does that host face tort liability? *See Ennabe v. Manosa*, 319 P.3d 201 (Cal. 2014) (yes, this can be considered a "sale").

Arizona law also specifically exempts social hosts from liability for harm caused by a drinker of legal age. But in *Gipson v. Kasey*, 150 P.3d 228 (Ariz. 2007), the court held that a man who gave prescription drugs to a female coworker at a company party, who in turn gave the drugs to her boyfriend, who died after taking them, owed a duty of care based largely on statutes criminalizing the distribution of prescription drugs. The court said that "Holding social hosts liable for harm caused by guests to whom they serve alcohol might curb desirable social exchanges. In contrast, no recognized social benefit flows from the illegal distribution of prescription drugs."

8. **Scope of risk, redux.** Even where a duty is owed by an alcohol provider, the defendant might still avoid liability in some cases because the injury is outside the scope of the risk created by the provision of alcohol—or, if you prefer, is not a proximate result of the breach. What if a bar serves alcohol to a visibly intoxicated patron, who leaves the bar and, without any apparent motive, fires a gun through the doorway of a nearby business, injuring the plaintiff? *See Chapman v. Mayfield*, 361 P.3d 566 (Or. 2015). Determining

scope of risk (proximate cause) is for a jury, remember, where reasonable people can differ.

NOTE: DRAM SHOP STATUTES

1. *Variations.* The traditional view is a statute regulating sales of alcohol—for example, a statute prohibiting sales to minors or intoxicated persons—does not create a private cause of action. *Robinson v. Matt Mary Moran, Inc.*, 525 S.E.2d 559 (Va. 2000). Now, however, many states have adopted statutes called dram shop statutes or civil damage acts that do not merely impose criminal penalties; instead, they expressly impose civil liability upon the dispenser of alcohol. There are many variations. Some statutes impose liability only for certain kinds of sales, such as sales to minors or intoxicated persons. Others require a higher showing than mere negligence. Some statutes apply only to those who sell alcohol for consumption on the premises, as opposed to stores selling packaged liquor. Others allow suits against those who sell closed or packaged liquor for off-site consumption, if the buyer is noticeably intoxicated and the seller knows he will soon be driving.

2. *Safety effects of statutes.* Dram shop liability has deterred alcohol providers from engaging in certain specific practices that lead to intoxication and drunk driving, such as serving multiple drinks at one time, and has reduced motor vehicle fatalities. *See* Ellen M. Bublick, *China's New Tort Law: The Promise of Reasonable Care*, 13 ASIAN-PAC. L. & POL'Y J. 36, 53 (2011).

3. *Exclusive remedy.* The dram shop statute may be the exclusive remedy against an alcohol provider, barring all common law claims relating to injuries caused by the defendant's sales. *See, e.g., Bauer v. Nesbitt*, 969 A.2d 1122 (N.J. 2009); *Delta Airlines, Inc. v. Townsend*, 614 S.E.2d 745 (Ga. 2005).

4. *Immunities.* At the other extreme, legislators in some states have immunized alcohol providers for negligence, even where they have served drunken customers who are likely to drive. *See, e.g.,* TENN. CODE ANN. §§ 57–10–101 *et seq.*; WIS. STAT. ANN. § 125.035.

NOTE: NEGLIGENT ENTRUSTMENT

1. *Basic contours.* The *Brigance* court cited with approval two sections of the Restatement Second that deal with what is commonly called "negligent entrustment." The thrust of this body of law is that a person in control of a chattel owes a responsibility not to entrust that chattel to a

person whom the entruster knows or should know, at the time of the entrustment, is likely to use it in a dangerous way. *See, e.g., Sheffer v. Carolina Forge Co.*, 306 P.3d 544 (Okla. 2013). Many courts have adopted the rules from section 390 of the Restatement Second, and hold that a plaintiff must prove (1) that the defendant entrusted a chattel, (2) to an incompetent entrustee, (3) with knowledge or reason to know of the entrustee's incompetence, and (4) the entrustee's incompetence while using the chattel caused the injury. *Martell v. Driscoll*, 302 P.3d 375 (Kan. 2013).

2.   *Theft of chattel.* Note that if a chattel is stolen from a defendant, the defendant has not "entrusted" the chattel to the thief and is thus not liable on this theory. *See, e.g., Estate of Kim ex rel. Alexander v. Coxe*, 295 P.3d 380 (Alaska 2013).

3.   *Kinds of chattels covered.* Most cases involve products that could be operated by the entrustee, such as cars, guns, or cigarette lighters. *See, e.g., Morin v. Moore*, 309 F.3d 316 (5th Cir. 2002) (making an AK–47 automatic rifle accessible to a dangerous person invested in Nazi ideology); *Shirley v. Glass*, 308 P.3d 1 (Kan. 2013) (entrusting shotgun to man known to have been convicted of attempted rape and attempted kidnapping, and "tended to lose control of himself when he was angry"); *Ardinger v. Hummell*, 982 P.2d 727 (Alaska 1999) (furnishing automobile to 15-year-old).

4.   *First-party negligent entrustment.* In most states a negligent entruster may be liable not only to third persons injured by the entrustee, but also to the entrustee himself. *See Herland v. Izatt* (Utah 2015) (entrustment of gun to intoxicated guest, who accidentally shot herself in the head); *Martell v. Driscoll*, 302 P.3d 375 (Kan. 2013) (entrustment of car to person known to have a suspended license, a history of DUI's, and a history of alcohol abuse).

REFERENCES: DOBBS, HAYDEN & BUBLICK, HORNBOOK ON TORTS §§ 26.1–26.12 (2d ed. 2016); 2 DOBBS, HAYDEN & BUBLICK, THE LAW OF TORTS §§ 413–424 (2d ed. 2011).

PART 7

SPECIAL TYPES OF HARM

■ ■ ■

Judicial attitudes about tort liability depend in part upon the relationships of the parties, as we saw in the last few chapters, but also in part upon the kind of harm the plaintiff claims she suffered.

In the absence of special relationships, courts are most receptive to tort claims when the defendant has risked and the plaintiff has suffered physical harm to her person or property. What tort cases do *not* involve physical harms? First, cases of stand-alone economic harm. For example, suppose a defendant negligently provides the plaintiff with information that leads the plaintiff to purchase a piece of property. The information proves erroneous, and the plaintiff loses money on the deal. No one or nothing is physically injured; the loss is purely economic. Second, cases of stand-alone emotional distress. For example, suppose the defendant negligently provides the plaintiff information leading the plaintiff believe that her child has been seriously injured. Before the plaintiff discovers that the information is false, she suffers serious emotional, but not physical, harm.

Several different torts besides the tort of negligence address emotional interests. Physical torts like battery, assault and false imprisonment obviously have the protection of emotional interests as one component. Defamation (libel and slander), malicious prosecution, the right to privacy and the nuisance tort also protect emotional interests tied to reputation, seclusion, and the enjoyment of land.

The three chapters that follow consider how courts treat negligence claims for emotional harm, prenatal injury and wrongful death.

CHAPTER 19

EMOTIONAL HARM

■ ■ ■

This chapter focuses on stand-alone claims for emotional distress. Such a claim can be for intentional infliction of emotional distress (IIED), or negligent infliction of emotional distress (NIED). As we will see, both claims are subject to significant restrictions.

Courts have long recognized that tortfeasors should be responsible for causing pain, anxiety, emotional distress, and similar intangible harms. But courts approach emotional distress damages in two quite different ways, depending on whether the emotional harm is considered a stand-alone claim—our focus here—or simply as a category of damages "parasitic" to another tort. When emotional distress damages are sought in connection with a tort claim such as negligence (as "pain and suffering") or assault (where the damages are for the mental distress resulting from being aware of an imminent battery), none of the limiting rules discussed in this chapter will apply. That is, the restrictions we see in this chapter have arisen to limit stand-alone emotional distress claims, not to limit the recovery of damages for pain or distress caused by the commission of some other tort. *See* DOBBS, HAYDEN & BUBLICK, HORNBOOK ON TORTS § 29.1 (2d ed. 2016).

§ 1. INTENTIONAL INFLICTION OF EMOTIONAL DISTRESS

CHANKO V. AMERICAN BROADCASTING COMPANIES, INC.
49 N.E.3d 1171 (N.Y. 2016)

STEIN, J. . . .

Mark Chanko (decedent) was brought into the emergency room of defendant The New York and Presbyterian Hospital (the Hospital). He had been hit by a vehicle, but was alert and responding to questions. Defendant Sebastian Schubl was the Hospital's chief surgical resident and was responsible for decedent's treatment. While decedent was being treated, employees of ABC News, a division of defendant American Broadcasting Companies, Inc. (ABC), were in the Hospital—with the Hospital's knowledge and permission—filming a documentary series (N.Y. Med) about medical trauma and the professionals who attend to the patients suffering from such trauma. No one informed decedent or any of the individual plaintiffs—most of whom were at the Hospital—that a camera crew was present and filming, nor was their consent obtained for filming or for the crew's presence.

Less than an hour after decedent arrived at the Hospital, Schubl declared him dead. That declaration was filmed by ABC, and decedent's prior treatment was apparently filmed as well. Schubl then informed the family of decedent's death, with that moment also being recorded without their knowledge.

Sixteen months later, decedent's widow, plaintiff Anita Chanko, watched an episode of N.Y. Med on her television at home. She recognized the scene, heard decedent's voice asking about her, saw him on a stretcher, heard him moaning, and watched him die. In addition, she saw, and relived, Schubl telling the family of his death. She then told the other plaintiffs, who also watched the episode. This was the first time plaintiffs became aware of the recording of decedent's medical treatment and death.

Plaintiffs commenced this action against, among others, ABC, the Hospital and Schubl. Defendants separately moved to dismiss the complaint. [The trial court partially granted the motions, dismissing the causes of action against all defendants for intentional infliction of emotional distress. The Appellate Division affirmed the dismissal of the these claims, and plaintiffs appealed.]

This Court has enumerated four elements of a cause of action for intentional infliction of emotional distress: (i) extreme and outrageous conduct; (ii) intent to cause, or disregard of a substantial probability of causing, severe emotional distress; (iii) a causal connection between the conduct and injury; and (iv) severe emotional distress. Liability has been found only where the conduct has been so outrageous in character and so extreme in degree, as to go beyond all possible bounds of decency, and to be regarded as atrocious, and utterly intolerable in a civilized community. Here, the complaint . . . alleges that the Hospital and Schubl allowed ABC to broadcast and disseminate the footage of the final moments of decedent's life, without the knowledge or consent of decedent or plaintiffs. The complaint alleges that plaintiffs watched the episode and were shocked and upset, that "[d]efendants acted intentionally, recklessly, willfully, maliciously and deliberately," and that it was foreseeable that plaintiffs would be caused to suffer emotional distress. Alternatively, the complaint alleges that "defendants acted with reckless disregard for the probability that they would cause plaintiffs to suffer emotional distress," and that defendants knew or should have known that emotional distress was a likely result of their actions. The complaint further alleges that plaintiffs experienced emotional distress due to defendants' conduct, and that "[d]efendants' conduct was extreme and outrageous, beyond all possible bounds of decency, utterly intolerable in a civilized community, and without privilege."

Although these allegations facially address all of the required elements, they are not sufficient to support this cause of action because they do not rise to the level necessary to satisfy the outrageousness element—the element most susceptible to a determination as a matter of law—which is designed to filter out petty complaints and assure that the emotional distress is genuine. Noting that "the requirements . . . are rigorous, and difficult to satisfy," we have commented that, "of the intentional infliction of emotional distress claims considered by this Court, *every one* has failed because the alleged conduct was not sufficiently outrageous".

The conduct at issue here . . .—the broadcasting of a recording of a patient's last moments of life without consent—would likely be considered reprehensible by most people, and we do not condone it. Nevertheless, it was not so extreme and outrageous as to satisfy our exceedingly high legal standard. The footage aired by ABC was edited so that it did not include decedent's name, his image was blurred, and the episode included less than three minutes devoted to decedent and his circumstances. We cannot conclude that defendants' conduct in allowing the broadcasting of that brief, edited segment is more outrageous than other conduct that this Court and the Appellate Division Departments have determined did not rise to the level required to establish "extreme and outrageous conduct" sufficient to state a cause of action for intentional infliction of emotional distress. For example, we did not deem a newspaper's conduct sufficiently outrageous when it published a picture of a person in a psychiatric facility—thereby informing the world that the photographed person was a patient at such a facility—even though the residents were photographed by someone trespassing on facility grounds and the facility had expressly requested that the newspaper not publish pictures of residents. Similarly, the conduct of a television station has been deemed insufficiently outrageous when the station displayed recognizable images of rape victims after repeatedly assuring them that they would not be identifiable.

We conclude that defendants' conduct here, while offensive, was not so atrocious and utterly intolerable as to support a cause of action in the context of this tort. Hence, there is no need to address whether the newsworthiness privilege is applicable.

[The order dismissing plaintiffs' claims for intentional infliction of emotional distress is affirmed.]

GTE SOUTHWEST, INC. V. BRUCE, 998 S.W.2d 605 (Tex. 1999). Several employees of GTE working under Morris Shields alleged that over a period of years, Shields engaged in a pattern of grossly abusive, threatening, and degrading conduct, regularly using the harshest vulgarity, verbally threatening and terrorizing them. He would physically charge at the employees, put his head down, ball his hands into fists, and walk quickly toward or lunge at the employees, stopping very close to their faces. A number of witnesses testified that Shields frequently yelled and screamed at the top of his voice, and pounded his fists when requesting the employees to do things. There was testimony that he often called one employee into his office and kept her standing there up to thirty minutes while he simply started at her. He required employees to vacuum their own offices daily despite the availability of regular janitorial services. A jury found for plaintiffs in their suit for intentional infliction of emotional distress. *Held*, affirmed.

"Generally, insensitive or even rude behavior does not constitute extreme and outrageous conduct. Similarly, mere insults, indignities, threats, annoyances, petty oppressions, or other trivialities do not rise to the level of extreme and outrageous conduct. In determining whether certain conduct is extreme and outrageous, courts consider the context and the relationship between the parties. . . . Shields's ongoing acts of harassment, intimidation, and humiliation and his daily obscene and vulgar behavior, which GTE defends as his 'management style,' went beyond the bounds of tolerable workplace conduct. . . . Occasional malicious and abusive incidents should not be condoned, but must often be tolerated in our society. But once conduct such as that shown here becomes a regular pattern of behavior and continues despite the victim's objection and attempts to remedy the situation, it can no longer be tolerated. It is the severity and regularity of Shields's abusive and threatening conduct that brings his behavior into the realm of extreme and outrageous conduct."

NOTES

1. **History of the tort.** The American Law Institute recognized the tort of intentional infliction of mental distress in the Restatement of Torts in 1948. The Second Restatement § 46 first employed the "extreme and outrageous conduct" standard and courts widely adopted it. To determine whether conduct is extreme and outrageous courts often ask "whether the recitation of the facts to an average member of the community would arouse her resentment against the defendant so that she would exclaim 'Outrageous!'" *Howerton v. Harbin Clinic, LLC,* 776 S.E.2d 288 (Ga. Ct. App. 2015) (using a test from the Second Restatement and holding that surgeon's lewd actions met the outrageousness threshold).

2. **The Restatement Third of Torts.** The elements under the Third Restatement are slightly different from those in *Chanko.* According to the Restatement, "[a]n actor who by extreme and outrageous conduct intentionally or recklessly causes severe emotional harm to another is subject to liability for

that emotional harm and, if the emotional harm causes bodily harm, also for the bodily harm." RESTATEMENT (THIRD) OF TORTS: LIABILITY FOR PHYSICAL AND EMOTIONAL HARM § 46 cmt. m (2012). In what way does the standard in *Chanko* seem easier to satisfy than the standard in the Restatement? *See Hill v. Cundiff*, 797 F.3d 948 (11th Cir. 2015).

3. **Judging extreme and outrageous conduct.** Courts are often called upon to determine whether conduct is "so outrageous in character, and so extreme in degree, as to go beyond all possible bounds of decency, and to be regarded as atrocious, and utterly intolerable in civilized society." *Tiller v. McLure*, 121 S.W.3d 709 (Tex. 2003). Or whether the conduct is only "unfortunate" or engenders "the mere disapproval" of the community. *Mik v. Federal Home Loan Mortgage Corp.*, 743 F.3d 149 (6th Cir. 2014); *see also Ortberg v. Goldman Sachs Group*, 64 A.3d 158 (D.C. 2013) (anti-Goldman Sachs protestors protesting outside employee's home and chanting "we know where you sleep at night," was not extreme and outrageous). According to the Restatement, the terms extreme and outrageous serve distinct roles. "Some conduct that may be outrageous—for example, marital infidelity—is sufficiently common that it could not be characterized as extreme." Moreover, "some extreme conduct—climbing Mt. Everest, for example—is not outrageous." RESTATEMENT (THIRD) OF TORTS: LIABILITY FOR PHYSICAL AND EMOTIONAL HARM § 46 cmt. d (2012). Could the conduct in *Chanko* and *GTE* be considered extreme and outrageous? Typically a court takes the question from the jury only when there is insufficient evidence to permit a jury to reach that conclusion, "[h]owever, the court plays a more substantial screening role on the questions of extreme and outrageous conduct." *Id.* cmt. g. Should the jury in *Chanko* have had an opportunity to evaluate whether the conduct was extreme or outrageous?

4. **Markers of outrage.** Perhaps the most common fact patterns involve conduct that is (a) repeated or carried out over a period of time, (b) an abuse of power by a person with some authority over the plaintiff, or (c) directed at a person known to be especially vulnerable. Which, if any, pattern does *Chanko* fit? Which pattern does *GTE* fit?

5. **Repeated conduct.** A single request for sexual contact might be offensive but is usually not sufficiently outrageous. *See Jones v. Clinton,* 990 F. Supp. 657 (E.D. Ark. 1998). On the other hand, repeated and harassing requests for sexual attention can be outrageous. Conduct that takes place over a long time can be actionable as well. *See Bratton v. McDonough*, 91 A.3d 1050 (Me. 2014) (landlord allowed tenants with young children to live for four years in a house containing toxic levels of lead, and delayed the tenants' relocation for four months after the State had declared the house a lead hazard; jury question); *Turley v. ISG Lackawanna, Inc.*, 774 F.3d 140 (2d Cir. 2014).

6. **Abuse of power.** Abuse of power by the defendant takes many forms. It might involve employers and employees, or public officials and those in a subordinate position. *See, e.g., Brandon v. County of Richardson*, 624 N.W.2d 604 (Neb. 2001) (sheriff crudely questioning rape victim soon after

rape); *Hysjulien v. Hill Top Home of Comfort, Inc.*, 827 N.W.2d 533 (N.D. 2013) (employee who, at a work conference, had fallen asleep after an evening of drinking with the boss and co-workers and awoke shortly after everyone else had left the room to find the boss naked on top of her trying to remove her clothes); *Hayward v. Cleveland Clinic Found.*, 759 F.3d 601 (6th Cir. 2014) (police officers arrested a man for a minor traffic infraction, and during arrest in front of parents, at 4 a.m. in their home, used excessive force, profanity and racial epithets, then dragged him from the home where they beat him severely and tased him numerous times).

7. **Knowledge of plaintiff's vulnerability.** This pattern may be seen as a subset of the abuse-of-power pattern. *See, e.g., Liberty Mut. Ins. Co. v. Steadman*, 968 So. 2d 592 (Fla. Dist. Ct. App. 2007) (insurance company's conduct was outrageous where it denied and delayed paying for treatment, knowing claimant had limited life expectancy); *Doe v. Corp. of President of Church of Jesus Christ of Latter-Day Saints*, 167 P.3d 1193 (Wash. Ct. App. 2007) (affirming jury verdict for plaintiff where church bishop acted with knowledge of teenaged church member's peculiar susceptibility to emotional distress).

8. **Exercising legal rights.** Cases and the Restatement emphasize that a person cannot be held liable for this tort merely for exercising a legal right, even where he is substantially certain that it will cause emotional distress—such as filing for a divorce, or firing an at-will employee, or seeking to collect a debt. RESTATEMENT (THIRD) OF TORTS: LIABILITY FOR PHYSICAL AND EMOTIONAL HARM § 46 cmt. e (2012). But a person is "not immunized from liability if the conduct goes so far beyond what is necessary to exercise the right that it is extreme and outrageous." *Id.* Thus a creditor would not be acting outrageously simply by demanding payment of an overdue debt, but might be liable for making harsh threats to a plaintiff known to be mentally fragile. *See MacDermid v. Discover Fin. Servs.*, 488 F.3d 731 (6th Cir. 2007).

9. **Causation.** A plaintiff must prove a sufficient causal link between the defendant's conduct and the plaintiff's distress. This is usually thought to mean factual causation, meaning that the plaintiff must show that but for the defendant's outrageous conduct, the severe distress would not have occurred. *See* RESTATEMENT (THIRD) OF TORTS: LIABILITY FOR PHYSICAL AND EMOTIONAL HARM § 46 cmt. k (2012). *See Turcios v. Debruler Co.*, 32 N.E.3d 1117 (Ill. 2015) (where plaintiff seeks to recover based on decedent's suicide as a result of the intentional infliction of emotional distress, plaintiff must plead facts demonstrating that the suicide was a likely result of defendant's conduct).

10. **Severity of emotional distress.** Although severe distress can be proved without showing physical symptoms, courts insist that the distress must be severe or even debilitating. *See, e.g., Rogers v. Louisville Land Co.*, 367 S.W.3d 196 (Tenn. 2012) (listing nonexclusive factors that are relevant to a determination that a plaintiff has suffered severe distress, including physiological manifestations; psychological manifestations such as depression, nightmares and anxiety; evidence of medical treatment and diagnosis;

evidence of the duration and intensity of the distress; proof that the distress caused significant impairment of day-to-day functioning; and the extreme and outrageous nature of the defendant's conduct itself). Is severe distress a useful requirement, or should a plaintiff be allowed to recover damages for lesser distress provably caused by a defendant's "extreme and outrageous" behavior?

11. **Overlap with other tort claims.** The tort of intentional infliction of emotional distress "originated as a catchall to permit recovery in the narrow instance when an actor's conduct exceeded all permissible bounds of a civilized society but an existing tort claim was unavailable." RESTATEMENT (THIRD) OF TORTS: LIABILITY FOR PHYSICAL AND EMOTIONAL HARM § 46 cmt. a (2012). Does the fact that the defendants in *Chanko* breached their fiduciary duty to the patient, and that that claim was permitted to proceed, make an intentional infliction of emotional distress claim on the part of the family members more or less essential? Would it matter if the two torts differed in terms of elements or measures of damage? Did some of the supervisor's actions in *GTE* constitute other intentional torts? Should a plaintiff be allowed to bring a claim for intentional infliction of emotional distress if a claim for battery or assault is stated as well?

12. **Constitutional limitations.** The First Amendment to the United States Constitution guarantees free speech and the free exercise of religion. These clauses may limit a variety of tort claims, including claims for intentional infliction of emotional distress, that are based on communicative or religiously motivated conduct. *See Snyder v. Phelps*, 562 U.S. 443 (2011) (barring claim of intentional infliction of emotional distress against defendant church members who picketed near military service member's funeral; anti-homosexual theme of the demonstration was a matter of public concern and therefore protected by the First Amendment although picketing caused father great distress); *Hustler Magazine v. Falwell*, 485 U.S. 46 (1998) (barring intentional infliction claim by a public figure on First Amendment free speech grounds). Could the *Chanko* court have said the conduct in that case was sufficient to establish extreme or outrageous conduct, but the media defendants had a privilege to publish it anyway because the story was newsworthy?

ROTH V. ISLAMIC REPUBLIC OF IRAN, 78 F. Supp. 3d 379 (D.D.C. 2015). American family members of 15-year-old Malka Roth, who died in a Hamas terrorist bombing at a Sbarro restaurant in Jerusalem, Israel, filed suit against the Islamic Republic of Iran and the Iranian Ministry of Information and Security, which played a role in supporting the terrorists. Family members sought damages pursuant to the Foreign Sovereign Immunities Act (FSIA). The family moved for a default judgment as to liability and damages. The district court held that the court had jurisdiction under the state-sponsored terrorism exception to the FSIA and awarded economic loss damages over $1 million, solatium damages (a form of damages intended to compensate persons for mental anguish, bereavement and grief that those with a close personal relationship to a decedent experience) of $5 million to each parent, and $2.5 million to each sibling (except for blind and intellectually disabled sibling for whom there was no evidence of mental anguish), and punitive damages of $112.5 million.

"Plaintiffs seek to recover solatium damages for defendants' intentional infliction of emotional distress. Relying principally on the Restatement (Second) of Torts, this Court has set out the following standard for recovery on a theory of IIED in section 1605A(c) cases: One who by extreme and outrageous conduct intentionally or recklessly causes severe emotional distress to another is subject to liability for such emotional distress, and if bodily harm to the other results from it, for such bodily harm. An actor may also be liable for IIED to a party against whom the extreme and outrageous conduct was not directed if that party is (1) a member of the victim's immediate family and (2) was present at the time of the extreme and outrageous conduct. The 'immediate family' requirement is strictly construed . . .; generally, only spouses, parents, siblings, and children are entitled to recover. As to the issue of presence, this Court has previously held that one need not be present at the time of a terrorist attack upon a third person to recover for severe emotional injuries suffered as a result. This is because terrorism is sufficiently extreme and outrageous to demonstrate that it is intended to inflict severe emotional harm on even those not present at the site of the act. The plaintiffs have stated a valid theory of recovery as to their IIED claims. . . . [A]lthough the family member plaintiffs do not allege that they were present at the site of the attack, this requirement is not imposed when the extreme and outrageous conduct is a terrorist attack such as this."

NOTES

1. **Liability to plaintiff when conduct is directed at another person.** As the *Roth* court noted, the Second Restatement (and the Third) limit recovery for intentional infliction of emotional distress when the defendant's extreme and outrageous conduct is directed at someone other than the plaintiff; in that situation, only immediate family members who are present at the time of the conduct, and who suffer severe distress, can recover. *See* RESTATEMENT (THIRD) OF TORTS: LIABILITY FOR PHYSICAL AND EMOTIONAL HARM § 46 cmt. m (2012) (emotional harm caused by harm to a third person). Why impose these limitations? The Third Restatement suggests they "might be justified by the practical necessity of drawing a line, since the number of persons who suffer emotional harm at the news of a homicide or other outrageous attack may be virtually unlimited." *Id.*

2. **Terrorism.** One recognized exception to the usual "presence" requirement occurs in cases of terrorism. *See Bettis v. Islamic Republic of Iran*, 315 F.3d 325 (D.C. Cir. 2003) (plaintiffs did not have to be present while their family member was kidnapped and tortured in order to state a claim); *Hatch*

v. Davis, 147 P.3d 383 (Utah 2006) ("a plaintiff must establish that the conduct was undertaken, in whole or in part, with the intention of inflicting injury to the absent plaintiff"). Why not preclude families of a terror victim not present at the abuse from recovering for intentional infliction of emotional distress as well? The *Roth* court wrote "acts of terrorism are by their very definition extreme and outrageous and intended to cause the highest degree of emotional distress." If a terrorist intended to cause widespread distress, should there be widespread recovery rather than recovery limited to family members? Absent evidence of mental distress, was the court right to limit recovery to the profoundly disabled sister?

3. **The FSIA.** The FSIA is the "sole basis for obtaining jurisdiction over a foreign state in our courts." *Argentine Republic v. Amerada Hess Shipping Corp.,* 488 U.S. 428, 434 (1989). It provides that federal district courts have original jurisdiction over (1) nonjury civil actions (2) for claims seeking relief *in personam* (3) against a foreign state (4) when the foreign state is not entitled to immunity. One exception to foreign sovereign immunity is the state-sponsored terrorism exception. Under that section, a foreign state has no immunity in any case "in which money damages are sought against a foreign state for personal injury or death that was caused by an act of torture, extrajudicial killing, aircraft sabotage, hostage taking, or the provision of material support or resources for such an act. . . . 28 U.S.C. § 1605A. After considering these elements, the court found the defendants in *Roth* were state sponsors of terrorism and could be held liable.

4. **Other exceptions to the presence requirement.** The Third Restatement notes that some courts have created an exception to the presence requirement in order to permit parents to recover for their emotional distress at the sexual abuse of their children. RESTATEMENT (THIRD) OF TORTS: LIABILITY FOR PHYSICAL AND EMOTIONAL HARM § 46 cmt. m (2012). Why create such an exception? Is there a principle that should be broader than these two specific types of cases? Some courts have broadened the definition of presence rather than creating an exception. *See, e.g., Bevan v. Fix*, 42 P.3d 1013 (Wyo. 2002) (children who did not actually witness attacks on their mother were "present" if they could show "sensory and contemporaneous" awareness). Does the presence requirement generally represent good policy? *See, e.g., Reid v. Pierce Cnty.*, 961 P.2d 333 (Wash. 1998) (barring claim where plaintiffs were not present while defendants used autopsy photos of their relatives for their own purposes).

§ 2. NEGLIGENT INFLICTION OF EMOTIONAL DISTRESS

A. EMOTIONAL DISTRESS FROM DIRECT RISKS OF PHYSICAL HARM

STACY V. REDERIET OTTO DANIELSEN, A.S., 609 F.3d 1033 (9th Cir. 2010). In dense fog, a small group of vessels fished for salmon. Stacy owned and operated a small vessel, the *Marja*. At 5 p.m., the *Marja*'s radar picked up a signal from a large freighter a mile away that was on a collision course directly toward the *Marja*. When Stacy realized that the freighter was heading straight for him, he feared for his life and felt sick to his stomach. He signaled the danger to the freighter, which passed by so close to the *Marja* that Stacy could hear its engines and feel its wake. Shortly thereafter, just out of Stacy's sight, the freighter collided with another small fishing vessel, causing the death of that ship's captain. Stacy sued the owner and operator of the freighter for negligent infliction of emotional distress. The trial court dismissed. → *Procedural Posture*

[Held, reversed and remanded. Under applicable maritime law, "a tort is committed by a defendant subjecting a plaintiff to emotional harm within 'the zone of danger' created by the conduct of the defendant." The zone of danger test allows recovery for those plaintiffs who . . . are placed in "immediate risk of physical harm" by defendant's negligence conduct. As a law review author put it, "those within the zone of danger of physical impact can recover for fright, and those outside of it cannot." Stacy alleged that he was within the zone of danger and that he suffered emotional distress from the fright caused by the negligent action of the defendants. Nothing more was required to assert a cause of action.

Holding

Emotional tranquility is something we value as a society. We will move to punish conduct that disturbs that.

No harm no foul

"physical" impact

MITCHELL V. ROCHESTER RAILWAY CO., 45 N.E. 354 (N.Y. 1896). In the spring of 1891, in Rochester, New York, the plaintiff was in the street about to board a street railway car when the defendant drove a team of horses at her. By the time the horses were stopped, the plaintiff found herself standing between the team, although never touched by them. The plaintiff suffered shock and a miscarriage as a result. The New York Court of Appeals held (1) there could be no recovery for fright alone and (2) as a corollary there could be no recovery for consequences of fright, even physical consequences like the miscarriage. Without a "physical injury," the negligence of the defendant would not be a proximate cause.

NOTES

1. **Recovery for direct stand-alone emotional harm.** The *Stacy* and *Mitchell* cases illustrate the distance the common law has travelled over the last century in permitting recovery for the defendant's negligent conduct that directly inflicts emotional harm on the plaintiff. Although *Mitchell* rejected plaintiff's claim, many courts, as in *Stacy*, would now permit a cause of action on the facts of *Mitchell*. The Third Restatement would also recognize a cause of action on facts like those in *Mitchell*. Under the Restatement: "An actor whose negligent conduct causes serious emotional harm to another is subject to liability to the other if the conduct: places the other in danger of immediate bodily harm and the emotional harm results from the danger." RESTATEMENT (THIRD) OF TORTS: LIABILITY FOR PHYSICAL AND EMOTIONAL HARM § 47 (2012).

A small number of courts still do not recognize the tort. *See Dowty v. Riggs*, 385 S.W.3d 117 (Ark. 2010) (on the ground that mental distress without a preceding physical injury is "too remote, uncertain and difficult of ascertainment"). And, as discussed in the note on development of a stand-alone claim below, some courts add restrictions to the Restatement limits.

2. **Stand-alone harm vs. parasitic damages.** Stand-alone emotional harm is to be distinguished from cases in which a plaintiff suffers both physical and emotional harm. Even under the traditional rule, if the defendant negligently causes physical injury to the plaintiff, the plaintiff can recover all damages that result, including damages for pain, suffering, and emotional harm. *See, e.g., Hagen Ins., Inc. v. Roller*, 139 P.3d 1216 (Alaska 2006) (distinguishing parasitic or "derivative" damages from stand-alone emotional harm claim). So if horses had actually run into Mitchell, causing some small physical harm, even under the older legal rules, she would ordinarily recover not only for that harm but for any immediately ensuing emotional harm as well.

3. **The fright or shock pattern.** Notice that *Stacy* and *Mitchell* involve a very definite pattern: (a) the defendant's negligent acts put the plaintiff at immediate risk of a personal injury at a very definite time and place and (b) the plaintiff's reaction to that risk was fright and shock.

4. **The zone of danger test.** The zone of danger test usually requires the plaintiff to prove that he was immediately threatened with physical injury, as the *Stacy* court says. The damages in negligent infliction of emotional distress cases are for the severe emotional distress suffered as a result of that situation. *See, e.g., Hedgepeth v. Whitman Walker Clinic*, 22 A.3d 789 (D.C. 2011) (recovery allowed for serious and verifiable mental distress "if the defendant's actions caused the plaintiff to be in danger of physical injury and if, as a result, the plaintiff feared for his own safety"); *Grube v. Union Pac. R.R.*, 886 P.2d 845 (Kan. 1994) (FELA case under federal law; the "essential elements for recovery under the zone of danger test are that plaintiff be within the zone of danger and suffer imminent apprehension of physical harm which causes or contributes to the emotional injury").

NOTE: DEVELOPMENT OF A STAND-ALONE CLAIM

1. *Impact.* The first step away from *Mitchell* and towards allowing a stand-alone negligent infliction claim was a small one. Courts began to drop the requirement of a preceding physical injury and substituting a requirement of "physical impact," even if it caused no physical injury at all. (Notice that *Mitchell* also required an "impact.") Most states have abandoned the impact rule. In *Battalla v. State*, 176 N.E.2d 729 (N.Y. 1961), the New York Court of Appeals overruled *Mitchell* entirely, observing that although some claims might be fraudulent, that would also be the case if the plaintiff could claim emotional harm after showing a

slight impact. Some speculative claims might be brought, the court said, but the solution to that is to deny those claims and not to exclude the entire class.

A handful of states retain the impact requirement today, with variations. *See, e.g., Atlantic Coast Airlines v. Cook*, 857 N.E.2d 989 (Ind. 2006); *Lee v. State Farm Mut. Ins. Co.*, 533 S.E.2d 82 (Ga. 2000).

2. *Physical manifestation of objective symptoms or medically diagnosable emotional disorder.* Other states adopted a different condition: The plaintiff can recover only if she produces evidence of some objective physical manifestation of the shock or fright occurring after the events in question. This approach, too, retains some currency today. *See Brueckner v. Norwich Univ.*, 730 A.2d 1086 (Vt. 1999). However, many states have abolished this requirement altogether. *See, e.g., Molien v. Kaiser Foundation Hospitals*, 616 P.2d 813 (Cal. 1980) (reasoning that the genuineness of emotional injury can be found in the facts of each case without such a rule). Other states have abolished the requirement in particular situations, or when facts provide some special guarantee that the harm is genuine. → States seem really divided on this!

Some courts have modified or diluted this requirement rather than rejecting it completely. A number have said that the emotional injury must be medically diagnosable as an emotional disorder, but not necessarily reflected in observable physical manifestations. *Paz v. Brush Engineered Materials, Inc.*, 949 So. 2d 1 (Miss. 2007).

3. *Zone of danger.* Other states developed a different rule that allows recovery only where the defendant's negligence placed the plaintiff in danger of physical injury, and because of that danger the plaintiff suffered emotional harm. *See, e.g., AALAR, Ltd. v. Francis*, 716 So. 2d 1141 (Ala. 1998). The zone of danger rule reappears in the *Catron* case below.

4. *Combinations.* States may combine the rules described above (and others) in myriad ways. *See, e.g., Willis v. Gami Golden Glades, LLC*, 967 So. 2d 846 (Fla. 2007) (plaintiff may recover either by showing impact or by proving that emotional distress is manifested in physical injury); *Catron v. Lewis*, 712 N.W.2d 245 (Neb. 2006) (plaintiff who fails to show impact or physical injury must be in zone of danger); *Atlantic Coast Airlines v. Cook*, 857 N.E.2d 989 (Ind. 2006) (plaintiff must show impact, and if the impact is "slight," must also show that the emotional distress is not "speculative, exaggerated, fictitious, or unforeseeable"); *Perrotti v. Gonicberg*, 877 A.2d 631 (R.I. 2005) (plaintiff must be in zone of danger, and must also suffer emotional harm "accompanied by physical symptomatology"); *Siegel v. Ridgewells, Inc.*, 511 F. Supp. 2d 188 (D.D.C. 2007) (plaintiff must suffer impact or be within zone of danger, and must prove "verifiable" emotional distress) (D.C. law). There is much state variation in this area of law.

5.   *Examples.* What result in the following cases, if you are in an "impact" state, a "physical manifestations" state, a "zone of danger" state, or a state that chooses to adopt the new Restatement rule?

(a) Defendant negligently performed surgery upon the plaintiff in such a way that the plaintiff lost the use or her right hand. She suffers periodic depression and a deep sense of loss, especially on bowling nights, but has no physical symptoms of the depression.

(b) Defendant, angry with a domestic partner, fired a pistol at random in an upscale restaurant. No one was hit, but one shot narrowly missed the plaintiff, breaking the back of his chair. The plaintiff was not touched and suffered no physical injury but wakes up with nightmares every night and has been unable to complete his college courses.

(c) Defendant negligently drove his car into the plaintiff's car, scratching the car but not physically touching or harming the plaintiff. Shortly thereafter, the plaintiff broke out in sweats and rashes, then fainted, all provably a result of the fright or shock.

B. EMOTIONAL DISTRESS RESULTING FROM INJURY TO ANOTHER

CATRON V. LEWIS
712 N.W.2d 245 (Neb. 2006)

McCORMACK, J.

[On July 5, 2002, Gaylen L. Catron took his boat out on Center Lake at a state recreation area, pulling two tubes ridden by two of his daughter's friends, Samantha Rader and Aimee Stuart. The towropes which attached the tubes that Rader and Stuart were riding to Catron's boat were approximately 61 feet long. After going around the lake twice, Catron decided to head for shore. Catron stated that as he was traveling straight east toward the shore, he noticed two jet skis heading north toward the right side of his boat. One of the jet skis was being ridden by 14-year-old Skylar Panek. The jet ski was owned by Marvin Lewis.]

Catron estimated that when he first saw them, the jet skis were 75 yards away going approximately 35 to 40 miles per hour. Catron then looked back behind his boat to confirm that the tubes were traveling straight behind his boat. Stuart confirmed in her deposition testimony that right before the accident, the ropes pulling the tubes were taut and that the tubes were traveling directly behind the boat, inside the wake.

In his deposition, Catron indicated that he feared for his safety "[j]ust when [the jet skis were] aiming at my boat." He subsequently explained during a psychiatric examination that he was not really afraid that the jet skis were going to hit his boat; he just did not know for sure what they were going to do. He was able to make eye contact with Panek and the other boy riding the jet skis before they turned, and he assumed they would either shut down or turn to avoid hitting his boat. Catron did not make any evasive maneuvers. When the jet skis turned, Catron became afraid they were going to hit the tubes Rader and Stuart were on.

Panek did in fact run into Rader, killing her. [Panek and Catron both testified that the accident occurred at least 61 feet from the rear of Catron's boat.] Catron testified that he saw Panek's jet ski hit the tube Rader was on and then saw Rader lying face down in the water "in a pool of blood." Catron jumped in, swam over to her, and floated her back to the boat. Rader was nonresponsive. With assistance, Catron was able to get Rader to shore.

[After the accident, a psychiatrist diagnosed Catron with major depression and anxiety disorder, and Catron was unable to work for three months. He was eventually diagnosed with post-traumatic stress disorder and continues to take antidepressants. He sued Panek, Lewis and the State.]

Catron's action sought damages for emotional distress stemming from his witnessing the accident and his unsuccessful attempt to rescue Rader. Catron alleged that such distress was a proximate result of the negligent acts or omission of the defendants, specifically, the negligent operation of the jet ski by the then 14-year-old Panek, the negligent entrustment of the jet ski to Panek by Lewis, and the failure of the State to operate the Bridgeport State Recreation Area in a manner reasonably safe for foreseeable users under foreseeable conditions.

The district court granted summary judgment in favor of the defendants, and Catron appeals. . . .

In Nebraska, where there is no impact or physical injury to the plaintiff, the plaintiff seeking to bring an action for negligent infliction of emotional distress must show either (1) that he or she is a reasonably foreseeable "bystander" victim based upon an intimate familial relationship with a seriously injured victim of the defendant's negligence or (2) that the plaintiff was a "direct victim" of the defendant's negligence because the plaintiff was within the zone of danger of the negligence in question. . . .

The zone of danger has been described as a complement to the basic requirement that persons exercise reasonable care to protect others from injury. "Those who breach their basic duty of care to others will be required to compensate those who are injured, even when the injuries are not caused by direct impact, but by the operation of foreseeable emotional distress." Hansen v. Sea Ray Boats, Inc., 830 P.2d 236 (Utah 1992). Persons in the zone of danger are clearly foreseeable plaintiffs to the negligent actor insofar as they have been placed at unreasonable risk of immediate bodily harm by the actor's negligence. The fact that the harm results solely through emotional distress should not protect the actor from liability for such conduct. . . .

Here, it is clear that Catron was not immediately threatened with physical injury as a result of the alleged negligence which resulted in Rader's death. While Catron described the jet skis at one point as coming directly toward him at a rapid speed, Catron admitted he was not in immediate danger. Rather, at that point, the jet skis were approximately 75 yards away, and Catron assumed the jet skis would either stop or turn in order to avoid a collision with the boat. This is what apparently happened, resulting in the collision with Rader, who was riding in the tube some 61 feet away from the rear of Catron's boat. . . .

NOTE

Direct victim or bystander? The *Catron* court notes that in Nebraska, plaintiffs can recover either under a "direct victim" rule or a "bystander" rule. Why isn't the father in *Catron* considered a direct victim and able to recover under the zone of danger test? Why can't the father recover as a bystander either?

DILLON V. LEGG, 441 P.2d 912 (Cal. 1968). A mother and infant sister saw a vehicle strike Erin Lee Dillon, a young child, as she crossed the road, causing her death. The mother and sister sued the driver for negligent infliction of emotional distress. The trial court granted defendant's motion for judgment on the mother's claim because she was not in the zone of danger, but denied the motion as it pertained to the sister, because she might have been. *Held*, reversed. "The instant case exposes the hopeless artificiality of the zone-of-danger rule. . . . [T]o rest upon the zone-of-danger rule when we have rejected the impact rule becomes even less defensible." The only reason for the zone-of-danger rule "lies in the fact that one within it will feel the danger of impact." While dropping this requirement may invite some fraudulent claims, this does not "justify a wholesale rejection of the entire class of claims." A defendant might owe a duty to protect not only the injured person but those who might foreseeably suffer emotional harm because of the injury.

Courts should henceforth take into account three factors in determining foreseeability: "(1) Whether plaintiff was located near the scene of the accident as contrasted with one who was a distance away from it. (2) Whether the shock resulted from a direct emotional impact upon the plaintiff from the sensory and contemporaneous observance of the accident, as contrasted with learning of the accident from others after its occurrence. (3) Whether plaintiff and the victim were "closely related." In this case, "the presence of all the above factors indicates that plaintiff has alleged a sufficient prima facie case."

NOTES

1. **Original denial of "bystander" claims.** *Dillon is* the classic case of emotional harm resulting from injury to another. A mother watches in horror as a car strikes her child. The mother's fear and shock is much like the fear and shock in *Mitchell*, but it is fear for her child rather than for herself. Courts originally denied these claims altogether.

2. **Bystander recoveries.** Today, most states have followed *Dillon* (or some variation of it), to allow plaintiffs who are not in the zone of danger to recover damages for the emotional distress of seeing another person injured or killed by a negligent defendant. The Restatement states the rule this way: A person who negligently causes "serious bodily injury" to a victim is liable for "serious emotional harm caused thereby to a person who: (a) perceives the event contemporaneously, and (b) is a close family member of the person suffering the bodily injury." RESTATEMENT (THIRD) OF TORTS: LIABILITY FOR PHYSICAL AND EMOTIONAL HARM § 48 (2012). Are there still reasons to retain special rules for bystanders? *See Lee v. State Farm Mut. Ins. Co.*, 533 S.E.2d 82 (Ga. 2000).

3. **Sensory perception.** The plaintiff's sensory perception of some sudden, injury-producing event when it happens or at least shortly thereafter is important as a factor under *Dillon*. In a later case, *Thing v. Lachusa*, 771 P.2d 814 (Cal. 1989), the California Supreme Court held that *Dillon's* guidelines had left too much uncertainty, and therefore limited recovery to situations in which a plaintiff is "present at the scene of the injury producing event at the time it occurs and is then aware that it is causing injury to the victim." New York courts have said that a person must either see the incident or be immediately aware of the incident at the time it occurred. *Coleson v. City of New York*, 24 N.E.3d 1074 (N.Y. 2014) (a boy saw his father with a knife and hid in a broom closet as his father attacked his mother; he heard her screams; "the child was not in the zone of danger because he was in a broom closet while his mother was stabbed, and thus neither saw the incident nor was immediately aware of the incident at the time it occurred").

4. **Delayed perception.** The clear case for recovery is one in which the plaintiff actually sees a serious bodily injury to a family member as it occurs. A parent who does not see the event itself but only sees the injured child later, in the hospital, is likely to be denied recovery. *Roitz v. Kidman*, 913 P.2d 431 (Wyo. 1996). What about all the times in between? Isn't it true, as the court said in *Gates v. Richardson*, 719 P.2d 193 (Wyo. 1986), that "the immediate aftermath may be more shocking than the actual impact"? So imagine that a family member arrives at the scene of the injury immediately afterwards. *Compare Entergy Miss., Inc. v. Acey*, 153 So. 3d 670 (Miss. 2014) (mother who learned that her daughter had been seriously injured from a 911 dispatcher, drove to the accident scene, and saw her daughter, who had been severely burned by electrocution, failed to meet the requirement that she must have contemporaneously observed the accident) *with Eskin v. Bartee*, 262 S.W.3d 727 (Tenn. 2008) (allowing claim by mother who saw her young child "lying in

a pool of blood in his school's driveway minutes after he had been struck by an automobile").

5. **Close relationship.** Whether courts use the rules as guidelines or as elements, they usually insist upon a close relationship—usually a close family relationship, in accord with the Restatement Third—between the plaintiff and the injured person. Should a fiancée who witnesses fatal injury to her partner be allowed to recover? *Grotts v. Zahner*, 989 P.2d 415 (Nev. 1999) (no); *Graves v. Estabrook*, 818 A.2d 1255 (N.H. 2003) (yes; unmarried cohabitants who have a "relationship that is stable, enduring, substantial, and mutually supportive . . . cemented by strong emotional bonds and provid[ing] a deep and pervasive emotional security" are "closely related" for this purpose). Is it problematic to make a right to recover turn on the particular "subjective emotional connection of the parties" as the *Graves* dissenters charged? *See also Smith v. Toney*, 862 N.E.2d 656 (Ind. 2007) (discussing problems with not having a bright-line rule). Or does the case-by-case approach better reflect the importance of the specific relationship? *See St. Onge v. MacDonald*, 917 A.2d 233 (N.H. 2007) (noting that the determination had to be made on a case-by-case basis, affirming judgment that a non-cohabiting girlfriend of six months was not in a close relationship with plaintiff). What about using a test like the one the California Supreme Court used in a take-home asbestos case which allowed for recovery of household members rather than family members? *Kesner v. Superior Court*, 384 P.3d 283 (Cal. 2016) ("Being a household member refers not only to the relationships among members of a family, but also to the bonds which may be found among unrelated persons adopting nontraditional and quasi-familial living arrangements").

6. **Beyond the family?** What about a "bystander" who is really a participant in the events, say a co-worker who attempts to rescue the primary victim but is forced to watch his horrible death instead? In *Michaud v. Great Northern Nekoosa Corp.*, 715 A.2d 955 (Me. 1998), the plaintiff, a diver, attempted to rescue another diver whose leg was trapped deep underwater and who watched as surface chains pulled him up, tearing his body apart. Similarly, in *Hislop v. Salt River Project Agric. Improvement & Power Dist.*, 5 P.3d 267 (Ariz. Ct. App. 2000), the primary victim was burned alive allegedly as a result of the defendant's negligence; the plaintiff pulled the burning man from the trench where he was engulfed with flames. Both courts denied recovery. However, English law may be more generous. *See M.H. Matthews, Negligent Infliction of Emotional Distress: A View of the Proposed Restatement (Third) Provisions from England*, 44 WAKE FOREST L. REV. 1177 (2009) (describing the case of *Dooley v. Cammell Laird & Co.*, in which the claimant was operating a crane when a piece of rope snapped and the load being carried fell into the hold of a ship where people were working. The claimant recovered damages for "nervous shock" that was suffered as a result of fear for the safety of his fellow workmen, whom he could not actually see from his position on the crane).

7. **A bystander who unwittingly causes the harm.** What about a plaintiff who, because of the defendant's negligence, becomes the unwilling

[handwritten margin note:] Case-by-case basis but will always evaluate actual closeness and the substance of the relationship if not directly family member

trigger of harm to another? In *Kallstrom v. United States,* 43 P.3d 162 (Alaska 2002), the defendant negligently placed a pitcher that appeared to be fruit juice on a kitchen counter; the pitcher actually contained caustic lye. The plaintiff poured a glass for a child, who suffered horrible injuries. The court rejected the plaintiff's claim for emotional harm. Are ordinary limitations sensible in such cases? England apparently allows recovery in a case like *Kallstrom.*

8. **Combining the rules.** States that have adopted special "bystander rules" apply them only to bystanders, of course—only to those claiming to have suffered emotional distress from witnessing an injury to someone else. That means that if the plaintiff is not a "bystander" at all—what some states would call a "direct victim"—a separate set of rules (as seen above in Part A of this Section) would apply. *See, e.g., Jarrett v. Jones*, 258 S.W.3d 442 (Mo. 2008) (bystander limitations not applicable to truck driver who was direct victim of car driver's negligence). Which "separate rules" apply depend, of course, on the state. *See, e.g., Helsel v. Hoosier Ins. Co.*, 827 N.E.2d 155 (Ind. Ct. App. 2005) (impact rule applies to direct victims, special bystander rules to bystanders); *Jablonowska v. Suther*, 948 A.2d 610 (N.J. 2008) (zone of danger rule applies to direct victims, special bystander rules to bystanders). The possible variations, while not endless, are certainly large.

NOTE: THE LOSS OF CONSORTIUM CLAIM

1. *Origins of the loss of consortium claim.* The loss of consortium claim is quite different from the emotional harm claim in its origin. In the earlier common law, the master of an apprentice had a claim against the tortfeasor when the apprentice was injured, since the master would lose the services of the apprentice and might still be bound to provide him with food and housing. The claim had a firm economic basis in such cases. By the 17th century, the idea was carried over to permit a husband to recover from the tortfeasor when the wife was injured, on analogy, then all too true, to the master-servant relationship. Originally the claim was for loss of services, but it gradually expanded to take in non-economic losses such as loss of society and sexual relations.

2. *Scope of consortium.* "The concept of consortium includes not only loss of support or services, it also embraces such elements as love, companionship, affection, society, sexual relations, solace and more." *Millington v. Southeastern Elevator Co., Inc.*, 239 N.E.2d 897 (N.Y. 1968). After 1950, courts began to permit the wife to recover for loss of consortium when the husband was injured, thus putting the marital partners on an equal footing in this respect. In doing so, they often emphasized the non-financial side of the claim.

3. *Bystander emotional distress claims compared.* Emphasis on the intangible losses inflicted upon one person when another person is injured

brings up the latent comparison to the bystander mental distress claim. Is the claim not one for a species of mental distress or emotional losses? The difference may lie in judicial attitudes. In the emotional distress claim, courts traditionally emphasized an acute moment—shock or fright. With the consortium claim, they recognize legal harm in a chronic, ongoing sense of loss. If emotional distress is the emotional equivalent of a stab wound, then loss of consortium is the emotional equivalent of carrying a large pack all day or living all your life in a cramped room. But both involve intangible and real losses in quality of life.

4. *Derivative nature of spousal consortium claims.* Consortium claims are traditionally said to derive from the claim of the physically injured spouse. This means that if the predicate injury claim of the loved one is extinguished, then the derivative claim for loss of consortium is also extinguished. *See, e.g., Voris v. Molinaro,* 31 A.3d 363 (Conn. 2011). It also means that a loss of consortium claim can rise no higher than the claim from which it is derived. *E.g., Wine-Settergren v. Lamey,* 716 N.E.2d 381 (Ind. 1999). For example, the contributory negligence of the injured spouse will bar or reduce the consortium claim just as it will bar or reduce the injured spouse's claim.

5. *Child and parent claims.* In 1980, Massachusetts permitted a claim by a child for loss of parental consortium following a serious injury to a father. *Ferriter v. Daniel O'Connell's Sons, Inc.,* 413 N.E.2d 690 (Mass. 1980) (later modified by statute). The court in *Campos v. Coleman,* 123 A.3d 854 (Conn. 2015), recognized a claim brought on behalf of minor children, finding that the "vast majority" of states now recognize a minor child's cause of action for loss of parental consortium where the parent is either injured or killed. Some states also allow a claim to be brought by adult children. See *Rolf v. Tri State Motor Transit Co.,* 745 N.E.2d 424 (Ohio 2001); *North Pac. Ins. Co. v. Stucky,* 338 P.3d 56 (Mont. 2014). A number of other cases, however, continue to reject any such extension of liability. *E.g., Harrington v. Brooks Drugs, Inc.,* 808 A.2d 532 (N.H. 2002). Parents of an injured child have not generally been allowed a recovery for intangible harm such as loss of society or companionship. *E.g., Vitro v. Mihelcic,* 806 N.E.2d 632 (Ill. 2004). A few courts, however, have allowed the parents' claim. In most of these, the child was severely injured or comatose and some of the courts emphasized that the injury was total and permanent, or even *E.g., United States v. Dempsey,* 635 So.2d 961 (Fla. 1994). There are a few statutes on point as well.

6. *Injuries to companion animals.* Might a pet owner have a claim for negligent infliction of emotional distress, or loss of consortium, against a defendant who negligently injures or kills the pet? Courts have been reluctant to allow such claims, on a variety of bases. *See, e.g., Strickland v. Medlen,* 397 S.W.3d 184 (Tenn. 2013) (dog owners cannot state claim for emotional, non-economic damages in case where shelter employee

negligently euthanized their dog); *McDougall v. Lamm*, 48 A.3d 312 (N.J. 2012) (reviewing many other cases, citing difficulties in line drawing and the possibility of inconsistent results); *Goodby v. Vetpharm, Inc.*, 974 A.2d 1269 (Vt. 2009) (pet owners could not recover for wrongful death of pet, and could not recover for negligent infliction of emotional distress because they were not in the zone of danger); *Kaufman v. Langhofer*, 222 P.3d 272 (Ariz. Ct. App. 2009) (animals are personal property, thus no loss of consortium claim, which is limited to spouses, parents and children; no recovery for emotional distress claim because plaintiff was not in the zone of danger). What about the argument that a veterinarian has undertaken an obligation that creates a likely risk that negligent performance of that obligation will cause the plaintiff serious emotional distress? *See McMahon v. Craig*, 97 Cal. Rptr. 3d 555 (Ct. App. 2009) (no).

C. DUTIES OF CARE TO PROTECT EMOTIONAL WELL-BEING INDEPENDENT OF PHYSICAL RISKS

BURGESS V. SUPERIOR COURT, 831 P.2d 1197 (Cal. 1992). The plaintiff, Julia Burgess, was given prenatal care by her obstetrician, Gupta, who also delivered her child, Joseph. During Burgess' labor, Gupta diagnosed a prolapsed cord, which meant that the child would receive insufficient oxygen. Burgess was aware of this and of the urgent comings and goings thereafter. She knew when she was sedated for the cesarean that followed that something was wrong with the child. By the time the child was taken by cesarean, he had been deprived of oxygen for a lengthy period. He suffered permanent brain damage. Joseph brought suit against Gupta and the hospital. Julia asserted a separate claim for her own emotional distress. *Held,* the special bystander rules do not apply. California recognizes two classes of emotional harm cases: In the first, the plaintiff is a bystander; in the second, the plaintiff is a "direct victim." A plaintiff who was in some kind of preexisting relationship with the defendant is a "direct victim," and the bystander rules are inapplicable to such a plaintiff. A "direct victim's" case is based on a breach of duty "assumed by the defendant or imposed on the defendant as a matter of law, or that arises out of a relationship between the two." Liability in this class of cases is not unlimited; it is limited by the relationship established by the parties themselves. Both parties here understood that the physician owes a duty to the pregnant woman, not merely to the fetus alone. If the mother were treated as a bystander, the physician would have an incentive to sedate her, so that she would not see or hear injury and thus would lose the case.] —> §48(a)

NOTES

1.   **Duty by undertaking.** The fright and shock cases normally involve strangers, that is, persons who had no particular relationship that might affect duties. Any number of people might be frightened by runaway horses and, if

you add the possibility of liability to bystanders, even more. *Burgess* is important because it recognizes that some claims are asserted against a defendant who has at least implicitly undertaken to protect the plaintiff and that such cases might call for quite different rules. *See* Dan B. Dobbs, *Undertakings and Special Relationships in Claims for Negligent Infliction of Emotional Distress*, 50 ARIZ. L. REV. 49 (2008).

2. **The growing impact of *Burgess*.** A number of courts have agreed that a defendant owes a general duty to avoid inflicting emotional distress where the defendant has undertaken some obligation to benefit the plaintiff, and that undertaking by its nature "creates not only a foreseeable, but an especially likely, risk that the defendant's negligent performance of the obligation will cause serious emotional distress." *Hedgepeth v. Whitman Walker Clinic*, 22 A.3d 789 (D.C. 2011). There is growing support for the concept that "justification exists to extend NIED liability to a subset of cases involving preexisting relationships . . . involving duties that obviously and objectively hold the potential of deep emotional harm in the event of breach." *Toney v. Chester Cnty. Hosp.*, 36 A.3d 83 (Pa. 2011).

3. **The Third Restatement approach**. The Third Restatement provides that a person whose negligent conduct causes "serious emotional harm" to another is liable if (a) the defendant's negligence places plaintiff in "danger of immediate bodily harm and the emotional harm results from the danger," [which we saw in section A] *or* (b) the negligence occurs "in the course of specified categories of activities, undertakings or relationships in which negligent conduct is especially likely to cause serious emotional harm." RESTATEMENT (THIRD) OF TORTS: LIABILITY FOR PHYSICAL AND EMOTIONAL HARM § 47 (2012). Comment f gives some examples of the kinds of activities, undertakings or relationships that might give rise to liability, including the erroneous delivery of a message that someone has died and the mishandling of dead bodies, while admitting that "courts have not provided clear guidance" in identifying guidelines for such categories.

4. **Undertakings that increase risk of emotional harm.** Wyoming has recognized a negligent emotional distress claim in a case involving two sisters who were negligently separated at birth by a hospital in 1954. In *Larsen v. Banner Health System*, 81 P.3d 196 (Wyo. 2003), the court said that "in the limited circumstances where a contractual relationship exists for services that carry with them deeply emotional responses in the event of breach," and that breach causes severe emotional distress, an action will lie. *See also Miranda v. Said*, 836 N.W.2d 8 (Iowa 2013) (immigration attorney recommended a course of action so flawed that it barred the clients from reentering the United States for ten years, and separated them from their children for that entire time; "when parties to a transaction should reasonably have contemplated that emotional distress will naturally flow from a breach of the contract, the foreseeable consequential damages the plaintiff could recover should include damages for emotional distress").

5.   **Undertakings that do not create a duty.** In *Guerra v. State*, 348 P.3d 423 (Ariz. 2015), public safety officers erroneously informed a family that their daughter had been killed in a car accident, when in fact she had survived. The question in the Arizona Supreme Court was whether the Department of Public Safety (DPS), by undertaking to provide a next-of-kin notification, assumed a duty of care to the family—at least as to the accuracy of the information conveyed. The majority held that it did not, in part based on policy concerns that such a duty might cause officers to delay or limit providing prompt information to family members. A dissent would have recognized the duty under the Third Restatement's category for duty in the course of undertakings especially likely to cause serious emotional harm. As with other undertakings cases, the scope of the defendant's undertaking determines the scope of its duty. *See, e.g., Destefano v. Children's Nat'l Med. Ctr.*, 121 A.3d 59 (D.C. 2015) (hospital treating 6-year-old patient; duty with respect to medical care but not air shaft in parking lot).

HEINER V. MORETUZZO, 652 N.E.2d 664 (Ohio 1995). Defendants tested the plaintiff for AIDS, but, according to allegations accepted as true, negligently and erroneously reported to the plaintiff that she was infected with that disease. They then did a re-test and erroneously confirmed the diagnosis and recommended a specialist in that disease. In fact the plaintiff later discovered that the diagnosis was wrong. She sued for negligent infliction of distress. *Held,* the plaintiff has no claim. "[T]he claimed negligent diagnosis never placed appellant or any other person in real physical peril, since appellant was, in fact, HIV negative. . . . [W]e hold that Ohio does not recognize a claim for negligent infliction of serious emotional distress where the distress is caused by the plaintiff's fear of a nonexistent physical peril."

NOTES

1.   **Extending *Heiner*.** Ohio reaffirmed and extended *Heiner* in *Dobran v. Franciscan Medical Center*, 806 N.E.2d 537 (Ohio 2004). The defendant gathered an irreplaceable tissue sample for a cancer test on the plaintiff and then lost it. The plaintiff feared that his cancer would metastasize, and that this fear was caused by the defendant's negligent act. The court, affirming a defense summary judgment, stressed that the plaintiff never faced an actual physical peril since his cancer has not, in fact, ever metastasized.

2.   **An analogy: the mishandling of dead bodies.** When a defendant (often a mortuary) mishandles a dead body, causing severe distress to relatives of the deceased, most modern courts have little trouble allowing recovery for the negligently inflicted emotional distress. This may be a logical application of the rule in *Burgess*, that no special rules constrain recovery when the defendant has undertaken an obligation that is likely to cause serious emotional distress to the plaintiff if the obligation is not fulfilled. *See, e.g., Guth*

v. Freeland, 28 P.3d 982 (Haw. 2001); *Christensen v. Superior Court,* 820 P.2d 181 (Cal. 1991) (plaintiffs could recover where defendants, who had contracted to provide dignified burials or cremations, instead harvested various human organs from the remains of deceased persons and sold them; defendants had "assumed a duty to the close relatives . . . for whose benefit they were to provide funeral and/or related services"). Distress in this context has long been actionable. *See Shipley v. City of New York,* 37 N.E.3d 58 (N.Y. 2015) (applying common-law "right of sepulcher," which affords deceased's next-of-kin the right to immediate possession of a decedent's body and allows an award of damages against any person who interferes with that right or improperly deals with the decedent's body). Do those cases, and that reasoning, undercut the result and reasoning in *Heiner?*

3. **Negligent misdiagnosis.** Some courts have upheld a right to recover in misdiagnosis cases. *Baker v. Dorfman,* 239 F.3d 415 (2d Cir. 2000); *Chizmar v. Mackie,* 896 P.2d 196 (Alaska 1995); *Bramer v. Dotson,* 437 S.E.2d 773 (W.Va.1993); *cf. Molien v. Kaiser Found. Hosps.,* 616 P.2d 813 (Cal. 1980) (wife misdiagnosed as having venereal disease, leading to emotional distress of husband).

4. **Death messages.** One kind of misinformation is treated as special in some courts. This is the message, usually carried by telegraph, erroneously announcing the death of a close relative. One group of cases has long permitted the plaintiff to recover for emotional harm in such cases. *E.g., Johnson v. State,* 334 N.E.2d 590 (N.Y. 1975).

BOYLES V. KERR, 855 S.W.2d 593 (Tex. 1993). Dan Boyles, then 17, secretly videotaped his sexual intercourse with 19-year-old Susan Kerr. The tape also included comments made by Boyles' friends. Boyles then showed the tape on several occasions to various friends. Kerr claimed negligent infliction of emotional distress resulting from the tape, its showing, and the gossip that ensued. *Held,* there is no general duty to avoid negligent infliction of distress. Texas will not recognize a cause of action for emotional distress except where the defendant creates a risk of physical harm. Thus bystander recovery is permissible under the rules of *Dillon v. Legg.* Some courts recognize a claim for serious or severe distress, but that standard is inadequate. "It is difficult to imagine how a set of rules could be developed and applied on a case-by-case basis to distinguish severe from nonsevere emotional harm. Severity is not an either/or proposition; it is rather a matter of degree. Thus, any attempt to formulate a general rule would almost inevitably result in a threshold requirement of severity so high that only a handful would meet it, or so low that it would be an ineffective screen. A middle-ground rule would be doomed, for it would call upon courts to distinguish between large numbers of cases factually too similar to warrant different treatment. Such a rule would, of course, be arbitrary in its application." [Quoting Richard N. Pearson, *Liability to Bystanders for*

Negligently Inflicted Emotional Harm—A Comment on the Nature of Arbitrary Rules, 34 U. FLA. L. REV. 477, 511 (1982).]

NOTES

1. **Relationships.** The *Kerr* majority said it would recognize a duty based upon special relationships of the parties, and cited the telegraphic death message cases and dead body cases as examples. But it went on to say, without much discussion, that there was no such relationship in this case. Is that right? If the phrase "betrayal of confidence" comes to mind, it surely suggests an important relationship was involved. Even so, however, it does not necessarily suggest that negligence is the proper basis for liability.

2. **Privacy.** Mental distress is often part of the harm associated with a number of torts that do not entail physical harms, or even risks of physical harms. For example, invasion of privacy, under some circumstances, can be a tort. Some invasions of privacy produce mental distress damages. *Boyles* might have been brought as a privacy invasion claim in some jurisdictions. *See Fontaine v. Roman Catholic Church of Archdiocese of New Orleans*, 625 So. 2d 548 (La. Ct. App. 1993) (allegation: a priest sexually abused a 17-year-old and later published photographs in a magazine and circulated video tapes; a privacy invasion claim is stated). But the privacy claim would be undesirable to the plaintiff if the defendant's liability insurance did not cover privacy claims.

D. NEGLIGENT INFLICTION OF EMOTIONAL DISTRESS AS AN ORDINARY NEGLIGENCE CLAIM?

CAMPER V. MINOR, 915 S.W.2d 437 (Tenn. 1996). Camper was driving a cement truck. Jennifer Taylor, 16, had been stopped at a stop sign, but suddenly pulled out in front of the plaintiff. "The vehicles collided, and Ms. Taylor was killed instantly. Camper exited his truck moments after the crash, walked around the front of his vehicle, and viewed Ms. Taylor's body in the wreckage from close range." Camper sued her estate, claiming negligent infliction of emotional distress, in the form of a post-traumatic stress syndrome. *Held* (1) The physical manifestation or injury rule will no longer be followed; (2) Negligent infliction of emotional distress claims should be analyzed under the general negligence approach, that is, no differently from any other negligence case. "[T]he plaintiff must present material evidence as to each of the five elements of general negligence— duty, breach of duty, injury or loss, causation in fact, and proximate, or legal, cause—in order to avoid summary judgment. [T]o guard against trivial or fraudulent actions, the law ought to provide a recovery only for serious or severe emotional injury. A serious or severe emotional injury occurs where a reasonable person, normally constituted, would be unable to adequately cope with the mental stress engendered by the circumstances of the case. Finally, we conclude that the claimed injury or impairment must be supported by expert medical or scientific proof."

NOTES

1. **End of the evolutionary line?** *Camper* appears to discard all the constraining rules for negligent infliction of emotional distress cases. Some other courts have also moved in this direction. *See, e.g., Carrol v. Allstate Ins. Co.,* 815 A.2d 119 (Conn. 2003); *Sacco v. High Country Indep. Press, Inc.,* 896 P.2d 411 (Mont. 1995). The Connecticut court in *Carrol* explained that a plaintiff must prove "that the defendant should have realized that its conduct involved an unreasonable risk of causing emotional distress." An appellate court interpreting *Carrol* affirmed a plaintiff's verdict in *Murphy v. Lord Thompson's Manor, Inc.,* 938 A.2d 1269 (Conn. App. Ct. 2008), where a wedding business negligently cancelled a bride's wedding date reservation. The court held that defendant's actions created an unreasonable risk of causing the bride emotional distress. Does such a case go too far?

2. **New constraints.** In discarding the older constraining rules, the *Camper* court substituted some new requirements—a severe emotional injury and expert medical proof. *See Rye v. Women's Care Ctr. of Memphis, MPLLC,* 477 S.W.3d 235 (Tenn. 2015) (NIED claim failed for lack of evidence of severe distress where there was no "expert proof" establishing it). *See also Sacco, supra* Note 1 (requiring "serious or severe" emotional harm and suggesting that expert testimony would often be helpful to prove that); *Squeo v. Norwalk Hosp. Ass'n,* 113 A.3d 932 (Conn. 2015) (parents who sued hospital for negligent infliction of emotional distress in connection with son-patient's suicide after he was discharged from the hospital did not produce sufficient evidence that their distress was "severe and debilitating"). Do such requirements fulfill the purposes of the earlier constraints we've seen in this Chapter? Is a requirement of expert testimony in all cases too formalistic? *See Thornton v. Garcini,* 928 N.E.2d 804 (Ill. 2010) (rejecting an expert witness requirement).

E. TOXIC EXPOSURES: FEAR OF FUTURE HARM

POTTER V. FIRESTONE TIRE & RUBBER CO., 2863 P.2d 795 (Cal. 1993). Firestone operated a tire manufacturing plant near Salinas. It contracted with Salinas Disposal Service and another company for disposal of industrial wastes in a class II sanitary landfill operated by the City. Class II landfills prohibit disposal of toxic substances because of the danger that they will leach into the groundwater. In addition, the disposal service prohibited solvents, oils and other substances. Firestone assured the service that no such waste would be sent to the landfill. For a while official plant policy required proper disposal of hazardous wastes in a Class I landfill, but that program was costly. A production manager, sent to California from Firestone's Akron, Ohio to make the plant more profitable, became angered over the costs of the hazardous waste disposal program.

As a consequence, Firestone's hazardous waste materials were once again deposited and these materials included serious toxins. The plaintiffs, including the Potters, lived near the landfill. They discovered that toxic chemicals had contaminated their domestic water wells. The plaintiffs sued Firestone on theories that included negligent infliction of emotional distress. The trial court awarded $269,500 for psychiatric illnesses and the cost of treating them, $142,975 for the cost of medical monitoring of the plaintiffs, and punitive damages of $2.6 million. The court of appeal modified the judgment in some respects, but affirmed the main elements. On appeal to the California Supreme Court, *held:* "in the absence of a present physical injury or illness, damages for fear of cancer may be recovered only if the plaintiff pleads and proves that (1) as a result of the defendant's negligent breach of a duty owed to the plaintiff, the plaintiff is exposed to a toxic substance which threatens cancer; and (2) the plaintiff's fear stems from a knowledge, corroborated by reliable medical or scientific opinion, that it is more likely than not that the plaintiff will develop the cancer in the future due to the toxic exposure. . . .) The plaintiff must further show that based upon reliable medical or scientific opinion, the plaintiff harbors a serious fear that the toxic ingestion or exposure was of such magnitude and proportion as to likely result in the feared cancer.

[But] we hold that a toxic exposure plaintiff need not meet the more likely than not threshold for fear of cancer recovery in a negligence action if the plaintiff pleads and proves that the defendant's conduct in causing the exposure amounts to 'oppression, fraud, or malice' as defined in Civil Code section 3294, which authorizes the imposition of punitive damages. Thus, for instance, fear of cancer damages may be recovered without demonstrating that cancer is probable where it is shown that the defendant is guilty of 'despicable conduct which is carried on by the defendant with a willful and conscious disregard of the rights or safety of others.' . . .

In our view, Firestone's conduct brings this case within the 'oppression, fraud or malice' exception for recovery of fear of cancer damages." [Remanded. Concurring and dissenting opinions omitted.]

NOTES

1. **Concern over unlimited liability.** In its opinion the court cited a number of significant policy concerns. In particular, it emphasized that 1) "all of us are potential fear of cancer plaintiffs," and "the enormity of the class of potential plaintiffs cannot be overstated," 2) unrestricted fear of liability could limit access to prescription drugs, 3) allowing fear of cancer claims may work to the detriment of those who ultimately develop cancer, and 4) consistency requires a definite and predictable threshold for recovery.

2. **An exception for oppression, fraud or malice.** In cases of oppression, fraud and malice, why make an exception to the general requirement that plaintiff must show fear of cancer is probable? Even if

defendant acted very badly, isn't there a need to show that the bad conduct was the actual cause and proximate cause of some harm? Could the rule be like the extended liability rule in intentional torts? Perhaps in this case, uncertainties should be borne by the culpable actor.

3. **Fear of disease.** Courts can have somewhat different rules. In *Exxon Mobil Corp. v. Albright*, 71 A.3d 30 (Md. 2013), the court held that to recover emotional distress damages for fear of contracting a latent disease because of exposure to some toxic substance, the plaintiff must show (1) actual exposure due to defendant's tortious conduct (2) which led him to objectively and reasonably fear that he would contact a disease, (3) and that as a result of that fear, he manifested some "physical injury" capable of objective determination. The second and third requirements of the fear-of future harm emotional distress case are closely related; unless the plaintiff suffers some physical injury as a result of the fear, the court may believe that the fear itself is not reasonable.

4. **Medical monitoring**. The *Exxon Mobil* court set up a different test for the recovery of medical monitoring costs resulting from toxic exposure. In that case, the plaintiff must show (1) exposure to a "proven hazardous substance" due to defendant's tortious conduct; (2) that, as a "proximate result of significant exposure, the plaintiff suffers a significantly increased risk of contracting a latent disease"; (3) that this increased risk makes periodic medical diagnoses "reasonably necessary"; and (4) that medical processes exist which make early diagnosis and treatment of the disease "possible and beneficial."

5. **Bodily harm.** What if a plaintiff develops asbestosis, a physical disease, as a result of exposure to asbestos, and also claims damages for fear of developing cancer? In *Norfolk & Western Railway v. Ayers*, 538 U.S. 135 (2003), the Court held 5–4 that such a plaintiff in a FELA case could recover for such a fear, which was simply a type of "pain and suffering." A physically harmed plaintiff, the Court said, need not prove any physical symptoms of his emotional distress, only that the emotional distress is both "genuine and serious." *Accord, CSX Transp., Inc. v. Hensley*, 129 S.Ct. 2139 (2009). Note that plaintiffs in almost all jurisdictions who seek damages for emotional harm for fear of contracting some disease have an incentive to plead their cases as involving actual physical injury, with the emotional distress as a parasitic element of damages. *See, e.g., Hartwig v. Oregon Trail Eye Clinic*, 580 N.W.2d 86 (Neb. 1998) (plaintiff stuck by needle who feared contracting AIDS did not need to bring a separate claim of negligent infliction of emotional distress to get compensation for such fear; the needle stick made it a "simple negligence" case in which pain and suffering damages were available).

REFERENCES: 2 DOBBS, HAYDEN & BUBLICK, THE LAW OF TORTS §§ 381–397 (2d ed. 2011); DOBBS, HAYDEN & BUBLICK, HORNBOOK ON TORTS ch. 29 (2d ed. 2016).

CHAPTER 20

PRENATAL HARMS

▪ ▪ ▪

§ 1. PRENATAL AND PRECONCEPTION INJURY

REMY V. MACDONALD
801 N.E.2d 260 (Mass. 2004)

GREANEY, J.

This case presents the issue whether a child, born alive, can maintain a cause of action in tort against her mother for personal injuries incurred before birth because of the mother's negligence. The plaintiff seeks to recover damages based on the alleged negligence of her mother, the defendant Christine MacDonald, in connection with a two-car automobile accident that occurred when the plaintiff was in utero. [At the time of the accident in 1999, MacDonald was 32 weeks pregnant with the plaintiff. The plaintiff was born by emergency caesarian section four days later. She continues to suffer from multiple breathing difficulties associated with her premature birth. The plaintiff claims that her mother's negligent driving caused the accident that led to the plaintiff's premature birth and subsequent related injuries. The trial court granted summary judgment for the defendant.]

In order to succeed on a claim of negligence, a plaintiff first must establish that the defendant owed a legal duty of care. We must decide whether a pregnant woman owes a legal duty of care to her unborn child to refrain from negligent conduct that may result in physical harm to that child. If no such duty exists, a claim of negligence cannot be brought.

Whether a duty exists is a question of common law, to be determined by "reference to existing social values and customs and appropriate social policy." As a general principle of tort law, every actor has a duty to exercise reasonable care to avoid physical harm to others. There are a limited number of situations, however, in which the other legal requirements of negligence may be satisfied, but the imposition of a precautionary duty is deemed to be either inadvisable or unworkable. This is such a case.

The [trial] judge ruled that the defendant did not owe a duty of care to the unborn plaintiff. In his memorandum of decision, the judge noted that no Massachusetts appellate court has recognized the existence of such a duty. Guiding himself by cases in other jurisdictions, the judge reasoned that, due to a "unique symbiotic relationship" between a mother and her unborn child, the judicial creation of such a duty, in this case, could raise a multitude of problematic issues, as well as potentially invade the personal choice of pregnant women. We, essentially, agree.

We begin by taking judicial notice of the fact that, during the period of gestation, almost all aspects of a woman's life may have an impact, for better or for worse, on her developing fetus. A fetus can be injured not only by physical force, but by the mother's exposure, unwitting or intentional, to chemicals and other substances, both dangerous and nondangerous, at home or in the workplace, or by the mother's voluntary ingestion of drugs, alcohol, or tobacco. A pregnant woman may place her fetus in danger by engaging in activities involving a risk of physical harm or by engaging in activities, such as most sports, that are generally not considered to be perilous. A pregnant woman may jeopardize the health of her fetus by taking medication (prescription or over-the-counter) or, in other cases, by not taking medication. She also may endanger the well-being of her fetus by not following her physician's advice with respect to prenatal care or by exercising her constitutional right not to receive medical treatment.

Recognizing a pregnant woman's legal duty of care in negligence to her unborn child would present an almost unlimited number of circumstances that would likely give rise to litigation. Courts would be challenged to refine the scope of such a duty, including the degree of knowledge expected of a mother in order to pinpoint when such a duty would arise (e.g., at the point of pregnancy; at the point of awareness of pregnancy; or at the point of awareness that pregnancy is a possibility) or the particular standard of conduct to which a reasonably careful pregnant woman, in a single case, should be held. There is no consensus on if and when a duty such as the one sought by the plaintiff should be imposed, and there is considerable debate with respect to a mother's civil liability for injuries to her unborn fetus, including disagreement over whether the rights of the child should supersede the legal rights of the mother. No set of clear existing social values and customs exist, and no settled social policy can be identified, to justify the maintenance of the present lawsuit. . . .

There are three appellate decisions in jurisdictions that have allowed a claim brought against one's mother for negligently inflicted prenatal injuries. See *National Cas. Co. v. Northern Trust Bank,* 807 So. 2d 86, 87 (Fla. App. 2002) (permitting claims only in context of motor vehicle accidents, up to limit of insurance); *Grodin v. Grodin,* 301 N.W.2d 869 (Mich. App. 1980) (permitting claim based on mother's ingestion of drug that caused child, when born, to develop discolored teeth); *Bonte v. Bonte,* 616 A.2d 464 (N.H.1992) (permitting claim based on mother's failure to use reasonable care in crossing street). These decisions uniformly were premised on the assumption that, because an unborn child, after birth, may recover for prenatal injuries negligently inflicted by another, and because parental immunity had been abolished in those jurisdictions, logic demands that a child's mother should bear the same liability for injurious, negligent conduct to a fetus as would any third party. The courts undertook no serious analysis of the unique relationship between a pregnant woman and the fetus she carries. The courts also failed to address the collateral social and other impacts of the imposition of a legal (as opposed to a moral) obligation that would hold a pregnant woman to a standard of care towards her unborn child. Because it is on these considerations that our decision rests, we find these cases unpersuasive.

The plaintiff contends that her mother, as the operator of a motor vehicle, had an existing duty of care that extended to all other persons to operate her automobile in a reasonably careful and prudent manner, and argues that, based on this existing duty, there is no legal reason, particularly in the context of motor vehicle negligence, to distinguish between an unborn fetus and a child already born. We do not agree.

This court has recognized the right of a plaintiff to maintain an independent cause of action for prenatal injuries sustained as the result of the negligence of another. See *Payton v. Abbott Labs,* 437 N.E.2d 171 (Mass. 1982) (allowing claim against drug manufacturer for prenatal injuries caused by mother's ingestion of drug). "If the tortious conduct and the legal causation of the harm can be satisfactorily established, there may be recovery for any injury occurring at any time after conception." *Id.,* quoting Restatement (Second) of Torts, § 869 comment d (1979). . . .

It is true that, had the plaintiff been injured while MacDonald was a passenger in an automobile negligently operated by another, the plaintiff (whether or not she survived) would have been able to recover damages against the operator of the vehicle. There is also no question that, had the plaintiff been born at the time of the accident, even if only one hour of age, she would have been able to recover against MacDonald for injuries sustained as a result of her mother's negligence. See *Stamboulis v. Stamboulis,* 519 N.E.2d 1299 (Mass. 1988) ("no absolute curtain of immunity protects a parent who negligently causes injury to his or her minor child"). . . . There is nothing in our statutes or case law, however, that addresses the situation before us.

We reject the plaintiff's argument that a rule permitting a child to recover for negligent injuries inflicted before birth by the child's mother could be restricted solely to a viable fetus claiming negligence in an automobile accident. Massachusetts law provides that there is nothing special about injuries incurred in automobile accidents that sets them apart from other negligently caused injuries, and the limitation sought by the plaintiff would be inconsistent with that law. The presence of automobile liability insurance does not create liability where none previously existed. Further, and more importantly, there is no meaningful way to limit such a rule to automobile accidents cases. It would be only a matter of time before the rule could be extended to a myriad of situations that would make pregnant women liable to their viable fetuses for all manner of allegedly negligent conduct.

We agree with the general principle expressed in Restatement (Second) of Torts § 869 (1979), that "[o]ne who tortiously causes harm to an unborn child is subject to liability to the child for the harm if the child is born alive." The quoted language emphasizes that it is not just a pregnant woman alone who may be harmed by the tortious act of a third party, but also the fetus, whose injuries become apparent at its birth. There is nothing in the Restatement text, or in comments to the text, to indicate that the drafters of § 869 intended to suggest a legal right, never before recognized in law, for a fetus to bring a claim of negligence against its own mother. . . . We have said that "[t]he evolution of the law of negligence has always required courts to make hard (and often fine) distinctions, and to assess and determine, in considering the existence of a duty, contemporary attitudes and public policy." *Cyran v. Ware,* 597 N.E.2d 1352 (Mass. 1992). We conclude that there are inherent and important differences between a fetus, in utero, and a child already born, that permits a bright line to be drawn around the zone of potential tort liability of one who is still biologically joined to an injured plaintiff.

Judgment affirmed.

NOTES

1. **Traditional rule.** A pregnant woman is injured by defendant's negligence. She herself may have a claim for her injury. If the fetus is also injured is there an additional claim? Suppose, for example, a physician negligently prescribes a drug to the mother and the child is born with serious defects. In *Dietrich v. Northhampton,* 138 Mass. 14 (1884), Justice Oliver Wendell Holmes took the view that there could be no action. The opinion suggested the absence of precedent, "remoteness," and the logical problem of injuring a being "before he became a person," but gave little justice or policy reasoning. In *Klutschkowski v. PeaceHealth,* 311 P.3d 461, 475–76 (Or. 2013), the Oregon Supreme Court distinguished Dietrich as a case that involved harm to the fetus through negligent injury to the mother, rather than injury to the fetus directly. In *Klutschkowski,* the fetus was injured during labor as a result of medical negligence. The jury awarded $1.3 million in noneconomic damages, which the lower court reduced to $500,000 under a statutory cap. Whether the cap was permissible hinged on the availability of a malpractice claim in 1857. The Court wrote "we are not aware of any nineteenth-century case that discusses one way or the other whether a child could maintain a cause of action for medical malpractice for independent physical injuries that the child sustains during delivery as a direct consequence of the defendant's acts or omissions. Whatever the reason for that absence of authority, our precedents

require us to decide whether a cause of action for the injuries Braedon sustained was recognized in 1857. Faced with that question, we follow the general principle that actions for medical malpractice and negligence were recognized in 1857 unless we are persuaded that an action comes within an exception to that rule." Accordingly, applying the cap to limit damages was unconstitutional.

2. **Contemporary rules: child born alive.** The *Dietrich* decision held sway for many years. Judicial reversals began shortly after the end of World War II and today most courts allow a tort claim by the child if the child is born alive. Some courts have insisted that the child must also be viable—capable of living independent of the mother—at the time of the injury. But that requirement seems strikingly unrelated to the reality of suffering after a live birth and most have rejected it. *See, e.g., Gonzales v. Mascarenas*, 190 P.3d 826 (Colo Ct. App. 2008) (listing states); *Leighton v. City of New York*, 830 N.Y.S.2d 749 (App. Div. 2007).

3. **Child born alive as the physician's patient.** Is the child who is injured before viability and subsequently born alive the physician's patient for the purpose of medical malpractice act limitations? In *Simpson v. Roberts*, 752 S.E.2d 801, 805 (Va. 2014), the court said: "The evidence presented at trial was that the amniocentesis was performed, at least in part, for Simpson's [the fetus's] benefit to determine whether her lungs were developed enough that she could be safely delivered. When Dr. Roberts performed this procedure, he was providing health care to Simpson and her mother. If Simpson had never been born alive, her mother would have been able to recover for the physical and emotional injuries associated with a stillbirth. However, once Simpson was born alive, she became a natural person under the Act. Upon birth, she became a patient of Dr. Roberts under the Act and had her own claim against Dr. Roberts. . . . Dr. Roberts' negligence in performing the amniocentesis 'caused the child, though born alive, to be seriously impaired . . . . the mother and child were both 'patients' of the defendant, each of whom was entitled to a separate statutory damage cap under the Virginia Medical Malpractice Act.' "

4. **Contemporary rules: child not born alive but viable at injury.** Most courts passing on the question now appear to hold that a wrongful death action is allowable when a fetus is stillborn, at least when the fetus was viable at the time of injury. *See, e.g., Pino v. United States*, 183 P.3d 1001 (Okla. 2008). A few states disagree. *See Shaw v. Jendzejec,* 717 A.2d 367 (Me. 1998).

5. **Contemporary rules: child not born alive and not viable at injury or thereafter.** Most courts reject liability if the fetus was not born alive and was never viable at any time. *See, e.g., Santana v. Zilog, Inc.*, 95 F.3d 780 (9th Cir. 1996); *Crosby v. Glasscock Trucking Co.,* Inc., 532 S.E.2d 856 (S.C. 2000). However, a few cases have supported liability under wrongful death statutes for loss of a fetus that was never viable. *See Mack v. Carmack*, 79 So.3d 597 (Ala. 2011) (noting that six other jurisdictions allow such claims). *Cf. Nealis v. Baird,* 996 P.2d 438 (Okla. 1999) (allowing recovery if fetus had "an instant of life outside the womb"); *66 Fed. Credit Union v. Tucker*, 853 So. 2d

104 (Miss. 2003) (allowing recovery if fetus was sufficiently developed to move in the womb).

6. **Emotional distress damages.** States are hardly uniform in their rules about recovery of stand-alone negligently-inflicted emotional distress. *See* Chapter 19. Should a mother be allowed to recover emotional distress damages for the negligently-caused death of a fetus when she has suffered no physical injury? The court in *Broadnax v. Gonzalez*, 809 N.E.2d 645 (N.Y. 2004), allowed such a claim. In *Sheppard-Mobley v. King*, 830 N.E.2d 301 (N.Y. 2005), the court held that *Broadnax* did not allow emotional distress recovery by the mother if the child was born alive, because in such a case the child herself can bring a medical malpractice action for physical injuries. Even where the fetus is not born alive, is there a risk of duplicative recovery if the mother sues for her own emotional harm and as a beneficiary for damages in a wrongful death suit? *See Smith v. Borello,* 804 A.2d 1151 (Md. 2002).

7. **Parental liability: some hard questions.** Should courts hold a mother liable to her child for ingesting dangerous substances while pregnant? Or for failing to get appropriate prenatal care? *See Stallman v. Youngquist,* 531 N.E.2d 355 (Ill. 1988); *Chenault v. Huie,* 989 S.W.2d 474 (Tex. App. 1999) (child suffering permanent and serious harm because of mother's use of cocaine during pregnancy). Do you agree with the *Remy* court's reasons for refusing to recognize a duty of care on the facts before it? Does a woman's right to decide whether to terminate a pregnancy during the first trimester as established in *Roe v. Wade*, 410 U.S. 113 (1973), bear on tort liability for an injury inflicted during that period?

RENSLOW V. MENNONITE HOSPITAL, 367 N.E.2d 1250 (Ill. 1977). When plaintiff's mother was 13 years of age, defendants negligently transfused her with Rh-positive blood. This was incompatible with her own blood, though she had no knowledge of this at the time. Years later when she became pregnant she discovered that her blood had become sensitized by this negligent transfusion. As a result of this her child, the plaintiff, was born jaundiced and suffering from hyperbilirubinemia. She has suffered various damages for which she here sues. The trial judge dismissed the claim because plaintiff had not been conceived at the time of the alleged negligence. *Held,* the plaintiff states a claim for relief. Although foreseeability alone does not establish a duty, a duty of care may be owed to one who may be foreseeably harmed, even if the person is unknown or is remote in time or place. The defendants argue a need for an end of liability somewhere and "raise the specter of successive generations of plaintiffs complaining against a single defendant for harm caused by genetic damage done an ancestor," but the judiciary "will effectively exercise its traditional role of drawing rational distinction, consonant with current perceptions of justice, between harms which are compensable and those which are not."

ALBALA V. CITY OF NEW YORK, 429 N.E.2d 786 (N.Y. 1981). Ruth Albala underwent an abortion at Bellevue Hospital during which her uterus was perforated. The plaintiff Jeffrey Albala was born some four years later. This action on his behalf claims he suffered brain damage as a result of the doctor's negligence in perforating his mother's uterus. *Held*, this does not state a claim. Although harm of this kind was foreseeable, foreseeability alone does not establish a duty to the plaintiff. And although New York recognizes prenatal injury claims, those cases are not controlling here because in those cases "there are two identifiable beings within the zone of danger each of whom is owed a duty independent of the other and each of whom may be directly injured." Were liability established in this case, it would be difficult to preclude liability "where a negligent motorist collides with another vehicle containing a female passenger who sustains a punctured uterus . . . and subsequently gives birth to a deformed child," and the "staggering implications are manifest. . . . [R]ecognition of a cause of action under the circumstances of this case would have the undesirable impact of encouraging the practice of 'defensive medicine.' A physician faced with the alternative of saving a patient's life by administering a treatment involving the possibility of adverse consequences to later conceived off-spring of that patient would, if exposed to liability of the magnitude considered in this case, undoubtedly be inclined to advise against treatment rather than risk the possibility of having to recompense a child born with a handicap." This would place "physicians in a direct conflict between their moral duty to patients and the proposed legal duty to those hypothetical future generations outside the immediate zone of danger."

NOTES

1.   **A hypo.** Suppose that, in 1970, D builds a defective building. At the time there is no other building around, though it is foreseeable that others will be built. In 1992 another building is completed adjacent to D's building. D's building, because of its defect, collapses and causes harm to the new building. Should New York allow a recovery if *Albala* is still recognized authority in that state?

2.   **The DES cases.** A number of manufacturers once marketed a drug, DES, for use by pregnant women. The drug turned out to cause cancers and a number of other problems for the daughters of the women who ingested the drug. In several ways, New York has recognized that the manufacturer of the drug would be liable to the DES daughter. *E.g., Hymowitz v. Lilly & Co.*, 539 N.E.2d 1069 (N.Y. 1989). Is that inconsistent with *Albala*? What if it is a DES granddaughter rather than a DES daughter who suffers? *See Enright v. Eli Lilly & Co.*, 570 N.E.2d 198 (N.Y. 1991).

3.   **Applying *Renslow*.** A number of cases are in accord with *Renslow* on various facts. *E.g., Lynch v. Scheininger*, 744 A.2d 113 (N.J. 2000); *see 2*

DOBBS, HAYDEN & BUBLICK, THE LAW OF TORTS § 368 (2d ed. 2011). In a state that follows *Renslow*, defendant negligently injures Christine Taylor in an auto accident. She requires hospitalization and operations twenty-five times as a result and still suffers some deformity of pelvic bones. Seven years later she gives birth to a child, whose head is damaged because during gestation it was shaped by the deformed pelvic bones. If the court would impose liability under *Renslow*, would it also impose liability on these facts? *Taylor v. Cutler,* 703 A.2d 294 (N.J. Super. Ct. App. Div. 1997), *aff'd,* 724 A.2d 793 (N.J. 1999). What of a claim brought by a woman who, because of malpractice, becomes Rh-sensitized but has not had a subsequent pregnancy? *See Rye v. Women's Care Ctr. of Memphis, MPLLC,* 477 S.W.3d 235, 265 (Tenn. 2015) (even if Rh-sensitization is considered a presently existing physical injury, the undisputed facts demonstrate that Mrs. Rye has not sustained any damages related to this injury and that no such damages are reasonably certain to occur").

§ 2. WRONGFUL BIRTH, CONCEPTION, OR LIFE

SHULL V. REID
258 P.3d 521 (Okla. 2011)

COMBS, J.

On June 8, 2009, the Shulls initiated an action sounding in medical malpractice seeking compensation for the injuries suffered as a result of the Appellees' alleged malpractice in failing to properly diagnose a Cytomegalovirus infection [a common herpes virus], that occurred during Patricia Shull's first trimester of pregnancy, and failing to inform the Shulls of the significant health risk to their unborn child. The Shulls alleged that, as a direct and proximate result of this failure to diagnose and inform, Shull's minor son was born on June 9, 2007, with the CMV infection and suffers significant complications rendering the child permanently and completely helpless. The Shulls do not claim Defendants could have treated CMV or that the Defendants were responsible for Mrs. Shull's exposure to CMV. The Shulls claim that, had they known of the virus, they would have terminated the pregnancy.

[Defendants moved for partial summary judgment, alleging that the Shulls may only recover damages for the medical cost of continuing the pregnancy, offset by the cost of terminating the pregnancy. The district court granted the motion in order to let this issue of first impression come to this Court.]

. . . This Court has previously addressed the question of wrongful conception in three separate cases. The first case was Morris v. Sanchez, 746 P.2d 184 (Okla. 1987), where this Court found the birth of a healthy child does not constitute a legal harm for which damages are recoverable. The next case was *Goforth v. Porter Medical Associates, Inc.,* 755 P.2d 678

(Okla. 1988), where again, this Court found that the birth of a normal, healthy child is not a compensable damage. However, this Court held:

> Morris, however, should not, and must not, be interpreted as precluding a claim for other forms of damages that may arise out of the negligent performance of sterilization operations. Insofar as the petition in this case alleges negligence and actual, ordinary damages arising out of the alleged negligence, to-wit: $2,000.00 in medical expenses incurred as result of the unplanned pregnancy, we are of the opinion that the petition adequately states a claim for which relief may be granted.

To reach that result we relied upon [a] Kansas case. . . . We again turn to another Kansas case for guidance. In Arche v. United States of America, Department of the Army, 798 P.2d 477 (Kan. 1990), the Kansas Supreme Court was requested to answer two questions. First, did Kansas law recognize a cause of action for wrongful birth of a permanently handicapped child, and if so, what is the extent of damages which may be recovered upon proper proof. The Kansas Court held:

> Wrongful birth plaintiffs typically desire a child and plan to support the child. Such support is, of course, the obligation of all parents. It is therefore reasonable to deny those normal and forseeable (sic) costs which accrue to all parents. We hold that those expenses caused by the child's handicaps may be recovered, but not those expenses natural to raising any child.

The Kansas Court then addressed the plaintiff's emotional damages and found that such damages were not allowable in this type of medical malpractice action. They held:

> We have thus far held that visibility of results as opposed to visibility of the tortious act does not give rise to a claim for emotional damages. The child's injury in this case occurred without human fault during development of the fetus; the parents were not aware of the injury at the time. . . . We see no reason why a wrongful birth case should be distinguished. We therefore hold that damages for emotional distress of the parents are not recoverable in a wrongful birth case.

Finally, the Kansas Supreme Court addressed the issue concerning allowable damages, and over what period of time such damages may be recovered. The Kansas Court found that recovery may be had only for the period of time of the child's life expectancy or until the child reaches the age of majority, whichever is the shorter period. . . .

Subsequent to the birth of the child in the instant case, the Oklahoma State Legislature passed [a statute] that recognized wrongful birth actions but does not allow a parent, or other person who is legally required to provide for the support of a child, to seek economic or noneconomic damages because of a condition that existed at the time of the child's birth, based on a claim that a person's act or omission contributed to the mother not terminating the pregnancy. This Statute, however, was passed after the birth of the child in the instant matter, and it does not affect our holding in the instant case. . . .

We . . . hold that in any case arising prior to the enactment of [this statute] in 2008, in a wrongful birth action alleging medical malpractice, the measure of damages allowable is the extraordinary medical expenses and other pecuniary losses proximately caused by the negligence. There is no cause of action for emotional distress as the child's injury in this case occurred without human fault during development of the fetus, and the parents were not aware of the injury at the time. Loss of consortium is also not allowable in the instant matter as Oklahoma law does not provide for this type of damage in the instant case. Finally, recovery may be had only for extraordinary expenses, not the normal and foreseeable costs of raising a normal, healthy child, for the period of time of the child's life expectancy or until the child reaches the age of majority, whichever is the shorter period. [This Court has previously held that a parent has a legal duty to support his or her child until the child reaches the age of majority.]

[Reversed and remanded.]

NOTES

1.   **"Wrongful birth" cases.** In a typical "wrongful birth" case, a doctor has negligently failed to diagnose a genetic difficulty, with resulting physical harm to the fetus and economic and emotional harm to the parents. Often, as in *Shull*, the parents argue that but for the doctor's negligence, they would have chosen to abort the fetus. Many courts have now upheld such claims. *See, e.g., Lininger v. Eisenbaum*, 764 P.2d 1202 (Colo. 1988); *Smith v. Cote*, 513 A.2d 341 (N.H. 1986); *Thornhill v. Midwest Physician Ctr.*, 787 N.E.2d 247 (Ill. App. Ct. 2003). Similarly, a physician who learns from genetic screening that any child conceived in the future is at risk may owe a duty to inform the prospective parents. *See Didato v. Strehler*, 554 S.E.2d 42 (Va. 2001). A few courts reject the wrongful birth claim entirely. *E.g., Etkind v. Suarez*, 519 S.E.2d 210 (Ga. 1999). A number of state statutes prohibit wrongful birth claims. *See Sernovitz v. Dershaw*, 127 A.3d 783, 792 (Pa. 2015).

2.   **Possible causal difficulties.** Does a wrongful birth claim present intrinsic causal problems, when the case may rest on the parents testifying that the fetus would have been aborted had they been non-negligently informed of problems? The court in *Wilson v. Kuenzi*, 751 S.W.2d 741 (Mo. 1988), thought so: "The percentage of women who under pressure refuse to consider abortion, whether for reasons of religious belief, strong motherly instincts, or for other reasons, is sometimes astounding. It would seem that testimony either more verifiable based upon experience or more verifiable by

some objective standard should be required as the basis for any action for substantial damages." Is the court right about this, or should credibility determinations simply be left to the trier of fact?

3. **Emotional distress damages.** In *Shull*, the court applied Oklahoma "bystander" rules to deny recovery for negligent infliction of emotional distress. Should the state's usual restrictions on the NIED claim be applied in wrongful birth cases, or should the plaintiff be able to state an ordinary negligence claim and recover emotional distress damages as part of a parasitic pain and suffering award? In *Bader v. Johnson,* 732 N.E.2d 1212 (Ind. 2000), the court held that so-called wrongful birth actions were merely medical malpractice actions, that general rules of negligence applied, and that all damages proximately caused by the defendant's negligence would be recoverable. Similarly, in *Clark v. Children's Memorial Hosp.*, 955 N.E.2d 1065 (Ill. 2011) (citing 2 DAN B. DOBBS, LAW OF REMEDIES § 8.2 (2d ed. 1993)), the court said that a prayer for emotional distress damages in a wrongful birth case did not require proof that the parents were in a zone of danger, as would normally be required in a stand-alone NIED claim. Such "special restrictions," said the court "have no logical bearing on a wrongful-birth claim, where a tort has already been committed against the parents. Wrongful-birth plaintiffs do not assert a freestanding emotional distress claim, but merely assert emotional distress as an element of damages for a personal tort."

4. **Damages for child-rearing costs.** Many courts recognizing a wrongful birth claim allow recovery for some of the expenses of rearing the now-impaired child. As the *Shull* court holds, recovery is usually limited to the "extraordinary" expenses over and above ordinary child-rearing expenses. Some states have limited the available damages to the expenses of pregnancy and delivery. *See Schirmer v. Mt. Auburn Obstetrics & Gynecology Assocs., Inc.*, 844 N.E.2d 1160 (Ohio 2006). The *Schirmer* court pointed to the "underlying but critical fact" that in such cases the mother is claiming she would have terminated the pregnancy, making "unimpaired life never a possibility in this situation." Does computing "extraordinary" child-rearing expenses require the trier of fact to assess the relative merits of "being versus nonbeing," as the *Shirmer* court concluded?

5. **Choice of law.** State laws in this area can vary significantly. Because of significant differences in New York's and New Jersey's wrongful birth actions, one court reviewed claims against each defendant based on the law in that defendant's jurisdiction. *Ginsberg v. Quest Diagnostics, Inc.*, 147 A.3d 434, 439–40 (N.J. 2016) ("New Jersey recognizes damages for 'the emotional injury of the parents' and 'the special medical expenses attributable to raising a child with a congenital impairment' but not damages for 'the birth defect or congenital impairment itself.' New York, in contrast, limits damages in wrongful birth cases to 'the pecuniary expense which [the parents] have borne, and . . . must continue to bear, for the care and treatment of their infants' and New York specifically bars damages for 'psychic or emotional harm' resulting from the birth of the child 'in an impaired state.' ").

6. **"Wrongful conception" cases.** Another kind of case, usually labeled "wrongful conception," often involves an allegation that a defendant physician failed to prevent conception because he negligently performed a sterilization procedure on the father or the mother. The child in such cases is normally healthy, but the parents, who had attempted to avoid pregnancy and childbirth, will now face financial costs because of the defendant's negligence. In addition, if they were emotionally unable to care for children, they will almost certainly have increased emotional difficulties. Some legislatures have forbidden courts to entertain these claims. *See Thibeault v. Larson*, 666 A.2d 112 (Me. 1995).

7. **Damages in wrongful conception cases: the healthy but unwanted child.** In wrongful conception cases, most courts have allowed recovery for the mother's pain in pregnancy, and medical costs of pregnancy, abortion, or birth, as well as any lost wages during this period. *See Dotson v. Bernstein*, 207 P.3d 911 (Colo. App. 2009) (negligent failure to terminate a pregnancy). However, the vast majority of courts have denied recovery for the cost of rearing the healthy child. *See, e.g., Chaffee v. Seslar*, 786 N.E.2d 705 (Ind. 2003) (listing states). "The parents of a normal, healthy child whom they now love have not suffered any injury or damage," the Kentucky Court said bluntly in *Schork v. Huber*, 648 S.W.2d 861 (Ky. 1983). In a small group of states, the parents of a child born after a botched sterilization procedure are allowed to recover all costs incurred in rearing the child, without any offset for the benefits that the child's presence may confer. *See, e.g., Zehr v. Haugen,* 871 P.2d 1006 (Or. 1994). A middle ground is to allow all damages that flow from the negligence, but reduce those damages by the benefits conferred on the parents by the child's birth. *See, e.g., Univ. of Ariz. Health Sciences Ctr. v. Superior Court*, 667 P.2d 1294 (Ariz. 1983). Which approach best fulfills the goals of tort law?

8. **"Wrongful life" cases.** There is no support in the cases for a general wrongful life claim, as distinct from a wrongful birth or wrongful conception claim. The child, in other words, cannot recover for being born. Statutes may prohibit such a claim. *See, e.g., B.D.H. v. Mickelson*, 792 N.W.2d 169 (N.D. 2010); *Sernovitz v. Dershaw*, 127 A.3d 783, 792 (Pa. 2015) (even if state statute prohibiting wrongful life and wrongful birth claims were unconstitutional, where reliance on that statute "has continued for more than 20 years, a presumption naturally arises that any process challenge is too stale to be cognizable regardless of whether the challengers exercised reasonable diligence"). However, several courts have permitted the child to recover the cost of extraordinary care in his own name.

REFERENCES: 2 DOBBS, HAYDEN & BUBLICK, THE LAW OF TORTS §§ 366–371 (2d ed. 2011); DOBBS, HAYDEN & BUBLICK, HORNBOOK ON TORTS CHAPTER 27 (2d ed. 2016).

CHAPTER 21

WRONGFUL DEATH
AND SURVIVAL ACTIONS

■ ■ ■

"In a civil Court, the death of a human being could not be complained of as an injury. . . ."

—Lord Ellenborough in *Baker v. Bolton*, 1 Camp. 493, 170 Eng. Rep. 1033 (1808).

Lord Ellenborough's statement meant or came to mean three separate things:

(1) If an injured person died before receiving judgment against the defendant, his cause of action died with him; put differently, the cause of action did not survive the death of the plaintiff.

(2) If an injured person remained alive after injury but the defendant died before a judgment was rendered against him, the plaintiff's cause of action died as well; put differently, the plaintiff's cause of action did not survive the death of the defendant.

(3) There was no separate cause of action on behalf of those who were dependent upon the deceased person.

In most states all of these rules have been changed; in all states one or more have been changed.[1] The first two rules have been changed by statutes generally known as "survival" statutes, because they provide that the cause of action survives the death of the plaintiff or the defendant or both. The third rule has been changed by statutes usually called "wrongful death" statutes, or "Lord Campbell's" Acts after the sponsor of the first such legislation.

Subject to a minor exception in federal maritime law, wrongful death and survival claims are entirely statutory. Statutes are amended from time to time and many have idiosyncratic elements. Lawyers must always

---

[1] A number of federal statutes also allow for death recoveries in some form. *See, e.g.*, Federal Employers' Liability Act, 45 U.S.C.A. § 51 (employees of interstate railroads); Jones Act, 46 U.S.C.A. § 688 (employees at sea).

consult the governing statute and should expect to find local variations in the general scheme described in this chapter.

§ 1. STATUTORY ACTIONS

WEIGEL V. LEE
752 N.W.2d 618 (N.D. 2008)

CROTHERS, JUSTICE.

[Darlyne Rogers died shortly after being admitted to a "regular" room in a hospital despite being critically ill. Her adult children (collectively "the Weigels") sued Dr. Lane Lee and the hospital (collectively "Lee") pursuant to the North Dakota wrongful death statute. The complaint sought damages for the Weigels' own emotional distress and loss of consortium. After a series of motions, orders, and reconsiderations, the trial court dismissed the Weigels' entire case. Ultimately the trial court reasoned that because under *Butz v. World Wide, Inc.*, 492 N.W.2d 88 (N.D. 1992), children do not have a cause of action for either loss of parental consortium or for their own emotional distress damages. The court further suggested that the Weigels could bring only a claim for the emotional distress suffered by Rogers before her death.]

. . . The district court erred by blending three distinct claims for tortious conduct. At various points in its orders, the district court discussed (1) loss of consortium claims arising out of personal injury actions, (2) survival actions and (3) wrongful death actions. This Court and North Dakota's statutes distinguish between these three claims, as we explain below.

[Historically, a loss of consortium claim was available only to husbands whose wives were injured.] In *Hastings,* this Court acknowledged both spouses' right to recover for loss of consortium, but refused to extend this type of recovery to children who suffer the loss of a parent's consortium. Nonetheless, this is not the basis of the Weigels' action, and as this Court importantly clarified in *Hastings,* the inability of children to recover for loss of consortium arising out of personal injury to a parent "should not be construed to prohibit recovery where a parent dies and recovery is allowed under the Wrongful Death Act."

The distinction between loss of consortium in personal injury and in wrongful death actions is important here because Lee argues this Court's decision in *Butz* indicates a decedent's children are not entitled to damages in a wrongful death action. Lee misapplies *Butz. Butz* was not a claim under the wrongful death act because the tortious conduct resulted in severe injury, not in death. . . . Because *Butz* does not address claims made under the wrongful death statutes, it is not applicable to the Weigels' claim.

Second, N.D.C.C. § 28–01–26.1 provides for survival actions: "No action or claim for relief, except for breach of promise, alienation of affections, libel, and slander, abates by the death of a party or of a person who might have been a party had such death not occurred." For example, in *Nodak Mut. Ins. Co. v. Stegman*, 647 N.W.2d 133 (N.D. 2002), an individual was seriously injured in an automobile accident. He underwent hospital treatment, but died approximately two weeks later. This Court stated, "Clearly a personal injury action existed on behalf of [the injured party] against [the tortfeasor] for various damages, including the medical expenses occasioned by the accident, and that action survived [the injured party's] death." Survival statutes "are remedial in nature, and are intended to permit recovery by the representatives of the deceased for damages the deceased could have recovered had he lived. . . . A survival action merely continues in existence an injured person's claim after death as an asset of his estate." Although they could have, the Weigels' complaint indicates they are not seeking damages on Rogers' behalf as part of a survival action. Instead, the Weigels brought a wrongful death action for their own injuries: "The Plaintiffs have sustained mental and emotional anguish as a result of the Defendants' negligence and their mother's death. Furthermore, the Plaintiffs have been denied the society, comfort, counsel and companionship of Darlyne Rogers, all to their injury and damage."

Third, N.D.C.C. ch. 32–21 provides for wrongful death actions. The Weigels offer the wrongful death act as the legal basis for their claim. We conclude the Weigels are entitled to seek compensation for Rogers' wrongful death for the reasons stated below.

There was no wrongful death claim at common law. Early wrongful death statutes severely limited compensable damages. Generally, only pecuniary losses were awarded, with no compensation available for mental anguish or loss of companionship. Contemporary wrongful death statutes tend to address a broader scope of injuries, including those considered non-pecuniary. Wrongful death actions are intended to compensate the survivors of the deceased for the losses they have sustained as a result of a wrongful killing. Dependent upon the specific statutory language, losses recoverable by survivors in wrongful death actions often include the prospective loss of earnings and contribution; prospective expenses; loss of services; loss of companionship, comfort, and consortium; and mental anguish and grief.

North Dakota's wrongful death act, N.D.C.C. ch. 32–21, provides:

"Whenever the death of a person shall be caused by a wrongful act, neglect, or default, and the act, neglect, or default is such as would have entitled the party injured, if death had not ensued, to maintain an action and recover damages in respect thereof, then and in every such case the person who, or the corporation, limited liability company, or company which, would have been liable if death had not ensued, shall be liable to an action for damages, notwithstanding the death of the person injured or of the tort-feasor, and although the death shall have been caused under such circumstances as amount in law to felony."

This statute is not a survival statute intended to increase the estate of the deceased, but its purpose is to give a measure of protection to those persons within a fixed degree of relationship to and dependency on the deceased because of actual injury sustained by them by reason of the wrongful killing of the deceased. Damages under the wrongful death act are based on the loss suffered by the beneficiaries, and not on the loss sustained by the decedent's estate. A jury determines the quantity of damages and "shall give such damages as it finds proportionate to the injury resulting from the death to the persons entitled to the recovery." N.D.C.C. § 32–21–02.

Compensable damages available in wrongful death actions are enumerated in N.D.C.C. § 32–03.2–04 [and specifically include both economic and non-economic damages. Included in the latter are mental anguish, emotional distress, and loss of consortium.]

Section 32–21–04, N.D.C.C., clarifies that intended recipients of damages under the wrongful death act are "the decedent's heirs at law." This Court has determined "heirs at law" for purposes of this statute are "those persons who by the laws of descent would succeed to the property of the decedent in case of intestacy, but in addition, that if members of a preferred class are precluded from recovery for reasons other than death those next entitled to inherit may be considered beneficiaries." A decedent's descendants are designated by the Uniform Probate Code to share in portions of the intestate estate and are therefore able to seek recovery of damages under the wrongful death act.

Persons entitled to recover damages under the wrongful death act should not be confused with persons statutorily authorized to bring an action. Section 32–21–03, N.D.C.C. [authorizes the following persons to bring an action, in the following order: "(1) The surviving husband or wife, if any; (2) The surviving children, if any; (3) The surviving mother or father; (4) A surviving grandparent; (5) The personal representative; (6) A person who has had primary physical custody of the decedent before the wrongful act."]

The distinction between persons eligible to seek damages from wrongful death actions and those entitled to bring such actions is important because the trial judge is charged with splitting the recovery among eligible heirs. . . . In specific wrongful death actions, overlap will likely exist between plaintiffs bringing the action under N.D.C.C. § 32–21–03 and those entitled to any damages. However, those with authority to bring the action do not have an absolute right to the damages recovered, and, instead, bring the action in a representative capacity for the exclusive benefit of the persons entitled to recover. The wrongful death act thus differentiates between the capacity to bring an action and the right to share in the damages recovered. Surviving children are eligible to bring a wrongful death action under N.D.C.C. § 32–21–03(2) if the decedent had no eligible spouse or if the spouse fails to bring an action for thirty days after the children made a demand. But this issue is separate from the children's ability to recover damages in a wrongful death action.

Because the wrongful death act does not exclude the decedent's children from parties entitled to damages and because the damages requested are permitted under N.D.C.C. § 32–03.2–04, the Weigels' claim should not have been dismissed.

[Reversed and remanded.]

NOTES

1. **Wrongful death and survival actions.** A survival action is the claim the decedent could have brought had the decedent lived. A wrongful death action is the claim of the decedent's survivors for losses they themselves have sustained. This means that a personal representative, say the surviving husband of a deceased wife, may bring one suit for the estate—the survival action; and may also bring a separate death action for the appropriate survivors. *See Spangler v. McQuitty*, 141 A.3d 156, 170 (Md. 2016) (a subsequent wrongful death action brought by a decedent's beneficiaries is not barred by the disposition of a decedent's personal injury claim); *Riggs v. Georgia-Pacific LLC*, 345 P.3d 1219 (Utah 2015) (the two causes of action "are aimed at compensating different types of loss" to different people). "Thus, '[i]n a survival action, a claim for lost earnings embraces only the earnings lost up to the time of death.' Future lost earnings are then recovered under a wrongful death statute." *Tembenis v. Sec'y of Health & Human Servs.*, 733 F.3d 1190, 1196 (Fed. Cir. 2013).

2. **Wrongful death: parties and procedure.** A wrongful death action does not involve a claim by the estate. Any recovery does not pass through the estate, but instead goes directly to the survivors. The action is often brought by survivors of the decedent; frequently one of them acts as a kind of informal trustee, suing for all of them. In some states the court appoints a trustee, who formally brings the action on behalf of all appropriate beneficiaries. Very often statutes provide that this person is to be the personal representative of the estate. But where this is so, the personal representative is a trustee for the survivors entitled to recover, not the representative of the estate generally. Many cases concern the appropriate wrongful death claimants and claims procedures. *See Ceja v. Rudolph & Sletten, Inc.*, 302 P.3d 211 (Cal. 2013) (second wife did not bar second wife from asserting subjective good faith).

3. **Survival statutes: parties and procedure.** The plaintiff in a survival claim is the personal representative of the decedent's estate. The

claim is a debt owed to the estate just as any other claim is, and any recovery is paid to the estate. The estate in turn pays the debts of the deceased person and the costs of administering the estate. If any funds are left, the estate pays those to heirs or the beneficiaries of the deceased's will.

§ 2. DAMAGES

LANEY V. VANCE
112 So. 3d 1079 (Miss. 2013)

PIERCE, J.

On July 13, 2005, Mamie Vance Hemphill began treatment at St. Dominic's Hospital. She was admitted with complaints of confusion, decreased appetite, and tremors, and also had end-stage renal disease, respiratory failure, pneumonia, and had been on dialysis. [A dialysis catheter may have been infected. Antibiotic treatment initially seemed to help, but then her condition worsened. Dialysis was attempted and tests were run. The doctors made plans to remove the catheter.] Dr. Anne B. Whitehurst, an infectious-disease specialist, was brought in, as well. By 1:45 p.m., on July 16, 2005, Hemphill went into cardiopulmonary arrest and could not be revived.

Martin Vance (individually and on behalf of wrongful-death beneficiaries of Mamie Vance Hemphill) complained (at trial) that Dr. Charles Laney failed to recognize Hemphill's medical problems and failed to move her to intensive care soon enough before she died. . . . The main issue to be resolved by the jury was whether Dr. Laney breached the applicable standard of care by deciding to treat the infection with antibiotics and to leave the allegedly infected catheter in place, since it was the only access for dialysis. The jury returned a verdict for $1,000,000, which included $200,000 in economic damages and $800,000 in noneconomic damages.

Dr. Laney has presented three issues to this Court. They include:

I. Whether the trial court erred in remitting the plaintiff's economic damage award to $103,688 when the substantial weight of the evidence proved that the award should be zero.

II. Whether the trial court erred in instructing the jury when the jury instructions are taken as a whole.

III. Whether Plaintiff's counsel's improper comments and arguments, including that the damages should represent "the value of a human life," when combined with the erroneous jury instructions, mandate reversal and a new trial.

Because we find that Issue Three (3) is dispositive, we will not address Issues One and Two. . . .

Dr. Laney alleges that the trial court erred in instructing the jury that an element of damages in this case is the "loss of the value of life of Ms. Hemphill."[1] Dr. Laney asserts that allowing the "value of life" to be considered as an element of damages is inconsistent with Mississippi Code Section 11–1–69(2), which states, "In any wrongful death action, there shall be no recovery for loss of enjoyment of life caused by death." Rather, damages are limited to: "(1) the present net cash value of the life expectancy of the deceased, (2) the loss of the companionship and society of the decedent, (3) the pain and suffering of the decedent between the time of injury and death, and (4) punitive damages."

This Court, in *Rebelwood Apts. RP, LP v. English,* held that "[i]n providing a framework for determination of lost future income, courts are not determining the 'value' of a person." Additionally, Mississippi Code Section 11–1–69(2) bars hedonic damages, which are:

> The damages for the loss of enjoyment of life, which purportedly compensate an injured person for the loss of quality of life or in the case of a wrongful death action for the value of life itself.

Vance asserts that the jury instructions were proper, because they were not objected to at trial and are correct under Mississippi law. . . .

The Legislature addressed this issue when it amended Mississippi Code Section 11–1–69(2) to include, "In any wrongful death action, there shall be no recovery for loss of enjoyment of life caused by death." . . . [W]e find that it was reversible error for the trial judge to instruct the jury that it might consider the "value of life" of the deceased in awarding damages.

Additionally, the statements made in Vance's attorney's closing argument were prejudicial to Dr. Laney. . . . During closing arguments, counsel for Vance stated the following to the jury:

> The first thing they do in a communist Nazi Country is destroy the jury system. Why do they want to destroy the jury system? Because you represent the line between tyranny and democracy, right and wrong. You have the power . . . You have more power today than the President of the United States. . . .

---

[1] The trial judge instructed the jury that if it returned a verdict in favor of Plaintiff, it was to award damages as follows:

1. The value of any physical pain and suffering suffered by Mamie Vance Hemphill;

2. The loss of income suffered by the death of Mamie Vance Hemphill, if any;

3. The value of any loss of companionship, love and society, past, present or future mental anguish and distress suffered by her wrongful death beneficiaries;

4. The value of the life of Mamie Vance Hemphill.

(Emphasis added.)

But the question is, will you have courage today? Do you have the God given courage. . . .

The value of the life of Mamie Hemphill. . . . I had to bring each one of the kids up here and ask them, what did your mother mean to you? What did she do with you? What did she do for you? The value of a loss.

Based on the prejudicial nature of the foregoing statements and other statements by counsel for Vance, which were presented to the jury during closing arguments, we reverse and remand for a new trial.

NOTES

Wrongful Death Statutes

1. **The value of a life.** Why do you think that plaintiff argued for the value of a life to be listed as an item of damages? Although the *Laney* court says the jury should not calculate the value of a life in a wrongful death action, is that, in essence, what a wrongful death action does?

2. **Measures of damages for wrongful death.** Wrongful death statutes traditionally aimed to replace pecuniary losses that would be suffered by others because of the decedent's death. "Apart from relatively minor items such as funeral expense, most states measure economic loss by the loss of support to dependents. Some measure it differently, by the loss of projected lifetime savings of the deceased. The first measure is usually called loss-to-survivors or loss-to-dependents measure, while the second is called the loss-to-the estate measure." "[M]ost of the states which use the loss-to-the estate measure calculate the loss by determining the deceased's probable lifetime earnings and then deducting the expenses the decedent would have had in maintaining himself." DAN B. DOBBS, LAW OF REMEDIES §§ 8.3(3) & 8.3(4) (2d ed. 1993). The statute in *Laney* is somewhat atypical in potentially allowing punitive damages in the wrongful death action.

3. **Pecuniary emphasis; loss to survivors' measure.** Wrongful death statutes originally limited the recovery to pecuniary losses suffered by dependents or those who would inherit. For example, under the loss to survivors' measure of damages, children of a decedent might recover for loss of support they received in the form of housing, food, and clothing. If the deceased person would not have contributed to any beneficiary during his lifetime, damages would be small or nonexistent. *See Armantrout v. Carlson*, 214 P.3d 914 (Wash. 2009) (in parents' suit for wrongful death of adult child, jury should consider services that have a monetary value when assessing the claimants' dependency on the decedent for support).

4. **Loss-to-estate measure.** The loss-to-estate measure might allow substantial damages even where the decedent was not contributing to the support of others. This measure would allow recovery for whatever sums the decedent would have earned and saved in her normal lifetime, even if she were

supporting no one. This would be helpful if decedent would have earned more than her self-support required. Under some circumstances might it lead to a zero award?

5. **Combining measures.** Several courts have now permitted death action plaintiffs to recover both the loss of support and a loss of inheritance. The loss of inheritance is essentially like the loss to the estate. The claimant must show that the decedent would have accumulated an estate (or an increase in his estate) and that the claimant would have inherited a share. When the claimants were receiving no support, as is often the case with adult children of the decedent, in such jurisdictions they could still recover for reasonably provable loss of inheritance. *See Schaefer v. Amer. Family Mut. Ins. Co.,* 531 N.W.2d 585 (Wis. 1995).

6. **Non-earning decedents.** Children, spouses who do not work in the labor market, retired persons, and others whose earnings are small or nonexistent create still another problem under the wrongful death statutes. It would be difficult to say that wrongful death has reduced their ultimate estate and equally difficult to say that they were supporting other persons. Thus neither measure of wrongful death damages is adequate for non-working decedents. In such cases, non-pecuniary damages become all-important. Does that seem like an issue in *Weigel* and *Laney?*

7. **Non-pecuniary claims generally.** At least three basic kinds of non-pecuniary loss might be claimed in death actions: (1) punitive damages; (2) damages for the mental anguish or grief of the survivors; (3) loss of consortium, which might include (a) loss of society or companionship, (b) loss of services, and (c) loss of guidance and care. As *Weigel* explains, claims like these were excluded under most original wrongful death statutes. The first two elements are generally rejected in wrongful death suits, though a few states permit their recovery. The third, loss of consortium, is usually recoverable. Courts stress that loss of consortium does not include emotional distress of the survivors, but that it does include a broad range of mutual benefits of family membership, including love, affection, care, companionship and the like. *See Reiser v. Coburn,* 587 N.W.2d 336 (Neb. 1998) (a zero award to parents of a young independent adult was inadequate, new trial required).

8. **Future losses.** Both the loss-to-survivors rule and the loss-to-the-estate rule require the court to estimate the earnings the decedent would have had but for the death. How many years would the decedent have lived to save money or make contributions to dependents? What would those earnings have been? These are difficult matters of proof and complicated by possible inflation and taxes. A discount must be made after all this to take into account the fact that the plaintiffs will recover all future losses now and can invest the sum at interest. *See generally* DAN B. DOBBS, LAW OF REMEDIES § 8.5 (2d ed. 1993).

9. **Damages caps.** Many states have a statutory cap on noneconomic damages in some types of cases. Limits on noneconomic damage recovery in wrongful death cases may violate state constitutional provisions. *See Smith v.*

United States, 356 P.3d 1249 (Utah 2015) ("The right of action to recover damages for injuries resulting in death, shall never be abrogated, and the amount recoverable shall not be subject to any statutory limitation, except in cases where compensation for injuries resulting in death is provided for by law."). If a doctor's negligence results in a wrongful death, should the medical malpractice damages cap be applied in the wrongful death case? *Compare DRD Pool Serv., Inc. v. Freed*, 5 A.3d 45 (Md. 2010), and *Jenkins v. Patel*, 684 N.W.2d 346 (Mich. 2004) (yes), *with Bartholomew v. Wisconsin Patient's Comp. Fund*, 717 N.W.2d 216 (Wis. 2006) (no).

Survival Statutes

10. **Survival of claim after plaintiff's death.** A tort victim might bring a suit to redress a tort, then die before the suit goes to judgment. In that case, the claim is "revived" and continued in the name of the personal representative. Or, the victim might die without having brought suit, so that the claim is brought by the personal representative in the first place. Either way, the claim is a survival action. It is a species of property which passes to the estate of the deceased person in the same way a share of stock or a bank account might pass.

11. **Survival of claim after defendant's death.** Survival statutes usually also provide for survival of the victim's claim after the defendant's death. In this setting, the living victim asserts the claim for all damages against the estate of the deceased tortfeasor. The case of the deceased victim is the more common one.

12. **Survival damages.** Since the survival action continues the claim held by the decedent for damages accruing up until his death, it may include any medical expenses, wages lost before death, and pain and suffering resulting from the injury. In some states it may also include funeral expenses. Most states allow for the recovery of punitive damages in these cases, on a rationale that "if a wrongdoer may be punished if his victim lives, then surely he should not escape retribution if his wrongful act causes a death." *Smith v. Whitaker*, 734 A.2d 243 (N.J. 1999).

13. **Special classes of damages.** Survival statutes can create new kinds of damages. A few states authorize "loss of life" damages, designed "to compensate a decedent for the loss of the value that the decedent would have placed on his or her life." *See Durham v. Marberry*, 156 S.W.3d 242 (Ark. 2004). Such damages are available even if the decedent died instantly, since it is not identical to an award for pain and suffering. *Id.*

Evaluating Death Damages

14. **Damages awarded.** Are death damages too low? In Eric A. Posner & Cass R. Sunstein, *Dollars and Death*, 72 U. CHI. L. REV. 537 (2005), the authors compare American regulation, which values life at a uniform number, recently $6 million, with tort law, which affords varied, but on average much lower, recoveries. One of Posner and Sunstein's conclusions is that "courts should move in the direction of administrative regulation by taking account of

the welfare loss to the decedent. This change would significantly alter wrongful death cases by producing far higher recoveries in many cases." What could be a benefit of higher recoveries?

15. **Individualized damages vs. presumptive awards.** In wrongful death cases, rather than calculate individualized damages in each case, Chinese tort law generally awards the decedent's beneficiaries twenty times the average earnings in the decedent's locality. This presumptive award can be decreased in certain circumstances, as in the case of old age, or increased in other circumstances, for example, when the decedent had been living in a city although registered as living in a rural area. *See* SPC Interpretation on Compensation for Personal Injury, cited in THE CHINA LAW CENTER, YALE LAW SCHOOL, TORT LAW IN CHINA: HISTORICAL DEVELOPMENT AND SELECTED ISSUES (2006). The 9/11 Fund also created presumed damage awards to be paid to victims. See FINAL REPORT OF THE SPECIAL MASTER FOR THE SEMPTEMBER 11TH VICTIM COMPENSATION FUND OF 2001, Report of Kenneth R. Feinberg, Esq., to U.S. Dep't of Justice (2004). Although presumptive awards have been criticized in China for creating unequal awards, would this type of system create more equal awards in the United States? Why permit widely-disparate individualized awards rather than more consistent awards?

§ 3. BENEFICIARIES

CHAVEZ V. CARPENTER, 111 Cal. Rptr. 2d 534 (Ct. App. 2001). Altie Chavez, 24, was killed by a drunk driver, the defendant here, in August. Though unmarried, Altie was the father of a two-year-old daughter, Jazmyne. Jazmyne died from unrelated causes in September. Altie had lived with and perhaps contributed monetary support to his parents, Jose and Elsa. They brought suit for his death. Maria Garcia, Jazmyne's mother, brought suit on behalf of Jazmyne's estate. Held: (1) the statute permits recovery by heirs, but the parents cannot recover as heirs of Altie because parents cannot be heirs if the decedent's child survived him, which Jazmyne did; (2) the statute now permits recovery by parents who were "dependents"; this is a factual question to be addressed at trial; and (3) Jazmyne, as an heir, had a cause of action for the wrongful death of her father, Altie, and that cause of action survived her and may be pursued by her estate.

NOTES

1. **Stepchildren.** Statutes may include "stepchildren" among those entitled to recover. *See, e.g., In re Estate of Blessing*, 273 P.3d 975 (Wash. 2012). Most courts interpreting statutes that allow "heirs" or "children" to recover, however, have held that stepchildren do not qualify. *See, e.g., Steed v. Imperial Airlines*, 524 P.2d 801 (Cal. 1974). The California Legislature responded to *Steed* by amending its Civil Procedure Code § 377 to provide that minors living with the decedent for six months or more and receiving more than half their support from decedent could recover for wrongful death. A recent case held

that an "in loco parentis" child was not decedent's child for purposes of the wrongful death statute. *Estate of Smith v. Smith ex rel. Rollins*, 130 So. 3d 508, 511 (Miss. 2014) (a person in loco parentis may be defined as one who has assumed the status and obligations of a parent without a formal adoption).

2. **Unmarried cohabitants.** Under statutes that distribute damages to heirs, or to named categories, such as "surviving spouse" or "children," there is no room for compensation to the surviving friend or lover. Some courts excluded not only unmarried partners, but partners of a civil union. *See, e.g., Langan v. St. Vincent's Hosp. of New York*, 802 N.Y.S.2d 476 (App. Div. 2005) (surviving partner of same-sex civil union not a "surviving spouse" under statute). Modern statutes may expressly provide for broader coverage, 15 VT. STAT. §§ 1204(a) & 1204(e)(2); CAL. CIV. PROC. CODE § 377.60, and the constitution may require it.

3. **Jury bias.** Along with distributional defects in the statutory wrongful death schemes, there are problems in jury awards. Studies show that jurors award much larger sums to the female spouse of a male decedent than to the male spouse of a female decedent, even when their earnings are the same. *See* Goodman, Loftus, Miller & Greene, *Money, Sex, and Death: Gender Bias in Wrongful Death Damage Awards*, 25 L. & SOC'Y REV. 263 (1991). Female decedents are worth less? Or female survivors need more? Is the disparity justified under either hypothesis?

4. **Distribution among beneficiaries.** Distribution of wrongful death proceeds is a frequent subject of litigation. *See In re Estate of Dezotell*, 140 A.3d 797 (Vt. 2016) (court entered distribution order, apportioning the amount between wife and children differently than it had in its previous two orders); *Estate of Eubanks v. Eubanks*, 197 So. 3d 861 (Miss. 2015) (Chancery Court was without authority to unequally divide wrongful-death settlement proceeds between decedent's wrongful death beneficiaries). What of a surviving spouse who was a spouse in name only? *Force v. American Family Mut. Ins. Co.*, 850 N.W.2d 866 (Wis. 2014) (estranged spouse).

NOTE: DEFENSES

1. *Decedent's contributory negligence or assumption of risk.* The rule under most death statutes is that the action could be brought for wrongful death only if the decedent could have sued had he lived. This language obviously means that the defendant is not liable unless he is guilty of conduct that would be tortious toward some individual.

It is sometimes argued, however, that the wrongful death action, always in theory a "new and independent action" for the protection of survivors, should be permitted in spite of the contributory negligence of the decedent. The survivors, it is argued, were guilty of no misconduct, and the defendant should not escape liability to these innocent victims of his wrongful conduct. Is this a sound argument? Most courts treat the decedent's contributory fault as a defense. *See Horwich v. Superior Court*, 980 P.2d 927 (Cal. 1999). In comparative fault systems, that means the damages in the wrongful death suit will be reduced by the percentage of fault attributable to the decedent. *E.g., Adamy v. Ziriakus*, 704 N.E.2d 216 (N.Y. 1998).

2. *Beneficiary's contributory negligence or assumption of risk.*

(a) *Survival claims.* Under survival statutes, the decedent's own claim is being pursued, not a claim for beneficiaries. This point is emphasized by the form of the claim, which is a suit by the estate of the decedent, with proceeds payable to the estate. The fact that an heir was guilty of contributory negligence will be of no direct relevance, even though the heir will inherit the estate, including the survival action recovery. However, in a joint and several liability system, the defendant may obtain contribution from the negligent heir, thus negating his recovery. The same result may be achieved in a several liability system in which each tortfeasor is responsible only for a percentage of damages equal to his percentage of fault.

(b) *Wrongful death claims.* If there was but one beneficiary, and he was guilty of contributory negligence, the common law rule barred his recovery for wrongful death. Where there were several beneficiaries, some guilty of contributory negligence and some not, a number of courts took the view that contributory negligence should not bar the entire death claim, but should bar only the claim of the negligent beneficiary. The comparative fault system seems to make this an easy case. Either by reducing damages or by contribution, the defendant can eliminate liability for the percentage share attributable to any negligent beneficiary. *See* 2 DOBBS, HAYDEN & BUBLICK, THE LAW OF TORTS § 378 (2d ed. 2011).

3. *Statutes of limitations.* Albert Weinberg was exposed to asbestos from 1941 to 1948. In 1975 a mesothelioma, or lung cancer, was discovered. This allegedly resulted from the asbestos exposure. Mr. Weinberg brought no action during his life and he died in 1977. Thereafter an action for his death was brought within two years. The death act prescribes two years from death as the limitation period. Is the claim nevertheless barred on the ground that no action for death can be brought unless the decedent could have maintained an action at the same time had he lived? Some courts have taken this view. *See Russell v. Ingersoll-Rand Co.*, 841 S.W.2d 343 (Tex. 1992); *Deggs v. Asbestos Corp. Ltd.*, 381 P.3d 32 (Wash. 2016). But many cases hold that the statute begins running at the time of death and that the death claim is not barred even if the decedent would be barred had he lived. *E.g., Chapman v. Cardiac Pacemakers, Inc.*, 673 P.2d 385 (Idaho 1983); *Mummert v. Alizadeh*, 77 A.3d 1049 (Md. 2013) (plaintiffs' right to

bring action was not contingent on patient's ability to bring negligence action prior to death).

REFERENCES: 2 DOBBS, HAYDEN & BUBLICK, THE LAW OF TORTS §§ 372–380 (2d ed. 2011); DOBBS, HAYDEN & BUBLICK, HANDBOOK ON TORTS CHAPTER 28 (2d ed. 2016).

PART 8

THE EBB AND FLOW OF COMMON LAW STRICT LIABILITY FOR PHYSICAL HARMS

• • •

In the materials covered so far, fault has been the keynote concept in liability. We now consider three areas involving complete or partial strict liability—liability without proof of the defendant's fault. Strict liability means that liability is imposed even without proof that the defendant acted intentionally or negligently.

In the last chapter in this Part, Chapter 24, the topic is products liability. Products liability law sometimes (but not always) imposes liability without proof of fault upon manufacturers and distributors of defective products.

In Chapter 23 we will see older forms of strict liability, those associated with certain problems of trespassing or dangerous animals, neighboring landowners (often making inconsistent uses of land), and with especially hazardous activities that tend to cause harm even when not carried out negligently.

In the first chapter in this Part, Chapter 22, we renew acquaintance with an idea introduced at the very beginning of the course—vicarious liability, which can be perceived as a form of strict liability in which one person or entity is held legally responsible for the fault-based torts of another.

CHAPTER 22

VICARIOUS LIABILITY

. . .

§ 1. RESPONDEAT SUPERIOR AND SCOPE OF EMPLOYMENT

We recognized early in the course that employers could be held liable for the torts of certain employees, provided those torts were committed within the scope of employment. This principle of liability is often called vicarious liability or the *respondeat superior* principle.

What is meant by the limitation that torts must be committed within the scope of employment? To a large extent the answer to this question turns on a much larger one—why hold the employer liable at all? The employer is not personally at fault, so that his liability is in a sense a kind of strict liability. One case summarized the [goals of vicarious liability succinctly as (a) the prevention of future injuries, (b) the assurance of compensation to victims, and (c) the equitable spreading of losses caused by an enterprise] *See Lisa M. v. Henry Mayo Newhall Mem. Hosp.*, 907 P.2d 358 (Cal. 1995).

RIVIELLO v. WALDRON, 391 N.E.2d 1278 (N.Y. 1979). Waldron, employed as a cook at the Pot Belly Pub, a Bronx bar and grill, was talking to a customer and flipping an open knife. [This accidentally struck the customer in the eye, causing a loss of its use] The customer sued the bar owner. [Held, the bar owner is liable;] Waldron was within the scope of employment. The scope of employment was originally defined narrowly "on the theory that the employer could exercise close control over his employees during the period of their service." But "social policy has wrought a measure of relaxation of the traditional confines of the doctrine." Reasons for this are that "the average innocent victim, when relegated to the pursuit of his claim against the employee, [most often will face a defendant too impecunious to meet the claim, and that modern economic devices, such as cost accounting and insurance coverage, permit most employers to spread the impact of such costs] So no longer is an employer necessarily excused merely because his employees, acting in furtherance of his interests, exhibit human failings and perform negligently or otherwise than in an authorized manner. Instead, the test has come to be [whether the act was

→ still scope of employment

done while the servant was doing his (master's work,) no matter how irregularly, or with what disregard of instructions.

Seems to have been expanded somewhat

FRUIT V. SCHREINER, 502 P.2d 133 (Alaska 1972). Fruit, a life insurance salesman, was attending a company sales convention where his employer required him to be. Events included morning business meetings and evening dinners and cocktail parties. Employees were encouraged to mix freely with out-of-state attendees to learn as much as possible about sales techniques. On the first night of the convention, Fruit and other sales agents went for dinner and drinks to a restaurant and bar in Homer, about five miles from the convention headquarters. The next evening, having slept through a scheduled dinner, Fruit drove back to the Homer restaurant, believing that out-of-state sales agents would be there. He left when he found no one there. It was 2:00 a.m. when, on his way back to the convention headquarters, Fruit skidded and struck Schreiner, whose legs were crushed. Schreiner sued Fruit and his employer. A jury found both liable; the employer was found liable because Fruit's negligent driving was within the scope of his employment. The employer appealed, claiming that the evidence did not support such a finding.

Procedural Posture ←

Held, affirmed. The jury could find that when Fruit made his fateful trip to Homer, "he was at least motivated in part by his desire to meet with the out-of-state guests and thus to benefit from their experience so as to improve his abilities as a salesman" . . . The basis of *respondeat superior* has been correctly stated as the desire to include in the costs of operation inevitable losses to third persons incident to carrying on an enterprise, and thus distribute the burden among those benefitted by the enterprise . . . Insurance is readily available for the employer so that the risk may be distributed among many like insured paying premiums and the extra cost of doing business may be reflected in the price of the product."

Juries resolve law questions when facts are in dispute; juries resolve those questions

Policy Rationale ?

NOTES

1. **Scope of employment.** In both *Riviello* and *Fruit*, the employees were found to have been acting within the scope of employment when they committed their torts. Whether an employee was acting within the scope of employment is a fact question for the jury, where reasonable people can differ. *See, e.g., Hecksher v. Fairwinds Baptist Church, Inc.*, 15 A.3d 1187 (Del. 2015). Traditionally, an employee's conduct is within the scope of employment if it is of the same general kind as authorized or expected, and the employee was acting within authorized time and space limits. The Agency Restatements, followed by many courts, additionally impose a kind of "purpose" or "motive" test—that the employee's action must have been motivated, at least in part, by a purpose to serve the employer. *See* RESTATEMENT (SECOND) OF AGENCY § 228(1)(c) (1959); RESTATEMENT (THIRD) OF AGENCY § 707(2) (2006). Thus some courts find no vicarious liability where the act is "too little actuated by a

purpose to serve the master." *See Doe v. Newbury Bible Church*, 933 A.2d 196 (Vt. 2007). However, a number of modern courts reject or minimize this "purpose" or "motive" test, and instead adopt a broader formulation. *See, e.g., Gina Chin & Associates v. First Union Bank*, 537 S.E.2d 573 (Va. 2000) (motive not determinative; issue is "whether the service itself, in which the tortious act is done, was within the ordinary course of such business"); *Sheffer v. Carolina Forge Co.*, 306 P.3d 544 (Okla. 2013) ("one acts within the scope of employment if engaged in work assigned, or if doing that which is proper, necessary and useful to accomplish the work assigned, or doing that which is customary within the particular trade or business"). While we will see some other definitions throughout this chapter, it is probably good to keep in mind the words of the Delaware Supreme Court: "The phrase, 'scope of employment' is, at best, indefinite. It is nothing more than a convenient means of defining those tortious acts of the servant not ordered by the master for which the policy of law imposes liability on the master." *Doe v. State*, 76 A.3d 774 (Del. 2013) (quoting *Draper v. Olivere Paving & Constr. Co.*, 181 A.2d 565 (Del. 1962)).

2. **Disregarding the employer's instructions or orders.** The *Riviello* court notes that vicarious liability may be found even where the employee disregards the employer's instructions in committing the injurious act. The general rule is that "the employer's vicarious liability extends to the negligent, willful, malicious, or even criminal acts of its employees when such acts are committed within the scope of the employment." *Adames v. Sheahan*, 909 N.E.2d 724 (Ill. 2009).

3. **Thinking about the rationales.** Do the New York and Alaska Courts in *Riviello* and *Fruit* give the same reasons for expansive liability of an employer? Is either court simply using the theory that the employer represents a "deep pocket"? What reasons can you give for holding an employer liable for the employee's negligence in causing harm to others?

4. **Vicarious liability and "fault."** When an employer is sued on a vicarious liability theory, the employer's own fault is irrelevant; in this way, it is accurate to call vicarious liability form of strict liability. But no one can be vicariously liable for another's tort unless that other person commits a tort—and as we have seen in this course, that will typically require the plaintiff to prove that the other person (such as an employee), was negligent or acted intentionally. In other words, where the employee has not committed a tort at all, the employer cannot be vicariously liable for whatever harm the employee may have caused. *See* DOBBS, HAYDEN & BUBLICK, HORNBOOK ON TORTS § 425, at 782 (2d ed. 2011).

Most states also hold that if the employee personally was not or could not be held *legally responsible* for an otherwise tortious act, the employer cannot be vicariously liable, either. *See, e.g., Ex Parte Labbe*, 156 So.3d 368 (Ala. 2014) (individual volunteer firefighters have statutory immunity, so their employer cannot be vicariously liable for the firefighters' negligent acts). Thus an employer will escape vicarious liability by proving that the employee either did not commit a tort at all, or could not be held legally responsible for a tort. *See, e.g., Strock v. Pressnell*, 527 N.E.2d 1235 (Ohio 1988) ("It is axiomatic that for the doctrine of respondeat superior to apply, an employee must be liable for a tort committed in the scope of his employment.").

5. **Employer's right of indemnity.** If an employer is held vicariously liable because of an employee's tort, the employer has a theoretical right of indemnity from the employee—that is, a right to recoup from the employee the damages the employer has paid to the plaintiff. That right is seldom asserted, however, partly because the employer's liability insurance is likely to protect both employer and employee.

NOTE: ENTERPRISE LIABILITY

As reflected in *Fruit*, the concept of enterprise liability is often close to the surface of any strict liability analysis. In his groundbreaking book, *The Costs of Accidents* (1970), Professor (now Judge) Guido Calabresi urged that tort law's principal function is to reduce the costs of accidents and the costs of avoiding them. We will see Calabresi's ideas in some more depth in Chapter 24, but some of his central conceptions are worth thinking about here.

One idea is that the price of goods and activities should accurately reflect the accident costs they cause. Holding an enterprise strictly liable for harms it causes facilitates this "internalization of costs," which in turn reduces the costs of accidents. How are accident costs reduced? Consumers are influenced by prices. If the price of a particular product or service actually reflects its total costs, including accident costs, the market will tend to favor the cheaper (safer) product or service. Companies will thus have an incentive to make their products and activities safer to compete in the marketplace. Do these ideas support holding an employer strictly liable for the torts of its employees, committed within the scope of employment?

How well does enterprise liability theory mix with accountability for fault? If there is a good reason to hold an employer strictly liable in these cases, why not hold all employers liable, regardless of employee negligence, when an act within the scope of employment causes harm?

HINMAN V. WESTINGHOUSE ELECTRIC CO.
471 P.2d 988 (Cal. 1970)

PETERS, JUSTICE.

Plaintiff, a Los Angeles policeman, was standing on the center divider of a freeway inspecting a possible road hazard when he was struck by a car driven by Frank Allen Herman, an employee of defendant Westinghouse. As a result of the accident he received permanent injuries. The city paid his medical expenses and disability pension. [Plaintiff sued Westinghouse on a vicarious liability theory.]

At the time of the accident, Herman was employed by Westinghouse as an elevator constructor's helper and was returning home from work from a job site. He had been working for Westinghouse for about four months. His work was assigned from the Westinghouse office. He did not go to the office before or after work but instead went from home directly to the job site and after work returned home from the job site. The particular job on which Herman was working was not completed at the time of the accident, and he would ordinarily return to the job site until the job was completed or he was told not to return.

The union contracts under which Herman worked provided for the payment of "carfare" and travel time in certain circumstances depending on the location of the job site in relation to the Los Angeles City Hall. As to this job, which was 15 to 20 miles from the city hall, Herman received an hour and a half per day as his roundtrip travel time and $1.30 for his travel expense. The employer had no control over the method or route of transportation used by Herman.

The trial judge refused instructions that Herman was acting within the scope of his employment at the time of the accident and instead instructed the jury that whether he was acting within the scope of his employment depended upon a number of factors including among others ["whether his conduct was authorized by his employer, either expressly or impliedly; the nature of the employment, its object and the duties imposed thereby; whether the employee was acting in his discharge thereof; whether his conduct occurred during the performance of services for the benefit of the employer, either directly or indirectly, or of himself; whether his conduct, even though not expressly or impliedly authorized, was an incidental event connected with his assigned work] . . ." [So instructed, the jury found that Herman was not within the scope of his employment and hence gave a verdict for Westinghouse.]

TC's jury instructions

? Jury found for defendant

Although earlier authorities sought to justify the *respondeat superior* doctrine on such theories as "control" by the master of the servant, the master's "privilege" in being permitted to employ another, the third party's innocence in comparison to the master's selection of the servant, or the master's "deep pocket" to pay for the loss, "the modern justification for vicarious liability is a rule of policy, a deliberate allocation of a risk. The losses caused by the torts of employees, which as a practical matter are sure to occur in the conduct of the employer's enterprise, are placed upon that enterprise itself, as a required cost of doing business. They are placed upon the employer because, having engaged in an enterprise which will, on the basis of past experience, involve harm to others through the torts of employees, and sought to profit by it, it is just that he, rather than the innocent injured plaintiff, should bear them; and because he is better able to absorb them, and to distribute them, through prices, rates or liability insurance, to the public, and so to shift them to society, to the community at large." . . .

Another leading authority also points out that the modern and proper basis of vicarious liability of the master is not his control or fault but the risks incident to his enterprise. "We are not here looking for the master's fault but rather for risks that may fairly be regarded as typical of or broadly incidental to the enterprise he has undertaken. . . ."

Liability of the employer may not be avoided on the basis of the "going and coming" rule. Under the "going and coming" rule, an employee going to and from work is ordinarily considered outside the scope of employment so that the employer is not liable for his torts. The "going and coming" rule is sometimes ascribed to the theory that the employment relationship is "suspended" from the time the employee leaves until he returns or that in commuting he is not rendering service to his employer. Nevertheless, there are exceptions to the rule.

Thus in Harvey v. D & L Construction Co., the court reversed a nonsuit for the employer where it was shown that because of the remote site of the construction project, the employer had asked the employee to recruit other employees, one such employee was riding at the time of the accident, and the employer was furnishing the gas for the trip to the employee's home. . . .

The above cases indicate that exceptions will be made to the "going and coming" rule where the trip involves an incidental benefit to the employer, not common to commute trips by ordinary members of the work force. The cases also indicate that the fact that the employee receives personal benefits is not determinative when there is also a benefit to the employer.

There is a substantial benefit to an employer in one area to be permitted to reach out to a labor market in another area or to enlarge the available labor market by providing travel expenses and payment for travel time. It cannot be denied that the employer's reaching out to the distant or larger labor market increases the risk of injury in transportation. In other words, the employer, having found it desirable in the interests of his enterprise to pay for travel time and for travel expenses and to go beyond the normal labor market or to have located his enterprise at a place remote from the labor market, should be required to pay for the risks inherent in his decision.

We are satisfied that, where, as here, the employer and employee have made the travel time part of the working day by their contract, the employer should be treated as such during the travel time, and it follows that so long as the employee is using the time for the designated purpose, to return home, the doctrine of *respondeat superior* is applicable. It is unnecessary to determine the appropriate rule to be applied if the employee had used the time for other purposes. We also need not decide now whether the mere payment of travel expenses without additional payment for the travel time of the employee . . . reflects a sufficient benefit to the employer so that he should bear responsibility to innocent third parties for the risks inherent in the travel.

The facts relating to the applicability of the doctrine of *respondeat superior* are undisputed in the instant case, and we conclude that as a matter of law the doctrine is applicable and that the trial court erred in its instructions in leaving the issue as one of fact to the jury. . . .

NOTES

1. **The going and coming rule.** The going and coming rule is widely, perhaps universally, accepted. *See Barclay v. Briscoe*, 47 A.3d 560 (Md. 2012). Does the rule make logical sense when you focus on the factors the *Hinman* court used to determine "scope of employment" more generally? Remember that many injuries will be caused by employees while driving their vehicles to and from work; does that fact give the going and coming rule a strong policy basis? *See Ahlstrom v. Salt Lake City Corp.*, 73 P.3d 315 (Utah 2003) ("The major premise of the 'going and coming' rule is that it is unfair to impose unlimited liability on an employer for conduct of its employees over which it has no control and from which it derives no benefit.").

2. **Exceptions.** Courts (and the Agency Restatements) have crafted some specific exceptions to the going and coming rule: (1) Where the employee is "on call," as long as the particular tortious act was otherwise within the scope of employment. (2) Where the employer requires the employee to drive his or her personal vehicle to work so that the vehicle may be used for work-related tasks. (3) Where the employer, either by general policy or specific directive, instructs the employee to carry out some job-related errand during the commute. (4) Where the commute serves a dual purpose for both the employer and the employee. These "exceptions" may not be entirely separable in a given case, and may be applied in combination as part of a broader analysis of scope of employment. *See Carter v. Reynolds,* 815 A.2d 460 (N.J. 2003). Which "exception" is being applied in *Hinman*?

EDGEWATER MOTELS, INC. V. GATZKE
277 N.W.2d 11 (Minn. 1979)

SCOTT, JUSTICE.

[Gatzke, a district manager for Walgreen's, stayed in plaintiff's motel while he was in Duluth, Minnesota supervising the opening of a Walgreen-owned restaurant. The motel was damaged by fire, allegedly the result of Gatzke's negligence while in his motel room. The motel sued both Gatzke and Walgreen's.]

[Gatzke] lived at the Edgewater at the company's expense. While in Duluth, Gatzke normally would arise at 6:00 a.m. and work at the restaurant from about 7:00 a.m. to 12:00 or 1:00 a.m. In addition to working at the restaurant, Gatzke remained on call 24 hours per day to handle problems arising in other Walgreen restaurants located in his district. Gatzke thought of himself as a "24-hour-a-day man." He received calls from other Walgreen restaurants in his district when problems arose. He was allowed to call home at company expense. His laundry, living expenses, and entertainment were items of reimbursement. There were no constraints as to where he would perform his duties or at what time of day they would be performed. . . .

[Around midnight or after, Gatzke left the work with others on the job; some went to their hotel rooms, but Gatzke and Hubbard went to the Bellows restaurant for a drink.]

In about an hour's time Gatzke consumed a total of four brandy Manhattans, three of which were "doubles." While at the Bellows, Gatzke and Hubbard spent part of the time discussing the operation of the newly-opened Walgreen restaurant. Additionally, Gatzke and the Bellows' bartender talked a little about the mixing and pricing of drinks. The testimony showed that Gatzke was interested in learning the bar business because the new Walgreen restaurant served liquor.

Between 1:15 and 1:30 a.m. Gatzke and Hubbard left the Bellows and walked back to the Edgewater. Witnesses testified that Gatzke acted normal and appeared sober. Gatzke went directly to his motel room, and then "probably" sat down at a desk to fill out his expense account because "that was [his] habit from traveling so much." The completion of the expense account had to be done in accordance with detailed instructions, and if the form was not filled out properly it would be returned to the employee unpaid. It took Gatzke no more than five minutes to fill out the expense form.

While Gatzke completed the expense account he "probably" smoked a cigarette. The record indicates Gatzke smoked about two packages of cigarettes per day. A maid testified that the ash trays in Gatzke's room would generally be full of cigarette butts and ashes when she cleaned the room. She also noticed at times that the plastic wastebasket next to the desk contained cigarette butts.

After filling out the expense account Gatzke went to bed, and soon thereafter a fire broke out. Gatzke escaped from the burning room, but the fire spread rapidly and caused extensive damage to the motel. The amount of damages was stipulated by the parties at $330,360.

One of plaintiff's expert witnesses, Dr. Ordean Anderson, a fire reconstruction specialist, testified that the fire started in, or next to, the plastic wastebasket located to the side of the desk in Gatzke's room. He also stated that the fire was caused by a burning cigarette or match. After the fire, the plastic wastebasket was a melted "blob." Dr. Anderson stated that X-ray examination of the remains of the basket disclosed the presence of cigarette filters and paper matches.

[The jury found Gatzke to be guilty of 60% of the negligence and the motel guilty of the remainder. The trial judge concluded, however, that Gatzke was not within the scope of his employment, and rendered judgment N.O.V. for Walgreen's]]

To support a finding that an employee's negligent act occurred within his scope of employment, it must be shown that his conduct was, to some degree, in furtherance of the interests of his employer. This principle is recognized by Restatement, Agency 2d, § 235, which states:

> An act of a servant is not within the scope of employment if it is done with no intention to perform it as a part of or incident to a service on account of which he is employed.

Other factors to be considered in the scope of employment determination are whether the conduct is of the kind that the employee is authorized to perform and whether the act occurs substantially within authorized time and space restrictions. No hard and fast rule can be applied to resolve the "scope of employment" inquiry. Rather, each case must be decided on its own individual facts.

The initial question raised by the instant factual situation is whether an employee's smoking of a cigarette can constitute conduct within his scope of employment. This issue has not been dealt with by this court. The courts which have considered the question have not agreed on its resolution. A number of courts which have dealt with the instant issue have ruled that the act of smoking, even when done simultaneously with work-related activity, is not within the employee's scope of employment because it is a matter personal to the employee which is not done in furtherance of the employer's interest.

Other courts which have considered the question have reasoned that the smoking of a cigarette, if done while engaged in the business of the employer, is within an employee's scope of employment because it is a minor deviation from the employee's work-related activities, and thus merely an act done incidental to general employment.

For example, in Wood v. Saunders, a gas station attendant negligently threw his lighted cigarette across an automobile's fuel tank opening while he was filling the vehicle with gasoline. The court, in finding this act to be within the employee's scope of employment, stated:

> In the case at bar, there was no abandonment by the employee of the master's purposes and business while the employee was smoking and carrying the lighted cigarette. There was merely a combining by the employee, with the carrying out of the master's

purposes, of an incidental and contemporaneous carrying out of the employee's private purposes. . . .

The question of whether smoking can be within an employee's scope of employment is a close one, but after careful consideration of the issue we are persuaded by the reasoning of the courts which hold that smoking can be an act within an employee's scope of employment. It seems only logical to conclude that an employee does not abandon his employment as a matter of law while temporarily acting for his personal comfort when such activities involve only slight deviations from work that are reasonable under the circumstances, such as eating, drinking, or smoking. . . .

We . . . hereby hold that an employer can be held vicariously liable for his employee's negligent smoking of a cigarette [if] he was otherwise acting in the scope of his employment at the time of the negligent act. . . . It appears that the district court felt that Gatzke was outside the scope of his employment while he was at the Bellows, and thus was similarly outside his scope of employment when he returned to his room to fill out his expense account. The record, however, contains a reasonable basis from which a jury could find that Gatzke was involved in serving his employer's interests at the time he was at the bar. Gatzke testified that, while at the Bellows, he discussed the operation of the newly-opened Walgreen's restaurant with Hubbard. Also, the bartender stated that on that night "[a] few times we [Gatzke and the bartender] would talk about his business and my business, how to make drinks, prices."

But more importantly, even assuming that Gatzke was outside the scope of his employment while he was at the bar, there is evidence from which a jury could reasonably find that Gatzke resumed his employment activities after he returned to his motel room and filled out his expense account. The expense account was, of course, completed so that Gatzke could be reimbursed by Walgreen's for his work-related expenses. In this sense, Gatzke is performing an act for his own personal benefit. However, the completion of the expense account also furthers the employer's business in that it provides detailed documentation of business expenses so that they are properly deductible for tax purposes. In this light, the filling out of the expense form can be viewed as serving a dual purpose; that of furthering Gatzke's personal interests and promoting his employer's business purposes. Accordingly, it is reasonable for the jury to find that the completion of the expense account is an act done in furtherance of the employer's business purposes.

Additionally, the record indicates that Gatzke was an executive type of employee who had no set working hours. He considered himself a 24-hour-a-day man; his room at the Edgewater Motel was his "office away from home." It was therefore also reasonable for the jury to determine that the filling out of his expense account was done within authorized time and space limits of his employment.

In light of the above, we hold that it was reasonable for the jury to find that Gatzke was acting within the scope of his employment when he completed his expense account. Accordingly, we set aside the trial court's grant of judgment for Walgreen's and reinstate the jury's determination that Gatzke was working within the scope of his employment at the time of his negligent act. . . .

NOTES

1. **Other issues?** Once the judges determined that the jury had a reasonable basis for concluding that Gatzke was acting within the *time and place* limits of his employment, was there any other issue left to be determined? Does the issue resemble the issue of scope of liability (proximate cause)?

2. **Temporary deviations.** The *Gatzke* court is not alone in finding that an employer may be held vicariously liable for an employee's actions in doing something "necessary to the comfort, convenience, health and welfare of the employee while at work, though strictly personal and not acts of service," as long as the employee is either "combining his own business with that of the employer, or attending to both at substantially the same time." *Farmers Ins. Group v. County of Santa Clara*, 906 P.2d 440 (Cal. 1995). *See also* RESTATEMENT (THIRD) OF AGENCY § 7.07, cmt. d (2006) ("Purely personal acts" such as "personal hygiene, smoking, and eating may be within the scope of employment because they are incidental to the employee's performance of assigned work"). Do you see adjudicative problems if that were not the rule?

3. **Frolic and detour.** A special factual category involves the employee who, during working hours, goes to a place not associated with employment for a purpose not associated with employment. Suppose an employee is instructed to deliver furniture to a town 30 miles north. After she has driven on the road 15 miles she turns to the east, intending to drive two miles in that direction to have a beer with a friend. She has a collision at a point one mile from the highway where she was supposed to be. Was she outside the scope of employment at the time of the accident? If this departure is seen as a "detour," as in cases of trivial departures from the job, the employer may be vicariously liable. If instead this is viewed as a "frolic" (as some courts say, "a personal mission"), then the employer is not vicariously liable. *See Nulle v. Krewer*, 872 N.E.2d 567 (Ill. App. Ct. 2007).

4. **Reentry into employment.** Suppose the employee sees her friend and starts back to the main highway and has a second collision at the same spot, but this time headed back to work. At what point has the employee reentered employment? "First, the employee must have formulated an intent to act in furtherance of the employer's business; second, the intent must be coupled with a reasonable connection in time and space with the work in which he should be engaged." *Prince* v. *Atchison, Topeka & Santa Fe Ry.*, 395 N.E.2d

592 (Ill. App. Ct. 1979). *See also* RESTATEMENT (THIRD) OF AGENCY § 7.07, cmt. e (2006) (a frolic ends "when an employee is once again performing assigned work and taking actions incidental to it," or when an employee "has taken action consistent with once again resuming work").

MONTAGUE V. AMN HEALTHCARE, INC.

223 Cal. App.4th 1515 (2014)

MCINTYRE, J. . . .

AMN Healthcare, Inc., doing business as Nursefinders (Nursefinders) is a staffing company that provides prescreened nurses and medical personnel to hospitals and other facilities. Nursefinders hired Theresa Drummond as a medical assistant. It later assigned Drummond to work at a Kaiser facility as a medical assistant. Plaintiff Sara Montague was also a medical assistant at Kaiser. At some point, Drummond and Montague had a disagreement at work regarding how rooms were to be stocked. At the end of the discussion Montague walked away. Montague did not consider the argument serious enough to report to a supervisor or anyone else. They also had a discussion regarding misplaced lab slips where Drummond raised her voice. A few weeks after that discussion, Montague left her water bottle at work. Montague later drank from her water bottle. Her tongue and throat started to burn and she vomited. Drummond admitted that she poured carbolic acid found in a Kaiser examination room into Montague's water bottle.

[Montague and her husband sued Drummond and Nursefinders, the latter on a vicarious liability theory. The trial court granted Nursefinders' motion for summary judgment, holding as a matter of law that Drummond's act of poisoning Montague was outside the scope of Drummond's employment.]

. . . For the employer to be liable for an intentional tort the employee's act must have a "causal nexus to the employee's work." Courts have used various terms to describe this causal nexus: the incident leading to the injury must be an "outgrowth" of the employment; the risk of tortious injury must be "inherent in the working environment"; the risk must be "typical" or "broadly incidental" to the employer's business; the tort was "a generally foreseeable consequence" of the employer's business.

One way to determine whether a risk is inherent in, or created by, an enterprise is to ask whether the actual occurrence was a generally foreseeable consequence of the activity. Foreseeability in the context of determining scope of employment merely means that in the context of the particular enterprise an employee's conduct is not so unusual or startling that it would seem unfair to include the loss resulting from it among other costs of the employer's business.

These various terms have been condensed into a two-prong disjunctive test. The conduct of an employee falls within the scope of his or her employment if the conduct either (1) is required by or incidental to the employee's duties, or (2) it is reasonably foreseeable in light of the employer's business . . .

employment scope test

We first consider whether Montague presented evidence showing that Drummond's acts were required by or incidental to her employment with Nursefinders. In evaluating this factor, occupational duties are broadly defined. The fact that an employee is not engaged in the ultimate object of his employment at the time of his wrongful act does not preclude attribution of liability to an employer. However, that is not to say, that employers are strictly liable for all actions of their employees during working hours. If an employee substantially deviates from his duties for personal purposes, the employer is not vicariously liable for the employee's actions.

Montague [presented] no evidence regarding the scope of Drummond's employment with either Nursefinders or Kaiser. While Drummond testified she generally knew that carbolic acid was used for patients with foot issues, it is unknown what specific job duties Drummond had at Kaiser and whether her duties involved the use of carbolic acid. It is also unknown whether Drummond committed the poisoning during working hours or what motivated Drummond to poison Montague.

We next consider whether Montague presented evidence showing Nursefinders could have reasonably foreseen that Drummond would poison a coworker at Kaiser. . . . An injury arising out of a work-related dispute has such a causal nexus, while an injury inflicted out of the employee's personal malice, not engendered by the employment, does not. Montague asserts summary judgment is not appropriate because the evidence shows the poisoning arose out of a work-related dispute. The evidence shows that a few weeks or months before the incident, Drummond and Montague had a disagreement at work regarding how rooms were to be stocked, but Montague did not consider the dispute to be serious. They also had a discussion regarding misplaced lab slips where Drummond raised her voice. A few weeks after that discussion, Drummond poisoned Montague's water bottle. Although Montague asserts the poisoning took place a day or two after she argued with Drummond about the misplaced paperwork, the evidence she cited does not support this assertion. Montague presented no evidence that these past work-related disputes, rather than Drummond's personal animosity toward Montague unrelated to Drummond's work for Kaiser, motivated her actions (Cf. *Carr v. Wm. C. Crowell Co.* (1946) 28 Cal.2d 652, 657, 171 P.2d 5 [the fact employee and coworker victim had never conversed before the dispute indicated dispute arose out of employment]; *Yamaguchi v. Harnsmut* (2003) 106 Cal.App.4th 472, 476, 486, 130 Cal.Rptr.2d 706 [trial court committed reversible error in ruling, as a matter of law, that restaurant worker's act of throwing hot oil at police officer there to break-up work-related dispute was within the scope of his employment for purposes of respondeat superior liability against restaurant]; *Rodgers v. Kemper Constr. Co.* (1975) 50 Cal.App.3d 608, 615, 621, 124 Cal.Rptr. 143 [when dispute arose, victims were complete strangers to assailants who worked at same job site, thus dispute was within the scope of employment].)

. . . Montague's attempt to establish respondeat superior liability for Nursefinders simply because she and Drummond worked together at Kaiser is misguided. The nexus required for respondeat superior liability—that the tort be engendered by or arise from the work—is to be distinguished from 'but for' causation. That the employment brought tortfeasor and victim together in time and place is not enough. The facts, construed most favorably for Montague, do not support liability against Nursefinders because Drummond's poisoning of Montague was highly unusual and startling.

Finally, the public policy factors underlying the doctrine of respondeat superior do not support the imposition of vicarious liability to Nursefinders under these facts. These public policy factors are: "(1) to prevent recurrence of the tortious conduct; (2) to give greater assurance of compensation for the victim; and (3) to ensure that the victim's losses will be equitably borne by those who benefit from the enterprise that gave rise to the injury." (*Farmers Ins. Group v. County of Santa Clara* (1995) 907 P.2d 440 (Cal. 1995).) Here, the potential for civil and criminal liability provides a deterrent to the type of aberrant conduct that Drummond committed. Additionally, while invoking vicarious liability under these facts would provide greater assurance of compensation to victims, Nursefinders derived no benefit from Drummond's conduct and it would be inequitable to shift the loss to Nursefinders. . . .

The judgment is affirmed . . .

NOTES

1. **Intentional torts of employees.** Intentional torts by employees do not usually give rise to vicarious liability of employers. *See* 2 DOBBS, HAYDEN & BUBLICK, THE LAW OF TORTS § 429 (2d ed. 2011). In a court that regards an employee's motive or purpose to serve the employer's interests as a key or determinative test, as both the Restatement Second and Third of Agency say, this is understandable. *See, e.g., Barnett v. Clark*, 889 N.E.2d 281 (Ind. 2008) (as a matter of law, town employee's false imprisonment and sexual assault of an applicant for public assistance was not within scope of his employment; the act did not "serve any purpose of the employer").

Vicarious liability is possible, however, even where a motive to serve the employer's interests is a highly relevant factor. *See, e.g., Patterson v. Blair*, 172

S.W.3d 361 (Ky. 2005) (affirming jury verdict for plaintiff against a car dealership, held vicariously liable for an employee's act of shooting a pistol at a car's tires in an attempt to repossess it while the plaintiff, a customer, was driving it away; the employee was "acting to further the business interests" of the dealership); *Kirlin v. Halverson*, 758 N.W.2d 436 (S.D. 2008) (issue of fact as to whether employee was motivated by a desire to further the employer's interest when he assaulted a competitor's employee). What if a person employed as a bouncer in a bar throws an unruly customer out of the door, breaking the customer's arm? Should vicarious liability attach?

2. **Broader tests for vicarious liability.** As we have already seen, many courts use broader (and sometimes looser) tests than one that turns centrally on the employee's motive or purpose. Often the main focus is on the reasonable foreseeability of the employee's act. *See Anderson v. Mandalay Corp.*, 358 P.3d 242 (Nev. 2015) (by statute, "reasonably foreseeable under the facts and circumstances considering the nature and scope of his or her employment"); *Farhrendorff v. North Homes, Inc.*, 597 N.W.2d 905 (Minn. 1999) (counselor in group home made sexual advances to a resident; "inappropriate sexual contact or abuse of power in these situations, although infrequent, is a *well known hazard*" in this kind of enterprise and thus may give rise to vicarious liability). If foreseeability is the ultimate issue for some courts, perhaps the strings of phrases we see in cases like *Montague* are not separate "tests" at all, but rather attempts to articulate relevant factors in the particular case.

3. **Motives connected to employment.** As we saw in *Montague*, it can be difficult to ascertain whether an employee's intentionally tortious acts were sufficiently connected to the employment so as to hold the employer vicariously liable. Not surprisingly, similar cases do not always produce similar outcomes. Compare two cases. In *Davis v. Devereux Foundation*, 37 A.3d 469 (N.J. 2012), the court affirmed a summary judgment for the employer, where the employee intentionally threw a cup of boiling water on a resident of a facility for the developmentally disabled, apparently in retaliation for the resident's aggressiveness towards the employee the previous day. The court regarded the motivation for this act as entirely personal. But in *Rodebush v. Oklahoma Nursing Homes, Ltd.*, 867 P.2d 1241 (Okla. 1993), a nurse's aide in a long-term care facility slapped an elderly Alzheimer's patient. Evidence showed the aide was intoxicated before 7:30 a.m. But the trial judge let the jury decide the case. Affirming the jury verdict for the plaintiff, the court said the jury could find that "the act [was] one which is fairly and naturally incident to the business, and [was] done while the servant was engaged upon the master's business and [arose] from some impulse of emotion which naturally grew out of or was incident to the attempt to perform the master's business."

In one prominent case, *Lisa M. v. Henry Mayo Newhall Memorial Hosp.*, 907 P.2d 358 (Cal. 1995), an ultrasound technician employed by the defendant hospital committed a sexual battery on an unsuspecting 19-year-old pregnant patient. Rejecting vicarious liability, the court held that the act lacked a sufficient "causal nexus" to the employee's job. For the act to be within the scope of employment, the employment "must be such as predictably to create the risk employees will commit intentional torts of the type for which liability is sought.... The flaw in plaintiff's case for Hospital's respondeat superior liability is not so much that [the employee's] actions were personally motivated, but that those personal motivations were not generated by or an outgrowth of workplace responsibilities, conditions or events."

4. **Caregivers.** Caregivers—those who have undertaken, at least implicitly, to care for the plaintiff who is relatively helpless—may be subject to some special rules of liability. Should special obligations of caregivers also affect vicarious liability? Illinois provides by statute that owners and licensees of nursing homes "are liable to a resident for any intentional or negligent act or omission of their agents or employees which injures the resident." 210 ILL. COMP. STAT. 45/3–601. Could courts develop special rules for this kind of setting as well? *See, e.g., Spurlock v. Townes*, 368 P.3d 1213 (N.M. 2016) (adopting the "aided-in-agency theory," under which "an employer may be held liable for the intentional torts of an employee acting outside the scope of his or her employment if the employee ... has by reason of his employment substantial power or authority to control important elements of a vulnerable tort victim's life or livelihood").

5. **Primary liability of employer as an alternative theory.** Where vicarious liability seems doubtful, especially where it appears that the employee's tort may be outside the scope of employment, plaintiffs often allege that the employer is liable for its own negligence in hiring, supervising or retaining the employee. *See Doe v. Guthrie Clinic, Ltd.*, 5 N.E.2d 578 (N.Y. 2014); *Doe v. Saint Francis Hosp. & Medical Center*, 72 A.3d 929 (Conn. 2013); *see generally* Chapter 18 § 2 (Note: A Duty to Control Employees?). This is not vicarious liability at all, but rather liability based on the employer's own fault. *See, e.g., Dragomir v. Spring Harbor Hosp.*, 970 A.2d 310 (Me. 2009) (no vicarious liability for employee's sexual misbehavior, but plaintiff stated a claim for negligent supervision); *James v. Kelly Trucking Co.*, 661 S.E.2d 329 (S.C. 2008). The two claims are often pursued in the same action.

§ 2. INDEPENDENT CONTRACTORS

MAVRIKIDIS V. PETULLO
707 A.2d 977 (N.J. 1998)

GARIBALDI, J. . . .

This case arose from an automobile accident that resulted in severe injury to plaintiff Alice Mavrikidis, including second-and third-degree burns over twenty-one percent of her body. On September 11, 1990, the intersection collision occurred after defendant Gerald Petullo, operating a dump truck registered to Petullo Brothers, Inc. (Petullo Brothers), drove through a red light, struck plaintiff's car, hit a telephone pole, and then overturned, spilling the truck's contents onto Mavrikidis's car. At the time of the accident, Gerald was transporting 10.99 tons of hot asphalt, which had been loaded onto the truck by Newark Asphalt Corporation (Newark Asphalt), to his job site at Clar Pine Servicenter (Clar Pine), a retail gasoline and automotive repair shop in Montclair.

[Clar Pine's owner, Karl Pascarello, was renovating the gas station.] Because Pascarello had no experience in the construction or paving business, he hired Gerald's father, Angelo Petullo, and Petullo Brothers to complete the asphalt and concrete work at the Clar Pine job site.] The Petullos supplied the labor, equipment, concrete, and most of the asphalt needed for the job. . . . Other than general supervision and periodic consultation, Pascarello's limited participation in the asphalt work consisted of payment for three loads of asphalt, including the one involved in this accident, as well as his direction to lay the asphalt in front of the service station's bay doors first to enable him to continue his automotive repairs while the gas station was out of service. . . .

On the morning of the accident, Gerald ordered twenty tons of asphalt from Newark Asphalt's plant. The employees of Newark Asphalt loaded 10.99 tons of asphalt, at a temperature between 300 and 310 degrees Fahrenheit, onto Gerald's truck and 9 tons onto a second truck. . . . [At trial, an expert testified that the trucks were overloaded and that had Gerald's truck not been overloaded, he would have had better control over the truck.]

[Mavrikidis sued Gerald, Angelo, Petullo Brothers, Newark Asphalt and Clar Pine, among others. In special interrogatories, the jury found that Gerald operated his truck negligently and that his negligence was a proximate cause of the accident; and that Gerald was acting as an employee of Angelo at the time of the accident. The jurors further found that Clar Pine retained control of the "manner and means" of performing the "inherently dangerous" activity of transporting and installing asphalt. The jury also found that Newark Asphalt was negligent in overloading Gerald's truck. The jury awarded the plaintiff $750,000, and fixed percentages of negligence on all liable defendants.] Based on the finding that Clar Pine was vicariously liable for its independent contractor, Angelo, the court entered a judgment against Clar Pine for 89% of the total damages awarded, including the 17% attributed directly to Clar Pine by the jury, the 24% attributed to Angelo, and the 48% attributed to Gerald. The court also entered judgment against Newark Asphalt for 11% of the total damages awarded. Clar Pine and Newark Asphalt appealed. [The Appellate Division reversed the judgment against Clar Pine, holding that there was insufficient evidence to support a finding of vicarious liability.]

The first question is whether Clar Pine is vicariously liable for plaintiff's injuries. As we explained in *Majestic Realty Associates, Inc. v. Toti Contracting Co.*, 153 A.2d 321 (N.J. 1959), the resolution of this issue must be approached with an awareness of the long settled doctrine that ordinarily where a person engages a contractor, who conducts an independent business by means of his own employees, to do work not in itself a nuisance (as our cases put it), he is not liable for the negligent acts of the contractor in the performance of the contract.

The initial inquiry in our analysis is to examine the status of the Petullos in relation to Clar Pine. Despite plaintiff's alternate theories to the contrary, the Petullos were independent contractors rather than servants of Clar Pine. [As we said in *Baldasarre*, 625 A.2d 458 (N.J. 1993),]

[Employee vs. Independent Contractor]

The important difference between an employee and an independent contractor is that one who hires an independent contractor "has no right of control over the manner in which the work is to be done, it is to be regarded as the contractor's own enterprise, and he, rather than the employer is the proper party to be charged with the responsibility for preventing the risk, and administering and distributing it."

In contrast, a servant is traditionally one who is "employed to perform services in the affairs of another, whose physical conduct in the performance of the service is controlled, or is subject to a right of control, by the other." W. Page Keeton, *Prosser & Keeton on Torts,* § 70 at 501.

In determining whether a contractee maintains the right of control, several factors are to be considered. The *Restatement (Second) of Agency* sets forth these factors, including:

[Determinative factors of whether a contractee maintains right of control]

(a) the extent of control which, by the agreement, the master may exercise over the details of the work; (b) whether or not the one employed is engaged in a distinct occupation or business; * * * (d) the skill required in the particular occupation; (e) whether the employer or the workman supplies the instrumentalities, tools, and the place of work for the person doing the work; (f) the length of time for which the person is employed; (g) the method of payment, whether by the time or by the job; (h) whether or not the work is a part of the regular business of the employer; [and] (i) whether or not the parties believe they are creating the relation of master and servant. . . . *→ less important, these classification will be made on an objective cases*

*[right to control + knowledge + Ex.
Door Dash
Driver who delivers food rather than restaurant makes it]*

Applying those Restatement factors, it is evident that neither Angelo nor Gerald was a servant of Clar Pine. The masonry work required a skilled individual. Although Pascarello paid for three loads of asphalt, the Petullos provided their own tools and the remainder of the needed materials, other than bolts and plywood supplied by Pascarello to install the canopies. Their work did not involve the regular business of Clar Pine. In addition, the period of employment spanned only the time it took to lay the asphalt and concrete. Following the accident, the Petullos continued the job for which they were hired, which was approved by the Building Inspector of Montclair. In exchange for their services, the Petullos were not paid by the hour or month. . . .

Based on that threshold determination, we now must determine whether this case falls within any exceptions to the general rule of nonliability of principals/contractees for the negligence of their independent contractors. There are three such exceptions, as delineated by the *Majestic* Court: "(a) where the landowner [or principal] retains control of the manner and means of the doing of the work which is the subject of the contract; (b) where he engages an incompetent contractor; or (c) where . . . the activity contracted for [is inherently dangerous]."

3 exceptions

. . . Under the first *Majestic* exception, the reservation of control "of the manner and means" of the contracted work by the principal permits the imposition of vicarious liability. "In such a case the employer is responsible for the negligence of the independent contractor even though the particular control exercised and its manner of exercise had no causal relationship with the hazard that led to the injury, just as in the case of a simple employer-employee situation." Under that test, the reservation of control over the equipment to be used, the manner or method of doing the work, or direction of the employees of the independent contractor may permit vicarious liability.

However, supervisory acts performed by the contractee will not give rise to vicarious liability under that exception. As indicated by the language of the exception, application of principles of *respondeat superior* are not warranted where the contractee's "supervisory interest relates [only] to the result to be accomplished, not to the means of accomplishing it."

Pascarello's actions did not exceed the scope of general supervisory powers so as to subject Clar Pine to vicarious liability for Gerald's negligence. Providing blueprints, paying for some of the asphalt, and directing that a portion of the concrete be completed first are clearly within the scope of a contractee's broad supervisory powers. . . . Pascarello's actions related to the overall renovations of the station and not to the specific work for which the Petullos were engaged. The Petullos were hired to do the paving for the station and were not involved in the renovation other than the paving. . . . When the evidence is viewed in the light most favorable to plaintiffs, Pascarello's actions arose from a general supervisory power over the result to be accomplished rather than the means of that accomplishment.

[Evidence did not support the application of either of the final two *Majestic* exceptions. There was no evidence that the Petrullos were unqualified to perform the masonry work for which they were hired. Further, the "inherently dangerous" exception has no application where the injury was caused merely by negligent driving, which is simply an ordinary risk associated with motor vehicles and the transport of materials.]

[Judgment of the Appellate Division affirmed; remanded for a determination of the liability percentages of the Petullos and Newark Asphalt.]

[Dissenting opinion omitted.]

NOTES

1.   **Vicarious liability for the torts of an independent contractor.** The *Mavrikidis* court states the general rule: subject to limited exceptions, a person who hires an independent contractor to perform work is not vicariously liable for the torts committed by that independent contractor. *See* RESTATEMENT (THIRD) OF TORTS: LIABILITY FOR PHYSICAL AND EMOTIONAL HARM § 57 (2012). The setting in *Mavrikidis* is the most common one, where one person (or business) hires another—the independent contractor—to do some particular work. Do the policy rationales for vicarious liability not apply with the same force when an injury is caused by the negligence of an independent contractor, as opposed to a servant?

2.   **Tests for status as independent contractor.** In determining whether an employee is a servant or an independent contractor, courts have often applied the multi-part test from the Restatement (Second) of Agency, as the *Mavrikidis* court did. But in the eyes of many courts, one factor—the right to control the details of the work—is the most important. As the West Virginia court said in *France v. Southern Equip. Co.*, 689 S.E.2d 1 (W.Va. 2010), four general factors bear on whether a master-servant relationship exists for purposes of respondeat superior: (1) selection and engagement of the servant; (2) payment of compensation; (3) power of dismissal; and (4) the power of control, and "[t]he first three factors are not essential to the existence of the relationship; the fourth, the power of control, is determinative." *See also* RESTATEMENT (THIRD) OF AGENCY § 7.07(3)(a) (2006) ("an employee is an agent whose principal controls or has the right to control the manner and means of the agent's performance of work").

To many courts, then, if the employer does have a right of control over the day-to-day operations of the worker, the worker is probably a servant; if not, the worker is probably an independent contractor. *See, e.g., Walderbach v. Archdiocese of Dubuque, Inc.*, 730 N.W.2d 198 (Iowa 2007). Yet regardless of its importance, control is only one factor of many. If the person being employed runs his own business and works for others as well as for the contractee, he is not likely to be a servant. If he provides his own tools or uses special skills, that is also likely to indicate that he is an independent contractor.

Suppose you have hired a professional painter to paint your house. You are paying him a set price for the job. He is supplying his own paint, brushes and other equipment (although you are paying for them as part of the price of the job). He decides when to come and go from the job. After the house is painted he will paint somewhere else. Is he your servant, so that any torts he commits will leave you vicariously liable?

3. **Structuring relationships by contract.** Employers often attempt to structure relationships with employees so that employees will be considered independent contractors. A newspaper may contract with scores or hundreds of home delivery drivers and describe the drivers in the contract as independent contractors. If the newspaper has the right to terminate their services for no reason at all, should the contractual label "independent contractor" determine a driver's status? *See Zirkle v. Winkler*, 585 S.E.2d 19 (W.Va. 2003); *see also Hill v. City of Horn Lake*, 160 So.3d 671 (Miss. 2015) (employer may not escape liability to third persons simply by drafting a contract that labels an employee an independent contractor).

4. **Retained control.** The *Mavrikidis* court applies an important rule (which it sees as an "exception" to the usual rule for independent contractors): employees who are ordinarily independent contractors—general building contractors and their subcontractors, for example—may become "servants" if sufficient control is retained by the employer. *See, e.g., Merit Energy Co. v. Horr*, 366 P.3d 489 (Wyo. 2016); *Gaytan v. Wal-Mart*, 853 N.W.2d 181 (Neb. 2014). What facts did the New Jersey court look at in determining that there was insufficient evidence of retained control to send the issue to the jury? Retained control may also show that the employer himself was negligent in not exercising the control he has to obtain appropriate safety. *See* RESTATEMENT (THIRD) OF TORTS: LIABILITY FOR PHYSICAL AND EMOTIONAL HARM § 56(b) (2012).

5. **The incompetent independent contractor.** *Mavrikidis* noted a second exception to the no-vicarious-liability rule: knowingly hiring an incompetent independent contractor. It has long been true in virtually all states that a defendant cannot insulate itself from liability by selecting or retaining an incompetent independent contractor. *See* RESTATEMENT (THIRD) OF AGENCY § 7.05(1) (2006). The incompetence can take many forms—for example, the contractor does not know how to do the job, or is known to be an alcohol abuser or someone with anger management problems.

Most courts appear to characterize this not as a vicarious liability theory at all, but rather a claim based on the employer's own negligence. *See, e.g., Basic Energy Services, L.P. v. Petroleum Resource Mgmt. Corp.*, 343 P.3d 783 (Wyo. 2015 (reviewing cases from many states, concluding that the claim for negligently hiring an incompetent independent contractor "has gained broad acceptance").

6. **The non-delegable duty rule: inherently dangerous activities and "peculiar risk."** The third exception to the general no-vicarious-liability rule for the torts of independent contractors mentioned in *Mavrikidis* is that principal cannot discharge a non-delegable duty to exercise reasonable care by hiring an independent contractor to undertake the activity. When courts say a duty is non-delegable, they mean only that the person who hires an

independent contractor does not escape liability under the independent contractor rules. The independent contractor himself is also liable for his own negligence. The Restatement Second of Torts applies the non-delegable duty rule to inherently dangerous activities in its § 427 and to cases of "peculiar risk" in § 416.

The two classes of cases (inherently dangerous and peculiar risk) are similar. Peculiar risk must be different in some way from ordinary risks. For example, transporting asphalt in *Mavrikidis* was held to be an ordinary, not a peculiar, risk. *See also King v. Lens Creek Ltd. Partnership*, 483 S.E.2d 265 (W.Va. 1996) (operation of empty logging trucks is not inherently dangerous). The Restatement Third of Torts reiterates that an actor who hires an independent contractor for an activity the actor knows or should know poses a peculiar risk may be vicariously liable where the contractor's negligence causes harm. RESTATEMENT (THIRD) OF TORTS: LIABILITY FOR PHYSICAL AND EMOTIONAL HARM § 59 (2012). The same Restatement would impose vicarious liability on an actor who hires an independent contractor to construct or maintain instrumentalities used in highly dangerous activities and the contractor's negligence in connection with those instrumentalities causes harm. *Id.* § 60. The case law is not entirely consistent, although courts readily find a duty non-delegable when poisons are sprayed and when explosives and strong acids are used—in other words, in cases on instrumentalities dangerous by nature. *See, e.g., Brandenburg v. Briarwood Forestry Services, LLC*, 847 N.W.2d 395 (Wis. 2014) (landowner vicariously liable for contractor's negligence in spraying herbicide).

§ 3. OTHER FORMS OF VICARIOUS RESPONSIBILITY

Respondeat superior liability of an employer is not the only form of vicarious liability. Other forms of vicarious liability that frequently occur in tort cases include the liability of a defendant for (1) acts of his business partner; (2) acts of a person engaged in a joint enterprise with the defendant, a kind of "temporary partnership" in which each has equal right of control; and (3) acts of one with whom the defendant acts "in concert" or to whose acts the defendant aids or abets.

REFERENCES: DOBBS, HAYDEN & BUBLICK, HORNBOOK ON TORTS §§ 31.1–31.8 (2d ed. 2016); 2 DOBBS, HAYDEN & BUBLICK, THE LAW OF TORTS §§ 425–436 (2d ed. 2011).

CHAPTER 23

COMMON LAW STRICT LIABILITY

*Strict Liability –
Liability w/o
proof of fault
⟶ required*

■ ■ ■

§ 1. HISTORICAL STRICT LIABILITY FOR TRESPASSORY TORTS AND THE ADVENT OF FAULT THEORY

The Trespass form of action. In medieval England, law suits in the King's courts were initiated by obtaining a "writ," a highly formal document giving jurisdiction to the King's court. The earliest, apart from cases involving rights in property and the like, was the writ called *Trespass.* This writ or form of action could be obtained whenever the plaintiff claimed an injury that was both (a) direct and (b) forcible. This form of action became the basis for torts we know today as battery, assault, false imprisonment, trespass to land and trespass to chattels. The judges in such cases asked only if a direct and forcible injury was inflicted. They did not ask whether the defendant acted with any particular intent or with negligence. Thus the *Trespass* writ imposed strict liability—liability without proof of fault.

The Case form of action. Eventually, plaintiffs were able to obtain a second kind of writ when the injury was indirect. This second writ (or form of action) was called *Trespass on the Case,* or more commonly, simply *Case.* When the plaintiff suffered indirect injury, *Case* and only *Case* would be the appropriate writ. When the writ of *Case* was used, one applicable rule was that the plaintiff was required to prove some kind of negligence or, later, "unlawful" act. So negligence came into the law of tort, but only when the writ of *Case* was used and injury was indirect.

Weaver v. Ward. In a famous case decided in 1616, the plaintiff and defendant were in bands of men practicing military exercises. The plaintiff was wounded when the defendant discharged his musket. The defendant argued that he did not intentionally cause the musket ball to strike the plaintiff. But the court held that this was no defense. The claim was based on the writ of *Trespass* (because injury was direct) and in *Trespass* the law awards damages for hurt or loss, that is, without requiring intent or negligence. The court did, however, recognize that if the plaintiff had run in front of the defendant's weapon as he fired, the defendant might not be liable. *Weaver v. Ward,* 80 Eng. Rep. 284 (K.B. 1616).

553

The shift to fault-based liability: Brown v. Kendall. In the next 200 years, for various reasons, plaintiffs brought more suits in *Case* for negligence. In 1850, in a blockbuster case, the Massachusetts high court finally held that negligence was required even in cases that fit the old *Trespass* form of action. In that case, *Brown v. Kendall,* 60 Mass. 292 (1850), a man was using a stick to separate two fighting dogs. Raising it over his head, he struck the plaintiff, who was behind him. This fit the *Trespass* pattern of direct injury. But the court held that proof of negligence would be *required* to establish liability for unintended harms and that the plaintiff had the burden of proving it. It defined negligence in terms we understand today: the care that would be used by persons of ordinary prudence in the circumstances. The "correct rule," said the court, is "that the plaintiff must come prepared with evidence to show either that the intention was unlawful, or that the defendant was in fault; for if the injury was unavoidable, and the conduct of the defendant was free from blame, he will not be liable." Rejecting the application of strict liability, the court concluded, "unless it also appears to the satisfaction of the jury, that the defendant is chargeable with some fault, negligence, carelessness, or want [of] prudence, the plaintiff fails to sustain the burden of proof, and is not entitled to recover."

Pockets of strict liability. After *Brown v. Kendall,* negligence, not strict liability, became the normal basis for liability for unintended harms. Despite this fundamental change in tort law to a fault-based system, particular pockets of strict liability survived *Brown v. Kendall,* and some other kinds of strict liability advanced. We explore some of the major areas in the remainder of this chapter. In the next, we will see the rise and partial fall of strict liability as a dominant theory in a purely modern area of law, products liability.

REFERENCE: 1 DOBBS, HAYDEN & BUBLICK, THE LAW OF TORTS § 17 (2d ed. 2011).

§ 2. STRICT LIABILITY TODAY

Liability without proof of fault remains the exception, not the rule. Some of the remaining areas of strict liability today predate *Brown v. Kendall's* revolutionary fault-based conception of tort law; others have developed more recently. In each area, the history of how and why they developed, while not always crystal clear, is important to understanding their scope today.

A. INJURIES CAUSED BY ANIMALS

1. Trespassing Animals

The Restatement Third provides that an[owner of livestock or other animals (other than dogs and cats) that intrude on another person's land, "is subject to strict liability for physical harm caused by the intrusion.] RESTATEMENT (THIRD) OF TORTS: LIABILITY FOR PHYSICAL AND EMOTIONAL HARM § 21 (2010). How did this become the rule?

Under the writ of *Trespass*, the plaintiff could redress all direct harms, even if the defendant was not at fault; and under the writ of *Case*, he would redress indirect harms, provided the defendant was at fault. But there was a period in which the only writ, or the dominant one, was *Trespass*. As an English legal historian has pointed out, a lawyer writing a book about torts in the late 14th century would have called the book *"Trespass,"* because at the time tort law was embodied in *Trespass*; *Case* developed later. S. MILSOM, HISTORICAL FOUNDATIONS OF THE COMMON LAW 261 (1969). What was done with claims for indirect injury before the writ of *Case* was developed?

As it happened, some of them were treated as *Trespass* cases and strict liability seems to have been imposed. If the defendant owned cattle and drove them onto the plaintiff's land, the writ of *Trespass* would be proper, or at least it could be argued. Such an entry would be reasonably "direct," and it might also meet the later test of "unlawfulness." However, suppose that the defendant's cattle merely strayed, or broke loose from an enclosure, and that they then entered the plaintiff's land and did harm such as crop damage. In such an instance, there seems to be no "direct" connection between the defendant's conduct and the harm—he did not "act"—and consequently the writ of *Trespass* would be inappropriate. But *Case* had not been developed, so the choice was to dismiss the claim or to entertain it under the writ of *Trespass*. The courts seem to have chosen the latter course, and since *Trespass* carried with it the rule of strict liability, cattle trespass became a strict liability tort. This rule, having gained its foothold in *Trespass*, remained the same even after *Case* was developed. As another English historian has said, if the claims had arisen later in time, *Case* would have been available and would have been used, with the result, presumably, that liability would have been based on negligence. G. WILLIAMS, LIABILITY FOR ANIMALS 133 (1939).

The cattle cases were apparently thought of as a special category of liability. Not only did the rule of strict liability for cattle trespass survive the advent of *Case*, to some degree it also survived the shift toward fault-based liability ushered in by *Brown v. Kendall*. That is, the "universal" fault formula in *Brown v. Kendall* found an exception in the trespassing cattle cases.

The rule for cattle included the barnyard beasts in general—cows, horses, sheep and others. It did not include pets, such as dogs, even though dogs might have important functions on a farm. There was also a special exception even as to cattle: if they strayed from a highway on which they were being driven, there was no strict liability for their trespass.

Under some cases and the earlier Restatement, strict liability for these barnyard animals would not apply to personal injury, only to "trespass" damage. *Cf. Hastings v. Sauve*, 989 N.E.2d 940 (N.Y. 2013) (negligence liability only for defendant whose cow strayed from property onto highway, where plaintiff collided with it and was injured). But the Restatement Third extends strict liability to any injury resulting from animal intrusion upon land that is a characteristic of such intrusion, which may include personal injuries. Thus being hurt trying to chase a bull off your property might give you a strict liability claim, but tripping over a goat sleeping on your land at night would not. *See* RESTATEMENT (THIRD) OF TORTS: LIABILITY FOR PHYSICAL AND EMOTIONAL HARM § 21 cmt. g (2010). Many states—especially those where large open grazing is feasible and desirable—have adopted different rules, often by statute; many of these statutes provide for a local option or a fencing district, giving counties or other districts the power to develop their own rules.

2. Abnormally Dangerous Animals

The Restatement Third provides for a form of strict but limited liability for the owner or possessor of an animal that has "dangerous tendencies abnormal for the animal's category." RESTATEMENT (THIRD) OF TORTS: LIABILITY FOR PHYSICAL AND EMOTIONAL HARM § 23 (2010). Strict liability is imposed if, but only if, the owner knows or has reason to know of the animal's abnormally dangerous tendencies (to attack without warning, for example), and liability attaches only "if the harm ensues from that dangerous tendency." *Id.* The Restatement recognizes that apart from wild animals, most animals are normally safe, but that particular animals might in fact present both "significant and abnormal dangers" to others. *Id.*, cmt. b. The rationale for strict liability is that it "gives the owner an incentive to consider whether the animal should be retained." Id. This strict-liability rule seems to apply to any kind of animal—that is, there is no strict liability where the owner does not know of the *particular* animal's abnormally dangerous propensities. *See, e.g., Bard v. Jahnke*, 848 N.E.2d 463 (N.Y. 2006) (bull); *Olier v. Bailey*, 164 So.3d 982 (Miss. 2015) (goose); *Knapton v. Monk*, 347 P.3d 1257 (Mont. 2015) (purebred pit bull).

Some states have rejected strict liability for harms caused by domestic animals, requiring proof of the owner's or keeper's negligent conduct. *See Vendrella v. Astriab Family Ltd. Parnership*, 87 A.3d 546 (Conn. 2014) (factual issue found as to whether bite injury was reasonably foreseeable to defendant who kept horse on farm; owner owes duty of reasonable care to prevent foreseeable injuries where animal belongs to a class that is naturally inclined to cause such injuries, without regard to whether the particular animal had previously caused an injury). Does the "strict liability" requirement that the owner knew or should have known of an animal's propensity to harm others actually create a negligence standard? *See Martin v. Christman*, 99 A.3d 1008 (Vt. 2014) (rejecting strict liability for dog bites, suggesting that an owner may be negligent where he knows of the dog's vicious tendencies and does not take reasonable steps to protect others).

Statutes and ordinances often impose additional liabilities on dog owners, through leash laws or otherwise. *See, e.g., Tracey v. Solesky*, 50 A.3d 1075 (Md. 2012) (applying statute to hold landlord strictly liable for harboring a tenant's pit bull that attacked the plaintiff); *Pawlowski v. American Family Mut. Ins. Co.*, 777 N.W.2d 67 (Wis. 2009) (applying statute to impose strict liability on homeowner who "harbored" a dog that did not belong to her).

3. Wild Animals

With respect to animals said to be "wild by nature," strict liability is usually imposed for injuries connected with the wild characteristics of the animal, so that the person in charge will be held liable in spite of all possible care. Animals in this "wild" category" include lions and tigers and bears that people have seen fit to import and exhibit. RESTATEMENT (THIRD) OF TORTS: LIABILITY FOR PHYSICAL AND EMOTIONAL HARM § 22 (2010).

B. IMPOUNDMENTS, NUISANCES AND BEYOND

RYLANDS V. FLETCHER
Exchequer: 3 Hurl & C. 774 (1865)
Exchequer Chamber: L.R. 1 Exch. 265 (1866)
House of Lords: L.R. 3 H.L. 330 (1868)

[Plaintiff operated a mine in the county of Lancaster. Defendants operated a mill in the vicinity, and had contractors build a reservoir or pond to supply water. The contractors did build such a pond, though in fact it was located immediately over some vertical shafts once used in mining. The shafts had been filled rather inadequately, but gave the appearance of solid earth. When the pond was filled with water, its weight caused the material in the shafts to give way, and the water flooded down the vertical shafts. From there it flowed through horizontal mine shafts of an intervening mine into the plaintiff's mine. This is an action by the plaintiff for damages caused by this flooding. A procedure was used in which an arbitrator stated a special case or found facts. The case was then considered in the Court of Exchequer, followed by review in the Exchequer Chamber and finally in the House of Lords. The style of the case is that used in the House of Lords.]

[IN THE COURT OF EXCHEQUER]

BRAMWELL, B. . . .

The plaintiff's right then has been infringed; the defendants in causing water to flow to the plaintiff have done that which they had no right to do; what difference in point of law does it make that they have done it unwittingly? I think none, and consequently that the action is maintainable. . . .

It is said there must be a trespass, a nuisance, or negligence. . . . But why is not this a trespass? Wilfulness is not material: Leame v. Bray (3 East, 593). Why is it not a nuisance? The nuisance is not in the reservoir, but in the water escaping. As in Backhouse v. Bonomi the act was lawful, the mischievous consequence is a wrong. . . .

MARTIN, B. . . .

First, I think there was no trespass. . . . I think the true criterion of trespass is laid down in the judgments in the former case, viz., that to constitute trespass the act doing the damage must be immediate, and that if the damage be mediate or consequential (which I think the present was), it is not a trespass. Secondly, I think there was no nuisance in the ordinary and generally understood meaning of that word, that is to say, something hurtful or injurious to the senses. The making a pond for holding water is a nuisance to no one. The digging a reservoir in a man's own land is a lawful act. . . . To hold the defendants liable would therefore make them insurers against the consequence of a lawful act upon their own land when they had no reason to believe or suspect that any damage was likely to ensue. . . .

[Pollock, C. B., agreed with Martin, B., that the facts found by the arbitrator were not a sufficient basis for relief.]

[IN THE EXCHEQUER CHAMBER]

May 14, 1866. BLACKBURN, J., read the following judgment of the court. . . .

We have come to the conclusion that the opinion of Bramwell, B., was right, and that the answer to the question should be that the plaintiff was entitled to recover damages from the defendants by reason of the matters stated in the Case . . .

What is the liability which the law casts upon a person who, like the defendants, lawfully brings on his land something which, though harmless while it remains there, will naturally do mischief if it escapes out of his land? It is agreed on all hands that he must take care to keep in that which he has brought on the land, and keep it there in order that it may not escape and damage his neighbor's, but the question arises whether the duty which the law casts upon him under such circumstances is an absolute duty to keep it in at his peril, or is, as the majority of the Court of Exchequer have thought, merely a duty to take all reasonable and prudent precautions in order to keep it in, but no more. . . .

We think that the true rule of law is that the person who, for his own purposes, brings on his land, and collects and keeps there anything likely to do mischief if it escapes, must keep it in at his peril, and, if he does not do so, he is prima facie answerable for all the damage which is the natural consequence of its escape. He can excuse himself by showing that the escape was owing to the plaintiff's default, or, perhaps, that the escape was the consequence of vis major, or the act of God; but, as nothing of this sort exists here, it is unnecessary to inquire what excuse would be sufficient. . . .

The case that has most commonly occurred, and which is most frequently to be found in the books, is as to the obligation of the owner of cattle which he has brought on his land to prevent their escaping and doing mischief. The law as to them seems to be perfectly settled from early times; the owner must keep them in at his peril, or he will be answerable for the natural consequences of their escape, that is, with regard to tame beasts, for the grass they eat and trample upon, although not for any injury to the person of others, for our ancestors have settled that it is not the general nature of horses to kick or bulls to gore, but if the owner knows that the beast has a vicious propensity to attack man he will be answerable for that too. . . . So in May v. Burdett, the court, after an elaborate examination of the old precedents and authorities, came to the conclusion that a person keeping a mischievous animal is bound to keep it secure at his peril. . . .

As has been already said, there does not appear to be any difference in principle between the extent of the duty cast on him who brings cattle on his land to keep them in, and the extent of the duty imposed on him who brings on his land water, filth, or stenches, or any other thing which will, if it escape, naturally do damage, to prevent their escaping and injuring his neighbor. Tenant v. Goldwin [a case decided in 1704 and reported in a number of places, including 1 Salk. 21 and 360, 91 Eng. Rep. 20 and 314, 2 Ld. Raym, 1089, 92 Eng. Rep. 222, and 6 Mod. Rep. 311, 87 Eng. Rep. 1051] is an express authority that the duty is the same, and is to keep them in at his peril. [In that case the defendant had a privy on his land and formerly had it enclosed by a wall. By reason of the defendant's failure to repair the wall, the filth of the privy flowed into the plaintiff's cellar.]

In the report in 6 Mod. Rep. at p. 314, it is stated:

"And at another day per totam curiam the declaration is good, for there is a sufficient cause of action appearing in it, but not upon the word solebat. If the defendant has a house or office enclosed with a wall which is his, he is, of common right, bound to use it so as not to annoy another. . . . The reason here is, that one must use his own so as thereby not to hurt another, and as of common right one is bound to keep his cattle from trespassing on his neighbor, so he is bound to use anything that is his so as not to hurt another by such use. . . ."

No case has been found in which the question of the liability for noxious vapours escaping from a man's works by inevitable accident has been discussed, but the following case will illustrate it. Some years ago several actions were brought against the occupiers of some alkali works at Liverpool for the damage alleged to be caused by the chlorine fumes of their works. The defendants proved that they had, at great expense, erected a contrivance by which the fumes of chlorine were condensed, and sold as muriatic acid, and they called a great body of scientific evidence to prove that this apparatus was so perfect that no fumes possible could escape from the defendant's chimneys. On this evidence it was pressed upon the juries that the plaintiff's damage must have been due to some of the numerous other chimneys in the neighborhood. The juries, however, being satisfied that the mischief was occasioned by chlorine, drew the conclusion that it had escaped from the defendant's works somehow, and in each case found for the plaintiff. No attempt was made to disturb these verdicts on the ground that the defendants had taken every precaution which prudence or skill could suggest to keep those fumes in, and that they could not be responsible unless negligence were shown, yet if the law be as laid down by the majority of the Court of Exchequer it would have been a very obvious defense. [T]he uniform course of pleading in actions for such nuisances is to say that the defendant caused the noisome vapours to arise on his premises and suffered them to come on the plaintiff's without stating that there was any want of care or skill on the defendant's part; and that Tenant v. Goldwin showed that this was founded on the general rule of law that he whose stuff it is must keep it so that it may not trespass. There is no difference in this respect between chlorine and water; both will, if they escape, do damage, the one by scorching and the other by drowning, and he who brings them on his land must at his peril see that they do not escape and do that mischief.

. . . But it was further said by Martin, B., that when damage is done to personal property, or even to the person by collision, either upon land or at sea, there must be negligence in the party doing the damage to render him legally responsible. This is no doubt true. . . . but we think these cases distinguishable from the present. Traffic on the highways, whether by land or sea, cannot be conducted without exposing those whose persons or property are near it to some inevitable risk; and, that being so, those who go on the highway, or have their property adjacent to it, may well be held to do so subject to their taking upon themselves the risk of injury from that inevitable danger . . . and it is believed that all the cases in which inevitable accident has been held an excuse for what prima facie was a trespass can be explained on the same principle, namely that the circumstances were such as to show that the plaintiff had taken the risk upon himself. But there is no ground for saying that the plaintiff here took upon himself any risk arising from the uses to which the defendants should choose to apply their land. He neither knew what there might be, nor could he in any way control the defendants. . . .

The view which we take of the first point renders it unnecessary to consider whether the defendants would or would not be responsible for the want of care and skill in the persons employed by them. We are of opinion that the plaintiff is entitled to recover. . . .

[IN THE HOUSE OF LORDS]

LORD CAIRNS, L.C. . . .

The principles on which this case must be determined appear to me to be extremely simple. The defendants, . . . might lawfully have used that close for any purpose for which it might, in the ordinary course of the enjoyment of land, be used, and if, in what I may term the natural user of that land, there had been any accumulation of water, either on the surface or underground, and if by the operation of the laws of nature that accumulation of water had passed off into the close occupied by the plaintiff, the plaintiff could not have complained that that result had taken place. If he had desired to guard himself against it, it would have lain on him to have done so. . . .

On the other hand, if the defendants, not stopping at the natural use of their close, had desired to use it for any purpose which I may term a non-natural use, for the purpose of introducing into the close that which, in its natural condition, was not in or upon it—for the purpose of introducing water, either above or below ground, in quantities and in a manner not the result of any work or operation on or under the land, and if in consequence of their doing so, or in consequence of any imperfection in the mode of their doing so, the water came to escape and to pass off into the close of the plaintiff, then it appears to me that that which the defendants were doing they were doing at their own peril. . . .

These simple principles, if they are well founded, as it appears to me they are, really dispose of this case. The same result is arrived at on the principles referred to by Blackburn, J., in his judgment in the Court of Exchequer Chamber . . .

In that opinion, I must say, I entirely concur. Therefore, I have to move your Lordships that the judgment of the Court of Exchequer Chamber be affirmed and that the present appeal be dismissed with costs.

LORD CRANWORTH.

I concur with my noble and learned friend in thinking that the rule of law was correctly stated by Blackburn, J., in delivering the opinion of the Exchequer chamber.[If a person brings or accumulates on his land anything which, if it should escape, may cause damage to his neighbor, he does so at his peril. If it does escape and cause damage, he is responsible, however careful he may have been, and whatever precautions he may have taken to prevent the damage.] In considering whether a defendant is liable to a plaintiff for damage which the plaintiff may have sustained, the question in general is, not whether the defendant has acted with due care and caution, but whether his acts have occasioned the damage. This is all well explained in the old case of Lambert and Olliot v. Bessey. The doctrine is founded on good sense, for when one person in managing his own affairs causes, however innocently, damage to another, it is obviously only just that he should be the party to suffer. He is bound sic uti suo ut non laedat alienum. This is the principle of law applicable to cases like the present, and I do not discover in the authorities which were cited anything conflicting with it. . . .

NOTES

1.   **Why strict liability in *Rylands*?** What is the scope of strict liability in *Rylands* and why is it imposed?

2.   **Special hazards in *Rylands*?** Does *Rylands* require any special hazard as a prerequisite to liability? Substances like dynamite may represent unusual hazards. Is water like that?

3.   ***Rylands* as an "escaping impoundments" case.** One central characteristic of *Rylands* is that it involved the escape of something that was held on the land by the defendant (water, in that case) that was likely to do harm to others if it escaped. How might this basis of strict liability apply today? In *Thomalen v. Marriott Corp.*, 845 F. Supp. 33 (D. Mass. 1994), a Marriott Hotel hosted a "Murder Mystery Weekend," in which a troupe of actors staged murder mystery entertainments. One member of the group, attempting to perform a fire-eating act, became engulfed in flames; another member ran to the stage to help but knocked over a can of lighter fluid. This ignited and caused burns to a guest close to the stage. The guest claimed Marriott was strictly liable under *Rylands*. The court disagreed. While Massachusetts has adopted *Rylands v. Fletcher* strict liability, the court said, there was "no escape of a dangerous instrumentality from Marriott's property," so that rule does not apply.

On the precise facts of *Rylands*—the sudden escape of ponded water—very few modern courts would impose strict liability. However, in two variants on the *Rylands* facts, strict liability may be imposed. The first is where the defendant impounds noxious substances that suddenly escape. *See, e.g., Cities Service Co. v. State*, 312 So. 2d 799 (Fla. Dist Ct. App. 1975) (escape of billions of gallons of phosphate slimes from a mine); *State Dept. of Envtl. Prot. v. Ventron Corp.*, 468 A.2d 150 (N.J. 1983) (escape of 268 tons of mercury). The second variation involves impounded liquids that do not escape suddenly, but merely percolate through the soil and contaminate a well or otherwise cause harm. These percolation cases almost always involve noxious impoundments, and may be traced to *Tenant v. Goldwin*, discussed in *Rylands*, where the judges appeared willing to impose strict liability for the escape of filth from a privy. *See Yommer* v. *McKenzie*, 257 A.2d 138 (Md. 1969) (gasoline); *Iverson v. Vint*, 54 N.W.2d 494 (Iowa 1952) (molasses dumped in ditch, percolation into farmer's well, strict liability). Some of these cases can be explained on other grounds, for example, that there was *Garratt v. Dailey* intent, or that there was a species of fault in carrying on an activity in an inappropriate place. Can there really be any principle, other than a whimsical one, that distinguishes damage caused by sudden escape from damage caused by percolation?

4. **Legitimate land uses endangering one another.** In one respect *Rylands* may be easy to understand. Suppose that thousands of acres of land in an agricultural area are devoted to farming Murg, a kind of grain that requires repeated aerial spraying. Into the midst of this great agricultural area move two new businesses: one is a beekeeper and one is a heavy industry. If, without fault, the aerial spraying of the Murg fields injures the bees or prevents them from finding usable pollen, should the beekeeper have a claim? If, without fault, the heavy industry discharges pollution that contaminates 3,000 acres of Murg growing in the fields, should the Murg owners have a claim?

5. **Does *Rylands* fit the inconsistent land uses pattern?** Cases like *Rylands*, and most nuisance cases today, can be seen as instances of inconsistent land uses. Though there is nothing "wrong" with moving a factory to the country, if it presents dangers to existing investments through its pollution, perhaps the most economical thing to do is to protect those investments without regard to "fault." Does this describe *Rylands*? After all, coal can be mined and that resource exploited only in places where the coal lies, but one could build a millpond almost anywhere in a pluvial country.

6. **A test case.** To test this idea, imagine that the coal mine in *Rylands* somehow caused damage to the mill owner or to nearby farmers. Would strict liability have been imposed then? Take an actual case: Salt water is used in oil well drilling, and must be stored in ponds. If the oil well driller's salt water pond collapsed without the driller's fault, would the farmer whose fields were ruined have an action based on strict liability? In *Turner v. Big Lake Oil Co.*, 96 S.W.2d 221 (Tex. 1936), the court rejected strict liability on such facts. While the court said it repudiated *Rylands,* is the result one *Rylands* might actually support? How?

7. **Coming to the nuisance.** There are similar ideas in pure nuisance cases. Although one who "comes to the nuisance" is not necessarily barred from recovery, since a number of factors must be weighed in nuisance cases, it seems clear that one who moves a home to a factory district cannot successfully enjoin

operation of the factories or even recover damages. Compare the situation of the beekeeper in Note 4. If the factory moves into a residential neighborhood, the situation is reversed and it may well be found to be a nuisance.

NOTE: NUISANCES TODAY

1. *Nuisance in context.* *Rylands* itself has been seen as a kind of "nuisance" case, although today nuisance cases are rarely a matter of truly strict liability. Contemporary cases require the plaintiff prove negligence, or intent to interfere with the plaintiff's interests, or the creation of a nuisance through abnormally dangerous activity, the subject of the next section below. *See, e.g., Ross v. Lowitz*, 120 A.3d 178 (N.J. 2015); *see also* 2 DOBBS, HAYDEN & BUBLICK, THE LAW OF TORTS § 400 (2d ed. 2011). Nuisance is an important tort claim when a defendant's acts—often a use by the defendant of his own land—substantially interfere with the plaintiff's use and enjoyment of her land. Often the invasions onto land that constitute nuisances are intangible—tangible invasions are often actionable as trespass to property—and almost always involve incompatible land uses. *See Wilson v. Interlake Steel Co.*, 649 P.2d 922 (Cal. 1982) (drawing this nuisance/trespass distinction). Nuisance cases often arise because the defendant's activity causes some kind of pollution, as by smoke, dust, chemicals, smells or noise. *See, e.g., Crosstex North Texas Pipeline, L.P. v. Gardiner*, 505 S.W.3d 580 (Tex. 2016) (compressor station that generated continuous loud noise and vibrations); *Sowers v. Forest Hills Subdivision*, 294 P.3d 427 (Nev. 2013) (wind turbine that would generate noise and shadow flicker).

2. *Substantial interference.* To constitute a nuisance, the interference with the plaintiff's use and enjoyment of her land must be *substantial*. This is a matter of degree, and a plaintiff's success will often turn on effective proof. *See Post and Beam Equities Group, LLC v. Sunne Village Development Property Owners Ass'n*, 124 A.3d 454 (Vt. 2015) (reviewing plaintiff's evidence proving that defendant's installation of a guardrail blocking access to restaurants over a subdivision's roadway caused substantial interference with plaintiff's use and enjoyment of land). A brief whiff of an unpleasant smell emanating from the yard next door will likely not suffice.

3. *Unreasonable invasion.* The invasion of the plaintiff's use and enjoyment of her land must be unreasonable, not in the sense that the defendant creates an unreasonable risk, but in the sense that given the time, place, and social expectations of the locale, it is unreasonable to expect the plaintiff to put up with the invasion without compensation. An intentional invasion may thus be permissible: defendant burns leaves in the fall, or operates a brick kiln that regularly causes odors, but not for

long. Other intended invasions may be actionable as nuisances if it is unreasonable to expect the plaintiff to put up with them. But this raises the question: how would you prove something is "unreasonable" if not by proving unreasonably risky conduct? The widely cited Restatement Second of Torts, in section 826, provides the traditional answer that the invasion is a nuisance if the gravity of the harm to the plaintiff "outweighs" the utility of the defendant's conduct. This would require a balancing of harm (not *risk* of harm) and utility of the conduct causing the invasion. *See, e.g., Lakey v. Puget Sound Energy, Inc.*, 296 P.3d 860 (Wash. 2013) (concluding that electromagnetic fields emanating from power company's substation was not a nuisance, where social utility of company's conduct outweighed interference with homeowners' enjoyment of their property). But the Restatement adds another alternative test: If the defendant could compensate the plaintiff and all others whose interests are invaded by the defendant's conduct, and could still stay in business, then compensation should be made. The idea is that it would be unreasonable to permit the defendant's activity to continue without paying, and the invasion will be regarded as a nuisance.

4. *Coming to the nuisance.* The fact that the plaintiff moved in next door to a nuisance is a significant fact in judging unreasonableness and hence in judging whether there is a nuisance at all. But no enterprise is allowed to create a noisome condition on its own land and insist that forever after anyone who comes into the area must be willing to tolerate such a condition. To permit this would be to allow an enterprise to condemn the land of others and to force a stasis on a dynamic and changing world. The fact that the plaintiff came to the nuisance is therefore only one factor to be considered in determining whether a nuisance exists. If the natural spread of a city brings it to the edge of the defendant's smelly feed lot, the lot, which was no nuisance at all when the area was devoted to farming, may become one when the area becomes suburban. On the other hand, the plaintiff who moves from Palm Springs to Bakersfield cannot complain about oil wells.

Another possibility when the plaintiff comes to the nuisance is that he has already been compensated for it. This is so because, if the nuisance is open and obvious, the plaintiff will probably have paid the former owner a smaller price because of the nuisance.

5. *Public nuisances.* Suppose the defendant, an industrial enterprise, dumps wastes on its own ground. These percolate through the soil and pollute a river, a lake, and even estuarine waters. All these bodies of water are public property. If the fish are killed or the waters become unusable, does anyone have a claim? Conceivably, landowners adjacent to these waters would have a nuisance claim on the principles stated above if the pollution substantially diminished the use and enjoyment of their land. What about a non-landowner who fishes for sport and can no longer catch

fish because they are dead? Or one who fishes commercially and can no longer catch them for the same reason? If the pollution constitutes a public nuisance because it substantially interferes with public health, safety, or convenience, the rule is that any person who has damages different in kind from the public generally may recover damages for the nuisance. The claimant who loses commercial fishing profits may thus have "standing to sue" because the claimant's injury differs from that of the public at large. The plaintiff who merely fishes for sport may be denied recovery, since her damages are not so different from those of other persons. In some states, a concern for environmental protection or enhancement may lead to a wider standing on the part of individuals. *See* DOBBS, HAYDEN & BUBLICK, HORNBOOK ON TORTS § 30.7 (2d ed. 2016).

6. *Environmental and zoning laws.* The common law of nuisance leads directly to contemporary legislation and administrative regulations aimed at pollution. It also leads to zoning laws, designed to maximize appropriate land-use. Although it would be theoretically possible to import a great deal of environmental and land-use law into a torts course, those fields have become major specialties of their own. Consequently, the bulk of nuisance law today may be better developed in connection with courses in property, land use, environmental protection, and public health and safety.

C. ABNORMALLY DANGEROUS ACTIVITIES

DYER v. MAINE DRILLING & BLASTING, INC.
984 A.2d 210 (Me. 2009)

SILVER, J.

[Vera Dyer and her sons sued Maine Drilling for damage to their home caused by the blasting of rock nearby in connection with a construction project to replace a bridge and bridge access roads. The Dyers asserted causes of action in strict liability and negligence. Maine Drilling moved for summary judgment on all claims. The court granted the motion. On the strict liability claim, the trial court relied on *Reynolds v. W.H. Hinman Co.*, 145 Me. 343, 75 A.2d 802 (1950), and other Maine precedent. The Dyers filed this appeal.]

DISCUSSION

. . . We [adopt today the Second Restatement's imposition of strict liability for abnormally dangerous activities, and remand to the court to determine if the blasting in this case was an abnormally dangerous activity under the Restatement's six-factor test] *See* Restatement (Second) of Torts

§§ 519–520 (1977).[4] In doing so, we overrule our prior opinions requiring proof of negligence in blasting cases.

Strict liability doctrine originated in the English case *Rylands v. Fletcher* (1868) 3 L.R. 330 (H.L.), where the court held that a defendant was liable regardless of negligence when he used his land in a way that was non-natural and likely to cause injury, and injury in fact resulted. ("If a person brings, or accumulates, on his land anything which, if it should escape, may cause damage to his neighbour, he does so at his peril. If it does escape, and cause damage, he is responsible, however careful he may have been."). This Court rejected *Rylands* in the 1950s, deciding that proof of negligence would be required in blasting cases.

In *Reynolds,* we noted that strict liability was the historic rule, but that the [majority of states had switched to a negligence approach in abnormally dangerous activities cases] Additionally, the opinion quoted a law review article arguing against strict liability based in part on the "difficulty of drawing the line between the danger which calls for care and the extra hazard. There are, as yet[,] no unanimously approved rules or criteria as to this subject." Finally, our *Reynolds* decision was supported by the conclusions that blasting is a reasonable and lawful use of land, and that plaintiffs would generally be able to recover under a negligence scheme.

These rationales have been undermined in the last half-century. Policy approaches have shifted nationwide, leading almost every other state to adopt strict liability in blasting and other abnormally dangerous activity cases, and leading Maine to apply strict liability in other contexts. Additionally, the Second Restatement has provided a scheme of clear criteria for delineating which activities require a strict liability approach. In light of these changes, we [overturn *Reynolds* and its progeny and adopt strict liability under the Restatement's six factor test]

---

[4]   The Second Restatement states:

§ 519. General Principle

(1) One who carries on an abnormally dangerous activity is subject to liability for harm to the person, land or chattels of another resulting from the activity, although he has exercised the utmost care to prevent the harm.

(2) This strict liability is limited to the kind of harm, the possibility of which makes the activity abnormally dangerous.

§ 520. Abnormally Dangerous Activities

In determining whether an activity is abnormally dangerous, the following factors are to be considered:

(a) existence of a high degree of risk of some harm to the person, land or chattels of others;

(b) likelihood that the harm that results from it will be great;

(c) inability to eliminate the risk by the exercise of reasonable care;

(d) extent to which the activity is not a matter of common usage;

(e) inappropriateness of the activity to the place where it is carried on; and

(f) extent to which its value to the community is outweighed by its dangerous attributes.

Reynolds operated on the assumption that negligence liability would allow most plaintiffs to recover in blasting cases. However, we have recognized that blasting is inherently dangerous, and most courts have recognized that this inherent danger cannot be eliminated by the exercise of care. The Dyers' expert testified that blasting may cause damage even when it is within the Bureau of Mines's guidelines. Consequently[although blasting is a lawful and often beneficial activity, the costs should fall on those who benefit from the blasting, rather than on an unfortunate neighbor.]

The negligence approach to abnormally dangerous activities initially taken by American courts was rooted in part in the idea that dangerous activities were essential to industrial development, "and it was considered that the interests of those in the vicinity of such enterprises must give way to them, and that too great a burden must not be placed upon them." But today, that attitude has changed, and[strict liability seeks to encourage both cost-spreading and incentives for the utmost safety when engaging in dangerous activities] Additionally, blasters are already required by the rules of the Maine Department of Public Safety and by many town ordinances to have liability insurance covering damages that result from blasting. Thus, a strict liability scheme should not greatly increase costs for these businesses.

At least forty-one states have adopted some form of strict liability for blasting, with only two of those clearly limiting it to damage caused by debris. . . .

Not only has the weight of authority shifted nationally, but we, acting pursuant to our common law authority, have applied forms of strict liability in certain circumstances. For example, we have adopted the Second Restatement approach to injuries caused by wild animals, analogizing those cases to blasting. *See Byram v. Main,* 523 A.2d 1387 (Me. 1987) ("The keeping of wild animals is categorized with such dangerous activities as blasting, pile driving, storing inflammable liquids, and accumulating sewage."). Owners of domestic animals may be held strictly liable as well. . . .

[The Restatement Second's approach] strikes the right balance of policy interests by considering on a case-by-case basis which activities are encompassed by the rule, and by taking account of the social desirability of the activity at issue. . . .

[A person who creates a substantial risk of severe harm to others while acting for his own gain should bear the costs of that activity] Most of the courts of the nation have recognized this policy, and we now do as well. For these reasons we adopt strict liability and remand for a determination whether the activity in this case subjected Maine Drilling to liability under the Second Restatement approach.

Under a strict liability analysis, <u>proof of a causal relationship between the blasting and the property damage is still required.</u> . . . [T]he Dyers produced sufficient evidence on the issue of causation to survive Maine Drilling's motion for summary judgment. . . . A fact-finder could reasonably find that the blasting was the . . . cause of damage to the Dyer home, because of: (1) the condition of the home observed before and after blasting commenced; (2) the temporal relationship between when the strongest blasting vibrations occurred and when damage was first observed; (3) evidence that the damage could have been caused by blasting; and (4) the reasonable inference that such damage was unlikely to be caused by other forces that typically cause cracking over longer periods of time. . . .

[Handwritten margin note: Proof of causal relationship between P + D]

[Judgment vacated. Remanded for further proceedings consistent with this opinion] *Holding*

[Concurring and dissenting opinions omitted.]

NOTES

1. **The Restatement Third.** The Restatement Third also recognizes that abnormally dangerous activities may subject a defendant to strict liability, but offers a simpler, two-part test for determining when an activity is abnormally dangerous: (1) the activity must create "a foreseeable and highly significant risk of physical harm even when reasonable care is exercised by all actors; and (2) the activity is not one of common usage." RESTATEMENT (THIRD) OF TORTS: LIABILITY FOR PHYSICAL AND EMOTIONAL HARM § 20 (2010).

[Handwritten margin note: Focus on Strict liability Restatement Third]

2. **Justifications for strict liability.** Why impose strict liability? (a) When the defendant engages in abnormally dangerous activities, knowing that he will reap the gains from the activity but that others may be harmed because it cannot be made safe by reasonable care, perhaps there is a moral basis for liability. If a defendant were *certain* that harm would result, you can make a moral case for liability. Is it so clear that the same is true when the defendant is not substantially certain of harm but merely knows of the high risk? Notice that, right or wrong, this idea is not to deter the activity—after all, it is not negligent—but to make it "pay its <u>own way</u>." (b) The Restatement Third suggests in § 20, comment b, that it is difficult to prove that an entire activity (like driving or building dams) is negligent and that some kinds of activity may involve negligence that cannot be detected or proved; strict liability, it suggests, is a good response to such cases.

[Handwritten margin note: P bears cost of non negligent activity]

3. **Risks or harms avoidable by reasonable care.** Notice that if reasonable care would reduce risks to a less-than-significant-level, strict liability does not apply. What if risks would be less than significant only if both the defendant and its potential victims were to exercise reasonable care? The Restatement Third provides in § 20, comment h, that the defendant's activity is not "unavoidably dangerous" and therefore not a matter of strict liability if potential victims can "commonly succeed in avoiding injuries." It is partially for this reason that the operation of a train that crosses a highway is not

considered "abnormally dangerous" activity; if both the defendant and the plaintiff exercise reasonable care, the likelihood of injuries is minimal. *Id.*

4. **When plaintiff or others contribute to the activity.** In another comment, the Restatement Third emphasizes an additional matter—that strict liability is appropriate where the activity, such as blasting, causes harm "without meaningful contribution from the conduct of the victim or of any other actors." In most cases, the victim is an uninvolved and innocent party who is doing nothing. *See Id.,* cmt. e. In *Pullen v. West,* 92 P.3d 584 (Kan. 2004), the plaintiff was helping with a fireworks display and suffered injury when struck by a fireworks rocket. The court rejected his strict liability claim because it said he participated in the activity. The court said he might still recover under negligence rules.

5. **Common usage.** If an activity is normal in the community—"a matter of common usage"—strict liability does not apply and liability is limited to cases in which the plaintiff can prove either negligence or intent. The common-usage rule certainly serves to limit the application of strict liability, but is a principle behind it? The Restatement Third in § 20, comment j, suggests two possibilities—first that the reason for strict liability might to some extent represent a concern for the acceptability of the activity and that when it is common, that concern tends to disappear. Second, when an activity is common, its benefits are likely to be distributed widely in the community and the basis for strict liability is stronger when benefits are concentrated among a few. *Cf.* Mark Geistfeld, *Should Enterprise Liability Replace the Rule of Strict Liability for Abnormally Dangerous Activities?*, 45 U.C.L.A. L. REV. 611 (1998). What do you think? If nuclear energy were not regulated by statutes, would you say that benefits of a nuclear power plant (a high risk activity) were concentrated among a few when electricity is distributed to virtually everyone?

6. **Factual cause.** Can a plaintiff prevail on a strict liability claim simply by proving that the defendant engaged in an abnormally dangerous activity? Of course not. As *Dyer* makes clear, a plaintiff must also prove that the defendant's activity was a factual cause of harm. The rules applied in this context are the same ones we saw in negligence cases in Chapter 7.

7. **Scope-of-liability limitations.** Under the Restatement Second § 519, the defendant is not strictly liable for *all* harms caused by his abnormally dangerous activity, but only those "the possibility of which makes the activity abnormally dangerous." This simply articulates the basic scope-of-liability (proximate cause) rule we saw in connection with negligence, doesn't it? *Accord,* RESTATEMENT (THIRD) OF TORTS: LIABILITY FOR PHYSICAL AND EMOTIONAL HARM § 29, cmt. l (2010).

Suppose a defendant engages in blasting, but the harm that results is neither harm from propelled objects, nor harm from vibrations. Instead the loud noises upset mother minks on nearby mink ranches and as a result they killed their kittens, resulting in loss to the breeder. This is not the kind of harm which led courts in the first place to consider blasting as abnormally dangerous, since it involves neither flying debris nor vibrations of the earth, and liability has been denied on facts like these. *See Foster v. Preston Mill Co.*, 268 P.2d 645 (Wash. 1954). *Cf. Indiana Harbor Belt Railroad Co. v. American Cyanamid Co.*, 916 F.2d 1174 (7th Cir. 1990) (toxic material leaked from railroad car, but not as a result of the inherent properties of the toxic material; no strict liability). This of course would not preclude liability for negligence or nuisance. *See Summit View, Inc. v. W. W. Clyde & Co.*, 403 P.2d 919 (Utah 1965).

So what role does foreseeability play? The Restatement Third § 20, comment i, suggests that a case for strict liability is "strengthened when the defendant has actual knowledge of the risky quality of the activity in which the defendant is engaging." In most cases of abnormally dangerous activities, of course, defendants do possess such knowledge. If a defendant "sincerely and reasonably believes" that his activity is not harmful, however, "there is inadequate reason to impose strict liability. *Id.*

8.   **History of strict liability for blasting.** The imposition of strict liability for abnormally dangerous activities may be traced back to *Rylands v. Fletcher*, as the *Dyer* court itself does. With respect to blasting activities in particular, the history is more recent. In a case from 1900, a 19-year-old girl was struck and killed by a stump that had been blasted out of the ground by the defendant. The court affirmed a verdict for her estate, not on the basis of abnormal danger, but on the ground that this was a "trespass to person" because the stump struck her on the fly. *Sullivan v. Dunham*, 55 N.E. 923 (N.Y. 1900). The court suggested that if the blasting had caused damage through a concussion or a shaking of the earth, no liability would be imposed. *Sullivan* seemed to distinguish between two claims that seemed morally indistinguishable—the injury from debris thrown up by a blaster and injury from the same blast but occurring through the medium of vibrations in the ground. In both cases, the defendant's act was the same and the plaintiff's injury equally real.

Some decades later, the Second Circuit faced the kind of alternative situation *Sullivan* had contemplated. In *Exner v. Sherman Power Construction Co.*, 54 F.2d 510 (2d Cir. 1931), defendant's blasting shook the plaintiff's house so violently that she was thrown out of bed. The court affirmed a jury verdict for her on the ground that the case was one of strict liability. Attacking the false distinction of "direct" versus "indirect" harms, the court said, "in every practical sense there can be no difference between a blasting which projects rocks in such a way as to injure persons or property and a blasting which, by creating a sudden vacuum, shatters buildings or knocks down people." The court also stressed the policy rationales behind its ruling:

"The extent to which one man in the lawful conduct of his business is liable for injuries to another involves an adjustment of conflicting interests. The solution of the problem . . . has never been dependent upon any universal criterion of liability (such as 'fault') applicable to all situations. If damage is inflicted, there ordinarily is liability, in the absence of excuse. When, as here, the defendant, though without fault, has engaged in the perilous activity of storing large quantities of a dangerous explosive for use in his business, we think there is no justification for relieving it of liability, and that the owner of the business, rather than a third person who has no relation to the explosion, other than that of injury, should bear the loss."

The first Restatement of Torts, drafted shortly after this decision was rendered, introduced a whole chapter on "Ultrahazardous Activities," which years later became the basis for the rules we have today.

NOTE: STRICT LIABILITY FOR OTHER ABNORMALLY DANGEROUS ACTIVITIES

1.   *Other high-energy activities.* The strict liability seen in explosives cases carries over to closely analogous activities where enormous force is involved, including the testing of rockets, *Smith v. Lockheed Propulsion Co.*, 247 Cal. App. 2d 774 (1967) (ground vibration damaged water well); the use of pile driving equipment, *Caporale v. C. W. Blakeslee & Sons, Inc.*, 175 A.2d 561 (Conn. 1961) ("intrinsically dangerous," strict liability for vibration damage); and even a "blow out" of an oil well in a populated area, *Green v. Gen. Petroleum Corp.*, 270 P. 952 (Cal. 1928).

2.   *Fireworks.* Is conducting a commercial firework display an abnormally dangerous activity, or is it "a matter of common usage?" Perhaps the answer depends on whether the focus is on how many people conduct professional fireworks displays (not many), or how many watch (millions). The court in *Toms v. Calvary Assembly of God, Inc.*, 132 A.3d 866 (Md. 2016), focused on the latter to reject strict liability in a case where the noise from a church-sponsored fireworks display conducted by a professional fireworks company allegedly caused a stampede inside plaintiff's dairy barn, resulting in the death of four cows and other damage. By contrast, in *Klein v. Pyrodyne Corp.*, 810 P.3d 917, *amended by* 817 P.3d 1359 (Wash. 1991), where a misfiring shell injured spectators at a public fireworks show, the court imposed strict liability, concluding that conducting fireworks displays was not a matter of common usage because various regulations prohibit members of the general public from engaging in such activities. Which approach best supports the goals of strict liability, do you think?

3.   *Poisons.* In *Loe v. Lenhardt,* 362 P.2d 312 (Or. 1961) strict liability was applied to crop-dusting activities. Might this be justified on a pure *Rylands v. Fletcher* rule, without resort to any "abnormally dangerous activity" rule? Courts have imposed strict liability for abnormally dangerous activity in pest control and fumigation cases. *Luthringer v. Moore*, 190 P.2d 1 (Cal. 1948); *Old Island Fumigation, Inc. v. Barbee*, 604 So.2d 1246 (Fla. Dist. Ct. App. 1992).

4. *Hazardous wastes.* Activities involving toxic substances are good candidates for strict liability based on abnormal danger. In *T & E Industries, Inc. v. Safety Light Corp.*, 587 A.2d 1249 (N.J. 1991), a plant used radium that left its own ground contaminated. Later it sold the property, which eventually passed to the plaintiff. Upon discovery of the contamination in the property it had purchased, the plaintiff sued. The court held that seller would be strictly liable not only to adjoining landowners who suffered harm, but also to purchasers like the plaintiff. The federal Superfund Act provides a fund, derived in part from taxes on industry, for the government to use to clean up substances released into the environment. Representatives of the fund may sue the responsible industry for reimbursement. Liability is strict and applies not only to one who actually released the substance but also to owners of the contaminated land whether they released the substance or not. *See* 42 U.S.C.A. § 9607(a).

5. *Lateral and subjacent support.* "Between adjacent landowners, the general principle . . . is that each has an absolute property right to have his land laterally supported by the soil of his neighbor, and if either in excavating on his own premises so disturbs the lateral support of his neighbor's land as to cause it, in its natural state, by the pressure of its own weight, to fall away or slide from its position, the one so excavating is liable." *Prete v. Cray*, 141 A. 609 (R.I. 1928). Can this form of strict liability be explained by the Restatement's "abnormally dangerous activity" theory? How does it compare, if at all, with other cases, such as those involving percolation, that appear to regulate property rights of near neighbors? *Cf.* RESTATEMENT (SECOND) OF TORTS § 817 (1979). The same rule is applied to "subjacent" support, that is, where an owner of minerals removes them so that the surface subsides. *See Id.* § 820.

NOTE: CONTRIBUTORY NEGLIGENCE AND ASSUMPTION OF RISK

1. *Traditional rule.* The traditional rule, still followed by some states and the one adopted by the Restatement Second, is that contributory negligence as such is no defense to a strict liability claim. The defendant, not at fault at all (because liability is strict), is thus held fully liable to a plaintiff who is guilty of negligence causing his own harm. At least a formal reason for this result can be found in the argument that since the defendant's liability is not based on negligence in the first place, his liability is not limited by contributory negligence of the plaintiff. Are you satisfied with this reasoning? The Restatement Second also takes the view that the plaintiff's "assumed risk," and also any contributory negligence in "knowingly" subjecting himself to risks of harm, *is* a defense. *See* RESTATEMENT (SECOND) OF TORTS § 524 (1977).

2. *Comparative responsibility and the Restatement Third.* The advent of comparative negligence (or "comparative responsibility," as the Restatement of Apportionment calls it) appears to call for a change in the traditional analysis. The Restatement of Apportionment, in § 8, provides that in all cases involving physical injury, the fact finder should assign shares of responsibility to each party, regardless of the legal theory of liability. That is, the Apportionment Restatement says that juries can and should assign percentages of responsibility even where one party is strictly liable and the other negligent. *Accord*, RESTATEMENT (THIRD) OF TORTS: LIABILITY FOR PHYSICAL AND EMOTIONAL HARM § 25 (2010) (if the plaintiff in a strict liability case is contributorily negligent "in failing to take reasonable precautions" his recovery should be reduced by his share of comparative responsibility).

With respect to assumption of risk, recall that in Chapter 10 we saw that that defense is no longer a unified one, and it is not self-evident what the label means without examining its context. Suppose, for example, in a comparative negligence state, that the defendant is blasting near or on a highway. Adequate signs are posted but the plaintiff negligently fails to observe them, drives into the danger area and is hurt by falling rocks from a blast. Should the plaintiff recover without any reduction in damages, or should a jury be allowed to compare the plaintiff's contributory negligence with the defendant's non-negligent activity? The Restatement Third (both of Apportionment and Liability for Physical and Emotional Harms) does not recognize a separate defense of implied assumption of risk at all. However, the Restatement rejects strict liability altogether if the plaintiff seeks contact with the abnormally dangerous activity to secure a benefit of his own, and states that if the risk of the defendant's activity can be reduced to a modest level by reasonable care of the plaintiff (or anyone else), the activity is not "abnormally dangerous" at all. RESTATEMENT (THIRD) OF TORTS: LIABILITY FOR PHYSICAL AND EMOTIONAL HARM §§ 24 & 20, cmt. h (2010).

REFERENCES: DOBBS, HAYDEN & BUBLICK, HORNBOOK ON TORTS §§ 32.1–32.9 (common law strict liability) & §§ 30.1–30.7 (nuisance) (2d ed. 2016); 2 DOBBS, HAYDEN & BUBLICK, THE LAW OF TORTS §§ 437–446 (common law strict liability) & §§ 398–404 (nuisance) (2d ed. 2011).

CHAPTER 24

TORT LIABILITY FOR
DEFECTIVE PRODUCTS

• • •

§ 1. HISTORY, RATIONALES, AND SCOPE
OF PRODUCTS LIABILITY

A. THE EVOLUTION OF LIABILTY THEORIES

Products liability law deals with the liabilities of those who manufacture or distribute harm-causing products. That law has undergone significant and sweeping change in the last several decades. Under today's law, those involved in commercial distribution of products are potentially liable for product-caused harm. Commercial distributors include manufacturers, wholesalers and retailers in the regular business of selling the particular product at issue. "Casual sellers" are not covered by special products liability rules; thus if you sell your car to a neighbor, the tort law discussed in this chapter would not apply to you—unless selling cars is your regular business.

The doctrine in this area is quite fluid, and the basis and extent of tort liability for injuries caused by faulty products continues to be debated. Indeed, the law of products liability is not limited to torts. A plaintiff may claim on a contract theory for breach of warranty, or on tort theories of negligence, strict liability, or even fraud. Tort theories dominate in cases of physical harm to person or property, but they cannot be understood in isolation from the law of contract and warranty.

The "Citadel of Privity" and Its Fall ⟶ "Contractual Relationship"

Negligence action—the privity requirement. The oldest products cases were brought on a negligence theory, some arising before negligence was regarded as a general theory or approach to tort liability. In these earlier cases, courts thought that the manufacturer's liability for an injury-causing product was derived from some kind of contractual undertaking to the purchaser. Since the basis for liability was not the general duty of reasonable care but the duty implicitly undertaken in a contract of sale, the manufacturer could be liable only to buyers who were in privity of contract—that is, a manufacturer who did not sell directly to the injured plaintiff could not be sued at all by that person. This rule insulated most manufacturers from liability.

In a leading New York case, *Losee v. Clute*, 51 N.Y. 494 (1873), the defendant Clute allegedly manufactured a boiler in a negligent way and sold it to Saratoga Paper Company. The boiler exploded and damaged, not Saratoga Paper, but the plaintiff's nearby property. The Court of Appeals of New York, following the privity rule, held that the complaint was properly dismissed. Defendants "contracted with the company . . . and when the boiler was accepted they ceased to have any further responsibility. . . ." Thus even active negligence was protected by the privity rule.

Courts did recognize exceptions for extreme cases. In *Thomas v. Winchester*, 6 N.Y. 397 (1852), the defendant mislabeled a jar of "belladonna, which is a deadly poison," and as a result the plaintiff, consuming it, became ill. Had the defendant sold the jar to the plaintiff, there would have been no privity problem. But the defendant had sold the jar to Aspinwall, who sold it to Ford, who sold it to the plaintiff. There was thus no privity between plaintiff and the defendant. Nevertheless, the court concluded that where death or great bodily harm would be "the natural and almost inevitable consequence of the sale" under a false label, privity would not be required.

Finally, in 1916, the New York Court of Appeals decided the landmark case of *MacPherson v. Buick Motor Co.*, 111 N.E. 1050 (N.Y. 1916). In *MacPherson* the wheel on an automobile collapsed. The plaintiff, who had purchased the car from a retail dealer, was injured. He sued the manufacturer of the car. Since he had purchased from the retailer, not the manufacturer, there was no privity between plaintiff and defendant. Judge Cardozo, writing for the court, said:

> We hold, then, that the principle of *Thomas v. Winchester* is not limited to poisons, explosives, and things of like nature, to things which in their normal operation are implements of destruction. If the nature of a thing is such that it is reasonably certain to place life and limb in peril when negligently made, it is then a thing of danger. . . . If [the manufacturer] is negligent where danger is to be foreseen, a liability will follow.

Cardozo in effect substituted foreseeability for contract or undertaking and thus applied general negligence principles to a case involving a defective product. Notice that *MacPherson* was definitely not a strict liability case—it simply permitted the application of negligence law to the products setting.

Misrepresentation. *MacPherson*'s rejection of the privity requirement for a products-liability negligence case, while it came to be accepted everywhere, did not assist every plaintiff. Some plaintiffs were injured by products that were not negligently made, and some simply could not prove negligence. Inventive lawyers attempted other theories to assist injured clients. One result was that it came to be held that a manufacturer would be liable for injuries resulting from conditions of the product that were misrepresented, even without privity. In *Baxter v. Ford Motor Co.*, 12 P.2d 409 (Wash. 1932), the plaintiff lost his eye when his windshield broke on impact from a pebble. The manufacturer had described its windshields as shatterproof. This was sufficient for liability, even though the manufacturer had not sold the car directly to the plaintiff. The misrepresentation approach can still aid plaintiffs and might even produce punitive damages awards. *See Williams v. Philip Morris Inc.*, 176 P.3d 1255 (Or. 2008) (on reconsideration after remand from the United States' Supreme Court) (tobacco industry statements about safety of smoking and industry research on safety, upholding $32 million in punitive damages).

Warranty. Another theory that plaintiffs could rely on when they could not prove negligence was *express warranty*. To take *Baxter*'s facts as an example, if Ford had sold the car to Baxter directly and had, as part of the contract, promised or guaranteed that the windshield was "shatterproof," this would be an express warranty, a kind of contract. Contract liability is usually strict liability; that is, proving breach of contract does not require proving that the breaching party is at fault. This contract theory is not often available, however, because manufacturers rarely make express guarantees about their products' safety directly to purchasing consumers.

Thus plaintiffs' lawyers began to argue to courts that the sale of goods gave rise to an *implied warranty*. For example, the act of selling a bottle of milk—whether it is sold by a retailer or by a manufacturer—seems to imply that it is not a bottle of belladonna, and also that it is not contaminated with human toes, dead flies, or unspeakable viruses. In other words, it should meet some kind of normal expectation as to quality and safety. Over the years, courts came to reject the maxim *caveat emptor*—let the buyer beware—and to accept the idea of a warranty implicit in the act of sale. The Uniform Commercial Code (UCC) Art. 2–314, which applies to any seller of goods, recognizes an implied warranty that goods are "fit for the ordinary purposes for which such goods are used"; and that they are as good as the seller claims they are.

The implied-warranty theory carries with it all the advantages and disadvantages of contract law—liability for breach is strict, but privity is required. While some courts created exceptions to the privity rule in cases involving such things as bad food and intimate products such as soaps, hair dyes and the like, these cases seemed to lack any underlying principle and they came to an evolutionary dead-end. About 1960, however, courts started off in an entirely new direction.

A leading case of the period was *Henningsen v. Bloomfield Motors, Inc.*, 161 A.2d 69 (N.J. 1960). *Henningsen* involved an automobile purchased by

Mr. Henningsen as a present for his wife. The car's steering failed, and the car crashed into a wall. The Henningsens sued the retailer and the manufacturer. The manufacturer and dealer had provided in the purchase contract that there were no warranties except that defective parts would be replaced within certain time limits. Since Mrs. Henningsen was badly injured, this was not helpful. The New Jersey Court held that there was an implied warranty in addition to this express warranty, that it ran to the ultimate purchaser and not merely to the retailer, and that the disclaimer of liability would be ineffective to protect the manufacturer. *Henningsen,* in other words, did for warranty about the same thing that *MacPherson* did for negligence.

Warranty remains a viable theory today in many products cases. However, to a very large extent the warranty theory has been displaced, or at least supplemented, by a theory of strict liability in tort, divorced from any conception of warranty.

The Development of Strict Products Liability

Strict tort liability emerged as a leading theory for products cases in *Greenman v. Yuba Power Products, Inc.*, 377 P.2d 897 (Cal. 1963). In that case, plaintiff's wife bought him a power tool that caused him serious injuries. Claiming the tool was defective, he sued the retailer and manufacturer on the two grounds then available to him: negligence and warranty. Affirming a jury verdict against the manufacturer, the court reasoned that in the case of defective products, "the liability is not one governed by the law of contract warranties but by the law of strict liability in tort." Justice Traynor wrote that the purpose of strict liability "is to insure that the costs of injuries resulting from defective products are borne by the manufacturers that put such products on the market rather than by the injured persons who are powerless to protect themselves."

Policy Purpose

Greenman was strongly influential in the drafting of the Restatement Second of Torts § 402A, promulgated in 1964. Section 402A quickly gained wide acceptance in the courts. By the mid-1960s, then, the developing law of strict products liability was freed from the older logic of the warranty theory and thus from the privity limitation. Section 402A became the lodestar of products liability discussion and development for a whole generation or more. Its essential provisions were simple: (a) sellers were strictly liable for physical injuries to persons or property other than the product itself; this meant that the injured consumer could recover without proving fault; (b) privity rules were abolished; this meant that the injured consumer could recovery without privity; and (c) strict liability attached to products that were "defective" because they were unreasonably dangerous to the consumer; and (d) the consumer's reasonable expectations defined what counted as a defective product.

The (Partial) Decline of Strict Products Liability

All of the arguments for broad strict products liability have been challenged, and as courts worked out the details of strict liability over a thirty-year period many critics asserted that strict liability for defectively-designed products was wrong in principle. Many states passed statutes in the 1980s limiting products liability cases in one respect or another as the criticisms reached critical mass.

A major turning point was the 1998 publication of the Restatement Third of Torts: Products Liability, which was by its own terms "an almost total overhaul of the Restatement Second as it concerns the liability of commercial sellers of products." RESTATEMENT OF PRODUCTS LIABILITY, Introduction (1998). The Products Restatement itself does not focus on the various theories of liability, but rather on whether products are proven to be "defective." Section 2 of the Products Restatement sets forth when a product is defective in manufacture, design, or because of inadequate instructions or warnings. The Products Restatement essentially retains strict liability only for products flawed in manufacture, and adopts a negligence standard or something very like it for design and warning defects.

The Products Restatement is increasingly influential, but many states continue to use some version of the Second Restatement for many if not all claims. Thus strict products liability may be said to be in decline, but it very much alive in a number of states.

> REFERENCES: 2 DOBBS, HAYDEN & BUBLICK, THE LAW OF TORTS §§ 448 & 450 (2d ed. 2011); DAVID G. OWEN, PRODUCTS LIABILITY LAW §§ 1.1–1.3 (2d ed. 2008).

B. RATIONALES FOR STRICT PRODUCTS LIABILITY

Strict products liability may be justified on one or more of the rationales discussed below. What do you think of them?

1. *Consumer expectations.* Manufacturers implicitly represent that the products they make are safe and healthy, and consumers are justified in relying on that implicit representation.

2. *Enterprise liability or "loss spreading."* Manufacturers and commercial sellers of goods can more easily spread the costs that result from injuries caused by defective products, by raising prices or purchasing insurance. Compensation is needed, and the most practical way to secure it is to have all consumers share the cost by paying more for the product. It has also been argued that strict liability justly imposes legal responsibility for injuries that are statistically associated with the enterprise of manufacturing and selling, making liability a cost of doing business that should be borne by someone other than injured individuals.

3. *Practicality.* Since a retailer in privity with the plaintiff may be held liable on warranty, and since if so held the retailer could have indemnity from the manufacturer, it would be cheaper to permit the plaintiff to sue the manufacturer directly. Another argument from "practicality" is that, since most defective products are that way because of negligence, imposing strict liability saves the legal system the time and expense of proving negligence.

4. *Fairness.* Another set of justifications stresses the basic *fairness* of a strict liability regime. First, because the manufacturer enjoys the advantages of sending its products into commerce, it should also take the disadvantages in the form of injury costs when the risks of such activity come to fruition. (On this argument, compare the reasons for the liability of a master for the torts of a servant.)

A second fairness-based justification is that the manufacturer imposes a special kind of risk—*nonreciprocal risks*—on the consumer. That is, the manufacturer imposes risks on the consumer that are quite different from any risks the consumer imposes on the manufacturer, and this fact justifies strict liability. George P. Fletcher developed the theory of nonreciprocal risks in a very influential article, *Fairness and Utility in Tort Theory*, 85 HARV. L. REV. 537 (1972). One example Fletcher uses of a non-reciprocal risk is the risk an airplane pilot imposes upon those on the ground. He imposes a risk of crashing into them but they impose no comparable risk upon him. To Fletcher, the crashing plane that causes ground damages represents a good case for strict liability in the absence of a defense.

5. *Deterrence.* If strict liability is imposed, manufacturers will tend to make products safer in order to avoid the increased costs resulting from liability. Liability of the manufacturer will drive the manufacturer to increase the price so as to cover the liability costs. As prices rise on unsafe products consumers will seek cheaper substitutes. These substitutes will usually be safer products; they are cheaper because they are not bearing the costs of tort liability. In addition, manufacturers, to avoid this loss of customers and the liability itself, will seek to find ways to make products more safe.

Guido Calabresi, in his 1970 book *The Cost of Accidents,* offered an economic analysis of the accident cost-reduction effects of strict liability. Much of his book is devoted to an idea he calls primary accident cost reduction or primary accident cost avoidance, focusing on reducing accident costs by reducing the number or severity of accidents themselves. This can be done in his view by using some combination of two major devices:

a. *Specific deterrence.* One way to reduce primary accident costs is to prohibit conduct that is excessively risky. This can be done by legislation or administrative regulation, for example. Specific prohibitions might be made because conduct is either "immoral" or because it does more harm than good. However, it is difficult to decide by political processes what risks are more harmful than useful. Calabresi believes that "the market" can make this judgment in a much better way.

b. *General deterrence.* [This is a technical term and an economic notion. The idea is that if a given activity, such as driving, causes accidents, that activity could be made to pay the costs.] Calabresi believes that if an activity is made to pay all the costs it really causes, this will in fact reduce accidents or the severity of accidents. Here's how. Suppose that convertibles are riskier than sedans, especially in turnover accidents. If manufacturers of convertibles had to pay all the costs of convertible injuries, they would raise the price of convertibles. Potential buyers will know comparative risks if the price of the convertibles reflect their true costs to society. Purchasers would not have to think about relative risks at all when they considered purchasing a convertible; they would have only to look at its price tag. Some people would buy the more expensive convertible even so. But others would reject it as too expensive. Even if they did not think about risks that were included in the price, their decision would be more informed because they would know the true costs of operating the convertible. Because a number of people would reject the more dangerous convertible, convertible-caused injuries would be reduced.

Athens and Sparta examples. Calabresi offered an example. He supposed that in Athens accident costs of an activity (like driving) were always charged to that activity so that insurance costs for an activity like driving would be higher than they would be otherwise. In Sparta, on the other hand, all injuries were compensated from general public funds raised by taxes. Taney is thinking of buying a second car. The costs of owning the second car would be $200 a year for operating plus another $200 for insurance. The alternative would be to take taxis occasionally, a cost of about $250 a year. In Athens he might reject the second car because its total cost, including the insurance which reflected accident costs, would be much greater than the cost of taxis. In Sparta, however, he would have no insurance costs, since injuries would be taken care of by public assistance. So his cost for the second car would be $200 a year as compared to taxis costing $250. He would buy the second car.

The Athens plan reduces accident costs by showing people like Taney the true cost of activities they are considering. The point is not that everyone would forgo the car, but that some people, getting the risk information through the price, would do so. Calabresi thought there was a second and maybe more important way that general deterrence would help reduce accident costs. He thought that it would encourage us to make activities safer if we knew the real costs of risks associated with them. If cars cause an average of $200 a year in accident costs but a new brake costing the equivalent of $50 a year can reduce those costs to $100, then Taney would install the new brake if he lived in Athens.

Cheapest cost avoider. Ideally, the costs of accidents should be borne by acts or activities that could avoid the accident costs most cheaply. A new car manufacturer might be a good choice, for example, if the manufacturer could add the $50 brake when it produces the car. If it is liable for car accidents, it will have the incentive to add the $50 brake.

REFERENCES: 2 DOBBS, HAYDEN & BUBLICK, THE LAW OF TORTS § 450 (2d ed. 2011); 1 MADDEN & OWEN ON PRODUCTS LIABILITY § 5:4 (3d ed. 2000).

C. EXCLUDING STAND-ALONE ECONOMIC HARM

NOTE: PURE ECONOMIC HARM
AND STRICT LIABILITY

1. *Pure economic harm.* A defective product can cause personal injury or death, but such a product might also cause pure economic harm, sometimes called "stand-alone economic harm." Economic harm is of course common in tort law. For instance, a person who is physically injured may have medical bills and lost wages as a result. That is economic harm, and it is recoverable in addition to non-economic harm like pain and suffering. However, in other cases, a defective product can cause a loss in value of the product itself and *no physical harm of any kind.* That would be a case of pure or stand-alone economic harm. For example, you buy a vacuum cleaner but it quits running after two days. That is a defective product and worth less because of its defect, but no property has been damaged and no person injured. It is a case of pure economic harm.

2. *Rule for pure economic harm.* The rule for pure economic harm resulting from a defective product is that tort actions are not available, even for negligence, much less for strict liability. The defendant may be liable, but if so, it will be under the contract—on the warranty. If warranty is excluded or the remedy on the warranty is limited by the terms of the contract, the plaintiff cannot in effect overrule the contract terms by suing in tort. This is in contrast with the rule for physical harms—strict liability in tort means that the defendant cannot avoid liability simply by contractually getting permission to provide a defective product that harms people or tangible property.

3. *Extending the economic loss rule.* Courts usually expand the economic loss rule a little by treating the product's self-damage as pure economic loss that must be sued for under the contract. If a defective garbage disposal unit will not turn off and grinds until it is burnt out, that is, literally, physical harm and not pure economic harm. However, the line is sometimes hard to draw, so courts have treated the product's self-damaging physical harm just like pure economic loss. *See East River Steamship Corp. v. Transamerica Delaval, Inc.,* 476 U.S. 858 (1986).

4. *Caveat.* In spite of the rules just recited, there are many tort claims for pure economic loss without personal injury or property damage. Examples are suits for fraud or misrepresentation that induces someone to enter into an agreement on the basis of material falsehoods, interference with contract by tortious means, and such torts as copyright or trademark infringement. Economic torts are covered primarily in advanced tort courses.

§ 2. ESTABLISHING A PRIMA FACIE CASE

Courts have recognized three types of product defects that may lead to liability: (1) Manufacturing defects (also called production flaws); (2) design defects; and (3) information defects. Perhaps the most crucial questions in products cases—and the focus of the Restatement of Products Liability—concern whether a product is "defective" in the first place, and what a plaintiff has to prove to establish such a defect.

A. MANUFACTURING DEFECTS

LEE v. CROOKSTON COCA-COLA BOTTLING CO.
188 N.W.2d 426 (Minn. 1971)

ROGOSHESKE, JUSTICE.

[Plaintiff, a waitress in the Norman Steak House at Ada, Minnesota, was injured when a Coca-Cola bottle exploded in her hand. The trial judge refused to submit a claim based on strict tort liability, and the jury, apparently finding no negligence and no breach of warranty, returned a defendant's verdict. Plaintiff appeals, arguing that the court should have submitted jury instructions on the strict liability claim.]

[Evidence showed the bottle exploded in the plaintiff's hand, that it had not struck anything, that it had not been subjected to temperature extremes or mishandling.]

The rule of strict liability, as revised and adopted by the American Law Institute in 1964, is embodied in Restatement, Torts (2d) § 402A. It imposes liability, without proof of negligence or privity of contract, upon a manufacturer or seller for injury caused by a dangerously defective product. To recover under the rule, the injured party must present evidence, direct or circumstantial, from which the jury can justifiably find that (1) the product was in fact in a defective condition, unreasonably dangerous for its intended use; (2) such defect existed when the product left defendant's control; and (3) the defect was the proximate cause of the injury sustained.

The greatest difficulty in establishing liability under this rule is in proving that the product was defective and that the defect existed when the product left defendant's control. While in conventional tort terms no proof of negligence is necessary, in many cases proof of a defect may simply be a substitute word for negligence. Thus, strict liability does not mean that the defendant is held liable as an insurer of his product regardless of circumstances. As is true in negligence cases with respect to the mere fact of an accident, the mere fact of injury during use of the product usually is insufficient proof to show existence of a defect at the time defendant relinquished control. . . . Also, liability is not imposed where the injured party has not eliminated the probability that improper handling by intermediate parties might have caused the defect. . . .

The narrow question presented here, however, is whether circumstantial evidence, the core of the res ipsa loquitur doctrine, is sufficient to take the case to the jury on the theory of strict liability as well as on the theory of negligence. . . .

It surely must be conceded that circumstantial evidence of the type present in . . . this case justifies submission of the issue of liability on the theory of res ipsa. . . . As testified to by defendant's expert, there are three fundamental causes of bottle failure: Thermo-shock, internal pressure, and external force. According to the expert's testimony, failure because of thermo-shock could only result from drastic changes in temperature applied to the outside of the bottle, such as would be produced by placing a bottle containing hot liquid in cold water. Failure caused by external force, of course, usually results from an impact, such as striking or dropping the bottle. Failure because of internal pressure due to excessive carbonation is ordinarily unlikely because the bottle is designed to withstand approximately four times the pressure created by the gas introduced, and after the carbonated liquid is added to the syrup mixture, any excessive carbonation is equalized by exposure to atmospheric pressure during the interval between carbonation and capping. The capacity of different bottles to withstand internal pressure varies, however, in part due to bottlers' customary reuse of bottles. Some bottles have been refilled for years and might have been subjected to "rough" handling numerous times, thereby increasing the probability that even though they are designed to withstand such handling, some could develop defects which would escape detection by the most careful bottler. This may be the only plausible explanation for the bottle's failure in this case, since there is uncontradicted evidence dispelling the probability that the failure was attributable to thermo-shock or external force. Absent expert opinion, as in a case of this type, circumstantial evidence may be the only available means of establishing a claim of either negligence or a defective product.

Under the theory of strict liability, the elements of proof as noted above are few and uncomplicated. The significant difference is that under strict liability the jury need not infer from the circumstantial evidence that defendant was negligent in order to impose liability. It is sufficient that the evidence establishes that the manufacturer placed a dangerously defective product on the market, knowing that it is to be used without inspection for defects. . . .

In short, under the theory of strict liability plaintiff should not be required to prove specifically what defect caused the incident, but may rely upon circumstantial evidence from which it can reasonably be inferred that it is more probable than not that the product was defective when it left defendant's control. . . .

The jury could properly have found on the evidence submitted that defendant was not causally negligent. This finding, of course, defeats plaintiffs' claim on the theory of negligence. As has been pointed out above, however, it would not necessarily preclude recovery under the theory of strict liability. Under instructions solely on negligence, a jury might conclude that the bottle was defective when it left defendant's control but that defendant was not liable because the defect did not result from negligence. Under instructions on strict liability, on the other hand, a finding that the bottle was defective when defendant put it on the market would *compel* a verdict *for plaintiffs*, absent the aforementioned defenses and without considering the question of negligence.

Thus, the trial court's refusal to submit plaintiffs' claim upon the theory of strict liability in tort must also be regarded as reversible error. The court's ruling deprived plaintiffs of a legitimate choice of theories on which to submit the case. Plaintiffs are entitled to attempt to prove their case on either or both theories—that defendant was negligent or that it put a dangerously defective product on the market.

It could be argued that the case in effect was submitted to the jury on strict liability, since the jury was instructed on implied warranty. Although strict liability in tort and in warranty are very similar, we cannot view the court's instructions as sufficient to constitute submission of the question of strict liability in tort to the jury. The jury was told that defendant warranted that the bottle of Coca-Cola "was reasonably fit for the ordinary and usual handling as it might reasonably anticipate in the exercise of reasonable care." This language falls short of conveying to the jury that if a defect existed in defendant's product when it left its control, defendant should be found liable for the injuries caused by such defect.

Reversed and new trial granted.

NOTES

1.   **Manufacturing defects.** A manufacturing defect can occur even if there is nothing at all wrong with the product's design—the product simply comes off the production line containing some flaw. Manufacturing defects typically affect only a small percentage of a manufacturer's products in a particular product line.

2.   **The consumer expectations test.** The Restatement Second § 402A in effect imposes strict liability when the product is defective and unreasonably dangerous. It tests defect/unreasonable danger by asking whether the product is "dangerous to an extent beyond that which would be contemplated by the ordinary consumer who purchases it, with the ordinary knowledge common to the community as to its characteristics." RESTATEMENT (SECOND) OF TORTS § 402A, cmt. i (1965). This is usually called the "consumer expectations" test.

3.   **The Products Liability Restatement's test.** The Products Liability Restatement states the test differently. It provides that "a product contains a manufacturing defect when the product departs from its intended design even though all possible care was exercised in the preparation and marketing of the product." RESTATEMENT OF PRODUCTS LIABILITY § 2(a) (1998). How does the newer Restatement's standard relate to the Second Restatement's "consumer expectations" standard?

4.   **Retaining the consumer expectations test.** Many courts today continue to apply the consumer expectations test in manufacturing defect cases, the more recent Products Restatement notwithstanding. *E.g., Potter v. Chicago Pneumatic Tool Co.*, 694 A.2d 1319 (Conn. 1997) (with other tests in some cases). Subject to qualification, the consumer expectations test is also widely used in the products liability law of countries in Europe, Asia, South America and elsewhere. *See* Mathias Reimann, *Liability for Defective Products at the Beginning of the Twenty-first Century: Emergence of a Worldwide Standard?*, 51 AM. J. COMP. LAW. 751, 768 (2003).

5.   **Elements of a strict liability claim.** To prevail on a strict liability claim, the plaintiff must prove not only that the product was defective, and that the defect was a factual and proximate cause of plaintiff's harm, but also that the product was defective when it left the defendant's hands. This latter part may not be easy to prove in a manufacturing defect case, particularly when the product has been in use for a long time before it fails. *See Barnish v. KWI Building Co.*, 980 A.2d 535 (Pa. 2009). Even where a manufacturing defect is proved, a plaintiff's evidence may fall short of proving that the defect actually caused the plaintiff's harm. This may be especially true where the manufacturing defect is only a small deviation from the intended design. *See, e.g., BIC Pen Corp. v. Carter*, 346 S.W.3d 533 (Tex. 2011).

6.   **Inferences from circumstantial evidence.** As *Lee* shows, drawing inferences is often necessary to make the plaintiff's case. The Restatement of Products Liability § 3 provides that it may be inferred that a product defect existing at the time of sale or distribution caused plaintiff's harm when the event (a) was of a kind that ordinarily occurs as a result of product defect; and (b) was not solely the result of causes other than product defect. What does the Restatement formulation remind you of?

7.   **Defect and negligence.** The use of *res ipsa* analogies, as in *Lee*, suggests a similarity between strict liability and negligence, as does the "unreasonable danger" phrase. One difference, however, is that a negligence claim focuses on the defendant's conduct, while a strict products liability claim

focuses on the product itself. Thus, as in *Lee,* a jury might find no negligence and still find a product defective. A defendant which has done the best anyone can do to produce a safe product is still liable for the inevitable defects that cause harm. But in the great bulk of cases, it can be inferred that negligence caused the manufacturing defect. Since this will so often be true, this kind of strict liability might be regarded as a "shortcut" to the same result a negligence rule would ordinarily achieve, but without the necessity of long, detailed trials over the fault issue. *See* Gary T. Schwartz, *Understanding Products Liability,* 67 CAL. L. REV. 435, 460–461 (1979). Under this view, strict liability differs from negligence because it is cheaper to use. But as to most defendants most of the time, it will add very little liability. What do you think of this analysis?

JACKSON V. NESTLE-BEICH, INC., 589 N.E.2d 547 (Ill. 1992). The plaintiff allegedly broke a tooth on a hard pecan shell embedded in a chocolate-covered pecan-caramel candy purchased in a sealed can and manufactured by Nestle. Nestle moved for summary judgment on the ground that the substance was natural to pecans, not foreign. *Held,* affirming the intermediate appellate court's decision, "the foreign-natural doctrine is unsound and should be abandoned." Instead, the consumer's reasonable expectation is the test of defectiveness under the Second Restatement's § 402A, cmt. i.

NOTES

1. **Food products and consumer expectations.** The Products Restatement provides that a harm-causing ingredient in a food product is a defect "if a reasonable consumer would not expect the food product to contain that ingredient." RESTATEMENT OF PRODUCTS LIABILITY § 7 (1998). Most courts in effect follow the rule seen in *Jackson* and adopted in the Restatement. However, in *Mexicali Rose v. Superior Court (Clark v. Mexicali Rose),* 822 P.2d 1292 (Cal. 1992), the court retained the "foreign-natural" doctrine rejected in *Jackson,* holding that a one-inch chicken bone in a chicken enchilada was "natural" to the food, and that strict liability could therefore not be imposed against the defendant. What if the chicken bone was in a beef enchilada?

2. **Proof.** Might a plaintiff have proof problems in some food cases? Suppose that a plaintiff purchases packaged food at a store, and later, upon eating it, gets sick. How does the plaintiff prove that the food was "defective," and that it was a defect in the food (as opposed to, say, improper storage or preparation of it) that made her sick? In *Massey v. Conagra Foods, Inc.,* 328 P.3d 46 (Idaho 2014), the plaintiff consumed the defendant's poultry pot pies, purchased frozen from a grocery store. She got violently sick and was diagnosed with salmonellosis. In response to defendant's motion for summary judgment, she testified that she ate at least one if not several of the pot pies, that she "always" followed the cooking instructions, and that the strain of salmonella that infected her had been found in defendant's pot pies. The trial

court granted defendant's motion, holding that her evidence on "defect" was insufficient. Reversing, the Idaho Supreme Court held that her testimony alone was sufficient to create a fact issue on whether the pot pie failed to meet the reasonable expectations of the ordinary consumer as to its safety.

> REFERENCES: DOBBS, HAYDEN & BUBLICK, HORNBOOK ON TORTS §§ 33.6–33.8 (2d ed. 2016); 2 DOBBS, HAYDEN & BUBLICK, THE LAW OF TORTS §§ 451–454 (2d ed. 2011).

B. DESIGN DEFECTS

LEICHTAMER V. AMERICAN MOTORS CO., 424 N.E.2d 568 (Ohio 1981). Plaintiffs were passengers in a Jeep driven by Paul Vance on an off-road facility. Vance was negotiating hills and terraces when he overturned the Jeep in a back-to-front flip over. The rollbar, attached to relatively thin metal housing, displaced toward the passengers when the housing collapsed. Vance and his wife were killed. The plaintiff Jeanne Leichtamer's legs were twisted through the front seat and she is now a paraplegic. The plaintiffs sued claiming that, though Vance was negligent, their injuries were enhanced because of the roll-bar's displacement. The jury found for the plaintiffs, awarding $1 million in compensatory and $1 million in punitive damages to Jeanne and $100,000 compensatory and $100,000 punitive to Carl Leichtamer. *Held*, affirmed.

"Appellees did not claim that there was any defect in the way the vehicle was manufactured in the sense of departure by the manufacturer from design specifications. The vehicle was manufactured precisely in the manner in which it was designed to be manufactured. It reached Paul Vance in that condition and was not changed. . . . [T]he vast weight of authority is in support of allowing an action in strict liability in tort . . . for design defects. . . . Strict liability in tort has been applied to design defect 'second collision' cases. While a manufacturer is under no obligation to design a 'crash proof' vehicle, an instruction may be given on the issue of strict liability in tort if the plaintiff adduces sufficient evidence that an unreasonably dangerous product design proximately caused or enhanced plaintiff's injuries in the course of a foreseeable use. . . . [A] product may be found defective in design if the plaintiff demonstrates that the product failed to perform as safely as an ordinary consumer would expect when used in an intended or reasonably foreseeable manner. . . . A product will be found unreasonably dangerous if it is dangerous to an extent beyond the expectations of an ordinary consumer when used in an intended or reasonably foreseeable manner." Since the roll-bar was designed for a side roll-over only and not a back-to-front roll-over, and since the company knew it had not provided tests for this kind of hazard when it advertised the Jeep for off-the-road use, punitive damages were warranted.

NOTES

1.   **Design defects.** Notice that the "defect" in *Leichtamer* was in the design of the product, and was not simply the result of some flaw in manufacture. Design defects are difficult to define and identify. In addition, design defect claims threaten manufacturers in ways that manufacturing defect claims do not. If a product is defective in manufacture, only a few products with flaws will be in circulation; but if a product is defectively designed, every one of the products represents a potential lawsuit against the manufacturer.

2.   **Consumer expectations and unreasonable danger.** As noted in § 2 above, the Restatement Second's § 402A provides that a product would be considered defective if it was more dangerous than the "ordinary consumer" would expect. When applied to design defect cases, this test raises many difficult questions. Cars do not provide roll-bars built into the roof. Does the consumer expectations test help decide whether such cars are defective? Would it be enough to show a defect if you could prove that consumers had a general expectation that cars would be safe? Or would it be necessary to show that consumer experience led to specific design expectations? *See Soule v. Gen. Motors Corp.*, 882 P.2d 298 (Cal. 1994) (requiring specific expectation based on everyday experience). Think about how consumer expectations might be proved in court. Would it be proved by (a) the plaintiff's testimony about her own expectations; (b) the jury's general knowledge about safety expectations; or (c) expert testimony? In *Wilson Sporting Goods Co. v. Hickox*, 59 A.3d 1267 (D.C. 2013), the plaintiff was a professional baseball umpire who was injured during a major league game when a foul-tipped ball struck his mask, which was manufactured by the defendant. The jury, instructed on the consumer expectations test, found for the plaintiff. *Held*, affirmed. The court stressed evidence that the plaintiff had been personally told by a manufacturer's representative that the mask was safer than other similar models; that, said the court, would lead an ordinary consumer to expect the mask to perform safely, which it did not.

3.   **Consumer expectations and obvious dangers.** Many commentators and courts consider the consumer expectations test of section 402A a "pro-plaintiff" test. But what if a product's danger is obvious? Wouldn't a plaintiff always lose such a case, because the product would not be "more dangerous than the ordinary consumer would expect?" *See Bourne v. Marty Gilman, Inc.*, 452 F.3d 632 (7th Cir. 2006); 2 DOBBS, HAYDEN & BUBLICK, THE LAW OF TORTS § 455 (2d ed. 2011).

4.   **Bystanders or strangers.** Suppose you are not using the product, but you are injured by it. You fall against an exercise machine and, quite surprisingly, a part pierces your thigh, cutting blood vessels and damaging nerves. *See Jones v. Nordictrack, Inc.*, 550 S.E.2d 101 (Ga. 2001). Or a defective lighter as used by one child causes burns to another child. See *Hernandez v. Tokai Corp.*, 2 S.W.3d 251 (Tex. 1999). Or you inhale asbestos fibers unknowingly brought into the house on the clothes of a worker who was

exposed to such toxic materials. *See Stegemoller v. ACandS, Inc.,* 767 N.E.2d 974 (Ind. 2002).

Courts impose liability in such cases, but how can a bystander have any expectation about the particular product's safety? In *Horst v. Deere & Co.,* 769 N.W.2d 536 (Wis. 2009), the court said that the focus remains on the expectations of the actual consumer, but that such a consumer may have safety expectations relating to bystanders, which can be taken into account by the jury in deciding whether the product is unreasonably dangerous in design. When the consumer expectations test is not used at all (see the next section below), there is no barrier to a bystander bringing a design defect claim. *See Berrier v. Simplicity Mfg., Inc.,* 563 F.3d 38 (3d Cir. 2009).

5.   **Crashworthiness.** At one time, a defendant in a case like *Leichtamer* could prevail on an argument that if a product was used in an unintended way—like getting involved in a car crash—then that unintended use, not any defect, was the sole cause of the harm. Such a restrictive view is no longer followed; manufacturers are liable for harms caused by defective products that are put to "foreseeable uses," even if unintended by the manufacturer. This is often called the "crashworthiness doctrine." *See, e.g., Malen v. MTD Products, Inc.,* 628 F.3d 296 (7th Cir. 2010) ("The premise underlying the crashworthiness doctrine is that some products, although not made for certain purposes—such as accidents—should nevertheless be reasonably designed to minimize the injury-producing effect of an accident.").

The crashworthiness doctrine allows a plaintiff to sue for the injuries that were *enhanced* by the product's defective design. For example, suppose the plaintiff is injured when a defectively designed airbag fails to deploy in an auto accident. The airbag defect, even if proved, did not cause the accident in the first place, right? Rather, what the defect caused was the enhanced injury— the injuries that would not have occurred without the product defect. How is that proved? Compare *Piltch v. Ford Motor Co.,* 778 F.3d 628 (7th Cir. 2015) (burden on plaintiff; plaintiff needed expert testimony on causation in order to separate the injuries caused by collision from those caused by the failure of the air bag), with *Polston v. Boomershine Pontiac-GMC Truck Inc.,* 423 S.E.2d 659 (Ga. 1992) (once plaintiff proves defect, burden shifts to defendant to prove which damages were not caused by the defect). Which approach represents sounder policy? *See* RESTATEMENT (THIRD) OF TORTS: PRODUCTS LIABILITY § 16 & cmt. d (1998) (if "proof does not support a determination . . . of the harm that would have resulted in the absence of the product defect, the product seller is liable for all of the plaintiff's harm"; "The defendant, a wrongdoer who in fact has caused harm to the plaintiff, should not escape liability because the nature of the harm makes such a determination impossible.").

KNITZ v. MINSTER MACHINE CO.
432 N.E.2d 814 (Ohio 1982)

[Defendant manufactured a press which delivered 60 tons of force in pressing die halves together. It was originally activated with a two-hand button tripping device, so that the operator's hands were necessarily outside the danger area. This press, with the button tripping device, was sold by defendant to Toledo Die and Manufacturing Company. Toledo, however, also purchased an optional foot pedal tripping device and it was in use at the time of the injury. Plaintiff, the press operator for Toledo, found it necessary to move the foot pedal with her foot; in doing so, she leaned on the bottom portion of the die with her hand. Her foot accidentally activated the foot pedal and the press descended, amputating two fingers. There was another safety device, intended to physically pull back the operator's hands, but it was not attached. The trial judge gave summary judgment for the manufacturer.]

WILLIAM B. BROWN, JUSTICE.

[The case presents us with the question of whether a motion for summary judgment pursuant to Civ. R. 56 should have been granted to appellee.] . . .

The focus of the inquiry in *Leichtamer* was what constituted a "defective condition unreasonably dangerous" as formulated by Section 402A of the Restatement of Torts. We adopted a variation of the familiar "consumer expectation test" of Comment *i* to Section 402: "A product is in a defective condition unreasonably dangerous to the user or consumer if it is more dangerous than an ordinary consumer would expect when used in an intended or reasonably foreseeable manner." This standard followed as a logical development from commercial warranty origins of strict liability in tort. It reflected "the commercial reality that '[i]mplicit in . . . [a product's] presence on the market . . . [is] a representation that it [will] safely do the jobs for which it was built.' "

Unlike the factual setting in *Leichtamer*, there are situations in which "the consumer would not know what to expect, because he would have no idea how safe the product could be made." Such is the case *sub judice*. Difficulty could arise, for example, where the injured party is an innocent bystander who is ignorant of the product and has no expectation of its safety, or where a new product is involved and no expectation of safety has developed. Conversely, liability could be barred hypothetically where industrial workmen "gradually learn of the dangers involved in the machinery they must use to make a living and come to 'expect' the dangers." In such cases, the policy underlying strict liability in tort, requires that "a product may be found defective in design, even if it satisfies ordinary consumer expectations, if through hindsight the jury determines that the product's design embodies 'excessive preventable danger,' or, in other words, if the jury finds that the risk of danger inherent in the challenged design outweighs the benefits of such design."

Accordingly, we hold that a product design is in a defective condition to the user or consumer if (1) it is more dangerous than an ordinary consumer would expect when used in an intended or reasonably foreseeable manner, or (2) if the benefits of the challenged design do not outweigh the risk inherent in such design. Factors relevant to the evaluation of the defectiveness of the product design are the likelihood that the product design will cause injury, the gravity of the danger posed, and the mechanical and economic feasibility of an improved design. . . . [W]e conclude that appellant has made out genuine issues of fact of whether appellee's press design was defective by allowing accidental tripping of the foot pedal control and in failing to provide a point of operation guard when the foot pedal is operative. Specifically, appellant provided an affidavit of James J. McCarthy, a former safety engineer for General Motors Corporation, involved with analysis of machine accident potential. McCarthy's affidavit states, *inter alia*, that in his opinion the press is defective "because of inadequate guarding at the point of operation caused by failure to attach a barrier or interlock gate guard to prevent entry of the operator's hands into the danger area while the ram is descending . . . the press is defective because of inadequate guarding of the foot pedal of the foot switch to prevent inadvertent entry and tripping."

NOTES

1.   **Different tests for design defects vs. manufacturing defects.** The distinction between design defects and manufacturing defects is fundamental in American law. The Restatement Second used the same test—consumer expectations—for both kinds of defects, and some courts continue to do that. *See, e.g., Aubin v. Union Carbide Corp.*, 177 So.3d 489 (Fla. 2015). The products liability laws of many other countries also apply the same rules to each type of defect. *See* Mathias Reimann, *Liability for Defective Products at the Beginning of the Twenty-first Century: Emergence of a Worldwide Standard?*, 51 AM. J. COMP. LAW. 751 (2003); Jane Stapleton, *Bugs in Anglo-American Products Liability*, 53 S.C. L. REV. 1225 (2002). But a great number of modern American courts utilize a different set of rules for each type of defect—frequently today using some form of strict liability for manufacturing defects (often using the consumer expectations test) and risk-utility balancing for design defects. The Restatement Third expressly "adopts a reasonableness ('risk-utility balancing') test as the standard for judging the defectiveness of product designs," but provides in a comment that consumer expectations, while they "do not constitute an independent standard for judging" design defects, "may substantially influence or even be ultimately determinative on risk-utility balancing," because they relate to foreseeability and frequency of the risks of harm. RESTATEMENT OF PRODUCTS LIABILITY § 2(b), cmts. d & g (1998). Does this preserve a useful role for both tests?

2.   **Using both tests for design defects.** Some jurisdictions use the consumer expectations and risk-utility balancing tests in combination, usually in the alternative, either leaving it to the parties' choice or choosing one or the other based on its suitability to the facts of the case. *See, e.g., Tincher v. Omega*

Flex, Inc., 104 A.3d 328 (Pa. 2014); *Soule v. Gen. Motors Corp.*, 882 P.2d 298 (Cal. 1994). The court in *Mikolajczyk v. Ford Motor Co.*, 901 N.E.2d 329 (Ill. 2008), said that where both parties argue a design-defect case based solely on consumer expectations, the jury should be instructed only on that test. However, "both the consumer-expectation test and the risk-utility test continue to have their place in the law of strict product liability based on design defect. Each party is entitled to choose its own method of proof, to present relevant evidence, and to request a corresponding jury instruction. If the evidence is sufficient to implicate the risk-utility test, the broader test, which incorporates the factor of consumer expectations, is to be applied by the finder of fact."

Would the flip-side work, as well? In other words, would it be possible to amalgamate the two tests by saying that consumer expectations is the test, but what a consumer expects is affected by the balance of risks and utilities? *McCathern v. Toyota Motor Corp.*, 23 P.3d 320 (Or. 2001). *See also Izzarelli v. R.J. Reynolds Tobacco Co.*, 136 A.3d 1232 (Conn. 2016) (applying its "modified consumer expectation test," under which "the jury would weigh the product's risks and utility and then inquire, in light of those factors, whether a reasonable consumer would consider the product design unreasonably dangerous").

3. **Negligence disguised as "strict liability"?** Where the consumer expectations test is discarded and the risk-utility test is adopted to control liability for design defects, does all this sound like *Carroll Towing* and thus like a regular negligence analysis? Sometimes courts have tried to distinguish risk-utility balancing on a negligence theory from the same balancing in strict liability cases by saying negligence is about conduct of the manufacturer, while strict products liability is about the defectiveness of the product itself. *E.g., Dart v. Wiebe Mfg., Inc.*, 709 P.2d 876 (Ariz. 1985). Yet behind every product's quality or lack of quality is the defendant's conduct. Is the distinction therefore illusory?

4. **"Negligent design" theory.** As Judge Posner put it in *Mesman v. Crane Pro Services*, 409 F.3d 846 (7th Cir. 2005), "*Expressly* requiring proof of negligence in a design-defect case, as Indiana law does, though unusual really isn't much of a legal innovation, since 'defect' always implied something that should not have been allowed into the product—something, in other words, that could have been removed at a reasonable cost in light of the risk that it created." A number of states allow a plaintiff to proceed on a "negligent design" theory, which requires proof of the same elements as any other negligence case. In *Reis v. Volvo Cars of North America*, 18 N.E.3d 383 (N.Y. 2014), the court said that in such cases, the reasonable-person standard "has been given more specific form: the question is whether the product is one as to which if the design defect were known at the time of manufacture, a reasonable person would conclude that the utility of the product did not outweigh the risk inherent" in marketing the product with that defect. *See also 5 Star, Inc. v. Ford Motor Co.*, 759 S.E.2d 139 (S.C. 2014) (plaintiff must establish that defendant failed to exercise due care in designing the product, based on what

the defendant knew or should have known at the time of manufacture; plaintiff must present evidence of a reasonable alternative design).

BARKER V. LULL ENGINEERING CO., 573 P.2d 443 (Cal. 1978). Plaintiff, an inexperienced operator of a high-lift industrial loader, lifted a load of lumber 10–18 feet off the ground. The ground was uneven and the loader began to vibrate as if it were about to tip over. Responding to warning shouts of fellow workers, the plaintiff scrambled out of the loader. He was hit and seriously injured by lumber falling from the load. The loader had no protective canopy and no outriggers to steady it. "We hold . . . that a product is defective in design (1) if the plaintiff demonstrates that the product failed to perform as safely as an ordinary consumer would expect when used in an intended or reasonably foreseeable manner or (2) if the plaintiff proves that the product's design proximately caused his injury and the defendant fails to prove . . . that on balance the benefits of the challenged design outweigh the risk of danger inherent in such design."

NOTES

1. **Burden-shifting.** Notice that *Barker* shifts the burden of proof to the defendant to justify its design by pointing to a suitable risk-utility balance. Only a few courts have embraced this burden-shifting idea. *See Quilez-Velar v. Ox Bodies, Inc.*, 823 F.3d 712 (1st Cir. 2016) (Puerto Rico law); *Shanks v. Upjohn Co.*, 835 P.2d 1189 (Alaska 1992). The shift occurs quite easily; all the plaintiff must do is prove that the design caused the harm. The burden of justifying the product's design then falls on the defendant. *See Mikolajczyk v. Ford Motor Co.*, 901 N.E.2d 329 (Ill. 2008) (expressly adopting *Barker*'s burden shift). If the defendant fails to prove that the benefits of the design outweigh the risks of the design, the plaintiff will prevail. How does *this* differ from the usual negligence case?

2. **Applying *Barker*.** In *Campbell v. General Motors Corp.*, 649 P.2d 224 (Cal. 1982), the plaintiff was a 62-year-old woman who was injured when thrown from her seat while riding on a city bus. She was sitting in the forward-most front-facing seat. The seats immediately behind the plaintiff had grab bars on them, so that if she had sat in one of them, she would have had something to hold onto. There was also a vertical bar in the aisle in front of the side seat immediately in front of the plaintiff, but she could not reach it from her own seat. After she settled with the city, she sued the manufacturer of the bus. *Held*, it can be fairly inferred that the design of the bus "caused" the injury, thus she prevails under the second test in *Barker*. Would this proof suffice in an ordinary negligence case, do you think?

3. **Limiting *Barker*'s application.** Strict liability under the consumer expectations test will not always be available under *Barker*, because California plaintiffs can choose the consumer expectations test only where the ordinary consumer, based on "everyday experience," could determine how safely a

product would have performed in the injury-causing event that occurred. *Soule v. Gen. Motors Corp.*, 882 P.2d 298 (Cal. 1994). The key factor is not the product's complexity, but whether "in the context of the facts and circumstances of its failure, the product is one about which the ordinary consumers can form minimum safety expectations." *McCabe v. Am. Honda Motor Co.*, 123 Cal. Rptr.2d 303 (Ct. App. 2002) (plaintiff allowed to proceed on consumer expectations test in case of non-deploying air bag); *see also Romine v. Johnson Controls, Inc.*, 169 Cal. Rptr.3d 208 (Ct. App. 2014) (consumer expectations test used in a case where vehicle driver's seat collapsed rearward in rear-end collision). Illinois, which also follows the *Barker* model, has said that "Nothing in our past decisions, even when we have applied the risk-utility test, has signaled a rejection of the consumer-expectation test merely because a complex product was involved." *Mikolajczyk, supra* Note 1. Are you troubled by allowing a jury to assess the defectiveness of a complex design using the consumer expectations test? The court in *Show v. Ford Motor Co.*, 659 F.3d 584 (7th Cir. 2011), held that a plaintiff was required under Illinois law to present expert evidence on the issue of defectiveness even when relying on the consumer expectations test. Does that solve the problem?

GENIE INDUSTRIES, INC. V. MATAK
462 S.W.3d 1 (Tex. 2015)

CHIEF JUSTICE HECHT delivered the opinion of the Court. . . .

[A product manufacturer is not liable for a design defect unless a safer alternative design exists and the defect renders the product unreasonably dangerous—that is, its risks outweigh its utility] . . .

[Genie Industries manufactures and sells aerial lifts throughout the world. An aerial lift is used to raise a worker on a platform to reach the ceilings of tall buildings or other high places. One of these lifts is the AWP–40S. The Cathedral in the Pines Church owns an AWP–40S, which it uses to reach the ceilings in its buildings. Matak and Boggan, employees of Gulf Coast Electric, were hired to run fiber optic cable in the ceiling at a church. They were safely using the church's lift to do the job when a church employee watching them suggested that rather than lowering the platform and having the man on the platform get off each time the lift needed to be moved, that they raise the stabilizing jacks, roll the lift to the new location, and then lower the jacks again, leaving the man at the top of the lift, fully extended, the entire time. One Gulf Coast worker expressed reservations about this method, but the church employee reassured him that it was safe. A sign on the machine itself displays an image of a man pushing the lift while elevated, with the text, "DANGER: Tip-over hazard. Attempting to move the machine with the platform raised will tip the machine over and cause death or serious injury." That is what happened; on the first attempt at moving the lift fully extended, it suddenly tipped over and crashed to the ground.]

Matak died of massive injuries to his head, and this action for wrongful death and survivor damages ensued. [The jury found for the plaintiff, and apportioned responsibility 55% to Genie, 20% to the Church, 20% to Gulf Coast, and 5% to Matak.] The trial court rendered judgment on the verdict, and Genie appealed. The court of appeals affirmed, holding that there was legally sufficient evidence to support the jury's design defect finding. We granted Genie's petition for review. . . .

[Safer alternative design]

. . . [The plaintiffs' evidence of a safer alternative design for the AWP–40S came from two sources.] Ken Zimmer, an expert on aerial lift design and manufacture, testified to three alternative designs, referred to as the "automatic drop-down" design, the "pothole protection" design, and the "chain and padlock" design. A fourth design—the "block" design—was suggested by Matak's attorney during direct examination of Genie's expert, Rick Curtin. . . .

Zimmer's automatic drop-down design idea is fairly simple. . . . Releasing an outrigger would trigger an alarm and automatically begin lowering the platform at one foot per second, reducing the height from which a worker would fall if the lift still tipped over. Zimmer testified that the design would have saved Matak's life. But nothing in the record indicates that the automatic drop-down design could have stabilized the lift or would have lowered the platform enough to prevent Matak's fall and serious injuries. Zimmer, himself, acknowledged that falls from 10 or 15 feet could be fatal, and the record, read generously, does not indicate that the platform could have reached a lower height. . . . But an even greater problem is the added danger that this design would cause. There was evidence that a sudden, unexpected movement of the platform could startle a worker, creating an even more dangerous situation when working with live electrical wires or leaving the worker hanging onto ceiling rafters as the platform suddenly descended. Even if the design could have prevented some or all of Matak's injuries, it could just as well have increased the risks of injury to himself and others.

Zimmer's pothole protection design would simply incorporate into the AWP–40S a feature on many mobile lifts. When a mobile lift is raised beyond a certain height, small stabilization bars—also called outriggers—automatically deploy from the vehicle, not all the way to the ground, but hovering just above it to reduce the machine's ground clearance. . . . If the modified pothole technology were incorporated to Genie's lift, the existing outriggers would need to be permanently attached to the lift so that they could be mechanized. Permanent attachment and mechanization would presumably add to the lift's weight and size, thereby diminishing one of the lift's key utility factors—its versatility. Furthermore, this design would still require that the user manually lower the leveling jacks for the lift to operate safely. . . . Zimmer's conclusion that the design would have been safer for Matak has little support in the evidence, and there is no evidence the design would be safer in other circumstances.

Zimmer's chain and padlock design was the simplest of all: the leveling jack handles would be chained and padlocked, and the key held by the worker on the platform, preventing the outriggers from being raised while the lift is extended. The obvious flaw in the design is that it would do little to prevent misuse. The key could simply be left with the person on the ground, or even thrown down to him by the worker on the platform. It cannot be imagined that users intent on disregarding multiple, plain, obvious warnings of danger would be stymied by the need for a key. Indeed, it is hard to imagine why users seeking to avoid the inconvenience of lowering the platform to move the lift would accept the inconvenience of chaining and locking the jack handles every time the outriggers were set.

Matak's counsel himself suggested a fourth design during his examination of Genie's expert: two of the lift's four wheels would be replaced by a block so that the lift could not be moved without tilting it back on its two wheels, and off its block, to roll the machine like a loaded dolly or a two-wheeled cart. This design would not directly ensure the proper deployment of the outriggers, but the obvious necessity of tilting the machine to move it would discourage attempts to move the machine while its platform was elevated. . . . While a two-wheel design would make it impossible to move a lift with the platform raised, a two-wheeled lift would also be much harder to move than a machine on four wheels. . . . If every move required putting a machine in that mode, every move would become that much more difficult. The impact of this design would be felt in the utility of the machine.

To impose liability on Genie, the plaintiffs must have presented evidence of an alternative design that (1) would have been safer for Matak and prevented or significantly reduced his risk of injury, (2) would not have been less safe in other circumstances and increased the risks to other users, (3) would not have substantially impaired the lift's utility, and (4) was economically and technologically feasible at the time. Genie argues that there was no evidence to support a design of this kind. We disagree. The evidence of a safer alternative design is weak, but we cannot say that it is less than a scintilla. Accordingly, we turn to Genie's second argument, that there is no evidence the AWP–40S is unreasonably dangerous.

[Risk-utility balancing]

Whether a defective design renders a product unreasonably dangerous depends on whether the product's risks outweigh its utility. . . . This balancing is for the jury unless the evidence allows but one reasonable conclusion. . . .

In the case before us, the evidence of the AWP–40S's utility is undisputed. The lift is designed to be small, lightweight, portable, and relatively inexpensive. To accommodate a wide variety of working environments, the lift uses outriggers with manual leveling jacks to stabilize the lift once it is positioned. This allows the lift to be used on surfaces that are not completely flat, such as the gradually sloped floor in this case, without having to sacrifice stability. Furthermore, the lift is designed so that the outriggers are removable in order to keep the lift as narrow as possible when being moved. This allows the AWP–40S to fit through standard door frames, therein expanding the range of uses for the machine. As previously explained, the lift also incorporates a mechanical interlock to make sure that all four outriggers are installed and the leveling jacks are firmly pressed against a given workspace. Until the outriggers are properly set, the lift cannot be operated. This maximizes the utility of the lift while still ensuring that it is used safely.

The risk is that a user will ignore the instructions in the user manual, the signs on the lift itself, and the danger, obvious to even a casual observer, that the lift will tip if the outriggers are removed when a person is on a fully elevated platform. So obvious is the risk of danger from misuse of the lift that the evidence does not reflect a single other accident involving a fully extended 40' lift. . . . The undisputed evidence is that Genie has sold more than 100,000 AWP model lifts all over the world, which have been used millions of times. But the record does not reflect a single misuse as egregious as that in this case.

The five factors to be considered in determining whether a product's risk outweighs its utility . . . conclusively establish that the AWP–40S is not, on this record, unreasonably dangerous. The first is whether the gravity and likelihood of injury outweighs the lift's utility. While misuse of the lift can result in the most serious injury, as this case illustrates, the likelihood of its occurrence is all but nonexistent. . . . [T]he danger was patent. The second factor asks whether there is a substitute that would meet the same need and not be unsafe or unreasonably expensive. There is no evidence of one. The third factor is whether there is a safer alternative design. As we have already explained at length, there is only slight evidence of such a design. The fourth factor is whether the danger of misuse is obvious and readily avoidable. The risk of tip-over is both. . . . The last factor considers ordinary consumers' expectations. Again, the danger of misuse is obvious, even to someone not trained in handling the AWP–40S. These factors require the conclusion that the AWP–40S is not unreasonably dangerous. . . .

[Accordingly, we reverse the judgment of the court of appeals and render judgment for Petitioner.]

[Dissenting judges argued that because there was "some evidence" in the record to support the jury verdict, the court should have affirmed.]

NOTES

1. **Reasonable alternative design ("RAD").** "Throughout the twentieth century, the great majority of design defect cases have involved proof by the plaintiff of a feasible alternative design—proof of some practicable, cost-effective, untaken design precaution that would have prevented the plaintiff's harm." DAVID G. OWEN, PRODUCTS LIABILITY LAW § 8.5, at 521 (2d ed. 2008). The Products Restatement says that a product is defective in design when the seller could have reduced or avoided the product's "foreseeable risks of harm" by "the adoption of a reasonable alternative design, and the omission of the alternative design renders the product not reasonably safe." RESTATEMENT OF PRODUCTS LIABILITY § 2 (1998). In other words, the Products Restatement requires RAD proof, with only very narrow exceptions. Does the *Genie Industries* court agree?

2. **Rejecting the RAD requirement.** Some courts have soundly rejected the Restatement Third's approach, and along with it, any requirement of proof of a reasonable alternative design. *See Aubin v. Union Carbide Corp.*, 177 So.3d 489 (Fla. 2015) (expressly rejected the Third Restatement on the ground that its test improperly "reintroduces principles of negligence into strict liability," and is insufficiently protective of plaintiffs). Logically, the consumer expectations test includes no requirement of RAD proof, so courts that reject risk-utility balancing generally also reject a RAD requirement. *See Delaney v. Deere & Co.*, 999 P.2d 930 (Kan. 2000); *Green v. Smith & Nephew AHP, Inc.* 629 N.W.2d 727 (Wis. 2001). Of course, that such proof is not *required* does not mean that it is not offered in many cases; certainly if the existence of RAD is a factor in a multi-part test, as in a number of states, it remains an important piece of evidence. Why would a plaintiff want to introduce evidence of RAD, regardless of the legal test used in the case? *See Tincher v. Omega Flex, Inc.*, 104 A.3d 328 (Pa. 2014).

3. **What is an "alternative" design?** A most intriguing question arises when you try to figure out what counts as an "alternative" design. Suppose there are three drugs on the market that, by different chemical formulas, help avoid some painful symptom like heartburn or rashes. All do the job, although by different means. The defendant manufactures a fourth drug, based on still a fourth formula. The defendant's drug, however, has serious side effects for a substantial number of people. Should the existing drugs be considered as alternatives, on the ground that they have the same end function? Or should they NOT be considered as alternatives on the ground that, whatever their function, their chemical formulas are widely different?

The Products Restatement poses a different set of facts for this problem. It supposes that the defendant manufactures a toy gun that shoots hard pellets at high velocity, presumably very dangerous to those who might be in close range of a child playing with the toy. The defendant could have manufactured a toy gun that is not harmful, say one that fires soft gelatin pellets or ping pong balls. Would a ping-pong-ball gun be an alternative for the hard-pellet gun? It depends how you characterize the product. If you think the product is "toy guns capable of doing injury," the ping-pong-ball gun will not be an alternative. You might think the pellet gun was defective because it should not be marketed at all, but you would not think it defective because it fails to achieve the safety of a ping-pong-ball gun. *See* RESTATEMENT OF PRODUCTS LIABILITY § 2, cmt. e (1998).

4. **When is an alternative design "reasonable?"** A number of courts have held that a plaintiff has proved the existence of a reasonable alternative design by adducing expert testimony that a specific improvement is safer and would not impair the product's usefulness or impose unreasonable costs. *See* DOBBS, HAYDEN & BUBLICK, HORNBOOK ON TORTS § 33.11, at 822 (2d ed. 2016).

Both technological and economic feasibility are also important components of plaintiff's RAD proof. In *Honda of America Mfg., Inc. v. Norman*, 104 S.W.3d 600 (Tex. Ct. App. 2003), survivors of Karen Norman, a motorist who drowned when the automatic seatbelt in her car malfunctioned and trapped her in her car, sued the car's manufacturer on a design-defect theory. Plaintiffs' experts testified that there were three alternative seatbelt designs that Honda could have used: (a) incorporation of a timer on the seatbelt-release button; (b) relocation of the release button to hip level, as used in Toyota vehicles; and (c) use of two release buttons. Reversing a jury verdict for plaintiff, the court held that this testimony was insufficient to prove RAD. There was no testimony to suggest that the timer—alternative (a)—was feasible, or that it would be safer than the challenged design. With respect to proposed alternative (b), there was no proof that the design "would have prevented or significantly reduced the risk of Karen's death without imposing an equal or greater risk of harm under all relevant circumstances"; further, the mere fact that Toyota used that design did not prove that it was safer, or that it would be *economically* feasible for Honda to adopt it. And on alternative (c), the court said there was no proof that it was technologically feasible; one of plaintiffs' experts even testified that it was not.

5. **Applying the RAD test.** Suppose that an automobile passenger was injured when the car in which she was riding was struck from the side by another vehicle traveling at high speed. The passenger sues the manufacturer of the car in which she was riding, claiming that the car was defectively designed, in that the doors should have protected her in the crash. Could the car be made safer for passengers if it was reinforced throughout with steel, and resembled a U.S. Army tank? Of course. But would that be found to be a *reasonable* alternative design? Perhaps it would weigh 30 tons, require super-premium fuel, get laughably awful gas mileage, look ugly, and cost $350,000. How would the *Genie Industries* court analyze whether the "tank-car" design would be a reasonable alternative?

6. **Already-existing alternatives.** Perhaps the clearest evidence of a reasonable alternative design is that similar products already on the market

have *safer* designs. RESTATEMENT OF PRODUCTS LIABILITY § 2, cmt. f (1998). However, mere proof that a competitor uses a *different* design does not by itself establish that the competitor's design is *safer* than the defendant's design, or that it would be economically feasible for the defendant to adopt it. *See Honda, supra* Note 4.

REFERENCES: DOBBS, HAYDEN & BUBLICK, HORNBOOK ON TORTS §§ 33.9–33.12 (2d ed. 2016); 2 DOBBS, HAYDEN & BUBLICK, THE LAW OF TORTS §§ 456–462 (2d ed. 2011).

C. WARNING OR INFORMATION DEFECTS

LIRIANO V. HOBART CORP.

170 F.3d 264 (2d Cir. 1999)

CALABRESI, CIRCUIT JUDGE:

[Luis Liriano was severely injured on the job when his hand was caught in a meat grinder manufactured by Hobart Corporation and owned by his employer, Super Associated. The meat grinder had been sold to Super with a safety guard, but the safety guard was removed while the machine was in Super's possession and was not on the meat grinder at the time of the accident. The machine bore no warning indicating that the grinder should be operated only with a safety guard attached.]

[Liriano sued Hobart, who brought a third-party claim against Super. The only claim that went to the jury was Liriano's failure to warn claim. The jury found for Liriano, attributing a degree responsibility to all three parties. Hobart and Super appealed, arguing (1) that there was no duty to warn, and (2) that even if there had been a duty to warn, the evidence presented was not sufficient to allow the failure-to-warn claim to reach the jury. The federal court certified both questions to the New York Court of Appeals, which rejected appellants' first argument but declined to address the second, leaving it for this court.]

More than a hundred years ago, a Boston woman named Maria Wirth profited from an argument about obviousness as a matter of law that is very similar to the one Hobart urges today. See Lorenzo v. Wirth, 170 Mass. 596, 49 N.E. 1010 (1898). Wirth was the owner of a house on whose property there was a coal hole. The hole abutted the street in front of the house, and casual observers would have no way of knowing that the area around the hole was not part of the public thoroughfare. A pedestrian called Lorenzo fell into the coal hole and sued for her injuries. Writing for a majority of the Supreme Judicial Court of Massachusetts, Oliver Wendell Holmes, Jr., held for the defendant. He noted that, at the time of the accident, there had been a heap of coal on the street next to the coal hole, and he argued that such a pile provided sufficient warning to passers-by that they were in the presence of an open hole. "A heap of coal on a sidewalk in Boston is an indication, according to common experience, that there very possibly may be a coal hole to receive it." And that was that.

It was true, Holmes acknowledged, that "blind men, and foreigners unused to our ways, have a right to walk in the streets," and that such people might not benefit from the warning that piles of coal provided to sighted Bostonians. But Holmes wrote that coal-hole cases were simple, common, and likely to be oft repeated, and he believed it would be better to establish a clear rule than to invite fact-specific inquiries in every such case. "In simple cases of this sort," he explained, "courts have felt able to determine what, in every case, however complex, defendants are bound at their peril to know." With the facts so limited, this was an uncomplicated case in which the defendant could, as a matter of law, rely on the plaintiff's responsibility to know what danger she faced.

Justice Knowlton disagreed. His opinion delved farther into the particular circumstances than did Holmes's opinion for the majority. In so doing, he showed that Lorenzo's failure to appreciate her peril might have been foreseen by Wirth and hence that Wirth's failure to warn might constitute negligence. He noted, for example, that the accident occurred after nightfall, when Lorenzo perhaps could not see, or recognize, the heap of coal for what it was. There was "a throng of persons" on the street, such that it would have been difficult even in daylight to see very far ahead of where one was walking. And the plaintiff was, in fact, a foreigner unused to Boston's ways. "[S]he had just come from Spain, and had never seen coal put into a cellar through a coal hole." In sum, the case was not the "simple" one that Holmes had made it out to be. What is more, none of the facts he recited was either unusual or unforeseeable by Wirth. "What kind of conduct is required under complex conditions, to reach the usual standard of due care, namely, the ordinary care of persons of common prudence, is a question of fact. . . . [and thus] a question for a jury." Even cases involving "obvious" dangers like coal holes, Knowlton believed, might not be resolvable as matters of law when viewed in the fullness of circumstances that rendered the issue less clear than it would be when posed in the abstract.

Holmes commanded the majority of the Supreme Judicial Court in 1898, but Knowlton's position has prevailed in the court of legal history. " '[T]he so-called Holmes view—that standards of conduct ought increasingly to be fixed by the court for the sake of certainty—has been largely rejected. . . . [The tendency has been away from fixed standards and towards enlarging the sphere of the jury.' " Fowler V. Harper, Fleming James, Jr., & Oscar S. Gray, The Law of Torts § 15.3, at 358–59 n. 16 (2d ed. 1986).

The courts of New York have several times endorsed Knowlton's approach and ruled that judges should be very wary of taking the issue of liability away from juries, even in situations where the relevant dangers might seem obvious. . . . [Even so] there have been situations in which New York state courts have deemed dangers to be sufficiently clear so that warnings were, as a matter of law, not necessary. See, e.g., . . . Caris v. Mele, 134 A.D.2d 475, 476, 521 N.Y.S.2d 260, 261 (1987) (holding that there is no duty to warn of the danger of diving headfirst into an above-ground swimming pool only four feet deep).

. . . Liriano was only seventeen years old at the time of his injury and had only recently immigrated to the United States. He had been on the job at Super for only one week. He had never been given instructions about how to use the meat grinder, and he had used the meat grinder only two or three times. And . . . the mechanism that injured Liriano would not have been visible to someone who was operating the grinder. It could be argued that such a combination of facts was not so unlikely that a court should say, as a matter of law, that the defendant could not have foreseen them or, if aware of them, need not have guarded against them by issuing a warning. . . .

Nevertheless, it remains the fact that meat grinders are widely known to be dangerous. . . . [W]e might well be of two minds as to whether a failure to warn that meat grinders are dangerous would be enough to raise a jury issue.

But to state the issue that way would be to misunderstand the complex functions of warnings. As two distinguished torts scholars have pointed out, a warning can do more than exhort its audience to be careful. It can also affect what activities the people warned choose to engage in. See James A. Henderson, Jr., and Aaron D. Twerski, Doctrinal Collapse in Products Liability: The Empty Shell of Failure to Warn, 65 N.Y.U. L.Rev. 265, 285 (1990). And where the function of a warning is to assist the reader in making choices, the value of the warning can lie as much in making known the existence of alternatives as in communicating the fact that a particular choice is dangerous. It follows that the duty to warn is not necessarily obviated merely because a danger is clear.

To be more concrete, a warning can convey at least two types of messages. One states that a particular place, object, or activity is dangerous. Another explains that people need not risk the danger posed by such a place, object, or activity in order to achieve the purpose for which they might have taken that risk. Thus, a highway sign that says "Danger— Steep Grade" says less than a sign that says "Steep Grade Ahead—Follow Suggested Detour to Avoid Dangerous Areas."

If the hills or mountains responsible for the steep grade are plainly visible, the first sign merely states what a reasonable person would know without having to be warned. The second sign tells drivers what they might not have otherwise known: that there is another road that is flatter and less hazardous. A driver who believes the road through the mountainous area to be the only way to reach her destination might well choose to drive on that road despite the steep grades, but a driver who knows herself to have an alternative might not, even though her understanding of the risks posed by the steep grade is exactly the same as those of the first driver. Accordingly, a certain level of obviousness as to the grade of a road might, in principle, eliminate the reason for posting a sign of the first variety. But no matter how patently steep the road, the second kind of sign might still have a beneficial effect. As a result, the duty to post a sign of the second variety may persist even when the danger of the road is obvious and a sign of the first type would not be warranted.

One who grinds meat, like one who drives on a steep road, can benefit not only from being told that his activity is dangerous but from being told of a safer way. . . . Given that attaching guards is feasible, does reasonable care require that meat workers be informed that they need not accept the risks of using unguarded grinders? Even if most ordinary users may—as a matter of law—know of the risk of using a guardless meat grinder, it does not follow that a sufficient number of them will—as a matter of law—also know that protective guards are available, that using them is a realistic possibility, and that they may ask that such guards be used. It is precisely these last pieces of information that a reasonable manufacturer may have a duty to convey even if the danger of using a grinder were itself deemed obvious.

. . . A jury could reasonably find that there exist people who are employed as meat grinders and who do not know (a) that it is feasible to reduce the risk with safety guards, (b) that such guards are made available with the grinders, and (c) that the grinders should be used only with the guards. Moreover, a jury can also reasonably find that there are enough such people, and that warning them is sufficiently inexpensive, that a reasonable manufacturer would inform them that safety guards exist and that the grinder is meant to be used only with such guards. Thus, even if New York would consider the danger of meat grinders to be obvious as a matter of law, that obviousness does not substitute for the warning. . . .

Hobart [also] raises the issue of causation. It maintains that Liriano "failed to present any evidence that Hobart's failure to place a warning [on the machine] was causally related to his injury." Whether or not there had been a warning, Hobart says, Liriano might well have operated the machine as he did and suffered the injuries that he suffered. Liriano introduced no evidence, Hobart notes, suggesting either that he would have refused to grind meat had the machine borne a warning or that a warning would have persuaded Super not to direct its employees to use the grinder without the safety attachment.

[Hobart's argument] assumes that the burden was on Liriano to introduce additional evidence showing that the failure to warn was a but-for cause of his injury. . . . But Liriano does not bear that burden. When a defendant's negligent act is deemed wrongful precisely because it has a strong propensity to cause the type of injury that ensued, that very causal tendency is evidence enough to establish a prima facie case of cause-in-fact. The burden then shifts to the defendant to come forward with evidence that its negligence was not such a but-for cause.

We know, as a general matter, that the kind of negligence that the jury attributed to the defendant tends to cause exactly the kind of injury that the plaintiff suffered. . . . In such situations, rather than requiring the plaintiff to bring in more evidence to demonstrate that his case is of the ordinary kind, the law presumes normality and requires the defendant to adduce evidence that the case is an exception. Accordingly, in a case like this, it is up to the defendant to bring in evidence tending to rebut the strong inference, arising from the accident, that the defendant's negligence was in fact a but-for cause of the plaintiff's injury.

This shifting of the onus procedendi has long been established in New York. Its classic statement was made more than seventy years ago, when the Court of Appeals decided a case in which a car collided with a buggy driving after sundown without lights. See Martin v. Herzog, 228 N.Y. 164, 170, 126 N.E. 814, 816 (1920). The driver of the buggy argued that his negligence in driving without lights had not been shown to be the cause-in-fact of the accident. Writing for the Court, Judge Cardozo reasoned that the legislature deemed driving without lights after sundown to be negligent precisely because not using lights tended to cause accidents of the sort that had occurred in the case. The simple fact of an accident under those conditions, he said, was enough to support the inference of but-for causal connection between the negligence and the particular accident. . . .

The words that Judge Cardozo applied to the buggy's failure to use lights are equally applicable to Hobart's failure to warn: "If nothing else is shown to break the connection, we have a case, prima facie sufficient, of negligence contributing to the result." . . . See Guido Calabresi, Concerning Cause and the Law of Torts: An Essay for Harry Kalven, Jr., 43 U. Chi. L.Rev. 69 (1975).

. . . The district court did not err. We affirm its decision in all respects.

[Concurring opinion omitted.]

NOTES

The Duty to Provide Information

1. **Information defects.** As indicated in *Liriano*, a manufacturer's failure to provide appropriate information about a product may make an

otherwise safe product dangerous and defective. Warnings about dangers represent one important kind of information necessary for some products. Thus, a product becomes defective when the product's foreseeable risks of harm could have been reduced or avoided by the provision of a reasonable warning, and the omission of such a warning renders the product "not reasonably safe." RESTATEMENT OF PRODUCTS LIABILITY § 2(c) (1998).

2.   **Functions of product information.** Necessary information to make a product reasonably safe may include directions for use, warnings, or some combination. Warnings may be needed either to alert users to risks that are not obvious, or to inform users of safer alternatives. *See* 2 DOBBS, HAYDEN & BUBLICK, THE LAW OF TORTS § 464 (2011).

Obvious Dangers

3.   **Warning of obvious dangers.** Because the cost of giving a warning is usually rather small, it may be easy to conclude that the risk-utility balance always calls for a warning. Even so, some warnings simply are not needed. Should a manufacturer of safety glasses warn that they will break under the force of a five-pound sledge-hammer dropped from a height of seven feet? *Amer. Optical Co. v. Weidenhamer*, 457 N.E.2d 181 (Ind. 1983). Should a pickup truck manufacturer be required to warn of the risks of riding unrestrained in the open cargo bed? *Josue v. Isuzu Motors Amer., Inc.*, 958 P.2d 535 (Haw. 1998). Should a BB gun manufacturer warn users that the gun could kill someone shot from close range? *Abney v. Crosman Corp.*, 919 So.2d 289 (Ala. 2005). Are consumers more likely to read a few important warnings, or a long list including warnings about trivial risks?

As the Restatement Third has it, "no duty exists" to warn of dangers that are obvious or should be obvious. RESTATEMENT OF PRODUCTS LIABILITY § 2, cmt. j (1998). Is this merely the logical outcome of risk-utility balancing? And isn't it even more clearly dictated by a consumer expectations test? *See Braswell v. Cincinnati Inc.*, 731 F.3d 1081 (10th Cir. 2013). Some states have codified a no-duty rule. *See, e.g.*, MICH.C.L. § 600.2948(2).

4.   **Obvious dangers and comparative fault.** Distinguish the no-duty rule from defenses based upon obvious danger. If the plaintiff is or should be actually aware of the specific danger and its magnitude, the defendant might avoid or limit liability under assumed risk or comparative negligence rules. See § 3, *infra*. Courts sometimes conflate the plaintiff-fault issue with the defendant-duty issue. In addition, courts may throw in proximate cause and "misuse" into the discussion. The straightforward explanation for most obvious danger problems, however, is simply that if the danger is foreseeably obvious in a significant degree, then the product is not defective at all for lack of a warning.

5.   **Obvious dangers and design defects.** A product that presents an obvious danger, and thus provides its own warning, may still be defectively designed. Diving into a pool of unknown depth is obviously dangerous, so no warning for that is required. However, if the manufacturer should foresee that

harm will befall users in spite of the obvious danger, the manufacturer may be liable for design defect if it could easily mark the depth and failed to do so.

6. **Obvious dangers and consumer expectations.** If the danger is truly obvious, the product could seldom be defective under the consumer expectations test, since the consumer could not expect safety in the face of obvious danger. What would the plaintiff's attorney argue in such a case? *See also Tabieros v. Clark Equip. Co.*, 944 P.2d 1279 (Haw. 1997) (open and obvious danger may prevent liability for failure to warn under consumer expectations test, but not necessarily under a risk-utility test).

Causation

7. **The "heeding presumption."** Suppose the plaintiff proves that the defendant failed to give a warning that was needed to make the product safe and that a safe warning would have been on the label of the product or on instructions accompanying it. Most case law says that unless the plaintiff would have read, understood and heeded the warning, the failure to warn cannot be a cause of the harm. But courts usually "presume" that the plaintiff would have read and heeded the warning, a phenomenon known as the "heeding presumption." *See, e.g., Moore v. Ford Motor Co.*, 332 S.W.3d 749 (Mo. 2011). This presumption is rebuttable by the defendant.

What result if the plaintiff admits that he did not read any of a product's accompanying instructions or warnings? *See Kirkbride v. Terex USA, LLC*, 798 F.3d 1343 (10th Cir. 2015) (when asked if he had read the safety manual for the front-loader on which he was injured, plaintiff responded, "Why would you read a manual?"); *see also Karst v. Shur-Co.*, 878 N.W.2d 604 (S.D. 2016).

CARRUTH V. PITTWAY CORP., 643 So. 2d 1340 (Ala. 1994). Seven family members were killed in a house fire. Their estates sued Pittway, a smoke-detector manufacturer, claiming that the deaths were caused by its negligence in providing insufficient installation instructions and warnings. Just two days before the fire, the victims' father had installed the smoke detector near a ceiling-wall junction. The device was accompanied by a seven-page pamphlet, set in small type. The pamphlet stated: "Dead air spaces are often . . . in the corners between ceilings and walls. Dead air may prevent smoke from reaching a detector." None of these statements was captioned by the words "warning," "caution," or "danger," as were other cautionary statements. The "dead air" statements were contained in a portion of the pamphlet that included numerous instructions and illustrations that together "could be viewed as confusing at best." A colored and highly visible diagram purported to show effective smoke detector locations, including the area immediately below a wall-ceiling junction. Ultimately, "from the pamphlet's format and print size, and the seemingly sufficient diagram on the box, a fair-minded person could reasonably infer that a user would be induced to only scan the pamphlet and thereby not get from the pamphlet the information about dead-air-space." A jury question was thus presented "as to whether the Pittway pamphlet provided a legally adequate warning about dead-air-space concerns."

NOTES

1. **Content or expression.** Warnings must be reasonably clear, and of sufficient force and intensity to convey the nature and extent of the risks to a reasonable person. "A manufacturer's techniques in promoting the product, inconsistencies or undue qualifications in stating the warning or directions, and depictions of uses that run counter to warnings may each nullify or dilute the warnings provided in printed literature. . . . When possible harm is severe, quite specific information may be required. A drug warning about possible blood clotting may disguise rather than reveal the possibility of a stroke." 2 DOBBS, HAYDEN & BUBLICK, THE LAW OF TORTS § 465 (2d ed. 2011).

2. **Form and location.** Placing a warning directly on a product can be effective, but a reasonable warning may be provided even in advertisements, posters or media releases; it is up to the jury to decide whether on the facts presented the warning's placement is reasonable. *See Patch v. Hillerich & Bradsby Co.,* 257 P.3d 383 (Mont. 2011). Can a warning be defective because it is in a form or location where it is not likely to be read? The father in *Carruth* admitted that he did not read the instruction pamphlet "in depth." Why wasn't this enough to support a summary judgment for the defense?

3. **Nature and seriousness of harm.** Sometimes the warning must not only alert the user to danger and how to avoid it but also to the extent of harm that can result. In *Pavlik v. Lane Ltd./Tobacco Exporters International,* 135 F.3d 876 (3d Cir. 1998), the estate of a man who died from self-administered butane inhalation sued the distributor, claiming that the single warning on the can ("DO NOT BREATHE SPRAY") was inadequate. The court left it to the trier to determine whether a more specific warning would have averted the harm. What might such a warning have said? In *Benjamin v. Wal-Mart Stores, Inc.,* 61 P.3d 257 (Or. Ct. App. 2002), a Coleman heater carried this: "WARNING: FOR OUTDOOR USE ONLY. Never use inside house, camper, tent, vehicle or other unventilated or enclosed areas." Deceased used it in his tent while camping; the heater depleted the oxygen and the user died as a result. Was the warning adequate?

4. **Language of the warning.** If the warning must be reasonably clear, should it be presented in any language besides English? *See Farias v. Mr. Heater, Inc.,* 684 F.3d 1231 (11th Cir. 2012). Suppose a manufacturer advertises in Spanish to buyers whose main or only language is Spanish. Should it even include symbols to help convey the message to non-readers? If a poison contains verbal warnings but no skull and crossbones or unhappy faces, is that adequate?

NOTE: LEARNED INTERMEDIARIES AND SOPHISTICATED USERS

1.   *Prescription drugs: The learned intermediary rule.* What warnings should accompany a prescription drug and to whom should the warnings be given? Most courts say the manufacturer must provide warnings only to the doctor who might prescribe, not directly to the patient. *See, e.g., Centocor, Inc. v. Hamilton*, 140 S.W.3d 140 (Tex. 2012) (recognizing only one state that has rejected the rule). When the manufacturer does in fact give appropriate warning or information to the physician, it is said that the physician is a "learned intermediary" upon whom the manufacturer can properly rely, and the warning can be couched in terms the physician can understand, not necessarily terms the consumer would grasp. And no warning at all is required if the physician already knows the danger.

2.   *The Products Restatement approach.* The Products Restatement provides that warnings about the health risks of prescription drugs and medical devices must be given directly to consumers only when the manufacturer knows or had reason to know that the learned intermediary "will not be in a position fo reduce the risks of harm in accordance with the instructions or warnings." RESTATEMENT OF PRODUCTS LIABILITY § 6(d) (1998). When might this occur? Comment e gives as an example the administration of mass inoculation, where health care providers are not in a position to evaluate individualized risks of the vaccine. Patients should be directly warned in that situation, if such warnings are feasible and would be effective.

3.   *Sophisticated users.* Similar rules apply to those who supply products to sophisticated users, meaning those users who are already aware or should be aware of the product's dangers, such as members of a trade or profession in which such knowledge is widespread. In such a case, the sophisticated users' knowledge of the product's dangers is the equivalent of prior notice. Is the "sophisticated user" rule merely a variant of the "open and obvious" rule? *See Webb v. Special Electric Co.*, 370 P.3d 1022 (Cal. 2016).

NOTE: POST-SALE WARNINGS

The Products Restatement provides that a seller or distributor is obliged to give a post-sale warning when a reasonable person would do so. A reasonable person would give such a warning if he knew or should know that the product poses a substantial risk of harm; those to whom a warning might be given can be identified and assumed to be unaware of the risk; a warning can be effectively communicated; and the risk of harm outweighs the burden of giving a warning. RESTATEMENT OF PRODUCTS LIABILITY § 10

(1998). The reasonable person standard means that a jury instruction on post-sale duty to warn should tell the jury to consider any factors that make it burdensome for the manufacturer to provide a warning. *Lovick v. Wil-Rich*, 588 N.W.2d 688 (Iowa 1999). Some courts, however, have firmly denied there is any post-sale duty at all, even to give a warning, where the product's defect was not known at the time of sale. *See, e.g., Jablonski v. Ford Motor Co.*, 955 N.E.2d 1138 (Ill. 2011).

In some situations, statutes or regulations may require post-sale warnings or repairs. Federal regulations set a number of standards for motor vehicles. If a manufacturer fails to comply with standards, the Secretary of Transportation may require the manufacturer to (a) give notice of the defect to purchasers and dealers and (b) to remedy the defect. 49 U.S.C.A. § 30118. The Consumer Products Safety Commission has the power to require a recall of dangerous products or to order their replacement. 15 U.S.C.A. § 2064 (d). The Products Restatement limits liability for failure to recall or repair to cases in which a recall obligation is imposed by statute or regulation or in which the manufacturer voluntarily undertakes a recall and fails to follow through in a reasonable way. RESTATEMENT OF PRODUCTS LIABILITY § 11 (1998).

> REFERENCES: DOBBS, HAYDEN & BUBLICK, HORNBOOK ON TORTS §§ 33.13–33.16 (2d ed. 2016); 2 DOBBS, HAYDEN & BUBLICK, THE LAW OF TORTS §§ 464–469 (2d ed. 2011).

§ 3. DEFENSES AND DEFEATS

A. COMPARATIVE FAULT AND ASSUMPTION OF RISK

BOWLING V. HEIL CO.
511 N.E.2d 373 (Ohio 1987)

HERBERT R. BROWN, JUSTICE.

[Heil manufactured a dump hoist system which was installed on a dump truck owned by Rogers. Brashear borrowed the truck for personal use. He and Bowling delivered gravel to Bowling's residence and dumped it, but the truck bed would not return to the down position after the load had been dumped. Bowling leaned underneath over the truck chassis to see what was wrong. This put him underneath the upraised truck bed. In this posture he grabbed the control lever on the pump valve assembly and manipulated it. The truck bed rapidly descended upon him, killing him instantly. Bowling sued Heil and various others involved in the hoist assembly and controls. The jury found that Bowling was guilty of contributory negligence but did not assume the risk of injury. Damages were assessed at $1.75 million. The trial court and the court of appeals treated Bowling's contributory negligence in different ways.]

... Currently, two affirmative defenses based upon a plaintiff's misconduct are recognized. First, an otherwise strictly liable defendant has a complete defense if the plaintiff voluntarily and knowingly assumed the risk occasioned by the defect. Second, such a defendant is also provided with a complete defense if the plaintiff misused the product in an unforeseeable manner. The court of appeals below, construing Comment n to Section 402A, attempted to distinguish between negligent "affirmative action" by a plaintiff and negligent passive conduct by him in failing either to discover a defect or to guard against the possibility of its existence. The court held that although a plaintiff's passive- contributory negligence provides no defense to a products liability action, his contributorily negligent "affirmative action" does provide a defense, and that such affirmative negligence should be compared by a jury to the fault of a strictly liable manufacturer of a defective product, in a manner similar to the principles of comparative negligence embodied in [the statute].

Comment n to Section 402A provides:

> "Contributory negligence. * * * Contributory negligence of the plaintiff is not a defense when such negligence consists merely in a failure to discover the defect in the product, or to guard against the possibility of its existence. On the other hand the form of contributory negligence which consists in voluntarily and unreasonably proceeding to encounter a known danger, and commonly passes under the name of assumption of risk, is a defense under this Section as in other cases of strict liability. If the user or consumer discovers the defect and is aware of the danger, and nevertheless proceeds unreasonably to make use of the product and is injured by it, he is barred from recovery."

The court of appeals has carved out a middle ground, to wit: contributory negligence consisting of "affirmative action," theoretically located between a plaintiff's failure to discover or guard against a defect and his voluntary assumption of a known risk. There is no such middle ground. Comment n covers the entire spectrum of conduct which can be termed "contributory negligence," as applicable to products liability actions. That spectrum begins with a mere failure to discover a defect in a product, continues with a failure to guard against the existence of a defect, and concludes with an assumption of the risk of a known defect. "Affirmative action" by the plaintiff is not left uncovered. Failure to guard against a defect can be "affirmative action." Indeed such would describe the conduct of David Bowling in this case.

Under Comment n, either a plaintiff's contributory negligence amounts to a voluntary assumption of a known risk, or it does not. If it does, then that conduct provides an otherwise strictly liable defendant with

[handwritten marginalia] the only affirmative defenses based on a P's conduct are 1) voluntarily and knowingly assumed the risk created by the product defect or

a complete defense. If it does not, the contributory negligence of the plaintiff provides no defense.

In the case sub judice, the jury found that Bowling was contributorily negligent but that he had not assumed a known risk. Therefore, his contributory negligence did not provide Heil with a defense to appellant's strict liability claim. . . .

The definitive statement of the policy and goals underlying the application of strict liability in tort to cases involving defective products is provided in Comment c to Section 402A, at 349–350:

"On whatever theory, the justification for the strict liability has been said to be that the seller, by marketing his product for use and consumption, has undertaken and assumed a special responsibility toward any member of the consuming public who may be injured by it; that the public has the right to and does expect, in the case of products which it needs and for which it is forced to rely upon the seller, that reputable sellers will stand behind their goods; that public policy demands that the burden of accidental injuries caused by products intended for consumption be placed upon those who market them, and be treated as a cost of production against which liability insurance can be obtained; and that the consumer of such products is entitled to the maximum of protection at the hands of someone, and the proper persons to afford it are those who market the products."

Dean Prosser has expressed this idea in slightly different terms:

"The costs of damaging events due to defectively dangerous products can best be borne by the enterprisers who make and sell these products. Those who are merchants and especially those engaged in the manufacturing enterprise have the capacity to distribute the losses of the few among the many who purchase the products. It is not a 'deep pocket' theory but rather a 'risk-bearing economic' theory. The assumption is that the manufacturer can shift the costs of accidents to purchasers for use by charging higher prices for the costs of products."

Prosser & Keeton, Law of Torts (5th Ed.1984) 692–693, Section 98.

Under negligence principles, on the other hand, liability is determined (and, under R.C. 2315.19, apportioned) according to fault. In negligence, we seek to make the person or persons responsible for causing a loss pay for it. In other words, we "blame" the loss on the negligent party or parties because it was they who could have avoided the loss by conforming to due care. Conversely, in strict liability in tort we hold the manufacturer or seller of a defective product responsible, not because it is "blameworthy," but because it is more able than the consumers to spread that loss among those who use and thereby benefit from the product.

We recognize that strict liability cannot be absolutely divorced from traditional concepts of fault. In a sense we "blame" the loss on the manufacturer or seller because it introduced the defective product into the marketplace. However, it must be reemphasized that strict liability is at odds with traditional notions of due care. . . .

Comparative negligence or comparative fault has been applied in products liability cases by a number of courts, both in states that have comparative negligence statutes and in states where comparative negligence was judicially adopted. On the other hand, numerous courts have refused to apply comparative negligence principles to products liability cases.

We believe that the better-reasoned decisions are those that decline to inject a plaintiff's negligence into the law of products liability. We agree with the court's holding in Kinard v. Coats Co., Inc. (1976), 37 Colo. App. 555, 557, 553 P.2d 835, 837, which states:

". . . Products liability under § 402A does not rest upon negligence principles, but rather is premised on the concept of enterprise liability for casting a defective product into the stream of commerce. * * * Thus, the focus is upon the nature of the product, and the consumer's reasonable expectations with regard to that product, rather than on the conduct either of the manufacturer or the person injured because of the product."

We agree with Justice Mosk of the California Supreme Court, who stated in his dissent in Daly v. General Motors Corp., supra:

"The defective product is comparable to a time bomb ready to explode; it maims its victims indiscriminately, the righteous and the evil, the careful and the careless. Thus when a faulty design or otherwise defective product is involved, the litigation should not be diverted to consideration of the negligence of the plaintiff. The liability issues are simple: was the product or its design faulty, did the defendant inject the defective product into the stream of commerce, and did the defect cause the injury? The conduct of the ultimate consumer-victim who used the product in the contemplated or foreseeable manner is wholly irrelevant to those issues."

Therefore, when we search the decisions from other jurisdictions, we find no rationale which persuades us that comparative negligence or comparative fault principles should be applied to products liability actions.

Based upon the foregoing analysis, we hold that principles of comparative negligence or comparative fault have no application to a products liability case based upon strict liability in tort. Strict liability, in focusing on the product rather than the conduct of its manufacturer or seller, does not seek to apportion a loss among all persons who have caused or contributed to it. Rather, it seeks to spread the loss among all users of the product. The concept of comparative fault is fundamentally inapplicable.

We therefore reverse the judgment of the court of appeals with respect to its reduction of appellant's verdict by the thirty percent found by the jury to be attributable to contributory negligence. . . .

[Concurring and dissenting opinions omitted.]

NOTES

1. **Comparative-fault reductions.** *Bowling* applies the traditional rule that some forms of contributory negligence of the plaintiff are not a defense to a strict liability claim. Some courts continue to hold these views. Most courts, however, apply comparative fault rules to strict products liability cases. *Daly v. General Motors Corp.*, 575 P.2d 1162 (Cal. 1978). The Products Restatement provides that whatever comparative responsibility system is used in a given state should apply to products liability claims as well. RESTATEMENT OF PRODUCTS LIABILITY § 17 (1998).

2. **Discovered vs. undiscovered defect.** Many states that do allow a contributory fault defense in products cases restrict that defense at times. In *Hernandez v. Barbo*, 957 P.2d 147 (Or. 1998), the plaintiff was a mechanic whose hand was partially amputated when it contacted a saw blade. He sued the saw's sellers and others, claiming that the product was defective because the on/off switch was inconspicuous. Defendants argued that the plaintiff was contributorily negligent. *Held*, a plaintiff's recovery will not be reduced when his negligence consisted solely of failure to discover or guard against the product's defect. Many courts agree with this rule. Texas has said that "a duty to discover defects, and to take precautions in constant anticipation that a product might have a defect, would defeat the purposes of strict liability." *Gen. Motors Corp. v. Sanchez*, 997 S.W.2d 584 (Tex. 1999). Does this distinction between failing to discover or guard against defects and other kinds of negligence make sense? Would it be better to formulate the rule by saying that a plaintiff is not negligent for trusting the defendant's product until there is some reason to distrust it?

3. **Obvious danger.** We have seen that a product is sometimes considered defective even when its danger is obvious and the plaintiff could be safe by taking the product's characteristics into account. In such a case, would a state adopting the Products Restatement's rule of comparative fault reduce the plaintiff's recovery? And would a court applying the *Bowling* rule allow full recovery?

4. **Assumption of the risk.** Recall that in a growing number of states, implied assumption of risk is subsumed within the comparative responsibility

rules, and is not regarded as a separate defense at all. *See* Chapter 10 § 2. Some states continue to agree with the *Bowling* court's view, however, that assumption of risk is a complete defense to a strict products liability suit, even if contributory negligence is not. *See* DOBBS, HAYDEN & BUBLICK, HORNBOOK ON TORTS § 33.17, at 835 (2d ed. 2016). Should courts distinguish between a plaintiff's negligence and "assumption of the risk," or should all forms of plaintiff "misconduct" enter into the comparison?

5.   ***Bexiga.*** If you would apply ordinary comparative negligence in products cases, maybe there are still cases in which you would not want to apply it. How would you feel about applying the comparative fault rule in *Bexiga v. Havir Mfg. Corp.*, 290 A.2d 281 (N.J. 1972), in Chapter 9 § 5—where the defendant was found to owe a duty to protect the plaintiff from his own carelessness? *Cf. Carrel v. Allied Prods. Corp.*, 677 N.E.2d 795 (Ohio 1997) (assumption of risk defense not available when the plaintiff "is required to encounter the risk while performing normal job duties").

B. MISUSE

HUGHES V. MAGIC CHEF, INC., 288 N.W.2d 542 (Iowa 1980). Plaintiff Vincent Hughes was severely burned when a propane-gas stove manufactured by defendant Magic Chef exploded in his mobile home. The propane tank that fueled the stove had been refilled that evening but one of the pilot lights in stove had not been relit. Experts testified that a resulting buildup of propane gas in the stove caused the explosion when Hughes attempted to use the stove. Hughes sued Magic Chef on a strict liability theory, claiming the stove was defective; Magic Chef raised the defenses of assumption of risk and misuse. The jury found for Magic Chef.

Held, reversed. First, the trial judge should not have given an instruction on assumption of risk at all, after the advent of comparative fault. Second, the trial court should not have characterized misuse as a *defense*. "Misuse of product is no longer to be considered an affirmative defense in products liability actions but is rather to be treated in connection with the plaintiff's burden of proving an unreasonably dangerous condition and legal cause. Regardless of whether a defendant does or does not plead misuse of the product, the burden is on the plaintiff to prove that the legal cause of the injury was a product defect which rendered the product unreasonably dangerous in a reasonably foreseeable use."

Further, the misuse instruction given by the trial court gave undue emphasis to what Hughes knew or should have known. "[T]he ordinary user's awareness that use of the product in a certain manner is dangerous does not conclusively establish that such use is not reasonably foreseeable, for the defendant may in a given case reasonably foresee that a given product will be used by persons such as children who do not possess the knowledge of the ordinary user. Hence knowledge which can be reasonably attributed to the ordinary user is to be considered as a factor in determining whether the manner in which the plaintiff used the product was reasonably foreseeable. . . . If on retrial Hughes proves by a preponderance of the evidence that the use made of the stove was reasonably foreseeable and that the stove was unreasonably dangerous when so used, then he will have established the first element of his case; otherwise the case is over."

NOTES

1.   **What "misuse" might mean.** What does the *Hughes* court think about unforeseeable misuse of a product that causes harm? (a) Unforeseeable misuse means the plaintiff is guilty of contributory negligence. (b) Unforeseeable misuse means the plaintiff assumed the risk. (c) Unforeseeable misuse means that, with respect to harms caused by the misuse and that would not have been caused by a properly used product, the product simply is not defective at all. *See Matthews v. Remington Arms Co.*, 641 F.3d 635 (5th Cir. 2011) (use of rifle without bolt-assembly pin was not a reasonably anticipated use, thus gun was not defective in design). In *Payne v. Gardner*, 56 So.3d 229 (La. 2011), a 13-year-old boy climbed onto the moving pendulum of an oil well pump and attempted to "ride" it. He was injured—thankfully not killed—and sued the manufacturer of the oil well pump, claiming a design defect. How should that case be analyzed?

2.   **Comparing contributory fault, assumed risk and no defect.** How can you determine whether the plaintiff's conduct is "misuse" on the one hand or contributory fault or assumed risk on the other? Is it more important to distinguish one kind of act from another, or foreseeable uses from unforeseeable ones? Note that many courts apply comparative fault principles to products strict liability cases and also treat misuse as merely one form of comparative fault. *Chapman v. Maytag Corp.*, 297 F.3d 682 (7th Cir. 2002). Presumably this rule applies to foreseeable misuse only. Can you see why that might be so?

3.   **Misuse as superseding cause.** Remember that regardless of the legal theory being used, the plaintiff must prove that the defect in the product (or, if negligence is the theory, the defendant's conduct) is both a factual and proximate cause of her injury. *See, e.g., Stahlecker v. Ford Motor Co.*, 667 N.W.2d 244 (Neb. 2003) (motorist was murdered after the tires on her car failed, stranding her in a dangerous area; manufacturer not liable because there was no "causal relationship" between any product defect and the murder). Might "misuse" be regarded as a type of superseding cause, thus causing a failure of the prima facie case on scope of liability (proximate cause) grounds? *See Moyer v. United Dominion Industries, Inc.*, 473 F.3d 532 (3d Cir. 2007) (Pa. law). Could the *Payne* case in Note 1, *supra*, be viewed this way?

4.   **Foreseeability of misuse.** In many states, the manufacturer must ordinarily design a product reasonably in the light of known or foreseeable misuses, not merely for "intended" use. Thus the usual rule of "crashworthiness" (see § 2.B, *supra*) is that if a car will collapse when it is in a

foreseeable collision, it may be defective, even though the manufacturer never intended it to be crashed. *Turner v. Gen. Motors Corp.*, 584 S.W.2d 844 (Tex. 1979); *Slone v. Gen. Motors Corp.*, 457 S.E.2d 51 (Va. 1995). Foreseeability has also become the test for bystander injury. When misuse is foreseeable and a reasonable alternative design would have prevented harm from the misuse, the manufacturer cannot avoid liability on the ground that the product was not defective or that the defect was not a proximate cause. *See, e.g., Perkins v. Wilkinson Sword, Inc.*, 700 N.E.2d 1247 (Ohio 1998) (rejecting argument by cigarette lighter manufacturer that because children are not the intended users of its lighters, it did not have to make its lighters childproof). Bear in mind, however, that in some cases a plaintiff's "misuse" might be regarded as a form of contributory fault or assumed risk, with whatever defensive advantage those doctrines might produce.

REFERENCE: 2 DOBBS, HAYDEN & BUBLICK, THE LAW OF TORTS § 470–472 (2d ed. 2011).

C. FEDERAL PREEMPTION

DOOMES V. BEST TRANSIT CORP.
958 N.E.2d 1183 (N.Y. 2011)

JONES, J. . . .

On April 23, 1994, a bus carrying approximately 21 passengers was returning from a visit to Adirondack Correctional Facility in Ray Brook, New York. The bus was equipped with a seatbelt for the driver, but not for the passengers. During the trip along the New York State Thruway, the driver, defendant Wagner M. Alcivar, "dozed off" while the bus was traveling approximately 60 miles per hour. The bus veered across the highway from the right-hand lane into the passing lane, and encountered a median strip and a sloping embankment. Alcivar awakened, but his belated attempts to regain control of the bus were futile as the vehicle rolled over several times, injuring many of the passengers.

[Three of the injured passengers, including Gloria Doomes, sued various defendants, including Warrick Industries, Inc., the manufacturer who completed the construction of the bus. Plaintiffs alleged, among other things, that the absence of passenger seatbelts was a cause of the injury. Warrick moved to preclude any evidence that the bus was defective or that it was negligent due to a lack of seatbelts on the ground that Federal Motor Vehicle Safety Standard (FMVSS) 208 (49 CFR § 571.208), which did not require the installation of passenger seatbelts, preempted any claims of liability for failure to install such seatbelts. The trial court declined to rule on the motion, and the jury found Warrick liable. The Appellate Division reversed, holding that plaintiffs' seatbelt claims were preempted, reasoning that these claims conflicted with the federal goal of establishing a uniform regulatory scheme for transit safety. Plaintiffs appealed.]

[handwritten margin notes: Preemption / Express / or / Implied / Field / Its / through regulator ...]

Under the Supremacy Clause of the United States Constitution (US Const, art VI, cl 2), preemption analysis requires us "to ascertain the intent of Congress." Express preemptive intent is discerned from the plain language of a statutory provision. Implied preemption may be found in two distinct ways when either "the Federal legislation is so comprehensive in its scope that it is inferable that Congress wished fully to occupy the field of its subject matter (field preemption), or because State law conflicts with the Federal law."

Plaintiffs contend that the Appellate Division erred in finding preemption because the relevant portions of FMVSS 208, compelling only the inclusion of a driver seatbelt, neither reflects a pervasive scheme of regulation nor makes compliance with federal and state standards impossible. Moreover, it is argued that the United States Supreme Court's recent decision in *Williamson v Mazda Motor of America, Inc.* (131 S Ct 1131 [2011]) disposes of this appeal in plaintiffs' favor. Warrick claims that the statute affords manufacturers the option to choose among different protective devices for installation at the driver's seat, and this availability of discretion places this appeal squarely within the holding of *Geier v American Honda Motor Co.* (529 US 861 [2000]).

First turning to express preemption, the pertinent statutory clause of the National Traffic and Motor Vehicle Safety Act (Safety Act) provides that

> "[w]hen a motor vehicle safety standard is in effect under this chapter, a State or a political subdivision of a State may prescribe or continue in effect a standard applicable to the same aspect of performance of a motor vehicle or motor vehicle equipment only if the standard is identical to the standard prescribed under this chapter. However, the United State Government, a State, or a political subdivision of a State may prescribe a standard for a motor vehicle or motor vehicle equipment obtained for its own use that imposes a higher performance requirement than that required by the otherwise applicable standard under this chapter" (49 USC § 30103 [b]).

In *Geier*, the Supreme Court considered the preemptive effect of a pre-1994 edition of the above preemption clause that similarly limited the authority of states to prescribe motor vehicle safety standards (*see* former 15 USC § 1392 [d]). However, rather than parsing the precise significance of the plain language of the provision, the Supreme Court concluded that Congress did not intend the preemption clause to be construed so broadly as to preclude state claims because the "saving" clause explicitly reserved a right to assert common-law claims.

As relevant here, the instant saving clause provides that "[c]ompliance with a motor vehicle safety standard prescribed under this chapter does not exempt a person from liability at common law." When read in conjunction with the preemption provision, the saving clause permits the commencement of common-law claims; compliance with applicable federal motor vehicle safety standards is not necessarily a preclusive bar. Accordingly, the presence of the saving clause limits a potentially broad reading of the preemption provision and does not expressly prohibit plaintiffs' seatbelt claims.

With respect to implied "field preemption," it does not appear that the federal statutes were intended to so greatly envelop the field of motor vehicle safety standards as to leave little room for state participation or operation. Certainly, the guidelines, as the Appellate Division noted, are consonant "with the federal goal of establishing uniform standards." And, the preemption clause constrains states from enacting guidelines that deviate from federal standards. However, the goal of uniformity cannot be singularly pursued at the expense of the Safety Act's primary purpose to "reduce traffic accidents and deaths and injuries to persons resulting from traffic accidents." This is evinced by the presence of the saving clause which expressly allows the commencement of state common-law claims. As the Supreme Court has reasoned previously, "the saving clause reflects a congressional determination that occasional nonuniformity is a small price to pay for a system in which juries not only create, but also enforce, safety standards" (*Geier*, 529 US at 871). Further, the saving clause represents a purposeful intent to allow meaningful state participation as a finding of preemption would "treat all such federal standards as if they were *maximum* standards, eliminating the possibility that the federal agency seeks only to set forth a *minimum* standard potentially supplemented through state tort law" (*Williamson*, 131 S Ct at 1139 [emphasis added]). Consequently, there is no implied "field preemption" as the explicit permission of common-law claims indicates that the federal statutes promulgated under the Safety Act are not so pervasive as to encompass the entire scheme of motor vehicle safety guidelines.

The significant point of contention between the parties is whether plaintiffs' seatbelt claims are barred under implied conflict preemption. We conclude they are not.

Implied conflict preemption can arise in two situations: when "it is "impossible for a private party to comply with both state and federal requirements' . . . or where state law 'stands as an obstacle to the accomplishment and execution of the full purposes and objectives of Congress'" (*Freightliner Corp. v Myrick*, 514 US 280, 287 [1995]). The Supreme Court has made clear that a state law will be preempted under the latter form of implied conflict preemption only where it would frustrate "a *significant objective* of the federal regulation" (*Williamson*, 562 US at ___, 131 S Ct at 1136 [emphasis added]).

. . . A plain reading of [the federal regulations here] shows that they only mandate the inclusion of protective devices at the driver's seat of a bus and are absolutely silent regarding the installation of passenger seatbelts. This does not make it impossible to comply with both the federal standards and the gravamen of plaintiffs' seatbelt claims, which seek liability for the failure to install such protective devices. Quite simply, Warrick could have installed passenger and driver seatbelts without running afoul of federal motor vehicle safety standards. Hence, plaintiffs' seatbelt claims are not preempted under the first category of implied conflict preemption. . . .

The NHTSA has consistently acknowledged the enhanced safety benefits of seatbelts, but it has neither imposed the installation of passenger seatbelts, nor expressed an intention to provide such an option to manufacturers of the type of bus involved in the instant appeal. . . .

Further, any contention that manufacturers impliedly had an option to install rear passenger seatbelts in buses over 10,000 pounds, because the NHTSA was cognizant of the safety benefits of rear passenger seatbelts, is belied by the plain language of FMVSS 208 and the federal regulations which simply do not consider the inclusion of such protective devices for vehicles of this type. [As such, like *Williamson*, there is simply no preemptive intent to be discerned from the regulations with respect to state common-law claims seeking the inclusion of passenger seatbelts in buses of this type.]

In sum, we find neither express nor implied preemption of plaintiffs' seatbelt claims. . . .

[Order reversed.]

NOTES

1. **Types of federal preemption.** The Supremacy Clause gives Congress the power to override state law, as long as it acts within the limits of its own constitutional powers. As the New York court explained in *Doomes*, Congress can effectively forbid the enforcement of state law not only when the state law would conflict directly with federal statutes or regulation, but also when Congress wishes to impose a single scheme of regulation or control. Congress might thus "preempt" state law by (1) occupying the field with heavy regulation so that there is no room left for state law; (2) by passing laws that actually conflict with state laws; or (3) by providing for preemption in particular cases, either expressly or by implication. Even when Congress has expressly provided for preemption, courts must construe the statute to determine what was and what was not preempted. In general, the Supreme Court is reluctant to find preemption of state powers unless the Congress has clearly manifested its purpose. *See Medtronic, Inc. v. Lohr*, 518 U.S. 470 (1996). Congress has exhibited such a preemptive purpose with increasing frequency, however.

2. **Effect in products cases.** Preemption is particularly important in products liability cases. Suppose a federal statute sets a minimum standard for warnings that must be contained on labels of a dangerous product. A state law that required a better warning or additional information would not actually conflict with the federal statute and would therefore not be preempted under the actual conflict rule. Nevertheless, the federal labeling statute might either expressly or impliedly preempt state law. If it did, the result would be that the manufacturer who complied with the federal statute would not be liable for failing to comply with the state statute. Common-law tort claims based on state law would also be preempted. *See, e.g., Brown v. Brown & Williamson Tobacco Corp.*, 479 F.3d 383 (5th Cir. 2007) (federal Cigarette Labeling and Advertising Act preempts state statutory and common-law claims concerning "light" cigarettes).

3. **Airbags and seatbelts.** Preemption has played an important role in claims against automobile manufacturers. In *Geier v. American Honda Motor Co.*, 529 U.S. 861 (2000), the plaintiff claimed that Honda was negligent in failing to equip its 1987 Accord with a driver's side airbag. The Court decided, 5–4, that plaintiff's state-law claim was impliedly preempted by federal regulations that had sought a "variety and mix of [restraint] devices" in cars in order to "help develop data on comparative effectiveness," to give "the industry time to overcome the safety problems and the high production costs associated with airbags," and to "facilitate the development of alternative, cheaper, and safer passive restraint systems." To allow the plaintiff to establish that Honda owed a duty under state law to install an airbag in its 1987 Accords would conflict with these federal goals; thus her claim was preempted.

4. **The growth of the preemption defense.** Arguments that federal law preempts state law products claims often reach the Supreme Court, and most of the decisions favor defendants. In *Riegel v. Medronic, Inc.*, 128 S.Ct. 999 552 U.S. 312 (2008), the Court held that where the Food and Drug Administration has given premarket approval to a particular medical device, federal law preempts common-law claims challenging the safety or effectiveness of such a device. In *PLIVA v. Mensing*, 564 U.S. 604 (2011), the Court held that federal law preempted state laws requiring generic drug manufacturers to warn of the risks of long-term use of their product, where it was impossible for the manufacturers to comply with both state and federal law on labeling. *See also Mutual Pharmaceutical Co. v. Bartlett*, 133 S.Ct. 2466 (2013) (similar). All design-defect claims against vaccine manufactures claiming injuries from side-effects were held preempted by the federal National Childhood Vaccine Act, in *Bruesewitz v. Wyeth LLC,* 562 U.S. 223 (2011). In *Kurns v. Railroad Friction Prods. Corp.*, 565 U.S. 625 (2012), the Court held that state-law claims of defective design and failure to warn about the dangers of asbestos brake pads used on railroad cars were preempted by the federal Locomotive Inspection Act. Do you see why manufacturers do not always see federal regulation in a negative light?

REFERENCES: DOBBS, HAYDEN & BUBLICK, HORNBOOK ON TORTS § 33.20 (2d ed. 2016); 2 DOBBS, HAYDEN & BUBLICK, THE LAW OF TORTS § 474 (2d ed. 2011).

PART 9

PRACTICALITIES AND VALUES

■ ■ ■

CHAPTER 25

APPORTIONMENT AND SETTLEMENT

∎ ∎ ∎

§ 1. APPORTIONMENT SYSTEMS

DOBBS, HAYDEN & BUBLICK, THE LAW OF TORTS
Vol. 3, § 487 (2d ed. 2011)

§ 487.   Apportionment of liability: an overview

Apportionment basics. When the tortious conduct of multiple parties causes a harm, questions arise about how to divide responsibility for damages among the various actors. This issue of damages division is addressed by the rules of apportionment of liability. There are two basic forms of liability apportionment: causal apportionment and fault or responsibility based apportionment.

Causal apportionment. When two or more tortfeasors cause divisible harms to the plaintiff, most authorities agree that causal apportionment should be employed. For example, if tortfeasor A negligently causes the plaintiff to suffer a broken leg and tortfeasor B negligently causes the plaintiff broken arm, each tortfeasor is normally liable for 100% of the damages that the tortfeasor separately caused. Causal apportionment . . . may also be required when the plaintiff suffers a single injury rather than distinct harms but the single injury is capable of being apportioned in some rational way. The principle of causal apportionment can apply between a plaintiff and a defendant as well as between defendants, as where the defendant's asbestos causes lung damage and the plaintiff's smoking causes a different lung damage, with both contributing to a shortness of breath. If evidence shows a basis for saying that the asbestos caused 90% of the disability, the defendant will be liable only for that portion of the harm. If no evidence shows a basis for causal apportionment, the court may allocate liability in proportion to fault or responsibility instead. On similar facts, but when no evidence permitted causal apportionment, the court upheld a jury award that apportioned 50% of the fault to the defendant as supplier of the asbestos. *Owens Corning Fiberglass Corp. v. Parrish,* 58 S.W.3d 467 (Ky. 2001).

Fault apportionment. Causal apportionment, is often contrasted with fault apportionment. Fault apportionment takes place when a plaintiff has suffered a single indivisible injury at the hands of two or more tortfeasors and the loss cannot be reasonably allocated by causal measures between the two. Instead, the loss is allocated based on percentages of fault. For example, suppose tortfeasor A, who is speeding, crashes into plaintiff's car. Tortfeasor B, who is sending a text message while driving, fails to keep a lookout and hits the plaintiff's car as well. The plaintiff emerges from the near-simultaneous accidents with a serious back injury. Experts attribute the injury to the combined impact of the crashes but cannot segregate the amount of harm caused by each. Because both defendants are factual causes of the plaintiff's single injury and no causal apportionment of the injury is possible, a jury would be asked to apportion liability by assigning a percentage of fault to each defendant.

Joint and several and several liability. Suppose the jury finds that defendant A is chargeable with 60% of the fault and defendant B with 40% of the fault. The jury also finds that the plaintiff has suffered $100,000 in damages: $50,000 in past and future medical expenses and $50,000 in pain and suffering. If joint and several liability applies, each defendant will be liable to the plaintiff for the full $100,000 in damages, subject to the caveat that the plaintiff can only receive one satisfaction of the judgment. Consequently, if the plaintiff recovers the full $100,000 from defendant B, she can recover nothing at all against defendant B. However, defendant A can call upon defendant B for contribution for the $40,000 owed by B. If on the other hand, several liability applies, the plaintiff can call on defendant A for payment of only $60,000 and defendant B for payment of $40,000. If either of the two negligent defendants cannot pay, it is the plaintiff who will bear the uncompensated loss.

Other ways to apportion liability. Although joint and several liability and several liability are two prominent options for sharing the loss, they are far from the only options. Some jurisdictions retain joint and several liability, but only for certain elements of the damages such as those based on the economic harm done to the plaintiff. In a jurisdiction like this, defendant A would be jointly and severally liable for the $20,000 of defendant B's liability to plaintiff for economic losses (40% of the plaintiff's $50,000 economic loss damages), but not jointly and severally liable for the $20,000 of defendant B's share that was due to pain and suffering. Similarly, some jurisdictions retain joint and several liability only if the defendant's percentage of responsibility exceeds a certain threshold percentage such as 50%. In a jurisdiction with this rule, defendant A, assigned 60% of the liability, would be jointly and severally liable for defendant B's uncollectible share. However, defendant B, assigned 40% of the total liability, would not be jointly and severally liable if defendant A's share were uncollectible. Other possibilities exist. Some jurisdictions have joint and several liability with reallocation. This means that if the plaintiff cannot collect a judgment from one of the parties, that portion of the judgment will be reallocated among the remaining parties on the basis of the remaining parties' fault. In the example with defendant A and B, because the plaintiff was assigned no fault, defendant A would bear the full cost of defendant B's insolvency. However, if instead the plaintiff had been assigned 30% of the fault and defendant A 30% of the fault, defendant B's uncollectible 40% share would be split by defendant A and the plaintiff 1:1—each would bear their assigned shares of the loss plus one-half of B's share.

The varied rules. As the variations in these illustrations suggest, apportionment of liability among multiple actors, once a fairly straightforward topic, has now become increasingly fragmented and complex. In fact, so divided is state law that when the Restatement Third of Torts was published at the start of the millennium, its provisions recognized five alternative "tracks" of liability apportionment that states might employ to address the situation of multiple tortfeasors who create indivisible harms—one for joint and several liability, another for several liability, one for joint and several liability with reallocation, another for hybrid liability based on a threshold percentage of comparative responsibility, and a final chapter on hybrid liability based on the type of damages. One English commentator has called the tracked sections of the Restatement of Apportionment "a trackless morass, Dismal Swamp, and Desolation of Smaug." Tony Weir, *All-or-nothing?*, 78 TUL. L. REV. 511, 534 n.63 (2004). And the [five Restatement] categories are not mutually exclusive. Indeed, given the varied apportionment-related statutes and case law in existence at the time the Restatement was enacted,[10] no single approach to the issue could have been followed in all jurisdictions. As is the case whenever statutes pervade and state case law varies, reference to the legislation and precedent of particular jurisdictions is essential. Despite jurisdictional differences, the issue of indivisible injury remains significant across the board. In joint and several liability the defendant is liable for that indivisible injury. In other types of apportionment of liability arrangements, the fact that the plaintiff suffered an indivisible injury remains significant because the defendant's percentage of liability is measured as a portion of the total of plaintiff's indivisible injury damages.

Issues within apportionment systems. The jurisdictional differences concerning joint and several liability and other types of liability is a significant divider. . . . However, many additional issues pervade the apportionment landscape. In joint and several liability systems, one of the most important questions is how joint liabilities are divided between multiple tortfeasors through contribution and indemnity. In several liability systems, contribution issues arise much less frequently, but courts have many other issues to resolve. Because several liability systems typically apportion liability into mutually exclusive portions, the key questions in these systems center on (1) which types of conduct and which

---

[10] Restatement (Third) of Torts: Apportionment of Liability § 17 Tables at 151–159 (2000).

types of actors can be a part of the apportionment percentages, (2) on what basis percentage apportionments are made, and (3) in what circumstances exceptions to the several liability rule are called for.

Apportionment and policy choices. Courts frequently address apportionment of liability as though the apportionment itself is a neutral issue—the defendant should be accountable for its fair share of responsibility and no more. However, the variation in state answers to the question of what constitutes a fair share of damages for which to hold a defendant to account, highlights just how important a policy question apportionment of liability has become.

Terminology. Unfortunately, there is no uniform nomenclature that marks which types of actionable conduct are included in a jurisdiction's apportionment of liability system. Because strict liability and negligence are types of conduct compared in some jurisdictions, the term comparative "negligence" or even comparative "fault" becomes problematic. When jurisdictions use the term comparative "responsibility," it is typically employed because the comparisons include at least one form of actionable conduct in addition to negligence, such as strict liability. A "comparative fault" system might include comparisons across types of actionable misconduct, or it might not. Comparative "negligence" systems are more likely to focus on negligent acts alone. The term "apportionment of liability" in this chapter is used as an umbrella term to encompass all forms of apportionment.

§ 2. APPORTIONMENT WITH JOINT AND SEVERAL LIABILITY

HILL V. RHINEHART
45 N.E.3d 427 (Ind. Ct. App. 2015)

RILEY, J.

[Patient John A. Hill (Hill) was admitted to Parkview Memorial Hospital (Parkview) for a coronary artery bypass surgery. Because of some complications after the surgery, several orders were placed to stop all administration of Heparin. However, on several occasions, plaintiff nevertheless was given heparin. Hill developed life threatening complications and ultimately had three limbs amputated as result of heparin-induced thrombocytopenia with thrombosis (HITT). Hill entered into settlements with Parkview Hospital and Indiana Patient's Compensation Fund for $250,000—the amount of the statutory cap for medical malpractice actions. He then brought a malpractice action against four doctors involved in his care. The physicians moved for summary judgment, arguing that the patient had received the maximum recovery under the Medical Malpractice Act, and filed a motion for judgment on the evidence. The trial court denied the motion for summary judgment on the ground that the three amputations might count as distinct injuries, but granted a motion for judgment on the evidence for two of the doctors after the close of patient's case-in-chief. The court subsequently entered judgment on a jury verdict in favor of the remaining doctors. Patient appealed.]

Hill . . . contends that the trial court erred by granting Drs. Lloyd and Csicsko's motion for judgment on the evidence because it prejudiced Hill by preventing the jury from "evaluating the liability of the doctors jointly and severally as a team." Hill maintains that after the directed verdict, the jury was unable to consider the actions of Drs. Lloyd and Csicsko, and consequently was prevented from considering the doctors "as collaborators and it prevented the failures of one of the doctors to be included with the failure of another." Therefore, Hill requests this court to grant him a new trial as to all parties, "so that all parties may be tried as joint tortfeasors."

It is well established that in medical malpractice actions, the Indiana Comparative Fault Act does not apply. Accordingly, the common law defenses remain available to defendants in cases alleging medical malpractice. At common law, joint tortfeasors are two or more persons jointly or severally liable in tort for the same injury to person or property. Their actions unite to cause a single injury.

When more than one unite in the commission of a wrong, each is responsible for the acts of all, and for the whole damage; also, where separate and independent acts of negligence by different persons concur in perpetrating a single injury, each is fully responsible for the trespass. Courts will not undertake to apportion the damage in such cases among the joint wrongdoers. The injured party has at his election his remedy against all, or any number.

Thus, to impose joint and several liability on Drs. Lloyd and Csicsko, it is imperative that these doctors contributed to the negligent actions which resulted in Hill's injury. In other words, joint and several liability does not impose liability on a defendant who is otherwise not liable. The fact that Drs. Csicsko and Lloyd contributed and collaborated with the two other doctors to jointly provide treatment to Hill does not equate to a transfer of liability of one doctor to the non-liable physicians simply by virtue of their collaboration. As we concluded that the directed verdicts in favor of Drs. Csicsko and Lloyd were properly entered, Hill cannot now avail himself of the doctrine of joint and several liability to transfer any perceived negligence of Drs. Ryan and Rhinehart onto Drs. Lloyd and Csicsko.

Moreover, the entry of the directed verdict did not prevent Hill from fully presenting his case. The doctors' motion for directed verdict was heard and ruled upon after Hill rested his case-in-chief. Accordingly, there was no prejudice to Hill in explaining the temporal relationship between the physicians and their respective collaborative actions with respect to Hill's care and treatment. Therefore, we deny Hill's request for a new trial.

NOTES

1. **Joint and several liability.** Under rules of joint and several liability, several defendants might be held liable together, jointly and severally, so that the plaintiff might enforce a judgment entirely against any one of them. In *Burg v. Dampier*, 346 S.W.3d 343, 360 (Mo. Ct. App. 2011), the court wrote: "A plaintiff may sue all or any of the joint or concurrent tortfeasors and obtain a judgment against all or any of them." But note, as in *Hill,* that it's not just any defendants who are sued who are jointly and severally liable. What else has to be true before a defendant can be held jointly and severally liable?

2. **Contribution.** What if the plaintiff tried to enforce a judgment against one tortfeasor for the full amount of the judgment? Could one defendant be forced to pay the full judgment? How might that defendant seek to share the costs with other defendants?

3. **One satisfaction.** Why does the total amount of money plaintiff is permitted to recover under the medical malpractice act matter? Recall that even if all four doctors had been negligent, and plaintiff could enforce his judgment against any or all of the tortfeasors, under the "one satisfaction rule," he cannot recover more than the total amount of his damages.

4. **Fairness.** Suppose the jury had found two of the doctors liable to the plaintiff for medical negligence. How could plaintiff argue it would be fair for either or both of the two doctors to pay plaintiff's full damage award? Would it be more fair for the non-negligent plaintiff to bear the loss?

5. **Applicability.** Joint and several liability was once the dominant rule for fault apportionment. Now it is the main rule in a small number of states, but, as in *Hill*, at times it still applies even in states with a general rule of several liability. Also, some federal statutes impose joint and several liability for matters within their scope. This is the rule under CERCLA, a statute imposing liabilities for hazardous substances. *See United States v. Stringfellow*, 661 F. Supp. 1053 (C.D. Cal. 1987). The Supreme Court has also retained joint and several liability in FELA cases. *Norfolk & W. Ry. v. Ayers,* 538 U.S. 135 (2003).

NOTE: TRADITIONAL CONTEXTS FOR JOINT AND SEVERAL LIABILITY

The rule of joint and several liability may apply in four distinct situations.

(1) *Concerted action.* Joint and several liability applies to true joint torts, those in which A and B act in concert to commit an unlawful act. This includes intentional torts pursued jointly, as where A and B agree, tacitly or formally, to beat the plaintiff. It also includes intended law violations, as where A and B agree to race on the public highway and in the course of the race A collides with the plaintiff.

(2) *Indivisible injury.* The rule of joint and several liability applies in cases of concurrent torts where there is no concert or agreement, but where the acts of A and B produce a single indivisible injury. For example, recall the *Landers* case, in which both defendants' toxins combined to kill the fish in plaintiff's lake.

(3) *A creates a risk of harm by B.* The rule of joint and several liability applies in part when A's negligence not only creates a harm to the plaintiff, but also creates a risk of further harm by reason of B's negligence. A negligently runs the plaintiff down and leaves him concussed and unconscious, but otherwise unharmed, in the street. B later negligently runs over and breaks the plaintiff's leg. Although B can only be held liable for the separate injury he caused, A is jointly and severally liable for the entire harm under the rules of "proximate cause, since he created a foreseeable risk of harm from B." Thus if B proved to be uninsured and insolvent, the plaintiff would be entitled to recover his entire damages from A. This is the import of the proximate cause rules. Similarly, if A does not directly harm the plaintiff but creates a risk that B will do so, joint and several liability is no doubt proper. For instance, in *Nallan v. Helmsley-Spear, Inc.*, 407 N.E.2d 451 (N.Y. 1980), a building owner failed to protect an invitee from a gunman. The building owner was held fully liable, not limited to its comparative share.

(4) *A defendant is vicariously liable.* An employer is liable for the torts of an employee committed in the scope of employment. The employee is also liable for his own torts. The result is that they are jointly and severally liable.

Why was joint and several liability at issue in *Hill*? Which of these four situations would be relevant to that case?

NOTE: CONTRIBUTION AND INDEMNITY

1. *Contribution.* (a) *General availability.* In Chapter 6, we saw that if one tortfeasor, A, paid more than his share of damages, he could recover contribution from the other tortfeasors to rectify their respective liabilities. The common law rule was opposed to contribution and contribution may still be denied among intentional tortfeasors. Otherwise, however, the

states generally permit contribution when A pays more than his share of a judgment for the plaintiff.

(b) *The common liability rule.* The person claiming contribution must show that both tortfeasors were liable to the plaintiff. Thus if one defendant is immune from suit, for example, no contribution could be had from him. *See, e.g., Crotta v. Home Depot, Inc.,* 732 A.2d 767 (Conn. 1999) (intra-familial immunity); *cf. Prince v. Pacific Gas & Elec. Co.,* 202 P.3d 1115 (Cal. 2009) (indemnity unavailable against a defendant who is immune from suit).

(c) *Payment in settlement.* In some states A can obtain contribution from B only when A has paid a judgment for the plaintiff. That rule would deny contribution if A paid the plaintiff's claim in a settlement rather than by paying off a final judgment. Such an approach is now outdated. If A settles with P for full compensation, A is usually entitled to contribution from B.

(d) *Traditional amount of contribution.* The amount of the appropriate share to be paid in contribution may not be obvious. However, the traditional rule is quite clear: if there is a single indivisible injury caused by two tortfeasors, each should pay one-half. Thus if A pays the entire $200,000, B would be liable to make contribution to A of $100,000. This rule is known as the pro rata share rule. The leading article is Robert A. Leflar, *Contribution and Indemnity Between Tortfeasors,* 81 U. PA. L. REV. 130 (1932). *See generally* 3 DOBBS, HAYDEN & BUBLICK, THE LAW OF TORTS § 489 (2d ed. 2011). Of course, now, most contribution claims are divided by percentages.

2. *Indemnity.* In a few situations, A may be technically liable to the plaintiff, but it may be that B is the only person really at fault. If A, because of a technical liability, pays the entire amount of the plaintiff's damages, A may recover, not merely a share from B, but the entire sum. This is known, traditionally, as indemnity. Thus while contribution involves a sharing of liability between the tortfeasors, indemnity involves a shifting of that liability.

There are not many occasions for indemnity in this sense. The chief example involves the negligence of the employee for which the employer is vicariously liable. In such a case the employer has a right of indemnity against the negligent employee, though it is not a right often exercised in practice. There is also a right of indemnity in some products cases, as where the retailer is held strictly liable for a defective product supplied by the manufacturer: the retailer will be entitled to recover indemnity from the manufacturer. *See generally* 3 DOBBS, HAYDEN & BUBLICK, THE LAW OF TORTS § 489 (2d ed. 2011).

§ 3. APPORTIONMENT ISSUES IN JURISDICTIONS WITH SEVERAL LIABILITY

A. ABOLISHING OR LIMITING JOINT AND SEVERAL LIABILITY

CAL. CIV. CODE § 1431.2

(a) In any action for personal injury, property damage, or wrongful death, based upon principles of comparative fault, the liability of each defendant for non-economic damages shall be several only and shall not be joint. Each defendant shall be liable only for the amount of non-economic damages allocated to that defendant in direct proportion to that defendant's percentage of fault, and a separate judgment shall be rendered against that defendant for that amount.

(b)(1) For purposes of this section, the term "economic damages" means objectively verifiable monetary losses including medical expenses, loss of earnings, burial costs, loss of use of property, costs of repair or replacement, cost of obtaining substitute domestic services, loss of employment and loss of business or employment opportunities.

(2) For the purposes of this section, the term "non-economic damages" means subjective, non-monetary losses including, but not limited to, pain, suffering, inconvenience, mental suffering, emotional distress, loss of society and companionship, loss of consortium, injury to reputation and humiliation.

NOTES

1. **Scope.** Remember that with the adoption of a comparative fault system, no defendant was liable to a plaintiff for the *plaintiff's* comparative fault share. Statutes abolishing joint and several liability do not affect that rule. Rather, they change the rule that defendants could be treated as a group so that each was liable for the comparative fault share of all defendants. Notice that the California statute applies only when an action is "based upon principles of comparative fault."

2. **Effects.** The most obvious effect of abolishing joint and several liability is that the plaintiff, not the tortfeasor, will bear the risk of a second tortfeasor's inability to pay. If A's share is 60% and B's is 40% but B is insolvent, the plaintiff will recover only 60% of her loss from A and none from B, even though A is a proximate cause of the entire harm. In *Vollaro v. Lispi*, 168 Cal. Rptr. 3d 323 (Ct. App. 2014), applying the statute, the court wrote: "under Proposition 51, an injured plaintiff bears the entire risk of loss for any unpaid noneconomic damages attributable to a tortfeasor who has not been sued or is statutorily immune. We therefore conclude that Vollaro bears the entire risk of loss for any unpaid noneconomic damages attributable to [a non-party], who was not sued."

3. **Adoption of several liability statutes.** By 1990 the tort reform lobbyists had obtained statutory change in the traditional joint and several liability rules in about half the states, relieving defendants of joint liability in a wide range of cases. More recent data suggests that only 15 states retain pure joint and several liability, and 4 more adopt it when the plaintiff is not at fault. RESTATEMENT (THIRD) OF TORTS: APPORTIONMENT OF LIABILITY § 17 Tables at 151–59 (2000).

4. **Constitutionality.** So far, courts have generally upheld statutes of this kind. *E.g., State Farm Ins. Cos. v. Premier Manufactured Sys., Inc.,* 172 P.3d 410 (Ariz. 2007); *Evangelatos v. Superior Court,* 753 P.2d 585 (Cal. 1988). However, other states have found them violative of various state constitutional provisions. *Best v. Taylor Mach. Works,* 689 N.E.2d 1057 (Ill. 1997); *State v. Sheward,* 715 N.E.2d 1062 (Ohio 1999).

5. **The economic/non-economic distinction.** The California statute is one of a group which *retains* joint and several liability for actual pecuniary ("economic") losses. New York is another such state. *See* N.Y. C.P.L.R. § 1601.

6. **The relative fault distinction.** Another kind of statute retains some joint and several liability when the plaintiff's fault is small or the defendant's is great. New York's statute, for example, limits a defendant's liability for non-economic damages to his comparative fault share but only when his liability is "fifty percent or less of the total liability assigned to all persons liable." N.Y. C.P.L.R. § 1601.

7. **Combination systems.** A number of statutes combine the non-economic loss distinction with the relative fault distinction in some way. For instance, Florida Statutes § 768.81(3), prescribes:

> In cases to which this section applies, the court shall enter judgment against each party liable on the basis of such party's percentage of fault and not on the basis of the doctrine of joint and several liability; provided that with respect to any party whose percentage of fault equals or exceeds that of a particular claimant, the court shall enter judgment with respect to economic damages against that party on the basis of the doctrine of joint and several liability.

8. **The more severe statutes.** Another group of statutes is more severe, abolishing joint and several liability as to all the plaintiff's damages, both pecuniary and non-pecuniary, and regardless of the plaintiff's lack of fault. *E.g.,* ARIZ. REV. STAT. § 12–2506. As with most other statutes, some of these exempt particular torts, such as those based on hazardous wastes or pollution.

9. **Judicial adoption of several liability.** Several state courts have rejected the traditional joint and several liability rule, setting up a judicially created several liability system, seemingly along the lines of the more severe statutes. *See, e.g., Volz v. Ledes,* 895 S.W.2d 677 (Tenn. 1995).

B. TYPES OF ACTIONABLE CONDUCT SUBJECT TO APPORTIONMENT

SAFEWAY STORES, INC. V. NEST-KART, 579 P.2d 441 (Cal. 1978). The plaintiff was injured when a shopping cart in Safeway broke and fell on her foot, requiring surgery. The jury found that the plaintiff was not at fault, that Safeway was strictly liable and also negligent, and that Nest-Kart, the manufacturer of the cart, was strictly liable. The jury also fixed the comparative responsibility of Safeway at 80% and the comparative responsibility of Nest-Kart at 20%. The trial court ordered each defendant ultimately to share payment of the judgment on a 50–50 basis, so that Nest-Kart would owe 50% in spite of the comparative responsibility finding. On appeal, *held*, the traditional contribution rule embodied in existing statutes does not prevent apportionment under "comparative indemnity" principles, even though one of the parties is negligent and the other strictly liable without proof of fault. Juries are competent to apportion between negligence and strict liability. And strictly liable defendants should be entitled to apportionment against negligent tortfeasors.

NOTES

1. **Apportioning contributory negligence and strict liability.** The principle that comparative fault can operate to reduce recovery from a person who is strictly liable is applied in *Safeway* on the contribution issue. If it is a valid principle there, then presumably it is equally valid to reduce the recovery of a faulty plaintiff under contributory negligence/comparative fault rules. *See Daly v. General Motors Corp.*, 575 P.2d 1162 (Cal. 1978).

2. **Apportioning tortfeasor fault and strict liability.** On its facts, *Safeway* operates to deny a negligent party any contribution from a non-negligent party who has paid its "comparative fault" share. But is this the legal significance of the case? Suppose Nest-Kart had paid the entire judgment in favor of the plaintiff and had sought contribution. Does the principle adopted in the case limit Nest-Kart's recovery from Safeway to 80%? If so, is this justified, given the fact that Nest-Kart is not shown to be guilty of any fault and Safeway is?

3. **Restatement of Apportionment.** Recognizing that comparing negligence, intentional wrongdoing, and activities that warrant strict liability requires the trier to compare incommensurable qualities, the Restatement of Apportionment rejects the terms comparative negligence and comparative fault altogether in favor of comparative responsibility. *See* RESTATEMENT (THIRD) OF TORTS: APPORTIONMENT OF LIABILITY § 8 cmt. a (2000). Under this section, the trier considers various factors in assigning responsibility. "The nature of each person's risk-creating conduct includes such things as how unreasonable the conduct was under the circumstances, the extent to which the conduct failed to meet the applicable legal standard, the circumstances surrounding the conduct, each person's abilities and disabilities, and each

person's awareness, intent, or indifference with respect to the risks." *Id*. cmt. c. Is this merely one way of saying the trier considers the *Carroll Towing* factors? If not, then does this approach invite the triers to exercise their biases? How can an appellate court review the sufficiency of evidence for any particular assignment of "responsibility?"

BOARD OF COUNTY COMMISSIONERS OF TETON COUNTY V. BASSETT

8 P.3d 1079 (Wyo. 2000)

GRANT, DISTRICT JUDGE. . . .

The Wyoming Highway Patrol pursued Ortega from Dubois at high speeds. [Ortega was wanted in two jurisdictions and considered to be armed and dangerous.] Ortega repeatedly swerved from his own lane toward oncoming traffic, and otherwise presented a menace to the traveling public in an apparent attempt to cause a crash which would divert the pursuing officers or involve them in a crash. These efforts failed, but the officers were unable to stop Ortega, making the roadblock necessary.

[Sheriff's deputies decided to establish the roadblock] beyond the intersection of U.S. Highway 89 and Antelope Flats Road. At that location, they placed improvised road spikes in the hope that Ortega would turn off of the highway onto the road and be stopped when the spikes disabled his vehicle. Ortega did not turn off of the highway, and continued on until he was stopped by the crash just on the Jackson side of the roadblock.

As these events were unfolding, appellees, Michael Coziah (Coziah) and Rayce Bassett (Bassett), were enroute home from fishing at Coulter Bay. As they approached Moran Junction, where they would turn south toward Jackson, they passed several officers who were at the right of the road. These were Sergeant Wilson of the Wyoming Highway Patrol and park police whom he was briefing. None of these officers made any effort to warn appellees of the hazardous situation developing on U.S. Highway 89 onto which appellees' vehicle turned.

As appellees approached the roadblock, surprised officers began frantically gesturing for them to go through as a deputy sheriff moved his car for their passage. Ortega, approaching at 100 miles per hour or more, went through the same opening, smashing into Coziah's car which was going approximately thirty miles per hour. Coziah and Bassett were injured, and Ortega was arrested.

. . . [Bassett and Coziah sued.] The jury allocated 0% fault to Coziah, 40% fault to the Wyoming Highway Patrol, 20% fault to the Sheriff's officers, and 40% fault to the National Park Service. . . .

Since it is dispositive, we turn first to the question of whether Ortega, whose conduct was willful and wanton or intentional, should have been included among the actors whose fault would be determined and compared with that of the other actors by the jury in apportioning fault among the actors as required by Wyo. Stat. Ann § 1–1–109. Appellees contend, and the district court held, that Ortega's willful and wanton or intentional conduct could not be compared with the conduct of appellants. . . .

Unlike the version before the 1994 amendment to Wyo. Stat. Ann. 1–1–109, which used "negligence," its present iteration introduces the more inclusive term "fault" and defines it as including conduct that is "in any measure negligent" eliminating degrees or varieties of negligence consistent with one of the purposes of the statute, that is to ameliorate the harshness of the doctrine of contributory negligence. The comparative negligence statute remedied the injustice of the doctrine of contributory negligence by stating that a plaintiff's negligence prevents recovery only in proportion as it causes plaintiff's damages.

The use of the word "includes" is significant because "includes" generally signifies an intent to enlarge a statute's application, rather than limit it, and it implies the conclusion that there are other items includable, though not specifically enumerated.

Appellees insist this is not so because the words "reckless," "wanton," "culpable" or "intentional" were stricken from the definition of "fault" in Senate File No. 35 evincing clear intent that they were not included in the definition of "fault" as conduct "in any measure negligent." This argument reads more into the deletion than we think justified. It leaves unexplained the legislature's expansion of "negligence" to "fault" which includes conduct "in any measure negligent." It may be as reasonable to attribute the deletions to a belief that the deleted words are subsumed in the phrase "in any measure negligent" as it would be to attribute them to other motives. . . .

Application of Wyo. Stat. Ann. § 1–1–109 in this case to include Ortega as an actor is also consistent with the other purpose of the statute, the elimination of joint and several liability. Subsection (e) provides that "[e]ach defendant is liable only to the extent of that defendant's proportion of the total fault * * *." To leave an actor such as Ortega out of the apportionment calculation exposes the remaining appellants to the possibility that they will be held to answer for his misconduct. Such a result does act as an incentive to those with a duty to protect against intentional harm, and "[a] number of courts therefore have concluded that persons who negligently fail to protect against the specific risk of an intentional tort should bear the risk that the intentional tortfeasor is insolvent." Restatement (Third) of Torts § 24 cmt. b at 164 (Proposed Final Draft (Revised) 3/22/99). The statutory elimination of joint and several liability, however, forecloses our consideration of the merits of such a policy. . . .

The exclusion of Ortega from the verdict form frustrates the legislature's expressed intent, and the defendants were entitled to have the causation rule of DeWald given as an instruction to the jury. We reverse and remand for a new trial.

NOTES

1. **Comparing negligence with intentional wrongdoing.** Several courts agree with the proposition that negligence of one defendant can be compared with intentional or willful wrongdoing of another. *Slack v. Farmers Ins. Exch.*, 5 P.3d 280 (Colo. 2000) (statute construed to require comparison of intentional wrong and negligence where defendant referred plaintiff to a chiropractor it should have known might sexually assault her); *see Barth v. Coleman*, 878 P.2d 319 (N.M. 1994) (bar owner negligently failed to oust or control a threatening attacker, he attacked plaintiff; fault must be apportioned between bar owner and attacker; held, bar owner liable only for his own percentage of fault); *Rodenburg v. Fargo-Moorhead Young Men's Christian Ass'n*, 632 N.W.2d 407 (N.D. 2001) ("A negligent tortfeasor's conduct is compared with an intentional tortfeasor's conduct."); *Berberich v. Jack*, 709 S.E.2d 607 (S.C. 2011) ("comparative negligence encompasses the comparison of ordinary negligence with heightened forms of misconduct"). For a different view, see the next case.

2. **Attributing less fault to an intentional tortfeasor.** Could a jury ever attribute less fault to an insolvent, intentional tortfeasor? In *Hutcherson v. City of Phoenix*, 961 P.2d 449 (Ariz. 1998), a woman made a 911 call reporting a credible threat that she would be killed in a few minutes. She was, and it could have been prevented if the dispatcher had categorized the call as a priority one call, which would have provided an immediate police response. The jury allocated 75% of the fault to the city based upon the dispatcher's negligence and only 25% to the killer. This was upheld by the court of appeals. The state Supreme Court avoided the issue by declaring that the defendant had no duty to plaintiffs. *See* Ellen M. Bublick, *Upside Down? Terrorists, Proprietors, and Civil Responsibility for Crime Prevention in the Post-9/11 Tort-Reform World*, 41 LOY. L.A. L. REV. 1483, 1521 (2008) (suggesting that these apportionments can be upheld if they are viewed as apportionments of civil responsibility rather than as apportionments of fault).

3. **Plaintiff-defendant comparisons.** Distinguish: plaintiff, chargeable with contributory fault, sues an intentional tortfeasor. Ellen M. Bublick, *The End Game of Tort Reform: Comparative Apportionment and Intentional Torts*, 78 NOTRE DAME L. REV. 355 (2003), notes that courts rarely call for apportionment of responsibility as between a contributorily negligent plaintiff and an intentionally wrongdoing defendant. In *Landry v. Bellanger*, 851 So. 2d 943 (La. 2003), the court, governed in part by a statute, held: (1) the plaintiff who negligently provokes an intentional tort will recover full damages against the intentional tortfeasor; (2) the plaintiff who is herself an intentional tortfeasor can recover against an intentional tortfeasor defendant with

damages reduced for comparative fault; (3) the plaintiff can recover nothing against a defendant whose intentional attack is privileged, as in the case of self-defense.

TURNER V. JORDAN, 957 S.W.2d 815 (Tenn. 1997). The plaintiff was a nurse and the defendant a psychiatrist at the same facility. One of the defendant's patients had a known history of violence, but the psychiatrist took no steps to protect those who might be attacked. He later said he did not know the patient's history of violence, but he himself had been attacked by the patient, and he had referred to that history in suggesting that the patient be encouraged to leave "against medical advice." The patient beat the plaintiff, causing a severe head injury. The jury attributed all the fault to the psychiatrist and awarded the plaintiff $1,186,000. The trial judge, however, thought the allocation of fault unjustified and ordered a new trial. *Held*, reversed and remanded for reinstatement of the jury verdict. The key issue is "whether the negligent act of a defendant should be compared with the intentional act of another in determining comparative fault. . . . [T]he concern in cases that compare the negligence of a defendant with the intentional act of a third party is not burdening the negligent tortfeasor with liability in excess of his or her fault; conversely, the primary concern in those cases that do not compare is that the plaintiff not be penalized by allowing the negligent party to use the intentional act it had a duty to prevent to reduce its liability. In our view, the conduct of a negligent defendant should not be compared with the intentional conduct of another in determining comparative fault where the intentional conduct is the foreseeable risk created by the negligent tortfeasor." Such a comparison presents practical difficulties in comparing acts that are different in both degree and kind and "reduces the negligent person's incentive to comply with the applicable duty of care." Further, a negligent defendant "should not be permitted to rely upon the foreseeable harm it had a duty to prevent so as to reduce its liability."

NOTES

1.   **Rejecting apportionment between intentional and negligent tortfeasors.** A number of cases or statutes side with *Turner* by holding or providing that apportionment between a negligent defendant and an intentional tortfeasor is not permitted, at least not in situations like the one reflected in *Bassett* and *Turner*. *See Bhinder v. Sun Co.*, 819 A.2d 822 (Conn. 2003); *Kansas State Bank & Trust Co. v. Specialized Transp. Servs., Inc.*, 819 P.2d 587 (Kan. 1991); *Veazey v. Elmwood Plantation Assocs., Ltd.*, 650 So. 2d 712 (La. 1994). In *Brandon v. County of Richardson*, 624 N.W.2d 604 (Neb. 2001), the court construed its statutes to exclude comparison between negligence and intent, but also observed that "it would be irrational to allow a party who negligently fails to discharge a duty to protect to reduce its liability

because there is an intervening intentional tort when the intervening intentional tort is exactly what the negligent party had a duty to protect against."

2. **Intent and negligence under the Restatement of Apportionment.** The Restatement of Apportionment favors comparison of all forms of culpability, so that the trier assigns a percentage of responsibility both to the negligent and to the intentional actor. However, when a negligent defendant specifically risks an intentional tort to the plaintiff, there is no apportionment to reduce the plaintiff's damages—the negligent defendant remains jointly and severally liable to the plaintiff. RESTATEMENT (THIRD) OF TORTS: APPORTIONMENT OF LIABILITY § 14 (2000). And the intentional tortfeasor is always jointly and severally liable for the entire damage. *Id.* § 12; *cf. Woods v. Cole,* 693 N.E.2d 333 (Ill. 1998) (joint and several liability remains for concerted action).

3. **Intentional tortfeasor's indemnity obligation.** If a negligent tortfeasor is held liable for the entire amount of the plaintiff's damages, could he obtain an indemnity judgment against the intentional tortfeasor? *See Degener v. Hall Contracting Corp.,* 27 S.W.3d 775 (Ky. 2000).

4. **Causal apportionment?** In *Welch v. Southland Corp.,* 952 P.2d 162 (Wash. 1998), the court held that apportionment of "fault" under the statute only includes some species of negligence, not intentional wrongdoing, so the defendant who negligently permits an intentional tortfeasor to harm the plaintiff is liable without apportionment. Yet in *Tegman v. Accident & Medical Investigations, Inc.,* 75 P.3d 497 (Wash. 2003), the same court said that while the negligent tortfeasor could not apportion "fault" to the intentional tortfeasor, the negligent tortfeasor would not be liable for damages caused by the intentional tortfeasor. Under standard concepts of causation, how could this work?

5. **Single, indivisible injury; either defendant's act is sufficient to cause harm.** Suppose two defendants negligently set separate fires. Each fire is blown by winds towards the plaintiff's farm. Either would suffice to burn the house down, but by happenstance of the winds, the two fires "combine" before they reach the plaintiff's farm. It is then burned down by the combined fire. Defendant A is fully insured but B has no insurance and no assets. Should A be liable for only one-half the damages? Notice that (a) his negligence is exactly the same as if B did not exist, and (b) the damage is exactly the same as if B did not exist.

6. **A's negligence creates B's opportunity for harm.** In one kind of traditional joint and several liability case, the first tortfeasor's negligence makes the second tortfeasor's fault possible. In *Hines v. Garrett*, 108 S.E. 690 (Va. 1921), the railroad was responsible for putting the plaintiff at risk of rape by unknown persons. She was in fact raped and the railroad was held liable. The railroad's fault is significant but obviously not in the category with that of the rapists. Does it really make any sense to apportion fault at all in this kind of case, and, if so, to limit the railroad's liability?

7. **A problem.** Suppose that Tenant leases premises from Landlord. The landlord's duty to the tenant is to warn of dangers of which the landlord actually knows and the tenant does not. The landlord knows the floor is flimsy and could collapse and he does warn the tenant. The tenant thereafter invites a social guest to the premises without warning the guest. The floor collapses with the guest, causing her injuries. What liabilities if any should be visited upon Landlord and Tenant in a state that has abolished joint and several liability? *Rittenour v. Gibson,* 656 N.W.2d 691 (N.D. 2003).

C. NON-PARTIES AT FAULT

CRAMER V. STARR
375 P.3d 69 (Ariz. 2016)

PELANDER, VICE CHIEF JUSTICE.

[Defendant Courtney Cramer rear-ended a car in which plaintiff Tammy Munguia was a passenger. Munguia had an MRI that revealed disc protrusions in her lumbar spine. Approximately eight months later, Dr. John Ehteshami, performed spinal fusion surgery, which did not cure Munguia's symptoms and might have exacerbated her condition. Munguia filed suit against Cramer. Cramer filed a notice naming Dr. Ehteshami as a non-party at fault. The trial court granted Munguia's motion for partial summary judgment to strike the notice, based on determination that the driver, as the original tortfeasor, was liable for foreseeable risks, including risk of negligently performed medical treatment. The Court of Appeals declined to exercise jurisdiction. Driver petitioned for and was granted review in the Arizona Supreme Court.]

Under Arizona's comparative fault regime, "[i]n assessing percentages of fault" in a personal injury action, "the trier of fact shall consider the fault of all persons who contributed to the alleged injury." A.R.S. § 12–2506(B). In allocating fault, the trier may consider a nonparty's negligence or fault if the defendant gives notice that "a nonparty was wholly or partially at fault." *Id.* . . .

Cramer argues that the trial court, by striking her notice, erroneously took the issue of comparative fault from the jury, in violation of A.R.S. § 12–2506. She also asserts that Second Restatement § 457, on which the trial court relied, could never trump that controlling Arizona statute and case law and, in any event, has been superseded by Restatement (Third) of Torts, Liability for Physical and Emotional Harm § 35 (Am. Law Inst. 2009) ("Third Restatement § 35").

Munguia counters that Arizona courts have long embraced the OTR [original tortfeasor rule] embodied in Second Restatement § 457 (as retained and broadened in Third Restatement § 35), a rule she characterizes as one of causation that was not displaced or abrogated by the Uniform Contribution among Tortfeasors Act ("UCATA"). A.R.S. §§ 12–2501 through—2509. Under the OTR, Munguia asserts, Cramer cannot escape or reduce her liability by claiming harm was caused by non-party Dr. Ehteshami, but rather she is independently liable for any and all enhanced harm proximately resulting from her actions and foreseeably caused by a successive tortfeasor.

We agree with Cramer that UCATA applies and controls the outcome here. As first enacted in 1984, the Act allowed a tortfeasor who paid more than the percentage of damages attributed to it by the factfinder to seek contribution from co-tortfeasors. The legislature amended the Act three years later by generally eliminating plaintiffs' ability to recover jointly from any or all liable defendants. With certain exceptions not applicable here, the liability of each defendant for damages is several only. Thus, Arizona's pure comparative fault scheme protects defendants from bearing more than their fair share of liability for a plaintiff's injuries under the harsh common-law rule of joint and several liability.

UCATA requires apportionment of damages based on degrees of fault. Under § 12–2506(A), "[e]ach defendant is liable only for the amount of damages allocated to that defendant in direct proportion to that defendant's percentage of fault." "Fault" is broadly defined as "an actionable breach of legal duty, act or omission proximately causing or contributing to injury or damages sustained by a person seeking recovery." UCATA is thus based on the concept of fault, which necessarily presupposes a duty, breach of duty, and causation.

Under A.R.S. § 12–2506(B), the trier of fact assesses percentages of fault after considering the fault of all persons who contributed to the alleged injury. That mandate applies "regardless of whether the person was, or could have been, named as a party to the suit." UCATA thus contemplates and permits the naming of nonparties whose alleged fault the trier of fact may consider in apportioning liability. . . . We have repeatedly held that under UCATA, the trier of fact must consider the fault of all parties and properly named nonparties in assessing and allocating percentages of fault. . . .

Neither the court's ruling nor Munguia's argument can be reconciled with UCATA's clear directives. Section 12–2506(D) identifies various circumstances under which "a party is responsible for the fault of another person, or for payment of the proportionate share of another person." But those exceptions do not apply here. And the statutes contain no exception to UCATA's several-liability rule when (1) a medical provider's post-accident services, even if medically necessary and foreseeable, are allegedly negligent and cause the claimant to sustain new or enhanced injury, or, more broadly, (2) when a non-party at fault is a medical practitioner.

Having named Dr. Ehteshami as a nonparty at fault, Cramer is entitled to have the trier of fact consider Dr. Ehteshami's alleged negligence in assessing percentages of fault. . . . As Cramer acknowledges, she bears the burden of proving any fault on Dr. Ehteshami's part. . . .

The trial court based its ruling on Second Restatement § 457, entitled "Additional Harm Resulting From Efforts to Mitigate Harm Caused by Negligence," which sets forth the OTR:

> If the negligent actor is liable for another's bodily injury, he is also subject to liability for any additional bodily harm resulting from normal efforts of third persons in rendering aid which the other's injury reasonably requires, irrespective of whether such acts are done in a proper or a negligent manner.

The comments to that section indicate that when a negligent actor causes an injury that may require medical services, it is reasonably foreseeable that such services could be performed negligently, thereby adding to the original injury. In such cases, the original tortfeasor is responsible for any additional injury resulting from the other's exposure to the risk of negligently performed medical services. Our court of appeals has referred to and arguably relied on, but not expressly adopted, Second Restatement § 457. . . .

In Arizona, if there is no statute or case law on a particular subject, we have traditionally followed the Restatement of Laws, and generally will embrace the Restatement if it prescribes a sound and sensible rule. Here, however, UCATA and our case law clearly permit Cramer's notice of nonparty at fault and, assuming evidentiary support exists, require the trier of fact to consider Dr. Ehteshami's alleged negligence in assessing and allocating fault and to determine liability. Thus, to the extent Second Restatement § 457 can be read to preclude those procedures and to support the trial court's ruling, it is directly contrary to Arizona law and we reject it. . . .

The Restatement (Second) of Torts has been updated and revised by the Restatement (Third) of Torts. As it relates to the OTR, the Third Restatement generally reiterates Second Restatement § 457. *See* Third Restatement § 35, cmt. a. Entitled "Enhanced Harm Due to Efforts to Render Medical or Other Aid," Third Restatement § 35 provides:

> An actor whose tortious conduct is a factual cause of harm to another is subject to liability for any enhanced harm the other suffers due to the efforts of third persons to render aid reasonably required by the other's injury, so long as the enhanced harm arises from a risk that inheres in the effort to render aid.

The Third Restatement emphasizes that adoption of several-only liability statutes like UCATA does not require or imply any change to the

OTR. As Comment (d) explains, this is because "[m]odern adoption of pure several liability *limits the liability* of each defendant liable for the same harm to that defendant's comparative share of the harm." Several liability, however, does not provide rules about *when* defendants are liable for harm that they caused. Instead, as Comment (d) clarifies, when the state's governing law imposes several liability, each of the defendants is held liable for the amount of damages reflecting the enhanced harm *discounted* by the comparative share of responsibility assigned by the factfinder to that defendant.

Thus, the OTR, now set forth in Third Restatement § 35, can be read in conjunction with the governing law of the state. When the state's law generally provides for several-only liability, as does UCATA, the OTR provides guidelines only regarding *when* a defendant may be subject to liability for future, enhanced harm that stems from the original negligent conduct—e.g., when the original tortfeasor's conduct created a reasonably foreseeable risk that future medical services may be necessary and that those services may be performed negligently. But the Third Restatement makes clear that the OTR yields to a state's law governing the apportionment of fault (and consequently, damages) based on the factfinder's determination of each potential tortfeasor's comparative share of responsibility. . . .

Subject to UCATA, the OTR can serve a useful purpose in cases like this. As stated earlier, the rule cannot be used to automatically impute to the original tortfeasor the subsequent negligence of a medical provider or other person who renders aid reasonably required by the original tortfeasor's act. But because UCATA defines fault as an actionable breach of duty that proximately caused the plaintiff's injury, plaintiffs remain free to argue under Third Restatement § 35 that an original tortfeasor proximately caused subsequent, enhanced injury and shares all or at least some responsibility for that injury. *See* Third Restatement § 35, cmt. d (noting that the "subsequent negligence of one rendering assistance to an injured person is not a superseding cause of any enhanced harm, thereby including such harm within the initial tortfeasor's scope of liability").

UCATA does not immunize or shield Cramer from liability for the enhanced harm allegedly caused by Dr. Ehteshami's negligence. If Munguia shows that the conditions of Third Restatement § 35 are met, Cramer will have proximately caused the enhanced harm, and her liability for such harm will be determined, consistent with UCATA, by the jury's assessment of comparative fault.

The trial court erred in striking Cramer's notice of nonparty at fault. . . .

PRICE V. KITSAP TRANSIT, 886 P.2d 556 (Wash. 1994). The plaintiff, already suffering from a whiplash in an earlier bus accident, was riding the defendant's bus. A four-year-old boy, walking in the aisle and holding his father's hand, suddenly reached into the driver's area and engaged an emergency stop switch, bringing the bus to a sudden halt and causing serious injury to the plaintiff. The jury found that the boy was guilty of 80% of the negligence, his father 10% and the bus company 10%. Tort reform legislation required the jury to apportion fault among "every entity which caused the claimant's damages, including the claimant or person suffering personal injury or incurring property damage, defendants, third-party defendants, entities released by the claimant, entities immune from liability to the claimant and entities with any other individual defense against the claimant. . . ." *Held,* no fault can be apportioned to the boy. Children under six years of age are incapable of negligence. Although fault of an immune entity is to be considered, the boy is not immune; rather, he is not at fault. "This interpretation agrees with the fundamental practice of not assigning fault to animals, inanimate objects, and forces of nature which are not considered 'entities' under the statute."

NOTES

1.   **UCATA.** The Uniform Contribution among Tortfeasors Act was a model act prepared by the National Commissioners on Uniform State Laws. The act was quite influential, and adopted by over 20 state legislatures. The Act shifted away from all-or-nothing contributory fault and provided for the division of responsibility between parties by percentages assigned by the jury. The Act retained joint and several liability. However, most legislatures, as in Arizona, changed the rule to several liability. The Uniform Law Commission replaced the Act with the Uniform Apportionment of Tort Responsibility Act ("The Uniform Apportionment Act"). This subsequent act would reapportion uncollectible shares between the parties. Though many commentators regard the later Act as more fair and coherent, most state legislatures have not changed their rules.

2.   **Apportioning fault to non-parties.** What happens if the jury apportions a large percentage of the fault to the surgeon? Does the driver have to pay it? Does the surgeon have to pay it? Who bears that portion of the loss? Why wouldn't the plaintiff just sue both the driver and the surgeon? If the defendant has to prove the doctor was a non-party at fault, should the defendant have to bring in expert testimony and comport with other burdens of proving medical negligence?

3.   **Effects of eliminating some defendants or non-parties from the calculus.** As *Price* suggests, the effects of abolishing joint and several liability may be mitigated if the negligence of some persons is disregarded in calculating comparative fault. Notice that the result in *Price* does not quite mimic the result of a joint and several liability system. The bus company is not liable for 90% but presumably only 50%.

4. **Phantom tortfeasors.** Plaintiffs have sometimes argued that the fault of any person who is not joined as a party in the suit should be ignored, so that only the fault of the plaintiff and the actual defendants should be compared. The plaintiff would not join an insolvent tortfeasor and could not join an unknown tortfeasor like a hit and run driver. Some courts have held that the fault of everyone, joined or not joined, is to be considered. However, the Uniform Apportionment Act allocates responsibility among those who are actual parties to the litigation and disregards the fault of all nonparties except released persons. *See* UNIFORM APPORTIONMENT OF TORT RESPONSIBILITY ACT, PREFACE, APPORTIONING TORT RESPONSIBILITY IN THIS ACT (2002).

5. **Immune tortfeasors.** One major area of current decision in the courts is whether liability should be apportioned to immune parties such as employers. Some cases oppose this apportionment. *See CSX Transp., Inc. v. Miller*, 46 So. 3d 434 (Ala. 2010) (FELA). However, others have held that the negligence of immune persons must be considered in determining the fault percentages of other tortfeasors. *E.g., Collins v. Plant Insulation Co.*, 110 Cal. Rptr. 3d 241 (Ct. App. 2010). The inevitable result of including the immune tortfeasors is that the amount of fault attributable to the solvent and non-immune defendant is reduced, and his liability along with it. Sometimes statutes so provides. *See* LA. CIV. CODE § 2324B. This is also the provision of the Uniform Apportionment Act.

6. **Settlement effects.** Suppose the plaintiff suffers $100,000 damages as a result of the combined negligence of A and B. A settles for $50,000. The plaintiff goes to trial against B and the jury finds her total damages to be $100,000 and B's negligence is 70%, while P's negligence is 10% of the total. If joint and several liability is abolished, isn't it clear that the plaintiff should recover $70,000 from B, even though that gives her a recovery in excess of the total damage? *See Wells v. Tallahassee Mem'l Reg'l Med. Ctr., Inc.*, 659 So. 2d 249 (Fla. 1995). The Uniform Apportionment Act considers the fault of and apportions responsibility to only those tortfeasors who are parties, *except* that it considers the fault of (a) immune persons and (b) persons who have settled with the plaintiff. Under this approach, if the plaintiff settles with A, then sues B, and the jury in the suit against B finds A's fault to be 75% and B's 25%, B owes only 25% of the damages. In contrast, Massachusetts has held that the fault of a settling tortfeasor is ignored in its joint and several liability system; the jury apportions 100% of the fault between the plaintiff and defendant. *Shantigar Found. v. Bear Mountain Builders,* 804 N.E.2d 324 (Mass. 2004).

§ 4. AN INTRODUCTION TO SETTLEMENTS

A. BEING AWARE OF INSURANCE

Knowledge of insurance and insurance law is extremely important in personal injury law practice. The subject usually gets a course to itself in law schools. We must omit details, but a few things must be understood.

One kind of insurance is "first party" insurance. You buy the coverage you want in case of harm to you or your property. Fire insurance and automobile collision insurance is like this. A common feature of first-party insurance policies is that the insured is entitled to recover upon proof of loss covered by the policy and it is not necessary to show fault on the part of anyone. Indeed, even the insured's own fault, short of intentional damage to his own property, is irrelevant.

A second general kind of insurance is "liability" insurance. You buy liability insurance in the amount you want or the amount you are legally required to have, but the insurance does not pay you. Instead it pays your *legal liability* to a person who claims you caused harm to him or to his property. Such insurance pays the claimant only if you are legally liable, so your insurance company has a right to your cooperation and a right to defend you. It also has a *duty* to defend you up to the amount of your policy.

The duty to defend carries with it the insurer's right to be involved in, if not to control, the investigation, negotiation and settlement of the case. It imposes upon the insurer the obligation to retain an attorney to defend the insured's interests. The result of all this is that to a very large extent the insurer is the *de facto* defendant, though in most states the named defendant in court is the insured, not the insurer. The lawyer, even if retained by the insurer, continues to owe his primary duty to the insured as the client, but must cooperate with the insurer except where the insurer and the insured's interests conflict.

The liability insurer's exact duties depend primarily on the contract between it and the insured, that is, upon the policy terms. The insurer can argue that under the terms of the policy it has a "policy defense"—some reason under the policy that the particular claim against the insured is excluded from insurance coverage. This creates a complex relationship between insured persons and their insurers, and sometimes serious conflicts. If the liability insurer fails to meet either its duty to defend or to pay on your behalf, it may become liable to you in tort. You can see an example in *State Farm Mut. Auto. Ins. Co. v. Campbell*, 538 U.S. 408 (2003).

An important effect of liability insurance is that it provides a fund available to pay judgments, without which legal liability might be meaningless. Over the years there has been an increased "socialization" of insurance, in which liability insurance is seen as a tool for financing injury loss. The existence of liability insurance encourages the expansion of tort liability, and could at times encourage excessive damages awards. KENNETH S. ABRAHAM, THE LIABILITY CENTURY: INSURANCE AND TORT LAW FROM THE PROGRESSIVE ERA TO 9/11 (2008). Does liability insurance protection undercut the idea of individual accountability and the effects of deterrence?

B. BASIC RULES

The vast majority of tort suits are settled without trial. The plaintiff accepts a sum of money and gives the defendant a document, usually a "release," the effect of which is to absolve the defendant of further liability. Consequently, settlement practice is part of the actual practice of tort law.

In general, settlement negotiations happen behind the scenes. Terms of proposed settlement offers cannot be admitted at trial either as an admission of fault or for any other purpose. Furthermore, statutes in a number of states provide that a defendant may make a written offer to settle a claim for a certain amount (called an "offer of judgment"). If the plaintiff rejects this offer and then fails to obtain a more favorable judgment at trial, the plaintiff must pay all of the defendant's costs, including attorney fees, from the time of the offer. *See, e.g.,* N.Y. C.P.L.R. § 3221; CAL. CIV. PROC. CODE § 998 (also applying, in a limited way, to plaintiffs' offers).

Settlements reflect the lawyers' estimates of how the facts will play out at trial and how legal issues will probably be decided. So the standard of care requires lawyers to prepare for settlement much as they would prepare for trial, with good development of the facts and clear understanding of the legal issues and arguments. Knowing the facts bearing on liability is not enough; lawyers must also know the facts about injury, its probable extent, and possible future effects. Settlement estimates cannot be made with certainty and sometimes settlement law involving multiple parties is itself complex.

The law and ethics rules pertaining to lawyers provides that it is the client's decision, not the lawyer's, whether and on what terms to settle a claim. The lawyer is obligated to explain the ramifications of settlement offers with sufficient clarity to allow the client to reach such a decision. This is both an ethical and a legal obligation. RESTATEMENT OF THE LAW GOVERNING LAWYERS § 22 (2000); ABA MODEL RULES OF PROFESSIONAL CONDUCT 1.2(a) & 1.4. The lawyer who fails fully to inform his client about acceptance of a settlement is subject to liability for malpractice. *Wood v. McGrath, North, Mullin & Kratz, P.C.,* 589 N.W.2d 103 (Neb. 1999). Moreover, a lawyer who negligently advises a client to settle may be subject to a legal malpractice claim as well. *See* PAUL T. HAYDEN, ETHICAL LAWYERING 91–97 (3d ed. 2012).

> REFERENCE: 3 DOBBS, HAYDEN & BUBLICK, THE LAW OF TORTS
> §§ 487–501 (2d ed. 2011); DOBBS, HAYDEN & BUBLICK, HORNBOOK ON
> TORTS Chapter 35 (2d ed. 2016).

CHAPTER 26

DAMAGES

■ ■ ■

§ 1. COMPENSATORY DAMAGES

Factors affecting settlement are largely factors that also affect the trial and ultimate award. As a plaintiff you don't accept an offer of $100 if you think the jury will award you $100,000. As a defendant you don't offer $100,000 if you think the jury will award nothing at all. Estimating probable jury awards is no easy matter. Lawyers must consider many matters, including the legal rules that guide, counsel, and constrain jurors' damage awards.

A. PROVING AND COMPUTING BASIC DAMAGES

The topic of tort damages is a small part of two larger fields. One field might be called "trial practice," which concerns itself with strategy, tactics, and rules of procedure and evidence governing trials. The trial tactics side of damages appears here only incidentally. The other field is that of "remedies," which includes not only the damages remedy but also the remedies of injunction and restitution. All three remedies are available in many tort cases. The field of remedies is a broad one, summarized in three volumes in DAN B. DOBBS, THE LAW OF REMEDIES (2d ed. 1993) (hereafter cited as DOBBS, REMEDIES), but some of the key rules are covered here.

Constitutional torts. We have seen that the plaintiff might have a personal injury or property damage claim under § 1983 based on the defendant's violation of plaintiff's constitutional rights. In such cases, courts apply the same damages rules that apply in any personal injury or property damage case. Some constitutional violations, though, cause no obvious physical injury to person or property. For instance, suppose you are denied the right to vote or your right to free speech is infringed in violation of the Constitution. In these cases the Supreme Court has so far insisted that you must prove actual damages, such as pecuniary loss or at least actual mental distress, in order to recover anything more than nominal ($1) damages. This problem is discussed in Jean C. Love, *Presumed General Compensatory Damages in Constitutional Tort Litigation: A Corrective Justice Perspective*, 49 WASH. & LEE L. REV. 67 (1992); 2 DOBBS, REMEDIES § 7.4.

Property torts. Quite a few torts involve physical injury to, or dispossession of, tangible property, real or personal. We have already seen that for total dispossession of personalty there is a conversion action, in which damages are measured by the full market value of the thing converted. When there is similar dispossession of real property, there is no analogous damages claim. Instead, the plaintiff recovers the rental value of the property during the time of dispossession. When physical harm is done to tangible property, the measure of damages is very often the diminished value of the property. Thus if A trespasses on Blackacre and damages a house, the owner or possessor will be entitled to recover a sum equal to the difference between the value immediately before and the value immediately after the damage. When the diminished value cannot be measured through this metric, because the property "has no commercial or market equivalent, its value, or plaintiff's damages, must be ascertained in some other rational way." *See U.S. v. CB & I Constructors, Inc.,* 685 F.3d 827 (9th Cir. 2012) (upholding a jury award of $28.2 million for intangible environmental harm to government property after defendants' negligence destroyed 18,000 acres of national forest).

For a number of reasons, the cost of repair may be substituted as a measure of damages in certain cases, especially where the repair will not likely enhance the damaged property to make it more valuable. *See Brooks v. City of Huntington,* 768 S.E.2d 97 (W.Va. 2014) (plaintiff may recover reasonable repair costs for damage to residential property, and may also recover related expenses caused by the inconvenience and loss of use of the property during the repair period).

The injunctive remedy is also important in certain tort cases. If the defendant repeatedly trespasses on the plaintiff's land, or threatens to trespass in some way that will cause irreparable harm, such as by cutting down old oak trees, the plaintiff may be entitled to an injunction prohibiting such a tort. Injunction is also important in many cases involving intangible property, such as a trademark, and in other business tort cases, such as those involving interference with contracts. *See generally* 1 DOBBS, REMEDIES, Chapter 5.

Personal injury torts. Personal injuries may occur through intentional torts, through negligence, or through strict liability torts. But the compensatory damages are theoretically the same for any given broken jaw without regard to whether the jaw was broken through intent, negligence, or wholly without fault. "The purpose of compensatory damages is to make the plaintiff whole for [the] injury." *Clausen v. Icicle Seafoods, Inc.,* 272 P.3d 827 (Wash. 2012). "[A]n award of damages to a person injured by the negligence of another is to compensate the victim, not to punish the wrongdoer. The goal is to restore the injured party, to the extent possible, to the position that would have been occupied had the wrong not occurred." *McDougald v. Garber,* 536 N.E.2d 372 (N.Y. 1989). The purpose of punitive damages is quite different. It is "to punish the defendant and deter similar conduct." *Clausen,* 272 P.3d at 832. Punitive damages may be warranted in some cases where the defendant's conduct is "malicious" or wanton.

The main elements of compensatory damages for personal injuries can be stated quite easily:

(1) Damages for reasonably incurred medical expenses resulting from the tort.

(2) Damages for lost earning capacity or wage loss resulting from the tort.

(3) Damages for pain and suffering resulting from the tort, including mental pain and suffering.

(4) In a limited number of cases, an award to pay for the cost of medical monitoring of the plaintiff's condition to intercept a prospective disease, such as cancer, that may develop in the future.

(5) Any other specifically identifiable harm that has resulted from the tort, such as special expenses necessary to travel for medical attention.

In each category, the plaintiff is also entitled to recover for future damages if they are reasonably certain to occur. How difficult is it to calculate these elements of damages?

MARTIN V. UNITED STATES
471 F. Supp. 6 (D. Ariz. 1979)

JAMES M. BURNS, DISTRICT JUDGE.

[Federal Tort Claims Act case tried to the judge. The plaintiffs, two school boys, riding a motorbike, struck a sagging power line negligently maintained by the government. Each "suffered tragically severe and permanent injuries" from the burns.

Plaintiff Melvin Burrows II sustained severe burns to his face, head, back, buttocks, arms, and legs. Medical expenses to Burrows to the time of trial came to $48,130.97, and future medical expenses will come to about $49,000 additional. $5,000 for psychological treatments, as recommended by a psychologist, is also appropriate. Loss of earnings evidence and calculations are as follows.]

Clarence Martin is principal of the Florence middle school, owner of a roofing business that employs Melvin Burrows' father, and uncle of the other plaintiff in this case. He testified upon the basis of his observation of Melvin during the seven years he has known him and the month and a half that Melvin had attended the middle school prior to the accident. He believed that Melvin was average or above average in intelligence and probably would have become a skilled worker, perhaps a mechanic or a carpenter. Dr. Glenn Wilt, an associate professor of finance at Arizona State University and an investment counselor stated:

[I]t can be reasonably presumed that, but for their injuries, both Melvin and Jeffrey would have gravitated into positions in one of the construction trades. Clearly, that is exactly what most of their uninjured classmates will do, and considering the general demand in this territory, due to the growth of population and need for attendant services in the construction field, a strong demand can be forecast for these jobs.

Dr. David Yandell, a clinical psychologist and vocational rehabilitation counselor called by the defendant, testified that the intelligence and aptitude tests administered by Dr. Donald [Guinourd] show that Melvin could not have pursued a career in the skilled crafts but instead probably would have become a laborer. Defendant's other witness, Dr. John Buehler, chairman of the department of economics at the University of Arizona, expressed his opinion that neither plaintiff probably would have become a worker in the skilled trades, but rather each would have earned average wages.

Based upon my evaluation of the testimony and the expertise and credibility of the witnesses, I conclude that Melvin Burrows probably would have become a skilled worker. Dr. Wilt stated that a carpenter would, at 1978 wage rates, earn about $9,450 per year during a four-year apprenticeship and during a subsequent 42-year career as a journeyman carpenter would earn about $18,900 annually in wages and $3,900 annually in fringe benefits. I accept these figures as reasonable approximations of Melvin's lifetime earnings had he not experienced this accident.

Dr. Guinourd testified that Melvin might be employable as a night watchman or night diesel mechanic not involved with the public interaction aspect of either business. Dr. Wilt concluded that, because of Melvin's disfigurement and intolerance to sunlight and perspiration, he would probably be unable to find a job suited to his handicap. Dr. Canter testified that Melvin would benefit psychologically from working even at a lowly position.

Based upon the testimony and my own observation of Melvin Burrows, I conclude that he probably will be able to work at an entry-level position for at least half of his normal working life. According to Dr. Wilt, such work would generate an annual income of $3,120 in 1978 dollars. Thus, Melvin is entitled to recover in 1978 dollars $6,330 per year for four years (apprenticeship period), then $19,680 per year for the following 42 years (journeyman period). . . .

I find that the award can presently be invested at very little risk and return 7.5% compounded annually. I find that 5.5% is a reasonable annual rate of wage inflation to be expected during Melvin's working lifetime.

I award an amount for the loss of Melvin's earning capacity sufficient when invested at a 7.5% annual rate of return to generate in 1978 dollars $6,330 per year for the four years 1983–1986 (hypothetical apprenticeship period) and $19,680 per year for the following 42 years 1987–2028 (hypothetical journeyman period). These amounts in 1978 dollars are to be converted to current dollars for each year by application of a 5.5% expected annual rate of wage inflation, then discounted at 7.5% per year back to 1979. By this method of calculation, the award for loss of Melvin's earning capacity amounts to $548,029.

The power line struck Melvin on the face, head and perhaps also on the back, causing severe and extensive burns on those areas and on "blowout holes" on his buttocks, legs, left arm and right hand, where the electric current left his body seeking the ground. More than 80% of his head and face was burned, 70% to the third degree or worse. He also suffered third degree burns on 40% of his back, on his entire left buttocks and on at least six blowout ulcers. Melvin regained consciousness soon after the accident and was found wandering in the desert near the scene. Dr. Williams Clemans, a general practitioner in Florence, treated Melvin briefly in the back of a pickup truck outside the local hospital before having him sent to the burn treatment unit at the Maricopa County Hospital in Phoenix. Dr. Clemans testified that Melvin appeared to be in critical condition. He doubted whether Melvin would survive long enough to reach the burn unit.

At the Maricopa County Hospital where Melvin remained for four months, the surgeons removed the charred layers of skin and tissue from Melvin's face, head, buttocks and other areas of his body. They performed numerous skin grafts and attempted to fashion a functioning right eyelid, which Melvin still cannot close. Melvin lost his right ear entirely and the top third of his left ear. To graft skin onto his left temple, which had been burned down to the skull, the doctors ground the skull down to granulation tissue that would accept a graft. Restoring hair growth to this area would require an additional series of scalp rotation operations. The operations have left Melvin's face and scalp severely scarred, his mouth permanently contorted into a sneer. Because his facial nerves and muscles have been burned away, even additional surgery will never restore to him the ability to smile.

Of the expected eleven future operations, Melvin will undergo eight additional operations to his face. Skin grafts not infrequently dry out, crack, become infected and ulcerated and must be replaced by new grafts. Sunlight darkens grafted skin permanently, highlighting the injured area.

Grafted areas are also more susceptible to skin cancer than normal tissue. Melvin testified that the grafted areas hurt and itch constantly. Dr. Sacks testified that additional plastic surgeries and skin grafts will not restore a normal appearance to Melvin.

Melvin has suffered psychologically as well as physically. At the burn unit Dr. Canter treated Melvin by hypnosis to relieve pain, prevent regurgitation of food and restore a will to live. Since emerging from the hospital Melvin has faced teasing and ridicule from his peers and startle reactions and revulsion from strangers.

For several months Melvin wore a mask to protect his healing face from further injury. His schoolmates labeled him "Maskatron." During a school outing children from another school saw him and ran away in horror. Strangers often ask, "What happened to you?" Clarence Martin testified that Melvin has become reclusive, reluctant to attend school. Dr. Canter stated that Melvin has become somewhat detached from life, blames himself for his father's heart trouble and may develop schizophrenic tendencies as a result of his injuries. Nor is it likely that Melvin will have a normal social or sexual life, given the severity of the injuries.

Based upon the testimony and my own observation of Melvin, I award $1,000,000 in compensation for pain and suffering.

[The claims made by plaintiff Martin warrant a similar analysis.]

I find that the plaintiffs are entitled to awards as follows:

	BURROWS	MARTIN
Past Medical	$48,130.97	$15,384.38
Future Medical	53,629.00	30,000.00
Loss of Earning Capacity	548,029.00	453,088.00
Pain and Suffering	1,000,000.00	750,000.00
Total	$1,649,788.97	$1,248,472.38

The foregoing shall constitute findings of fact and conclusions pursuant to Rule 52, Fed. R. Civ. P., together with earlier findings and conclusions set out in my oral opinion on February 14, 1979.

NOTES

1. **Inflation and reduction to present value.** Notice that the judge had to make an upward adjustment in the award for future loss in order to account for expected inflation. The judge also made a downward adjustment to account for the fact that although the loss will take place over many years in

the future, all of the money to compensate the plaintiff will be paid now and can be invested. This reduction to present value requires the judge or the trier to determine the amount the plaintiff can earn in safe investments of the award. Any reduction may require expert testimony. *See* 1 DOBBS, REMEDIES §§ 3.7, 8.5.

2. **Periodic payments.** These adjustments would not be necessary if, instead of a lump sum award, future loss were compensated in periodic payments that could be varied as inflation occurred. Some states authorize such payments in a limited class of cases. *See* Roger Henderson, *Designing a Responsible Periodic Payment System for Tort Awards*, 32 ARIZ. L. REV. 21 (1990). At least two courts have held periodic payments statutes unconstitutional under state constitutional provisions against denial of due process and limitation of damages.

3. **The scope of pain and suffering.** The pain and suffering recovery includes all forms of pain, including mental or emotional distress. *Wald v. Grainger*, 64 So. 3d 1201 (Fla. 2011) (pain and suffering includes evidence of sensitivity and discomfort). The pain and suffering recovery includes the negative emotional reactions to pain as well as the pain itself. For example, a disfiguring injury, no longer physically painful, may cause a plaintiff to become self-conscious or even to withdraw from social contact. If so, such reactions count as part of the pain for which damages may be assessed. *See Engquist v. Loyas*, 787 N.W.2d 220 (Minn. Ct. App. 2010) (young girl injured after a dog bit her face, leaving permanent scars; court affirmed $15,000 award for past pain and suffering, disability, disfigurement, and emotional distress); 2 DOBBS, REMEDIES § 8.1(4). In *Martin,* how would you value never being able to smile?

4. **Proving and evaluating pain.** Pain is notoriously difficult to measure or even to talk about meaningfully. In *District of Columbia v. Howell*, 607 A.2d 501 (D.C. 1992), a nine-year-old boy was badly burned in a chemical explosion in school. "The chemicals burned at 5000 degrees Fahrenheit, and Dedrick was burned over 25% of his body including his hands, arms, chest, and face." The jury awarded $8 million in pain and suffering damages. If this award and Martin's had been made in the same year, could you say that one was wrong or even that one was closer to the mark than the other? In *Surette v. Islamic Republic of Iran,* 231 F. Supp. 2d 260 (D.D.C. 2002), a group encouraged by the Republic of Iran tortured Buckley for a long period before he died of his mistreatment. In a suit for his death and for his pre-death pain and suffering, the court said: "Subject to adjustment for cases deviating from the more common experience of victims, this Court typically has awarded former hostages or their estates roughly $10,000 for each day of captivity." *See also Estate of Brown v. Islamic Republic of Iran*, 872 F. Supp. 2d 37 (D.D.C. 2012) (case on behalf of victims of 1983 terrorist bombing of military barracks in Beirut, Lebanon, calculating pain and suffering among other damages).

5. **Argumentation.** Lawyers have developed some effective jury arguments, one of which is called the per diem or unit-of-time argument. It asks the jury to consider the value of pain by the minute or hour and then to

multiply by the number of hours the plaintiff will continue to suffer pain over his lifetime. Federal circuit courts are divided on whether this type of argument is admissible. *Rodriguez v. Señior Frog's de la Isla, Inc.*, 642 F.3d 28, 37 n.3 (1st Cir. 2011).

6. **Pain and suffering pays attorney's fees.** One important thing to bear in mind when you judge pain and suffering awards is the American Rule that each side pays its own attorney. *See* 1 DOBBS, REMEDIES § 3.10. That rule explains why the contingent percentage fee is so important in personal injury cases. Lawyers for injured people must recover their fee from the damages award, since hardly any individual would be able to pay a guaranteed hourly fee for the lawyer's services. If there were no substantial pain and suffering award, lawyers would often be unable to pursue the claim with the vigor it requires simply because damages equal to the plaintiff's pecuniary loss would not bring enough money to justify the time invested.

B. PAIN AND SUFFERING

AVERYT V. WAL-MART STORES, INC.

265 P.3d 456 (Colo. 2011)

JUSTICE RICE delivered the Opinion of the Court. . . .

I. Facts and Proceedings Below

On December 13, 2007, petitioner, Holly Averyt, a commercial truck driver, slipped in grease while making a delivery to Wal-Mart Store # 980 in Greeley. The grease had accumulated in the grocery receiving area. As a result of her fall, Averyt ruptured a disc in her spine and injured her shoulder and neck. These injuries ended her career as a truck driver and have left her unable to perform many daily functions.

[Averyt sued Wal-Mart, alleging that its negligence in failing to clean up the grease spill caused her significant injuries. After a jury verdict for Averyt, Wal-Mart moved for a new trial, arguing among other things that the evidence did not support the amount of damages the jury awarded. The trial judge granted Wal-Mart's motion, and Averyt appealed pursuant to a statute allowing a direct appeal to the state Supreme Court under these circumstances.]

II. Analysis

Generally, this Court will review a decision by the trial court to grant a new trial for an abuse of discretion. A trial court abuses its discretion if its decision is manifestly arbitrary, unreasonable, or unfair. . . .

The jury ultimately found in favor of Averyt and awarded her $15 million in damages, including: $4.5 million in economic damages; $5.5 million in non-economic damages [which the trial court reduced to $366,250 pursuant to a statutory cap; and $5 million for physical impairment. The trial court found the award excessive and granted a new trial. We find] sufficient evidence in the record to support the jury's award. . . .

With regard to non-economic damages, the court found that the damages awarded "exceeded even the amount asked for in Plaintiff's final argument." The trial court described non-economic damages as past and future physical and mental pain and suffering, inconvenience, emotional stress, and impairment of the quality of life. Regardless of the amount that was requested, evidence in the record suggests that Averyt has and will suffer vast non-economic losses. Doctors testified that Averyt suffers from chronic pain and that such pain induces personality changes including depression, difficulty sleeping, and difficulty concentrating. Friends and fellow truck drivers testified that Averyt is now in constant pain, always looks tired and run down, and looks like she has aged ten years from the time of the accident. They further acknowledged her depression and testified that Averyt's most concerning issues were that she could no longer drive her truck, which she enjoyed doing, and a feeling that she could no longer be a productive member of society. A nurse, who was certified as an expert in life-care planning, testified that Averyt was emotional and cried when discussing losing her truck and not being able to do the job that she loved and was good at, as well as when describing the many tasks that she could no longer perform. Another witness, an expert in vocational rehabilitation, testified that when she interviewed Averyt, she "recall[ed] seeing a person in a lot of pain. It was visual, not just on her face, but also her presence." Lastly, Averyt herself testified that she misses the independence that she had in her job as a truck driver. We believe that this is sufficient evidence to support the jury's award of non-economic damages and will not reverse the jury's award. . . .

Averyt's attorney asked for $6.2 million in damages for physical impairment. The trial court specifically instructed the jury that in determining damages for physical impairment, it should not include the economic or non-economic damages already considered. We must assume that the jury followed the court's instructions. . . . Testimony in this case indicated that, as a result of her injuries, Averyt has difficulty walking, falls often, has bladder and bowel incontinence, likely cannot work in any kind of job, and has trouble performing simple everyday tasks such as cooking, carrying groceries, cleaning, and basic hygiene. We believe that the jury's award is supported by the evidence and is not the result of prejudice. Thus, we refuse to reverse the jury's award and grant a new trial.

For the reasons discussed above, we . . . reverse the trial court's order granting a new trial.

NOTES

1. **Noneconomic damages.** Compensatory damages are typically divided into two categories—economic or pecuniary, and noneconomic or nonpecuniary damages. Pecuniary damages compensate the victim for the economic consequences of the injury, such as medical expenses and lost earnings. Nonpecuniary damages are awarded to compensate for the physical and emotional consequences of the injury, such as pain and suffering and the loss of the ability to engage in certain activities. Noncompensatory damages are often the more controversial of the two groups. What is the purpose of these damages? Why not just award pecuniary damages?

2. **Physical disfigurement.** You can see that *Averyt* adds a distinct category of damage. According to the Colorado Supreme Court in *Pringle v. Valdez,* 171 P.3d 624 (Colo. 2007), "under Colorado common law, damages for physical impairment and disfigurement have historically been recognized as a separate element of damages. . . . 'If someone tortiously inflicts a permanent injury on another he or she has taken away something valuable which is independent and different from other recognized elements of damages such as pain and suffering and loss of earning capacity. For this invasion the plaintiff should be awarded a separate sum in addition to the compensation for the other elements and such recovery should be proportional to the severity of the injury.' . . .The principle that a victim is entitled 'to have a sound body and mind throughout his or her life' provides the rationale for this distinction. . . . Physical impairment and disfigurement constitute a permanent injury irrespective of any pain or inconvenience." Do you think courts should recognize some intrinsic value of a sound body and mind in *Averyt*? Does Colorado's cap on pain and suffering damages influence whether you approve of a separate category for physical impairment and disfigurement?

3. **Hedonic damages: the terminology.** In the 1980s, plaintiffs' lawyers and some judges began to use the term hedonic damages from the Greek word referring to pleasure or happiness. The term has acquired ambiguity because those who use it sometimes seem to suggest: (a) a right of recovery for the plaintiff's awareness of lost pleasures; (b) a right of recovery for lost pleasures even when the plaintiff is *not* aware of the loss or, in fact, has died; or (c) a certain type of economic evidence. To avoid misunderstanding, the term is avoided here. For concerns about hedonic damages as a separate category, see Victor E. Schwartz & Carly Silverman, *Hedonic Damages: The Rapidly Bubbling Cauldron*, 69 BROOK. L. REV. 1037 (2004).

4. **Plaintiff's awareness of loss.** When the plaintiff has lost the ability to pursue life's pleasures and knows it, that knowledge or awareness is itself a source of unpleasant feelings, a sense of loss, and even anguish. Recovery is allowed now in most courts without hesitation. *See Maldonado v. Sinai Med. Group, Inc.,* 706 F. Supp. 2d 882 (N.D. Ill. 2010) ($6.7 million noneconomic award not excessive in light of plaintiff's impaired ability to perform necessary life functions like bathing and dressing as well as pleasures such as walking and dancing); *Kenton v. Hyatt Hotels Corp.,* 693 S.W.2d 83 (Mo. 1985)

(reinstating an award of $4 million which included plaintiff's loss of ability to play tennis, ski, jog, and carry on other athletic activities).

Two categories or one—should a jury be instructed that the plaintiff can recover both for pain and suffering and loss of enjoyment of life as separate sets of damages? Some courts have approved this idea. *See, e.g., Guillory v. Saucier*, 79 So.3d 1188 (La. Ct. App. 2011). Would it be less confusing to the jury to instruct broadly on pain and suffering and to make it clear that consciousness of lost enjoyment is a part of that pain and suffering? *See Gregory v. Carey*, 791 P.2d 1329 (Kan. 1990) (concluding lost enjoyment is inextricably included in damages for pain and suffering).

5. **Plaintiff's lack of awareness of loss.** When the plaintiff is unaware of her loss there is no tradition of awarding damages for that "loss." Recent cases have gone both ways, however.

6. **Proof.** How can a plaintiff prove loss of enjoyment damages to the jury? Could an expert testify about the value of the loss of enjoyment of life? *See Mercado v. Ahmed*, 974 F.2d 863 (7th Cir. 1992) (affirming trial judge's refusal to admit such testimony). *Montalvo v. Lapez,* 884 P.2d 345, 367 (Haw. 1994), commented that valuing the joy of life is "a uniquely human endeavor . . . requiring the trier of fact to draw upon the virtually unlimited factors unique to us as human beings."

7. **Variation.** You have now seen a number of jury awards in very significant injury cases. Awards can vary. In *Maldonado v. Sinai Med.Group, Inc.*, 706 F. Supp. 2d 882 (N.D. Ill. 2010), the plaintiff suffered a bacterial infection in his spine after improper hospital treatment, which left him permanently paralyzed below the waist. Based on the facts of this case and range of awards in comparable cases ($0.5 to $8 million), the court awarded $6.7 million in non-economic damages. Appellate courts must give significant deference to the trier of fact's calculation of damages. Once the jury or trial judge has fixed damages, the aggrieved party cannot win simply by arguing that the jury got the amount wrong. Is this variation an appropriate function of a jury process, or should there be more standardization?

8. **Considering comparable awards.** Could the jury consider awards in comparable cases to fix the amount of noneconomic damages? Many courts have disapproved of this kind of evidence at trial. *See, e.g., Richardson v. Chapman*, 676 N.E.2d 621 (Ill. 1997). Where the trial judge is the trier of fact, however, a number of appellate courts approve of, and perhaps even require, the consideration of such information, usually on the ground that the trial judge is required to explain the basis for her decision. *Arpin v. United States*, 521 F.3d 769 (7th Cir. 2008) (reversing trial judge's award of damages where he did not consider awards in similar cases). On appeal, many appellate courts also consider comparable cases when determining whether an award is excessive. *See, e.g., Okraynets v. Metropolitan Transp. Auth.*, 555 F. Supp. 2d 420 (S.D.N.Y. 2008) (applying New York law that requires reviewing courts to "compare verdicts sustained by New York courts in similar cases"); *Meals v. Ford Motor Co.*, 417 S.W.3d 414 (Tenn. 2013) (reinstating jury verdict for $43.8

million in favor of six-year-old car passenger who suffered spinal fracture and internal injuries from lap belt in collision with another vehicle; court detailed child's severe injuries and looked at awards in other cases involving paralysis of a young child).

But not all courts employ such evidence. *See Gonzalez v. United States*, 681 F.3d 949 (8th Cir. 2012); *Allied Concrete Co. v. Lester*, 736 S.E.2d 699 (Va. 2013) ("Although a trial court may grant remittitur on the grounds that the award is disproportionate to the injuries suffered, we have specifically rejected comparing damage awards as a means of measuring excessiveness;" remittitur of $6.22 million jury award for wrongful death of wife in accident with cement truck was an abuse of discretion because it compared award to award in case for same victim brought by her parents). Do you see any problems with allowing a jury to consider awards in prior cases? Do all of those problems disappear when a trial judge is making the determination? Do you see any problem with not comparing?

9. **Presumptive awards.** What about creating some sort of guidelines with respect to presumptive awards? In setting up the 9/11 Victim's Compensation fund, the special master created a presumptive pain and suffering award that applied to all victims regardless of their particular situation. Would something like that be a good idea? At what amount would you set the award? Would someone with temporary but severe pain receive more or less than someone with moderate chronic pain?

NOTE: THE SPECIAL CASE OF MEDICAL MONITORING DAMAGES

The plaintiffs—sometimes whole neighborhoods or an entire workforce—are exposed to a toxic substance which increases the likelihood of a disease, usually some form of cancer. However, the plaintiffs have no demonstrable physical injury at present. They might conceivably claim either an increased risk of cancer or emotional harm resulting from their fear of future disease. But, courts have typically denied both of those claims.

If the plaintiffs suffer from any physical harm because of the toxic exposure, the defendant would be liable for that harm and damages for the costs of periodic medical checks that could detect future cancers in early stages so as to permit early intervention. *See Donovan v. Philip Morris USA, Inc.*, 914 N.E.2d 891 (Mass. 2009) (where plaintiffs alleged that they had sustained present injury resulting in substantially increased risk of cancer, they stated a claim for medical monitoring expenses).

Some courts have gone further by allowing medical monitoring damages even when no physical harm has been done and no emotional harm claim is allowable. *See, e.g., Sadler v. PacifiCare of Nev.*, 340 P.3d

1264 (Nev. 2014) (plaintiff can state a cause of action for negligence with medical monitoring without asserting any present physical injury; negligence on the part of health maintenance organizations in failing to monitor medical providers who used unsafe injection practices, resulting in the plaintiffs being placed at risk of contracting, blood-borne diseases); *Perrine v. E.I. du Pont de Nemours & Co.*, 694 S.E.2d 815, 879 (W. Va. 2010) (permitting medical monitoring claim); *Burns v. Jaquays Mining Corp.*, 752 P.2d 28 (Ariz. Ct. App. 1987) (exposure to asbestos). But other courts have insisted that medical monitoring costs are not "actual harm" that supports a claim; instead, the plaintiff must prove actionable physical harm before medical monitoring costs can be recovered. *See, e.g., Alsteen v. Wauleco, Inc.*, 802 N.W.2d 212 (Wis. Ct. App. 2012) (plaintiffs exposed to hazardous chemicals for approximately 40 years); *Henry v. Dow Chem. Co.*, 701 N.W.2d 684 (Mich. 2005) (refusing to recognize a common law negligence claim in the absence of a present injury). Two commentators have suggested that any other rule would be judicial "madness." James A. Henderson, Jr. & Aaron D. Twerski, *Asbestos Litigation Gone Mad: Exposure-based Recovery for Increased Risk, Mental Distress, and Medical Monitoring*, 53 S.C. L. REV. 815 (2002). Do you agree?

NOTE: THE COLLATERAL SOURCE RULE AND ITS COUSINS

1. *The collateral source rule.* Suppose the injured plaintiff, as a result of his injury, collects medical insurance, continues to receive full pay from his job while he is in the hospital, and is a recipient of a donation from sympathetic neighbors. The general rule is that in figuring the defendant's liability, all these "collateral benefits" to the plaintiff must be ignored. *See* 1 DOBBS, REMEDIES §§ 3.8, 8.6; *Mariani v. State ex rel. Okla. State Univ.*, 348 P.3d 194 (Okla. 2015) (retaining collateral source rule). The defendant pays the full medical expenses of the plaintiff even though they may have been paid already by the medical insurance. The defendant pays full lost earnings or lost earning capacity even though the plaintiff collected full pay as a gift from his employer or as part of his job benefits.

2. *The windfall effect.* As perceived by many, the collateral source rule sometimes gives the plaintiff a kind of windfall: in effect, plaintiff may collect twice for the medical expenses and the "lost" wages. In *Covington v. George*, 597 S.E.2d 142 (S.C. 2004), the plaintiff's hospital bills came to about $4,000, which were claimed as damages. The defendant offered evidence that the hospital actually accepted payments, apparently from Medicare, of about $700 in full payment. This evidence was excluded, even though it suggested that the reasonable value of the medical services was much less than the nominal value of $4,000. The court said: "While a defendant is permitted to attack the necessity and reasonableness of

medical care and costs, he cannot do so using evidence of payments made by a collateral source." Some jurisdictions have a different rule. *Meek v. Montana Eighth Judicial Dist. Court*, 349 P.3d 493 (Mont. 2015) (evidence of the amount Medicare or other insurance paid towards plaintiff's medical expenses were admissible on the issue of the reasonableness of plaintiff's medical bills, to be considered by the court after a verdict).

3.   *The subrogation protection effect.* At other times the collateral source rule merely preserves the subrogation right of the insurer who paid the plaintiff to recover back its loss from the tortfeasor. For instance, suppose that the plaintiff's car is damaged by defendant's negligence. The plaintiff's own collision insurer pays for repairs. In the ordinary case, the collision insurer is subrogated to the plaintiff's claim against the defendant to the extent that it has paid for the car damage. In such a case the plaintiff would be entitled to recover against the defendant for the plaintiff's personal injuries and also for the car damage, but the recovery for car damage goes, by way of subrogation, to the plaintiff's collision insurance company. This can be done only because the collateral source rule allows the plaintiff to recover in spite of the fact that he has been paid.

4.   *Criticizing the collateral source rule.*

(a)   *Eliminating subrogation to eliminate transaction costs.* The collateral source rule has many critics. In the best case, it protects an insurer's subrogation recovery. But even in this best case, it merely sets up a system where one insurer recovers from another. Since this shift of the loss entails costs, it might be better to abolish the collateral source rule.

(b)   *Eliminating windfalls to eliminate windfall costs.* When the collateral source rule does not merely protect a subrogation right, it may be seen as a windfall to the plaintiff. This is not entirely so, because, in the case of insurance at least, the plaintiff has paid for the right to the insurance proceeds. Still, if the plaintiff is to recover twice for some elements of damages, the total cost is excessive. The excess is charged against insurers who must reflect it sooner or later in premiums.

5.   *Abolishing the collateral source rule.* The tort reform movement of the 1980s sought to limit defendants' liabilities in a number of ways, one of them by abolishing or substantially altering the collateral source rule in selective cases, usually medical malpractice claims, or those against public entities. The collateral source rule has been abolished or limited in something like half the states or more. *E.g.,* CAL. CIV. CODE § 3333.1; N.Y. C.P.L.R. § 4545 (a). Some of the limiting statutes have been upheld against constitutional attack, *see, e.g., Eastin v. Broomfield*, 570 P.2d 744 (Ariz. 1977), while others have been struck down, *see, e.g., Farley v. Engelken*, 740 P.2d 1058 (Kan. 1987).

C. CAPPING AND LIMITING DAMAGES

CAL. CIV. CODE § 3333.2

(a) In any action for injury against a health care provider based on professional negligence, the injured plaintiff shall be entitled to recover noneconomic losses to compensate for pain, suffering, inconvenience, physical impairment, disfigurement and other nonpecuniary damage.

(b) In no action shall the amount of damages for noneconomic losses exceed two hundred fifty thousand dollars ($250,000).

MD. CODE ANN., CTS. & JUD. PROC. § 11–108

(a) In this section: (2)(i)(1) "noneconomic damages" means pain, suffering, inconvenience, physical impairment, disfigurement, loss of consortium, or other nonpecuniary injury; and (2)(ii) "Noneconomic damages" does not include punitive damages.

(b) In any action for damages for personal injury in which the cause of action arises on or after July 1, 1986, an award for noneconomic damages may not exceed $350,000. . . .

(d)(1) In a jury trial, the jury may not be informed of the limitation established under subsection (b) of this section. (2) If the jury awards an amount for noneconomic damages that exceeds the limitation established under subsection (b) of this section, the court shall reduce the amount to conform to the limitation.

NOTES

1. **Caps on pain and suffering awards.** In theory, damages are compensatory. For this reason, customarily, tort damages have been limited only by the evidence, not by any arbitrary dollar amount or by any formula.

2. **Two statutory waves.** Two waves of statutes have been passed changing this common law tradition. The first resulted from the supposed medical malpractice insurance "crisis" of the 1970s. The second resulted from a supposed "crisis" in the 1980s. This second wave, however, was the product of long and persistent efforts by a much wider group of defendants and insurers who felt threatened by tort law. The statutory limits were based on a perception that there was a crisis in the affordability and availability of insurance, especially for target groups like health care providers and public entities, or sometimes simply on the claim that juries had gone wild.

3. **Line-up of the states.** Some kind of cap or limit has been enacted in well over half of the states. Some have been held unconstitutional, some are applied to only one particular kind of claim, and some are overridden by statutes such as California's Elder Abuse Act, which allows recovery for

reckless neglect of the elderly without a cap. As to this last point, *see Delaney v. Baker,* 971 P.2d 986 (Cal. 1999).

4. **Capping plaintiffs vs. capping defendants.** Suppose the cap is $250,000 but the plaintiff has damages of $500,000. If two defendants are liable, could the plaintiff recover up to $250,000 from each? *General Elec. Co. v. Niemet,* 866 P.2d 1361 (Colo. 1994) (yes, as a matter of statutory construction, Colorado's cap applies to individual defendants, not to plaintiffs). A somewhat similar question arises when a person dies and children bring a wrongful death action. Does the cap apply to the childrens' claims as a unit, or could each child recover a sum up to the cap's limit? See *THI of Tex. at Lubbock I, LLC v. Perea,* 329 S.W.3d 548, 586 (Tex. App. 2010).

5. **Caps and comparative fault.** Suppose the plaintiff has $300,000 in nonpecuniary damages as well as pecuniary loss that can be separately calculated. The state has a cap on nonpecuniary damages of $250,000 and a pure comparative fault statute. The jury finds the plaintiff to be chargeable with 20% of the negligence. What should the plaintiff recover? Consider:

(a) $300,000 reduced to the cap of $250,000, minus 20% of the $300,000 or $60,000 = a net of $190,000 for nonpecuniary damages.

(b) $300,000 reduced to the cap of $250,000, minus 20% of the damages as capped, or $50,000 = a net recovery of $200,000.

(c) $300,000 minus 20% = $240,000; since this falls below the cap, no further reduction is required.

See McAdory v. Rogers, 264 Cal. Rptr. 71 (Ct. App. 1989) ("There is no legitimate or logical reason for reducing that award to the $250,000 cap prescribed by section 3333.2 before reducing it further due to Ms. McAdory's 22 percent comparative fault.").

6. **Caps unconstitutional.** Several courts have found the capping statutes to be unconstitutional under various provisions of their respective state constitutions. *See, e.g., Klutschkowski v. PeaceHealth,* 311 P.3d 461 (Or. 2013) (cap on non-economic damages in medical malpractice and negligence actions unconstitutional under jury trial provision of Oregon Constitution because causes of action preexisted adoption of the Oregon Constitution). Broad themes discussed in opinions finding caps unconstitutional include some version of these ideas:

(a) the injured plaintiff cannot be made to bear the burden of reducing insurance costs for others or for society as a whole;

(b) it is arbitrary to select the particular group of defendants for special attention;

(c) no alternative redress or even assistance is provided for the injured plaintiff; the plaintiff shoulders the burden others are feeling without a quid pro quo;

(d)   caps are in themselves arbitrary, especially when injuries may be quite different among those affected;

(e)   no showing is made that the caps will actually resolve the supposed insurance crisis.

7.   **Caps constitutional.** The California statute set out above was upheld in *Fein v. Permanente Medical Group*, 695 P.2d 665 (Cal. 1985). A number of other decisions have upheld caps against arguments that the caps violated jury trial rights, due process, equal protection, or various analogous state constitutional provisions, or that they contravened the Americans with Disability Act. *See, e.g., Samples v. Florida Birth-Related Neurological Injury Comp. Ass'n*, 114 So. 3d 912 (Fla. 2013) (infants found to have birth-related neurological injury; statute provides no-fault compensation via an alternative plan, and lifts the cap where clear and convincing evidence shows bad faith, malice, or willful and wanton disregard of human rights, safety or property); *Espina v. Jackson,* 112 A.3d 442 (Md. 2015) (state cap on damages against public entities, set at $200,000 per individual claim); *Dixon v. Ford Motor Co.*, 70 A.3d 328 (Md. 2013) (lump sum statutory maximum on damages from asbestos exposure); *Tam v. Eighth Judicial Dist. Court,* 358 P.3d 234 (Nev. 2015) (cap on non-economic damages in suits against a healthcare provider); *Howell v. Boyle*, 298 P.3d 1 (Or. 2013) ($200,000 maximum for governmental entity under Oregon Tort Claims Act). Will caps on the pain and suffering award shortchange the most seriously-injured plaintiffs or remove just claims from the judicial system?

8.   **Discrimination against women and children?** Certain kinds of cases produce noneconomic (but real) harms. Some sexual abuse, for example, may be so harmful that the victim is actually unable to work effectively, but very often the main component of damages is noneconomic. Most, but not all, sexual abuse victims are women. Does this mean that if tort reformers cap pain and suffering damages, they are discriminating against women? *See* Lucinda Finley, *The Hidden Victims of Tort Reform: Women, Children, and the Elderly,* 53 EMORY L. REV. 1263 (2004); Thomas Koenig & Michael Rustad, *His and Her Tort Reform: Gender Injustice in Disguise*, 70 WASH. L. REV. 1 (1995). Similarly, statutory caps on noneconomic damages may dramatically reduce claims of the families of deceased children. For example, in *DRD Pool Service, Inc. v. Freed*, 5 A.3d 45 (Md. 2010), a five-year-old child drowned in a country club swimming pool. In a suit against the pool maintenance service, the jury awarded over $4 million in damages. However, pursuant to state caps on non-economic damages, which the Maryland Court of Appeals found constitutional, the verdict was reduced to approximately $1 million.

9.   **Side effects of caps.** Maybe caps will have some unintended side effects. Would judges or juries be more inclined to resolve close questions of *liability* for the plaintiff where caps limit the *damages*? After the 9/11 terrorist attacks, Congress set up a victims' compensation scheme but permitted victims to opt for tort suits instead. If they opted for tort suits, however, damages were capped (except in suits against terrorist-associated defendants) at the total of

the defendants' liability insurance. In *In re September 11 Litigation*, 280 F. Supp. 2d 279 (S.D.N.Y. 2003), one question was whether the airlines owed a duty of care to potential victims on the ground. The court held that they did. One factor: there would be no limitless liability because of the caps. ·

REFERENCE: 3 DOBBS, HAYDEN & BUBLICK, THE LAW OF TORTS §§ 479–81 (2d ed. 2011); DOBBS, HAYDEN & BUBLICK, HORNBOOK ON TORTS §§ 34.1–34.3 (2d ed. 2016).

§ 2. PUNITIVE DAMAGES

A. GENERAL RULES

DAN B. DOBBS, THE LAW OF REMEDIES
§ 3.11(1) (2d ed. 1993)

1.   Punitive damages are awarded only for . . . misconduct coupled with a bad state of mind involving malice or at least a reckless disregard for the rights of others.

2.   The stated purposes of punitive damages almost always include (a) punishment or retribution and (b) deterrence. Sometimes the purpose also encompasses (c) the desire to assist in financing useful litigation by providing a source from which fees and costs can be paid. The purposes are somewhat conflicting in that they do not necessarily call for the same amount of punitive recovery.

3.   If the judge decides that the facts warrant submission of the case to the jury on the punitive damages issue, the jury's discretion determines (a) whether to make the award at all and (b) the amount of the award, as limited by its purposes, subject only to review as other awards are reviewed.

4.   Punitive damages are not per se unconstitutional under the double jeopardy, excessive fines, or due process provisions of the United States Constitution. However, extreme awards, given without appropriate guidance to the jury and without adequate review by judges, may violate due process.

5.   Statutes in some states now limit the amount of punitive damages that can be awarded, or, alternatively, direct a portion of the award to some public entity. In addition, some double and treble damages statutes may have the effect of precluding ordinary punitive damages.

6.   Punitive damages were traditionally proven by the ordinary civil standard of proof, a preponderance of the evidence. Some courts now demand clear and convincing evidence.

7. The jury is normally allowed to hear evidence about the defendant's wealth, income, or profits as a basis for determining an appropriate amount of punitive damages.

8. [Under one rule, punitive awards may be levied against defendants who are only vicariously responsible.] Under another rule, employers and others can be responsible for punitive damages for torts of agents or servants only if the employer participated in, encouraged, or ratified the tort.

9. Under one view, probably the majority, liability insurers whose policies do not eliminate coverage for punitive damages are liable for punitive damages judgments against the insured. Under another view, the "punishment" will not be effective if the wrongdoer can insure, so insurance coverage for such awards is against public policy.

10. A defendant whose wrongs have caused many harms to different people may be subjected to more than one punitive liability.

11. Courts sometimes say that punitive damages cannot be awarded unless the plaintiff suffers actual harm or recovers actual damages. Some courts now read this rule to mean only that the plaintiff cannot recover punitive damages unless she first establishes a cause of action.

12. [Courts sometimes say that the amount of punitive damages must be in some reasonable proportion to actual damages.] . . .

OWENS-CORNING FIBERGLASS CORP. V. BALLARD, 749 So. 2d 483 (Fla. 1999). Ballard proved that he had developed mesothelioma, a cancer of the chest lining, due to thirty years of exposure to asbestos in the defendant's product, Kaylo. Evidence showed that "for more than thirty (30) years Owens-Corning concealed what it knew about the dangers of asbestos. In fact, Owens-Corning's conduct was even worse than concealment, it also included intentional and knowing misrepresentations concerning the danger of its asbestos-containing product, Kaylo. For instance, in 1956, Owens-Corning, after having been told by the Saranac Laboratory that Kaylo dust was 'toxic,' and that asbestos was a carcinogen, advertised Kaylo as being 'non-toxic.' In 1972, after Owens-Corning developed an asbestos-free version of the Kaylo product, Owens-Corning knowingly and intentionally contaminated the new product with asbestos containing debris from its old Kaylo, and then intentionally and knowingly claimed falsely that the new Kaylo product was asbestos[-]free." The jury awarded compensatory damages of $1.8 million and punitive damages of $31 million. *Held,* affirmed.

NOTES

1. **Deterrence function.** This case represents the tort-for-profit punitive damage case in contrast to the bully case. The defendant in such cases has a motive to continue its tortious activity unless the total expected damages liability will be greater than the profit. Although the courts always focus on the defendant's bad state of mind as a justification for awarding punitive damages, *Ford Motor Co. v. Washington*, 431 S.W.3d 210 (Ark. 2013), deterrence seems to be the major goal in many cases.

2. **Illustration.** Suppose the defendant is making so much money from the sale of the product that compensatory damages awards will never induce the defendant to take it off the market. That might be because, although damages are high, some victims do not discover that the defendant caused their harm. A national products manufacturer which deliberately markets a dangerous product like the Dalkon Shield after its dangers are known may continue to do so (as the Robins company did) unless punitive damages are enough to deny it any profit. See the shocking behavior of the manufacturer as described in *Tetuan v. A.H. Robins Co.*, 738 P.2d 1210 (Kan. 1987). *See also* Thomas Galligan, *Augmented Awards: The Efficient Evolution of Punitive Damages*, 51 LA. L. REV. 3 (1990). [Or perhaps the right amount of punitive damages would be to bring the manufacturer's total liability up to the level it would have paid in ordinary compensatory damages if all victims had appropriately recovered.] *See* A. Mitchell Polinsky & Steven Shavell, *Punitive Damages: an Economic Analysis,* 111 HARV. L. REV. 869, 888–96 (1998).

3. **Strict liability cases.** Defendants used to argue that punitive awards could not be made in strict liability claims, even if the underlying conduct involved the kind of knowing wrong seen in cases like *Owens-Corning Fiberglas Corp. v. Ballard*. This has now changed, and punitive damages are understood to be warranted by conduct and state of mind, not by the name of the legal theory used. The classic article is David G. Owen, *Punitive Damages in Products Liability Litigation*, 74 MICH. L. REV. 1257 (1976).

B. MEASUREMENT OF PUNITIVE DAMAGES

NOTE: TRADITIONAL FACTORS IN MEASURING PUNITIVE DAMAGES

1. *Reprehensibility of the defendant's misconduct.* If punitive damages are warranted by the defendant's serious misconduct, courts must then identify an appropriate sum. You might think that the most important consideration would be to identify the amount necessary to ensure that the defendant does not repeat the wrong. However, courts have often said that the degree of reprehensibility of the defendant's conduct is the most important single consideration. *State Farm Mut. Auto. Ins. Co. v. Campbell*, 538 U.S. 408 (2003). At the same time, courts identify other factors, not necessarily consistent.

2. *Wealth.* Courts have traditionally admitted evidence of the defendant's wealth as bearing on punitive damages, on the theory that a person of great wealth might not be deterred by a small award. *See, e.g., Tarr v. Bob Ciasulli's Mack Auto Mall, Inc.*, 943 A.2d 866 (N.J. 2008). If the tort itself is profitable, profits from the wrongdoing would also be highly relevant. *Must* the plaintiff introduce wealth evidence to warrant punitive damages? *Compare Adams v. Murakami,* 813 P.2d 1348 (Cal. 1991), *with Kemezy v. Peters,* 79 F.3d 33 (7th Cir. 1996) (wealth evidence risks prejudice to the wealthy defendant). Partially because of this problem, it is now common to bifurcate the trial so that the punitive damages evidence is excluded until the jury has already found fault.

3. *Ratio rules.* Courts have long said that punitive damages should bear some kind of reasonable comparison to the compensatory damages, or to actual or potential harm done. In its crudest form, this ratio rule suggests limits incompatible with the purposes of punitive damages in the first place. Suppose the defendant malevolently and repeatedly fires his rifle at the plaintiff, but has so far only chipped the plaintiff's $10 sunglasses. If the jury awards $10 compensatory damages, the ratio rule suggests that punitive awards should be some modest multiple of that sum. It is apparent that this cannot be right under either a punitive or deterrence rationale and it is even less right if the defendant's conduct is profitable even after he pays compensatory damages. The more sophisticated form of the rule does not compare punitive awards to compensatory awards. It compares punitive awards to the potential actual harm that could have resulted from the defendant's conduct. This form of the ratio rule is in fact merely a way of measuring the seriousness of the defendant's misconduct.

Some other factors are sketched in discussing the constitutional decisions in the next Note.

NOTE: LIMITING PUNITIVE AWARDS

1. *Moves to limit punitive awards.* There is a perception that punitive damages awards are common, but recent studies show that punitive damages are awarded in only 2–5% of all cases in which plaintiffs prevail. Remember that most cases do not even go to trial. "Thus, for every 1,000 tort claims filed, typically only 50 are resolved by trial, only 25 produce trial outcomes favorable to the plaintiff, and only 1.25 have a punitive damages award." Thomas A. Eaton, David B. Mustard & Susette M. Talarico, *The Effects of Seeking Punitive Damages on the Processing of Tort Claims,* 34 J. LEGAL STUD. 343, 344 (2005). Another common misperception is that punitive damages awards are primarily a problem produced by "runaway juries." Studies show that judges award such

damages at about the same rate as juries. *See* Theodore Eisenberg, Neil LaFountain, Brian Ostrom, David Rottman & Martin T. Wells, *Juries, Judges, and Punitive Damages: An Empirical Study*, 87 CORNELL L. REV. 743 (2002). However, repeat defendants greatly fear punitive awards. As punitive damages have sometimes run into the millions of dollars, defendant-oriented lobbies have tried to find ways to limit those awards in statutes and by more restrictive judicial decisions.

2. *Two types of limitations.* Although several means have been used to limit punitive awards, they fall mainly into two large categories. Because the main problem with punitive damages is to find a suitable measure or standard for guiding the award and evaluating it afterward, some legal changes attempt to enhance the methods for measuring the awards. A second and much broader way to limit total damages awarded is to limit the number of cases in which punitive damages may be awarded.

3. *Increased proof standards.* One way to filter out potential punitive damages claims is to increase the plaintiff's burden of proof. A number of courts and legislatures have done this, usually requiring the plaintiff to prove grounds for punitive damages by clear and convincing evidence rather than by a mere preponderance. *E.g., Hester v. Vision Airlines, Inc.*, 687 F.3d 1162 (9th Cir. 2012).

4. *Single liability statute.* Georgia enacted a statute that immunized a product liability defendant from all punitive liability for a given product, once the defendant had been vaccinated by a single punitive award. So the first plaintiff to recover was the only one to do so. GA. CODE ANN. § 51–12–5.1(e)(1).

5. *Specific malice requirement.* Another effort to cut punitive damages off at the pass requires the plaintiff to prove some specific malice or oppressive intent toward the plaintiff, eliminating wanton and reckless misconduct as a basis. *See* NEV. REV. STAT. § 42.005.

6. *Redirection of awards and the problem of financing tort suits.* A fourth line of legislative attack intended to cut down the number of claims redirects a portion of any punitive award from the plaintiff (or the plaintiff's attorney) to the state or some designated beneficiary. *E.g.,* IOWA CODE ANN. § 668A.1. In *Kirk v. Denver Public Co.*, 818 P.2d 262 (Colo. 1991), the court held one such statute unconstitutional as a taking of property without just compensation. *Cheatham v. Pohle*, 789 N.E.2d 467 (Ind. 2003), disagreed, upholding the statute.

7. *Statutory ratios, multiples, or caps.* With the push for tort reform, some states have enacted ratio cap statutes. For instance, Colorado limited punitive awards to no more than actual damages, with the added possibility of punitive damages up to three times actual damages if the defendant's misconduct continued during the trial. WEST'S COLO. REV. STAT. ANN. § 13–21–102. In Ohio, the statute caps damages at twice the

amount of compensatory damages awarded. *See Sivit v. Village Green of Beachwood*, 143 Ohio 3d 168 (2015). Utah, by court decision, has produced a kind of sliding scale ratio rule that varies according to whether the compensatory damages awarded are low or high. *Crookston v. Fire Ins. Exch.*, 817 P.2d 789 (Utah 1991) (3–1 ratio for punitive awards under $100,000, much closer ratio for higher awards). Georgia enacted a flat cap limiting punitive damages in some cases to $250,000. GA. CODE ANN. § 51–12–5.1. Indiana limits punitive damages to three times compensatory damages or $50,000, requiring that 75% of the amount goes to violent crime victim charities. *State v. Doe*, 987 N.E.2d 1066 (Ind. 2013) (remand for reduction in damages awarded to sexual abuse victim in lawsuit against clergyman). Some limitations on punitive damages have been struck down as unconstitutional. *See, e.g., Bayer Cropscience LP v. Schafer*, 385 S.W.3d 822 (Ark. 2011) (Arkansas Constitution prohibits the legislature from limiting the amount to be recovered for injuries resulting in death or for injuries to persons or property); *Lewellen v. Franklin*, 441 S.W.3d 136 (Mo. 2014) (statute capping punitive damages violated the state constitutional right to a jury).

8. *Assessing the filters.* What is your assessment of these efforts? Do they help the problem of measurement? Is there a good chance, in your view, that the deterrence or litigation finance function of punitive awards needed in some of the cases will be filtered out by these rules?

MATHIAS V. ACCOR ECONOMY LODGING, INC.
347 F.3d 672 (7th Cir. 2003)

POSNER, CIRCUIT JUDGE.

[The plaintiffs, a brother and sister, were guests at a Motel 6 hotel where they were bitten by bedbugs. Evidence showed that the hotel's exterminating service discovered bedbugs in 1998 and offered to spray every room, for which it would charge only $500. The hotel refused and year by year the bedbug problem grew.]

The infestation continued and began to reach farcical proportions, as when a guest, after complaining of having been bitten repeatedly by insects while asleep in his room in the hotel, was moved to another room only to discover insects there; and within 18 minutes of being moved to a third room he discovered insects in that room as well and had to be moved still again. . . . [Desk clerks were instructed to call the "bedbugs" "ticks," apparently on the theory that customers would be less alarmed, though in fact ticks are more dangerous than bedbugs because they spread Lyme Disease and Rocky Mountain Spotted Fever.] Rooms that the motel had placed on "Do not rent, bugs in room" status nevertheless were rented.

[The plaintiffs sued the defendant for "willful and wanton conduct." The jury awarded each plaintiff $186,000 in punitive damages though only

$5,000 in compensatory damages. The defendant appeals, complaining primarily that the punitive damages award was excessive and that any award in excess of $20,000 to each plaintiff deprives the defendant of its property without due process of law.

Motel 6 could not have rented any rooms at the prices it charged had it informed guests that the risk of being bitten by bedbugs was appreciable. Its failure either to warn guests or to take effective measures to eliminate the bedbugs amounted to fraud and probably to battery as well as in the famous case of *Garratt v. Dailey,* 46 Wash.2d 197, 279 P.2d 1091, 1093–94 (1955), which held that the defendant would be guilty of battery if he knew with substantial certainty that when he moved a chair the plaintiff would try to sit down where the chair had been and would land on the floor instead. There was, in short, sufficient evidence of 'willful and wanton conduct' . . . to permit an award of punitive damages in this case.

But in what amount? In arguing that $20,000 was the maximum amount of punitive damages that a jury could constitutionally have awarded each plaintiff, the defendant points to the U.S. Supreme Court's recent statement that "few awards [of punitive damages] exceeding a single-digit ratio between punitive and compensatory damages, to a significant degree, will satisfy due process." *State Farm Mutual Automobile Ins. Co. v. Campbell,* 538 U.S. 408, 123 S.Ct. 1513, 1524, 155 L.Ed.2d 585 (2003). . . . The ratio of punitive to compensatory damages determined by the jury was, in contrast, 37.2 to 1.

The Supreme Court did not, however, lay down a 4-to-1 or single-digit-ratio rule-it said merely that "there is a presumption against an award that has a 145-to-1 ratio," *State Farm Mutual Automobile Ins. Co. v. Campbell, supra,* 123 S.Ct. at 1524—and it would be unreasonable to do so. We must consider why punitive damages are awarded and why the Court has decided that due process requires that such awards be limited. The second question is easier to answer than the first. The term "punitive damages" implies punishment, and a standard principle of penal theory is that "the punishment should fit the crime" in the sense of being proportional to the wrongfulness of the defendant's action, though the principle is modified when the probability of detection is very low (a familiar example is the heavy fines for littering) or the crime is potentially lucrative (as in the case of trafficking in illegal drugs). Hence, with these qualifications, which in fact will figure in our analysis of this case, punitive damages should be proportional to the wrongfulness of the defendant's actions.

Another penal precept is that a defendant should have reasonable notice of the sanction for unlawful acts, so that he can make a rational determination of how to act; and so there have to be reasonably clear standards for determining the amount of punitive damages for particular wrongs.

And a third precept, the core of the Aristotelian notion of corrective justice, and more broadly of the principle of the rule of law, is that sanctions should be based on the wrong done rather than on the status of the defendant; a person is punished for what he does, not for who he is, even if the who is a huge corporation.

— Formalistic manner

[What follows from these principles, however, is that punitive damages should be admeasured by standards or rules] rather than in a completely ad hoc manner, and this does not tell us what the maximum ratio of punitive to compensatory damages should be in a particular case. To determine that, we have to consider why punitive damages are awarded in the first place. See *Kemezy v. Peters,* 79 F.3d 33, 34–35 (7th Cir.1996).

England's common law courts first confirmed their authority to award punitive damages in the eighteenth century, see Dorsey D. Ellis, Jr., "Fairness and Efficiency in the Law of Punitive Damages," 56 *S. Cal. L. Rev.* 1, 12–20 (1982), at a time when the institutional structure of criminal law enforcement was primitive and it made sense to leave certain minor crimes to be dealt with by the civil law. And still today one function of punitive-damages awards is to relieve the pressures on an overloaded system of criminal justice by providing a civil alternative to criminal prosecution of minor crimes. An example is deliberately spitting in a person's face, a criminal assault but because minor readily deterrable by the levying of what amounts to a civil fine through a suit for damages for the tort of battery. Compensatory damages would not do the trick in such a case, and this for three reasons: because they are difficult to determine in the case of acts that inflict largely dignitary harms; because in the spitting case they would be too slight to give the victim an incentive to sue, and he might decide instead to respond with violence-and an age-old purpose of the law of torts is to provide a substitute for violent retaliation against wrongful injury-and because to limit the plaintiff to compensatory damages would enable the defendant to commit the offensive act with impunity provided that he was willing to pay, and again there would be a danger that his act would incite a breach of the peace by his victim.

When punitive damages are sought for billion-dollar oil spills and other huge economic injuries, the considerations that we have just canvassed fade. As the Court emphasized in *Campbell,* the fact that the plaintiffs in that case had been awarded very substantial compensatory damages—$1 million for a dispute over insurance coverage—greatly reduced the need for giving them a huge award of punitive damages ($145 million) as well in order to provide an effective remedy. Our case is closer to the spitting case. The defendant's behavior was outrageous but the compensable harm done was slight and at the same time difficult to quantify because a large element of it was emotional. And the defendant may well have profited from its misconduct because by concealing the infestation it was able to keep renting rooms. Refunds were frequent but may have cost less than the cost of closing the hotel for a thorough fumigation. The hotel's attempt to pass off the bedbugs as ticks, which some guests might ignorantly have thought less unhealthful, may have postponed the instituting of litigation to rectify the hotel's misconduct. The award of punitive damages in this case thus serves the additional purpose of limiting the defendant's ability to profit from its fraud by escaping detection and (private) prosecution. If a tortfeasor is "caught" only half the time he commits torts, then when he is caught he should be punished twice as heavily in order to make up for the times he gets away.

Finally, if the total stakes in the case were capped at $50,000 (2 × [$5,000 + $20,000]), the plaintiffs might well have had difficulty financing this lawsuit. It is here that the defendant's aggregate net worth of $1.6 billion becomes relevant. A defendant's wealth is not a sufficient basis for awarding punitive damages. That would be discriminatory and would violate the rule of law, as we explained earlier, by making punishment depend on status rather than conduct. Where wealth in the sense of resources enters is in enabling the defendant to mount an extremely aggressive defense against suits such as this and by doing so to make litigating against it very costly, which in turn may make it difficult for the plaintiffs to find a lawyer willing to handle their case, involving as it does only modest stakes, for the usual 33–40 percent contingent fee.

In other words, the defendant is investing in developing a reputation intended to deter plaintiffs. It is difficult otherwise to explain the great stubbornness with which it has defended this case, making a host of frivolous evidentiary arguments despite the very modest stakes even when the punitive damages awarded by the jury are included. . . .

All things considered, we cannot say that the award of punitive damages was excessive, albeit the precise number chosen by the jury was arbitrary. It is probably not a coincidence that $5,000 + $186,000 = $191,000/191 = $1,000: i.e., $1,000 per room in the hotel. But as there are no punitive-damages guidelines, corresponding to the federal and state sentencing guidelines, it is inevitable that the specific amount of punitive damages awarded whether by a judge or by a jury will be arbitrary. (Which is perhaps why the plaintiffs' lawyer did not suggest a number to the jury.) The judicial function is to police a range, not a point.

But it would have been helpful had the parties presented evidence concerning the regulatory or criminal penalties to which the defendant exposed itself by deliberately exposing its customers to a substantial risk of being bitten by bedbugs. That is an inquiry recommended by the Supreme Court. But we do not think its omission invalidates the award. We can take judicial notice that deliberate exposure of hotel guests to the health risks created by insect infestations exposes the hotel's owner to sanctions under Illinois and Chicago law that in the aggregate are comparable in severity to the punitive damage award in this case.

"A person who causes bodily harm to or endangers the bodily safety of an individual by any means, commits reckless conduct if he performs recklessly the acts which cause the harm or endanger safety, whether they otherwise are lawful or unlawful." 720 ILCS 5/12–5(a). This is a misdemeanor, punishable by up to a year's imprisonment or a fine of $2,500, or both. Of course a corporation cannot be sent to prison, and $2,500 is obviously much less than the $186,000 awarded to each plaintiff in this case as punitive damages. But this is just the beginning. Other guests of the hotel were endangered besides these two plaintiffs. And, what is much more important, a Chicago hotel that permits unsanitary conditions to exist is subject to revocation of its license, without which it cannot operate. Chi. Munic. Code §§ 4–4–280, 4–208–020, 050, 060, 110. We are sure that the defendant would prefer to pay the punitive damages assessed in this case than to lose its license.

NOTES

1. **Wrongdoing.** Recall *Garratt v. Daily* (Chapter 3), cited by Judge Posner in *Mathias*. What would be the prima facie case for battery here? Fraud is an intentional material misrepresentation of fact that is intended to and does induce justifiable reliance and proximately causes harm. 3 DOBBS, HAYDEN & BUBLICK, THE LAW OF TORTS § 664 (2d ed. 2011). What is the intentional, material misrepresentation that Motel 6 made to its guests?

2. **Ratio rule limitations.** After the Supreme Court's decision in *State Farm Mut. Auto. Ins. Co. v. Campbell*, 538 U.S. 408 (2003), courts have limited punitive damages claims. *See Kimble v. Land Concepts, Inc.*, 845 N.W.2d 395 (Wis. 2014) (jury awarded plaintiffs $50,000 in compensatory damages and $1 million in punitive damages in claim against insurance company for bad faith and breach of contract; relying on *Campbell*, punitive damages award was excessive and reduced to $210,000). Courts have struggled to draw a ratio-based constitutional line. *See, e.g., Goddard v. Farmers Ins. Co.*, 179 P.3d 645 (Or. 2008) (as a general rule, the constitution prohibits a punitive award more than four times the compensatory award, at least where the injuries to the plaintiff are economic rather than physical); *Flax v. DaimlerChrysler Corp.*, 272 S.W.3d 521 (Tenn. 2008) (upholding a punitive award 5.35 times greater than the compensatory award in a products liability suit involving a child's death); *Bennett v. Reynolds*, 315 S.W.3d 867 (Tex. 2010) (punitive damages in cattle theft case excessive; remanded to lower court for remittitur consistent with ratio analysis). Is there really any basis for saying that punitive awards should bear some more or less specific ratio to compensatory awards?

3. **Ratios.** Do you agree with Judge Posner's assessment that high punitive damages to compensatory damage ratios are more acceptable in some types of cases than others? The Texas Supreme Court noted that several

significant ratio cases have involved intangible rights, for example concerning discrimination. *See Bennett v. Reynolds*, 315 S.W.3d 867 (Tex. 2010) (discussing cases that had upheld even triple-digit ratios); *see also Goff v. Elmo Greer & Sons Constr. Co.*, 297 S.W.3d 175 (Tenn. 2009) (nuisance case against company that buried waste tires on owners' property). In the billion-dollar oil spill cases, do compensatory awards more fully account for harm such that the incentives function of punitive damages is less relevant?

4.   **Institutional profit from harm.** Why didn't the hotel in *Mathias* eradicate the problem? Judge Posner suggests it must have been more profitable for the hotel to operate in that way. Judge Posner frames this case as more of an intentional tort than a significant economic injury. But looking at the defendant's unjust gains, rather than the plaintiffs' losses, isn't it clear that significant economic interests are at stake? The major modern cases involve the wrongdoer who engages in wrong in order to make a large profit. Shouldn't profit from the wrong be far more relevant than any ratio between compensatory and punitive awards? The point would be to retain full deterrence by eliminating the profits and to retain the capacity of the punitive award to provide appropriate incentives to sue. *See* Dan B. Dobbs, *Ending Punishment in "Punitive" Damages: Deterrence-Measured Remedies*, 40 ALA. L. REV. 831 (1989).

5.   **Revisiting *Owens*.** The *Owens-Corning* asbestos case involved significant harm to the plaintiff, who had developed mesothelioma. Yet, as a later court noted, the ratio of punitive damages to compensatory damages in *Owens* is 18:1. *Sun Int'l. Bahamas, Ltd. v. Wagner*, 758 So. 2d 1190 (Fla. Dist. Ct. App. 2000). *Owens* justified that award on the on the basis that "it would be difficult to envision a more egregious set of circumstances than those found herein by the trial court to constitute a blatant disregard for human safety involving large numbers of people put at life-threatening risk." Should *Owens* be considered outside constitutional bounds after *Campbell*?

6.   **Litigation finance function.** As Judge Posner's discussion in *Mathias* highlights, punitive damages may serve societal goals, for example by acting as a deterrent to the defendant by providing source for payment of attorney fees. *See Estate of Hoch v. Stifel*, 16 A.3d 137, 154 (Me. 2011). Punitive damages may encourage lawyers to invest the time, effort and expense necessary to prevail in cases that require investigation and evidence. If punitive damages had not been awarded in *Mathias*, would the case have been worth pursuing?

PHILIP MORRIS USA V. WILLIAMS, 549 U.S. 346 (2007). The widow of a heavy cigarette smoker sued the cigarette manufacturer for negligence and deceit, seeking both compensatory and punitive damages after her husband died of lung cancer. The jury found in her favor and awarded $821,000 in compensatory damages and $79.5 million in punitives. The trial judge reduced the compensatory damages to $500,000 and the punitive award to

$32 million. After several interim rulings and decisions after remand, the case came to this Court. Defendant now argues that the trial judge should have instructed the jury that it could not punish the defendant for injury to persons not parties before the court. *Held*, a punitive damages award based in part on a jury's desire to punish a defendant for harming nonparties violates due process. A state may properly impose punitive damages, but it must do so in a way to cabin the jury's discretionary authority, and give the defendant "fair notice . . . of the severity of the penalty." Penalizing a defendant for misconduct towards nonparties who are "strangers to the litigation" adds a nearly standardless dimension to the punitive damages equation, and magnifies this Court's due process concerns in these cases: arbitrariness, uncertainty, and lack of notice. There is no authority at all for using punitive damages awards to punish a defendant for harming persons not before the court. While evidence of harm to nonparties may show that a defendant's conduct was particularly reprehensible, a jury may not go further and use a punitive damages award to punish a defendant directly for harms to such nonparties. States must develop procedures to insure that harm to nonparties is considered only on the reprehensibility issue and does not form the basis of the amount of the punitive award itself.

NOTES

1. ***Williams* results on remand.** The Court did not reach the issue of whether the amount of punitive damages was excessive, but instead remanded for further proceedings. On remand, the Oregon Supreme Court held that the trial court did not err in refusing to give the particular jury instruction the defendant had requested, and remanded for further proceedings. *Williams v. Philip Morris Inc.*, 176 P.3d 1255 (Or. 2008). Subsequently, defendant paid compensatory damages and part of the punitive damages award (which had been reduced to $32 million), but contested the state's statutory share of punitive damages. In *Williams v. RJ Reynolds Tobacco Co.*, 271 P.3d 103 (Or. 2011), the court ruled that the state had a right to pursue its statutory share of punitive damages.

2. **Another view.** Four justices (Stevens, Thomas, Scalia and Ginsburg) dissented in the U.S. Supreme Court's *Williams* decision. Justice Stevens commented on the majority's distinction between using harm to nonparties as evidence of reprehensibility but not to punish the defendant, "This nuance eludes me." He added, "A murderer who kills his victim by throwing a bomb that injures dozens of bystanders should be punished more severely than one who harms no one other than his intended victim." Thus, in his view, the jury should be free not only to take conduct towards nonparties into account on the reprehensibility issue, but also to punish the defendant on that very basis. Do you agree?

3. **Magnitude of risks to others.** Does it matter that in *Mathias* harm to others was so small that they could not have been reasonably expected to

sue about it, while in *Williams* the harm to others may have been significant and the subject of separate suits? This distinction has been important in some class action consumer fraud and civil RICO cases.

REFERENCES: 3 DOBBS, HAYDEN & BUBLICK, THE LAW OF TORTS §§ 479–86 (2d ed. 2011); DOBBS, HAYDEN & BUBLICK, HORNBOOK ON TORTS §§ 34.4–34.7 (2d ed. 2016).

CHAPTER 27

EVALUATING TORT LAW

• • •

How good are tort systems at coping with the problem of injury in modern American life? Any system used to deal with the injury problem will be severely strained. According to the National Safety Council, Americans suffer

- about 27.6 million nonfatal injuries per year, of which more than 2.6 million are from motor vehicle accidents.

- 121,902 accidental deaths a year; about 35,500 from motor vehicle accidents alone.

- 5 million work-related injuries.

- economic impact of unintended injury of $730.7 billion in 2010.

- lost quality of life from unintended injury valued at an additional $3,706.6 billion.

- economic costs of $258 billion from motor vehicles alone equivalent to about $1,200 per licensed driver.

Despite this staggering number of injuries, injury rates have declined substantially over the last century. National Safety Council statistics show that "Between 1912 and 2007, unintentional-injury deaths per 100,000 of population were reduced 53% . . . from 82.4 to 38.8. The reduction in the overall rate during a period when the nation's population tripled has resulted in 5,500,000 fewer people being killed due to unintentional injuries than there would have been if the rate had not been reduced." National Safety Council, Injury Facts 2010 and 2012.

§ 1. TORT WARS

The New Tort Reform

Major Criticisms Advanced by the Tort Reformers

According to a common complaint of critics, a litigation explosion occurred in the 1980s; suddenly, everyone was suing everyone else. Critics say the tort system is running amok; liability is everywhere; the American public wants to sue whenever anything goes wrong; and lawyers' greed has brought the country to the brink of disaster. Some of these charges lead to long battles about whether litigation really has increased.

More soberly, tort reformers say that the tort system as presently administered has caused specific problems because of the costs it imposes on defendants and insurers:

(1) liability insurance costs too much, especially for certain defendants like malpractice defendants (the affordability crisis);

(2) insurance has or may become unavailable for some defendants (the availability crisis);

(3) some goods or services of vast importance may become unavailable because the threat of tort liability is driving some producers out of the market, as perhaps the diminished availability of certain vaccines suggests.

Evaluating the Criticisms

The data suggest that injured people actually should be claiming redress more often than they do and that juries, far from running amok, award recoveries less often than judges do. Here are some major items of information.

- Most suits filed, around 86 million a year, deal with crimes, divorce, juvenile proceedings, debt claims, and traffic and parking infractions. Although the total number of cases filed has increased somewhat in recent years, the number of tort claims is a small percentage of courts' incoming civil litigation—about 5%. 69% percent of the state courts' civil litigation claims are contract-based. *See* R. LaFountain, R. Schauffler, S. Strickland, S. Gibson, & A. Mason, *Examining the Work of State Courts: An Analysis of 2009 State Court Caseloads* (National Center for State Courts 2011). An earlier study found that a full 60% of the tort cases filed stem from automobile accidents. *See* B. Ostrom, N. Kauder, N. LaFountain, *Examining the Work of State Courts 2002* (National Center for State Courts 2003).

- Only about 10% of injured people make any claim at all; probably many more could justly assert claims. *See* Marc Galanter, *Real World Torts: An Antidote to Anecdote*, 55 MD. L. REV. 1093 (1996).

- Settlements, which constitute the great majority of tort dispositions, on the average probably undercompensate. *See* Deborah L. Rhode, *Frivolous Litigation and Civil Justice Reform: Miscasting the Problem, Recasting the Solution*, 54 DUKE L. J., 447, 460 (2004) (contending that "although excessive litigation is the pathology dominating public discussion and policy agendas, systematic research reveals that the more serious problems are undercompensation of victims").

- A Bureau of Justice Statistics study showed that the median total award in a sample of tort cases was only $24,000, although the National Safety Council estimates that the average economic cost (apart from human cost) of incapacitating injury in automobile cases is much greater— about $70,200. *See* Bureau of Justice Statistics, Civil Bench and Jury Trials in State Courts, 2005 (October 2008); and National Safety Council, Estimating the Costs of Unintentional Injuries (2012).

- Juries have not run amok; in a Bureau of Justice Statistics sample, juries found for the plaintiff in only 52% of the cases. Judges found for the plaintiff only a little more often. When judges act as triers of fact, their awards resemble those of juries, even with punitive damages. *See* Theodore Eisenberg, Neil LaFountain, Brian Ostrom, David Rottman & Martin T. Wells, *Juries, Judges, and Punitive Damages: an Empirical Study*, 87 CORNELL L. REV. 743 (2002).

- Some torts, with disastrous consequences to human beings, really are being committed. Litigation should be perceived as a problem only if litigation outruns actionable injury. Striking studies show that in fact many more tortious injuries are caused than are sued for. *See* Michael J. Saks, *Do We Really Know Anything About the Behavior of the Tort Litigation System—And Why Not?*, 140 U. PA. L. REV. 1147 (1992); Localio, et al., *Relation between Malpractice Claims and Adverse Events Due to Negligence*, 325 N. ENG. J. MED. 245 (July 25, 1991).

Frank Cross, a professor of Business, Law and Government at the University of Texas recently examined whether states that had pro-defendant tort law as judged by Chamber of Commerce indices enjoyed greater economic growth or other benefits. Professor Cross concluded that "Contrary to conventional wisdom, evidence shows no negative economic effects from more pro-plaintiff tort law. . . . More pro-plaintiff law is associated with higher economic growth. . . . The finding [with respect to tort costs and economic growth] is powerful evidence that tort law is at least not harming states' economies." This finding accorded with the theory that tort law should be economically beneficial because it forces firms to internalize costs imposed on others and expands the number of economic transactions. Frank B. Cross, *Tort Law and the American Economy*, 96

MINN. L. REV. 28, 86–89 (2011). In light of the data, why have some people claimed that the courts are giving money away in ridiculous cases?

In part, this may reflect bias against courts—which, after all, are independent and on the whole not subject to political pressure or legislative control. Recent analysis suggests that restrictions on tort actions may also reflect racial bias. *See* Donald G. Gifford & Brian Jones, *Keeping Cases from Black Juries: An Empirical Analysis of How Race, Income Inequality, and Regional History Affect Tort Law*, 73 WASH. & LEE L. REV. 557 (2016) (based on data analysis, concluding: "Even in the twenty-first century, supreme courts in a number of states with substantial percentages of African-Americans in their largest cities, particularly those in the South, continue to follow outmoded substantive doctrines of tort law that make it more difficult for personal injury plaintiffs to have their cases decided by juries. These tort doctrines are but the latest iteration of various means used by courts during the past 150 years to keep African-Americans from participating as jurors in personal injury cases.").

Anti-tort law opinion also has been molded by anecdotes that shamefully distort the cases they purport to report. For example: (1) The story was that a burglar recovered when he fell through a skylight of a building he was trying to burglarize; the fact was that it was a student who fell when he was on the roof of a school to fix a floodlight. (2) The story was that a man who was struck by a car while he was in a telephone booth recovered from the phone company; the fact was that he tried desperately to get out of the booth when he saw the car coming, but the door jammed and he was trapped. Even if anecdotes were correct, they would tell us little about the system as a whole. When they are so terribly misleading, they generate conflict but not information. On the anecdotes, see Joseph Page, *Deforming Tort Reform*, 78 GEO. L. J. 649 (1990) (book review of Peter W. Huber, Liability: The Legal Revolution and Its Consequences (1988)). To read about the campaigns to shape public opinion in a misleading way, see Elizabeth G. Thornburg, *Judicial Hellholes, Lawsuit Climates and Bad Social Science: Lessons from West Virginia*, 110 W. VA. L. REV. 1097 (2008). For a thorough review of many empirical studies, see John T. Nockelby, *How to Manufacture a Crisis: Empirical Claims Behind "Tort Reform,"* 86 OR. L. REV. 533 (2007).

§ 2. THE IMPACT OF TORT LAW ON THE INJURY PROBLEM

The Old Tort Reform

The tort reform movement discussed above was and is fueled mainly by industries, insurers and others who wish to see greater protection for defendants. The first tort reformers approached tort law with different questions and a different orientation. They were not focused on liability reduction, but asked in part: How well does the tort system work in the real world? Does it cope adequately with the problem of massive injury? Does it adequately deter wrongdoing? Compensate the injured? Encourage rehabilitation and otherwise minimize economic loss?

Problems with the Tort System?

1. *Undercompensation.* Studies have repeatedly shown that many claimants are not fully compensated. This point has three parts: (a) undercompensation is itself a failure of the tort system to achieve its own goals; (b) undercompensation has social consequences—the hardships on the injured and their families may be translated into welfare claims on society, or into crime and juvenile delinquency; (c) undercompensation of some groups of claimants is part of a larger picture in which some other groups are—according to many thinkers—overcompensated, with the result that the system not only fails its goals, but also provides a "maldistribution" of the insurance pie and fails to treat people equally.

How does undercompensation come about under the tort systems? Consider these possibilities: (1) The cost of going to court is such that settlement is imperative; in many ranges of injury, lawyers will encourage settlement and, with or without encouragement, plaintiffs will be compelled to accept a fraction of their actual losses. (2) Delay in trial may force the claimant to accept a settlement now. (3) Other factors would encourage a settlement for less-than-loss. These include estimates of liability, and estimates about problems in proof, effectiveness of witnesses and the bias of juries. (4) In spite of compulsory insurance laws, one in five or six drivers is uninsured and often insolvent, so that their victims have little chance of collecting any compensation, much less adequate compensation. This is a very serious problem the states have not dealt with adequately.

One of the earliest studies was Conard, Morgan, Pratt, Volz & Bombaugh, Automobile Accident Costs and Payments (1964), hereafter cited as Conard. Of 86,000 persons who suffered economic loss, some 20,000 received no compensation from any source. Of those who were compensated, the majority received compensation from their own insurance, workers' compensation or the like—not from the tort system. More recent figures suggest that more than two-thirds of those injured in vehicle accidents receive at least some compensation, although because of the problem of uninsured motorists, that compensation may be from their own uninsured motorist coverage. *See* Gary T. Schwartz, *Auto No-fault and First-party Insurance: Advantages and Problems*, 73 S. CAL. L. REV. 611, 624 (2000). Recent evidence suggests that post-tort reform, fewer injured people are bringing actions. Stephen Daniels & Joanne Martin, *Where Have All the Cases Gone? The Strange Success of Tort Reform Revisited*, 65 EMORY L.J. 1445 (2016) ("it is not that jury trials are vanishing, it is the cases themselves"). In the area of intentional torts, victims may be particularly likely to go without compensation. In his article, *Uncompensated Torts*, 28 GA. ST. U. L. REV. 721 (2012), Rick Swedloff outlines the reasons that victims of intentional acts, acts causing more than $460 billion of damages each year, have few practical remedies.

Are the individual and social consequences of these facts significant enough to warrant changing the tort system if this is the only objection?

2. *Overcompensation.* Students of accident compensation have repeatedly found that some claimants are grossly overcompensated. Although one expects that many claimants will recover more than their financial losses—because of pain and suffering recoveries—this does not seem to explain the enormous overcompensation at the lower end of the scale. The Department of Transportation completed an extensive study of the auto accident problem in the early 1970s. This showed, in line with some other studies, that where the economic loss was low, the average recovery might more than double the loss. For instance, if the average economic loss was $330, the average recovery was $829. Westat Research Corp., Economic Consequences of Automobile Accident Injuries 38 (Department of Transportation Automobile Ins. & Compensation Study 1970) (hereafter cited as Economic Consequences). At the upper end of the scale, where pain and suffering would likely be more, the reverse was true, and undercompensation was common.

Knowing what you do about the tort system and how it works, what is your best guess as to the reason for this overcompensation feature?

What impact does this overcompensation have? Is it, standing alone, sufficient to warrant changing the tort system?

3. *Misuse of limited resources.* The DOT study concluded that the personal economic losses from auto accidents in the year 1967 were between $5 and $9 billion. *See* Economic Consequences at 40. That figure did not include either pain and suffering or social losses, such as lost production. The same study concluded that the tort-insurance system paid net compensation of about .8 billion dollars or less than 20% of the actual economic losses. *See id.* at 146. More recent estimates of the total economic cost of motor vehicle crashes placed the cost at $230.6 billion. "Lost market productivity accounted for $61 billion of this total, while property damage accounted for nearly as much-$59 billion. Medical expenses totaled $32.6 billion. . . Each fatality resulted in an average discounted lifetime cost of $977,000. Public revenues paid for roughly 9 percent of all motor vehicle crash costs, costing tax payers $21 billion in 2000." U.S. Department of Transportation, National Highway Traffic Safety Administration, *The Economic Impact of Motor Vehicle Crashes 2000* (2002).

Do figures showing that only a small portion of individual economic losses are compensated by insurance funds reflect any misuse of resources?

Some of the division of the "insurance pie" goes for pain and suffering claims. Every dollar paid for pain and suffering is a dollar that cannot be used to pay basic economic loss. The result is that while some claimants recover for pain, other claimants don't even get their medical bills or lost wages paid. There simply is not enough in the premium fund to go around.

Is this, as some critics argue, a misuse of the limited resources available? If it is, would this be ground, standing alone, for changing the tort system in any substantial way? Would you, instead, favor multiplying liability insurance premiums several fold in order to cover all economic losses?

Notice that the misuse of resources argument as it is cast here could be resolved in part by eliminating the pain and suffering recovery in tort. Would that be desirable, neutral, or undesirable?

4. *Inefficiency of the tort-liability insurance system.* Without liability insurance there would be no tort system as we know it in auto accident cases. The liability insurance system is, however, a three-party system, in which you buy insurance from the company, who will pay a third person— the plaintiff. This builds in certain costs and the tort system itself builds in more. The insurer must investigate fault, cause, damage, and, sometimes, complex legal issues as well. Given fault as a trigger of liability, much of the premium dollar must be devoted to administration costs.

In addition to the costs of the parties and the insurer, the tort system imposes costs on the public because it entails the cost of judges, courthouses, juries, clerks and other apparatus of the judicial system. Special problems appear in class actions, which literally involve hundreds of thousands of claims.

Would the inefficiencies suggested in these paragraphs be enough, standing alone, to warrant any attempt to find substitutes for the tort system in auto accident cases?

5. *Delay in payment under the tort system.* If a claimant is entitled to recover but cannot be paid for months or even years, a number of harmful consequences come about. This is not a problem peculiar to torts. All law attempts to make a careful investigation into the facts and to give full opportunity to debate the legal issues. These good points of law, however, carry a heavy price in forcing delay. In tort cases, the substantive rules requiring proof of fault, cause and damage, along with the ambiguities of many rules, require especially intensive investigation and especially intensive trials. Delay seems unavoidable.

Delay is also due to the fact that the claimant must assert all claims for the future in one legal action. This may require a period of waiting to better estimate future losses and it certainly requires extensive proof about the future.

Delay may also be used strategically by defendants. The procedural system, aimed at supporting the law's aim of full investigation and complete opportunity to be heard, is readily manipulated to delay trial. Defendants can, within the ethics of the system, often delay trial and hence delay settlement or payment. This is useful from the defendant's point of view, since the plaintiff, deprived of wages, will feel more and more pressure to accept smaller and smaller settlements as time goes by.

Would these problems of delay warrant making a substantial change in the tort system if they stood alone? Could you eliminate some of the problems of delay without eliminating the tort system?

6. *The failure to deter or compensate.* The tort system begins with a determination to fix fault. It assumes that fault can be determined in a rational way, and that when it is determined, the imposition of liability in accord with fault will accomplish two purposes: (a) it will administer justice by imposing liability upon faulty persons, and (b) it will deter similar faulty conduct in others. To some, the justice argument itself fails. We have all been faulty in driving at one time or another, quite probably very often by today's standards of negligence in auto cases. Since we are all at fault, according to this view, it is largely a matter of fortuity that some of us get involved in an accident because of fault and some escape an accident. It is even more a matter of fortuity that some of us may cause large damages and some may cause quite small damages. *Cf.* Marc Franklin, *Replacing the Negligence Lottery*, 53 VA. L. REV. 774 (1967). Under these circumstances, it is less than clear that imposing liability in accord with fault is truly "just."

Whatever may be said about the justice side of the argument, the deterrent effect of tort liability is undercut by the presence of liability insurance. When a defendant is held liable, that defendant does not ordinarily make payments to the injured plaintiff in the tort system. The liability insurer does so. In many states, punitive as well as compensatory damages are covered by insurance, so that insurance may protect even a reckless defendant from any personal accountability in money. In addition, the court's desire to compensate the plaintiff has led to many cases in which "fault" is found in a defendant who has behaved in a way that, but for insurance, most people would not find faulty at all. In this view, then, the tort system fails to accomplish one of its main purposes—deterrence.

Is it true that the tort system does not accomplish any of its main goals—justice, deterrence, compensation? If it is true, would this criticism standing alone lead you to seek a substitute system?

7. *Participation in the insurance fund—lack of reciprocity.* Although the tort system is fueled on liability insurance, not everyone purchases such insurance. Among those who do purchase it, many have procured only low-limit policies, inadequate to protect a seriously injured plaintiff. A

person who purchases only minimal insurance protection or none at all may nevertheless be the beneficiary of a high-limits policy purchased by someone else.

A second problem of reciprocity in the participation in insurance funds can be seen if one imagines that poor people as a class will draw less of the insurance pie than others because for any given injury they will have less wage loss. Yet they will pay the same premiums paid by wealthier persons. Again, this is a result of the fact that injury is compensated through the insurance of others, not through one's own insurance.

Do these observations amount to a criticism of the tort system? If so, would this criticism standing alone warrant an effort to change the tort system?

8. *Is the tort system a lottery?* Some lawyers think so. There are at least three senses in which this may be so.

(a) There is a large element of fortuity from the injured person's point of view. If a woman is injured in an ordinary car collision, she will have to prove negligence to recover. If the collision occurs while she is in the course of employment, she will not be required to prove negligence, though her workers' compensation recovery will be limited to economic losses. If the collision occurs because of a defective steering apparatus, she will be entitled to recover from the manufacturer without proving negligence and she will not be limited to economic losses. From her point of view, her legal rights depend almost wholly on the luck of the case—whether she was working or not, whether her injury was caused by the manufacturer or by another driver. There are a number of these fortuitous elements in the negligence case. Consider: The defendant is negligent, but by luck he causes no harm at all; or the defendant is negligent, but by luck the plaintiff was also guilty of substantial negligence, though the defendant would have caused the same harm to a non-negligent plaintiff. See Franklin, supra.

(b) The torts system may be viewed as a lottery for more quotidian reasons. Consider: the plaintiff is injured, but as luck would have it, the plaintiff herself is not very attractive and does not capture the jury's sympathy; or the only witness is quite truthful, but has an abrasive personality and makes a bad impression; or there is no witness at all; or defendant's witnesses have been packaged and stage managed to create the best impression; or the defendant is a sympathetic local person and the plaintiff is an outsider. Similarly, lawyers' abilities to deal with complex issues vary greatly; some plaintiffs lose because their lawyers were not up to the demands of the particular case, not because the case itself was unworthy.

Are any of these "lottery" reasons ground for reconsidering the tort system?

9. *Are the lump-sum award and pain and suffering compensation justifiable?* The instinctive answer of almost everyone is that something should be paid for pain and suffering, at least when that pain is caused by wrongdoing of others. Yet the pain and suffering award does not compensate in the ordinary sense. If wages are lost, money can repay that loss. If one is in pain, the money award cannot relieve the pain. (Pain relievers are covered under medical expense awards.) To the extent these awards are used to pay lawyers' fees, they are explicable in practical terms; but lawyers are needed in the first place chiefly because the tort system requires detailed analysis of fault, cause and damage. If the system were changed, the role of lawyers would be very different, as it is in workers' compensation systems. Perhaps pain awards are symbolically important and important in deterrence. What do you think?

If you think there is something wrong with pain awards, do you also think that is ground standing alone to reconsider the whole tort system?

New Directions

If either the old or the new tort reformers are right or partly right in their central perceptions, would it be a good idea to find alternatives to some or all parts of the tort system?

Many of the criticisms summarized above are reviewed by Professor Sugarman, who insists that tort law fails in the goal of inducing safety, providing compensation, or doing justice if you look at the system as a whole and consider alternatives. STEPHEN SUGARMAN, DOING AWAY WITH PERSONAL INJURY LAW (1989). Sugarman proposes a comprehensive welfare program that would take care of injuries as well as any other misfortune. Employers would cover short term needs, government the rest. Safety incentives would be provided by regulation, not by threat of liability.

Other critics have suggested that society should allocate certain kinds of injury problems to some institutions other than tort law, but that tort law should be retained for at least some kinds of cases. *E.g.,* Richard B. Stewart, *Crisis in Tort Law? The Institutional Perspective*, 54 U. CHI. L. REV. 184 (1987); W. Kip Viscusi, *Toward a Diminished Role for Tort Liability: Social Insurance, Government Regulation, and Contemporary Risks to Health and Safety*, 6 YALE J. REG. 65 (1989). See also the good short discussion as to toxic torts in Robert Rabin, *Book Review*, 98 YALE L. J. 813 (1989) (reviewing Peter Schuck, Tort System on Trial: The Burden of Mass Toxics Litigation (1987)).

Some of the major ones other than regulation or contract are considered next.

PART 10

ALTERNATIVES TO TORT LAW

■ ■ ■

For many, including many legislatures, the disadvantages of the tort system have outweighed its advantages, at least in particular settings. As a consequence, legal thinkers and state and federal legislatures have provided several non-tort alternatives to the tort system. All of these, however, have limited application, for example, to employment injuries or automobile accidents.

This Part briefly introduces some of these alternatives. In many ways they are enormously different from tort systems. But this should not obscure the similarities. In considering these alternatives, consider whether the same issues must be resolved in both systems, and whether similar problems arise (perhaps in new language) for the judiciary in deciding claims. More importantly, consider whether any of these alternative systems is better than the tort system. If they are not to wholly supplant the tort system, can they be satisfactorily meshed with tort law?

CHAPTER 28

BEING AWARE OF
COMPENSATION OPTIONS

■ ■ ■

In evaluating tort law from a public policy point of view, awareness of some major options is important. Apart from alternatives like forced apology instead of accountability for harm done, or mediation or arbitration, three general models stand out.

Workers' Compensation

The first major option to tort law could be a general adoption of a plan like that used at present only for certain on-the-job injuries. Workers' compensation statutes adopted in all states provide that employers must carry insurance to provide some basic levels of compensation for workers injured on the job. The levels of compensation vary from state to state. Sometimes the compensation is quite inadequate, but at other times it seems to be sufficient, particularly considering the fact that the worker is often paid automatically and even if she is herself at fault and the employer is not. Here are the main characteristics of workers' compensation systems:

1. *Strict liability.* Employers are made strictly liable for on-the-job injury of employees. Thus a worker injured on the job is entitled to compensation even if the employer is not negligent.

2. *Defenses are abolished.* Contributory negligence, assumed risk and fellow-servant defenses are abolished completely.

3. *Limited liability.* The employer's liability is limited. The compensation provided is not common law damages, but rather fixed and limited amounts, expressed as specific sums for certain injuries like the loss of a thumb, or as a percentage of average wages where there is total disability. Liability includes compensation for medical needs and wage loss, but nothing for pain and suffering.

4. *Immediate and periodic payment.* An injured worker is entitled, after a short waiting period, to immediate periodic payments, which continue as long as the disability exists, subject to any statutory maximum amounts.

5. *Enforcement and administration.* Where there is no dispute, the employer (or its insurer) pays money directly to the worker on a periodic basis. If there is a dispute, the worker reports the claim to an

administrative agency. The statutes contemplated that there would be no need for lawyers, but today lawyers do in fact appear in many of these hearings. However, the procedure is relaxed and informal, and there are no rules of evidence, so it remains true at least in theory that lawyers are not required.

6. *Financing.* The scheme is essentially a compulsory insurance scheme, with the employer required to purchase insurance which must provide the coverage specified by the statute.

7. *Courts.* Courts have a most limited role in workers' compensation. They do, however, decide the meaning of the statute and whether evidence is sufficient to warrant the decisions of the administrators who decide disputes under the statute.

8. *Exclusive remedy and third-party claims.* With few exceptions, there is no tort action against the employer. The employee injured on the job by a third person, such as a manufacturer of a machine used on the job, still has a tort suit against that third person, however.

Public Compensation

A second option would be to substitute public compensation for tort law. Several public compensation systems are in effect on a limited scale. One of them taxes vaccine manufacturers, then uses the tax to pay specified compensation for certain vaccine-caused injuries. This is handled bureaucratically, with fixed and limited damages.

Another public compensation system encouraged all victims of the 9–11 attacks to claim against the special public fund, again with limits and bureaucratically fixed rules that gave only a little attention to individual variations in the claims.

Another bureaucratic system is administered by the most successful of all federal agencies, the Social Security Administration. Although most of social security benefits are associated with retirement and Medicare or Medicaid, the social security statutes also provide payments to totally disabled persons, if the disability is permanent or expected to last a long time. The benefits paid are more or less equivalent to early retirement benefits, not keyed to, say, loss of wages, much less to pain and suffering. Many people who receive these social security disability benefits suffer disabilities unrelated to tort-type injuries. However, the benefits are payable to those who qualify even if the disability resulted from an injury rather than, say, a genetic problem.

Private Insurance

A third model option that could conceivably replace substantial parts of the tort system is based on private insurance. No-fault insurance plans originated for automobile accidents. The gist of the plan was that everyone would be covered by insurance which drivers were compelled to purchase for the benefit of themselves, occupants of their cars, and pedestrians. This insurance would take the place of tort liability. In theory it could take the place of *all* tort liability, so that no drunken driver ever need fear civil liability. And by the same token, the drunken driver who injured himself would have compensation from his own insurer. In practice, even the most expansive no-fault plans allow the tort system to kick in once injuries are severe or involve high amounts of loss. Thus in existing no-fault systems, no-fault applies only to relatively small injuries and only to those arising from automobile accidents. Part of the savings created by this plan come from the limitations on liability of the insurer and part from the limited amounts of compensation payable. For example, pain and suffering is excluded.

Evaluating the Options

How would you evaluate the major options? Would you like to see one or more of them used to displace tort law entirely? Would you worry about incentives for the right amount of safety? On that point, might automobile accident cases warrant different treatment from, say, products liability or medical malpractice cases?

PART 11

ECONOMIC AND DIGNITARY TORTS

■ ■ ■

CHAPTER 29

BEING AWARE OF DIGNITARY
AND ECONOMIC TORTS

■ ■ ■

This edition is focused on torts involving physical harms to persons or tangible property. But there are a number of other torts, common law and statutory, that address other kinds of legal harm. These fall into two groups: (1) dignitary torts and (2) pure economic torts. In both groups, specific rules govern the torts. Analysis therefore does not much resemble the analysis in negligence cases with emphasis on duty, breach, cause-in-fact and scope of risk or proximate cause.

Dignitary torts are concerned with recognition and preservation of intangible human interests, including reputation, privacy, and family integrity.

Reputational interests are redressed under the law of defamation, broken down into libel and slander. The tort of libel applies when a defendant communicates something seriously negative (defamatory) about the plaintiff to someone other than the plaintiff herself, and does so in writing or in some more or less permanent medium, such as a movie or television. Slander is similar, but is usually oral. The common law of libel imposed liability even if the defendant reasonably thought was he was communicating was true, but truth was an affirmative defense. Constitutional free speech rules heavily impact the contemporary law of libel, so that in many cases, but not quite all, the plaintiff must nowadays prove some kind of fault, negligence or even knowing falsehood, in order to establish liability.

Reputational and other interests are also protected by the rules of malicious prosecution and several similar torts. These torts provide redress for persons who have been prosecuted or sued civilly without probable cause. Because it is important to protect the defendant's right to sue or prosecute the plaintiff, however, courts impose several restrictions on the right to maintain tort suits for malicious prosecution and its sister torts.

Privacy interests are quite varied, and include protection from prying, physically or otherwise, and may also some kinds of publication about private facts.

Interference with family relations was once generally tortious if the defendant either had sexual relations with the plaintiff's spouse or, with or without sexual relations, alienated the spouse's affection, for example, by inducing the spouse to leave the plaintiff. These alienation of affections and criminal conversation actions have been abolished in many states.

Pure economic torts are like dignitary torts in that neither is based on personal injury or damage to tangible property. A number of economic torts fill a number of small niches, with each tort, like the dignitary torts, having its own set of rules. Two large categories of economic torts are (1) intentional interference with contractual relations (in some states a sister tort, intentional interference with business prospects, is also recognized); and (2) misrepresentation that induces the plaintiff to enter into an unfavorable economic transaction.

Courts have generally, but not invariably, held that negligent interference with economic interests is not a ground for liability. This is usually called the economic loss rule. In some cases this rule is applied even when the plaintiff and defendant have no contractual relationship, partly because it is difficult to constrain liability within reasonable bounds. In other cases, the economic loss rule applies when the plaintiff and defendant have contracted about the subject matter. In these cases, the rule aims to hold the plaintiff to his contract rights, providing he can sue for whatever contract rights he has and would not undermine the contract limits by suing in tort.

INDEX

Using the Index

This index refers to key words, legal rules or ideas, legal issues, key parties, and important factual settings. It is not a concordance or a computer-generated word list. Hence not every instance of a word is listed. Equally, the referenced page may discuss or exemplify the legal idea indexed without using the indexing word. References are to pages. When indexed material appears in a main case, only the first page of the case is given, unless inclusive references are more practical. Similarly, only the first page is typically given when a broad topic covers many succeeding pages. When indexed material appears in notes, the first page of an inclusive reference is the page on which the note begins.

EMPLOYERS
See also Vicarious Liability
Common law duties to employees, 418, 443,
446
Consent and, 77
Emotional harm intentionally inflicted, 477

ESTOPPEL
Statute of limitations and, 300, 301

EVIDENCE
See also Res Ipsa Loquitur
Available evidence not introduced, 172, 173
Circumstantial, generally, 151
Credibility rule, 152
Defendant's safety rules as evidence on
standard of care, 158
Expert testimony
emotional distress, to prove, 498–99
medical malpractice cases, 341
not required, when, 153, 344
permitted when, 153
required, when, 341
Inferences, generally, 151
Negligence generally, 149
Opinion testimony, 152
Presumption,
meanings, 169
warning would have been heeded if
given, 607
Statistical evidence, 172, 195

EXTENDED LIABILITY
See also Transferred Intent
Limits on, 43, 53
Principle of, transferred intent as, 43
Trespass to land cases, 53

FACTUAL CAUSE
See also Apportionment
Generally, 179
Alternative causation, 192, 194
Apportionment to causes, 184, 194, 625,
640
Burden of proof, 179
But-for test
alternatives to, 188
applied, 180
Causation obscured by defendants'
negligent acts, 192
Causation without fault, 8–10
Comparative causation, 625, 640
Comparative fault, only causal fault
compared, 254
Concurrent causes, 184
Divisible injury, 187
"Duplicative" causation, 187
Duty to preserve plaintiff's chance of life or
health, 195
Duty-to-try analysis, 201
Element of plaintiff's negligence claim, 179
Evidence of causation, increased risk as,
190
Existing injury, aggravation of, 185

Increased risk and, 190
Indivisible injury, 184, 625
Inference or burden shifting when injury is
within the risk, 190, 601, 606
Liability without causation, 185
Loss of chance, 195
Multiple actors, 184
"Preemptive" causation, 187
Preexisting injury or probability of harm,
185
Probabilistic or proportionate causation
Generally, 186
Product liability, warnings, causation
issues, 607
Proximate cause and, 183
Relaxed causation requirement, 200
Res ipsa loquitur and, 184
Single indivisible injury, 184
Substantial factor test, 188
Value of the chance, 195

FALSE IMPRISONMENT
Generally, 48
Confinement, 50
Damages, 51
Duress or threat, by, 50
Elements, 50
Exclusion as, 50
False arrest compared, 51
Privileged or not, 69

FAMILY MEMBERS
See also Children; Consortium;
Prenatal Harms
Federal Tort Claims Act, *Feres* rule,
application to, 390
Immunity
Generally, 365
family relationship terminated, 366
foster parents, 371
intentional torts, 366
negligent supervision immunity, 367
rejection of immunities, 367
retention of immunities, parental
care and authority, 367
violation of duty to larger class
injures family, 366
Interference with family
actions for abolished, 998–99
common law actions for, 998–99
Mother, duty to fetus or not, 503, 508
Negligent supervision, 367
Parental liability, child's tort
common law, 36
duty to control known violent child,
458
statutes, 36
Rejection of immunities, 367
Spousal abuse, see domestic abuse, this
topic
Spouse, duty to control, 458